AN INTRODUCTION TO SOCIOLOGY

SECOND EDITION

CONTRIBUTORS

David V.J. Bell, York University

Wallace Clement, Carleton University

Lawrence F. Felt, Memorial University

Sid N. Gilbert, University of Guelph

Ian M. Gomme, Memorial University

Hubert Guindon, Concordia University

Alfred A. Hunter, McMaster University

Linda Hunter, York University

Frank E. Jones, McMaster University

Wayne W. McVey, Jr., University of Alberta

Nancy Mandell, York University

Peter C. Pineo, McMaster University

Judith Posner, York University

M. Michael Rosenberg, Dawson College

Stuart Schoenfeld, York University

William B. Shaffir, McMaster University

Michael R. Smith, McGill University

Robert A. Stebbins, University of Calgary

R.A. Sydie, University of Alberta

Allan Turowetz, Dawson College

Morton Weinfeld, McGill University

AN INTRODUCTION TO
SOCIOLOGY
SECOND EDITION

M. Michael Rosenberg

William B. Shaffir

Allan Turowetz

Morton Weinfeld

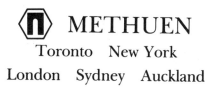 METHUEN

Toronto   New York

London   Sydney   Auckland

Canadian Cataloguing in Publication Data

Main entry under title:
    An Introduction to Sociology

Includes index.
Bibliography: p.
ISBN 0-458-99020-5

1. Sociology. 2. Canada—Social conditions.
I. Rosenberg, M. Michael

HM51.I67 1987   301   C86-094580-4

61,384

This book is dedicated to:
Rebecca, Rachel, and Samuel from M.R.
Rivka, Yael, Elichai, and Ariel from W.S.
Gail, Jason, and Mark from A.T.
Phyllis, Rebecca, and David from M.W.

Editor: Lenore d'Anjou
Managing Editor: Anita Miecznikowski
Executive Editor: R. Peter Milroy
Picture Research: Cathy Munro
Copy Editor: Kathleen Hamilton
Production Editor: Kate Forster
Cover Design: Falcom Design & Communications

Printed and bound in Canada

1 2 3 4   87   91 90 89 88

CONTENTS

CONTENTS IN DETAIL

ACKNOWLEDGMENTS

This second edition, like the first, is the result of a collaborative effort in which we have benefitted from the wisdom, expertise, and generosity of many people. Obviously, the real heart of this book has been the work of the contributors who produced the high-quality chapters of which this book is composed. We would also like to thank the many reviewers who worked on both the first and second editions of this book. Without their critical readings and valuable suggestions this book would have been a much poorer one. In addition to those who worked on the first edition we thank Neil Guppy, Les Laczko, Meg Luxton, Ralph Matthews, Carolyn Miller, Joseph Smucker, Daiva Stasiulis, Kenneth Stoddart, and Ivan Varga for their work on this new edition.

All of us, editors and contributors, would like to express profound thanks to Lee d'Anjou for her outstanding work in translating our writing into English from its original sociologese. We also thank Anita Mieczni-kowski of Methuen Publications for making our work on this edition so much easier by virtue of her talents for organizing and coordinating such a complex project.

PREFACE

Only a few short years ago the publication of a new Canadian introductory sociology textbook was a rare event. Most teachers (many of whom had been trained in the United States) used American textbooks, secure in the knowledge that they were providing their students with material that was "state of the art."

Nevertheless, it gradually became apparent to many instructors that these American texts, while often excellent books, failed in several respects as introductions to sociology for Canadian students. A textbook must reflect the experiences of students if it is to be successful in introducing them to a new way of thinking. It must point to the most familiar features of its readers' lives and point out that these are neither as familiar nor as clear-cut as the readers had supposed.

It is not that Canadian sociologists are engaged in a different enterprise from that of American sociologists; the two groups share a wide range of similar concerns. What differs is the focus, the emphasis on those issues that are significant to Canadians. For example, American textbooks typically deal with the concept of ethnicity as an adjunct to a discussion of race relations. While the subject of race relations is relevant to Canada, it must be understood in the historical and social context of Canadian ethnicity, which is very different from the dynamics of race relations in the United States. Additionally, American textbooks abound with references to the American political system, social problems, and cultural concerns, but never mention Canada's new Constitution, provincial regionalism and separatism, or the unique problems of multiculturalism.

Some of these problems are being solved as Canadian sociology textbooks have begun to appear; students are now learning how sociology can lead them to an understanding of their own society. Yet many of the new textbooks have only inserted Canadian data into a book that imitates the format, style, and choice of topics of the American texts. Indeed, some of the texts, while of excellent quality, are little more than Canadianized versions of American texts.

We, the editors, have aimed to produce a book that not only contains Canadian data as illustrative material but that reflects as well the specific concerns and accomplishments of Canadian sociologists. Organizationally, the table of contents indicates our commitment to trying something new: providing a comprehensive review of basic sociological concepts while integrating these concepts within a framework appropriate to an understanding of Canadian society. Thus, you will find chapters on essential sociological topics such as the family, socialization, gender, education, deviance, demography, and urbanism, each written by a specialist in the field and each examining the relevance of these concepts to an understanding of Canada. But we have also included chapters rarely found in such a book, or which have been given a new or somewhat different format.

We have included three chapters on topics that we consider necessary to an understanding of Canadian society: regionalism, Quebec, and political economy. The chapter on political economy by Wallace Clement takes this difficult topic and provides the student with an overview of the history, methodology, and achievements of this perspective. In doing so, Professor Clement indicates why the political-economy perspective has been so central to the evolution of sociology in Canada. While this perspective can be applied or described for each of the substantive chapters in the book, we feel that it is itself a distinctive feature of Canadian sociology and merits separate treatment.

The lengthy political struggles surrounding Canada's adoption of the new Constitution have made most Canadians aware of the enormous influence of regionalism on this nation—not only politically, but economically, socially, and culturally (the appearance of a dictionary of Newfoundland terms and phrases is illustrative of this last). In his chapter on regionalism, David Bell illustrates some of the most important sociopolitical processes in contemporary Canada and displays for students the insights that social scientists can provide into sociopolitical events.

The chapter on Quebec by Hubert Guindon is a departure from textbook tradition in two senses. Guindon examines the place of Quebec in Canadian society (from a Quebecker's point of view) and shows the clear connections between fundamental social processes of change and modernization and the emergent political culture of Quebec. Because Quebec is, frankly, unfamiliar territory to many anglophone Canadian students (and sociologists), we asked Professor Guindon not to write a chapter in the standard introductory textbook style. Instead he has produced an incisive and powerful essay that is not only a valuable asset to this book but that also stands, we think, as a major contribution to the sociological study of Quebec.

The chapter on ethnicity is yet another example of how a topic usually covered in the American textbooks has a very different format within a book oriented to Canada. If the United States was founded by people who attempted to make ethnicity irrelevant to the body politic, Canada was founded as a union of two ethnic groups; the result has been that ethnicity pervades Canadian society in a way that it does not the American. Our chapter shows how ethnicity is intimately tied into the political, cultural, and economic realities of what has come to be called a multicultural society. Additionally, we devoted space in the chapter to a consideration of the policy implications that arise from a sociological understanding of ethnicity in Canada.

Overall we have attempted to produce an introductory textbook that is Canadian without being self-consciously so. Contributors were under no orders to be Canadian at all costs or to avoid American or other comparative data. The time is past for any such narrowness of vision. It is a sign of the maturity of Canadian sociology that there is so much to be said and shown about how sociology is being done in Canada and what it is achieving.

But what have we left out? Inevitably, choices had to be made in selecting topics for chapters; when we decided to add chapters on topics not usually found in introductory textbooks we had to exclude other topics. There is no chapter on social movements, for example. Nevertheless we believe that enough references can be found in other chapters, as in Guindon's discussion of modernization in Quebec, to allow instructors to emphasize these elements.

At the end of each chapter is a set of further readings, to which the student can refer for more information on the topic. Each set was prepared by the author of the chapter and reflects his or her sources, interests, or preferences. In the chapter on religion, for example, Stuart Schoenfeld presents a reading list limited to Canadian materials because he felt, given the much greater volume of American and British publications, that the Canadian materials are somewhat hard to find.

Finally, we have been concerned throughout this book to ensure that it is directed to *students*—that it is readable, interesting, and even, we hope, at times exciting. Yet we have insisted that these traits not be at the expense of competence or thoroughness. Thus, the reader of the chapters on population and sociological method may find them heavy going at times. These are, frankly, difficult chapters. But these two topics are essential points of grounding in sociology; they are foundations for much of the rest in this book and much that comes later in the career of a sociologist. This fact allows for no compromise. We have included a preliminary discussion entitled "What Is Sociology?" to provide some background and ease the student into the discussion found in these chapters.

In conclusion, we call on all those who use this textbook to feel free to address their comments on it to the editors. No piece of work is perfect and there are doubtless many ways in which this book could be improved. We would be delighted to hear from you, for it would be a sign that this book is being read and evaluated seriously.

PART I

THE DISCIPLINE OF SOCIOLOGY

Sociologists may agree on basic principles, but they subscribe to several different and competing images of society—theoretical perspectives that reflect a wide variety of assumptions about the nature of human beings and society. These perspectives serve to shape both the problems that particular sociologists choose for investigation and the methods they use to organize and conduct research—in short, the manner in which they attempt to describe, understand, and explain a society and behaviour within it.

Students are often perplexed by this diversity of viewpoints. "Can't these guys get their act together?" they wonder. "Which perspective is right?" But what at first appears to be a failing soon comes to be understood as one of sociology's greatest strengths. The existence of different perspectives in sociology encourages students to use a variety of viewpoints in re-examining their assumptions about

the world and how it works, to think these ideas through, and to come to some resolution for themselves. For sociologists, the constant criticism generated by competing perspectives helps to keep the discipline alive, vigorous, and interesting. Moreover, it may well be that the variety of social phenomena in society—the many different sorts of things going on—and the different levels of analysis at which sociologists work require a variety of approaches to be made understandable.

In Chapter 1, "What Is Sociology?", we present some basic ideas and concepts shared by most sociologists, as well as some brief examples of the ways in which sociologists engage in sociological work. These points are developed more systematically throughout the text. We also try to answer some of the initial questions students ask about the discipline, such as "What do sociologists do?" and "What can

1

I do with a background in sociology?" In this way we hope that students, whatever their career plans, will come to see the value of a background in sociology and will become familiar with some of the diverse ways in which sociologists themselves understand their enterprise.

In Chapter 2, Alfred A. Hunter introduces a broad range of the methodological techniques sociologists use to conduct research on the full spectrum of social phenomena. Again, students often wonder at the variety of methods used by sociologists (and at their disagreements as to relative merits). A natural science, such as chemistry, makes use of a far more restricted set of methods. But a fairer comparison would be that between sociology and the natural sciences. Just as the methods used by a geographer differ from those of a chemist, and the methods of a paleontologist will differ from those of a physicist, so too the methods suitable for research on the family differ from those used to study political movements, and the methods appropriate to examining differences of status found in a bureaucracy are not appropriate for research on heroin addicts.

CHAPTER 1

WHAT IS SOCIOLOGY?

M. Michael Rosenberg
and Morton Weinfeld

As a student beginning a sociology course, you already know a great deal about the workings of society. Parents, peers, the media, and your own experience have taught you much about how people are likely to behave and what you can expect to happen in a wide variety of situations. This knowledge, a rudimentary form of sociology, is made up of maxims, common-sense assumptions, and everyday experiences. For most people most of the time, it provides a perfectly adequate understanding of how to live your lives in the social world. However, it differs from the discipline of sociology, which you will be learning about in this book, in one crucial respect: sociology, unlike everyday knowledge, is scientific knowledge.

WHAT IS SCIENCE?

Despite the extraordinary transformations that modern science has effected in human lives (and can be expected to continue effecting), few people are aware of what science is really all about. When most people think of science, they think of the study of molecules, nuclear fission, dinosaur bones, and other such phenomena. However, modern science is characterized not by what it studies but by how it goes about studying something. In other words, science is a method. This method can be applied to studying the structure of molecules or the structure of society. Both types of study are scientific to the degree that they use the scientific method.

The philosopher of science Ernest Nagel describes the **scientific method** as the "persistent critique of arguments, in the light of tried canons for judging the reliability of the procedures by which evidential data are obtained, and for assessing the probative force of the evidence on which conclusions are based" (1961,13). This is method not in the sense of using particular procedures, such as experiments, or instruments, such as test tubes, but in the sense of principles for evaluating procedures, instruments, and results. To illustrate, we contrast the scientific method with common sense:

1. People using common sense take truth for granted. Short of major upheavals, most people do not question their assumptions about how the world works and what everybody "knows" to be true. Thus everybody "knew" for many centuries that the sun went around the earth, and anyone who thought otherwise was considered either foolish or insane. Science, by contrast, treats all its accomplishments as **hypotheses**, possible explanations that may be found to be false. This constant questioning of basic assumptions provides science with its dynamism and challenge.
2. Common-sense knowledge is pragmatic. People see a problem and seek a solution that "works"; they are unconcerned with how or why it works. Calling this type of knowledge "recipe knowledge," the philosopher Alfred Schütz explains:

> This kind of knowledge is concerned only with the regularity as such of events. . . . Because of this regularity it can be reasonably expected that the sun will rise tomorrow morning . . . that the bus will bring me to my office if I choose the right one and pay my fare. (1964,74)

In contrast, science is primarily directed toward understanding both why and how things work. Science, in other words, is systematic.

3. Finally, common-sense knowledge is subjective—that is, it is based on and altered by the personal experiences, biases, interests, and expectations of each individual. And although many people are easily swayed by public opinion, they still insist that seeing is believing and that their beliefs are validated in their own experiences. The scientist, in contrast, seeks to be objective: the validity of his or her findings is based on the presentation of evidence to others, rather than on the believability of the findings to that particular scientist. Although subjectivity (bias) remains a problem in science and although there is some disagreement about what "objectivity" means (for example, the two philosophers of science already mentioned, Ernest Nagel and Alfred Schütz, have conflicting views on this point), objectivity remains the goal of the scientific method.

None of this should be seen as denigrating common sense. Common-sense knowledge is itself an accomplishment that displays the subtleties, sophistication, and reasoning of people in everyday life. Scientist or non-scientist, we all depend on common-sense knowledge to make our way in the world.

SOCIOLOGY AND SCIENCE

All the sciences share the principles of the scientific method, but each makes use of the procedures that are best suited to its particular subject matter. (See Chapter 2 for a detailed discussion of the methods used by sociologists.) As a social science, sociology differs in a crucial respect from the natural sciences such as physics or chemistry: its subject matter is human beings, people as thinking, reasoning, willing social actors. This fact provides sociology with some major advantages over the natural sciences, but it also leads to problems for a scientific discipline.

On the plus side, sociologists study people, and people, unlike molecules, can talk back. Natural scientists must base their theories of how the world works solely on the recording of observed events. They are thus limited by their ability to observe and record these events and by their need to have some clear idea in advance about what sort of events to look for. People as subjects, on the other hand, can give sociologists answers to their questions and provide the information needed to generate theories. Many of the research methods that you will be reading about in this book—for example, questionnaires, interviews, and interactional methods such as participant observation—are directed to asking people to explain, evaluate, or comment on their own lives and on their own understanding of society.

But sociology is not merely a summary of people's opinions or a compendium of what everyone already knows. People often have a mistaken or confused understanding of social events; they may also purposely conceal, distort, or misrepresent their views. (Statistical tests are no protection against such distortions, for if everyone conceals in a similar manner the results will be statistically reliable, but untrue.) Like all scientists, sociologists must be prepared to question their data rather than to accept them at face value. "Debunking," "unmasking," and "engaging in critical thought" are among the terms that sociologists use to describe that all-important step of getting past the appearance to uncover what is really going on. Only then can they try to understand why things work this way, and how.

We can illustrate this point by looking at the work of two sociologists, Erving Goffman and Robert Merton.

Goffman was a master at investigating the nuances of social interaction. In his classic work, *The Presentation of Self in Everyday Life*, he describes the enormous amount of work people put into presenting themselves to other people in ordinary interaction. He explains the role of "dramatic realization," whereby individuals, in order to show themselves as they want to be seen, "dramatically highlight and portray confirmatory facts that might otherwise remain unapparent or obscure" (1959, 30). For example, in his discussion of presenting to others an atmosphere of tasteful simplicity, Goffman comments:

> To furnish a house so that it will express simple, quiet dignity, the householder may have to race to auction sales, haggle with antique dealers, and doggedly canvas all the local shops for proper wallpaper and curtain material. To give a radio talk that will sound genuinely informal, spontaneous, and relaxed, the speaker may have to design his script with painstaking care, testing one phrase after another, in order to follow the content, language, rhythm and pace of everyday talk. (1959, 32)

We all know that everyday appearances result from complex interactions; as described in Chapter 4, Goffman has developed this knowledge into a systematic vision of the nature of social interaction.

While Goffman's work makes clear the insights that can be found by examining in detail what everyone already knows (or thinks they know), Robert Merton has devoted himself to overturning people's assumptions about what they are doing and why it is they are doing it. He seeks to uncover the hidden, unarticulated reasons that lead people to engage in seemingly inexplicable social behaviour. According to Merton, **manifest functions** are the generally recognized and accepted consequences of social behaviour and **latent functions** are the "unintended and unrecognized consequences" (1968, 117).

Robert Merton maintained that while rituals such as the Hopi snake dance may not produce rain they do reinforce group identity.

Merton applies this distinction to an analysis of the rain ceremony of the Hopi Indians in the American southwest:

> Hopi ceremonials designed to produce abundant rainfall may be labelled a superstitious practice of primitive folk. . . . Were one to confine himself to the problem of whether a manifest (proposed) function occurs, it becomes a problem, not for the sociologist, but for the meteorologist. And to be sure, our meteorologists agree that the rain ceremonial does not produce rain. . . . But . . . ceremonials may fulfill the latent function of reinforcing the group identity by providing a periodic occasion on which the scattered members of a group assemble to engage in common activity.

Thus the seemingly irrational behaviour of the Hopis can be seen as a quite rational solution to a problem—not the problem of lack of rain, but the need to maintain group identity.

In the work of Goffman and Merton then, we see two ways in which sociology can deal with the common-sense knowledge and assumptions that are its data: by making explicit all that common sense takes for granted and by looking for the hidden meaning in what for common sense is inexplicable.

APPROACHES TO UNDERSTANDING SOCIETY

There are many different approaches to understanding society and discovering the "truth" about human behaviour and the social world. Fiction, informed journalism, and social science are examples of such approaches. Four boxed inserts in this chapter illustrate several approaches.

Franz Kafka's description of the bureaucratic maze involving departments A and B was written to be humorous, but it confirms the experience of many people with bureaucracy. Kafka's satirical fiction is, well, Kafkaesque and methodically takes us to the borders of the irrational as we chuckle.

In contrast, Mordecai Richler's humour relies largely on one-liners. Richler is criticizing what he sees as the sterility of modern Reform Judaism compared to the more traditional religious expressions of Orthodox Judaism. (His critique implicitly applies to modern Christianity as well.) Like Kafka, Richler makes no pretence to objectivity; you know where he stands. Nor does he make any effort to offer the other side of the story—that is, any possible defence of Reform Judaism—nor any explanation of why or how the Reform movement originated.

Alexis de Tocqueville's analysis of American society and political culture is based on his observations and discussions with Americans during a visit of several months to the United States in the 1830s. His judgments are based on his distillation of a large amount of evidence. Generations have marvelled at the astuteness of his generalizations and the sharpness of his vision, which were, perhaps, a result of his being a foreigner and possibly free of the biases of a native-born American observer. For example, in the brief selection quoted here, de Tocqueville describes an anti-aristocratic egalitarianism and an undervalued or underdeveloped intellectual class as characteristics of the America of the mid-19th century. Some observers might argue that these societal traits persist to the present.

The brief selection from John Porter's *The Vertical Mosaic* is a good example of modern sociological work. Porter here is arguing that Canadian university students in the 1950s were likely to come from higher-income families. Unlike de Tocqueville, Porter presents his evidence clearly for the reader's own evaluation. Moreover, his evidence is quantitatively expressed and is presumed to be representative of Canadian society, because it is taken from a scientific, government-sponsored national sample survey. The writing style is typically social scientific. Porter prefers to let the facts speak for themselves and presents them in a straightforward, sober manner. We have an inkling of his personal feelings about the research only in his use of terms like "class-biased" and "privilege of upper middle classes."

In this book, we hope to point out the strengths and benefits of the sociological approach to understanding society.

From IN THE MAZE OF BUREAUCRACY

Kafka's grotesque absurdities, written early in the 20th century in what is now Czechoslovakia, exemplify a satirical, fictional approach to describing the everyday social world.

We replied with thanks to the order that I've mentioned already, saying that we didn't need a land-surveyor. But this reply doesn't appear to have reached the original department—I'll call it A—but by mistake went to another department, B. So Department A remained without an answer, but unfortunately our full reply didn't reach B either; whether it was that the order itself was not enclosed by us, or whether it got lost on the way—it was certainly not lost in my department, that I can vouch for—in any case all that arrived at Department B was the covering letter, in which was merely noted that the enclosed order, unfortunately an impractical one, was concerned with the engagement of a landsurveyor. Meanwhile Department A was waiting for our answer; they had, of course, made a memorandum of the case, but as, excusably enough, often happens and is bound to happen even under the most efficient handling, our correspondent trusted to the fact that we would answer him, after which he would either summon the Land-Surveyor or else, if need be, write us further about the matter. As a result he never thought of referring to his memorandum, and the whole thing fell into oblivion. But in De-partment B the covering letter came into the hands of a correspondent famed for his conscientiousness, Sordini by name, an Italian; it is incomprehensible even to me, though I am one of the initiated, why a man of his capacities is left in an almost subordinate position. This Sordini naturally sent us back the unaccompanied covering letter for completion. Now months, if not years, had passed by this time since that first communication from Department A, which is understandable enough, for when—as is the rule—a document goes the proper route, it reaches the department at the outside in a day and is settled that day, but when it once in a while loses its way, then in an organization so efficient as ours its proper destination might be sought for literally with desperation; otherwise it mightn't be found; and then—well, then the search may last really for a long time. Accordingly, when we got Sordini's note we had only a vague memory of the affair; there were only two of us to do the work at that time, Mizzi and myself, the teacher hadn't yet been assigned to us; we only kept copies in the most important instances, so we could only reply in the most vague terms that we knew nothing of this engagement of a landsurveyor and that as far as we knew there was no need for one. . . .

—FRANZ KAFKA

From THE APPRENTICESHIP OF DUDDY KRAVITZ

Richler's fiction, drawing on his Montreal boyhood, is another kind of humorous approach to describing social realities.

The Cohen boy's bar-mitzvah was a big affair in a modern synagogue. The synagogue in fact was so modern that it was not called a synagogue any more. It was called a temple. Duddy had never seen anything like it in his life. There was a choir and an organ and a parking lot next door. The men not only did not wear hats but they sat together with the women. All these things were forbidden by traditional Jewish law, but those who attended the temple were so-called Reform Jews and they had modernized the law to suit life in America. The temple prayer services were conducted in English by Rabbi Harvey Goldstone, M.A., and Cantor "Sonny" Brown. Aside from his weekly sermon, the marriage clinic, the Sunday school, and so on, the rabbi, a most energetic man, was very active in the community at large. He was a fervent supporter of Jewish and Gentile Brotherhood, and a man who unfailingly offered his time to radio stations as a spokesman for the Jewish point of view on subjects that ranged from "Does Israel Mean Divided Loyalties?" to "The Jewish Attitude to Household Pets." He also wrote articles for magazines and a weekly column of religious comfort for the *Tely.* There was a big demand for Rabbi Goldstone as a public speaker and he always made sure to send copies of his speeches to all the newspapers and radio stations.

Mr. Cohen, who was on the temple executive, was one of the rabbi's most enthusiastic supporters, but there were some who did not approve. He was, as one magazine writer had put it, a controversial figure.

"The few times I stepped inside there," Dingleman once said, "I felt like a Jesuit in a whorehouse." . . .

Another dissenter was Uncle Benjy. "There used to be," he said, "some dignity in being against the synagogue. With a severe Orthodox rabbi there were things to quarrel about. There was some pleasure. But this cream puff of a synagogue, this religious drugstore, you might as well spend your life being against the *Reader's Digest.* They've taken all the mystery out of religion."

—Mordecai Richler

From DEMOCRACY IN AMERICA

De Tocqueville was a 19th-century French historian; he made what is often considered the first systematic and impartial study of the United States. This passage exemplifies the essayist's approach to describing social reality.

It is not only the fortunes of men which are equal in America; even their acquirements partake in some degree of the same uniformity. I do not believe that there is a country in the world where, in proportion to the population, there are so few ignorant, and at the same time so few learned, individuals. Primary instruction is within the reach of everybody; superior instruction is scarcely to be obtained by any. This is not surprising; it is, in fact, the necessary consequence of what we have advanced above. Almost all the Americans are in easy circumstances, and can, therefore, obtain the first elements of human knowledge.

In America, there are but few wealthy persons; nearly all Americans have to take a profession. Now, every profession requires an apprenticeship. The Americans can devote to general education only the early years of life. At fifteen, they enter upon their calling, and thus their education generally ends at the age when ours begins. Whatever is done afterwards is with a view to some special and lucrative object; a science is taken up as a matter of business, and the only branch of it which is attended to is such as admits of an immediate practical application.

In America, most of the rich men were formerly poor; most of those who now enjoy leisure were absorbed in business during their youth; the consequence of which is, that, when they might have had a taste for study, they had no time for it, and when the time is at their disposal, they have no longer the inclination. There is no class, then, in America, in which the taste for intellectual pleasures is transmitted with hereditary fortune and leisure, and by which the labors of the intellect are held in honour. Accordingly, there is an equal want of the desire and the power of application to these objects. A middling standard is fixed in America for human knowledge. All approach as near to it as they can; some as they rise, others as they descend. Of course, a multitude of persons are to be found who entertain the same number of ideas on religion, history, science, political economy, legislation, and government. The gifts of intellect proceed directly from God, and man cannot prevent their unequal distribution. But it is at least a consequence of what we have just said, that although the capacities of men are different, as the Creator intended they should be, Americans find the means of putting them to use are equal.

—ALEXIS DE TOCQUEVILLE

From THE VERTICAL MOSAIC

Porter was one of Canada's outstanding sociologists until his death in 1979. This passage, on the class origins of Canadian university students, is a lucid example of the social science approach to describing society.

If social class position with its sociological and psychological elements is an important factor in attendance at high school, it follows that university students would be an even more class-biased group. Motives for the longer educational haul must be transmitted, and the higher cost, which includes immediate income lost, must be met. Some evidence is available on the relationship between university attendance and social class position.

In 1956 the Dominion Bureau of Statistics conducted a national sample survey of university students' income and expenditure. The students included in the study were in various faculties, at various levels of their university careers, from all regions in Canada, and of both sexes. Two of the questions asked in the survey—occupation of chief wage-earner in the parental family and parental family's total yearly income—can be taken as indications of the social class position of the respondents.

Although a student's knowledge of his parental family's total yearly income may not be too accurate, it is interesting that just over one-half of those surveyed reported incomes of less than $5,000. In 1956 seven-tenths of Canadian families had incomes of less than that amount. In the D.B.S. survey

Percentage Distribution of University Student Families and All Canadian Families, by Family Income Groups, 1956

Family Income ($)	Student Families	All Canadian Families
10 000 and over	15.2	3.3
7000–9999	12.2	8.4
5000–6999	21.3	18.7
4000–4999	14.8	15.7
3000–3999	17.5	22.9
2000–2999	11.6	17.0
Under 2000	7.4*	14.0
Total	100.0	100.0

Adapted from D.B.S., *University Student Expenditure and Income in Canada, 1956-57* (Ottawa, 1959), 15, Table 6.

*Includes families where persons are on pension or out of work, where father is deceased and mother working, etc.

more than one-quarter of the students stated that their families had more than $7,000 a year, whereas just over one-tenth of Canadian families fell into this income class. The tendency for university students to be drawn from higher income families can be seen from the table, which shows the distribution of students by family income groups. The median family income of all students was $4,908.

Education for the higher professions is even more a privilege of upper income classes. In law and medicine the median family incomes of student's families were $6,293 and $5,663 respectively. Twenty-eight per cent of the law students and 22 per cent of the medical students came from families with incomes of more than $10,000 compared to 15 per cent of all students in the survey. Only 3.3 per cent of Canadian families

had incomes greater than $10,000 in 1956. The lowest median family income was for the faculties of education which would suggest that greater student aid in these faculties makes it possible to recruit students from lower down the income scale. Women students on the average came from higher income groups than did men. As the class position of the family determines to a great extent whether or not a young person will go to university, it also has an influence on the kind of course he will take when he gets there.

*D.B.S., *University Student Expenditure and Income in Canada, 1956-57* (Ottawa: 1959). The details of the sampling procedures used are given in Appendix B of the foregoing document.

—JOHN PORTER

THE DEVELOPMENT OF SOCIOLOGY

Sociology and the other social sciences emerged from a common tradition of reflection on social phenomena. Although interest in the nature of society and social behaviour has probably always existed, most people in most past societies saw their culture and social organization as fixed and absolute, as given by the gods and therefore both inevitable and perfect. If things went wrong, the fault lay with human beings. Had the rituals not been performed properly? Had the gods not been propitiated? Had the natural order been disturbed in some way? The world in which people lived—a world in which they might suffer poverty or disease, a world in which a few might command or benefit from the many—was a world determined by fate. Generation after generation was born into this world to suffer and die.

By the 17th or 18th century, such views had undergone a fundamental change in Western Europe. Trade with foreign cultures, the discovery of a new world, the religious ferment between Protestants and Catholics, the beginnings of new forms of economic behaviour, the emergence of science and technology, and the creation of new political structures in which laws were seen as made by humans, not God—all of these occurrences had served to make people aware that their world was not an inevitable fate, but a society created by and serving the interests of human beings.

This new awareness was revolutionary in its scope and liberating in its consequences. The point is made particularly well by the German sociologist Max Weber:

> There is a great difference between the fact that a . . . peasant is hungry and knows the while that the deity is unfavorable to him or the spirits are disturbed and consequently nature does not give rain or sunshine at the right time, and the fact that the social order itself may be held responsible for the crisis, even to the poorest laborer. In the first case, men turn to religion; in the second, the work of men is held at fault and the laboring man draws the conclusion it must be changed. ([1927] 1961, 217-18)

Once the order of the world was seen to be a social order, created by human beings, rather than a natural order imposed by God, two questions inevitably arose:

1. What is the nature of the social order, and how did it come into being?
2. How can the social order be changed to eliminate its evident faults?

At first, those interested in what are today called the social sciences were philosophers, historians, or chroniclers. Most of what they wrote was descriptive or prescriptive, moral in tone, and neither analytical nor scientific by modern standards.

The first significant answer to the first question was developed by British and French philosophers such as Thomas Hobbes and Jean-Jacques Rousseau. Essentially their idea was that of the "social contract," the notion that society is the outcome of a rational process whereby people get together and agree to a society designed in the best interest of all.

That those attempting to understand society were philosophers should not tempt you to believe that these issues were academic. The philosophers were merely expressing in more systematic form issues that were being debated, as Weber put it, by even the poorest labourer. These debates led naturally to an attempt to answer the second question, how society could and should be changed. The revolutions in England and Scotland, America, France, the German states, Austria, Hungary and elsewhere in Europe from the mid-17th century through much of 19th were the outcome of this kind of questioning.

By the middle of the 19th century it was obvious that the social philosophy of the 18th century and the political revolutions it had spawned had failed to meet their primary aims of explaining society and making the social order more just and equitable. It was then that some people thought to look to science rather than philosophy for solutions to social problems. The view became common that just as the natural sciences had begun to progress with the development of the scientific method, so too the study of society called for the development of a scientific approach.

In this respect, the work of Auguste Comte (1798–1857) can be seen as important. Although his writings are not much read today, and although his philosophy of positivism (which is based on the tenet that only knowledge garnered by the scientific method is real) is not now seen as relevant, Comte had a profound impact upon the development of the social sciences. It was he who coined the term "sociology" to refer to the science of society, and although his sociology has little similarity to today's science, many sociologists still consider him the first of their number. It is more appropriate, however, to view Comte as being the first to express clearly the new attitude that favoured a science of society, rather than as being the first practising sociologist.

The Founders of Sociology

Modern sociology derives from the work of three men: Karl Marx, Max Weber, and Emile Durkheim. You will see their names appear again and again throughout this text, a testament to the wide range of subjects in which they made contributions and also a sign that their work remains as relevant today as it was when they were alive.

Karl Marx

Karl Marx (1818–1883) was the great social scientist of the 19th century. His work defined what is meant today by economics, political science, history, and sociology (and, of course, more than half the world's present population lives in political states that proclaim themselves to be following Marx's political ideals). Marx's contributions to all the social sciences are too numerous to mention here, and you will find many of his key concepts and views discussed in other chapters of this text. It is difficult to single out one feature of his thought as more crucial than others. One can say, however, that his work broke with the past in that no one before had expressed so fully, rigorously, and systematically the implications of seeing human beings as the creators of their own world and the makers of their own history. That this process is fundamentally a social one, that the world created by and inhabited by people is society, was the starting point for modern sociology.

Marx went beyond this crucial insight, of course; he sought to show how the social world is made, what laws underpin its development, what sort of a society people really live in, and where the social world is heading. Although Marx believed that economic factors were the most important

Karl Marx

in determining these—hence his focus on the concept of class (see Chapter 8)—it was social processes, such as class conflict, that he saw as providing the dynamic of social change. Marx's account is succinctly summarized in an often-quoted passage from the *Communist Manifesto*:

> The history of all hitherto existing society is the history of class struggles. . . . Freedman and slave, patrician and plebian, lord and serf, guildmaster and journeyman, in a word oppressor and oppressed, stood in constant opposition to one another, carried on an uninterrupted, now hidden, now open fight, a fight that each time ended, either in a revolutionary reconstitution of society at large, or in the common ruin of the contending classes. (Marx and Engels [1848] 1969, 9)

Max Weber

Like Marx, Max Weber (1864–1920) was a universal social scientist: an economic and legal historian, political scientist, sociologist, and social science methodologist. The sociologies of religion, power, stratification, organization, and law—in fact, almost every branch of sociology one can think of—have been enriched by Weber's work. And many of Weber's terms, like Marx's, have entered the general vocabulary and become part of the way in which ordinary people see our modern world. For example, Weber gave the modern meanings to such terms as charisma, authority, status, and the Protestant ethic.

Although his range of interests was encyclopedic, Weber focused much of his attention on the social institutions of which society is composed. (The sociological concept of institutions is discussed later in this chapter.) It was Weber who first showed how these institutions are built up from the social relations among people. For Weber, institutions are always

Max Weber   *Emile Durkheim*

processual: they are always composed of acting individuals engaged in social relationships. This insight made Weber sensitive to such forms of power as charisma and to the importance of subjective attitudes and values in the transformation of society.

Weber's most famous work was *The Protestant Ethic and the Spirit of Capitalism*. Still as controversial today as when it was first published in 1905, it suggests that the extraordinary economic, political, and technological transformations of the modern world had their origins, in part, in changing religious attitudes brought about by the Protestant Reformation.

Emile Durkheim

Emile Durkheim (1858–1917) sought to institutionalize sociology as a legitimate discipline. When Durkheim began his university studies, there were no departments of sociology, and he was officially trained in philosophy. Durkheim's determination to change this state of affairs led him to engage in a series of studies designed to prove that sociology deserves separate status as an academic discipline in its own right. He achieved his goal, and by the time he died sociology had become an accepted discipline throughout Europe and North America. Durkheim's works, such as his fascinating book, *Suicide*, are still used today to teach students how to go about the study of sociology.

Sociology and the Other Social Sciences

Durkheim and various counterparts succeeded so well in establishing their areas of interest as legitimate disciplines that the social sciences today, although they emerged from a common tradition, are characterized by rather rigid boundaries, dividing up the tasks of dealing with social phenomena. By the early 20th century, many scholars had a vested interest in separating the social sciences, claiming each could make a unique contribution to a better understanding of society. They were, of course, also enhancing their status, protecting their turf from encroachment, and defending the intrinsic worth of their new disciplines.

This differentiation of the study of social affairs into various disciplines is reflected in the structure of present-day university departments and related academic institutions. In addition to sociology (which is defined later in this chapter), the social sciences are usually understood to comprise anthropology, economics, geography, history (though there is some debate here), psychology, political science, and sociology:

1. **Anthropology** is in many ways the social science closest to sociology. (Many universities have combined anthropology and sociology departments.) Anthropology is the science of culture, with **culture** defined as a set of symbols shared by a group. Until recently, most anthropologists studied pre-industrial or traditional societies. In the past few decades, however, the field has been diversified rapidly to include the study of certain aspects of modern societies, such as urban anthropology. Anthropology includes such subareas as archaeology, physical anthropology, and cultural anthropology.

2. **Economics** is the science of the production and consumption of goods and services. It is perhaps the most quantitatively sophisticated of the social sciences, in part because it has the largest sets of data for analysis (partly in the form of mountains of government statistics); moreover, the fundamental unit of measurement—a country's basic unit of currency—can be used to link up or represent a variety of economic variables. Economics includes several subdivisions of economic theory, econometrics (the development and study of quantitative economic models of economic activity), labour economics, international trade, and money and banking (finance), as well as public-policy and welfare economics. The economic difficulties and policy disagreements of the 1980s suggest that, for all the mathematical sophistication of economics, the science has far to go to develop an accurate understanding of our economy.

3. **Geography** is the study of the relationship between human beings and their natural or physical environment, which ranges from a barren desert to an urban red-light district. Geographers, whose discipline is a relatively new addition to the set of social sciences, straddle the boundary between social and natural science, since much of their work deals with climate, land formations, and so on.

4. **History** is the study of past human interactions and their results. This discipline pre-dates the social sciences. For a long time, it was considered one of the humanities, and great emphasis was placed on the

literary abilities of individual historians to interpret the significance of past events and, with the skills of journalists and essayists, to capture the moods of given events and periods. In this century, historians have become more and more concerned with basing observations not only on traditional historical materials, such as government documents, letters, and memoirs, but also on quantitative evidence, which permits conclusions to be made with more confidence. **Social history** is a subdiscipline concerned with social conditions or large, often non-elite groups in a society; many social historians are using the quantitative methods of sociology to analyze large bodies of data. For example, analysis of the records of early Ontario school inspectors and turn-of-the-century city directories enables social historians to discover the incidence of French as the language of instruction and how much mobility there was in New England in the early 20th century.

5. **Psychology** can be described as the science of the human mind and personality, and used to be an integral part of philosophy. Modern psychologists attempt to understand such processes as learning, perception, emotion, and motivation. Although most academic psychologists engage in some form of experimental research, the field is divided between those whose approach is physiological (many of whom are involved in animal studies) and those whose approach is more social psychological. **Social psychology** is the subdiscipline that studies how psychological characteristics (attitudes and behaviour) are influenced by social background. Both sociologists and psychologists claim this subdiscipline as their own.

6. **Political science**, broadly defined, is the study of political behaviour and institutions, such as voting, political participation, political parties, protest movements, revolutions, legislatures, and courts. It includes the subfields of comparative politics, international relations, and political theory.

Despite this differentiation, you may sense something artificial about a rigid separation of the social sciences. For example, can anyone fully understand political behaviour in isolation from the economic structure of a given society? Can a social phenomenon as complex as a city be studied without reference to the concerns and methodologies of a number of social sciences? By and large, the answer is no.

Indeed, there has been a growing recognition of the interdependence of the social sciences and of the benefit of studying issues from a multidisciplinary approach. This acknowledgment, not surprisingly, developed after practitioners of each of the social sciences had won their battle for its independent status and had begun to feel secure in its niche in academic life. Thus the study of political economy has re-emerged as a field of some importance; other hybrid areas are also recognized. Political sociology, which focuses on the social structural correlates of political behaviour, is a subdivision of sociology that also attracts many political scientists. Social history, as already suggested, combines sociology and history. Moreover, there have emerged area studies such as urban studies, native studies, and developing-area studies, that integrate concerns and approaches of many social sciences (and even the humanities) in examining a single, complex phenomenon.

SOCIOLOGY: SOME BASIC CONCEPTS

We have said that sociology is the scientific study of how the social world works, but this statement is not a formal definition of sociology. It is difficult to know how to proceed here. For many years, every textbook seemed to have yet another definition of its own. Recently, some authors and editors have given up trying to present a short and succinct definition, preferring to let the book as a whole "define" sociology. Nevertheless, a definition has its uses as a guide to the sort of issues or terms a discipline takes as its foundations. Moreover, although sociologists may not be able to agree on a description of what they are doing, most of them do seem to be engaged in more or less the same enterprise, the same sorts of things. Even though they may disagree on where to place the emphasis or on the implications of their research, almost all would agree that their primary task—the one that precedes all their other goals—is that of uncovering what is really going on in society, how the social world really works.

Thus, for our purposes, we can define **sociology** as the scientific study of society and the social relationships of which it is composed. Although this definition does not include all that sociology is concerned with, it provides a guide to the field and to some of the basic terms used by sociologists in the course of their activities.

Society is a highly abstract term that requires some clarification; it can be understood as referring to a set of social institutions that channel behaviour in everyday life. The term social institution is used in sociology in a special sense. Most people think of institutions as places—banks, universities, prisons—identifiable as a building or group of buildings dedicated to some task. For sociologists, **institutions** are reciprocal sets of patterned social relationships. Thus, the family is a social institution because it is composed of such relationships—as are banks but also peer groups and ethnic groups, prisons but also the legal system as a whole. Institutions are found wherever regular reciprocal relationships engage any set of people, for example: mother, father, son, daughter; teller, customer, branch manager; warden, guard, prisoner.

Social institutions are themselves composed of two essential elements, which can be examined separately: (1) the people who engage in interaction with one another, and (2) the patterns that develop when this interaction becomes habitualized, routinized, or regulated. Institutions exist only because people act in terms of them. Anyone who has ever been in a classroom in which one of the participants refused to act like a student (or the instructor failed to act like a teacher) knows how easily disrupted social institutions can be. Being a mother or a father, a teacher or a student, or fulfilling almost any other institutional role is in large measure determined by others' willingness to accept the individual in that role and thus to participate properly in the social relationship. The study of how persons interact to create, sustain, or transform social relationships is referred to as **microsociology**, and it covers a large field of sociological research.

Although individuals have a measure of choice as to whether or not to act out institutional roles, they have very little choice as to how to act out these roles. Institutions channel behaviour; they "predefine" for people how to be a mother, a student, a bank teller, or a prison inmate. Most institutions precede the individual, and people learn, through socialization, how to participate in them properly. Thus, the patterns of interaction have a reality independent of the persons who enact them. Studying these patterns and the ways in which they fit together to create a society is referred to as **macrosociology**, and this term also covers a large field of sociological research.

To sum up, society comprises sets of social institutions that in turn comprise sets of social relationships. While institutions guide and predefine people's behaviour in particular settings, society is the sum of these institutions, and it channels most human behaviour in almost all aspects of everyday life. To be a member of society is to participate in social institutions.

SOCIOLOGICAL PERSPECTIVES

Although most sociologists would agree with the description of sociology just given, the discipline is today characterized by the existence of several very different and competing perspectives. Three of these perspectives, structural functionalism, conflict theory, and symbolic interactionism, are referred to often in this text. A brief introduction to each is in order here.

Structural Functionalism

A perspective that emphasizes the ways in which society is integrated to act as a coherent and consistent whole is **structural functionalism** (sometimes simply referred to as **functionalism**). Key concepts in this perspective are function, structure, and norm.

Functionalism has been described as based on three assumptions:

> (1) One necessary condition for survival of a society is minimal integration of its parts; (2) the term **function** refers to those processes that maintain this necessary integration or solidarity; (3) thus, in each society structural features can be shown to contribute to the maintenance of necessary solidarity. (Turner 1986, 29, italics added)

We saw an example of function in the discussion of Merton's manifest and latent functions. **Structural features** refers to the patterned ways in which social institutions are integrated to make up and stabilize the society. Essentially, functionalists look for the consequences that particular social institutions and the actions of the people within them have for the integration of society.

A question remains: Why do people act in ways that contribute to the integration of society? The functionalists' answer focuses upon **norms**— that is, upon sets of socially derived expectations about appropriate behaviour in particular settings. The most important of these norms are learned in childhood during socialization. It is at this time that individuals learn the behaviour expected of them from parents, relatives, peers, teachers, and the media. Later in life, people continue to act in those ways that are socially approved. They also enter new social institutions, such as universities or occupations, and learn new norms there. People in different institutions have different norms. For example, the norms that guide the behaviour of a doctor in a hospital during the course of the day are quite different from those that guide a convict in a penal institution. Those norms that are particularly important to the integration of a society are the **values** of the society, and the functionalists see values as shared by almost everyone. Such a view of norms and values is referred to as a **consensus model** of society. (Norms, values, and a variety of other common sociological terms are further described in Chapter 3; socialization is examined at length in Chapter 4.)

Conflict Theory

Whereas functionalists look at how societies remain stable, **conflict theorists** focus on the dynamic processes that promote change. Derived in large part from the views of Marx, this perspective sees group conflict as the key to understanding society. Collins provides a succinct summary of the conflict position:

> For conflict theory, the basic insight is that human beings are sociable but conflict prone animals. Why is there conflict? Above all else, there is conflict because violent coercion is always a potential resource, and it is a zero-sum sort. This does not imply anything about the inherence of drives to dominate; what we do know firmly is that being coerced is an intrinsically unpleasant experience, and hence that any use of coercion, even by a small minority, calls forth conflict in the form of antagonism to being dominated. Add to this the fact that coercive power, especially as represented in the state, can be used to bring one economic goods and emotional gratification—and to deny them to others—and we can see that the availability of coercion as a resource ramifies conflicts throughout the entire society. The simultaneous existence of emotional bases for solidarity—which may well be the basis of cooperation, as Durkheim emphasized—only adds group divisions and tactical resources to be used in these conflicts. (1975, 59)

It is worth noting that although some people use the terms Marxism and conflict theory interchangeably, many conflict theorists reject this equation. Some follow Marx in seeing the basic social conflict as one of class; others identify it as one of cultures, historical groups, and so on.

Symbolic Interactionism

The sociological perspective that focuses on the microsociological processes of everyday life is **symbolic interactionism**. Derived in large part from the work of the American philosopher George Herbert Mead (discussed in detail in Chapter 4), symbolic interactionism looks for the meanings that guide people's understanding of everyday life interactions. Whereas functionalists focus on social institutions and societal integration, and whereas conflict theorists focus on groups and their conflicting interests, interactionist sociologists are particularly interested in studying the microsociological processes whereby individuals develop a sense of self and interact with others through symbolic processes. The most important of these processes to the interactionists is **taking the role of the other**, the process in which individuals try to see themselves as others see them and adjust their behaviour accordingly. The efforts of people to try to control the perception of themselves by others, as described above by Erving Goffman, requires just such a process of taking the role of the other.

Which Perspective Is "Right"?

All three perspectives have many variations, and all three have made important contributions to sociological understanding. Most sociologists have no firm commitment to any one of these perspectives but simply make use of whichever set of ideas, theories, or research findings are most helpful for their own work. Students sometimes complain that sociologists cannot seem to make up their minds about which perspective is "right"; the truth is that social phenomena are so complex that sociologists find much that is "right" in all three perspectives.

From THE SOCIOLOGICAL IMAGINATION

The sociological imagination enables its possessor to understand the larger historical scene in terms of its meaning for the inner life and the external career of a variety of individuals. It enables him to take into account how individuals, in the welter of their daily experience, often become falsely conscious of their social positions. Within that welter, the framework of modern society is sought, and within that framework the psychologies of a variety of men and women are formulated. By such means the personal uneasiness of individuals is focused upon explicit troubles and the indifference of publics is transformed into involvement with public issues.

The first fruit of this imagination—and the first lesson of the social science that embodies it—is the idea that the individual can understand his own experience and gauge his own fate only by locating himself within his period, that he can know his own chances in life only by becoming aware of those of all individuals in his circumstances. In many ways it is a terrible lesson; in many ways a magnificent one. We do not know the limits of man's capacities for supreme effort or willing degradation, for agony or glee, for pleasurable brutality or the sweetness of reason. But in our time we have come to know that the limits of "human nature" are frighteningly broad. We have come to know that every individual lives, from one generation to the next, in some society; that he lives out a biography, and that he lives it out within some historical sequence. By the fact of his living he contributes, however minutely, to the shaping of this society and to the course of its history, even as he is made by society and by its historical push and shove.

The sociological imagination enables us to grasp history and biography and the relations between the two within society. That is its task and its promise. To recognize this task and this promise is the mark of the classic social analyst.

It is characteristic of Herbert Spencer—turgid, polysyllabic, comprehensive; of E.A. Ross—graceful, muckraking, upright; of Auguste Comte and Emile Durkheim; of the intricate and subtle Karl Mannheim. It is the quality of all that is intellectually excellent in Karl Marx; it is the clue to Thorstein Veblen's brilliant and ironic insight, to Joseph Schumpeter's many-sided constructions of reality; it is the basis of the psychological sweep of W.E.H. Lecky no less than of the profundity and clarity of Max Weber. And it is the signal of what is best in contemporary studies of man and society.

No social study that does not come back to the problems of biography, of history, and of their intersections within a society has completed its intellectual journey. Whatever the specific problems of the classic social analysts, however limited or however broad the features of social reality they have examined, those who have been imaginatively aware of the promise of their work have consistently asked three sorts of questions:

1. What is the structure of this particular society as a whole? What are its essential components, and how are they related to one another? How does it differ from other varieties of social order? Within it, what is the meaning of any particular feature for its continuance and for its change?

2. Where does this society stand in human history? What are the mechanics by which it is changing? What is its place within and its meaning for the development of humanity as a whole? How does any particular feature we are examining affect, and how is it affected by, the historical period in which it moves? And this period—what are its essential features? How does it differ from other periods? What are its characteristic ways of history-making?

3. What varieties of men and women now prevail in this society and in this period? And what varieties are coming to prevail? In what ways are they selected and formed, liberated and repressed, made sensitive and blunted? What kinds of "human nature" are revealed in the conduct and character we observe in this society in this period? And what is the meaning for "human nature" of each and every feature of the society we are examining?

Whether the point of interest is a great power state or a minor literary mood, a family, a prison, a creed—these are the kinds of questions the best social analysts have asked. They are the intellectual pivots of classic studies of man in society—and they are the questions inevitably raised by any mind possessing the sociological imagination. For that imagination is the capacity to shift from one perspective to another—from the political to the psychological; from examination of a single family to comparative assessment of the national budgets of the world; from the theological school to the military establishment; from considerations of an oil industry to studies of contemporary poetry. It is the capacity to range from the most impersonal and remote transformations to the most intimate features of the human self—and to see the relations between the two. Back of its use there is always the urge to know the social and historical meaning of the individual in the society and in the period in which he has his quality and his being.

That, in brief, is why it is by means of the sociological imagination that men now hope to grasp what is going on in the world, and to understand what is happening in themselves as minute points of the intersections of biography and history within society. In large part, contemporary man's self-conscious view of himself as at least an outsider, if not a permanent stranger, rests upon an absorbed realization of social relativity and of the transformative power of history. The sociological imagination is the most fruitful form of this self-consciousness. By its use men whose mentalities have swept only a series of limited orbits often come to feel as if suddenly awakened in a house with which they had only supposed themselves to be familiar. Correctly or incorrectly, they often come to feel that they can now provide themselves with adequate summations, cohesive assessments, comprehensive orientations. Older decisions that once appeared sound now seem to them products of a mind unaccountably dense. Their capacity for astonishment is made lively again. They acquire a new way of thinking, they experience a transvaluation of values: in a word, by their reflection and by their sensibility, they realize the cultural meaning of the social sciences.

—C. WRIGHT MILLS

APPLYING SOCIOLOGY

What role does sociology play in the world? Why should sociology be studied?

Like the natural sciences, sociology has both a basic (sometimes called pure) and an applied dimension. **Basic (pure) sociology** is concerned with increasing theoretical understanding of society. This is knowledge for its own sake. Basic sociological work is often of primary concern to other professional sociologists, who take seriously the theoretical and methodological disputes that typify sociology (as these disputes do any other academic discipline). The settling of these disputes—and the inevitable discovery of new ones—is the way in which the formal discipline can be said to progress (or at least evolve). An example of such an issue is whether the fundamental social processes of industrialization and modernization tend to reduce or exacerbate ethnic tensions, and why.

Applied sociology or research is concerned with applying sociological knowledge or methods to solving real problems. It deals with the problems that policy-makers have to solve or with which people are confronted in their daily lives. At times people want some factual information best obtained by using sociological instruments: say, is there discrimination against blacks in professional sports and, if so, of what kind? At times they want to solve a clearly specified problem: how can we lower the rates of teenage pregnancies? At times they want to explore an issue, such as the relationship between alcoholism and child abuse in families. These kinds of questions, most of which are seen as problems, are investigated with an ultimate view to using the information gathered as a basis for some kind of policy or intervention. The decision resulting from sociological information may range from a new piece of legislation passed by a government to a change in the guidelines used by an alcohol treatment centre.

Researchers may raise or treat the issues in a number of ways. **Evaluation research** involves the study of the effectiveness of a project or a program after it has been initiated. A **social experiment** means setting up a research design before a program is initiated, again to study its effects—namely, to test whether it has achieved the desired results. Both these approaches use similar methods, notably the comparison of an experimental group that experienced the program with a control group that did not.

Another type of research is the large **policy-oriented study** designed to generate data that relate to specific topics; these data can then be used to examine relationships and explore or test hypotheses about these relationships. Such large-scale surveys may be the basis for designing policies and programs and for establishing subsequent experiments or evaluations. These studies of social problems, in other words, suggest possible remedies that can then be studied using more precise methods. An example of such a study is the one by John Porter et al. on the impact of social and cultural mileux on educational aspirations.

CAREERS IN SOCIOLOGY

What do sociologists do? Relatively few people work as professional sociologists, and the majority of them are college or university teachers. Such academic sociologists not only teach but also conduct research, and many engage in criticism on social and political issues of the day or work as consultants of various kinds, often in fields of social policy. Other professional sociologists are employed directly by governments, corporations, and survey-research firms where sociological skills are in demand. A few are branching out into the area of **clinical sociology** where, like clinical psychologists, they offer professional advice to people or organizations with "social" problems. Thus, large-scale organizations such as business firms, hospitals, and sports teams may use the services of sociologists to enable them to accomplish their goals more efficiently.

It is important to recognize that most people who study sociology will never work as professional sociologists. However, their sociological training will stand them in good stead whatever their occupational future.

First, many sociological courses that are part of an undergraduate program are directly relevant to possible choices for further graduate or professional study. Some examples are offered below. Second and equally important, many sociological skills—such as data analysis, research design, statistics, the writing of research papers, and library and archival research—are useful for practically any job that relies on informed, rational decision-making or problem-solving. Knowing how to find, assemble, and interpret data and to draw appropriate conclusions—in other words, how to test theories on the basis of evidence—are skills valuable in any career.

Finally, sociologists like to think that the study of sociology may yield valuable personal benefits to the student. Students of sociology have increased their understanding of the society in which they live. They know how "the system" works and may, as a result, be better able to cope with or change it successfully. The words of politicians or messages on the TV screen will be scrutinized more rigorously. People who are familiar with some of the results or findings of sociology may be sceptical of quick-fix "sloganeered" solutions to complex social problems. In short, sociological study can help to produce more competent, effective citizens. In addition, it may lead students to understand the conditions of their own lives and to develop insight into their own personalities and relationships. Family life, relations with friends and lovers, the courses and consequence of health-related behaviours and so on may come into clearer focus.

People with graduate training in sociology are also increasingly found in many areas of government and industry, such as social work, family and employment counselling, urban research and planning, **demography** (the study of the distribution and growth of population), probation and parole work, public-opinion polling, advertising and market research, personnel work, health-services planning, recreation work, cultural exchange programs, and so on.

Clearly, as suggested earlier, university studies can be successfully integrated into the preparation for many careers. Here are a few examples of undergraduate courses related to occupational interests. The list of courses in each area is not exhaustive, but does give an idea of the range of areas covered and their practical benefits.

For those interested in careers in a *health-related field*:

1. Medicine and Health in Modern Society
2. Deviance
3. Modern Social Psychology
4. Sociology of Health and Illness
5. Sociology of Mental Disorder
6. The Professions
7. Applied Sociology
8. The Sociology of Medicine

For those interested in careers in *law, law enforcement, or criminology*:

1. Deviance
2. Social Problems
3. The Professions
4. The Sociology of Law
5. Crime

For those interested in careers in the *business world or management*:

1. Technology and Society
2. Industrial Sociology
3. The Professions
4. Women and Work
5. Applied Sociology

For those interested in careers in *social work, education, government or counselling*:

1. Population and Society
2. Family and Kinship
3. Social Problems
4. Socialization
5. Sociology of Education
6. Personal Service Organizations

For those interested in careers in *communications, the media, or the arts*:

1. Canadian Mass Communications
2. Sociology of Innovation and Cultural Change
3. Research on Women and the Media
4. Television in Society
5. Sociology of Popular Culture

For *many careers*, including those already described, some familiarity with statistics and qualitative and quantitative social-research methods are required so as, at the very least, to understand the findings of social science and research. Many sociology courses provide these tools:

1. Elementary Statistics in Sociology
2. Introduction to Quantitative Analysis
3. Networks and Social Structures
4. Field Methods in Sociology
5. Survey Analysis
6. Quantitative Methods of Social Research

For those in the *physical or natural sciences* who are interested in the social aspects of science:

1. Sociology of Innovation and Cultural Change
2. Technology and Society
3. Sociology of Science

For those interested in *comparative studies of diverse societies and groups* as a substantive field:

1. Class and Politics in the United States
2. Class, Ethnicity, and Politics
3. Canadian Society
4. Social Change
5. Comparative Ethnic Relations
6. Social and Political Movements
7. Sociology of the Jews in North America
8. Social Change in the Caribbean
9. Society and Politics of Germany

FOR FURTHER READING

Berger, Peter L.
    1963 *Invitation to Sociology*. Garden City, N.Y.: Doubleday Anchor.
    Berger provides an absorbing and entertaining introduction to the main ideas of the sociological perspective.
Durkheim, Emile
    1951 *Suicide*. New York: Free Press.
    This is a classic sociological work that, as the text notes, is still on the list of required reading for every aspiring sociologist.
Marx, Karl, and Friedrich Engels
    [1848] 1969 *The Communist Manifesto*. New York: Regnery.
    Nowhere else do Marx and Engels present as clear and systematic an analysis of the nature and dynamics of social change.
Mills, C. Wright
    1959 *The Sociological Imagination*. New York: Oxford University Press.
    This book is a clever critique of some major perspectives in sociology and an inspiring call for a sociology that makes a real difference in the lives of ordinary people.
Weber, Max
    1958 *The Protestant Ethic and the Spirit of Capitalism*. New York: Charles Scribner's Sons.
    Perhaps the most controversial work ever produced by a sociologist, this closely argued essay is one of Weber's most accessible works.

CHAPTER 2

SOCIOLOGICAL METHODS

Alfred A. Hunter

While you and i have lips and voices which
are for kissing and to sing with
who cares if some oneeyed son of a bitch
invents an instrument to measure Spring with? . . .

                    (cummings 1972, 264, xxxiii)

Be it cause for delight or despair, sociologists seldom agree on much or for long. And sociologists in different countries tend to disagree about different things. This divergence may always have been so, but it has not always been seen to be so. A generation ago, the Canadian sociologist Kaspar Naegele could claim, "The study of society as a cumulative and, therefore, scientific enterprise is under way" (1961, 3). Today, Canadian sociologists are as likely to see a "sociology galloping off madly in all directions" (Clark 1976, 141)—some of them scientific, others not.

Within the field of sociology in Canada—and indeed, throughout the Western world—there has been a recent flowering of disparate theoretical points of view. Where once there was the functionalist perspective and little else, many schools of thought now contend, including a resurgent Marxism in several varieties. Analysts have revived methodological debates that were pronounced dead even before sociology became firmly established in Canadian universities in the 1960s. In 1959, the American sociologist Robert Bierstedt observed:

> The methodological controversies that disturbed the sociological scene both a hundred years ago . . . in Germany and twenty-five years ago in the pages of the American journals have now largely subsided. No one argues any more whether or not sociology is or ought to be a science and whether or not the scientific method is applicable to the study of social phenomena. (xviii)

No one then, maybe. But some do now.

SOCIOLOGY AS SCIENCE

Is sociology science? If what we mean by **science** is systematic observation of the real world for the purpose of developing theories to describe the occurrence of certain events as originating in the prior occurrence of certain other events, then much sociology is science. That is, most sociologists pose questions of the form: "How does this event (getting divorced, committing suicide, moving from one place to another, voting for a socialist party) come about?" They then seek answers by careful study of people or groups to see if the event in question seems regularly to follow certain other event(s) (say, unemployment), as proposed in a theory. If the answer is yes, the theory is retained as a potentially accurate description of how the event occurs; if the answer is no, the theory is either revised for future use or discarded altogether in favour of some other theory.

If much sociology is science, however, it has not proceeded very far in building up a well-tested body of explanatory theory, which is the essential criterion of the success of a science. In this regard, though, some sciences (such as geology) have never been very successful; others (such as biology) languished for centuries before achieving success, and still others (such as physics) almost define what we mean by success. So scientific sociology's uncertain progress in developing theory does not mean that the effort will ultimately fail.

A more serious objection comes from those who think that social life cannot be understood through the pairing of systematic observation with explanatory theory. It is not possible here to list all the arguments for this position, which calls into question the fundamental assumptions of a scientific sociology. The following are some of the more important arguments:

1. Since social behaviour differs across cultures and over time, universal social theories cannot be developed.
2. Objectivity is impossible in social inquiry; sociologists' own values influence what they choose to study, how they feel about what they observe, what they take to be facts, and how they analyze their data.
3. Observational techniques are inadequate for the study of social life, which involves such subjective phenomena as meanings, motives, and goals.

I will begin with the first two arguments, which are easier to deal with than the third. The fact that social behaviour differs outwardly across cultures and over time does not necessarily mean that it cannot conform to a single set of underlying principles. There are many instances in the physical sciences in which phenomena that appear very different to the eye can be explained in terms of the same physical laws; examples are falling leaves and flowing rivers (theory of gravity), or the aurora borealis and the dreaded static cling of clothes in winter (theory of electro-magnetism). Although examples in the social sciences may be more difficult to find, they do exist. For example, it has been discovered that, regardless of the language they speak, people everywhere judge objects and events in terms of three fundamental dimensions of connotative meaning: evaluation, potency, and activity. That is, despite the enormous variety of words, in many different languages, that people use to give their impressions of things, these descriptions largely boil down to assessments of objects or events as good or bad (evaluation), strong or weak (potency), and active or passive (activity).

Second, values undeniably influence what sociologists do. But this fact is also true of physicists, chemists, and biologists. If it makes impossible a science of society, it also makes impossible the sciences of physics, chemistry, and biology.

To address the third argument, it is true that social life involves meanings, motives, goals, and other mental states directly accessible only to those who experience them, and that some aspects of human conduct can probably be explained only by reference to these states. How can states internal to individuals be studied scientifically? If they are purely private experiences, they are of no scientific interest, since science provides explanations only for observable events. However, if they are not entirely private but are expressed through people's behaviour, then this behaviour (including people's verbal descriptions of their mental states) can be studied, just as any other actions can. (This point is parodied by the one-liner about two social scientists—probably psychologists—greeting each other: "Hi, how am I? You are fine.")

Nothing in these arguments, then, refutes the possibility of a successful scientific sociology. At the same time, our answers do not prove that the only good sociology is scientific sociology. If most sociologists, in their own individual ways, are working to develop a scientific sociology, not all of them are. Because the methodology of scientific sociology is the most advanced, however, this chapter will concentrate on its essential features, leaving to others the description of the methodologies of non-scientific sociologies.

PURPOSES OF SOCIAL RESEARCH

Social research is not all of a piece; it varies in its purpose and, hence, in its relationship to sociology as science. In particular, it is important to distinguish between basic and applied research and between exploratory research and hypothesis testing.

Basic research is carried out for the ultimate purpose of developing explanatory theory. For example, a hypothesis may be tested ("Does economic recession make the young more career-minded?") or a new phenomenon that does not easily fit into existing scientific categories may be described so that those categories can be refined or redefined ("Does Western separatism seem to be a left-wing, a right-wing, or some other kind of political movement?"). **Applied research** is undertaken to satisfy some practical concern. For example, a public-opinion poll may be commissioned by a political party planning its election strategy; the relative effectiveness of different kinds of French-as-a-second-language programs might be assessed by a ministry of education wishing to improve teaching methods.

Basic research and applied research are not antithetical but complementary: the former is concerned with theory and the latter with practice. They often make use of the same research techniques (measurement scales, research designs, statistical procedures, and so on), and the results from one are sometimes useful to the other. For example, a way of finding that one approach to second-language instruction is more effective than another may also constitute a test of the theories of language acquisition embodied in these approaches. In this chapter we will describe only the methodology associated with basic research.

Exploratory research is preliminary research in that it involves observing relatively unstudied phenomena in order to identify their important features. Since exploratory research is devoted to discovering the new, there are few reliable rules for discovery. This is not to say that it is unimportant; even the most determinedly scientific sociologists engage in it continually. **Hypothesis-testing research** aims to check proposed explanations against real-world observations, which implies the existence of a set of "rules for demonstration" (Coser 1975). These rules are the methodology of science and the major topic of this chapter.

ELEMENTS OF A SCIENTIFIC THEORY

What are the elements of a scientific theory? First, a theory refers to a particular **unit of analysis**: the objects or events which the investigator observes and whose characteristics the theory purports to explain. For example, in a social theory referring to individual people, individuals are the unit of analysis. The wide variety of units of analysis includes families, business firms, cities, social classes, countries, elections, riots, revolutions, and wars.

Second, theories contain statements about **variables**, aspects of a unit of analysis that differ in degree or form from one object or event to another or that change over time. That is, variables are features of objects or events—not entire objects or events as a whole—that are not the same for all cases or that do not remain constant from day to day. Moreover, variables identify elements common to a number of observations; thus, they are abstractions from the real world of concrete things. Exhibit 2-1 depicts the relationships between an abstract, theoretical variable, A, and a number of specific phenomena, the as, which have the underlying element A in common. For example, say the unit of analysis is countries and the theoretical variable labour unrest. Strikes, lockouts, and absenteeism may all be concrete phenomena with labour unrest as the common underlying element. If the unit of analysis is individuals, and the theoretical variable job satisfaction, particular observations relating to this attribute might include contentment with salary, pleasure derived from the tasks involved, happiness with co-workers, and optimism about opportunities for promotion. It is important to remember that theoretical variables are abstractions from the empirical world; they are never entirely embodied in any single, concrete thing.

Variables are of two kinds: quantitative and qualitative. **Quantitative variables** show differences in degree or magnitude; familiar physical examples are distance, weight, and temperature. **Qualitative variables** show variation in form or type, such as whether matter is organic or inorganic, whether animals are vertebrates or invertebrates, or whether trees are coniferous or deciduous. Both labour unrest and job satisfaction

Exhibit 2-1
A Theoretical Variable and Some Specific Observations

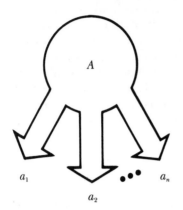

Theoretical variable
(e.g., labour unrest)

Specific observations
(e.g., strikes, lockouts, absenteeism)

are quantitative variables, since they may exist to varying degrees. Other common quantitative variables are self-esteem, wealth, power, and socio-economic status. Gender, on the other hand, is a good example of a qualitative variable. Gender differences are generally thought of as differences of kind, not degree; a person is either male or female. Other common qualitative variables are ethnicity (Scottish, Jewish, native Indian, and so on), region of residence (Atlantic provinces, Quebec, Ontario, the Prairies, British Columbia), marital status (married, separated, widowed, divorced, single), and the Marxian class categories (bourgeoisie, petite bourgeoisie, and proletariat).

Scientific theories provide potentially testable explanations in the form of hypotheses. In its simplest form, a **hypothesis** is a statement that certain differences or changes in one variable (known as the **independent variable**) precede in time and result in particular changes in another variable (known as the **dependent variable**). So, for example, one might hypothesize (on the basis of Marxist theory) that individuals (unit of analysis) who move from the bourgeoisie or petite bourgeoisie into the proletariat (a change in an independent variable) tend to become more radical in their political attitudes (a change in a dependent variable). Or it might be proposed (from Max Weber's analysis) that business firms (unit of analysis) that become more bureaucratized (a change in an independent variable) tend to become more efficient (a change in a dependent variable).

In considering hypotheses, a number of points should be noted. Hypotheses must be potentially testable, which means (1) that the relevant variables are, at least in principle, capable of being measured, and (2) that the hypotheses themselves are not true by definition and could conceivably be shown to be false. A good test for this latter is simply to assert the negative of the hypothesis and then to ask if this negation is illogical. For example, one can say that movement into the proletariat is not followed by radicalism, or that bureaucratization does not lead to efficiency.

These statements may be true or false, but they are not illogical. Consider, on the other hand, Howard Becker's famous "theory" (1963) of how one can use marijuana for pleasure. It posits as a necessary condition that one must first enjoy the effects. Yet how could one use marijuana for pleasure if the effects were not enjoyed?

The idea that the occurrence of one event results in the occurrence of another resides in theories, not in the real-world objects or events that the theories describe. That is, we attempt to give order and meaning to what we see by viewing things as if changes in one variable led to changes in another; we do not seek to prove that such relationships actually obtain in social life. The most important reason for this is that such relationships can be disproved, but can never be conclusively proved, since we can never examine all cases of a phenomenon at one time, and some case observed in the future may disprove a hypothesized causal relationship. Consequently, science advances not by proving hypotheses but by a process of disproving or failing to disprove them.

A hypothesis proposes, not just that a change in one variable accompanies a change in another, but that one change both precedes and results in the second. Thus, it is important to distinguish between asymmetric relationships between variables over time and simple empirical associations (accompanying changes in variables). An absurd example may help to illustrate the distinction. Space shuttle voyages began in the 1980s. The 1980s also marked the first time a Canadian baseball team reached the World Series semifinals. This association proves neither that Canadian baseball teams benefit from the existence of space shuttles nor that shuttle travel is more likely when Canadian baseball teams play well.

Everything in the real world is probably related, however remotely, to everything else. For this reason, hypotheses that simply state that a change in one variable leads to a change in another are not very informative and are difficult to disprove. That is, since the kind of change is not specified, almost any empirical association between two variables can be used to support the hypothesis (except where it can be shown that the hypothesis proposes a time ordering between the variables that is inconsistent with what is actually found). It is necessary, then, that a scientific hypothesis specify just what kind of change in the dependent variable is expected to follow a particular change in the independent variable.

The form this specification takes depends on whether the variables are quantitative or qualitative. There are four possibilities:

1. Quantitative-quantitative. For hypotheses in which the independent and dependent variables are both quantitative, increases in the independent are specified to lead to increases (or decreases) in the dependent. For example, "The higher the status of an individual's occupation [*quantitative, independent*], the higher his or her job satisfaction will be [*quantitative, dependent*]."

2. Qualitative-quantitative. For hypotheses in which the independent variable is qualitative and the dependent variable quantitative, movement between certain categories of the independent variable is specified to lead to increases (or decreases) in the dependent variable. "Persons who enter age-segregated communities, such as boarding schools and retirement homes [*qualitative, independent*], experience reduced levels of social contact [*quantitative, dependent*]" is an example of such a hypothesis.

3. Quantitative-qualitative. If the independent variable is quantitative and the dependent variable qualitative, an increase (or decrease) in the independent variable leads to movement between certain categories of the dependent. An example of such a hypothesis is "The lower one's level of self-esteem [*quantitative, independent*], the more likely one will be to commit suicide [*qualitative, dependent*]."

4. Qualitative-qualitative. If both the independent and dependent variables are qualitative, movement between certain categories of the former is specified to lead to movement between certain categories of the latter. For example: "People who experience involuntary loss of employment [*qualitative, independent*] are more likely to separate from their spouses [*qualitative, dependent*]."

Exhibit 2-2 shows how hypotheses are often represented in the form of a diagram. *A* is the independent variable (and the *a*s are specific observations having *A* in common), *B* is the dependent variable (and the *b*s are specific observations having *B* in common), and the straight, one-headed arrow indicates that it is changes in *A* that result in changes in

Exhibit 2-2
Relationships between an Independent and a Dependent Variable

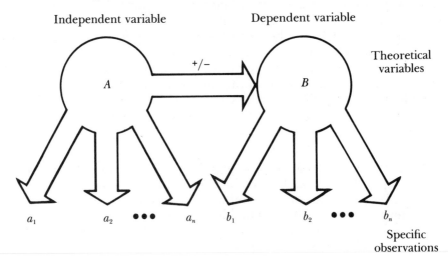

B, not vice versa. If both variables are quantitative, a plus or minus sign next to the arrow is frequently used to indicate that increases in *A* are specified to lead to increases or decreases in *B*.

PRINCIPLES OF MEASUREMENT

To test hypotheses is to assess whether they are consistent with what we can observe of the real world. The first step is to measure the variables involved. (Measurement is, in fact, so important to sociologists that they are sometimes facetiously described as "anthropologists who can count.") To **measure** means to assign numbers to objects or events according to certain rules. In general, it involves applying some calibrated instrument to an object or event to determine its membership in a particular category or its location along some continuum. Litmus paper (calibrated in the colours of red and blue) can be dipped into your favourite lake to identify whether it is acidic (red) or basic (blue). Audiometers (calibrated in decibels) can be used to gauge how loud the party down the hall is. Rulers (calibrated in centimetres) can be laid against objects to estimate their physical dimensions. Thermometers (calibrated in degrees Celsius) can be inserted into substances to measure temperatures.

In sociology as in any other science, the principles of measurement involve expressing theoretical variables in terms of real-world observations. And as in any science, there is no strictly logical way to do this, since theoretical variables are abstractions from the real world. The problem then is to find a set of concrete operations that corresponds plausibly to the definition of a theoretical variable but is not directly implied by it. For this reason, a scale to measure a theoretical variable is often referred to as an **operational definition** or **indicator** of that variable; the act of measuring a variable is referred to as operationalizing it.

Qualitative theoretical variables are abstractly defined as sets of mutually exclusive, all-inclusive categories into which every member of a set of units of analysis can be classified. Sex, for example, is defined as the categories male and female; every individual—dead, living, or yet to be born—can be regarded as fitting into one or the other, but not both, of these categories. Such theoretical definitions do not, however, always tell us exactly how real cases are to be classified into categories. So we must develop empirical rules for the classification of actual cases; these rules constitute the operational definitions of the variables in question. In the case of sex, these rules might involve a question in a questionnaire, a chromosome count (as is done for the Olympic games), or simple observation by an interviewer (when asked in a face-to-face interview, this question can provoke hostility). Finally, each category is given a unique identifying code—usually a number—(for example, 1 for male, 2 for female), and each unit actually studied is assigned the number of the category to which it is judged to belong; for instance, those persons operationally defined as male are scored 1 on the sex variable and those defined as female are scored 2. Since the categories involved are qualitatively but not quantitatively distinct, it does not matter which numbers are given to which categories—only that no two categories have the same number. Such instruments to measure qualitative variables are referred to as **nominal scales** because objects or events are named in terms of their category memberships.

Quantitative theoretical variables are abstractly defined as continua along which all members of a set of units of analysis can be placed. Job satisfaction, for example, is a quantitative variable. All employed individuals can be thought of as located at points along a continuum of job satisfaction; the location varies depending on how positively they evaluate their work. Again, such abstract conceptions do not tell us directly where real cases are to be placed. So again we must establish some concrete criteria for measurement. In the case of job satisfaction, people might be asked to respond to a number of questions about their attitudes toward their work, using a set of graded categories ("excellent," "very good," "average," "fair," "poor"). Or trained observers might watch people at their work and then rate the positiveness of the workers' attitudes. There are all sorts of other possibilities. Finally, the possible judgments that people can make of themselves, that others can make of them, and so on, are assigned numerical values, depending on how far along the continuum they are seen to fall; each real unit observed is given the number corresponding to the judgment actually made. Continuing the example of job satisfaction, the response "excellent" might be assigned a score of 5, "very good" a score of 4, and all the way down to a score of 1 for "poor." Then a person who described his or her salary as "average" would be assigned a score of 3 for this aspect. On this type of instrument, called a **quantitative scale**, the numbers are not arbitrary; rather, they are assigned according to the magnitude of the characteristic.

Although the principles involved in measurement are universal, sociological measurement is not very advanced in some respects. First, in the physical examples cited above, decibels, centimetres, and degrees Celsius are generally accepted units for measuring sound, distance, and temperature, respectively; their meanings are the same everywhere. Few, if any, sociological variables, however, are measured in such a **standard metric**. In the case of job satisfaction, for example, the five-point scale described above is only one of many possible scales that might be (and have been) used. The same situation prevails for most sociological variables.

Second, some scales for measuring physical variables (most notably those for distance and weight) have the property of **equal intervals**—a unit of measurement represents a constant amount of whatever is being measured, no matter where along the scale it is found. Thus, the difference between four metres and three metres is one metre—the same distance as the difference between eight metres and seven metres. Few, if any, sociological scales can be shown to have equal intervals. For instance, it remains to be demonstrated that the difference in job satisfaction between "excellent" and "average"—5 − 3 = 2—is actually the same quantity as the difference between "average" and "poor"—3 − 1 = 2.

Finally, some scales for measuring physical variables (such as those for distance and weight) have an **absolute zero point**, so that the total absence of the variable can be observed. Few if any sociological scales, however, have a zero point. In the case of job satisfaction, for example, the lowest point on the scale—"poor" (1)—may not indicate a total absence of satisfaction in the job aspect being assessed.

It would be good if all sociological scales had standard metrics, equal intervals, and absolute zero points. Still, the lack of them creates fewer difficulties than might be imagined. These properties can, in fact, be demonstrated for very few scales of any kind (those for distance and weight being perhaps the only ones). Sciences such as physics and chemistry have been very successful without completely resolving issues of measurement. There are no grounds to think that sociology is an exception.

In summary, science uses both an abstract language of theoretical definitions and a concrete language of operational ones, and there is no simple, one-to-one correspondence between them. Just as we need sociological theory to suggest relationships among variables, we need measurement theory to describe how these variables might be linked to their indicators.

Reliability of Measurement

A basic concept in measurement theory is **reliability**, the extent to which a scale yields consistent results when applied repeatedly to the same objects or events within a short space of time. For example, imagine sitting in an automobile, engine off, and continually turning the ignition key just far enough to activate the gasoline gauge. If the needle invariably ends up at the same location, then you can conclude that the gauge is a reliable indicator of how much gasoline is in the tank. If, however, the gauge does not always end up in the same place, you may decide that it is unreliable and that a more accurate reading of how much gasoline is in the tank would be obtained by turning the key several times in a row and taking an average of the results. Of course, if you become obsessed with your task and continue it over an extended period, the battery will begin to wear down and the readings will start to change. This is an instance of **instrument decay**.

The act of measuring something usually changes it, however imperceptibly. If you repeatedly measure your gasoline level by using a stick of wood, the results will change over time since each measurement will remove some small amount of the fluid from the tank. This is a **testing effect**. Although the same kinds of reliability checks can be run on indicators of sociological variables as on the gasoline gauge, overcoming problems of instrument decay and testing effects sometimes requires real ingenuity.

THE MEDIAN ISN'T THE MESSAGE

My life has recently intersected, in a most personal way, two of Mark Twain's famous quips. One I shall defer to the end of this essay. The other (sometimes attributed to Disraeli) identifies three species of mendacity, each worse than the one before—lies, damned lies, and statistics.

Consider the standard example of stretching truth with numbers—a case quite relevant to my story. Statistics recognizes different measures of an "average," or central tendency. The *mean* is our usual concept of an overall average—add up the items and divide them by the number of sharers (100 candy bars collected for five kids next Halloween will yield 20 for each in a just world). The *median*, a different measure of central tendency, is the halfway point. If I line up five kids by height, the median child is shorter than two and taller than the other two (who might have trouble getting their mean share of the candy). A politician in power might say with pride, "The mean income of our citizens is $15,000 per year." The leader of the opposition might retort, "But half our citizens make less than $10,000 per year." Both are right, but neither cites a statistic with impassive objectivity. The first invokes a mean, the second a median. (Means are higher than medians in such cases because one millionaire may outweigh hundreds of poor people in setting a mean; but he can balance only one mendicant in calculating a median).

The larger issue that creates a common distrust or contempt for statistics is more troubling. Many people make an unfortunate and invalid separation between heart and mind, or feeling and intellect. In some contemporary traditions, abetted by attitudes stereotypically centered upon Southern California, feelings are exalted as more "real" and the only proper basis for action—if it feels good, do it—while intellect gets short shrift as a hang-up of outmoded elitism. Statistics, in this absurd dichotomy, often become the symbol of the enemy. As Hilaire Belloc wrote, "Statistics are the triumph of the quantitative method, and the quantitative method is the victory of sterility and death."

This is a personal story of statistics, properly interpreted, as profoundly nurturant and life-giving. It declares holy war on the downgrading of intellect by telling a small story about the utility of dry, academic knowledge about science. Heart and head are focal points of one body, one personality.

In July 1982, I learned that I was suffering from abdominal mesothelioma, a rare and serious cancer usually associated with exposure to asbestos. When I revived after surgery, I asked my first question of my doctor and chemotherapist: "What is the best technical literature about mesothelioma?" She replied, with a touch of diplomacy (the only departure she has ever made from direct frankness), that the medical literature contained nothing really worth reading.

Of course, trying to keep an intellectual away from literature works about as well as recommending chastity to *Homo sapiens*, the sexiest primate of all. As soon as I could walk, I made a beeline for Harvard's Countway medical library and punched mesothelioma into the computer's bibliographic search program. An hour later, surrounded by the latest literature on abdominal mesothelioma, I realized with a gulp why my doctor had offered that humane advice. The literature couldn't have been more brutally clear: mesothelioma is incurable, with a median mortality of only eight months after discovery. I sat stunned for about fifteen minutes, then smiled and said to myself: so that's why they didn't give me anything to read. Then my mind started to work again, thank goodness.

If a little learning could ever be a dangerous thing, I had encountered a classic example. Attitude clearly matters in fighting cancer. We don't know why (from my old-style materialistic perspective, I suspect that mental states feed back upon the immune system). But match people with the same cancer for age, class, health, socioeconomic status, and, in general, those with positive attitudes, with a strong will and purpose for living, with commitment to struggle, with an active response to aiding their own treatment and not just a passive acceptance of anything doctors say, tend to live longer. A few months later I asked Sir Peter Medawar, my personal scientific guru and a Nobelist in immunology, what the best prescription for success against cancer might be. "A sanguine personality," he replied. Fortunately (since one can't reconstruct oneself at short notice and for a definite purpose), I am, if anything, even-tempered and confident in just this manner.

Hence the dilemma for humane doctors: since attitude matters so critically, should such a sombre conclusion be advertised, especially since few people have sufficient understanding of statistics to evaluate what the statements really mean? From years of experience with the small-scale evolution of Bahamian land snails treated quantitatively, I have developed this technical knowledge—and I am convinced that it played a major role in saving my life. Knowledge is indeed power, in Bacon's proverb.

The problem may be briefly stated: What does "median mortality of eight months" signify in our vernacular? I suspect that most people, without training in statistics, would read such a statement as "I will probably be dead in eight months"—the very conclusion that must be avoided, since it isn't so, and since attitude matters so much.

I was not, of course, overjoyed, but I didn't read the statement in this vernacular way either. My technical training enjoined a different perspective on "eight months median mortality." The point is a subtle one, but profound—for it embodies the distinctive way of thinking in my own field of evolutionary biology and natural history.

We still carry the historical baggage of a Platonic heritage that seeks sharp essences and definite boundaries. (Thus we hope to find an unambiguous "beginning of life" or "definition of death," although nature often comes to us as irreducible continua.) This Platonic heritage, with its emphasis on clear distinctions and separated immutable entities, leads us to view statistical measures of central tendency wrongly, indeed opposite to the appropriate interpretation in our actual world of variation, shadings, and continua. In short, we view means and medians as the hard "realities," and the variation that permits their calculation as a set of transient and imperfect measurements of this hidden essence. If the median is the reality and variation around the median just a device for its calculation, the "I will probably be dead in eight months" may pass as a reasonable interpretation.

But all evolutionary biologists know that variation itself is nature's only irreducible essence. Variation is the hard reality, not a set of imperfect measures for a central tendency. Means and medians are the abstractions. Therefore, I looked at the mesothelioma statistics quite differently—and not only because I am an optimist who tends to see the doughnut instead of the hole, but primarily because I know that variation itself is the reality. I had to place myself amidst the variation.

When I learned about the eight-month median, my first intellectual reaction was: fine, half the people will live longer; now what are my chances of being in that half. I read for a furious and nervous hour and concluded, with relief: damned good. I possessed every one of the characteristics conferring a probability of longer life: I was young; my disease had been recognized in a relatively early stage; I would receive the nation's best medical treatment; I had the world to live for; I knew how to read the data properly and not despair.

Another technical point then added even more solace. I immediately recognized that the distribution of variation about the eight-month median would almost surely be what statisticians call "right skewed." (In a symmetrical distribution, the profile of variation to the left of the central tendency is a mirror image of variation to the right. In skewed distributions, variation to one side of the central tendency is more stretched out—left skewed if extended to the left, right skewed if stretched out to the right.) The distribution of variation had to be right skewed, I reasoned. After all, the left of the distribution contains an irrevocable lower boundary of zero (since mesothelioma can only be identified at death or before). Thus there isn't much room for the distribution's lower (or left) half—it must be scrunched up between zero and eight months. But the upper (or right) half can extend out for years and years, even if nobody ultimately survives. The distribution must be right skewed, and I needed to know how long the extended tail ran—for I had already concluded that my favorable profile made me a good candidate for that part of the curve.

The distribution was, indeed, strongly right skewed, with a long tail (however small) that extended for several years above the eight month median. I saw no reason why I shouldn't be in that small tail, and I breathed a very long sigh of relief. My technical knowledge had helped. I had read the graph correctly. I had asked the right question and found the answers. I had obtained, in all probability, that most precious of all possible gifts in the circumstances—substantial time. I didn't have to stop and immediately follow Isaiah's injunction to Hezekiah—set thine house in order: for thou shalt die, and not live. I would have time to think, to plan, and to fight.

One final point about statistical distributions. They apply only to a prescribed set of circumstances—in this case to survival with mesothelioma under conventional modes of treatment. If circumstances change, the distribution may alter. I was placed on an experimental protocol of treatment and, if fortune holds, will be in the first cohort of a new distribution with high median and a right tail extending to death by natural causes at advanced old age.

It has become, in my view, a bit too trendy to regard the acceptance of death as something tantamount to intrinsic dignity. Of course I agree with the preacher of Ecclesiastes that there is a time to love and a time to die—and when my skein runs out I hope to face the end calmly and in my own way. For most situations, however, I prefer the more martial view that death is the ultimate enemy—and I find nothing reproachable in those who rage mightily against the dying of the light.

The swords of battle are numerous, and none more effective than humour. My death was announced at a meeting of my colleagues in Scotland, and I almost experienced the delicious pleasure of reading my obituary penned by one of my best friends (the so-and-so got suspicious and checked; he too is a statistician, and didn't expect to find me so far out on the left tail). Still, the incident provided my first good laugh after the diagnosis. Just think, I almost got to repeat Mark Twain's most famous line of all: the reports of my death are greatly exaggerated.

—STEPHEN JAY GOULD

There are basically two approaches to the assessment of reliability. In the first, the same scale is applied to the same objects or events at two or more points in time. This is the **test-retest approach**. For instance, people might be asked in successive interviews how old they are, and their answers compared for consistency. In another approach, two or more similar (but not identical) scales are applied to the same objects or events at essentially the same point in time. This is the **internal consistency approach**. For example, people might be asked at the beginning of an interview how old they are and, at some later point, what their birthdate is.

Each of these two approaches has its strengths and weaknesses. The major strength of the test-retest method is that since the same scale is used each time, differences between readings cannot be attributed to differences in the indicators, unless one suspects instrument decay. (The meaning of words, for example, can change over time, seriously changing the meaning of questions that contain them. "Gay divorcees" are not what they used to be, "grass" is sometimes smoked as well as mowed, and "cruising" no longer requires the use of a vehicle.) The principal weakness of the test-retest method is that, because the readings are taken at different times, real changes can occur in the objects or events being measured; these changes can be distinguished from unreliability only if the scale is applied at more than two points in time. Also, if individuals are answering questions in a questionnaire or interview, they may recall earlier answers to the same question, thereby causing reliability to be overestimated (a testing effect). The strength of the internal-consistency approach is that changes in what is being measured cannot become confused with unreliability, since effectively no time elapses between the readings. The main weakness of this approach is that, because the scales are not exactly the same, unreliability cannot be distinguished from indicator differences unless more than two indicators are used.

Validity of Measurement

A second basic concept in measurement theory is **validity**, the degree to which a scale actually measures what it is intended to measure. If a scale is unreliable, it is necessarily invalid, since what is measures is random error. But a reliable scale may still not measure what it is intended to, as when you run out of gasoline even though the gauge reliably tells you the tank is half full. Validity must therefore be assessed, in addition to reliability. The simplest method is face validation; the most important is the method of construct validation. **Face validation** involves the agreement of a number of experts that a scale appears (hence "face") to measure a certain theoretical variable. For example, a group of sociolinguists might agree that a question in a survey asking respondents which language they customarily speak in the home (English, French, other) is a valid measure of whether a Canadian is an anglophone, a francophone, or neither. **Construct validation** is more complex. It works like this:

This famous photograph shows a smiling American President Truman holding up a false report in a Chicago newspaper that he had been defeated by his rival for the presidency, Dewey. The newspaper printed the headline before the election results were in, relying on polls and early election returns. Events such as this taught pollsters and other survey researchers the importance of random sampling and refined statistical tests.

1. A considerable accumulation of prior research gives good reason to think that changes in variable or construct *A* precede and result in changes in construct *B*.
2. Several available scales can measure *A* (or *B*), but no one scale is universally preferred.
3. A scale to measure *A* is construct validated if subsequent research shows that this scale is associated positively with other scales for *A* and that it relates to scales for *B* as if changes in *A* lead to changes in *B*.

For example, say a researcher wishes to measure self-esteem and introduces a new scale on which people are asked to rate themselves; this scale ranges from "pleasant" (7) to "unpleasant" (1). Now suppose there is a hypothesis that "an increase in a person's socioeconomic status leads to an increase in his or her self-esteem," in which socioeconomic status has been measured by level of education, prestige of occupation, and income, and self-esteem by self-ratings on two seven-point scales as "good" (7) vs. "bad" (1) and "positive" (7) vs. "negative" (1). Let us say that previous studies all conclude that this hypothesis—tested using indicators identical or similar to these—cannot be rejected. The new scale is construct validated if people who tend to rate themselves as "good" and "positive" also tend to rate themselves as "pleasant," and if people who are well educated and have high-prestige occupations and good incomes tend to rate themselves as "pleasant."

Multiple Indicators

Because theoretical variables have no direct counterparts in empirical indicators and because scales are always to some extent unreliable, research is most convincing when it incorporates multiple indicators, as in the example above. Multiple indicators permit researchers to detect unreliability and make corrections for it; then checks can be made for construct validity. Without such checks, research results are interpreted on the assumption that the indicator is both perfectly reliable and completely valid. But such an assumption can be highly unrealistic; thus, interpretations of results based on single-item indicators of unknown reliability and uncertain validity can be grossly in error.

Exactly how are multiple indicators used? Some uses are very sophisticated and some are quite simple. One method is just to express all of the indicators in a common metric and then to add them together to form a scale called a **composite indicator**. Note that all of the indicators must be converted to a common measure; one cannot add metres to centilitres or litres to millimetres. Since each of the self-rating scales in our example has a metric of values from 1 to 7, one could form a composite indicator of self-esteem by simply adding together each person's scores on the "good" versus "bad," "positive" versus "negative," and "pleasant" versus "unpleasant" scales. In terms of what is known about measurement, this would be a rather crude way to go about it, but it would yield much the same results as would more sophisticated approaches.

METHODS OF DATA COLLECTION

How do researchers actually go about gathering information? The choice of strategies depends on many factors: whether a research project is purely exploratory or designed to test hypotheses, the unit of analysis to be studied, the nature of the variables, the time and money available, and ethical considerations. A researcher may use a single strategy or two or more in tandem. Since each strategy has characteristic strengths and weaknesses—and the strong points of one are sometimes the weak points of another—a **multimethod approach** is often best.

Participant Observation

In **participant observation**, a method of gathering information adapted from anthropology, an investigator actually becomes, to some extent, a member of a group for the purpose of studying it. This method has the advantage of putting the researcher in direct contact with the research subjects. Moreover, if the group is relatively small, the researcher may be able to view all parts of it first-hand. While participant observation is most often employed to study groups in natural settings, it is sometimes used for groups assembled in experimental environments, such as small groups observed in laboratories.

In scientific sociology, participant observation is especially useful for exploratory research, in which the theoretical variables remain unknown or ill-defined and hypotheses are at best only vaguely formed. This method can yield richly detailed information on individuals and their relationships with one another. Hence, it is often an invaluable source of clues for defining variables and generating hypotheses.

Participant observation is not, however, an easy method in practice. For one thing, however delicately the matter is handled, a researcher who joins a group to study it changes its nature simply by the act of joining. Participant observers, therefore, sometimes do not reveal themselves as researchers to their subjects. In a well-known study of a doomsday group (Festinger et al. 1956) for example, the researchers formed a significant fraction of the group's total membership by the time it was clear that the earth was not about to end; the group might have disbanded much earlier had the researchers not given the others encouragement by continuing to act out their membership roles.

For another thing, there is always some danger that the investigator, after sustained contact and shared experiences with the group being studied, will uncritically take its point of view. If the researcher remains aware of this possibility, some counter-measures can be taken; otherwise, the result can be extreme. For example, the researcher may become a full-fledged member of the group and abandon his or her research goals. (On one occasion, several researchers delivered themselves up to be saved at a Billy Graham Crusade for Christ meeting in Madison Square Garden.)

Participant observation is a difficult method to use for gathering information to test hypotheses. If the hypotheses are suggested in the course of the research itself, the data collected cannot be used to test them, since circular logic proves nothing. Furthermore, participant observation does not allow for truly independent interpretations of the observations because it typically fuses observation and interpretation. The investigator is both the instrument that measures the variables and the interpreter of those measurements. This method is also prone to unsystematic and incomplete data collection, since the participant observers are usually vastly outnumbered by the group members and must normally be discreet in recording their observations. A final limitation is that since relatively long-term, face-to-face contact between researcher and subjects is required, usually only a small number of different groups can be studied.

Of course, as with all data-gathering methods, the advantages and disadvantages of participant observation depend on the uses to which the information is to be put. In general, participant observation is the method of choice for exploratory research in which the unit of analysis is the individual in face-to-face interaction with others or a small group of individuals in direct contact with one another.

Structured Observation

In **structured observation**, a non-participant observer, using a predetermined schedule, systematically notes the occurrence of certain aspects of individuals' behaviour. This method differs from participant observation in two important ways: (1) the observer is socially—and perhaps, to some extent, physically—detached from his or her subjects, and (2) the observer knows beforehand just what information is to be recorded. Structured observation is often used in laboratory settings to study people participating in experiments. It is also used in such natural environments as school classrooms (say, to study pedagogical styles), industrial shops (for example, to gather information on the frequency and content of workers' interactions), and even streetcorners (to monitor traffic flow, for instance).

Because researchers using this method do not participate in group activities, they are free to use trained observers to gather the required information. Data on many different people and groups can be gathered, and observation can be kept separate from interpretation. Structured observation can also reduce the effects on subjects of being observed, since the investigator can be quite unobtrusive, even if the subjects are told that they are being studied. (This is generally necessary if the research is conducted anywhere but in a public place or if the subjects are manipulated in any way.) Since certain selected behaviour is recorded systematically, the data collected are often in the form of tallies of the occurrences of different acts, which are easily adapted to the testing of hypotheses. This is the principal advantage of structured observation. However, because observers are typically limited to what they can see or hear directly, structured observation works best for subjects located within a very circumscribed area. This limitation is the principal disadvantage of the method.

Interviews and Questionnaires

The interview and the questionnaire are both devices to elicit information or opinions from individuals by having them respond to questions. In the interview, these questions may be decided on beforehand and presented to each respondent in exactly the same way (**standardized questions**) or they may be allowed to arise and take form in the context of the interview (**unstandardized questions**). In the questionnaire, the questions are necessarily always standardized.

Either form may use **open-ended questions**, with respondents free to answer as they choose, or **closed-ended questions**, which ask respondents to select from a set of categories predetermined by the researcher. For example, there are literally thousands of distinct occupations in the Canadian labour force, so it is impractical to use a closed-ended question to determine people's occupations. Instead, researchers customarily use open-ended questions of the following kind:

> Would you mind telling me what your occupation is? This involves what kind of work?

Then, trained coders, often using a manual such as the *Canadian Classification and Dictionary of Occupations*, take the answers to these questions and attempt to identify them with occupational categories. (Having two questions is useful. Many people give uninformative answers, such as "salesperson," "manager," or "self-employed," to the first. Another common example of the open-ended question is the Who Am I? test, in which respondents are asked to list "twenty words or phrases which you think best describe who you are." Again, trained coders take respondents' answers ("a woman," "an insurance broker," "a friend," "a lily on a pond") and systematically record their content and form, noting, for example, how many answers are in the form of nouns, how many are adjectives, whether gender, occupation, or marital status is mentioned, and so on.

A common variety of the closed-ended question is the **Likert-type item**, in which respondents are asked to react to some statement in terms of graded response categories: "strongly agree," "agree," "neutral," "disagree," and "strongly disagree." Usually, the categories are assigned numeric values, from 5 for "strongly agree" through to 1 for "strongly disagree." For example, Breton (1972) compared anglophone and francophone secondary-school students in terms of their sense of control over their lives, using two Likert-type items with the statements:

> Making plans only makes a person unhappy because plans hardly work out anyway;

and

> When a man is born, the success he's going to have is already in the cards, so he might as well accept it and not fight against it.

Another common type of closed-ended question is the seven-point bipolar adjectival type used in the **semantic differential** (Osgood et al. 1975). With this kind of scale, respondents are asked to indicate the number that best describes some concept (in the following example, Canada), using a format like this:

	Canada	
strong	1 2 3 4 5 6 7	weak
active	1 2 3 4 5 6 7	passive
good	1 2 3 4 5 6 7	bad

Both Likert-type and semantic-differential items are widely used in attitude research.

The advantage of standardized questions is that the responses given by different people can be compared easily. This is essential for testing hypotheses, although standardization does not guarantee that all respondents will interpret a question the same way. Unstandardized questions, on the other hand, have the advantage of permitting free adaptation to the flow of an interview. The interviewer can choose how to phrase a question and can follow up responses that seem important or unclear. This flexibility is important to a researcher seeking to discover what the important variables seem to be and how they may be related to one another. It is especially useful in exploring areas of human experience that are not well understood. Unstandardized questions do not, however, yield results to test hypotheses; since the question is put somewhat differently to each person, there is no basis for comparison of answers.

The advantage of closed-ended questions is that comparing different people's answers is relatively simple and inexpensive. In fact, sometimes optical scanning machines can read information directly from interview schedules or questionnaires into a computer, without human intervention. The advantage of open-ended questions is that people can answer in their own fashion. Thus, their answers are not distorted by the imposition of a limited set of arbitrary categories that may be unfamiliar or unnatural to them. If responses to open-ended questions are to be used in testing hypotheses, however, they must be processed from their raw form into some qualitative or quantitative scale; this is almost always an expensive process.

Composing a standardized question is a minor art form. But there is a body of questions that have been used in empirical studies so often that their strong and weak points are widely known. New questions are seldom used in the field unless they have been pre-tested on a sample group to check for ambiguities in wording and sometimes for reliability and validity. Improvising unstandardized questions in an interview is a craft for which there are few firm rules; it is best learned by observing seasoned interviewers at work and by supervised practice.

Canada's bilingual, multicultural character poses problems for the use of interviews and questionnaires in social research. Any national survey in Canada must have separate interview schedules or questionnaires in English and French and sometimes in several other languages as well. Especially if standardized or closed-ended questions are used, the researcher must ensure that the questions and response categories have the same meaning in all languages used. A common and effective check is **back translation**, in which a question is first translated from one language to another by one translator and then translated back to the original language by another. If the back translation does not differ materially from the original question, the researcher can be confident that both versions have the same meaning. If it does differ, revisions are required.

Finally, what are the relative advantages of interviews and question-naires? Questionnaires cost much less. It is very expensive to hire, train, and supervise interviewers and to pay their wages, travel, and other costs. (In 1986, the typical completed interview cost more than $75, not in-cluding sampling, coding, and data entry expenses.) Questionnaires can often be simply delivered to respondents by hand or through the mails. Interviewers also represent a potential source of error not present with questionnaires; no matter how careful and lengthy the training period has been, every interviewer conducts an interview somewhat differently. Interviews, however, can reach people who are illiterate or otherwise unable or unwilling to complete a questionnaire. Partly as a consequence, the proportion of people contacted who actually end up participating in a study is typically higher when interviews are used. Up to 90 percent, or even more, of the people contacted may give interviews. Much lower participation rates are expected with questionnaires. Also, if there are ambiguities in questions, an interviewer can clarify them; ambiguities in a questionnaire may result in unanswered questions. Finally, an inter-viewer can follow up certain answers with a further question. In general, where both methods are feasible, interviews are usually the better choice.

Telephone interviewing is increasingly used by researchers since most Canadians can now be reached by telephone. A recent innovation is computer-aided telephone interviewing (CATI). Interviewers read ques-tions from a video display and enter responses directly into a computer. By eliminating both travel time and manual coding, this method cuts down on research costs and reduces errors in the recording of data.

With participant and structured observation, it is often possible to con-duct an investigation without the knowledge of the subjects, although ethical considerations may prevent this from actually being done. With questionnaires and interviews, this is seldom possible (at least with adults) so the ethical imperative to inform research subjects of their involvement is rarely at issue. (Most sociologists would probably agree that children should not be studied without the permission of parents, guardians, or other responsible adults, such as school officials.)

Unobtrusive Measures

All the methods of data collection reviewed to this point involve some risk that the research act itself may intrude on the subject of study, generating false findings. Subjects being observed in an experiment may act out idealized versions of themselves. Or they may try to act as they think the experimenter expects them to. Attempts to measure some var-iable may cause it to change. A question phrased positively may elicit different responses than the same question phrased negatively. People may respond to the characteristics of an interviewer or to the packaging of a mailed questionnaire. Over time, interviewers and observers may tire or, conversely, become more proficient. The meaning of questions may change between one measurement point and the next.

To overcome these risks of distortion, sociologists have devised **unobtrusive measures**—techniques that do not interfere with the objects or events studied (Webb et al. 1966). In comings and goings, people leave many physical traces that can often be used as the basis for measurement. They litter the streets, leave garbage outside their dwellings, wear down sidewalks, steps, floors, and grass, sign their names, leave their radio or television sets at particular locations on the dial, deposit fingerprints, borrow library books, and write messages on the walls of public washrooms. All these traces and many others can be measured.

Another category of unobtrusive measures is natural observation: structured observation in a natural setting. Simple facts about people's comings and goings in public places can often be easily recorded. There are ready, if under-used, sources of information everywhere: how people dress and decorate themselves (for example, with cosmetics or tatoos), how they stand or sit relative to others, how they drive their automobiles, what verbal or non-verbal expressions they use, and so on. Tape recorders, videotape cameras, galvanic skin-response recorders, electric eyes, and the like can be used to observe signals, such as facial expressions, hand and eye movements, and vocal tremors, that are too subtle or fleeting to be recorded systematically by the unaided eye or ear.

Yet another source of unobtrusive measures is official statistics. Governments at all levels keep records, some of which are public documents and some of which are systematically tabulated and periodically published. Government records of births, deaths, marriages, probated wills, land transfers, adoptions, name changes, divorces, arrests, criminal charges and convictions, welfare allowances, unemployment insurance payments, and automobile licences are potentially useful sources of informaton. A wealth of data is contained in the Census of Canada, which is taken every five years (a major one at the beginning of each decade and a minor one in the middle). Unlike physical traces and natural observations, official statistics are highly refined and processed pieces of information designed for administrative, not research, purposes. Gathered and reported in accordance with bureaucratic or political needs and legal requirements, government statistics are often difficult for researchers to use. Official categories (of crime, occupations, or income, for instance) seldom match sociological ones. Moreover, government regulations usually mean that information is made available only in summary form for highly aggregated groups. Detailed information on anonymous individuals—the kind much sociological research requires—is rarely available. It is often very difficult to determine how official statistics have been compiled and thus how accurate they are. For these reasons, Canadian government data are less likely to be used for basic research than are data gathered by governments in some other countries. (In the United States, the federal government and several state governments have, on occasion, even given social scientists access to individuals' income tax records for research

Census Canada gathers data for official statistics from Canadian households every five years.

purposes.) Consequently, Canadian sociologists must sometimes design and carry out their own research studies—which ironically, are largely funded by public agencies such as municipal, provincial, and federal governments, the Social Sciences and Humanities Research Council, and by universities, which operate largely on public funds.

Finally, information may be collected from documents of various kinds, such as diaries, biographies, novels, lyrics of popular songs, magazines, tapes of radio and television broadcasts, and newspapers. These materials are made useful for research through the technique of **content analysis**, in which the frequency of occurrence of certain kinds of information is systematically recorded. For example, a researcher might document the changing character of problems in male-female relationships by analyzing the lyrics of popular songs over time. Or an investigator might compare and contrast images of a war as portrayed in the television newscasts of countries on opposing sides. Such research has rarely been used because it has traditionally been very time-consuming. Increasingly, however, it is possible for researchers to analyze certain kinds of documents (most notably written records) using computerized systems to read, classify, and tabulate the information.

Serious ethical issues are fairly unlikely to arise in connection with unobtrusive measures. Observing physical traces or people in public places, using official statistics, or analyzing published materials rarely compromises the privacy of the subjects or violates the law. Still, such issues do arise. In one widely publicized and debated case, a sociologist observed homosexual encounters between men in public washrooms, took note of the men's automobile licence plate numbers when they left, and later interviewed them on a pretext (Humphreys 1970).

RESEARCH DESIGN

The term **research design** refers to the procedures used in selecting the objects or events studied and the schedules under which they are observed. These procedures and schedules are very important because they determine how the investigator will answer the two questions that must be asked of any hypothesis-testing research.

1. For the particular units selected and observed, are there any plausible interpretations of the data other than that changes in A lead to changes in B? For example, could it be that changes in B result in changes in A? Research must be very carefully designed to exclude such rival interpretations.

2. Does the interpretation apply only to the particular units studied or can it be extended, or **generalized**, to other units of the same kind? For example, data from a national sample of 2000 Canadian adults may support the hypothesis that conventionally attractive persons tend to be somewhat more successful in their careers than are the less attractive. But does this result apply to Canadians generally, or only to the 2000 actually studied? Again, if the researcher is not very careful in designing the research, it may be that findings cannot be generalized.

Research can be judged a failure if it generates results that can be given no clear interpretation; research that does not yield generalizable data is less than a success.

One can distinguish two categories of research design. In true experimental design, the investigator decides which units will be exposed to the independent variable and when they will be exposed. In quasi-experimental and non-experimental designs, the investigator simply observes this exposure to take place (or not) naturally. In either case, results will be generalizable only if the units studied are selected, using random procedures, from some larger category of units. Where true experimental designs are involved, cases must also be randomly assigned to exposure to the change in the independent variable.

Random Selection

In studying large groups of objects or events, it is not necessary to measure every case. Very accurate inferences can be made about large groups based on the observation of a small number of cases. This is only possible, however, if these cases have been drawn from the larger **population**, or group, at random. In this context, "random" has a precise meaning. It does not mean haphazard or accidental. It means that cases have been selected from the population using a purely probabilistic procedure, which can be as folksy as drawing well-mixed names from a hat or as sophisticated as a computerized random-number generator. A set of cases selected from a population is called a **sample**; a sample drawn from a population in which each case has an equal probability of being chosen is a **simple random sample**.

To draw a simple random sample from a population one must:

1. Carefully define the population to be studied: all residents of Canada, all homeowners in Saskatchewan, all high-school students in the Atlantic provinces, or some other group.
2. Obtain a complete listing of all the cases in this population and give each case a unique identifying number from 1 to N (N being the total number of cases in the population). An example of this might be the tax-roll assessment lists for the entire province of Saskatchewan, with each homeowner assigned a number from 1 to N (N being the number of homeowners in that province).
3. Using some purely random procedure, select a sample of numbers. The cases on the list bearing these numbers make up the simple random sample.

Simple random samples are rarely drawn in social research. First, a listing of the cases in the population is seldom available. At best, a researcher may have only such out-of-date and incomplete lists as telephone or city directories. At worst, the researcher may have to begin by sampling large areas on a map, then sampling smaller areas within them, then buildings within these areas, then dwelling units within these buildings, then people within these dwelling units, and so on, creating a final sample whose relationship to the population from which it was drawn is unknown. Moreover, large areas of low population, most notably in Canada the Yukon and the Northwest Territories, are usually not included when "national" samples are drawn, and the residents of small communities and rural areas are usually under-represented. These problems have led to the practice of **weighting samples** to make them representative of the entire country. Weighting a sample usually involves counting each member of each under-represented group as more than one member. The gain in doing this is that the weighted sample is made to appear representative of the larger population; the loss is that the probability theory used to make inferences about populations from sample data no longer strictly applies.

RANDOMLY SELECTED

Two techniques often used in sampling are clustering and stratifying. A **cluster sample** is one in which groups of units—for instance, areas in cities, schools, or business establishments—are enumerated and selected, even though the individual unit is the object of study. Clustering is almost always a matter of necessity rather than choice; perhaps no enumeration of the individual members of the population is available, or a simple random sample is too expensive. Clustering greatly complicates attempts to make inferences about populations from sample data. A **stratified sample** is one in which individual units are first classified into categories or strata; for example, people might be grouped into those who have at least a high-school education and those who have less. Separate samples are then drawn from within each stratum. Stratifying, like clustering, is usually a response to difficulties in drawing a simple random sample, such as inadequate resources to draw a large enough simple random sample to meet the researcher's needs. Stratified samples can often yield the same quality of information as simple random samples, but with a smaller total sample size. But stratifying, like clustering, usually creates problems in making inferences about populations. Finally, a **multistage sample** is one in which sampling is carried out in two or more phases: a sample of clusters is selected, then units within each cluster are selected, and so on until a sample of individual units has been drawn.

Random Assignment

Random assignment is used to ensure that two or more groups differ initially only in ways that could be expected to occur by chance alone. That is, it is a means of equating groups in terms of the characteristics of their members. Its most common use is in experiments in which different groups of units are to be exposed to different levels of an independent variable, in order to observe the consequences on a dependent variable. Such a test can be convincing only if the groups are the same at the outset. The researcher therefore assigns units at random to the different groups. An intuitively appealing alternative to random assignment is **matching**—taking two units that are the same in some respect, assigning one to one group and the other to the other group. Unfortunately, since units differ from one another in an infinite number of ways and can be matched only in terms of a small number of characteristics, this practice cannot ensure identical groups. Moreover, random assignment allows one to use probability theory to assess the effects of experimental manipulations, where matching does not. That is, when random assignment is used, one can always ask what the probability of obtaining a particular experimental result is. This question is inappropriate when matching is used.

Experiments

In the simplest form of the true experiment (see Exhibit 2-3), cases are first assigned at random to either the experimental or the control group. Then, the members of the **experimental group** are exposed to a change in the independent variable, while those in the **control group** are not. Both groups are subsequently measured for their scores on the dependent variable. If the average score in one group differs in the predicted direction from that in the other, the hypothesis is supported.

From a logical point of view, the true experiment is the most powerful design for testing the hypothesis that a change in one variable results in a change in another. It thus provides a standard against which other

Exhibit 2-3
Simplification of a True Experiment Design

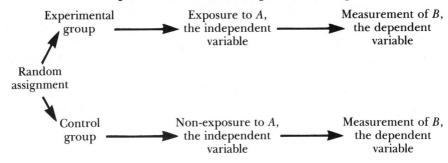

designs can be judged. First, because the true experiment uses random assignment, one can be very confident that a difference in the dependent variable between the experimental and control groups arose in the course of the experiment, not because the two groups differed beforehand. Second, because the experimenter manipulates the change in the independent variable, differences in this exposure are by far the most likely source of any differences in the dependent variable—assuming that great care has been taken to make sure that the members of the experimental and control groups have otherwise been treated exactly alike.

It is not, however, always possible to use the true experiment. Its logical strengths are to some extent counterbalanced by its limited ability to model social processes. Many sociological variables do not lend themselves to experimental manipulation at all; for instance, an experimenter cannot alter the sex or ethnicity of subjects in order to assess the effects of such changes on, say, a person's influence on other group members in reaching a collective decision. Many other variables cannot be manipulated for ethical reasons; it would be unacceptable, for instance, for an experimenter to cause subjects to lose their jobs in an experiment to test for the effects of unemployment on marital harmony. Even when the experiment can be used, the subjects must still be randomly selected for the results to be generalizable to a larger population. And random selection is no guarantee of generalizability, since the highly controlled (usually laboratory) settings in which experiments are typically conducted are sometimes far removed from the environments in which people live, and serious questions can be raised about the value of experiments for informing us about the long-term nature of relationships between variables outside the laboratory. If experiments are the best way to test whether changes in one variable result in changes in another, they are probably not the best way to show that these effects are important or enduring ones, since the period of observation is generally short. Other designs (most notably panel studies and time series, which are described below) may be preferable for studying long-term effects.

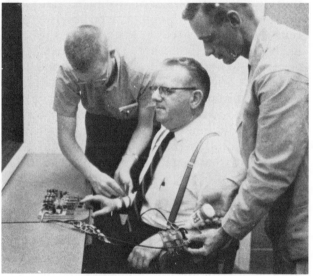

In an experiment by Stanley Milgram at Yale University to test levels of obedience, subjects were encouraged to administer what they thought were electric shocks to volunteers. The more switches they pushed on the impressive-looking but fake "shock generator" (top), the more obedient they were judged to be. Below, a "volunteer" (actually an associate of Milgram's) is strapped in and wired up. At his fingertips is a set of switches that light up numbers on an "answer box." The associate would purposely make errors to see if the subjects would continue to administer "shocks."

Researchers must be very careful to avoid ethical problems in using experiments to test hypotheses. Should subjects ever be induced to do things they would never do on their own? (In one infamous experiment [Milgram 1963], the researcher encouraged subjects to administer what they thought were lethal electrical shocks to people.) If an experimenter has good reason to believe that exposure to a change in the independent variable (say, taking a dose of a drug) has very beneficial effects (cures cancer, for instance), can *not* exposing subjects to it ever be justified? While this hardly exhausts the list of ethical problems that can arise in conducting experiments on human subjects, it indicates how serious they can be.

Panel Studies

In a **panel study**, measurements of a set of variables are taken on a sample of cases at two or more points in time. The relationships among the indicators are then checked to see if increases over time in the independent variable seem to be systematically associated with increases or decreases over time in the dependent variable. If the relationships found are consistent with the relationship specified in the hypothesis, then the hypothesis is supported.

Random assignment is not done, and researchers must observe changes in the independent variables as they occur naturally rather than inducing changes themselves. The results of a panel study are therefore more often open to plausible alternative interpretations than the results from an experiment. The particular weakness of the panel-study design is that evidence of a causal relationship between two variables may be either grossly exaggerated or entirely obscured as a consequence of additional, unobserved variables. For instance, many sociologists are interested in the question of how people's aspirations (educational, for instance) either retard or lead to greater achievements (for example, occupational). It is likely, however, that other variables, such as aspects of social background, are prior to and influence both aspirations and achievements. Since subjects in a panel study are not randomly assigned to two groups and then either inspired or not inspired to achieve by an experimenter, it is not possible to specify the exact relationship between aspirations and achievements. One can never be certain that high and low achievers do not differ from one another in other ways that might also influence achievements. All one can do is to gather as much additional information on the subjects as possible in order to rule out plausible alternative interpretations.

Time-Series Analysis

In a **time-series analysis** to test a hypothesis, observations are taken on two or more variables for a single case on several separate occasions. The associations among the indicators are then examined to see if increases over time in the independent variable seem to be systematically related to increases or decreases over time in the dependent variable. If the associations found are in line with those predicted in the hypothesis, then the hypothesis is supported.

Time-series analysis shares with the panel study the problem of additional unobserved variables. As well, since only one case is studied, it is not possible to generalize the results to a larger population; that is, there is no basis for inferring that evidence supporting the existence of a causal relationship between two variables applies to other cases. For example, Fox and Hartnagel (1979) show that, for Canada, changes over time in women's social roles (as measured by rates of fertility, graduation from post-secondary educational institutions, and labour-force participation) are related to increases over time in the incidence of female crime (as evidenced in conviction rates), but this relationship provides no basis to infer that the same process has occurred elsewhere.

One-Shot Surveys

A one-shot survey involves taking a single set of measurements on a number of variables for a sample of cases. The associations among the indicators are then checked to see if high values for the independent variable correspond systematically to high (or low) values for the dependent variable. If the relationships among the indicators are consistent with the hypothesis, the hypothesis is supported.

The one-shot survey is the weakest design for generating data to test an explanatory hypothesis. There is no random assignment, no manipulation of the independent variable, and no observation over time. The assumption is that the influences of one variable on another over time will be revealed in associations among their indicators at any one time. For example, if high aspirations lead to high achievements, people with high aspirations might be expected to have higher achievements at any particular time than do those with low aspirations. But an association between these two variables, if found, could arise from several sources. Perhaps changes in aspirations are prior to changes in achievements, as hypothesized. But it could be that additional, unobserved factors led to the finding or that changes in achievements precede and result in changes in aspirations (that is, that people who do well are, by that fact, inspired to do even better). If observations are taken at just one point in time, it is often not obvious which variable is the independent and which is the dependent. Observations taken over time are likely to be more revealing.

DATA ANALYSIS

The analysis of data gathered in a research project typically proceeds in two distinct but related sets of steps. First, the investigator calculates **descriptive statistics** to represent the form and magnitude of the relationships among variables in the study. Second, the researcher usually wishes to know if the relationships revealed in the sample can be generalized to the population from which the sample was drawn. The tool here is known as **inferential statistics**.

Descriptive Statistics: Cross-Tabulation

In terms of actual data, what does it mean to say that "the greater the *A*, the greater (or lesser) the *B*" or that "members of one category of *A* are higher (or lower) on *B* than are members of another category of *A*"? In the simplest case, data collected in support of such a hypothesis can be represented in a 2 × 2 table, so called because the two variables involved are each defined as if they exist in two categories and then **cross-tabulated** with one another. For example, let us examine the relationship between father's occupational status (in two categories, "high" and "low") and the son's educational attainment (again, in two categories, "high-school graduation or more" and "less than high-school graduation"). The results, as recalculated from Ornstein (1981) for a sample of Ontario men, can be displayed as in Exhibit 2-4, where the number in the upper-left cell (346) is the number of fathers with high occupational status whose sons achieved high-school graduation or more, the number in the lower-right cell (1122) is the number of fathers with low occupational status whose sons achieved less than high-school graduation, and the total sample size is 2036.

Just staring at raw numbers, or **frequencies**, in a table is seldom very enlightening. The immediate goal here is to use these frequencies to reveal how the independent variable (father's occupational status) and the dependent variable (son's educational attainment) are related to one another. One way is to calculate percentages within categories of the independent variable. The frequency of educational attainments can be expressed as a percentage of the total number of cases for each category of father's occupational status, as in Exhibit 2-5. The strength and direction of the association between the two variables can then be gauged by subtracting the number in the upper-right from the number in the upper-left cell—that is, $49.9 - 16.4 = 33.5$ percent more fathers with high occupational status than fathers with low occupational status had sons who achieved high-school graduation or more.

This finding suggests a moderate association between the two variables. A perfect association would have been revealed in a **percentage difference** of 100.00 between the upper-right and upper-left cells, while no association at all would have been shown in a percentage difference of 0. Notice that the percentage difference, and thus the type of association, may be positive or negative. The association between father's occupational status and son's educational attainment is positive, with high values for the independent variable tending to be associated with high values for the dependent variable. In a negative association, high values of the independent variable are found along with low values of the dependent variable.

The percentage difference is a **measure of association**—a statistic that indicates the strength and, if relevant, direction of the relationship(s) among two or more variables—and a very informative one with a clear interpretation, but it cannot be used with tables larger than 2×2. Partly for this reason, a variety of other measures of association have been developed, including two common measures arbitrarily named after Greek letters. Where both of the variables involved are qualitative, tau is a very useful measure of association for tables of any size; where both variables are quantitative, the statistic gamma is often employed. **Tau** (τ) can have a range of values from 0.00 (indicating no association at all between the

Exhibit 2-4
Respondents' Education
by Fathers' Occupation, Raw Frequencies

	Father's Occupational Status		
Respondent's Education	High	Low	Total
High-school graduation or more	346	220	566
Less than high-school graduation	348	1 122	1 470
Total	694	1 342	2 036

Note: Raw frequencies may contain small rounding errors.
Source: Recomputed from Ornstein (1981, table 3).

Exhibit 2-5
Respondents' Education
by Fathers' Occupation, Percentages

	Father's Occupational Status		
Respondent's Education	High	Low	Total
High-school graduation or more	49.9%	16.4%	27.8%
Less than high-school graduation	50.1	83.6	72.2
Total	100.0	100.0	100.0
			(No. = 2036)

Note: Percentages may contain small rounding errors.
Source: Recomputed from Ornstein (1981, table 3).

variables) to 1.00 (indicating a perfect association between them). Since the variables are qualitative, it makes no sense to have negative values of tau. **Gamma** (γ), however, can take on a range of values from -1.00 (perfect negative association), through 0.00 (no association at all), to $+1.00$ (perfect positive association), since the variables are quantitative.

Both tau and gamma yield values that can be given what is known as a **proportional reduction in error** interpretation. Consider, for example, Exhibit 2-4 and imagine that you know only how many sons achieved high-school graduation ($N = 566$) and how many did not ($N = 1470$). Now suppose that you have to guess which category each individual member of the sample falls into. You will, of course, make many errors. But now imagine that you have some additional information. Suppose you also know how many of the 566 had fathers with high occupational status ($N = 346$) and how many of the 1470 had the same ($N = 348$). You will now make fewer errors in your guessing game. The new information helps you because the two variables in the table are related to one another. For this table, gamma, which is known as Yule's Q in 2×2 tables, is equal to 0.67, which indicates that knowledge of the independent variable reduces the errors in guessing values on the dependent variable by a proportion of 0.45. ($0.67 \times 0.67 = 0.45$. For reasons too complicated to go into here, the interpretation goes to the squared term. Actually, this interpretation of gamma, or Q, is subject to complex qualifications. The important point here is to understand the principle of proportional reduction in error interpretation.)

Descriptive Statistics: Correlation and Regression

For hypotheses in which the dependent variable is quantitative, it is almost always more informative to use **correlation and regression analysis** (CRA) than to cross-tabulate the data. When quantitative variables are defined in terms of a limited number of categories (in the extreme case, the dichotomies of "high" and "low"), information is always lost. CRA requires no categories. Briefly, CRA is a body of statistical procedures for describing how accurately values of a dependent variable can be predicted from knowledge of the values of one or more independent variables (correlation) and what the rules are for making such predictions (regression).

The **Pearson product-moment correlation coefficient** (denoted by r) is the CRA statistic that measures the strength, or predictive power, of the relationship between two quantitative scales. In order to use r, we must first have a set of units on which measurements have been taken on two or more quantitative variables, as in Exhibit 2-6. If only two variables are involved, the data can be represented geometrically by plotting each unit as a point in a two-dimensional space in which the horizontal axis stands for values of variable A and the vertical axis for values of variable B, as in the first panel of Exhibit 2-7. A unit's score on A determines how far to the right its point is located, while its score on B determines how far up it is placed.

Having plotted each unit as a point, we can then find the straight line— hence, "linear relationship"—that best fits this scatter of points. (This is done mathematically for computational purposes, but an eyeball guess is often very close.) Correlation now involves finding r, a measure of how good this fit actually is. If all the points fall exactly on a line sloping upward from the left, the relationship between the two variables is perfect and positive and $r = 1.00$ (panel 2 of Exhibit 2-7). If they all fall exactly on a line sloping downward from the left, the relationship is perfect and negative and $r = 1.00$ (panel 3 of Exhibit 2-7). If no straight line fits this scatter of points better than other lines, there is no relationship at all between the two variables and $r = 0.00$ (panel 4 of Exhibit 2-7). Almost always, though, one straight line does best fit the scatter of points, even though it does not fit perfectly, in which case r takes on some non-zero value between -1.00 and $+1.00$.

Exhibit 2-6
Average Annual Earnings (1980)
and Prestige, Twelve Selected Occupations

	Earnings	Prestige
Physicians and surgeons	$57 495	87.2
University teachers	31 833	84.6
Veterinarians	30 660	66.7
Architects	28 111	78.1
Civil engineers	25 917	73.1
Commercial travellers	21 705	40.2
Insurance agents	21 441	47.3
Funeral directors and embalmers	17 995	54.9
Net, trap, and line fishing occupations	9 701	23.4
Chefs and cooks	8 143	29.7
Bartenders	8 091	20.2
Newspaper carriers and vendors	3 751	14.8

Note: Data on earnings and data on prestige come from separate sources in which the occupational titles are not always identical.

Sources: Earnings: Statistics Canada, *1981 Census of Canada*, cat. no. 92-930, table 1; prestige: Pineo and Porter (1967).

Values of r are nicely interpretable when they are squared. Specifically, r^2 is the proportion of variation in one variable that is explained by variation in the other. So if we wish to test an explanation in which changes in A are hypothesized to result in changes in B and the product-moment correlation coefficient between the measures for A and B is calculated to be 0.50, we can say that 0.25, or one-quarter, of the variation in B is explained by variation in A.

The regression part of CRA involves a set of rules for predicting a unit's score on B from knowledge of its score on A. We use a statistic known as an **unstandardized regression coefficient** (denoted by b). Briefly, values of b tell us how many units of change in B occur as a consequence of one unit of change in A. To phrase the point somewhat differently, a value of b is the slope of the best-fitting straight line drawn through the scatter of points. The unstandardized regression coefficient (b) tells us exactly how to predict changes in B on the basis of changes in A. The Pearson product-moment correlation coefficient (r) measures the accuracy of this linear prediction. For the two sets of values in Exhibit 2-6 (plotted in panel 1 of Exhibit 2-7), the unstandardized regression coefficient is 0.0016, and the Pearson product-moment correlation coefficient is 0.88. In this case, then, variation in occupational income explains 0.77 of the variation in prestige ($r^2 = 0.88^2 = 0.77$), while an increase of $1 in annual income predicts an increase of 0.0016 in occupational prestige.

Exhibit 2-7
Correlations Represented Graphically

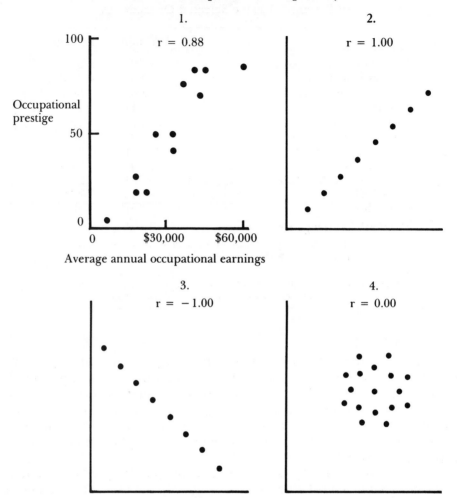

Average annual occupational earnings

Inferential Statistics: Testing the Null Hypothesis

Inferential statistics is a body of techniques that draws on probability theory to enable generalizations about populations based on data from samples of units drawn from those populations. Typically, a researcher has information known to be true for a sample of units. The interest, however, is seldom in the sample as such but in the population from which it was drawn. If the sample is a simple random sample, probability theory offers a way to extrapolate from sample to population.

Statistical inference often involves using tests of statistical significance to reject or fail to reject **null hypotheses**:

1. The starting point is a hypothesis, such as Marx's contention, "religion is the opiate of the masses," which can be read to mean that the more involved people are in formal religious activities, the more conservative they tend to be in their political beliefs. This is the research hypothesis, but it is not the one actually tested. Instead, researchers aim to reject or fail to reject the **null hypothesis** that one variable is not (hence "null") related to another.

2. The investigator develops scales to measure the independent variable (in this case, involvement in formal religious activities) and the dependent variable (here, conservatism in political belief).

3. The researcher defines the population in question, enumerates it, draws (let us say) a simple random sample from it, takes measurements, and calculates the appropriate statistics (unstandardized regression coefficients, for instance).

4. Now one can ask, "How often would samples of this size be drawn from this population to yield a statistical result of this magnitude, if the true value for this statistic in the population is zero?" Before making any calculations, it is usual to define a sufficiently small frequency as one or five times in 100 samples—that is, probabilities of 0.01 or 0.05. If the test results meet this definition, one can reject the null hypothesis that involvement in formal religious activities is not related to conservatism in political belief. If results are not sufficiently small—that is, if the probability is greater than the level decided on beforehand as the criterion—one has failed to reject the null hypothesis.

Such a test is known as a test of statistical significance, and the probability level chosen as the **level of statistical significance**. It should be pointed out that tests of statistical significance are technical criteria applied to empirical data and should not be confused with judgments of substantive importance. A result is statistically significant if it would rarely be found in a sample drawn from a population in which the null hypothesis is true. It is substantively important if it is of consequence for the development of theory.

Considering "Third" Variables

Social theories are rarely restricted to hypotheses about the relationship of two abstract variables in isolation from all others. Consequently, data analysis to test a hypothesis is seldom confined to an examination of how two sets of empirical measurements are connected. Whether in proposing theories or in testing them, sociologists must almost always consider one or more additional, or **third**, **variables**.

Essentially the same principles apply to theorizing about or analyzing the relationships among three variables as among many variables. Thus, a few observations on the three-variable case can illustrate some of the issues that arise in connection with larger systems.

Just how a third variable is incorporated into an empirical analysis depends on how the hypothesis relates it to the independent variable. The hypothesized relationship can take one of two distinct forms:

1. *C* as simultaneous or prior variable. The first and second panels of Exhibit 2-8 show *C* as prior to *B*, where *C* is either simply associated with *A* (as shown by the two-headed, curved arrow in panel 1) or prior to *A* (as shown by the one-headed, straight arrow in panel 2). In either case, because *C* is both related to *A* and prior to *B*, the nature and magnitude of the relationship between *A* and *B* cannot be precisely determined unless *C* is systematically analyzed in relation to both of them. For example, "better-educated people tend to move into higher-status occupations than do the less well educated." But better-educated people and those with higher-status occupations tend to have fathers with higher-status occupations than do people with less education or those with lower-status occupations. So studies of the relationship between level of education (*A*) and occupational status (*B*) will yield inflated estimates of the influence of the former on the latter if the

Exhibit 2-8
Causal Relationships among Three Variables

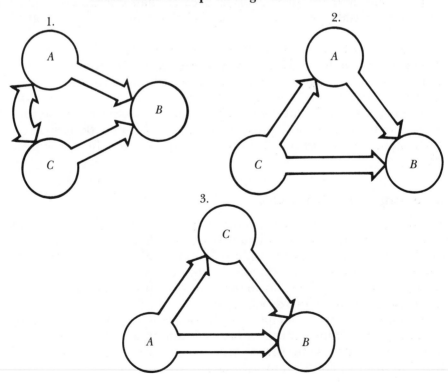

father's occupational status (*C*) is not analyzed in relation to the other two variables.

2. *C* as intervening variable. Panel 3 of Exhibit 2-8 shows a third variable, *C*, as **intervening** between *A* and *B*, so that all or part of the relationship between these latter two variables is channelled through *C*. If all of this relationship is mediated by *C*, the relationship between *A* and *B* is entirely indirect (via *C*). If only part of this relationship is channelled through *C*, the relationship between the two is both indirect and direct. For example, although people whose parents have high-status occupations tend to have higher-status occupations than do those whose parents have low-status occupations, part of the influence of parents' occupational statuses (*A*) is by way of the children's educational attainment (*C*). That is, parents with high occupational status have children who tend to go farther in school than do parents with low occupational status and, partly as a consequence, the children of the former tend to obtain higher-status occupations than do those of the latter.

Analysis of the relationships of multiple variables, some of which are wholly or partially intervening variables, is called multiple variable causal analysis. A common and useful technique for showing the results is called a path diagram; Chapters 6 and 8 of this book have good examples.

CONCLUSION

This chapter has been a fast run over the topic of sociological methodology, emphasizing the principles of social research rather than the technical details. The rules for demonstration are, after all, more important than the techniques. These rules are few and relatively constant, while the particular techniques used to implement them are many and in continuous flux. But:

> who cares if some oneeyed son of a bitch
> invents an instrument to measure Spring with?

My answer is that we should all care. Kissing and singing and measuring Spring are not at all unrelated. A scientific approach to the study of a phenomenon holds the promise of eventually enabling us to explain, predict, and control it. And the implications of this ability for the quality of our lives can be enormous. For, if knowledge is preferable to ignorance, it does matter greatly who has that knowledge and who determines how it is used, since the same truth can just as readily enslave you as set you free. It is better, then, that you care how sociology develops and is used or misused; your kissing and singing may depend on it.

FOR FURTHER READING

Broad, William, and Nicholas Wade
  1982 *Betrayers of the Truth: Fraud and Deceit in the Halls of Science.* New York: Touchstone.
  This book is a healthy corrective to conventional views of how scientists proceed.
Bulmer, Martin, ed.
  1984 *Sociological Research Methods: An Introduction.* 2nd ed. London: Macmillan.
  This well-chosen collection of readings focuses on current issues in empirical research in sociology.
Easthope, Gary
  1974 *History of Social Research Methods.* London: Longman.
  Easthope provides a short and straightforward account of the evolution of social science methodology.
Erickson, B.H., and T.A. Nosanchuk
  1977 *Understanding Data.* Toronto: McGraw-Hill Ryerson.
  This approach to the analysis of quantitative data emphasizes innovative, descriptive procedures.
Halfpenny, Peter
  1982 *Positivism and Sociology.* London: George Allen & Unwin.
  Halfpenny gives an abbreviated but lucid discussion of the philosophical foundations of empirical social research.

PART II
CULTURE AND SOCIETY

Although the term environment most often refers to the natural world of grass, trees, clouds, and sky, for most people the real environment in which they live is a world of their own creation. This humanly constructed world, whether one of earthen pottery and feather headdresses or of air conditioners and astroturf, is not one given by nature. Rather, it is a product of society. Another word for this humanly constructed world is culture. Understanding culture is essential to understanding oneself and it is just as central to understanding others. A society cannot be understood adequately without knowing its culture, and a culture cannot be understood without knowing the society that shapes it— the two concepts are the cornerstones of an understanding of human behaviour. Because of culture, the way Canadians live differs from the ways in which people live in the Amazon forests, the rice paddies of China, and the highlands of New Guinea.

Though variously defined, the term culture usually refers to the socially shared and transmitted knowledge of a society as reflected in its norms, beliefs, practices, and objects. The organization of behaviour in a society is largely influenced by and mediated through the symbolic meanings available in the culture. Culture also provides the acceptable boundaries within which members of the society channel their behaviour. In short, it is the glue of human organization.

Nevertheless, the concept of culture, as Linda Hunter and Judith Posner show in Chapter 3, is a somewhat amorphous one in the social sciences. Perhaps because it is so intimately tied in with the concept of society, the notion of culture must encompass the extraordinary variety of ways in which people in different societies organize their lives. A concept that covers such a broad range of phenomena tends to lose precision. Furthermore, as Hunter and Posner indicate, it is questionable

whether a complex modern industrial society such as Canada really has one common culture. Perhaps such a society can best be understood as a cluster of subcultures—cultures specific to particular groups.

Generally, the role of culture is most obvious in the more intimate of social institutions. It is within families, schools, and relationships with friends that norms, beliefs, and practices are the most powerful and most often manipulated; these norms, beliefs, and practices may also be at odds with those of others. Culture pervades all of human life and all social institutions.

One of sociologists' perennial concerns is the attempt to discover the ways in which society and culture serve to channel the behaviour of individuals. Why do people follow the norms, customs, and beliefs of their society? At one time it was believed that people behave as they do because it was "natural" for them to do so, because God had commanded it, or because different races had different tendencies. Today, sociologists use the term socialization to refer to the means whereby individuals come to learn and adopt the norms, values, beliefs, and attitudes of their society. In Chapter 4, "Socialization and the Self," William Shaffir and Allan Turowetz examine the processes whereby individuals internalize the symbolic meanings of their society as a crucial component of their sense of self. Using the symbolic interactionist perspective, the authors show that the development of the self is not a result of passively accepting bits and pieces of the surrounding culture, but the outcome of an active, ongoing process of interaction with others.

Much of this socialization occurs in the family, and it is the family—one of the central social institutions of society—that is the most important transmitter of culture from one generation to the other. Given the crucial role that the family performs in society, the dramatic changes that it has undergone in recent years and is continuing to undergo have important implications for understanding present-day Canadian society. As Nancy Mandell shows in Chapter 5, most Canadians are members of a family, but the image of the typical family does not conform to the reality of family life in today's Canada.

Chapter 6, by Sid Gilbert and Ian Gomme, deals with the other major agent of socialization in Canadian society—education. As provincial finance ministers are quick to point out, the education system is the single largest expenditure in most provincial budgets. Yet many people are asking whether that system really benefits either the students or the public that pays the bills. Of particular concern in recent years has been the question of equality—that is, whether the education system prepares everyone equally well and gives everyone an equal chance to take his or her place in society.

The final chapter in this section, Stuart Schoenfeld's look at the sociology of religion (Chapter 7) focuses on the links between systems of cultural symbols and their implications for social behaviour. Traditionally, religion has been the major source of symbols that give individuals a sense of purpose and hope in life. Just as important, religion has served to legitimate and justify the norms and values of a society, to explain pain and suffering, and to make sense of death. Since the 19th century, sociologists have been fascinated by the ways in which such systems of cultural meanings are institutionalized in church and sect, profoundly affecting behaviour. Just as studying the family helps one to understand individuals, and studying the education system reveals the processes underlying the ways individuals take on their roles in society, so studying religion sheds light on the powerful social movements through which individuals collectively change their society.

CHAPTER 3

CULTURE AS POPULAR CULTURE

Linda Hunter and Judith Posner

CULTURE: EVERYBODY TALKS ABOUT IT BUT . . .
What Isn't Culture

CULTURE AS CODE: THE SYMBOL

CULTURE AND THE INDIVIDUAL

SUBCULTURES: VARIATIONS ON A THEME
Studying Cultures on Their Own Terms

STYLE AND CULTURAL PATTERNS
Fashion: A Study in Custom, Costume, and History

TECHNOLOGY AND CULTURE
Media Culture

CANADIAN CULTURE: DOES IT EXIST?

Summary
For Further Reading
Audio-Visual Resources

CULTURE: EVERYBODY TALKS ABOUT IT BUT . . .

Almost every introductory sociology or anthropology text includes a chapter or section on the concept of culture. And yet, after wading through a set of definitions that reads more like a dictionary entry than an essay, the reader/student is probably left as puzzled as ever. Intuitively, we all know that culture is an important concept because we use it in our everyday speech, but it is difficult to put into words. In short, culture is one of those maddening concepts that everybody takes for granted but that is usually a gloss for some unresolved analysis. In this chapter we will attempt to come to terms with unexamined notions about culture.

The concept of culture is actually less abstract than some of the descriptions of it in the literature would indicate. Unfortunately, there are almost as many definitions of culture as there are anthropologists and sociologists. To list a few:

> Culture is that complex whole which includes knowledge, belief, art, morals, law, custom, and any other capabilities and habits acquired by man as a member of society. (E.B. Tylor 1871, 1)

> A culture consists of the acquired or cultivated behavior and thought of individuals within a society, as well as the intellectual, artistic and social ideals and institutions which the members of the society profess and to which they strive to conform. (D. Bidney 1953, 104).

> We may view culture as "the sum total of the ways in which human beings live, transmitted from generation to generation by learning." It includes "the relations between people in pairs and in groups, man's work activities involving actual materials, and his expenditure of energy in the realm of symbols, including speech, music, the visual arts, and the human body itself. (C.S. Coon 1954, 5)

> Culture consists of the sum total of skills, beliefs, knowledge and products that are shared by a number of people and transmitted to their children. (D. Dressler and W. Willis Jr. 1976, 33)

These definitions, vague and wide-ranging as they are, all make two things clear:

1. Culture subsumes society as well as the individual. It is the broadest of concepts.
2. Culture involves both material and ideological aspects of a group's existence.

Culture, as discussed by sociologists, embodies a number of subconcepts. Some of these are useful. Others are archaic. And still others are less relevant to sociology than to anthropology, the field in which they originated. Familiarity with the vocabulary defined in the box on the next page is, however, necessary for comprehension of much of the material on culture.

SUBCONCEPTS
OF CULTURE: DEFINITIONS

Society: A self-perpetuating group of people who are engaged in interaction according to a pattern of social organization.

Status: A culturally defined position in the social structure. Each individual may occupy many statuses.

Ascribed status: A status usually assigned to an individual at birth.

Achieved status: A status attained by an individual through his or her actions.

Role: The pattern of behaviour associated with a particular status.

Symbol: Anything taken by a group of people as a representation of something else—a word, gesture, or object for example.

Values: The criteria people use in assessing behaviour and in determining appropriate goals.

Norms: Formal or informal rules telling members of society how they are expected to behave in particular situations; the concrete ways in which values are applied.

Mores: Traditional important ethical rules that, although regarded as extremely important for members of the society, are informally enforced. Also called salient norms.

Laws: Norms that are institutionalized, maintained, and enforced by a legislative body.

Folkways: Traditional norms about customary ways of behaving that are shared and informally enforced by members of a society. Folkways change fairly often. Violation may bring criticism or reprimand but is not as harshly sanctioned as violation of mores.

Sanction: An action that punishes non-conformity to norms and/or rewards conformity to norms.

Stigma: A mark of discredit or unworthiness. A person who violates a norm may be stigmatized.

Ideologies: Sets of normative beliefs, values, and ideas used in defining what is desirable and undesirable in society.

Material culture: The level of culture that includes the products of the interaction of human beings— the physical artifacts.

Non-material culture: The level of culture that includes the meanings, values, norms, and beliefs of the members—the ideologies.

Subculture: A social group whose norms, values, and ideologies differ in some respects from those of the dominant culture.

Counterculture: A subculture that is opposed to or in conflict with the norms and values of the dominant culture.

Cultural trait: A particular characteristic of members of a culture; the smallest meaningful unit of culture.

Ethnocentrism: The tendency to evaluate the norms and values of other cultures by the standards of one's own culture; the belief that one's own culture is superior to other cultures.

Cultural relativity: The principle that all cultures are equally valid and that every culture must be judged on its own terms.

What Isn't Culture

The greatest difficulty in defining culture is to distinguish it from any-thing (everything) else. It is useful to think of culture as a residual cat-egory; that is, **culture** is anything related to human behaviour that cannot be directly attributed to biology and/or instinct. This dichotomy sounds neat and is often treated as quite simple. Unfortunately, distinguishing culture from biology—or, in anthropological terms, nature from nur-ture—is not as easy as we might like. Researchers have devoted a great deal of energy to delineating the biological determinants of social be-haviour (see Chapter 4). For example, the popular books of zoologist Desmond Morris (1965; 1983) have aroused heated debate because they view people as merely a species of animal, and most social behaviour as biologically determined. The study of gender or sex-role behaviour is a case in point (see Chapter 9). In recent years, especially since the rise of modern feminism, many studies have dealt with the nature/nurture aspect of gender socialization. For example, one set looked at how adult reactions to a baby varied with the baby's reported gender.

> Sidorowicz and Lunney (1980) observed how adults interacted with Baby X, an infant variously introduced as a boy, a girl or without any gender infor-mation. The university student subjects were told that the study concerned the responses of infants to strangers, and were encouraged to talk with and touch the baby. In the room there were a small toy football, a doll and a teething ring (gender-neutral). When the baby was designated as male, 65% of the subjects chose the football. When it was designated as female, 80% of the subjects chose the doll. When no gender was assigned, 25% chose the football, 40% chose the doll, and 35% the teething ring. These adults then acted in sex-stereotypical ways with the *same* infant, depending on the label provided. (Mackie 1983, 86)

Notice that culture is not merely **high culture**—the forms of expression defined as high art by an elite. Ballet, symphony music, painting, and poetry—Culture with a capital C—are a part of culture. But they are no more important to the study of human behaviour than any other aspect of a people's existence. In fact, one could argue the reverse—that popular art, advertising, rock music, and so on are more suitable topics for so-ciological analysis than the history of painting or classical music. (We examine the phenomenon of advertising later in this chapter.) We do not suggest, however, that high art is altogether irrelevant. Recently a number of researchers have turned their attention to parallels between high culture and popular culture. For example, John Berger's excellent (1972) series of books and films, *Ways of Seeing*, examines the nude in Western painting, relating classical poses to the depiction of woman in modern advertising. One of the authors of this chapter does similar work and finds, for example, that seductive female modesty, often used in classical paintings, is a pervasive theme in today's print ads and fashion

The pose may be similar but the depiction of feminine beauty has changed.

photography (see the photographs on page 84). Such visual depictions are important manifestations of cultural values—in this case, assumptions about values and beliefs related to one's gender.

CULTURE AS CODE: THE SYMBOL

What makes human beings different from other animals? Anthropologists often refer to the use of the symbol. Whereas other members of the animal kingdom communicate through signs with inherent, concrete meanings, humans have in their culture a richly interpretive meaning system made possible by **symbols**—things that stand for other things. Symbols can be either verbal, as in the case of language (a highly codified system of phonetic sounds), or non-verbal, including the use of space, gestures, and facial expressions.

One of the most dramatic statements on the significance of the symbol is the Sapir/Whorf hypothesis. Less a hypothesis than an elaborate statement on the relationship of language to thought, it has become a classic contribution to the way we think about society, culture, and communication:

> Human beings do not live in the objective world alone, nor alone in the world of social activity as ordinarily understood, but are very much at the mercy of the particular language which has become the medium of expression for their society. It is quite an illusion to imagine that one adjusts to reality essentially without the use of language and that language is merely an incidental means of solving specific problems of communication or reflection, . . . we see and hear and otherwise experience very largely as we do because the language habits of our community predispose certain choices of interpretation. (Edward Sapir [1929] 1962, 294)

This statement emphasizes how difficult it is to think outside of culture. Culture in turn is shaped by the semantic patterns of a specific language. Probably the most widely cited example is the Inuit perception and naming of snow. Because snow is highly relevant to their way of life, the Inuit use many words to differentiate various types of snow. Concomitantly, because of this linguistic and cognitive ability to differentiate, they tend to observe many nuances or variations in snow. In a similar vein, the more students develop a sociological vocabulary for talking about human behaviour, the more sensitive they become to behavioural nuances. The relationship between language and culture is reciprocal; since it is impossible to say which comes first, it is important to view them together.

Non-verbal communication is equally important. Anthropologist Edward Hall has contributed many dramatic examples of the importance of proxemics (concepts and use of space), kinesics (gestures), and attitudes toward time. In his world travels as a diplomatic consultant, he observed non-verbal cultural codes. He noticed particularly the way that different cultures use and define space. For example, North Americans generally like to stand about 60 to 120 cm apart during social conversations, while

Arabs prefer to be 30 cm apart (see Hall 1966, 154-64). This discrepancy leads to an odd sort of dance at social occasions that bring together people of different cultures. One party to a conversation pursues the other, who retreats, as each unconsciously tries to establish a comfortable speaking distance. In recent years social psychologists and psychologists have paid considerable attention to verbal and non-verbal codes in studies of small-group interaction. The box on this page gives an excellent example of the analysis of verbal and non-verbal nuance.

WORD PLAY: WHAT HAPPENS WHEN PEOPLE TALK

Even the simplest statement may convey meanings through para-language that a sensitive listener detects without quite realizing how he does it. To examine the meanings often hidden in utterances, a team of linguists and psychiatrists collaborated on a remarkable project—a microscopic analysis of the speech interaction between a young woman and a psychiatrist, the words they used, their tone of voice and stress patterns, their pauses and coughs and hesitations. So detailed was the analysis that only the first five minutes of the interaction filled an entire book. This is what took place in merely the first few seconds:

> The scene is a psychiatrist's office. A young woman enters and he says to her, "What brings you here?" The woman hesitates for a moment, then emits a brief, throaty sigh; she drawls her words as she replies, "Everything's wrong. I get so— irritable, tense, depressed."

Since the psychiatrist is trained in the strategies of the language game, presumably his utterances are calculated. When he says *What brings you here?* he apparently intends to evoke a certain kind of response from the young woman. His first statement does indeed set the tone for the interaction. Three of the four words he uses—*what, you,* and *here*—are words that linguists call substitute, or pronominal, forms. They can easily be substituted for other words, and therefore they are basically non-committal. Instead of these pronominal forms, the psychiatrist might have said *What problems bring you so upset to a psychiatrist's office?* But if he had begun the conversation that way, he would clearly be starting off on the wrong track. He would appear to be saying that he already concluded the woman has problems, that her face plainly reveals the intensity of her emotions, and that she is in an office that treats mentally ill people—which is certainly too much for him to convey before the woman has even spoken. Instead, he chose to use neutral pronominal forms and allow the story to emerge from the woman.

A close look at the stress pattern of the psychiatrist's opening sentence is revealing. He placed stress only on the word *here*, and even that was very slight. If the stress had been very strong—*What brings you HERE?*—he might have appeared to express surprise that the woman was seeing a psychiatrist, which would have been unfitting, since he did not yet know anything about her. If he had chosen to place stress elsewhere in the sentence—such as *WHAT brings you here?* or *What brings YOU here?*—he might have seemed to imply amazement that the woman had the same sort of problems as the disturbed people he treats. The word *you* also is significant. He uses it as the object of the sentence, sympathetically indicating that the woman may have come to him because of external pressures that were victimizing her rather than because of problems in her own personality. If, instead, he had used *you* as the subject of the sentence—such as *Why have you come here?*—he would appear to be blaming the woman for having the leading role in whatever her problems are.

It is now the woman's turn to speak. She hesitates, emits a sigh, and finally says *Everything's wrong.* She drawls her words slightly, which is not the way someone who speaks spontaneously would utter them. Like most people who visit a psychiatrist for the first time—or who go to an interview for a job, meet with a client or customer, or even testify in a law case—she has rehearsed the opening of her story. She no doubt thinks she is being very clever, but her hesitation, sigh, and drawl have given her away.

Her next sentence confirms that she is dramatizing a conversation opener she has memorized. The way she utters the words *I get so* is particularly important. She clips the *so* by closing her vocal cords, then holds a pause before she speaks the three adjectives that are her symptoms: *irritable, tense, depressed.* The absence of *and* between the last two adjectives is a further indication that she is delivering a prepared speech; spontaneous conversation surely would insert an *and* in a string of adjectives. The psychiatrist's first question had been carefully posed to leave open the possibility that the woman had come to see him because of external pressures rather than because of problems stemming from her own personality. But the woman does not accept this opportunity to appear blameless. Instead of making external forces the subject of her sentence—such as *People make me irritable, tense, depressed*—she acknowledges at least partial responsibility for whatever is troubling her by saying *I get so.*

In only a few seconds and through the utterance of a total of a dozen words, two people have entered fully into a speech interaction. Each has heard the sound of the other's voice. The psychiatrist has shown himself to be open-minded, fair, willing to listen. The woman had come to the office with her mind made up to play a part in a drama she had written in advance, yet she displays a willingness to face up to her problems. The rest of the conversation can now proceed fruitfully, as in fact it did.

—PETER FARB

CULTURE AND THE INDIVIDUAL

Perhaps the central issue for the social sciences is the precise relationship between individual behaviour and culture. Because culture is such a wide-ranging concept, it is difficult to imagine anything that does not impinge upon individual behaviour. Yet we do not want to suggest that the individual is an automaton. We believe in the notion of free will, but we also acknowledge that the individual does not exist outside of culture. Like a tree in a forest, the individual is both an autonomous being and a part of a larger whole, subject to the influence of that whole. People act and make choices within a web of social relationships and rules of which they may not even be aware.

Individuals play **roles** within a social organization; they behave in patterns that fit their positions and fit the expectations of others. Position within the social system may also be referred to as **status**. Each individual has many statuses. A person might be, for example, a chartered accountant, a mother, a sister, a wife, a church committee member, and an amateur musician. Each of these statuses requires that the individual be involved in relationships with others and encounter various role expectations. Each status affects the way a person is seen by others and sees him or herself, and each carries with it specific duties and obligations. When these obligations are in opposition to one another or when obligations of different statuses surface simultaneously, individuals suffer from **role conflict**. For example, a man may be a dedicated father, husband, and successful lawyer in a large law firm. When work consumes too much time, he may feel guilty for what he sees as irresponsibility in family life, and hence experience role conflict.

People choose their statuses only to a certain extent. Within all societies, some statuses are **ascribed**: that is, a person is simply born with them. One is male or female, belongs to a given race or ethnic group, and is part of a particular family. Other statuses are **achieved** by an individual through education, occupation, or voluntary association with particular groups. Societies value certain statuses more than others, although this changes as social values change.

The expectations of a given society are based on the **values** accepted by its culture—the basic definitions of what is good and bad, important and trivial. Values are translated into **norms**, or rules of behaviour, which may be codified into laws and enforced by the power of the state, or merely informal and generally accepted.

The most important rules, close to the heart of a culture, are called **mores**. These may include prohibitions against murder, armed robbery, and sexual violations such as incest. While they are the basis of most laws, not all breaches of mores are illegal. Breaches of law, of course, bring penalties enforced by the state and police. But beatings, lynchings, or intense ostracism may also punish certain violations.

Folkways, on the other hand, are informal norms, not usually encoded in law, and less serious than mores. Folkways include rules of politeness, dress, and manner. Without perhaps thinking much about it, people realize that some things that may not be illegal or considered immoral are simply not done. For example, although it is quite acceptable to belch after a meal in some countries, it is certainly not acceptable behaviour in North American dining rooms.

Yet what was unacceptable even a few years ago may be commonplace today, while what was perfectly all right in earlier generations may now be frowned upon. For example, couples are no longer ostracized for living together without getting married. On the other hand, marriage between an adult man and a girl of 16 or 17, which was not uncommon in pre-Confederation Canada, is now outside the norm.

Generally, sanctions for violating folkways are relatively subtle. They may consist merely of tacit disapproval, a facial expression of disgust, an uncontrollable chuckle, a snide comment, or a verbal reprimand.

This brief analysis sounds cut and dried when, in fact, the matter is much debated and the links between cultures and individuals are complex and subtle.

How do all these general rules and regulations—norms, mores, folkways, and the like—get translated into social behaviour? This we take to be the central question of any humanistic sociology, and the subject not only of this chapter but of this entire book.

SUBCULTURES: VARIATIONS ON A THEME

When sociologists or anthropologists find it difficult to account for behaviour that is marginal to the normative framework, they sometimes employ the concept of **subculture**, which refers to a social group whose norms, values, and ideology differ in some respects from those of the dominant culture.

The concept of subculture is useful, yet it can be as nebulous and riddled with contradiction as the concept of culture itself. Moreover, the line of distinction between culture and subculture is not always clear. In a pluralistic society such as Canada, it can be argued that there is no dominant culture. Canada is a blend of many groups, alike in some ways but different in others. Except at the institutional or legal level, people do not live in Canadian society or culture as a whole. They live in various milieus—in a large city, in a small town, on a farm, or on a reserve; in a relatively homogeneous or highly heterogeneous area; in a French-, English-, or Italian-speaking neighbourhood. In short, each person's day-to-day existence is more strongly influenced by a specific cultural context than by any general national demographic profile. This point, which we discuss at the end of this chapter, is important to an understanding of Canadian culture.

The word subculture may evoke images of the bizarre, mysterious, and exotic. It suggests the underworld and the deviant. The sociology of deviance, which focuses on behaviour that violates society's norms, makes frequent use of the subculture concept to explain the creation and maintenance of deviant groups, from Alcoholics Anonymous to female impersonators (see Chapter 12). The theory of differential association holds that individuals take up deviant lifestyles through their membership in a subculture (Becker 1964). Within Canada, various regions can also be considered to have their own subcultures, with distinctive styles of architecture, foods, and social and political orientations. Particular classes, age groups, and religious, ethnic, racial, and gender groups can also be viewed as subcultures. In a work-oriented society such as ours, occupational groups also form subcultures. Entering a trade or profession may entail learning not only skills but a code of ethics, a dress code, and a special vocabulary not usually understood by people outside the group. Occupational subcultures use a special language and set of symbols to communicate, control, or define situations. Police officers, doctors, musicians, and actors, for example, all use special vocabulary to talk shop.

A novice in one of these occupations learning its highly specialized language, is also being taught how to perceive the social world and how to act accordingly. In a similar vein, it is sometimes argued that men and women live in different worlds and use different argots.

Cabby-ese and the Social World

Cab drivers have their own special problems to deal with in their work. They have developed an argot that James Henslin, who has studied them, calls Cabby-ese. In the following table, he demonstrates how it both shapes their perceptions of their work world and helps them to communicate these perceptions to one another. (The words shown in quotation marks are additional terms in the argot.)

Term	Some effects on how cabbies perceive the world	Indication of appropriate action
Ace man	a. Some cabbies are legitimately eligible to make money on the next order, while others must wait. b. The world is highly structured into persons who have rights or access to something and others who do not have rights or access to it. c. People must take their turns in this highly structured world.	a. Try to "ace out" fellow cabbies by getting to "cab stands" before they do. b. As orders are given according to "ace position," be on the alert for other "empty cabs" as you are returning to a "cab stand." c. Stay near the radio if you are in "ace position" so you don't miss out on your order. d. Wait your turn if you've been "aced out." e. If there are too many cabs at a "stand," go to another "stand" or "cruise" for passengers.

Bucket load	a. Most passengers pay willingly. b. Some passengers try to skip out on their "fare" if they get the chance.	a. Be suspicious of a passenger's intentions. b. Always guard against giving a passenger the opportunity to leave your sight before paying.
Flag load	a. Some people who want a cab haven't telephoned for one. b. Flag loads are, in general, to be less trusted than are "dispatched orders."	a. Constantly be on the look-out for flag loads ("cruise"). b. Drive near the curb so you can quickly pull over if someone "flags you down." c. Be suspicious of persons who try to "flag you down," especially if it is a man at night or in a "bad neighborhood."
Liner	a. Some men who desire prostitutes don't know where to find them. b. Liners have ready money to spend.	a. Find out where prostitutes work. b. Help a liner out in order to make extra money. c. Charge a liner his "fare" plus whatever else you can get out of him for giving him this service. d. Work out *in advance* your financial arrangement with a liner. e. Be careful of the "cab squad" if you work with liners.
No go	a. Some people who "call in" for a cab will not be at their location when you arrive. b. Others will have changed their minds about taking a cab by the time you get there. c. You never know if you have an order for sure until a passenger actually gets into your cab.	a. Rush to your order before the caller changes his mind about wanting a cab. b. Don't be overconfident. c. If you get a no go, radio the dispatcher so you can be given "ace position."
Stiff	a. Some passengers never tip. b. Passengers can be "sized up" as to whether they are stiffs or not. c. You can be wrong in "sizing someone up." d. If a passenger is a stiff, what you do won't affect your tip. e. If you didn't get a tip, it probably had nothing to do with your services. f. If you don't treat passengers right, you can make stiffs out of them.	a. Figure out whether your passenger is a stiff or not. b. If he is a stiff, do nothing extra for him: Don't even be polite if you don't feel like it. c. If he isn't a stiff, be your usual self, or even do extra things in order to increase the size of the tip. d. As you can't tell for sure until after the trip, err on the side of giving the passenger the benefit of the doubt.

From LANGUAGE AND WOMAN'S PLACE

Aside from specific lexical items like color names, we find differences between the speech of women and that of men in the use of particles that grammarians often describe as "meaningless." There may be no referent for them, but they are far from meaningless: they define the social context of an utterance, indicate the relationship the speaker feels between himself and his addressee, between himself and what he is talking about.

As an experiment, one might present native speakers of standard American English with pairs of sentences, identical syntactically and in terms of referential lexical items, and differing merely in the choice of "meaningless" particle, and ask them which was spoken by a man, which a woman. Consider:

(a) Oh dear, you've put the peanut butter in the refrigerator again.

(b) Shit, you've put the peanut butter in the refrigerator again.

It is safe to predict that people would classify the first sentence as part of "women's language," the second as "men's language." It is true that many self-respecting women are becoming able to use sentences like *(b)* publicly without flinching, but this is a relatively recent development, and while perhaps the majority of Middle America might condone the use of *(b)* for men, they would still disapprove of its use by women. (It is of interest, by the way, to note that men's language is increasingly being used by women, but women's language is not being adopted by men, apart from those who reject the American masculine image [for example, homosexuals]. This is analogous to the fact that men's jobs are being sought by women, but few men are rushing to become housewives or secretaries. The language of the favored group, the group that holds the power, along with its nonlinguistic behavior, is generally adopted by the other group, not vice versa. In any event, it is a truism to state that the "stronger" expletives are reserved for men, and the "weaker" ones for women.)

—ROBIN LAKOFF

Studying Cultures on Their Own Terms

The roots of North American sociology lie in the field studies of marginal and/or deviant subcultures in the urban milieu. Earlier in this century the students of the Chicago School became noted for studying the social world by living alongside their subjects. Robert Park, W.I. Thomas, Clifford Shaw, Everett Hughes, Oswald Hall, Howard Becker and William Foote Whyte, to name some of the best known, recorded at first hand the "definition of the situation" of Polish peasants, jackrollers, factory workers, jazz musicians, dancehall patrons, professional boxers, and medical students, among others. Their discoveries confirmed the value of fieldwork.

Today the tenets of the Chicago School have been developed by sociologists espousing the labelling perspective on deviance (see Chapter 12). These theorists emphasize the complexity and diversity of social life, pointing out that the practices of any subculture, whether it is made up of the poor, the very rich, female impersonators, or debutantes, can only be fully understood by reference to its own norms and values. An **ethnocentric approach**, one that starts with the assumption that one's own culture is right and others wrong or odd in their differences from it, will reveal little about either culture. How can one culture hope to understand another when there is so much confusion and misunderstanding within cultures? Yet the very essence of both anthropology and comparative sociology is the quest to find cultural universals and to compare and contrast cultural patterns. Social scientists have adopted the concept of **cultural relativism** to acknowledge the fact that culture can only be understood from the inside, from the actor's viewpoint. Because symbols, codes, language, and norms are meaningful only in context, to understand them one must become intimately familiar with the specific cultural setting.

STYLE AND CULTURAL PATTERNS

Style, which is represented in even the simplest material object, always has cultural meaning. Dress style, for example, has a symbolic dimension, marking identity in a particular group and conveying information about the wearer. Dick Hebdige (1979) argues that tensions between dominant and subordinate groups are reflected in style. The expressive forms and rituals of groups such as the teddy boys, the mods and rockers, the skinheads and the punks are represented in style, music, and dress, making them visible and often disturbing to the dominant culture. He describes the implications of style for British subcultures of the late 1970s:

> Glam rock contributed narcissism, nihilism and gender confusion. American punk offered a minimalist aesthetic (e.g., the "Ramones" "Pinhead" or Crime's "I Stupid"), the cult of the street and a penchant for self-laceration. Northern Soul (a genuinely secret subculture of working-class youngsters dedicated to

acrobatic dancing and fast American soul of the 60's, which centres on clubs like the Wigan Casino) brought its subterranean tradition of fast, jerky rhythms, solo dance styles and amphetamines; reggae its exotic and dangerous aura of forbidden identity, its conscience, its dread and its cool . . . . (Hebdige 1979, 25)

To shed some light on the relationship between cultural artifacts and cultural norms, we offer the following exploration of fashion.

Fashion: A Study in Custom, Costume, and History

Since material and non-material culture are closely linked, fashions and fads intrinsic to a particular culture and time provide insight into socio-political ideology and sentiment. The flapper dress of the early 1920s, for example, represented a prosperous and carefree age. The punk look of the 1980s speaks to the lack of naturalness in the contemporary environment.

When sociologists think of fashion, they think of the variety of trends in clothing and body image that reflect rapidly changing social attitudes. As Lakoff and Scherr (1984, 86) maintain, "The pendulum of beauty swings along with the pendulum of politics." At the end of the 1930s, beauty became patriotic as war became a reality. In its 1 November 1939 issue, *Vogue* commented on how the war had changed fashion. In Paris, it reported, "Gas masks are worn nonchalantly, snoods are almost uniform, knickers are possible, boots ideal." In Britain, women wore "a spate of white accessories" in order "to avoid head-on collisions while going through . . . blackouts," low-heeled shoes because gas rationing forced them to walk, and "special dresses called A.R.P. (Air Raid Precaution) for nocturnal diving into air raid shelters" (Lakoff and Scherr 1984, 87).

Post-war styles in the late 1940s shifted from the practical and comfortable to the ultrafeminine. As if to compensate for the hardships of the war, elaborate frilly dresses became popular once more. The 1950s fashion industry marketed cuteness and innocence. These years of affluence brought the celebration of leisure and of youth. Rolled-up jeans, ponytails, saddle shoes, and wide skirts were worn by many teenagers as they attempted to mimic the carefree, spunky style of Hayley Mills, Annette Funicello, and Sandra Dee.

The youth theme became even more popular in the 1960s. Young men grew longer hair and wore beaded necklaces. Young women imitated Twiggy and Penelope Tree; their thin, curveless bodies honoured the androgynous, "unisex" look. Unlike the fashions of the 1950s, which expressed an ease with accepted values, the styles of the 1960s reflected the desire of young people to challenge the status quo. "Beautiful people" and flower children demonstrated for peace, for black rights, for women's and gay liberation. Flowers were painted on bodies in psychedelic colours to celebrate "flower power."

Responding to the popularity of exotic and ethnic looks, and to the growing awareness of the presence of minorities in the country, black and oriental models became a part of *Vogue* fantasy. Bejewelled and painted bodies, bared breasts, heads of hair turned rainbow-colored fantasies, animal-masked leopard-lean figures, androgynous Greek boys, all helped to give beauty a Felliniesque look. Beauty became bizarre. (Lakoff and Scherr 1984, 99)

Thus fashion in the 1960s symbolized the ideological values of that time—freedom and liberation. In the 1970s, things changed considerably. The new theme was reality, as people shared concerns about a fragile ecology and an economic recession. The American mood, which spread to Canada, was one of disillusionment at the bitter end to the Vietnam War as well as the Watergate affair, which revealed amorality and politically inspired dishonesty reaching as high as the office of the president of the United States. Women now wanted to look natural—without the mask of makeup or the restriction of bras. In fact the first wave of the modern feminist movement was humorously epitomized by the popular slogan, "Burn your bra!"

Woman in the 1980s: Mixed Messages

In the 1980s, fashion and beauty shock the public once more. In shop window displays (the showplaces of our culture) and in the pages of fashion magazines one sees a fundamental paradox in the model meant to represent the modern woman. Her ghostly thinness and childlike guise contradict the pouty, erotic expression on her face. This woman-child, portraying both innocence and sexuality, embodies the essential contradiction in woman's role today. When millions of women are enrolled in diet organizations and tens of thousands more are suffering from anorexia nervosa and bulimia, one cannot help but notice that our culture seems to prefer female bodies that look undeveloped, childlike, and dependent. This trend is also reflected in the tendency of pornographic magazines to use models who look (and often are) younger and younger.

But the 1980s also pay tribute to health and fitness. The fitness boom cannot be ignored. Exercise, aerobics, and body building have become recognized as legitimate activities for women. The cover story of a 1982 issue of *Time* magazine analyzes that year's fitness rage among women:

As a comely by-product of the fitness phenomenon, women have begun literally to reshape themselves, and with themselves, the American notion of female beauty, . . . A new form is emerging. . . . It is a body that speaks assurance, in itself, and in the woman who, through will power and muscle power, has created it. (Corliss 1982, 72)

The article salutes women's achievement in this domain. However, as Lakoff and Scherr (1984, 110) point out, the model on the cover is so

This recent photograph suggests that the notion of the ideal feminine physique and demeanor is ever changing. Does this look represent North America's newest standard of feminity? To put the question simply, should "girls" have muscles and, if so, how many?

Although focusing on the female form as an object is common enough in modern Western culture, the passive objectification has been more familiar than the aggressive. If gender differences are about power, nothing could be more effectively symbolic of the closing gender gap than women's becoming just as muscular as men.

fragile and thin that she seems "to have barely enough stamina to stroll from the cover of *Vogue* to the cover of *Time*." *Chatelaine* recently selected the "10 best bodies in Canada" to illustrate the desired vibrant glow of health that reflects the ideology of fitness pervasive in today's culture. However, *Chatelaine*, like many fashion magazines, is quick to remind readers that an active body can still be glamorous. The message is clear: the primary goal is not health, but appeal—through conformity to the demanded image.

The Culture Lag

Material items are often diffused much faster and also persist much longer than ideas or ideologies. Thus one sees the perpetuation of styles of dress associated with various sociopolitical movements, long after the movement's initial impact has faded. For example, one still sees long-haired, bearded men wearing the faded blue jeans and psychedelic shirts popularized in the 1960s, when flower children and the back-to-nature movement represented a popular opposition to the establishment. But this style of dress no longer carries the same ideological meaning. Now the leading countercultural crusaders are the punks. They demonstrate their contempt for the establishment with a shocking, unnatural look— spiked hair dyed pink, purple, green, or orange, exaggerated makeup, metallic studded jewellery (belts, bracelets, chains, spurs), and safety pins or razor blades stuck through the nose, cheeks, ears, or lips. In costumes and behaviour, they demonstrate their anti-establishment ideology of unnaturalness in perverse and startling ways. It has been argued, however, that many North American youths active in the punk movement have merely borrowed the material cultural traits—the remnants of the punk image—from the working-class British youth who originated the movement, but have not necessarily adopted their ideology. The result is "fashion punk"; the forms developed to express a working-class ideology are co-opted by the upper-class establishment. This process culminates in the appearance of punk-like fashion and demeanour in the pages of magazines such as *Vogue*—a phenomenon that might be called "punk without a cause."

Fashion and Class

Today, all over the world, countless fashion magazines reveal changing material trends and hint at the cultural ideas they reflect. Beautiful people in beautiful clothes beckon from the covers. Each model helps to delineate current aesthetic standards and thus to convince readers of what fashions (and what sizes) should be in their closets.

Fashion, however, has not always symbolized popular sentiment; fashion magazines were not always geared to selling clothes and style to the masses. High society magazines, such as *Vogue*, began by catering to an exclusive and elite audience. In the early 1900s, women from the nobility, royalty, and the upper class appeared in *Vogue*. They set fashion standards simply by wearing their own clothing in their own homes. As Lakoff and Scherr explain:

> Their beauty is not ready-made for the camera, nor a perfection of feature and figure. It is not typically a beauty of high cheekbones and ghostly thinness but rather a beauty born of poise and refinement. It divides the "haves" from the "have nots." (1984, 77)

Material culture reflected the appearance and behaviour of respected and wealthy people, whom society at large admired, envied, and emulated. Because the elite was recognized as sophisticated and wise, their styles determined prevailing taste. Thus they could disregard certain societal norms and dictate new trends in fashion and attitude. The women of the *Vogue* elite broke rules: they were the first to wear shorter hair and shorter skirts, and to appear in public in bathing suits or holding cigarettes.

Today *Vogue* and other fashion magazines no longer cater exclusively to upper-class women. Beauty has become big business, and the fashion industry has developed schemes to appeal to all. Readers are promised a beauty and a style that can transcend their background and socioeconomic status. This rapid and widespread proliferation of images is a distinctive feature of modern cultural life. It both reflects and contributes to the democratization of social values.

ADVERTISING,
THE UNEASY PERSUASION

The democratization of goods—and a reaction to it—may help account for the stunning popularity of designer jeans in the late 1970s. People spend less money, as a percentage of their income, on clothing today than they did ten years ago. A low-budget family spent 11.6 percent of its budget on clothing and personal care in 1970, 9.0 percent in 1980; an intermediate-budget family's clothing allocation dropped from 10.7 percent to 7.6 percent; and a high-budget family dropped from 10.7 percent to 7.4 percent. The stunning fact of designer jeans was not that the jeans were expensive beyond all reason but that people could "get away with" wearing them in semiformal situations and posh surroundings. The important trend of dress in the 1970s was toward informality. Consequently, today men no longer wear hats at all, ties are no longer required, dress slacks are not de rigueur, women need not wear dresses or skirts on "dress" occasions. This does not mean one can wear just anything. But it is much easier to dress acceptably with a limited wardrobe than it once was. For people who do not know by training or instinct what it is to dress well, "brand name" goods are themselves a democratization. People took to designer jeans as a reaction against Levis, a revolt against dressing down, and yet, they did not return to previous standards of dressing up. Designer jeans grew popular, they were imitated in cheaper versions, and fashion was democratized again.

—MICHAEL SCHUDSON

TECHNOLOGY AND CULTURE

In anthropology it is traditional to classify cultures according to their technological level: hunting and gathering, agricultural, peasant, or industrial. Sociologists tend to find similar patterns of social organization in cultures that are at a similar level of economic development. Although many societies today are still largely engaged in farming or early industrialization, Canada, like other first-world nations, has moved into a new era, called the **post-industrial** or **information age**. More and more, Canada imports manufactured goods, while the centre of its economy is becoming not production but the transfer of information.

Technology today offers a wide variety of information and communication resources. It is important for people to question the extent to which the proliferation of mass media and new technology will change society, communication, and their daily lives. The information age may transform culture and social relations as thoroughly as did the industrial revolution; some scholars predict even greater changes.

It is only in the 20th century that people have become acutely aware of the complexity and intricacy of communication systems. Harold Innis and Marshall McLuhan both emphasize the technology of communications in their works. Innis, an economic historian, demonstrates how use of the written word influences the culture of a society. He claims that societies that depend on oral communication are quite unlike societies that have mastered the technique of writing (Innis 1972). Most important, a literate society, like Canada's, is able to spread out over a large area, whereas oral societies are restricted. And what happens when the printed page is overtaken by the video screen and the modem? Does the nature of what is communicated change? Industrial technology encouraged the build-up of big cities. When much work consists of information processing and the modem makes it possible for people to work anywhere, will the population become more evenly dispersed?

McLuhan views technology, whether simple or complex, as an extension of the human body. He refers to wheels as extensions of the feet, cameras as extensions of the eyes, and microphones as extensions of the ears (McLuhan 1964). Extending outward, from their bodies into the environment, allows humans to do a number of things. For example, they can expand their mobility through the wheel, the engine, and the rocket. They can communicate with each other through books, newspapers, radio, television, and computers. Each invention increases people's ability to change and to react to natural and artificial alterations in the environment. But the inventions also affect the nature of their actions and their communications.

The technology of communication influences the culture of a given society and the personality characteristics of its people. Agricultural societies, for example, often use farming images to speak of themselves. (Biblical images spring to mind: "The Lord is my shepherd"; the seed that falls on stony ground.) In the 20th century many people have come to visualize society as an enormous, impersonal machine, in which they are mere cogs. But perhaps the personal computer will suggest new images, as more and more people acquire one.

Today the change in technology is extremely rapid. Already, the telephone and telegraph, which themselves replaced letters and messengers, are being supplanted or extended by electronic mail and phone answering and calling machines. By the end of the century, many analysts say, a common piece of technology will be the television-computer hook-up that allows people to shop, pay bills, deal with government offices, seek information, and give feedback to broadcasters. Will two-way television allow more opportunity for personal choice? Or will these sophisticated systems merely allow those who control them to manipulate those who use them? Policy decisions based on future patterns of communication and information are extremely serious. Information technologies can increase human knowledge and extend the reach of human intelligence, but at what cost? Are the mass media and the close relationship of people to computers endangering personal identity? Will data bases make privacy and confidentiality impossible? How much information can humans handle?

The stumbling block to realizing the potential of the electronic text is fear. The Western world is divided between those who support an increase in information technology and those who feel there is already too much. According to Statistics Canada, 98 percent of Canadian households have radios and 96 percent have television sets. Sociologists are still evaluating the profound effects of these relatively simple technologies on modern social life. As video games and portable stereos are joined by still newer forms of mass media, one can only guess at the continuing alteration of cultural values.

Media Culture

> For the past twenty years, the Annenberg School of Communications at the University of Pennsylvania has been studying the impact of television on society. More than ten years ago, I first read their given conclusion that television is not *part* of our culture; it *is* our culture. . . . Now all our children are the children of McLuhan and their values are shaped by the thousands of hours of cops-and-robbers shows they watch. (Landsberg 1985, 3)

The academic community's interest in the mass media has risen dramatically in the past few decades. This interest is reflected in the proliferation of new journals and new and popular courses in communications and mass media. The general public also appears to be more sensitive to the effects of the mass media, due to the popularizing of the ideas of important theorists like Marshall McLuhan. Few people now who watch television are unaware of its mesmerizing, stultifying effects. People are also concerned about the content of the medium. Submissions to the Canadian Radio-television and Telecommunications Commission (CRTC) and to self-regulation hearings of the broadcasting and advertising industries have, for example, decried the proliferation of violence and commercials aimed at children.

The Debate on Pornography

The most dramatic example of media awareness is the intense debate about pornography, a debate that has helped to sensitize the public to the entertainment media and their effects on social values. Throughout the Western world, feminist groups in particular have been vociferous in the campaign against the proliferation of pornography. They argue that the portrayal of women as objects, and often victims, in the mass media leads to a general debasement of women—an influence clearly at odds with the egalitarian rhetoric of government policies such as affirmative action programs.

The revolution in communications technology has raised many controversial issues and crystallized disparate viewpoints. Video machines have made pornography an easily accessible commodity, but have also united feminists and their supporters determined to put an end to the sexual exploitation of women.

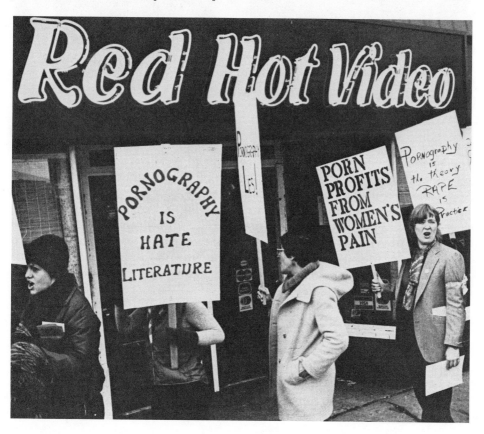

Increasing use of sexual imagery in many forms of media makes one question whether the sexual exploitation gap is diminishing.

In the United States the controversial Minneapolis Ordinance has provided one model for dealing with this contentious issue. Debated throughout North America and emulated in a number of American cities, this law enables civilians to charge purveyors of pornography. Another interesting example is recent hearings in the United States about the sexual and violent content of popular music; these hearings have produced a system of record ratings similar to the rating system for films (whether at commercial movie theatres or on video cassettes) that exists in Ontario and other provinces. In Canada, legislation was proposed in 1986 to ban pornography (defined very broadly); this brought applause from fundamentalist churches and condemnation from many other groups, including many feminists.

Censorship is hotly debated both within and without the feminist community. Some feminists believe that only censorship can protect women and children from violent and exploitive pornography. Others, while concerned about pornography, feel that further government intervention would stifle legitimate self-expression and put more power in the hands of the (exploitive) establishment. Some argue that pornography is not the cause but the reflection of violent social attitudes.

Mass education—sometimes called **media literacy**—has been proposed

SEX ROLE STEREOTYPING IN THE BROADCAST MEDIA
A REPORT ON INDUSTRY SELF-REGULATION, 1986—SOME CONCLUSIONS

1. There are fewer women than men in almost all areas of Canadian television and radio broadcasting.

2. On television, women make up only 16 percent of the characters in children's cartoons, 41 percent in adult drama, 29 percent in news and public affairs, and 21 percent among those interviewed in news and public affairs.

3. The roles of women and men differ in each major area of broadcasting and advertising. In television news, 89 percent of the experts interviewed are men. In TV drama, women are most often associated with home and family roles and men with paid employment roles.

4. Women are much more likely than men to be shown partially clothed, in swimsuits, underwear or skin-tight clothing. Researchers found that women accounted for 63 percent of the instances of scanty clothing although they make up just 41 percent of the characters.

as an alternate response. The theory is that people need to learn to respond critically to media messages if they are not to be manipulated by them. Some school boards have acknowledged the significance of this issue by organizing professional development days on the topic and by bringing media experts into the classroom. Teachers at an experimental high school in Toronto have started a group, The Association for Media Literacy, which publishes a journal and promotes classroom teaching on the media. Particularly controversial, of course, is the sexual content of such genres as rock videos and high-fashion advertising. Other Canadian organizations responding to media messages include the Saskatchewan Department of Consumer Affairs, which has produced excellent educational materials dealing with sex-role stereotyping in the media, and ACTRA (Alliance of Canadian Cinema, Television and Radio Artists), which monitors the depiction of women in the media with particular attention to the use of male voiceovers. A Vancouver-based national organization called Media Watch provides a vigilant feminist perspective.

Yet a 1986 CRTC summary of more than 700 industry reports shows that the depiction of women has changed very little in recent years. What has changed somewhat is the portrayal of men in the mass media. The recent trend to erotic—even objectified—male images in advertising, in television shows such as "Magnum P.I.," and in magazines such as *Gentlemen's Quarterly* raises the intricate question of the relationship of image to ideology. In short, is the sexual exploitation gap diminishing? A comparison of two images from a Toronto magazine (see page 102) illustrates the increasing use of sexual imagery in advertising. Although both models are promoting the same product, the gender gap remains: the female is more exploited and more passive than the male.

CANADIAN CULTURE: DOES IT EXIST?

Discussions of popular culture evoke an important question for Canadians: what is Canadian culture? Does Canada have a discrete culture, separate from that of the United States? Inundated as Canadians are with American culture, similar as the two lifestyles are in many respects, some people find it difficult to see Canada as different from its larger, commercially dominant neighbour. Yet there is a small but significant body of literature supporting the notion of a separate Canadian identity, ranging from Susan Crean's 1976 classic (*Who's Afraid of Canadian Culture?*), which focuses on arts and the media, to the more broadly defined works of political scientist Gad Horowitz. The quest for a Canadian identity, especially one distinct from that of the United States, has been controversial and perplexing for academia, the arts world, and the government.

A sociological study by Seymour Lipset (1965, 174) focused on distinctions between American and Canadian culture. "Those distinctions which seem particularly suitable for the analysis of Canada and the United States are achievement–ascription, universalism–particularism, self-orientation–collectivity-orientation, and egalitarianism–elitism."

This study echoes a still earlier work called *Patterns of Culture*, an anthropological classic by Ruth Benedict (1934). Benedict proposed a holistic, psychological perspective for looking at cultures. She argued that cultures are more than the sum of their parts—that is, of the various institutions they comprise. Rather, they hang together in a characteristic pattern, which can be described simply. Using the terms of historian Oswald Spengler (borrowed in turn from Nietzsche), Benedict grouped cultures into two basic types—the Apollonian and the Dionysian. The former refers to the quiet, low-key, collective lifestyle of cultures such as that of the Pueblo of the American Southwest. The latter refers to the more aggressive, competitive cultures of the American Northwest Coast.

Benedict's model, although it was developed for more homogeneous cultures, describes the American/Canadian dichotomy very well. Despite regional, ethnic, and subcultural differences, Canada as a whole presents a neutral, affable face that distinguishes the country from its more exuberant and aggressive neighbour. In an age in which aggressive, patriarchal values are being challenged by a burgeoning feminist movement, Canada's gentler cultural presence may be ahead of its time.

Canada's media image is dominated by the Hollywood view of Canadians as Mounties, trappers, and Eskimos. Canadians' own view of themselves, as the photo of the McKenzie brothers shows, tends to be self-deprecating and unflattering.

SUMMARY

Although culture is an important concept in social science, it is difficult to put into words. Defined negatively, culture is anything related to human behaviour that cannot be directly attributed to biology and/or instinct. Culture embodies a richly interpretive meaning system made possible by symbols.

One important aspect of culture is the web of social relationships whereby individuals are tied into their society. Status, or position in the social system, may be ascribed at birth or achieved by one's own efforts. Social behaviour expresses values, or cultural expectations of what is good. These values are translated into norms or rules of behaviour.

The integration of the individual or of sets of individuals into the system of values and norms in a society is never complete. The concept of subculture was developed to help account for behaviour that does not fit a normative framework. This concept has been particularly helpful in the development of the sociology of deviance.

A dynamic model of culture helps us to understand the role of culture in social change. Applied to fashion, it illustrates the role culture plays in the contemporary world. Similarly, recognizing the close link between culture and technology in the modern world helps us to look for the manipulation and creation of symbols in the mass media.

FOR FURTHER READING

Crean, Susan M.
1976 *Who's Afraid of Canadian Culture?* Don Mills, Ont.: General Publishing. This timely and informative book explains how Canadian arts organizations, educational institutions, and mass media have excluded Canadian culture, and how Americanization has resulted in a suppression of Canadian culture and independence.

Hall, Edward
1966 *The Hidden Dimension.* Garden City, N.Y.: Doubleday. A well-known anthropologist, Hall gives a perceptive account of the importance of space, gestures, time, and other non-verbal expressions of culture. The book discusses how communication can be effective across cultural boundaries and how the use of space can affect personal and business relationships.

Hebdige, Dick
1979 *Subculture: The Meaning of Style.* London: Methuen. Hebdige gives an extremely detailed account of the lives of teddy boys, mods, rockers, skinheads, and punks. He describes the process by which objects take on a symbolic dimension and hence develop significant meanings. From the subtlest gesture to the most overt dress code, symbols become meaningful for a culture or subculture.

Lakoff, R.T., and Scherr, R.L.
1984 *Face Value: The Politics of Beauty.* London: Routledge and Kegan Paul. This insightful book comes to terms with taken-for-granted notions about the concept of beauty in various cultures. The history, psychology, and politics of this concept are presented so as to satisfy both academic and general readers. Lakoff and Scherr question the devastating power that beauty has come to possess, and the universal fear of women that they may be undesirable.

McLuhan, Herbert Marshall
1964 *Understanding Media: The Extensions of Man.* New York: McGraw-Hill. McLuhan views technology, simple and complex, as an extension of the human body. The Western world is undergoing incredible changes with the advent of technological innovations.

AUDIO-VISUAL RESOURCES

Bathing Babies in Three Cultures. Produced by Gregory Bateson and Margaret Mead, New York University, 1952. This short film is now dated but remains a useful cross-cultural statement on body language and child-rearing practices. It illustrates non-verbal communication of cultural values.

Killing Us Softly. Jean Kilbourne. Produced by Cambridge Documentary Films, released in 1979. Distributed by Kinetic Films Canada.

This excellent film depicts the image of women in advertising. A narrated lecture accompanies Jean Kilbourne's slide collection.

Micro Cultural Incidents at Ten Zoos

Ray L. Birdwhistell, Department of Studies in Human Communication, Eastern Pennsylvania Psychiatric Institute. Made by Jacques D. Van Vlack. University Park, Pa: Psychological Cinema Register, 1971.

This wonderful film by the father of kinesics looks at the subtlety of nonverbal communication in a cultural context.

Not a Love Story. Produced by Studio D, the National Film Board of Canada, 1981. Distributed by the National Film Board of Canada.

This now-famous documentary is an excellent chronicle of the changing face of pornography and the sex trade, which aptly reflect cultural conceptions of women.

Ways of Seeing. John Berger. Produced by the BBC, 1972. Distributed by BBC Canada.

This four-part film is a teaching device useful in helping students learn to decode visual imagery. Part II on the nude in painting and Part IV on advertising are particularly germane.

CHAPTER 4

SOCIALIZATION AND THE SELF

William B. Shaffir and Allan Turowetz

Some societies, such as those of bees and ants, are maintained almost entirely by the exercise of instincts. The young are born programmed to adapt to their places and their obligations. By contrast, the human infant is a helpless organism. At birth, it understands nothing and cannot survive for more than a few hours without the help and support of other people. Moreover, it has few inborn guides to later behaviour within the human group. Yet somehow this helpless being must be transformed into a person who is able to participate effectively in society. The study of socialization focuses on the process by which this lengthy and complex transformation occurs.

"NATURE VERSUS NURTURE"

The understanding of socialization has undergone several revolutions in the past century or so. Much of the change has centred on what is sometimes called the **"nature versus nurture" debate**: do individuals become what they are primarily because of biology and genetic inheritance ("nature") or because of their environment—how others behave toward them and what opportunities they have ("nurture").

In the latter part of the 19th century, many people believed in **biological determinism**—the idea that human beings are what they are and behave as they do because of their biological inheritance alone. Human nature and personality, it was maintained, developed from the "baggage" babies bring with them into the world. According to the biological determinists, human behaviour is simply an expression or unfolding of inborn drives and tendencies, such as instincts, needs, and constitutional makeup. To support this claim, theorists looked to the work on evolution by Charles Darwin and others, who had reasoned that those members of a species who are biologically best suited to survive in their environment are the ones most likely to reproduce; over many generations, the characteristics best adapted to the way a species fits into its ecological niche thus become more common. The claim of **Social Darwinism** was that human societies evolve in the same manner as other living species.

This theory was certainly useful to many late 19th-century opinion-setters. The wealthy used it to maintain that their success was due to a natural, biological superiority. The upper classes of powerful industrial countries used it to justify the colonization of less-developed parts of the world. Moreover, casual observation supported the belief that personality is biologically determined. There were "good" families that regularly produced statesmen, church leaders, and scholars, and bad families that just as regularly produced thieves and rogues. Drawing on the early studies of genetics, social scientists concluded that people inherit their talents and character from their parents. Crime, alcoholism, addiction, and other socially undesirable behaviour were attributed to "bad blood."

Then, near the end of the century, Ivan Pavlov, a Russian physiologist, upset the entire scheme by demonstrating that much behaviour, even among lower animals, is learned. A hungry dog salivates instinctively when it sees food. Pavlov showed that it could learn to associate the ringing of a bell with food; then it salivated whenever it heard a bell, whether it saw food or not.

In time the idea that the infant is a *tabula rasa* (a "blank slate")—and thus that the individual is the product of the environment—gained a following. In the early 1920s, John B. Watson, a psychologist, challenged the biological determinists this way:

> Give me a dozen healthy infants, well-formed, and my own specific world to bring them up in, and I'll guarantee to take any one at random and train him to become any type of specialist I might select—a doctor, lawyer, artist, merchant chief, yes even a beggerman and thief, regardless of his talents, penchants, tendencies, abilities, vocations, and race of his ancestors. (1924, 104)

Soon many sociologists also argued that environment determined the differences among human beings. Other people—the social environment—were seen as especially important. Using this basic premise, social scientists developed theories of **cultural determinism**: that human nature and personality depend on the society into which the individual happens to be born. Biology is unimportant. As one sociologist put it, the human being is "merely the instrument through which cultures express themselves. . . . Culture makes man what he is and at the same time makes itself" (White 1949; 340, 353).

Today, social scientists no longer seriously debate the "nature versus nurture" question. Although they differ in their emphasis, almost all recognize that neither heredity nor environment alone can explain the behaviour patterns that distinguish one person from another and members of one society from those of another. Instead, it is understood that the interaction of biological and environmental factors shapes individual behaviour.

Clearly, the process of becoming socialized occurs within a cultural context. Social interaction follows the norms—standards of conduct—and values of the culture in question. Thus, one must expect the content of socialization to differ greatly from one society to another. People in different parts of the world learn different norms, values, and lifestyles and are likely to approach their environment from different perspectives. As well, each society develops distinctive personality patterns—characteristic patterns that result from a common socialization experienc in a unique culture. At the same time, however, within every society, each person is also different. These differences are also the product of socialization. The unique personal history of each individual permits sharing not only in the larger society but also in specific parts of it. Each is influenced by distinctive subcultures of family, friends, class, and religion, and no one encounters exactly the same set of them. Thus, the socialization process helps to explain the similarities of peoples' behaviour in a particular society as well as the behavioural differences among both individuals and groups.

Biological and Cultural Interaction

From the earliest moments of life, biological and emotional needs are closely intertwined. Dependency is a biological given for humans. Newborns must be provided with food and shelter (warmth). But meeting only these needs is insufficient. Babies also require human presence, both physical and emotional. Human contact, although less tangible than the necessities of food and shelter, is no less significant for their development and even for their survival.

Researchers often find that the most practical way to support a hypothesis of need for some factor is to test its absence. Psychologist Harry F. Harlow demonstrated the need for body contact and interaction in experiments with rhesus monkeys. Harlow took infant monkeys away from their mothers and raised them in isolation. When placed in a cage with two substitute "mothers," one made only of wire and the other covered with soft cloth, the monkeys spent most of their time clinging to the soft one. Even if they received food from the wire "mother," they preferred the soft cloth "mother." Most significant, however, was the fact that none of the animals raised in isolation developed normally. When given the chance to associate with others of their species, all were frightened and hostile (Harlow and Zimmerman 1959).

Human development experts believe that human babies, like the infant monkeys, have a basic need, biological as well as emotional, to cling to and to interact with a warm, sheltering mother figure. A part of this necessary contact is some form of communication—not necessarily verbal communication but at least smiles, laughs, and touches. Without this attachment, socialization is impaired, and irreversible damage may be done to the personality and even to the body. Evidence for this view comes not only from recurring reports of children allegedly raised by wild animals, but also from studies of children deliberately raised in isolation and of children in institutions, particularly those of the first half of the 20th century, whose organizers tended to meet physical needs quite efficiently but knew little of psychological and social requirements.

One of the best descriptions of what such children lack comes from a medieval historian. In the 13th century, Frederick II, emperor of the Holy Roman Empire, conducted an experiment with human infants.

His . . . folly was that he wanted to find out what kind of speech and what manners of speech children would have when they grew up, if they spoke to no one beforehand. So he bade foster mothers and nurses to suckle children, to bathe and wash them, but in no way to prattle with them or to speak to them, for he wanted to learn whether they would speak the Hebrew language, which was the oldest, or Greek, or Latin, or Arabic, or perhaps the language of their parents, of whom they had been born. But he labored in vain, because the children all died. For they could not live without the patting and joyful faces and loving words of their foster mothers. (Quoted in Ross and McLaughlin 1949)

FERAL CHILDREN

Children raised in isolation or near-isolated conditions are termed **feral children**. Throughout the centuries have come occasional reports of children allegedly raised by wild beasts. The evidence is highly dramatic, though quite unreliable. In the late 19th and early 20th centuries, a few reports came from India and elsewhere of the discovery of children whose behaviour seemed more like that of animals than human beings (Singh and Zingg 1942). Efforts to socialize these children were said to have met with little success, and all died at a young age.

More convincing evidence comes from studies of children intentionally raised in isolation from their families. Kingsley Davis (1940; 1947; 1948) reports two such instances, both of which occurred in the United States.

One of the classic cases of a feral child was "Anna of the Attic." Discovered at the age of six, Anna had been born illegitimate—a fact so displeasing to her grandfather that he insisted she be confined in a small, dark attic and be given the bare minimum of physical care to keep her alive, but nothing more. When discovered by social workers, she could not talk, walk, keep herself clean, or feed herself. Initially, it was thought that she was also blind and deaf. Efforts to socialize Anna met with only limited success. With special care and training, she learned to coordinate her body and to use language in a limited way. Unfortunately, Anna died four and a half years after she was discovered.

Isabelle was another case. Also an illegitimate child, she spent most of her early childhood in a dark room shared with her mother, a deaf-mute. Like Anna, Isabelle had no opportunity to develop language, as she and her mother communicated by gestures. When she was discovered, it was incorrectly thought she was deaf, and the specialist working with her pronounced her feeble-minded. With systematic and intense training, however, Isabelle soon began making substantial progress. By the time she was eight and a half years old, specialists concluded that she had overcome the consequences of her years in isolation and had reached an apparently normal level of intellectual development.

SOCIALIZATION

Although sociologists now agree that socialization is the product of a complex interaction of heredity and environment, they assign the concept of socialization two fairly distinct meanings. One group, mostly those who take the structural-functionalist perspective—a view that emphasizes the ways in which a society is integrated—focuses on the individual's adaptation and conformity, how he or she learns the ways of the society in order to be able to function within it. The viewpoint is the societal viewpoint of the group to which the individual belongs. Thus, the concept refers to the learning of expectations, habits, values, motives, skills, beliefs, and other requirements necessary for effective participation in the social groups that link the individual and society. **Socialization**, in this definition, is a learning process brought about by interaction with other people. The individual becomes aware of others when he or she acts and learns to modify behaviour in accord with those others' responses. In short, the process of socialization familiarizes people with and makes them skilled at the rules for living.

An alternative conception uses the viewpoint of the individual, rather than the group, emphasizing the development of the person. This concept of socialization refers to the process of development or change that the person experiences as a consequence of social influences. "Its focus tends to be the development of self-concept, identity and various attitudes, dispositions, and behaviors of the individual" (Gecas 1981, 165). Symbolic interactionism, which is described at length in the next section of this chapter, is the framework most closely associated with this way of understanding socialization as a continuous process of shaping self-concepts.

Notice that the two concepts are not antithetical. Rather, they differ in viewpoint and emphasis, and both are surely true. At the level of society, socialization is basic to group continuity and stability. Through socialization, the individual becomes familiar with the group's language, beliefs, norms, and standards of judgment required for social living. Socialization helps account for the continuity of society through successive generations because it enables the group to reproduce itself socially and biologically. At the individual level, socialization is accompanied by the emergence or development of a **social self**—that is, an awareness of others and their expectations. Through this acquisition, the individual is able to take on someone else's point of view and to look at the world the way others see it.

Thus, socialization can be seen as a shaping or moulding. This imagery is correct only up to a point, however. Although the child is shaped by society, the process does not work merely in one direction. The individual, even the very young child, is not a passive victim of socialization; rather, he or she can resist it, or collaborate with it in varying degrees. Indeed, socialization is best viewed as a process that is reciprocal, in that not only the socialized but also the socializers are affected by it. This phenomenon

Humans have the ability to take the role of the other and thus to attribute a self to others. Some people treat pets as if they were human, giving them "surprise" birthday parties for example, despite the inability of animals to develop a social self.

can be observed quite readily in everyday life. While parents generally succeed in moulding the child in accord with certain generally accepted patterns, they are changed by the experience of parenthood.

Socialization as a Lifelong Process

So far we have spoken of socialization as something aimed at children. Yet the mention of the effects on parents raises another important point: the socialization process is continuous throughout life, beginning as soon as the infant is born and going on until death. Perhaps it is best understood as occurring at two levels—primary and secondary. **Primary socialization** refers to the socialization an individual experiences in childhood, the process through which the child becomes familiar with and a member of society. It usually occurs within the family, and the individual almost automatically accepts and internalizes the parents' and other caregivers' view of the world. As the process proceeds, children's referents expand until they are able to abstract and thus understand what others in general expect of them. **Secondary socialization** refers to any subsequent process that initiates a person into a new or different dimension of life—raising a family, entering medical school, moving to a new area, and so on. Since it need not presuppose a high degree of identification, the individual can remain more objective than in primary socialization. (Primary and secondary socialization are dealt with in more detail later in this chapter.)

SYMBOLIC INTERACTIONISM

Today, many of the concepts and terms used by students of socialization come from symbolic interactionism. That framework in sociology and social psychology owes its intellectual debts to Charles H. Cooley, George H. Mead, and John Dewey, who all found keys to their work in one or more aspects of socialization. Therefore, before proceeding, we need to define and examine some of the key ideas of this perspective.

The phrase **symbolic interaction** was coined by Herbert Blumer to refer to the distinctive character of interaction between human beings—the fact that "human beings interpret or 'define' each other's action" (1962, 19).

A central concept of symbolic interactionism is **definition of the situation**—a phrase coined for a sociological study titled *The Child in America* by W.I. and Dorothy Swaine Thomas (1928) and sharpened and refined by McHugh (1968) and Robert A. Stebbins (1967). The Thomases introduced this concept by saying, "If men define situations as real, they are real in their consequence" (1928, 572). This dictum underscores the idea that reality is socially constructed and that people respond as much or more to the meaning a situation has for them as to the objective features of the situation. People do not interpret prayer, say, in the abstract, but within particular situations in which they have come to expect that certain things are likely to occur. Thus, an individual in a dialogue with God while sitting in a restaurant may be regarded as a candidate for a mental institution, yet the same behaviour in a house of worship is expected.

According to symbolic interactionism, human behaviour is to be viewed as a conscious and rational interpretation of situations and events. To have a basis for these interpretations, people define and construct their social situations by using sets of cultural meanings and understandings. In such interactions, individuals convey to one another what they ought or are expected to do. By symbolically communicating a series of definitions or expectations to each other, they define the situation.

For the most part, people have the same definition of a given situation. Social life would be impossible without this similarity of understanding. But it is not always present, and the degree to which it is present can vary. In order to share a definition of a situation to any meaningful extent, individuals and groups must be able to **take the role of the other**—to look through one another's eyes. The sharing of meanings is most likely to occur during interaction that is extended and continuous, particularly by individuals who occupy similar positions or face similar situations.

From the Thomases' theorem, notes Merton (1968), is derived the social process of the **self-fulfilling prophecy**. It involves a definition of the situation that is false but that sets into motion several mechanisms leading to behaviour that makes the prediction come true. To illustrate the notion of self-fulfilling prophecy, Robert Rosenthal and Lenore Jacobsen (1968) pretended to test the intelligence of some elementary-school children in San Francisco. Saying that the tests had identified 20 percent of the children as "academic spurters," they provided the children's teachers with names of the youngsters "expected" to do well in school. In fact, the "spurters" had been selected at random. Yet when the children were tested later in the year, the teachers described the "spurters" as happier than the other students, more curious, more appealing, and better adjusted; moreover, they showed greater gains in academic achievement than the other students. The teachers had acted on their definition of the situation—what they thought to be true—and behaved so that what they expected to occur did occur.

In his summary of the basic position of symbolic interaction, Blumer outlines three propositions, or what he calls three "simple" premises:

1. "Human beings act toward things on the basis of the meanings that the things have for them" (1969, 2). Human behaviour cannot be understood as merely a direct response to external stimuli or a reflection of a pervasive system of culture. Rather, in contrast to non-human animals and to the view of humans set forth by other theoretical perspectives, people act toward and in response to objects depending on the meaning of those objects.

2. "The meaning of such things is derived from, and arises out of, the social interaction that one has with one's fellows" (1969, 2). An object or a situation does not have an inherent meaning that is imposed on the individual. Rather, the meaning is derived through social interaction. Objects or situations can be given a variety of meanings; so can the language symbols used to describe them. Thus, the meaning of objects, their symbols, and people's actions toward them evolve largely out of contexts of interactions with others. For instance, if you are stopped by a cruising police officer while driving down the highway, the situation may be defined along various lines of action. But it has no automatic meaning; rather, the meaning will emerge from the nature of the interaction between you and the police officer. Perhaps it becomes an angry confrontation, in which you receive a ticket for speeding while insisting that a few kilometres over the limit shouldn't count. Or perhaps the officer gives you a warning and you solemnly agree to be more careful. Or perhaps it turns out that the problem is not your speed at all but a washed-out bridge around the next bend. (Notice too the considerable sharing of meaning implied by the facts that each of you understands the other's words, that you know the symbolism of the flashing lights and uniform, and that rules of the road exist at all.)

3. "Meanings are handled in, and modified through, an interpretive process used by the person in dealing with things he encounters" (1969, 2). Individuals use sets of cultural meanings to indicate to themselves the possible courses of action in a particular situation. In other words, people do not apply acquired meanings automatically; precisely because they have selves, they are able to engage in an internal dialogue, interacting with themselves and indicating to themselves relevant meanings. Thus the individual does not routinely use the same meanings but selects, shapes, and modifies them in terms of perceived demands of the situation. Interpretation is "a matter of handling meanings," says Blumer (1969, 5), emphasizing the fluid, and emergent nature of human behaviour, the way it involves process.

That symbolic interactionism continues to loom so large in modern sociology serves as a testament to this framework's value and credibility for widening our understanding of social interaction and human behaviour and to the efforts of numerous scholars (see Stone and Farberman 1970; Manis and Meltzer 1967) who through their writings have added to the theoretical corpus as well as refined, clarified, and extended it.

SELF AND SOCIALIZATION

In the course of interaction between parents and children, the latter are learning to define themselves as persons, in the social sense of the word. They are developing a personality, the core of which is the self. (Psychologists are more inclined to use the term personality; sociologists generally prefer to use self.) **Self** refers to an individual's awareness of ideas and attitudes about his or her own personal and social identity. The self can be viewed as a reference centre for planning and orientation, for sorting and assessing life's situations in terms of their relative importance.

The development of a sense of self, or **self-image**, greatly depends on social interaction. The newborn does not differentiate itself from its mother. Gradually, however, the baby learns to see its mother as one person and itself as another. Then, over time and through social interaction, the young child acquires the ability to see itself reflected in the eyes of others and thus to sense its own identity. (As we have seen, it is precisely this ability that children reared in social isolation are lacking.) The need for social interaction to define the self continues throughout life. Individuals continually learn new roles and, by interpreting others' responses in the course of social interaction, may alter their self-images. Thus, self-conception is a social product: it arises in social interaction and is continually tested and then confirmed or changed in further social interaction.

How does the self emerge in childhood and how is it continually modified throughout the life cycle? These questions are of great interest to sociologists, psychologists, and social psychologists, as well as to parents, educators, and almost everyone. To gain some understanding of the process of the growth of self, we will examine the theories of three individuals—Charles H. Cooley, George H. Mead, and Jean Piaget. Their contributions, although different in detail, all emphasize that the self emerges through social interaction with others.

The Looking-Glass Self: Cooley

Charles Horton Cooley (1864–1929), an economist turned social psychologist, formulated a theory about the emergence of the self through a process of social interaction. His most sensitive insights concerned the ways in which people establish and maintain a sense of personal identity. Cooley believed that the structure and contents of the self are derived from the society as represented in the groups and **significant others** (people emotionally or symbolically important to a person) surrounding the individual. A self-image emerges as a product of group involvement and communication with others.

Cooley used the image of a looking glass to explain how others influence the way one sees oneself. The conception of self—feelings about who and what one is—are organized around one's evaluation of how one sees oneself as judged by others:

> As we see our face, figure and dress in the glass, and are interested in them because they are ours, and pleased or otherwise with them according as they do or do not answer to what we should like them to be; so in imagination we perceive in another's mind some thought of our appearance, manners, aims, characters, friends, and so on, and are variously affected by it. (1964: 184)

The **looking-glass self**, for Cooley, has three major elements: one's imagination of how one's physical appearance, friends, manners, goals, and self-presentation are seen in the mind of another person whose opinions one values; perception of the other's judgment about these items; and some sort of reaction about this judgment, such as pride or disgust at being seen this way. In Cooley's view, a person's self-image and self-esteem are directly related to the feedback received from others. In the course of interaction with the significant people in the environment, through the repeated process of imagination and identification, the self-concept is built and organized. Without the social mirror, there can be no sense of self.

Much of Cooley's theorizing was based on the observation of his own children, and he emphasized the childhood years as the most critical for the development of the looking-glass self. It should be understood, however, that the process of self-evaluation continues throughout life. As the individual moves through the various phases of the life cycle, the social mirror changes; he or she must learn to evaluate successive looking glasses and to continually redefine the self appropriately as each new stage is reached. Moreover, given that most people engage daily in a complex set of social arrangements, performing for different audiences with different and at times competing expectations, most people must learn to anticipate skilfully and evaluate accurately the images received from various looking glasses.

The Theory of Self: Mead

For Cooley, self and society constituted an inseparable, harmonious unity: society would not exist without interacting individuals and the individual would not develop without society. George Herbert Mead (1863–1931), a philosopher, followed this lead, concentrating his analysis of human nature on the importance of the interplay between society and the individual. His major contribution was a theory of the relationship between the mind, self, and society (which became the foundation of symbolic interactionism).

Mead emphasized the importance of symbolic communication, especially language, in all human relations. For Mead, the ability to use symbols was the most distinctive attribute differentiating people from animals. In particular the use of symbolic behaviour enables the child to conceive of itself in relation to others and is at the core of all stages of the socialization process.

Mead pointed to communication as essential to the development process. People first communicate, like other animals, through gestures. Even at this rudimentary level, most human interaction is symbolic, depending on shared understandings about the meanings of gestures. Non-verbal gestures provide simple communication. They also lay the foundation for the development of language, which makes possible the replacement of gestures with ideas. The essence of language is that its symbols are conventions. The sounds of the word *horse*, for example, mean nothing in themselves. In fact, people in various societies have agreed that the quite different sounds of *cheval, caballo, loshad'*, and *Pferd* mean exactly the same thing. To restate the point: the cluster of sounds that make a word is a significant symbol if and only if it has for the speaker roughly the same meaning that it has for the listener.

For Mead, the key process in the human capacity to organize behaviour to correspond to particular social situations is what he referred to as the capacity to take the role of the other—to see or attempt to appreciate the perspective of someone else in a particular situation. Indeed, the distinguishing characteristic of selfhood rests in the capacity of individuals to be an object to themselves. Doing so involves putting oneself in someone else's position to imagine how the other will respond to one's actions. One observes the conduct and reactions of the other people, learns their expectations and point of view, and at the same time is able to interpret one's own behaviour from their point of view. This distinctively human ability provides the opportunity to construct action while taking into account the perspectives of others.

George Herbert Mead

The identity of these others suggests the sophistication of socialization. In any situation, specific others are actually present, and the individual must take their presence into account in organizing behaviour. A partially socialized person is able to internalize the expectations of particular others—specific individuals, such as members of the family. Most adults are also able to assume the role of the other in a broader sense, assuming the perspective of what Mead called "the generalized other." Thus, the individual's behaviour is oriented not merely to the expectations of people who are physically present but also to the general expectations of the group to which he or she belongs.

Mead saw the essence of the socialization process as this ability to anticipate what others expect and to organize behaviour accordingly. This ability, he said, is acquired in three stages as the self is developed. First is the imitative stage. Children aged two, three, and four spend much of their time in the world of make-believe. For hours they may play at being mothers and fathers, doctors and firefighters. At this stage of development, however, children have no real conception of themselves as separate social beings. What they are doing is not true role playing but only imitations of actions.

The second major developmental stage is the play stage in which children play more creatively and do actually begin to adopt social roles. They learn to imagine how people will respond to them without actually having to act out the situation. Having reached a level of verbal organization, the child can manipulate the various roles without physical action. The roles adopted during this stage are those of significant others—a parent, a sports star, a storybook hero. Role playing is fluid, subject only to the limitation of the child's own comprehension of the role. At this stage, the role need not be firmly rooted in reality but can be defined

Anticipatory socialization — the acting out of anticipated future roles — is an important part of learning many social roles.

according to the child's own specifications. Children do not yet see role playing as a social necessity—they merely play at social roles of life.

The third and final stage in the development of the self is the game stage. It is characterized by the child's ability to develop a generalized impression of the behaviour people expect as well as an awareness of his or her own importance to the group and vice versa. Mead used the metaphor of a game to describe the complex behaviour that is required in this stage. In an organized game such as baseball, a player must continually adjust behaviour to the needs of the team as a whole and to the specific situations that arise in the game. Moreover, the meaning of the player's role lies solely in its relation to the other roles; it has no meaning outside that relation. At this point, Mead contended, children are responding to the generalized other—the organized group or community that provides them their unity of self.

Mead claimed, however, that the socialization process is neither perfect nor complete. He saw the self as composed of two parts: the active, spontaneous, unsocialized part, which he called the "I," and the social self, conscious of norms, expectations, and social responsibility, which he named the "me." The development of the self, he suggested, involves a continuing conversation between the "me" and the "I."

Cognitive Development: Piaget

Jean Piaget (1896–1980) was a Swiss psychologist who pioneered the scientific study of children's mental and social development. The first to show that cognitive development is as much a social as a psychological process, he described development as proceeding through specific stages (somewhat different ones from Mead's) and showed how the organization of children's behaviour changed as they moved through these stages.

Of particular interest for sociologists is Piaget's research on the development of morality. "All morality consists in a system of rules and the essence of morality is to be sought for in the respect the individual acquires for these rules" ([1932] 1965, 13). His focus was not so much the content of rules as the child's obligation to them. As the young child begins to appreciate the authority figure associated with rules, he or she perceives them as absolute laws, to be followed to the letter no matter what the circumstances. Since rules are absolute givens, their rationality is not nearly as significant as the respect offered to the person enunciating them. Later the child perceives other kinds of rules, involving peer relationships, as far more rational; he or she is as much concerned with the effect their violation has on others as with the punishment derived from them. Thus, Piaget delineated two specific stages in the development of children's moral judgment. The first (at about ages three to eight) is marked by respect for authority, while the second (at about ages nine to twelve) is characterized by the development of mutual respect and the notion of cooperation. Essentially, the younger group perceives rules as fixed and beyond debate; the child learns to respect the rules given and does not take issue with the ways in which they are presented. After the age of eight, this morality of constraint is replaced by the morality of cooperation. For example, Piaget asked children for their opinions on just punishments for specific violations. He noticed that younger children were more apt to choose severe punishments for violations while older children exhibited a greater fairness in evaluating the violation and any extenuating circumstances.

Role-Taking: A Summary

In their efforts to account for socialization, sociologists continue to rely on Mead's explanation of the emergence and development of the self. The distinguishing trait of selfhood resides in human beings' capacity to be objects to themselves. The mechanism by which the individual self-consciously views himself or herself from the standpoint of others is role-taking.

Human beings are able to understand each other because they can imagine how others feel and think—a process of empathizing, or vicariously assuming others' points of view. Because an individual can see social situations from the perspective of others, he or she is able to anticipate and weigh their possible reactions to behaviour. He or she can assess a situation from different viewpoints, consider several alternative courses of action, and act in ways that seem most appropriate.

This process of definition is continuous and dynamic. As human beings move through new situations, they acquire new definitions; as their relationships with others change, so does behaviour toward them. Over time, each individual learns a host of definitions, meanings, and expectations; in a complex, heterogeneous society such as ours, some of these expectations may conflict. Thus, the understanding of human behaviour is always problematic.

Since human beings are born into social groups, any understanding of who each is must be related to the group of which he or she is a part. By the same token, one cannot conceive of self without considering the people interacted with, directly or indirectly. The responses of others necessarily play an important role in the construction of self-image. This self-image, or self-conception, may be regarded as personal identity. Whatever else it may be, identity is connected to the ongoing evaluation of oneself by oneself and by others.

Cooperation and teamwork are possible because human socialization involves coming to appreciate and/or understand others' points of view. Out of interactions with others, shared meanings emerge. In a process that is most intensive in childhood but lasts a lifetime, the human being is socialized to understand meanings created by others and to create meanings that can be understood by others. The capacity to learn meanings and develop humanness results from the ability to communicate by taking the role of others.

THE SELF IN EVERYDAY LIFE: LIFE AS THEATRE

Socialization is one of the most powerful concepts available to social scientists to explain social behaviour. Most sociologists assume that the vast bulk of human behaviour is social in origin and intention. Although there always exists what Dennis Wrong (1961) calls the danger of "oversocializing" the nature of the individual, the concept of socialization helps them to see that most behaviour is created, sustained, and modified in the course of interacting with other people.

A Shakespearean character says that all the world's a stage on which people merely act out roles. Borrowing Shakespeare's metaphor, American sociologist Erving Goffman proposes the **dramaturgical model**, which focuses on the ways in which people act and interact in everyday life. Goffman uses Mead's notion of taking on the role of the other, but extends it, arguing that people try not only to see with others' eyes but also to manage and control how others define the situation. Goffman argues that the basic unit of activity in everyday life is the face-to-face encounter because it generates and sustains social definitions and social realities. It is

a type of social arrangement that occurs when persons are in one another's immediate physical presence.... For the participant this involves: a single visual and cognitive focus of attention; a mutual and preferential openness to verbal communication; a heightened mutual relevance of acts; an eye-to-eye ecological huddle that maximizes each participant's opportunity to perceive the other participant's monitoring of him. (1961b, 17-18)

In short, encounters are organized by means of a special set of acts and gestures that function as communication about communication. One of the interactants makes an initial move; the other provides a response. Thus, following the lead of the symbolic interactionists, Goffman suggests that situations are socially created phenomena. As meaning emerges, so too do the selves that the participants present to each other. The definition of the situation, then, is created on the basis of external "resources" (race, sex, and so on) and the sets of meanings advanced by the actors in the situation. Communication is never perfect, however, so actors are never sure they share a definition of a situation. Thus interaction is vulnerable to disruption. Since disruptions endanger not only the situation but also the selves being sustained therein, the actors attempt to control information and impressions in a manner that will sustain a desired self and preserve the encounter.

Using this dramaturgical model, one can come to terms with two central images: that of the society and that of the person. As Cooley suggested, society is not to be seen as something separate from the individual. It exists only in the form of interactive situations, which simultaneously make manifest the existence of individuals. Thus, both individual and society are created by situations, and the key to understanding society is in recurrent social situations.

Goffman's basic assumption is that each human being is constantly seeking control over others. The individual seeks to manipulate situations, impressions, and information in order to sustain a self he or she can cherish in this respect. Power is crucial; actors who have it can make claims about themselves and be reasonably sure that their claims will be validated. Thus, every person—every actor—struggles to maintain a valued self that is as fragile and tentative as the situations that engender it.

Goffman suggests that the individual is capable of manipulation in two different ways: as an individual and as part of a team. The individual can manage another person's definition of the situation by using strategies such as dramatic realization and misrepresentation.

Dramatic realization refers to the successful expression, during interaction, of qualities and attributes claimed by the performer—in short, the actor's ability to convey a sense of sincerity. For example, suppose you are sitting in a class and the professor suddenly calls on you to respond. If you respond enthusiastically and energetically, you will convey the impression of being a sincere classroom actor. If, on the other hand, you are not paying attention to the question, you will present the opposite impression. The notion of dramatic realization includes even greater subtleties. It conveys the total presentation of self that organizes the other person's perspective about what the individual is like as the actor. Furthermore, dramatic realization permits the continued presentation of ideas, beliefs, and attitudes that will more likely be accepted than rejected.

Misrepresentation, on the other hand, entails the creation of a false impression through impersonation, innuendo, strategic ambiguity, crucial omissions, and lies, white or otherwise. Misrepresentation is probably the most widely practised form of manipulation, and some degree of it is inevitable in interaction; as most people are taught in childhood and adolescent socialization, to be absolutely candid is to be absolutely tactless. Thus misrepresentation protects the individual from potential danger and provides a wide range of social masks to assist in the management of another person's definition of the situation. From subtle little white lies uttered to avoid offending a colleague or friend to more major forms of cheating and withholding information from others, persons in all walks of life seem to engage in this sort of role performance.

On many occasions, actors work as teams to sustain a specific image. A **performance team** is a set of individuals who cooperate in staging a single routine. Since any member of the team has the power to disrupt the projected definition of the situation, it is of prime importance that they demonstrate intragroup solidarity. Each team, as in a play in a theatre, has a director who is given the right to direct and control the progress of the performance. The team performance, although consolidated and unified in social action, opposes another team—the audience. The audience, in effect, constitutes a heterogeneous group that is also performing throughout the interaction. For that reason, all team members must maintain a uniform attitude and support each other at all times during the encounter.

Teamwork is present in all spheres of social life. In business, marriage, religion, and all forms of bureaucracy, people often work together to convey a perspective or belief system to those around them. Be it a group of social workers convincing clients of their feelings of compassion or officers, sergeants, and squad leaders exhorting the infantry to battle, everyone is subject to team performance frequently; for the performers, the act may well be routine but for the one being socialized it is often a new and perhaps misunderstood event.

To summarize, Goffman suggests that individuals use specific types of strategies to attempt to control and manage a social encounter as well as to project a desired definition of the situation to the other interactants. Implicit in this concept of control is the idea that individuals process and assign identities to one another.

Individuals bring to a situation their own identity kits filled with personal data (ethnic background, age, sex, style of speech and dress, and so on) as well as a whole range of beliefs, attitudes, and motives. The more astute and creative individuals are the more successful in the process of manipulation. The only difficulty is to determine which self will best suit a specific interaction and purpose.

SOCIALIZATION OF MALE STRIPPERS

Because male stripping is a relatively new phenomenon and because most male strip clubs prohibit men from being in the audience, our interviewees had only vague expectations about what the stripper role entails. What preliminary knowledge they did have was derived from their attendance at female strip shows, their friendships with female strippers, information from girlfriends, sisters, and female coworkers who had attended a male strip show, or the brief glimpses the men themselves had had of male strippers.

Prejob socialization experiences among our strippers were extremely limited. None of the interviewees had received professional training in dancing or related fields such as music. In addition, previous employment in some other facet of entertainment work was limited to one dancer who had past experience as a singer and dancer as well as a stripper in nightclubs. One other dancer, however, although self-taught in dancing, was skillful enough to have had previous work experience as an instructor in a dance studio.

For the rest of our dancers a strong avocational interest in dancing existed, and they reported frequent attendance at night clubs and discotheques. The typical presocialization experiences are exemplified in the comments of one respondent:

Most of the stuff is things I've learned in discos. I watch people all the time; *that's how I've learned. I've never had any training. I started watching American Bandstand. That's how I first learned to dance.*

Because of minimal anticipatory socialization the dancers' first performances generated uncertainty and anxiety. A number of respondents reported being taken to the club by a friend to inquire about the possibility of becoming a stripper. Instead, it was a typical occurrence that they were asked to dance that same night without even auditioning. The comments of one dancer illustrate the nature of first night experiences:

I figured I'd have to be completely drunk to do it. I can remember everything—the music, my dress, everything. I was nervous as I could be. I had one glass of vodka on the rocks and when I came on [the stage], I needed another. I wore what I wore down to the club. [Another dancer] handed me a G-string. I did two singles [dance numbers] and tabletopped. I guess I made about $30 that night.

The nature of these dancers' initial stripping experiences was not uncommon: They did not expect to dance that first night, they were not prepared with costume or G-string, and they required alcohol to loosen themselves up in order to get on the stage and remove their clothes. However, since the first performances were rewarding in terms of money and audience response, our strippers appeared for work on subsequent nights. . . .

To be a successful stripper one must acquire certain work skills, techniques, and tricks of the trade. As we have already noted, although strippers have not had formal training in dance, they do enter the occupation with a certain level of dance skills. Our dancers report that they are expected to be fairly self-reliant in terms of dance skills. Nevertheless, some informal socialization does occur, as they also indicate that they spend considerable time watching others perform to pick up cues and that they occasionally ask other dancers for advice about specific moves.

Another area in which dancers are expected by their coworkers to be relatively self-sufficient is that of the selection of specific costumes, music, and gimmicks. Those strippers who used costumes were apparently socialized to the idea of the use of costumes and gimmicks and the coordination of these with music by noticing their success when utilized by other dancers. Beyond the general idea of coordination, however, dancers were expected to develop the specific content of their costumes, music, and gimmicks on their own and not to imitate other dancers.

The acquisition of certain other work skills occurs for the neophyte stripper almost entirely on the job under the tutelage of the experienced dancers. Through informal conversations, and in a more limited way through observations, new strippers learn about the appropriate way to remove one's clothes, how to wear a G-string properly, and various tips about grooming and other factors in presenting oneself to the audience. Although not trying to eschew the provocative nature of the act, it is important to male strippers to get down to the G-string as quickly as possible. Since tipping almost universally occurs by the customer placing money in the dancer's G-string, it is in the dancer's financial interest to maximize the time during his performance that he is accessible for tips. An essential part of the stripper's act includes proper placement of the G-string so that exposure of his genitals does not occur accidentally while he is dancing. In addition, strippers are cautioned to hold their G-string in place when receiving tips. Dancers are also socialized to the need for maximizing their attractiveness to the audience and for maintaining the manifest heterosexuality of the show (Petersen and Dressel, forthcoming). To do this, they learn to employ a number of specific techniques to enhance their desirability to audience members including using makeup to diminish the glare of the lights against their features, trimming what they felt was excessive body hair, keeping in shape physically, and establishing eye contact with as many audience members as possible to break down social distance.

Besides acquiring job skills, a stripper must learn a certain occupational code of ethics. Although the code is not formalized, it provides dancers with guidelines regarding their relationships to the work organization, to the customers, and to fellow dancers. With regard to the code as it governs strippers in the work organization, expectations include reporting for work on time; being alert to when one's individual performance is scheduled; not bringing women or glassware into the dressing room; keeping one's genitals covered at all times and not touching that area during the performance; and not mingling with the audience during the course of the show. The latter norm was important to protect dancers from charges of solicitation.

Norms relative to interaction with the audience are directed to manipulating the audience to the dancer's advantage and to ways of maintaining physical distance between the dancer and his audience. With regard to the former, dancers learn from one another who the good and the bad tippers are. It is also important for a dancer after receiving his tip to know how to initiate physical contact with an audience member in a manner which prevents the customer from feeling shortchanged but which allows him to move quickly to other audience members to maximize his tips. In addition, it was thought detrimental to potential club attendance for a dancer to date more than one female from the same group who attended the show. Among the norms regarding the maintenance of physical distance are that dancers should not allow audience members to touch their genitals, that they should not "feel girls up," and that they should not have sex with customers on the premises.

Several norms pertain to strippers' interactions with fellow dancers. The most important of these norms centered around the stripper's act. One was not to use another dancer's gimmick or duplicate another stripper's costume. Moreover, it was acknowledged that certain songs "belonged" to particular dancers and that another dancer could not use the same song for his routine without permission from the original user. Finally, there was the understanding that strippers should not discuss their own or other dancers' sexual preferences with anyone in the audience.

—PAULA DRESSEL AND
DAVID PETERSEN

The theme of management and control is a major concern for Goffman in all of his work. In *Asylums* (1961a), he deals with identity—maintaining equipment or how the person maintains the self. In *Stigma* (1962), he indicates how a person controls or manages the tension that results from being discredited or stigmatized. In *Behavior in Public Places* (1963), he relates the way in which a person manages allocation of involvement to fit the size of the social occasion.

In reading Goffman, one begins to realize just how complex ordinary, everyday interactions among people really are. Learning these complex processes and how to make use of them is an important part of socialization in our society.

AGENTS OF SOCIALIZATION

To this point, we have examined the ways in which individuals learn about both their society and their culture. We have looked at the ways in which individuals develop the beliefs, attitudes, and motives that govern their social lives as participants in an ongoing culture. But who are the **agents of socialization**—the people who initiate the socialization process? Who is responsible for shaping the young person's thinking about self and the social world? For the young, the answers include the family, the peer group, the school, and the mass media. For most adults, the influence of these agents continues in some way or other and is joined by influence from superiors, peers, and subordinates in the workplace as well as from various other kinds of social groups.

It is interesting to note that some agents of socialization, such as the family and school, have a clear mandate from society to train the next generation—to transmit the group's cultural heritage so that the young may become full-fledged participants. By contrast, other agents, such as the mass media, do much of their teaching less directly, yet they actively influence how the individual perceives and responds to the social environment.

The Family

The family is probably the most significant agent of socialization. A young child's first contact with the social world is through the eyes, beliefs, and understandings of parents. Family members, including older siblings, are familiar with the ways of the surrounding culture, and they impart to children the accepted ways of thinking, feeling, and acting. From the first days of life, the individual is moulded; significant others impart a wide range of meanings about norms and values related to the kinds of behaviour the individual will experience during the course of his or her life. (Notice that in modern Canadian society, these significant others often include babysitters and day-care workers, who act as surrogates for the family.)

In addition to the interpersonal and personal skills the family provides, it also naturally gives the child a range of roles and statuses. The family of birth largely determines the individual's place in society by bestowing various **ascribed statuses**—social positions, such as those linked to ethnicity, race, religion, social class, and placement within the family (first born, youngest, eldest, or so on) over which the individual has no control. These ascribed characteristics significantly affect the individual's life and sense of self, including how others respond to it. These social characteristics limit the opportunities the individual has in life. (See, for example, Chapters 6, 8, and 15, which suggest how the effects of educational opportunity, social class, and ethnicity, respectively, extend into adulthood.)

Through the dominant set of beliefs communicated to young children, they come to understand their place and to appropriate and announce

Old-order Amish co-exist with technological change, but they strive to transmit their traditional culture from generation to generation.

their identity in terms of those beliefs. For example, a person growing up in a ghetto comes to understand upward mobility, personal achievement, and wealth in a very different way than a child reared in a middle-class milieu.

The family also orchestrates the transmission to children of sentiments such as love, honesty, idealism, and integrity. A young child learns to respect authority, begins to understand the value of sharing and expressing thoughts, and eventually comes to self-discipline.

Clearly, the family serves as a critical agent of socialization. Yet the contents of what it transmits and the manner of transmission vary across families differentiated by ethnicity, religion, and social class, as well as by other factors including rural or urban location, the occupations of the parents, and the presence or absence of either parent.

The Peer Groups

The **peer group**—a grouping of individuals of the same general age with approximately the same interests—is the only agency of socialization of the child that is not controlled mainly by adults. In fact, the child usually belongs to several peer groups; for example, a girl may have schoolmates, may have made other friends among neighbourhood children, belong to the Girl Guides, and interact with yet other peers within a church group, at summer camp, and during ballet classes.

Some sociologists have suggested that in contemporary Western societies the peer group has become the most important agent of socialization. David Riesman is one of the leading proponents of this view. In his book *The Lonely Crowd* (1950), he concludes that modern society, in contrast to primitive and traditional societies, produces people who tend to be "other directed"; that is, they look to their peers for guidelines and ideas on how they should behave. According to Riesman, peer-group approval is for many youngsters and adults the most important motivating factor in social behaviour.

The peer group contributes to socialization by enabling children to engage in experiences that may not be provided in the family. Here they can engage in give-and-take relationships—relationships involving exchange, conflict, competition, and cooperation—not always possible at home. In this manner, children are provided with opportunities for self-direction and self-expression.

Sharing in the peer group has numerous advantages. For the most part, the young person is here able to examine feelings, beliefs, and ideas that are in some way not acceptable to the family structure. Friends tend to share a good deal about how they see the world, how they come to experience relationships with the opposite sex, and how they understand developments within, say, their school and the friendship circle.

The peer group also helps to promote independence from parents, by introducing the child to ways of thinking and acting that differ from those offered by parents. In fact by the time the child is a teenager, the peer group may demand behaviour that conflicts sharply with the norms and values of the parental generation. During adolescence, the peer group is undoubtedly the major socialization agent, and individuals may value its opinions more highly than those of the family, the school, or the larger society. The conflict of values between parents and their children is sometimes referred to as the "generation gap."

Although the "generation gap" is common in the contemporary Western world, adolescence is not a period of conflict in every society. In a

As women enter the labour force in increasing numbers, day-care centres have become a major socializing agency for the very young child, with consequences we cannot yet foresee.

number of societies studied by social scientists, it is a time of increased interaction with adults, a period of gradually assuming adult roles. By contrast, the generations have become compartmentalized in Western society. Adolescence is a period during which young people decrease their involvement with adults. Some analysts see this difference as a result of shifting considerable responsibility for socialization from the family to other agencies. Coleman (1961), for example, suggests that since children are isolated from adult society by being set apart in school for much of their pre-adult lives, they come to depend increasingly on one another. By adolescence, he claims, they form a subculture complete with its own mode of dress, speech, rituals, norms, and values. Another factor contributing to this adolescent subculture is that many parents spend much of their time away from home—commuting to work, attending social events, and so on. As a result, adolescents and even younger children tend to spend more time with their peers than they do with their parents.

The School

Schools are formally charged with the task of passing on many of the culture's symbols, beliefs, values, and norms. Writing of the United States, Denzin says:

> Schools are best seen not as educational settings but as places where fate, morality and personal careers are created and shaped. Schools are moral institutions. They have assumed the responsibility of shaping children, of whatever race or income level, into right and proper participants in American society, pursuing with equal vigor the abstract goals of that society. (1979, 3)

In Canada and elsewhere, the socialization process in school also involves more than the formal teaching of skills and subject matter. Accompanying the formal goals of schools is what has come to be known as the **hidden curriculum**—the informal teachings that they inculcate to help ensure students' successful integration into society. Students learn what is expected of them not only academically but also as members of their group and as responsible citizens of their society. The hidden curriculum exposes students to such matters as discipline, conformity, authority structures, and cooperation; it rewards them for the acquisition and display of "desirable" attitudes and behaviour. (For more discussion of the hidden curriculum, see Chapter 6.)

Interpersonal skills are also learned at school. Discipline, schedules, and regime are important. The child is assessed by outsiders and, most important, develops a specific reputation about the kind of person he or she is.

In some instances, the socialization received from the school reinforces and extends the learning from within the family. If, however, the family's values and beliefs run contrary to those of the dominant culture, school can modify or even reverse the socialization received in the family. This kind of cross-cutting is, for example, said to create considerable difficulty for many immigrants and their children. Thus, too, some religious groups seek to establish their own schools. In his study of secular education in a Hassidic community near Montreal, Shaffir (1974) observes that administrators devoted meticulous attention to hiring only certain kinds of teachers, to excluding some subjects from the curriculum, and to screening the teaching to ensure that it did not depart markedly from the group's religious beliefs. It was all an attempt to control the content of the socialization to which the group's children were exposed.

The Mass Media

Academic institutions are in constant competition with a pervasive form of information distribution—the mass media. The influence of newspapers, magazines, radio, television, and motion pictures is overwhelming. They not only provide entertainment and information, they also help children to begin the process of role modelling. With a wide range of stereotypes and experiences available through the popular culture, young children begin to build on a whole series of folk heroes, imagining themselves to be Hulk Hogan or Wonder Woman. They begin to experience what Klapp (1969) refers to as "identity voyages," fantasies in which they place themselves in contexts and even develop a set of values consistent with the presentations of folk heroes. Sometimes the values conveyed to young people by Indiana Jones and Luke Skywalker have a far more pervasive influence than those of parents and teachers.

A frequent and significant sociological question concerns how adults monitor what children internalize from the particular performances they see through the mass media. Feshbach and Singer (1971) suggest that televised violence may have a more important function for lower-class audience participants than for middle-class ones. They note that the socialization of children in middle-class families leaves them better equipped to control their aggressive impulses. In contrast, lower-class children often have poorly developed internal-control mechanisms and are thus more dependent on the external catharsis provided by television violence.

Yet the impact of the mass media goes well beyond impressions fostered in children. De Fleur and Ball-Rokeach suggest that audiences in urban-industrial societies are dependent on mass media information resources:

> We assume that the ultimate basis of media influence lies in the nature of the three-way relationship among the larger social system, the media's role in that system, and audience relationships to the media. . . . [The media] operate as a fourth estate delivering information about the actions of government; they serve as the primary signaling system in case of emergencies; they constitute the principal source of the ordinary citizen's conceptions of national and world events. (1976, 262)

Thus, the socialization experience is to a large degree influenced by relationships between society and the mass media.

Many of the values and norms current in a society are transmitted by a reference model — someone who is held up as an example of desirable behaviour. In this photograph we see how values related to sports, success, certain clothes, and popularity are all being transmitted simultaneously.

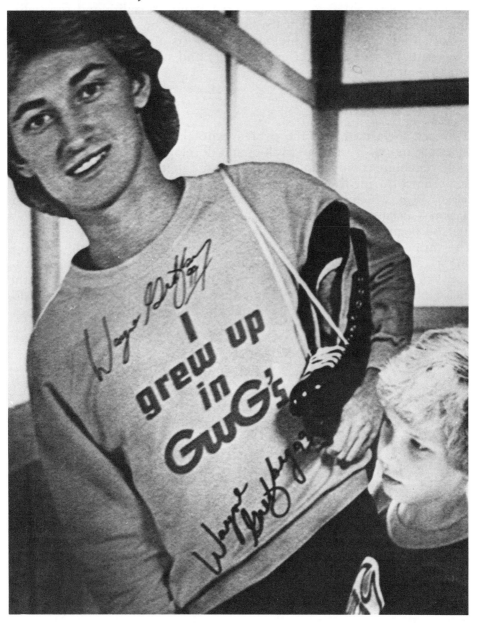

SOCIALIZATION AND THE LIFE CYCLE

As we have seen, socialization occurs primarily within the family, in peer groups, in schools, and through the mass media. It is important to note, however, that socialization does not terminate when a student graduates from school or leaves home. The mass media continue their influence, and usually the family does too, in some way. Peer groups, in the form of friends and neighbours, various organizations, such as service clubs and political societies, and occupational groups socialize and resocialize individuals throughout their lives.

Socialization, then, is a lifelong process. As already mentioned, sociologists have categorized it into primary and secondary phases. Each is worth a bit more discussion.

Primary Socialization

Primary socialization is the process whereby children learn language, symbols, mores, norms, and values and develop a diverse set of cognitive skills, enabling them to cope with the wide range of interactions they will experience during their lifetime. Some primary socialization is *anticipatory socialization*, which some social scientists refer to as preparatory socialization—socialization for what lies ahead. It includes the ways in which a person begins to understand—for example, through the mass media—the variety of opportunities available for personal growth and development. The young person who aspires to be, say, a professional athlete can learn a good deal from the kinds of information imparted by the mass media, such as televised interviews and games. In a sense, the potential athlete is developing an orientation, a perspective about the professional athlete, which will be useful whether he or she achieves that role or not.

The variety of training programs that teenagers and young adults engage in to prepare themselves for the world of work are yet another example of anticipatory socialization. By learning about the ways in which a specific industry operates, the individual develops the cognitive skills and vocabulary appropriate to it. He or she also learns coping strategies—how to manage impressions and be perceived as someone in the know. In a general sense, then, anticipatory socialization is the preparatory phase in which a person acquires some of the specifics of a craft or pursuit in order to function effectively later on.

Secondary Socialization

Adult socialization is an ongoing process of learning, communicating, and sharing information. According to Rosow:

> Adult socialization is the process of inculcating new values and appropriate behaviour to adult positions and group memberships. These changes are

normally internalized in the course of the induction or training procedures, whether formal or informal. They result in new images, expectations, skills and norms as the person defines himself and as others view him. (1974, 31)

Each time people step into a new role, learn about a new set of beliefs through another person, or exchange ideas in a new social setting, they are becoming socialized, they are adapting, they are learning about new and varied ways of looking at the world.

Closely linked with the process of adult socialization is the concept of career. Everett C. Hughes (1958) has suggested that people's work identities are one of the most important parts of their social identities and that people are judged to a large extent by the ways in which they do their jobs and how successful they are at achieving their goals. In this regard, occupational socialization is a very important part of adult socialization.

During the apprenticeship period of occupational socialization, the individual goes through a process of learning the ropes, which includes appropriate presentation of self, the language of the occupation, and the rules and regulations (**vocabularies of motive**) that govern the organization. Whether the training period is measured in days or years, it involves a learning process whereby individuals come to make sense of organizational and work arrangements. For example, with whom is it important to associate, and with whom should one maintain some kind of social distance? Who is the powerful decision maker in the organization and who is the person who defers? What is expected of the individual as a worker? To whom is loyalty to be given? Only after these questions have been answered can the individual move through a maintenance process, meeting obligations and carrying out responsibilities.

The young student attempting to assume the responsibility of a career in medicine must at the same time become resocialized—must adopt new skills and new attitudes that will replace the old ones. Davis (1966) speaks about nurses going through a process of "doctrinal conversion"—that is, they put aside the lay imagery they have of the practising profession and take on the professional symbols. Lovell (1964) describes how newcomers to the armed forces are required to reshape not only their life routine but also some of their thinking, beliefs, and values and to develop a new vocabulary of motive around the new experience. Few people in Canadian society are used to the kind of hierarchy of responsibility and sense of power exercised in the military. Therefore, in boot camp the recruit has to begin to internalize the norms and values of the military system and to adopt a perspective consistent with the ideological and social arrangements conveyed by the military system to the larger society.

It is possible that a good deal of the information absorbed during adolescent and adult socialization will, in fact, serve the individual well, but some of the significant components of that learning will have to be transformed so that the individual's perceptions fit the new system within which he or she must operate. To oppose the system would be to create conflict, resulting in grave problems for both the novice and those involved in his or her supervision.

Entrance to a career is not the only time of occupational resocialization. Take, for example, the long-time worker who is offered a management position. Overnight that person must begin to understand the perspective of management; it is not uncommon to witness a former representative of the workforce suddenly take a pro-management position in general conversation as well as in labour-related matters. As Becker (1965) points out, that kind of resocialization has to do with personal survival: individuals in that position decide to cover their side bets to ensure that their particular role performance and place in the organization are sustained over time.

Socialization is, in other words, an ongoing process. Human beings are constantly learning about themselves through interaction with others. Through these experiences, they develop the kinds of commitments that help to shape their thinking about how they are going to cooperate in the social world.

THE FATE OF IDEALISM IN MEDICAL SCHOOL

(NOTE: *In the almost 20 years since this article was written, women have entered medical school in increasing numbers, so that a gender-inclusive language would be used today.)*

Professional schools often receive a major share of the blame for producing cynicism—and none more than the medical school. The idealistic young freshman changes into a tough, hardened, unfeeling doctor; or so the popular view has it. Teachers of medicine sometimes rephrase the distinction between the clinical and preclinical years into one between the "cynical" and "precynical" years. Psychological research supports this view, presenting attitude surveys which show medical students year by year scoring lower on "idealism" and higher on "cynicism." Typically, this cynicism is seen as developing in response to the shattering of ideals consequent on coming face-to-face with the realities of professional practice.

The Freshmen

The medical students enter school with what we may think of as the idealistic notion, implicit in lay culture, that the practice of medicine is a wonderful thing and that they are going to devote their lives to service to mankind. They believe that medicine is made up of a great body of well-established facts that they will be taught from the first day and and that these facts will be of immediate practical use to them as physicians. They enter school expecting to work industriously and expecting that if they work hard enough they will be able to master this body of fact and thus become good doctors.

In several ways the first year of medical school does not live up to their expectations. They are disillusioned when they find they will not be near patients at all, that the first year will be just like another year of college. The freshmen are further disillusioned when the faculty tells them in a variety of ways that there is more to medicine than they can possibly learn. They realize it may be impossible for them to learn all they need to know in order to practice medicine properly. Their disillusionment becomes more profound when they discover that this statement of the faculty is literally true. Experience in trying to master the details of the anatomy of the extremities convinces them that they cannot do so in the time they have. Their expectation of hard work is not disappointed; they put in an eight-hour day of classes and laboratories, and study four or five hours a night and most of the weekend as well.

Some of the students, the brightest, continue to attempt to learn it all, but succeed only in getting more and more worried about their work. The majority decide that, since they can't learn it all, they must select from among all the facts presented to them those they will attempt to learn. There are two ways of making this selection. On the one hand, the student may decide on the basis of his own uninformed notions about the nature of medical practice that many facts are not important, since they relate to things which seldom come up in the actual practice of medicine; therefore, he reasons, it is useless to learn them. On the other hand, the student can decide that the important thing is to pass his examinations and, therefore, that the important facts are those which are likely to be asked on an examination; he uses this as a basis for selecting both facts to memorize and courses for intensive study. For example, the work in physiology is dismissed on both of these grounds, being considered neither relevant to the facts of medical life nor important in terms of the amount of time the faculty devotes to it and the number of examinations in the subject.

A student may use either or both of these bases of selection at the beginning of the year, before many tests have been given. But after a few tests have been taken, the student makes "what the faculty wants" the chief basis of his selection of what to learn, for he now has a better idea of what this is and also has become aware that it is possible to fail examinations and that he therefore must learn the expectations of the faculty if he wishes to stay in school. The fact that one group of students, that with the highest prestige in the class, took this view early and did well on examinations was decisive in swinging the whole class around to this position. The students were equally influenced to become "test-wise" by the fact that, although they had all been in the upper range in their colleges, the class average on the first examination was frighteningly low.

In becoming test-wise, the students begin to develop systems for discovering the faculty wishes and learning them. These systems are both methods for studying their texts and short-cuts that can be taken in laboratory work. For instance, they begin to select facts for memorization by looking over the files of old examinations maintained in each of the medical fraternity houses. They share tip-offs from the lectures and offhand remarks of the faculty as to what will be on the examinations. In anatomy, they agree not to bother to dissect out subcutaneous nerves, reasoning that it is both difficult and time consuming and the information can be secured from books with less effort. The interaction involved in the development of such systems and short-cuts helps to create a social group of a class which had previously been only an aggregation of smaller and less organized groups.

In this medical school, the students learn in this way to distinguish between the activities of the first year and their original view that everything that happens to them in medical school will be important. Thus, they become cynical about the value of their activities in the first year. They feel that the real thing—learning which will help them to help mankind—has been postponed perhaps until the second year, or perhaps even further, at which time they will be able again to act on idealistic premises. They believe that what they do in their later years in school under supervision will be about the same thing they will do, as physicians, on their own; the first year had disappointed this expectation.

Later Years

The sophomore year does not differ greatly from the freshman year. Both the work load and anxiety over examinations probably increase. Though they begin some medical activities, as in their attendance at autopsies and particularly in their introductory course in physical diagnosis, most of what they do continues to repeat the pattern of the college science curriculum. Their attention still centers on the problem of getting through school by doing well in examinations.

During the third and fourth, or clinical years, teaching takes a new form. In place of lectures and laboratories, the students' work now consists of the study of actual patients admitted to the hospital or seen in the clinic. Each patient who enters the hospital is assigned to a student who interviews him about his illnesses, past and present, and performs a physical examination. He writes this up for the patient's chart, and appends the diagnosis and the treatment that he would use were he allowed actually to treat the patient. During conferences with faculty physicians, often held at the patient's bedside, the student is quizzed about items of his report and called upon to defend them or to explain their significance. Most of the teaching in the clinical years is of this order.

Contact with patients brings a new set of circumstances with which the student must deal. He no longer feels the great pressure created by tests, for he is told by the faculty, and this is confirmed by his daily experience, that examinations are now less important. His problems now become those of coping with a steady stream of patients in a way that will please the staff man under whom he is working, and of handling what is sometimes a tremendous load of clinical work so as to allow himself time for studying diseases and treatments that interest him and for play and family life.

The students earlier have expected that once they reach the clinical years they will be able to realize their idealistic ambitions to help people and to learn those things immediately useful in aiding people who are ill. But they find themselves working to understand cases as medical problems rather than working to help the sick and memorizing the relevant available facts so that these can be produced immediately for a questioning staff man. When they make ward rounds with a faculty member they are likely to be quizzed about any of the seemingly countless facts possibly related to the condition of the patient for whom they are "caring."

Observers speak of the cynicism that overtakes the student and the lack of concern for his patients as human beings. This change does take place, but it is not produced solely by "the anxiety brought about by the presence of death and suffering." The student becomes preoccupied with the technical aspects of the cases with which he deals because the faculty requires him to do so. He is questioned about so many technical details that he must spend most of his time learning them.

As a result of the increasingly technical emphasis of his thinking the student appears cynical to the nonmedical outsider, though from his own point of view he is simply seeing what is "really important." Instead of reacting with the layman's horror and sympathy for the patient to the sight of a cancerous organ that has been surgically removed, the student is more likely to regret that he was not allowed to close the incision at the completion of the operation, and to rue the hours that he must spend searching in the fatty flesh for the lymph nodes that will reveal how far the disease has spread. As in other lines of work, he drops lay attitudes for those more relevant to the way the event affects someone in his position.

Their original medical idealism reasserts itself as the end of school approaches. Seniors show more interest than students in earlier years in serious ethical dilemmas of the kind they expect to face in practice. They have become aware of ethical problems laymen often see as crucial for the physician—whether it is right to keep patients with fatal diseases alive as long as possible, or what should be done if an influential patient demands an [illegal treatment]—and worry about them. As they near graduation and student culture begins to break down as the soon-to-be doctors are about to go their separate ways, these questions are more and more openly discussed.

—HOWARD S. BECKER AND
BLANCHE GEER

SUMMARY

In this chapter we have examined socialization, which refers (1) to the process by which the individual learns the ways of a group or society in order to become a functioning participant and, (2) to the changes experienced by an individual as a result of social influences. Traditionally, the literature has focused on childhood socialization and the development of the concept of self, especially because a person's first contact with individuals, groups, and organizations is most likely to have a significant impact on all subsequent phases of that person's socialization. Socialization should not, however, be thought of as confined primarily to the first years of life. Rather, it occurs throughout the lifespan; the individual must constantly learn to adapt to and deal with new and changing experiences. Although anticipatory socialization may help the individual prepare for future roles, movement through life's different stages rarely offers much continuity in role requirements and performance.

Viewed as a lifelong process rather than a passing period in the life cycle, socialization occurs in relationships with various agents of socialization: some of them assume a greater influence than others, and relative importance often depends on the stage of the process. In the earliest stage of socialization, the family is usually the most significant agent; it and the school are charged by society with the formal task of imparting to the new generations the attitudes, values, knowledge, and skills required for effective participation as an individual and as a group member. Peer groups and the media are two other influential agents, influencing the shape and direction of the individual's movement through the life cycle. Both the influence and significance of these agents of socialization and others—for example, organizations and institutions—are related to the person's particular stage of development, social situation, and subjective appreciation thereof.

In the socialization process the individual must be regarded not as a passive learner but rather as a dynamic agent. The individual is not merely an object responding willy-nilly to environmental forces and conditions. In fact, the opposite is more accurate. As an actor capable of anticipating others' reactions, the individual defines and interprets situations and, using his or her best judgment, organizes a line of behaviour. At the same time, however, the individual's behaviour must be coordinated with the general bounds of the culture within which experiences have been shaped. Thus, socialization is best seen as a two-way process: the individual, exposed to societal influences, learns a series of appropriate modes of orientation and behaviour and, through the formation and development of a social self, in turn helps shape and mould the nature and significance of those influences.

FOR FURTHER READING

Becker, Howard S., Blanche Geer, Everett C. Hughes, and Anselm Strauss
1961 *Boys in White: Student Culture in Medical School.* Chicago: University of Chicago Press.
This study of students in medical school, based on participant observation and informal interviews, examines the transition from layperson to practising professional. The study focuses on the various influences affecting the pace and direction of medical student socialization.

Elkin, Frederick, and Gerald Handel
1972 *The Child and Society.* New York: Random House.
This book, which incorporates both sociological and social-psychological material and is largely based on role theory, provides an overview of the socialization process.

Erikson, Erik H.
1963 *Childhood and Society*, 2nd ed. New York: W.W. Norton.
This classic statement about socialization in childhood details how the personality develops through eight stages of ego development.

Goffman, Erving
1961 *Asylums: Essays on the Social Situation of Mental Patients and Other Inmates.* New York: Anchor Books, Doubleday.
This work, consisting of four essays, is an analysis of life in total institutions. The essays describe the effects of institutionalization on the inmates, the process of resocialization within institutions, and how inmates learn to adapt.

Lindesmith, Alfred R., Anselm L. Strauss, and Norman K. Denzin
1975 *Social Psychology*, 4th ed. Hinsdale, Ill.: Dryden Press.
One of the major social psychology textbooks, this volume approaches socialization and social interaction almost exclusively from a symbolic-interactionist perspective.

Mead, George Herbert
1934 *Mind, Self and Society.* Charles W. Morris, ed. Chicago: University of Chicago Press.
The material in this book is compiled from Mead's lectures and published writings. It provides a detailed analysis of the origins and development of the social self.

Piaget, Jean
1954 *The Construction of Reality in the Child.* Margaret Cook, trans. New York: Basic Books.
In this detailed study of childhood learning, Piaget chronicles the process through which young children make sense of their physical world.

Shibutani, Tamotsu
1961 *Society and Personality.* Englewood Cliffs, N.J.: Prentice-Hall.
The book examines the relationship between social interaction and personality, with emphasis on the emergence of the self.

Williams, Thomas Rhys
1983 *Socialization.* Englewood Cliffs, N.J.: Prentice-Hall.
This text provides a discussion of the nature and major features of the socialization process. It is written in a manner that enables readers to understand socialization irrespective of their level of study.

CHAPTER 5

THE FAMILY

Nancy Mandell

Families are the social arenas in which North Americans spend the largest part of their lives. For most people, the family evokes conflicting images and experiences. Potentially, it is both oppressive and supportive, abusive and nurturing. Understanding various patterns and structures of family life gives you a glimpse of how intimate interactions are constructed and imbued with symbolic meaning.

In addition to providing important personal insights, the sociological study of the family also contributes to your grasp of how society works. The family is a basic institution embedded in the social, political, and economic conditions of society. Family life is strongly affected by the economic system—how poor or affluent the society is and whether production is based in the family or in outside workplaces. Such economic events as layoffs, high youth unemployment, and an increase in the proportion of women working outside the home all have enormous consequences for the family. Moreover, discerning the family's relationship with the larger society illuminates the process of state policy enactment. Welfare policies, tax reforms, and educational funding are among the many government programs modelled by a particular conception of family life.

In addition to its private and public nature, the family is an ideological and historical creation. Most aspects of the family, including child-rearing patterns and the contributions—financial and otherwise—expected from various members, are not universals; rather, they vary from one culture to another, one period to another, one class to another.

OBSTACLES TO UNDERSTANDING FAMILIES

Despite their public and private significance, families are unusually difficult to study. The problems include the usual existence of a norm of privacy, discrepancies between people's ideal of the family and actual behaviour in families, and the difficulty of obtaining a definition of "family" that is generally accepted and useful.

The Norm of Privacy

As intimate havens, families are intensely private affairs, "backstages" in Goffman's (1959) phrase, where individuals relax and let their hair down. Privacy has become a **norm**—an unwritten rule or expectation based on accepted values—and is jealously guarded by Canadians, who resent public interference.

The ideological construction of the family as an invulnerable, unassailable refuge makes it one of the most difficult social organizations to study. People are reluctant to allow researchers to investigate (and perhaps evaluate) their private lives. Most do not want to reveal their sexual patterns, late-night television-viewing habits, or parent-child arguments. The cherished ideal of privacy both restricts the type of family research carried out and makes one cautious about the validity of interview data.

Research on family decision-making is a typical example of methodological inconsistencies. Assessing who is really the boss was of considerable interest to researchers in the 1960s and 1970s, yet their studies consistently revealed internally inconsistent results. Husbands and wives gave remarkably different answers when asked who makes decisions on purchasing a car, taking a vacation, or going to the movies. This discrepancy prompted Jessie Bernard (1972) to coin the phrase " 'His' and 'Her' marriage," referring to a husband's and wife's quite different experiences and interpretations of the same marriage. Even when researchers interview spouses together, different realities often prevail.

Respondents also tend to answer according to societal expectations. Before the enormous movement of married women into the labour force, most women perceived their primary role to be that of mother-wife, a "junior partner" to the husband (Scanzoni and Scanzoni 1981). By 1983, when almost three-quarters of young women (age 20 to 24) were in the labour force, married women tended to see themselves as equal to their spouses. In a 1966 Gallup poll, 63 percent of Canadian men and women agreed with the statement "Fathers should be top boss in the family in this country"; by 1981, the same poll found that only 36 percent agreed, showing a trend toward egalitarian marital relationships. However, studies continue to reveal an unequal division of household tasks, suggesting that behavioural patterns have not caught up with attitudinal changes.

Ideal and Actual Norms

This difference between attitudes and actions is one example of what sociologists call the discrepancy between ideal norms and actual behaviour. Other dichotomies within family life include equality-inequality, nurturance-abuse, private-public, and female-male. (For more on these dichotomies, see Chapter 9.) Recent family research reveals that myths, secrets, and information-processing rules determine how families communicate with themselves and others. Privately, people know how their own family stands relative to ideal norms—the way family life is supposed to be. But they do not know where they fit into statistical norms—that is, to what extent their family differs from others. Families often present a unified, content, and loving image. Yet estimates suggest that a quarter of all Canadian women and a tenth of men were sexually abused as children or youths (Badgley 1984) and that one in ten married or cohabiting women is battered by her partner (MacLeod 1980). Behind closed doors, people may say and do ugly things, which they tend to conceal from researchers.

Both the norm of privacy and the discrepancy between ideal and actual behaviour conspire to keep social scientists relatively ill informed about family life. This state of what Skolnick (1983) calls pluralistic ignorance means that, while everyone is an expert about his or her own family, no one knows much about what goes on in other people's lives.

Defining the Family

What is a family? It is difficult to compose a list of features that distinguish a family group from a non-family group. Yet legal, sociopolitical, and ethical decisions are based on definitions of the family. "Who is your family?" is a frequent question, but the "right" answer varies according to whether the respondent is filling out an income tax form, applying for social welfare benefits, dividing up family property or applying for a student loan. Often these differentiations are blurred in sociological definitions.

The most commonly accepted definition in Canada is provided by the census. A **family** is

> a group of persons consisting of a husband and wife (with or without children who have never been married, regardless of age) or a parent with one or more children never married, living in the same dwelling. A family may consist, also, of a man or woman living with a guardianship child or ward under 21 years of age for whom no pay was received.

However, Canada has (as it has always had) a variety of family types—common-law, single-parent, and reconstituted families—that do not conform statistically or ideologically to this or other traditional definitions. This variety has led sociologists to distinguish between a family and a household. A family refers to a relatively durable unit of two or more members considered to be related to each other by blood or marriage (Nett 1983, 332). A **household** refers to people living within the same dwelling place and can include unrelated roommates, a single person, or a family with a boarder or a domestic servant (Baker 1984, 2).

This concern for definitions is no mere word game. The attempt to define the Canadian family as an undifferentiated whole represents what Eichler (1983, 9) calls the "monolithic bias." It emphasizes not the multiplicity of family structures, experiences, members, and functions, but the universal sameness of families. Such emphasis reinforces the notion of an ideal family that all families should resemble.

Ideological constructions of the ideal family are powerful influences on family life. Ideal norms prescribe appropriate gender roles, parent-child interactions, and relationships with relatives. Often the media perpetuate these images. The 1950s television program *Leave It to Beaver* exemplified the ideal family: a father who worked outside the home and was unquestioned leader of the family, a stay-at-home wife, and mischievous but respectful children following in their footsteps. Today, television shows depict single parents, reconstituted or **blended families** (one or both spouses bring to the union children from a previous marriage), and homosexual unions, but some of the most popular family programs, such as *The Cosby Show*, give images that are basically conservative, harmonious, and monolithic.

To what extent do media depictions accurately reflect current family forms? For example, the large family portrayed in *The Cosby Show* is more representative of the 1950s than of the 1980s, when the fertility rate has dropped to 1.7 children. The relationship between Canadian family ideology and statistical realities will be explored later in this chapter.

THE CHANGING FAMILY

Back in the 1950s, everyone knew what a typical family was. It was, of course, the Anderson family in *Father Knows Best*, or Ozzie and Harriet Nelson and their two sons, David and Ricky, who lived at 822 Sycamore Road in Hillsdale, Televisionland.

The Adventures of Ozzie and Harriet—TV's longest-running situation comedy—seemed to epitomize family life in the 1950s. The Nelson's suburban household was a peaceful and prosperous nest in which the family members' roles were clearly defined: Ozzie was the breadwinning husband, Harriet was the homemaking wife, and David and Ricky were the well-adjusted children destined, it seemed, to carry on their parents' stable values and homey lifestyle when they grew up and married. Between 1952 and 1966, 435 episodes of *Ozzie and Harriet* were beamed into North American

households. Over the years, lovable little David and Ricky grew up and got married—and their real-life wives were incorporated into the all-in-the-family show. By September 3, 1966, however, the date of the final episode, the Nelsons had become something of an oddity as a family. What they once typified was no longer the norm.

In the 1960s, social, economic and technological forces began to shape the so-called nuclear family the Nelsons represented (mother, father and children living together) into a remarkably diverse number of family forms. As a result of this transforming process, which carried on throughout the 1970s and is still making its effects felt today, family units are not at all as predictable in 1986 as they were two or three decades ago.

If a television crew were to visit Hillsdale in 1986, who might they find living in Ozzie and Harriet's old house at 822 Sycamore? Quite possibly it would be husband, wife and two children. The mother, however, would spend her weekdays in the workplace and not, as Harriet did, in the kitchen. Perhaps the house would be occupied by a couple with three children: one of them his by a previous marriage, one of them hers by a previous marriage and one of them theirs. Or perhaps the family in residence would comprise a 30-year-old, single, working woman and her pre-school daughter. Or an older couple whose children had grown up and left home. Or a separated woman and her unemployed, 25-year-old son, widowed mother and retired uncle.

The likelihood of finding an Ozzie-and-Harriet-style family in the Hillsdale house today is slim. According to most sources, less than 7 per cent of the North American population now lives in the once-classic family unit of a breadwinning father, homemaking mother and two children.

THEORETICAL APPROACHES

Sociologists differ in their theoretical conceptualizations of the family. Researchers have structured their study of the family around three concepts: structure, interaction, and gender.

Structure

Structure is a key concept for the structural-functionalists' and the materialists' analyses of the family. Both of these theoretical perspectives assume a macroanalysis of the family as an institution linked to other institutions in society. An **institution** is an organized aspect of social existence that is established and perpetuated by various norms and rules. The family is one of the most basic institutions in society, laying the foundation for the emergence of other institutions. Typical macro questions include "What does the family do for society?" and "How is the family interrelated with the society's economy, political structure, and religious organizations?" Sociologists from both perspectives analyze the norms, beliefs, structures, and social processes that control and define the social environment within which families exist. Functionalists view the family as fitting comfortably into the social structure, while materialists see its relationship to society as contradictory and riddled with inherent conflict.

The Structural-Functionalist Approach

The two approaches differ markedly. **Structural functionalism**, the dominant school, treats the family as a conservative, harmonious, and integrated whole, interesting for its effects on other institutions. Within the society, the family assumes the function of socialization of children, sexual regulation, reproduction, economic cooperation, affection, intimacy, emotional support and status placement. Integration, solidarity, and **social control** (mechanisms to support desired forms of behaviour and discourage undesirable ones) are achieved through mass adherence to cultural norms and values.

Much of functionalist research centres on changes in the functions performed by the family. Writing in the 1930s, William Ogburn (1933) described the changes in these functions that have resulted from industrialization and urbanization: economic production was transferred from the family to the factory and office; education to the schoolroom; religion almost entirely to the church or synagogue; recreation to the theatre and stadium; health care to the doctor's office and the hospital. The family is left to provide little but affection and understanding.

Rather than viewing these changes as net losses, some functionalists see the process as one of expansion and parcelling out. For example, although the family may no longer be an economic producing unit, its function as consumer has been heightened. And the family is now free to specialize in two areas: providing emotional support and socializing children. Recent functionalist writings tend to be analyses of the effects of this specialization of functions, criticizing the role of the welfare state, which distributes social rewards differentially. For example, the income tax exemption for dependent children is usually claimed by the parent with the higher income, who is most often the father. In contrast, the child-care deduction can only be claimed by a "working" mother, and the maximum set is usually below her actual cost. Moreover, a "working" mother can claim child-care expenses if her husband is unemployed or a student but not if she herself is unemployed or a student (Eichler 1983, 311).

The Materialist Approach

Materialists, influenced by the thought of Karl Marx and his intellectual successors, discuss comparable family issues but are more caustic in their explanation of change. **Materialists** begin with the economic system, which, as they see it, conditions social relationships within the familial, political, and cultural arenas. People's productive activity—work—influences their family life, daily schedules, needs, interests, ideas, and interactions. Shift work, unemployment, and career commitment all affect family relationships. Moreover, productive activity structures class relations within the society. Materialists view the family as in *dialectical* relationship with the society's other institutions, all of them preconditioned by the economic system.

Materialists are critical of the interplay between the family and the economy. The growth of industrial capitalism ensured the subordination of women to men by assigning productive activity on the basis of gender. Men became identified as family breadwinners and women as domestic caretakers. Marx suggests that people's ideas, or consciousness, grow from their daily productive activity and are transmitted through the generations. Gender differences in consciousness, skills and self-perceptions emerge from the distinctions made in men's and women's daily work. This rigid dichotomization reflects an economic reality but creates a *false consciousness* of the desires, skills, and possible contributions of women and men to the family. Women's primary identification with domestic labour and child care has come to be viewed by society, and by many women, not as a false label, created by capitalist development, but as something natural and inevitable. Similarly, women's work as wives and mothers has until recently served as both an explanation and a justification for the segregation and subordination of women in the labour force. As Marx and Engels point out (see Tucker 1978), since the ruling class controls the means of productive activity, their ideas dominate and act to preserve the existing social reality. People perceiving their class or gender subordination are likely to conclude it is inevitable.

Interaction

The concept of interaction is central in family research. Usually **interaction** refers to the public interplay, verbal or non-verbal, between two or more individuals or groups. **Private interaction** refers to the individual's inner conversation with him or herself, the self-reflection in which the individual engages. Intimate relationships are often assessed privately for their current meaning and purpose. (For more on this "mirror image" process, see Chapter 4.)

Following G.H. Mead (1938), **symbolic interactionists** base their theoretical approach to family studies on the concept of interaction. They explore such questions as how family relationships are negotiated and maintained, how family groups develop shared symbols and meanings, and how situations are defined by family members. Typically, their approach is micro, humanistic, and reflective, using **qualitative data** (data on variations in type, as opposed to variations in quantity—see Chapter

2) garnered from participant observation and long interviews. For example, using in-depth interviews with married women about the effects of their employment on family life, Mandell and Hutchens (1986) reveal the strains and conflicts women encounter in juggling their multiple responsibilities of domestic and wage labour. Qualitative interviews allow the women to speak in their own voices, explaining how they allocate time, space, and energy to various family members and tasks.

Symbolic interactionists focus on the definition and creation of group meanings, the processes by which these meanings are communicated, and the mechanisms individuals use to manage tension. How family members perceive situations is considered as important as what they actually do. For example, more fascinating to interactionists than the inequity in the division of household labour is the finding that women do not interpret this inequity as unfair. Wives, it seems, have internalized the ideology associating women with domestic labour and willingly carry out these chores even when they are engaged in full-time wage labour.

Gender

Beginning in the late 1960s **gender**—the social, cultural, and psychological characteristics assumed appropriate to being male or female—emerged as a key variable in family research. Barrie Thorne (1982,2) identifies five themes central to a feminist rethinking of the family:

1. Feminists challenge as not functional, biological, or natural the prevalent assumptions about the family as composed of a breadwinner husband and a stay-at-home mother. Traditional family ideology reinforces the economic exploitation of all women by typifying women as mothers who neither need nor want to work outside the home.

2. Feminists seek to reclaim family studies—including such topics as the sexual division of labour, heterosexuality, male dominance, and motherhood—for social and historical analyses. Nancy Chodorow (1978), for example, explores the consequences of the fact that women mother. This gender-based division of labour sets up a developmental experience that differs for girls and boys, encourages men's devaluation of women, and creates gender-specific personalities, with men undervaluing connections with others and women excessively preoccupied with social relations.

3. Since families are structured around gender and age, women, men, boys, and girls do not experience their families in the same way. Studies of children's help in the household show gender distinctions in the type of chores performed. Boys assume gardening, repair, and maintenance tasks while girls do cooking, cleaning, laundering, and babysitting.

4. Feminists raise questions about family boundaries, challenging a series of dichotomies—private and public, family and society—that are often taken for granted. Dorothy Smith (1985) demonstrates that there are ongoing relations between home and paid work. For example, middle-class mothers, by monitoring their children's educational careers, friends, and activities, and by taking the youngsters to lessons, plays, and cultural events, create middle-class children, reinforce status distinctions, and reproduce capitalist relations.

5. These dichotomies are often linked to an ambivalence between individualism and equality. The family is often seen as the encapsulation of nurturing, enduring, non-contingent relations, in contrast to the impersonal, competitive, contractual, and temporary relations characteristic of market relations. Feminists question these assumptions by asking not "What do women do for the family?" but "What does the family do to women?"

Gender is crucial both to structures and to interactions. A feminist analysis of family structure reveals how the childhood socialization of young boys attempts to train them in "male inexpressiveness" (Sattel 1982), an emotional impassivity they learn to display regardless of crisis. For adults, being neutral and rational is associated with the ability to dominate, control, and make important decisions.

The rest of this chapter will discuss historical and current treatments of structure, interaction, and gender.

HISTORICAL TRANSFORMATIONS IN THE CANADIAN FAMILY

Most studies, current and past, employ the functionalist view of the family as a universal social institution. Although researchers today are aware of the variety of family forms, cross-cultural research continues to search for commonalities in family functions.

Anthropologist Bronislaw Malinowski (1913) is credited with establishing the view of the family as performing the universal function of:

> nurturing young children mapped onto (a) a bounded set of people who recognized one another and who were distinguishable from other like groups (b) a definite physical space, a hearth and home (c) a particular set of emotions, family love. (Collier et al. 1982, 27)

Thus the functionalist ideology constructs the image of the family as monolithic, universal, and unchanging in its core purpose. Yet no one family structure has ever been common to most societies. Various kinds of organization have characterized family life in the past, as they do today, when singles, commuting couples, one-parent households and group arrangements are all part of the mosaic of society.

Throughout history, individuals have always expected to have special connections with their genealogically closest relatives. When one searches for "the family" in past and present societies, one finds kinship groups of people who interact daily and share material resources. However, what form these relationships take—how people share their daily lives—and what these relationships mean to group members vary according to socioeconomic conditions.

Despite the multiplicity of family forms, Gough (1986) identifies three universal elements common to all: rules forbid sexual relations and marriage between close relatives; men and women cooperate through a division of labour based on gender; and marriage exists as a socially recognized, durable relationship between men and women, giving rise to the concept of social fatherhood.

Hunting and Agricultural Societies

No one knows exactly when the family originated, but Gough (1986, 32) suggests that it "built up around tool use, the use of language, cookery and a sexual division of labor . . . sometime between 500,000 and 200,000 years ago." In these hunting and gathering societies, a band of 20 to 200 individuals comprised numerous families. The household was the main unit of economic cooperation. Nuclear families were common, mating was individualized, and economic life was built on a division of labour by gender (Gough 1986). Women nursing children stayed close to their caves, foraging for small game, berries, and plants. This food provided the household's only dependable mainstay since the men, who hunted larger game, were frequently unsuccessful. Resources were owned communally, and economic reciprocity between spouses led to relatively egalitarian gender relations.

With the domestication of plants and animals, perhaps 8,000 to 10,000 years ago, equality was eroded. Once the bands were concentrated in one physical location, they tended to grow into clans of several thousand people. Centralized state organizations gradually developed to facilitate the production and distribution of food and to provide judicious laws. The accumulation of property—agricultural products, tools, animals, land, houses—required the protection of the state. Engels ([1884] 1902) associates the rise of privately owned property with individual families' becoming the basic economic unit within society. Property, since it was owned and exchanged for commodities, constituted the basis of male supremacy; although women shared in consuming the surplus from production, men controlled *access* to the surplus and hence power over nonowners. As private property increasingly differentiated power and class, it became important for men to recognize and provide for their children. Strict lineage rules ensured the secondary status of women. Living in extended kinship systems also helped to consolidate and maintain power. (Nuclear and extended families are defined and described a little later in this chapter.)

"TRADITIONALISM" VS. "MODERNISM" IN FAMILY FORM, FUNCTION, AND IDEOLOGY

"Traditionalism"	"Modernism"
1. Kinship is organized principle of society; almost everything a person does is done as a member of a kinship group.	Kinship is differentiated from economic, political, and social life; recruitment to jobs is independent of one's relatives.
2. Sons inherit father's status and occupation.	Individual mobility based on "merit."
3. Low geographic and social mobility.	High geographic and social mobility.
4. The extended or complex family may be basic unit of residence and domestic functions—e.g., meals and child care.	Conjugal or nuclear family is basic unit of residence and domestic functions.
5. Most adults work at home; the home is workshop as well as school, hospital, old-age home.	Separation of home and work; household consumes rather than produces.
6. Dominance of parents over children, men over women.	Relatively egalitarian relations within nuclear family in ideals and practice.
7. Kinship bonds override economic efficiency and maximization of individual gain.	Advancement and economic gain of individuals prevails over kin obligations.
8. Ideology of duty, tradition, individual submission to authority and to fate.	Ideology of individual rights, equality, freedom, self-realization.
9. Little emphasis on emotional involvement within nuclear family; marriage not based on love; predominant loyalty of individual is to blood kin, rather than spouse; children are economic rather than emotional assets, but subordination and dependency of children on parents may continue as long as parent lives—in Europe parent-child bonds may be reduced further by practice of apprenticing children to other families at an early age.	Intense involvement of spouses, parents, and children with each other; ideologies of marital happiness and adjustment; great concern with child's development, current adjustment, and future potential, but sharp break with parental authority on attaining adulthood.

10. Little or no psychological separation between home and community; broad communal sociability; no large-scale institutions.	Sharp line of demarcation between home and outside world; home is a private retreat and outside world is impersonal, competitive, threatening.
11. High fertility and high death rates, especially in infancy; rapid population turnover—death a constant presence in families.	Low, controlled fertility and low death rates, especially low in infancy; death a phenomenon of old age.

Modernization

The family patterns established in agricultural societies are still common in what are called traditional societies. For the Western world, sociologists, although aware of the dangers of oversimplification, have concentrated on the past 400 years of family history by comparing pre-industrial and industrial societies. **Modernization** is the process of enormous change, including industrialization, urbanization, and technological innovations, that has substantially altered public and private relationships and transformed Western society in the past two centuries.

Goode (1963), in his classic discussion of the effects of modernization on the family, shows that today, for the first time in history, a common set of influences (industrialization and urbanization) are affecting every known society. These trends include a weakened extended kinship system, dissolving lineage patterns, movement toward an independent and mobile conjugal system, emphasis on individual success based on performance rather than family ties, and the allocation of resources to personal ends.

In this functionalist view, the conjugal family neatly fits into industrialization's demands for a small, compact, and mobile family. Burgess extends the concept, suggesting that modernization has led to a

> transition from a traditional, family system based on family members playing a traditional role to a companionship family system based on mutual affection, intimate communication and mutual acceptance of a division of labour and procedures of decision-making. ([1945] quoted in Nett 1979, 61)

With the emergence of modernization, the nuclear family structure became very common; the average number of children declined; home and workplace were separated; arranged marriages were replaced by romantic love relationships; family life became intensely emotional; and families developed more privacy and hence less community life. (For more emphasis on these trends and especially their demographic aspects, see Chapter 14.)

The Modern Conjugal Unit

The **nuclear** or **conjugal family** refers to the smallest form of family unit. Usually it includes a husband, a wife, and their children. A nuclear family may or may not include marriage partners, but it does consist of two or more people related to one another by blood, marriage or adoption, assuming they are of the same or adjoining generations (Eshleman 1985, 87). (Although the terms "nuclear" and "conjugal" are used interchangeably, technically a conjugal unit must contain a husband and wife. Single parents with children or siblings are nuclear but not conjugal families). According to the last census, 77.3 percent of Canadian households are nuclear.

True **extended families** (see the box on the next page) are the largest kind of family yet represent only 2 percent of Canadian households. Various ethnic groups live in modified extended families. The smallest form of extended family is the **stem family**, which comprises two nuclear families generationally and economically linked and co-residing. The Dutch residing in the Holland Marsh area of Ontario are an example of parents living in the same household with a married child. Before Newfoundland modernized, the fishing industry was organized around stem family households. Government institutionalization of a planned and rationalized economy eroded family fishing enterprises and the stem family has practically disappeared.

The extent to which modernization replaced extended families with nuclear units is controversial. Historian Peter Laslett (1970) insists that the extended family is a sociological myth and that the nuclear family has been the predominant family form in England since the 16th century. Similarly, Frank Furstenberg (1966) maintains that in the United States the nuclear family existed before industrialization and urbanization and that the effect of the industrial system on the family has been greatly exaggerated. The kinds of family conflicts usually attributed to industrialization—undisciplined children, confusion about choosing a marital partner, women's subordination in marriage, and their discontent with housework—existed before modernization.

Changing Economic Functions

Throughout history, economic conditions have influenced family organization and interaction. Pre-industrial societies are associated with the **family economy**, in which families operated as mini-manufacturing units. In Canada, the economy was pre-industrial until the mid- to late 19th century (Gaffield 1984). Most Canadians lived on farms and engaged in agriculture, fishing, lumbering, and fur trading. Production was small-scale and labour-intensive, and it required all members of the family to participate. Families functioned as economic workshops, as well as schools, churches, nursing homes, and day-care centres.

With the introduction of manufacturing in the 1850s and 1860s, the first stage in **industrialization** included the mechanization and centralization of certain productive activities. Traditional home crafts disappeared into the factories. By the end of the 19th century, families could purchase every household good that they used to make. Although families continued to be economic units, they now were units for sharing the wages men, women, and children earned in manufacturing centres. Household production became an increasingly supplementary economic activity.

The shift from a family economy to a **family wage economy** took place slowly over a period of many years in Canada. One of the most decisive features was the separation of home and the workplace, as wage labour and business replaced agriculture as a way of life. The household was no longer a self-contained unit binding its members together in common work.

During this transition, women and children made essential contributions to the household economy. Bryan Palmer explores how conditions of the Canadian workplace affected family life and heightened class distinctions between working-class and non–working-class families; of central importance was "the expanding employment of women and children ushered into the workplace by expansions in plant size, mechanization of trades and dilution of skill" (1983, 82). Textile production, shoemaking, and bakeries particularly relied on the labour of women and children. In Montreal, for example, the number of children employed in the shoemaking and clothing industries increased 50 and 70 percent, respectively, between 1861 and 1871. By the 1880s entire families were recruited to work settings. Families subsisted not on the husband's inadequate wage but on the earnings of the husband, wife, and children, as well as their unpaid work in the home.

The transferral of productive activity from the home to an outside location changed the family from a unit of production to a unit of consumption. In the new **family consumer economy**, family life revolved around decisions and activities related to the purchase and use of goods produced in specialized workplaces (Gaffield 1984). As the economic role of the household changed, the roles of men, women, and children became increasingly differentiated. By the end of the 19th century, children were no longer viewed as economic assets because they were squeezed out of labour markets. Teenage workers, however, were in demand well into the 20th century. Fertility declined with children's decreasing economic value. In Hamilton, Ontario, an urban centre extensively studied by social historians, the records show that between 1851 and 1871 fertility fell for the families of merchants, professionals, master craftsmen, and clerks, but rose among the working class. These contradictory trends were a reflection of class needs. Middle-class parents were the first to have smaller families—in the hope of being able to offer their children more education

A TYPOLOGY OF FAMILY STRUCTURES

Nuclear	Modified nuclear	Modified extended	Extended
Completely self-sufficient; economically no help	Largely self-sufficient economically; recreation and friendship ties; occasional help in emergencies	Independent economic resources in nuclear family units, but daily exchange of goods and services	Complete economic interdependence of kin network—common ownership of economic resources, occupational cooperation, daily exchange of goods and services.
Nuclear family, friends, experts, distant models exclusive agents of socialization, emotional support, and protection	Weak kin network role in socialization, emotional support, and protection	Strong kin network psychological interdependence, but more reliance on non-kin for socialization, emotional support, and protection	Psychological interdependence—socialization, emotional support, protection—almost completely confined to kin network
Complete nuclear family autonomy; kin network influence absent	Nuclear family autonomy, weak kin network influence	Nuclear family autonomy, but strong kin network influence in decision-making and resolving conflicts	Arbitrary, linear, intergenerational authority
Minimal contact; geographic isolation; visits on holidays or for family rituals; contact primarily by letter or telephone in literate societies	Regular but not daily contact; kin network within easy visiting distance	Daily contact, geographic proximity	Daily contact, geographic proximity

and consumer goods—while the social classes most constrained by economic necessity responded positively to the opportunity of an expanding teenage labour market (Palmer 1983). By the 1890s, the majority of women and children had returned to work in the home.

Changing Emotional Aspects

The shift from the pre-industrial to the industrial economic functions of the family were accompanied by changes in the psychological or emotional aspects of family life. It became more intense, emotional, private, subjective, and disassociated from the larger community. Zaretsky (1976) correlates these changes with the advent of the family consumer economy. Capitalism separated family life from direct economic production, and hence personal relationships were separated from commodity production. Historian Lawrence Stone (1977) calls this **affective individualism**: in the late 17th and early 18th centuries, individuals altered their views of themselves in relationship to society (individualism) and changed their feelings and behaviour toward other individuals, especially their parents, kin, and children (affect). The growth of individualism and introspection and the demand for privacy, self-expression, and autonomy placed the individual above the family, as opposed to earlier emphasis on subverting individual wishes for the well-being of the group.

Aries (1962, 400-401) describes this change in the quality of modern family life as the rise of domesticity. The house became a private living space in which members could develop intimacy and affection for each other. Community interaction declined as the family moved behind closed doors.

At the same time, there emerged the ideal of love as the basis of a marriage contract. The cult of courtly love, which had begun in the 12th century as an aristocratic posture involving neither marriage nor extra-marital sex, gradually became diffused and assimilated to all classes and to marriage, producing the absurd notion of free choice for life. Marriage became redefined less as an economic contract and more as a voluntary love match. In reality, it contains both elements.

Firestone (1970) points to the tension created by the ideology of romantic love. The idea of spontaneous, uncontrollable passion between equals contrasts with the voluntary, contractual, and unequal nature of marriage. Even today, marriage patterns continue to be **homogamous** with most matches occurring between spouses of similar geographic origins, class, ethnic, income, and educational backgrounds. Romance is the ideal— but only with socially appropriate partners.

Changing Roles for Men, Women, and Children

Industrialization encouraged objectivity, rationality, and emotional detachment. In contrast, family relations stressed subjectivity, intuitive response, and emotional expressiveness. Rather than being integrated with the competitive, hostile, and brutal work environment, the family was privatized and idealized as a retreat.

In functionalist terms, the family specialized in providing the affective functions of nurturance, child-rearing, and regeneration of the work-force. Women's purpose as mothers and wives—as "love experts"—was to mediate the tension between the harsh and competitive social relations of the work world and the revitalizing and soothing nature of the home. By the time of the later phases of industrialization, women became the domestic experts and men assumed the breadwinner role. This role specialization legitimated economic reality. Married women, excluded from the workplace, retreated into their homes. Sole-provider husbands were forced to work long hours, in often hazardous circumstances, to earn a wage that was rarely sufficient to support the entire family. By the 20th century, gender dichotomies had emerged as an ideological norm. Experts proclaimed it inevitable, essential, and biologically natural for women to mother and men to labour.

Thus the 19th century fostered contradictory images for women. Industrialization created the housewife, whose unpaid contributions in labour and service were belittled. Being outside the market economy, women's work was seen as a labour of love due the paid worker. At the same time, middle-class women were glorified in their domestic roles as paragons of virtue, patience, tenderness, devotion, and gentleness. Ironically, this idealized image was adopted by middle-class mothers at the same time that immigrant and rural women were being recruited into expanding manufacturing factories. Upward social mobility for women meant adopting this middle-class domestic cult. A labour force survey suggests that in Canada in 1901, some 14.4 percent of adult women were engaged in wage labour, primarily in working-class jobs—as servants, dressmakers, teachers, farmers, seamstresses, saleswomen, housekeepers, laundresses, and milliners (Wilson 1986, 80). It is ironic that the cult of domesticity became entrenched during this period, when more than one woman in ten was employed outside the home.

The ideological exclusion of married women from the labour force was a harbinger of the changing status of children. The enactment of child labour laws and compulsory education signalled the exclusion of young children from wage labour. In 1881, about 11 percent of the Canadian labour force was under age 16. Ten years later, only 5 percent were children.

Despite the shrinking employment of children, their earnings, like those of their mothers, proved essential in working-class households. Teenagers continued to move into the labour market as soon as laws allowed. In 1900, the majority of working-class children in Hamilton, Ontario, were wage earners by age 14, and 1911 census data from Hamilton indicate that employed children from families of general labourers contributed more than 44 percent of total family income. Gaffield (1984) suggests that adolescents could be students only in financially secure families.

The income that child labour earned was one incentive to large family size and helped maintain high birth rates.

During the late 19th and early 20th centuries, middle-class children were idealized and transformed into emotional assets, as their lives were gradually divorced from the marketplace. It should be noted, however, that the Victorian idealization of children as helpless innocents in need of solicitous guidance extended only to children of means. Working-class children contributed essential earnings and services to the family economy. Many lived in a state of semi-independence from their families as servants, apprentices, or student boarders.

No doubt class continues to differentiate familial expectations of children. As labour market conditions worsened for youth, children of all classes acquired the role of consumers rather than producers. "The prolonged dependency of young people upon their parents and their increased education in specialized age-segregated institutions formed the basis for adolescence" (Katz and Davey 1978, 117).

To put the point another way, economic, familial, and cultural changes transformed the experience of growing up. In pre-industrial times, adolescence did not exist, and childhood was a brief preparatory period terminated by apprenticeship and the commencement of work, generally before puberty. Children had such craft occupations as farming, baking, and shoemaking. They could be apprentices to lawyers, merchants, pharmacists, or churchmen, and they could enter college at age 12. With the beginning of prolonged education and the removal of children from the labour market, the idea appeared that there was something not quite right about children doing adult things until they were "ready." Psychological theorists of the early 1900s proposed that children were not able to participate in adult life until they had completed a series of developmental tasks lasting into their twenties. Adolescence emerged as a critical stage of development. Stay-at-home mothers assumed the role of moral custodians, focusing family activities on the perceived needs and interests of their children.

Aries dramatically proclaimed in 1980 that the days of the "child-king" were over. Couples no longer plan their life in terms of their children. Rather, children are expected to fit into life plans. Although children are seen individually as socially and emotionally priceless, as a group they now occupy a smaller place within a family's life course. Declining birth rates, increasing longevity, and women's multiple involvements are moving children from the centre to the margin of the family's lifetime pursuits.

MARRIAGE AND THE FAMILY IN THE 1980s

What is the Canadian family of the 1980s like? The following section lists some of its typical characteristics.

1. Marriage is declining in popularity. One of the most remarkable trends in Canadian history is the current decline in *nuptiality* (the occurrence of the married state in a society). In 1972, 97 percent of Canadian men and 93 percent of Canadian women were married or had been married at some time during their lives. Ten years later, it was approximately 66 percent for both sexes, breaking the previous low recorded in 1932 during the Depression.

    Despite a brief upswing in 1979 and 1980, the total number of marriages has been dropping by an average of 1200 per year since 1972. Many couples are postponing marriage, some permanently. People are living in alternative household structures as singles, cohabiting in heterosexual or homosexual relationships, acting as heads of lone-parent households (see Exhibit 5-1). Despite these downward trends, marriage is still the choice of the majority.

2. Canadian families are diverse. The Canadian census distinguishes between a **family household** (the people in it are closely related by blood or marriage) and a **non-family household** (a dwelling place with one person or with "unrelated" persons). As shown in Exhibit 5-2, in 1981, 74.1 percent of all households were one (nuclear) family households, including those with single parents, and 1.1 percent were multiple (extended) family households. About 20.3 percent were non-familial households of one person (a sharp rise over the previous decade).

The remaining 4.5 percent were the dwellings of two or more people classified as a non-family household, but these groupings included cohabitors, homosexual relationships, and group homes, which some people would list as families.

Exhibit 5-1
Marital Status of Heads of
Lone-Parent Families, Canada, 1981

	Men	Women	Both
Single (never married)			
No.	5 115	65 175	70 290
%	4.1	11.0	9.8
Separated			
No.	49 775	172 845	222 620
%	40.0	29.3	31.2
Divorced			
No.	32 010	154 950	186 960
%	25.7	26.3	26.2
Widowed			
No.	37 480	196 465	233 945
%	30.1	33.3	32.8
Total			
No.	124 380	589 435	713 815
%	100.0	100.0	100.0

Note: Percentages do not total 100 because of rounding.
Source: Statistics Canada, *1981 Census Report*, cat. no. 92-935, table 15.

Exhibit 5-2
Family and Non-Family Households,
1971, 1976, and 1981

	1971 %	1976 %	1981 %
Family households	81.7	78.6	75.2
One family	79.7	77.3	74.1
Two or more families	2.0	1.3	1.1
Non-family households	18.3	21.4	24.8
One person	13.4	16.8	20.3
Two or more persons	4.9	4.6	4.5
Total	100.0	100.0	100.0

Sources: Statistics Canada, *1971 Census of Canada*, cat. no. 93-703; Statistics Canada, *1976 Census of Canada*, cat. no. 93-806; Statistics Canada, *1981 Census of Canada*, cat. no. 92-904.

This kind of multiformity is also characteristic of American and Western European families, suggesting that Canada's particular ethnic, religious, geographic, and social class patterns alone do not account for the trend toward diversity. Rather, it results from decreased birth rates, the increased divorce rate, the movement of women into the labour force, and the liberalization of Canadian family law. Consider, for example, the changes of a single decade shown in Exhibit 5-3.

3. Families are getting smaller. Canada has moved from a baby boom to a baby bust. Today, the typical intact Canadian family is smaller, with no more than two children, born later in their parents' lives and spaced further apart than at any previous time. One useful measure here is the **total fertility rate**, the average number of children that would be born to a hypothetical woman if she survived through her reproductive years and bore children in accordance with the age-specific fertility rates observed in a given year. This rate has been declining dramatically in recent years: from a high of 3.9 per thousand women in 1959 to a low of 1.7 in 1978—a rate that would not replace the current population. A downward trend is found throughout Canada in every social class, ethnic and linguistic group, and geographic location. Fertility rates are depressed even among groups with traditionally high fertility, such as the Québécois and the Indians. Moreover, the rate

Exhibit 5-3
Husband-Wife and Lone-Parent Families, 1971 and 1981

	1971		1981		Increase 1971–81	
	No.	%	No.	%	No.	%
Husband-wife[a]	4 605 485	90.7	5 611 500	88.7	1 006 015	21.8
With children	3 146 165	62.0	3 598 860	56.9	452 695	14.4
Without children						
at home	1 359 320	28.7	2 012 640	31.8	553 320	37.9
Childless	[b]	[b]	921 810	14.6	[b]	[b]
Lone-parent	470 605	9.3	713 820	11.3	243 215	51.7
Female parent	370 820	7.3	589 435	9.3	218 615	59.0
Male parent	99 785	2.0	124 380	2.0	24 595	24.6
Total	5 076 090	100.0	6 325 315	100.0	1 249 225	24.6

[a]In 1971, children at home included never-married children under 25 living at home. In 1981, children at home included all never-married children living at home regardless of age.
[b]Figures not available.
Sources: Statistics Canada, *1971 Census of Canada*, cat. no. 93-720 and 93-721; Statistics Canada, *1981 Census of Canada*, cat. no. 92-935.

of childlessness is increasing. Of the Canadian women who were born early in this century and were ever married, about 17 percent were childless. The rate dropped to a low of 5 to 7 percent for women born between 1937 and 1944, but it is now rising, and a figure of 16 percent is projected for today's young Canadian women.

(For more on the demographic aspects of modern trends in nuptiality, divorce and remarriage, and birth rates, see Chapter 14.)

The basic nuclear family.

While most Quebec families were not as large as this one, the strong norms among French Canadians for large families gave Quebec one of the highest birth rates in the world. Since the 1960s, however, Quebec's birth rate has declined dramatically.

4. Most families now have two wage earners. Unlike their **families of orientation**, the ones into which they were born or adopted, the young **family of procreation** today, the one a new couple creates, is likely to be a dual-earner family, which is now the typical form in North America (see Exhibit 5-4). In 1984, 53.7 percent of married Canadian women were employed either full- or part-time in the labour force, a substantial increase in the past few years (see Exhibit 5-5). An unusual factor in this rise is the entry of women with children, especially preschoolers, into wage labour (see Exhibit 5-6). In 1941, all married women represented only 4 percent of the labour market. In 1984, 54.0 percent of Canadian women with husbands and preschoolers were employed outside the home. Until recently, the norm was that once their children were born, married women left the labour force and contributed to the family economy by producing goods and services in the home. Certainly they worked, but they did not work for direct wage remuneration, as more and more women do now. Projections call for a steady increase in female employment, with women constituting approximately half of all workers by the year 2000.

5. Families are pseudoegalitarian. Since the turn of the century, North American family relations have become less traditional and more egalitarian. Husbands and wives, parents and children are increasingly engaging in flexible, negotiable, and democratic relationships. Yet, most of these relationships are less flexible than they seem. They tend to be only moderately or quasi-egalitarian. Husbands usually come first in terms of money earned and influence on household decisions, and they maintain the ultimate veto power. Wives are viewed ideologically as equal partners, but they do more household labour and have less marital power. Similarly, although children are treated socially more as companions than as subordinates, they remain economically and emotionally dependent on their parents for longer periods of time than in earlier eras.

6. Families are subject to disruption. The number of divorces in Canada more than doubled between 1971 and 1982, with the largest increase occurring between 1972 and 1975. The proportion of remarriages has also climbed steadily. In 1982, 20.6 percent of men marrying were marrying for the second time; 18.8 percent of women getting married were entering a second marriage. In other words, almost one marriage in five was a remarriage.

7. Families are prone to violence. Studies of domestic violence in Canada estimate that one in ten married or cohabiting women are physically battered each year, and that one-third to one-half of all adult men and women were sexually abused as children. More than half of the sexual assaults against children occur in their own homes or those of the suspected assaulters—in households, which are "usually considered to be safe and which are not open to scrutiny by the public"—and a large proportion of the perpetrators are family members (Badg-

Exhibit 5-4
Family Types by Income Earners

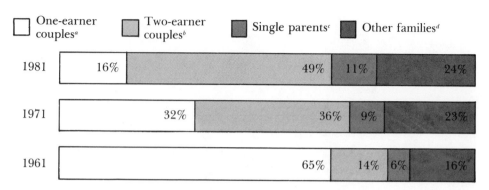

Notes: Because of rounding, not all totals are 100 percent.
   ᵃOne-earner couples are married couples, with or without children, in which only
   the husband is an income earner.
   ᵇTwo-earner couples are married couples, with or without children, in which both
   spouses are income earners.
   ᶜSingle parents are single adults, either male or female, with at least one child.
   The adult need not be an "income" earner; that is, the data include single parents on government support.
   ᵈOther families include husband-wife families in which neither spouse is an income earner and also families with more than two income earners.

Sources: Statistics Canada (1985), *Women in Canada: A Statistical Report*, 1971 and 1981,
   cat. no. 89-503E, p. 6 and 69;
   Dominion Bureau of Statistics (1964), *Census of Canada, 1961: Households and
   Families*, p. 93-1 and 73-1.

Exhibit 5-5
Married Women in the Labour Force, Canada, 1961–84

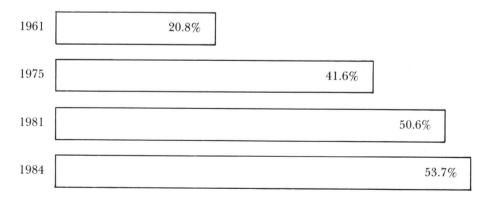

Source: *The Royal Bank Reporter* (1986, 19).

Exhibit 5-6
Labour Force Participation Rates of Women with Children,
1976, 1980, 1984

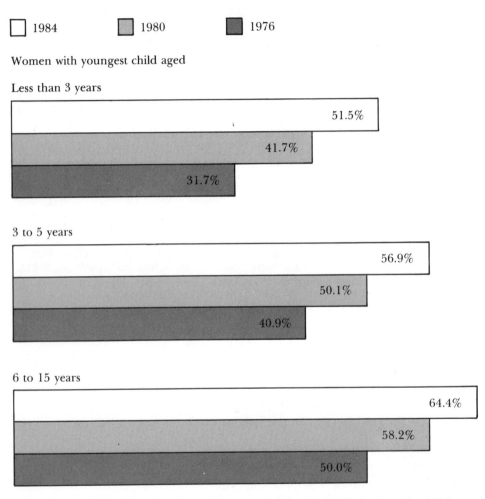

☐ 1984 ▨ 1980 ▪ 1976

Women with youngest child aged

Less than 3 years

51.5%

41.7%

31.7%

3 to 5 years

56.9%

50.1%

40.9%

6 to 15 years

64.4%

58.2%

50.0%

Sources: Statistics Canada (1984), *The Labour Force*, p. 100; Statistics Canada (1982), *The Labour Force*, p. 106.

ley 1984, 201). These figures are beginning to reveal the brutality of family relationships.

8. Families are aging. Because of increased longevity, a newlywed couple today could potentially experience 50 years of marital bliss. As the baby boom generation ages, an increasing proportion of families are composed of middle-aged and aging persons, a fact that is already

affecting social planning and policy and will do so even more in the future.

9. Families are protected by the law. The Canadian family is bound by provincial and federal strictures. Marriage is a legally sanctioned ceremony. All the provinces stipulate minimum ages for marriage with and without parental consent, require a religious or a civil ceremony, prohibit marriage between certain people including those of the same sex, those already married, and those within prohibited degrees of consanguinity.

The state also prescribes the relationship between parents and children. Parents are obliged to maintain their children and are responsible for their actions. In return, children are under the authority of their parents until they reach the age of majority (usually age 18). Some provinces—Ontario, Quebec, and New Brunswick—no longer distinguish between legitimate and illegitimate children with respect to the father's obligation to provide support and inheritance, but others continue to do so.

MARRIAGE AND FAMILY INTERACTIONS

In the last section we said that the typical Canadian family today is smaller than in the past and is more likely to have a wage-earning mother and father—if both parents are present. (Though the marriage could last for 50 years, there's a one-in-three chance that the couple will divorce, and that one or both parties will remarry.) This demographic portrait tells little about the nature of interaction within the family—the reality of daily life for husbands, wives, and children.

The Process of Getting Married

About 85 percent of Canadians marry at least once (Baker 1984). Marriage, in one form or another, is a universal pattern. Its traditional purpose has been to regulate sexual behaviour, to provide a social unit for bearing and rearing children, and to serve as a basic economic unit. Today, people marry for love, companionship, and self-fulfilment; marriage is designed to meet the psychological needs of the partners, providing emotional support, friendship, sexual satisfaction, freedom to pursue a career, sharing of the provider role, and the protection of children, if any.

Rating and Dating

Prepare a "shopping list" of the characteristics you would like to see in an ideal mate. List items relating to personal appearance; personality traits; economic potential or worth; attitudes, beliefs, and philosophies; special interests and abilities; and your secret desires. Then divide this list into two columns: absolute necessities and luxury features.

Why do people marry? Because they are in love, most of us reply. This photograph of 2200 couples being married by Reverend Sun Myung Moon gives a different answer. Many of these people barely know their partners; the disciples of Reverend Moon believe marriage to have a religious rather than an emotional significance.

This exercise is a blatant but precise summary of the traditional view of mate selection as **courtship bargaining** (Waller [1938] 1951). Dating is seen as a complicated male/female game: one acknowledges what one has to offer and what the other person can get. At some level, participants in the game are aware of its purpose—the exchange of awards and this awareness is embedded in an understanding of the rules, goals, strategies, and counter-strategies. The market-oriented bargaining, based on the enactment of prescribed gender roles, will be carried over into the marital script.

Underlying traditional dating is a gender-based double standard. For men, the courtship game involves progressing toward sexual intimacy, while for women the goal is to move the relationship toward commitment. The spending of money by males is presumably rewarded with the acceptance of sex by the female. In marriage, this double standard translates into men's financially providing for their wives in return for domestic and sexual subservience.

Sociologists note that dating among young adults is an American invention that emerged after the First World War, and many think that its traditional form is dying or dead (see, for example Eshleman 1985, 329). Group activities performed in a less structured fashion characterize youths' leisure patterns in the 1980s. Shifts to a later age of marriage, more flexible gender roles, and new methods of mate selection (computer match-ups, videotape selections, newspaper ads, single clubs, and bars) are contributing to less formal dating procedures. But dating still fulfils the functions of recreation, socialization, courtship selection, and status grading and status achievement (Korman 1983).

Types of Mate Selection

All societies have socially approved patterns of mate selection. They range from highly structured and formally arranged patterns to relatively open and flexible systems of free choice. North Americans normatively endorse the **free choice model**, which implies the freedom to choose a mate without regard to money, occupation, education, age, sex, or family desires. In reality, Canadians and Americans operate within a **limited free choice model** that takes account of these sociocultural factors. The widely accepted **theory of social and cultural homogamy** suggests that "like marries like" with regard to age, education, social class, race, religion, and area of residence. In the United States, only about 1.4 percent of marriages occurred between blacks and whites, and interreligious marriages (those that did not stay within the broad grouping of Protestant, Jew, or Catholic) were an estimated 15 to 20 percent.

In contrast to free choice models, **arranged marriages** involve mate selections in which the parents or kin make the selection for the couple. Arranged marriages preserve family property, lineage, and economic status, and maintain social control over the couple's behaviour. Personal

MATE SELECTION VIA NEWSPAPER ADS

Attractive blonde professional lady, 32, seeks compatible male for fine dining, theatre, and quiet times. Photo appreciated. Box 0000.

Sincere, responsible gent, widower, seeks female companion, 25-35, for dancing, travel, etc. Must like children. Tel. 000-0000.

We are five lively, classy, professional ladies with interests ranging from cuisine minceur to Mahler to Shinto shrines and ranging in age from 27 to 34. We are offering an invitation to Sunday brunch to 5 educated, lively, classy men. Drop us a line at Box 0000. Photo appreciated.

A male, 25, built, seeks female. Race, weight unimportant. Tel. 000-0000.

Affectionate male with country estate seeks slim blond female, to 29. Must like horses, fishing. Box 0000. Photo.

Are you a man of quality and class, with a taste for quiet times by the fireplace and long walks in the rain? If so, this slim, quiet, affectionate lady, 39, educated, would like to hear from you. Box 0000.

Gemini male, 28, seeks affectionate black lady for dancing, dining, etc. Tel. 000-0000.

Gay male, professional, 27, seeks mature masculine man for friendship, evenings at the opera, and summer travel. Box 0000.

Tall stunning redhead, 33, loves travel, fine food, jazz, racquet sports. Still hoping to find that exceptional man who is warm, witty, considerate, educated, and secure. Box 0000.

preferences such as sexual predilections, compatible expectations, and passion are not consulted. Rather, the choice is made on the basis of social and economic concerns, such as traditional customs, patriarchal family authority structures, and the bride's price. Many families of Indian, Pakistani, and Middle-Eastern origin still use a form of **arranged free choice**, in which parents arrange the marriage but the children have some sort of veto power.

Violence during courtship is a phenomenon that has not been studied much. This lack is unfortunate since such violence likely precedes and forms a pattern for spousal violence in marriage. Makepeace (1983) estimates that one in five people has had direct experience of courtship violence, and that a majority of dating individuals know someone personally involved in a violent relationship. (In dating, milder forms of violence, such as slapping and punching, are more common than the more extreme forms of assault with a weapon that may occur within abusive marriages.) Similarly, Cate et al. (1982) found that 22 percent of students at Oregon State University had experienced violence in dating. In more than two-thirds of the cases, the violence was reciprocal: each partner both assaulted and was assaulted.

Economic and Social Connections

The effects of female employment on family life are hotly debated. Marital roles, power, and satisfaction have altered as women have become providers. This section considers how the shift to a predominance of dual-worker families has changed family life in North America.

Models of Marital Interaction

Existing literature contrasts two models of marital interaction: the traditional and the egalitarian. (These models are, of course, **ideal types**— that is, they are general prototypes drawn from observation of and research on many actual relationships in various societies and situations. No real-life situation is likely to be as simple as the model or to match it in every respect.) Each model defines the marital relationship as a set of social, economic, legal, and ideological responsibilities, and specifies the rights, duties, and privileges of spouses.

The **traditional model of marriage** assumes a rigid division of labour by gender, with the man assuming total responsibility for financial provision and the woman for homemaking. Considerable power and privilege are accorded the sole provider. The husband is the head of household and assumes a benign but firm control over all family decisions. The scheduling of daily household routines, the location of the family home, and the relationship of the wife and children to the husband all revolve around the demands of the husband's work.

The wife, as a non-economic contributor to the family, is a junior partner. She has complete control over daily household management and child care, delegating the chores of repair and maintenance to her husband. Each spouse guards his or her traditional sphere of duty and influence. Although the model calls for the wife not to work for wages, many women in traditional marriages do work, often from financial necessity. But they are still considered junior partners, and do not give up their household obligations. Traditional employed wives thus maintain two full-time jobs while their husbands have one. This situation has been ironically referred to by Kay (1965) as the "triple-career family."

In the **egalitarian model of marriage**, tasks, responsibilities, and privileges are shared equally, and none is considered inherently male or female. Both spouses accept responsibility for earning money, caring for

---

TRADITIONAL VERSUS EGALITARIAN MARITAL SCRIPTS

Traditional marriage is based on the male breadwinner/female homemaker model; egalitarian marriage is based on contemporary views of sex-role equality and changes in marital expectations. These two different scripts can be compared and contrasted as follows:

Traditional Script	*Egalitarian Script*
Husband as provider, wife as homemaker and child rearer	Sharing of provider, homemaker and child-rearing roles
Fixed sex roles following traditional masculine and feminine models	Flexible sex roles determined in part by experience and by choice
Husband as primary decision-maker	Decisions made jointly by marital partners
Sex is initiated by husband; the wife submits	Sex is initiated by either partner, with emphasis on mutual enjoyment
The husband is strong and silent, the wife is nurturant	Both partners share feelings and provide mutual emotional support
Conflict resolution is dominated by the husband	Conflicts are negotiated by the partners
Residence is determined by the husband's occupation	Residence takes into account the work of both partners
Personal growth is important for the husband, not the wife	Personal growth is important for both partners

Most marriages fall somewhere on a continuum between the extremes of the two types, although the trend is toward more egalitarian marriages, which John Pollack (1981) has referred to as "the new marital ideal."

the children, and looking after the house. Consequently, both have comparable access to decision-making and control over family resources. The financial independence of each partner means that the marriage specializes in providing emotional intimacy, support, and companionship. Presumably this emotional interdependence leads to greater flexibility in marital roles.

The traditional and the egalitarian models are each based on a concept of gender relations. The egalitarian marriage rests on a view of sex-role equality and shared roles. Male/female worlds are portrayed as equal and integrated, with the degree of involvement in household and employment determined by individual choice. Traditional marriages are based on segregation of chores by sex role. Male and female endeavours are portrayed as separate but complementary.

Data suggest that the typical Canadian family is neither traditional nor egalitarian, but somewhere in between these two poles. **Neotraditional marriage**, also called quasi- or pseudoegalitarian marriage, is a marital relationship in which the spouses endorse egalitarian principles but relate to each other unequally. Canadian marriages have moved from open discrimination sanctioned by law and ideology, to covert discrimination. Adams (1980, 280) suggests that this pseudoegalitarianism functions in several ways.

1. Women in the labour force cluster in low-status occupations, such as teaching, nursing, and office work.
2. Women have greater influence in the home than men, but at a time when the home is under attack and domestic work is devalued.
3. Traditional roles have given way not to role sharing but to neotraditional roles (Poloma and Garland 1971) in which both the husband and wife can work "if they wish" but the husband's work comes first in terms of the amount earned, family influence, and location of family residence. The wife may work but only if she is capable of holding two jobs.

Today, although serious male/female differentials exist in paid labour, women contribute about 40 percent of total family income. Yet, despite the ideological stress on equality and companionship, Canadian wives in neotraditional relationships do not have a comparable share of power, decision-making, or workloads with the family.

This pattern is found throughout North America as well as Western and Eastern Europe. Material from places as diverse as the Soviet Union, China, Scandinavia, and Australia suggest that marital relationships are becoming increasingly symmetrical as societies move toward an egalitarian marital ideal (Pollack 1981). Some sociologists believe the change is along a continuum, that marital roles are moving linearly, away from the traditional model with its highly differentiated division of labour based on gender, toward a model of flexible, negotiated sharing of wage and domestic labour (Szinovacz 1984). But some disagree; they stress the neotraditional aspects of current marital interactions. Given women's low wages, wives remain economically dependent on their husbands. Men's greater earning power and ascendancy in the labour market insulates them from female demands for increased involvement in parenting and household chores. In other words, while women's responsibilities expand, men's remain the same (Yogev 1981).

Definitions of Dual-Earner Families

The term **dual-career marriage** was coined by Rapoport and Rapoport (1971) to refer to the marital arrangement in which both partners are committed to pursuing a career and to maintaining a family. These relationships deviate from traditional ones in two ways: (1) the wife values her career as much as her family; and (2) the husband values his family as much as his career (Coleman 1984, 388). Although these couples are still in the minority, Rice (1979) estimates that their incidence in the United States is rising by 7 percent a year; if homosexual and cohabiting couples are included, the rise is even higher.

Studies, such as that of Acock and Edwards (1982) indicate that women, especially those who are university educated, are more likely than men to prefer a dual-career arrangement. This finding is not surprising: subordinate groups are always more interested in structural change than the power brokers. Presumably the media, schooling, and role-model exposure are socializing young women to seek sex-role parity in marriage and work.

Men's commitment to their wives' careers is equivocal. Cross-cultural data (Cherlin and Walters 1981; Thornton et al. 1983) indicate increased acceptance of female employment by both men and women, but little specific male support for daily tasks such as housework and child care (Eshleman 1985, 116). In other words, husbands seem to support their wives' right to work for wages as long as this employment does not alter significantly the balance of power.

Some sociologists distinguish between the dual-worker family and the dual-career family. In the former, women get "jobs" for financial reasons, and the household division of labour is traditional. Career women, on the other hand, are committed to careers, and seek their intrinsic rewards. But since both working-class and middle-class women seem to derive considerable psychological and financial benefits from paid employment, this distinction may be largely artificial and rooted in class-based assumptions. Myra Feree (1984), for example, criticizes this bias, stating, "Not only do we idealize the employment of the few, we apologize for the employment of the many." Women of all classes rank money as a prime reason for working. Working-class women use employment as a way to secure necessities. Middle-class women may work to maintain their class position for themselves and their offspring. To depict the employment of women of any class as supplementary ensures that they will be limited to occupational ghettos, undermines their claims on family resources, and denigrates the energy they exert when employed.

Hunt and Hunt (1982) predict that as careers for women become more accepted, careers and family will become not more integrated but more polarized, with growing institutional separation of work and family. Families will become more of a liability than before for men and women seeking career success.

Changing Roles and Changing Workloads

Although Canadians say they support role-sharing in the family (in a 1981 Gallup poll, 72 percent of men and women agreed that husbands should share in domestic labour) and Americans do the same, most North American studies show that behaviour has changed little. Married women with children increase their weekly workload by 50 percent when they take on full-time employment, without any corresponding shift in their husband's workload (Mandell [in press]). On average, women reduce the time spent on housekeeping from 50 to 28 hours a week when they take paid employment, but their husbands maintain a steady 8 hours in domestic, repair, and maintenance chores. Pleck (1979) optimistically suggests that "non-trivial increments" in a husband's family work are associated with a wife's employment and that this represents the beginning of a major shift in men's family roles, but other researchers have found little such evidence. The reduction in women's housekeeping time comes from lowering standards, hiring help, or getting assistance from friends or neighbours, rather than from obtaining help from the husband or children.

Clearly, the largest part of household labour still comes from women. Berheide (1984) estimates that wives take responsibility for 74 to 92 percent of the tasks done in eight major areas: meal preparation, cleaning the kitchen, laundry, straightening, ironing, outside errands, child care, and other household tasks. Women also make community links and take on kinship obligations, including buying gifts, writing letters, and arranging visits. **Time budget studies** (studies, often using self-reports, of how much time respondents devote to particular tasks) from various industrialized countries estimate that employed women with household responsibilities average a 70-hour work week. Similarly, two recent surveys of Toronto women—Wellman's (1985) survey in East York and Crysdale's (in press) in Riverdale—give pictures of wives with too much to do and too little time to do it in.

Interestingly, the total time that women spend on housework did not decline significantly from the 1920s to the 1970s, despite rapid technological change (Vanek 1974). Standards of cleanliness, child care, and emotional support have risen (Hartmann 1981). The decline in time spent on meal preparation and laundry is offset by increased involvement in shopping, record keeping, and child care.

Despite the enormous amount of time women spend on housework, it is socially denigrated. People assume that it is less time-consuming and physically strenuous than paid labour (Vanek 1974) and has little productive value. This degradation indicates the subservience of "mother-work" (Bernard 1974) and the uneasy relationship between the family and the state. Capitalism has pushed the production of goods (food, clothing) and services (education, health care, nursing, psychotherapy, childbirth) into the market. Housewives are both consumers and domestic labourers; they also work for wages that enable them to purchase the items they require in their job as mothers (see Exhibit 5-7 for an analysis of the costs of raising a child). Women produce economically beneficial goods and services, provide free domestic labour, and work in the labour market to reinforce their work as mothers in the home. In invisible ways, their double burden of labour reproduces class and gender relations.

Stresses and Strains

Most of the literature on the effects of women's employment on family life seems to assume that until recently women stayed home. In fact, the ideal of the housewife was a middle-class one. In discussing the stress and coping strategies of middle-class women, sociologists seem to have forgotten that working-class women have always combined paid labour and family roles. This glaring omission reflects the current ideology, which focuses on promoting egalitarian changes in the work lives of middle-class women.

In the egalitarian model, the switch from full-time homemaker to employed wife and mother presumably realigns the spousal balance of power. If the couple fails to share roles equally, conflicts result. Skinner (1980) refers to external and internal stresses. External stresses result from the conflict between the dual-career family and other societal structures: work demands geographic mobility, which is difficult to achieve when two jobs are at stake; a career requires long working hours, but the family demands intimate interaction. Internal stresses are conflicts that arise within the family, including work overload, identity confusion, and dilemmas about when to have children, and whose career should take priority. When parenting young children coincides with the heavy time commitments of early stages of career development, these strains are exacerbated.

Both spouses in a two-job family experience role strain and depression, but women suffer significantly more than men (Keith and Schafer 1980). Yet employed wives appear to be in better physical health than stay-at-home wives and are more likely to enjoy their relationships with their children. They reveal more positive and fewer negative feelings about themselves, project an image of ability and confidence, and evaluate their community as a satisfactory place to live (Kessler and McRae 1982).

The husbands of working women experience both the stress and the rewards of increased intimacy with children. The wife's employment reduces the amount of personal care the husband receives, increases his

Exhibit 5-7

The Cost of Raising a Child, 1984

(in 1984 dollars)

	Food	Clothing	Personal Care	Public Transportation	School Needs	Recreation	Housing	Health and Home Maintenance	Baby Sitting	Total without Day-Care	Day-Care	Total with Day-Care
Infant	$ 791	$ 951[b]	$ 33				$ 788	$ 290		$ 2 853	$ 3 862	$ 6 715
1–3 Boy	865	197	55	8		101	788	290	577	2 881	5 062	7 943
1–3 Girl	865	212	55	8		101	788	290	577	2 896	5 062	7 958
4–6 Boy	1 018	232	68	22	35	101	788	290	487	3 041	3 908	6 949
4–6 Girl	1 018	247	68	22	35	101	788	290	487	3 056	3 908	6 964
7–9 Boy	1 200	298	72	27	71	240	824	290	307	3 329	2 916	6 245
7–9 Girl	1 200	348	72	27	71	240	824	290	307	3 379	2 916	6 295
10–12 Boy	1 414	340	80	32	71	259	860	290	197	3 543		3 543
10–12 Girl	1 414	387	117	32	71	259	860	290	197	3 627		3 627
13–15 Boy	1 727	445	94	203	110	326	860	290		4 055		4 055
13–15 Girl	1 450	536	205	203	110	326	860	290		3 980		3 980
16–18 Boy	1 894	486	155	203	178	382	860	290		4 448		4 448
16–18 Girl	1 400	676	253	203	178	382	860	290		4 242		4 242
Total Boy	25 145	6 945	1 605	1 485	1 395	4 227	15 728	5 510	4 704	66 744	39 520	106 264
Total Girl	22 832	8 169	2 343	1 485	1 395	4 227	15 728	5 510	4 704	66 393	39 520	105 913
Average Increase % 1981–1984	21.3%	17.2%	23.4%	28.5%	30.0%	20.8%	20.4%	22.4%	4.5%	19.7%	44.2%	25.6%
Total Gov't Aid[c]										$14 947	$5 600[d]	$20 547[a]

Notes: Costs, figured in 1984 dollars for a two-parent family in Metropolitan Toronto, are conservative in that they exclude luxuries and unusual expenses.

[a] Assumes no eligibility for day-care subsidies, which can reduce costs substantially.

[b] Includes furniture, equipment, and toys.

[c] Estimated 1984 government aid: maximum child tax credit, family allowance, and income tax deduction for dependent child, calculated at a marginal income tax rate of 28 percent.

[d] Includes child-care income tax deduction, calculated at a marginal income tax rate of 28 percent.

Source: Social Planning Council of Metropolitan Toronto, as quoted in *The Royal Bank Reporter* (1986, 18).

responsibility for child care and household tasks, decreases his responsibility for financial provision, and sometimes requires a modification in his career plans (Booth 1977).

Studies suggest that maternal employment has no detrimental effect on children. Differences between the children of employed mothers and those whose mothers stay home are often explained by other factors, such as social class, age of the children, and the mother's attitude toward employment (Eshleman 1985, 133). However, the employment of mothers has focused attention on the severe shortage of child-care facilities in North America. By 1984, according to the recent report of the federal Task Force on Child Care (1986, 326) 52 percent of mothers with children under three years of age were in the labour force, compared to 32 percent in 1976.

One consequence of the high and growing percentage of labour force participation by the mothers of young children, says the report, is a need to rethink policy toward parenting and child care. It recommends extending parental leaves up to one year from the birth or adoption of a child, permitting parental leave to be shared between the mother and the father, giving employees five days' annual paid leave for family-related responsibilities, expanding both full-time and part-time day-care facilities, including those for handicapped children, and retaining in the Income Tax Act, at least in the short term, the child-care expense deduction.

Married women with children increase their workload by 50 percent when they take on full time employment without any corresponding shift in their husbands' workload.

Marital Power

Does having dual earners affect the authority structure of the family? Female employment seems to lead to increased power for wives in small families, in families without preschool children, and in lower-class families. In all other family arrangements, women's wage labour does not affect gender roles as much as might be expected. Moreover, the effects diminish as the gap between the husband's and wife's incomes increases. The more money a man earns, the more it insulates him from family demands. Research (Bahr 1974) also suggests that employment brings wives increases in power primarily in external decisions (finances or the provider role, rather than internal household areas.

A recent Canadian study (Brinkerhoff and Lupri 1983) reports a high degree of equality between husbands and wives. Wives say they have slightly more power than their husbands, though in areas considered unimportant by men, such as household and child-care decisions. Although women still occupy a subordinate position in the family, some sociologists detect the emergence of a new norm of marital power—the **interdependence norm**, which implies both mutual dependence and the capacity to be independent (Weingarten 1978). Neither spouse holds the dominant position at all times. Rather, both rely on or support each other as personal, professional, and family needs require. This shifting definition of marital power relations no doubt reflects the finding that egalitarian marriages are the happiest and most satisfying.

Statistics Canada estimates that at least 70 percent of married women will be employed by the year 2000. Given the prevalence of dual-earner families, the traditional models of family interaction, power, division of labour, and authority structures seem quite out of date.

(For more discussion of family models and women's roles, see Chapter 9.)

Family Violence

Violence is defined as any act carried out with the intention of injuring another person. Such acts include sexual molestation, physical abuse, and verbal aggression. Of these types, sociological studies have given the most attention to physical violence, which includes throwing something, pushing, grabbing, shoving, slapping, spanking, kicking, biting, hitting, making threats, and using a weapon. Physical abuse is sometimes categorized as mild or severe, based on the risk of serious injury.

Canadian and American data alike reveal that violence is a pervasive feature of North American family life. The abuse of a spouse, siblings, and children is a common practice in many Canadian homes. American studies conclude that family fights are the largest single cause of police calls; that 84 to 97 percent of parents use physical punishment at some point in their children's lives; that 26 percent of men and 19 percent of women approve of slapping a husband; and that one in four men and one in six women approve of slapping a wife under certain conditions (Eshleman 1985, 569). Canadian statistics are sketchy, but the Badgley Report (1984) notes that in 1980 provincial child protection services knew of or suspected sexual abuse cases for three out of every 1000 children, and most experts put the actual incidence much higher. From information on physically battered women in transition houses and statistics on the number of divorces filed on grounds of physical cruelty in 1978, MacLeod (1980) extrapolates that one out of every ten married or cohabiting women are battered.

Steinmetz and Strauss (1974) analyze the features of families that predispose members to use violence to resolve difficulties. Structural elements include economic and health strains, institutionalized gender discrimination, lack of deterrents for the abuser, and lack of alternatives for the victims. Sociocultural norms legitimating the use of physical violence are perpetuated through the media, the association of sex and violence, language, and the denigration of women and children. Interpersonal qualities include the individual characteristics of family members, immediate stressful precipitating factors, and a history of childhood abuse on the part of the abuser.

Abuse is disproportionately directed toward the powerless—women and children—and tends to be perpetuated through early childhood socialization into a subculture of family violence. Through the adult years, society's endorsement of violence reinforces these experiences as legitimate responses to structural and individual strain.

Battered women and children are often trapped in abusive situations by the desperate lack of alternative living arrangements. This situation has been alleviated slightly in recent years by the building of a number of temporary shelters across the country. Women are able to leave their homes and live for short periods in these shelters until they can organize more permanent accommodation.

EMERGING FAMILY FORMS

The nuclear families discussed in this chapter are not the only form of family life in 20th century Canada. Modern Western societies are pluralistic: a range of lifestyles co-exist. Although most people seek some more or less stable household arrangement within which they can meet their needs for companionship and confirmation of self-worth, there is no single model of family structure to which all Canadians aspire.

Today a number of alternative family forms have emerged. Increasing numbers of couples choose to remain childless. A significant percentage of Canadians never marry; they include single-person households, people living in platonic shared living arrangements, and cohabiting and homosexual couples. Changing demographics are also making more common the pattern of the empty-nest couple, middle-aged spouses whose children have left home.

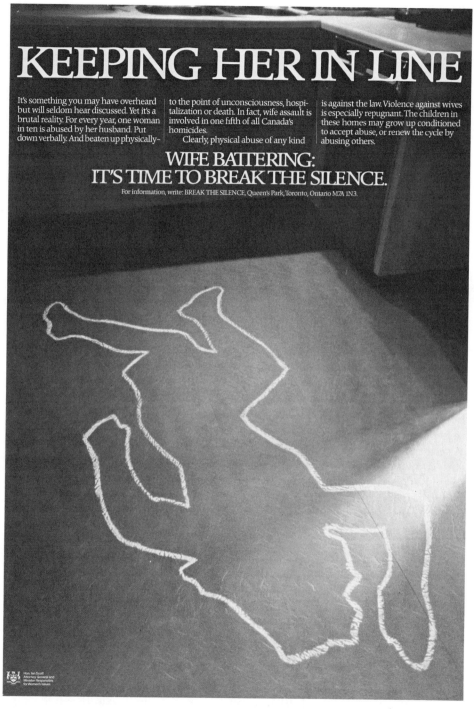

KEEPING HER IN LINE

It's something you may have overheard but will seldom hear discussed. Yet it's a brutal reality. For every year, one woman in ten is abused by her husband. Put down verbally. And beaten up physically— to the point of unconsciousness, hospitalization or death. In fact, wife assault is involved in one fifth of all Canada's homicides.

Clearly, physical abuse of any kind is against the law. Violence against wives is especially repugnant. The children in these homes may grow up conditioned to accept abuse, or renew the cycle by abusing others.

WIFE BATTERING: IT'S TIME TO BREAK THE SILENCE.

For information, write: BREAK THE SILENCE, Queen's Park, Toronto, Ontario M7A 1N3.

Hon. Ian Scott
Attorney General and
Minister Responsible
for Women's Issues

The cultural ideal of blissful married life does not reflect the harsh and sometimes violent reality faced by many women — and some men.

These household models are no longer rare arrangements engaged in by the individual eccentric or social outcast. They have all become common enough to take a more or less accepted place in the social mosaic of Canada.

Childless Couples

The recent report of the Task Force on Child Care (1986) notes the gradual, long-term trend toward lowered fertility in North America and other industrialized nations. Childless couples rose from 27 percent in 1961 to 32 percent in 1981. The baby boomers, those born between 1946 and 1966, are having fewer children than their parents and some of them are having no children at all.

Statisticians are cautious in interpreting the current trend toward decreased fertility. Are couples postponing having children? Or will they remain childless? Divorce, sterility, and careers may prevent women who want children from bearing them. Yet data from surveys of women's childbearing plans, as well as studies of fertility trends, predict a significant rise in voluntary childlessness in the future. Projections estimate that 16 percent of Canadian women and as many as 25 percent of American women may forego maternity (Statistics Canada 1985c, 33). Given Canada's 15-year trend of decreased fertility, childless couples seem to represent a significant alternative to traditional family patterns.

Why are people having smaller families or remaining childless? The answers are economic, technical, ideological, and demographic. The drop in fertility occurred at the same time as high rates of inflation, spiralling housing costs, high unemployment, deteriorating relative incomes, and increased female labour force participation (Statistics Canada 1984a). Women's expanding economic role corresponds with their higher educational attainment and lowered fertility. Role incompatibility theory, discussed earlier in the chapter, points out how working and mothering compete for women's time and energy. Women may forego having children to concentrate on careers or may delay childbearing until their careers are established.

Technological innovations in birth control have reduced the incidence of unwanted and unplanned pregnancies. Social alterations include the decline in the marriage rate and the rise in divorce and remarriage, the postponement of childbearing, the preference for smaller families, and the changing status of children. According to one theory, the chief cause of the decline in Western fertility is that children have become the focal point of family aspirations for higher social status. Families have fewer children so they can afford to provide them with a better education and thus improve their chances for social ascension (Statistics Canada 1984a, 64). Another interpretation suggests that it is demographic changes, such as later marriage, later child-rearing, increased divorce and remarriage, and lowered fertility, that have altered the status and treatment of children (Statistics Canada 1984a, 96).

No doubt low fertility, changing household arrangements, and shifts in ideological approaches to children are factors that affect each other. Low fertility does not seem to imply an opposition to children. In West Germany, Romania, Czechoslovakia, Hungary, and Bulgaria, fertility rates too low to replace the population have prompted successful state interventions to encourage childbirth: access to abortion has been restricted, paternity leave prolonged, family allowances and fiscal exemptions increased.

One explanation for falling birth rates is that women no longer feel compelled to have children to prove their femininity. In today's world, motherhood no longer automatically assures a woman's identity and maturity. Rather, women are increasingly judged by male standards of work performance, with parenting assuming a subordinate status.

Moreover, the literature on childlessness portrays childless couples as happier with their marriages than couples with children, more likely to have egalitarian marital relationships, and more likely to make joint decisions (Veevers 1979). Perhaps couples are having fewer children because they feel that increased marital happiness, greater career advancement for women, and the reduction of expense and stress are more important than the rewards of having children: emotional pleasure, companionship, vicarious social advancement, the perpetuation of the family, and the possibility of support in old age.

(For a more detailed discussion of falling birth rates and their effects, see Chapter 14.)

Singlehood

In recent years, the rates of marriage have fallen, marriage breakdown has become more common, and more single people have been living away from their family of orientation (Statistics Canada 1984a, 97). Singlehood is statistically on the rise and is becoming an acceptable family form.

Macklin (1980) gives three reasons for the growth of singlehood: (1) the increased number of women in higher education and the expanding range of lifestyle and employment options for women; (2) the fact that there are more women than men of marriageable age; and (3) the increasing ease with which singles can enjoy an active social and sexual life. Of course, many adults are single at some point in their life cycle, but 10.2 percent of women and 9.6 percent of men now remain permanently single, and Stein (1983) estimates that 8 to 9 percent of adults now in their twenties will remain single. Stein distinguishes between voluntary and involuntary singleness and between stable and temporary singles. All singles face the tasks of achieving and maintaining friendships, achieving intimacy and fulfilling sexuality, maintaining emotional and physical well-being, making satisfactory living arrangements, and seeking and finding productive work. Stein finds single women to be better off than single men in terms of education, occupation, and mental health.

Single men tend to have lower levels of intelligence and occupational achievement than married men. These statistics confirm Jessie Bernard's (1972) contention that marriage benefits men more than women.

In a survey in southern Ontario (Peters 1983) single women cited the advantages of singlehood as being able to travel (36 percent), participation in hobbies (13 percent), independence (13 percent), pursuit of a career (11 percent) and education (9 percent). As disadvantages, more than half the respondents (53 percent) cited having no companion to share feelings with; other disadvantages included having to live alone and having to pay more taxes.

Historically, attitudes toward single men and women have been negative. Single men are stereotyped as swingers and women as lonely spinsters. Cargan (1981) shows that most singles are neither lonely nor swingers. They are also more likely to be divorced than never married.

Unmarried Cohabitation

Few changes relating to marriage and family life have been as dramatic as the rapid increase in unmarried cohabitation (Glick and Spanier 1981, 65). **Cohabitation** is defined as a "more or less permanent relationship in which two unmarried persons of the opposite sex share a living facility without legal contract" (Cole 1977, 67). In the United States in 1981, unmarried men and women living together made up about 4 percent of all couple households—twice the incidence of five years earlier (Spanier 1980). Of these, 28 percent had at least one child in the household. In Sweden, 15 percent of all couples living together under marriage-like conditions are not legally married (Macklin 1980). In Canada, the proportion of non-familial households is expected to reach 25 percent by 1991 (Statistics Canada 1981b, 49).

Spanier (1980) attributes most of the increase in unmarried cohabitation among relatively young adults to the recent increase in the average age at first marriage and to society's increasing tolerance for non-traditional living arrangements. Stein (1983, 37) also notes financial considerations, including the high cost of living alone, housing shortages in urban areas, as well as the greater acceptance of premarital sex and changing gender role definitions.

Two recent Canadian studies categorize types of cohabitators and attempt to explain their perceptions of their relationships. Clarke (1978) identifies cohabitation as a form of trial marriage, providing a means of assessing a prospective marriage partner. And Fels (1981, 32) notes that living together has become an intermediate stage of the courtship process, between dating and marriage.

The effects of cohabitation vary. Although cohabitors view themselves as playing untraditional sex roles, there is little evidence that their relationships are less traditional than those of married couples (Macklin 1983, 61). Unmarried and married couples have similar levels of marital satisfaction, emotional closeness, and egalitarianism. They have the same sorts of problems and conflicts. Nor does living together affect the marriage or divorce rate. The hypothesis that cohabitation prepares couples for marriage seems not to have been borne out.

The most significant effects of non-marital unions have been on the legal system. In Canada, legislation governing non-marital cohabitation is a provincial affair. Since 1978, the provinces have recognized limited legal rights of common-law spouses, including the right to support after a certain period of co-residence (the length of time varies by province, but one year is common). This change is intended to protect women from potentially exploitive relationships and to protect the community from the burden of supporting people otherwise entitled to social assistance. The state has effectively shifted responsibility from its public assistance programs to individuals.

THE CHILDREN OF DIVORCE

More often than not, the pain, disappointment and heartbreak of a marriage breakup involve children. Within the last decade, about half a million young Canadians have become "divorced kids." A hundred years ago in England, it was common for mothers and fathers to work away from home during the day. Children were given a house key to wear on a chain around the neck. They were called "latchkey children," and they were on their own. Today's escalating divorce rate has created a new key club—a new generation of latchkey children.

The family in Canada was once a stable unit within a stable society. Children grew up in a closely knit, clearly defined world of immediate families, relatives, neighborhoods, traditions and customs. Over time the extended family gave way to the more limited nuclear family. Then in the 1960s both society and families began to explode with even more dramatic changes. Because people started to move regularly and often, neighborhoods were no longer stable, and our family ties became stretched around the planet as we moved farther and farther away from our relations. Within this world of explosive change, however, the family seemed the basic unit of organization and stability. It's no wonder, then, that the impact of divorce on children can be devastating

On [my radio program] *Discovery* I discussed this impact with four psychologists and psychiatrists who worked with children of divorced parents. One was Mary Gendler, a counselling psychologist with the Andover, Massachusetts, school system and the innovator of puppet therapy for children of divorce. I recall vividly her description of a play a group of Grade 6 students staged .... The first scene, which they called "Tug of Kids," featured a judge, who was depicted as a unicorn puppet, asking the children which parent they wanted to go with. One child said, "I want to go with Mommy," while another said, "I want to go with Daddy." The third child said, "Cut me in half, so half can go with Mommy and half can go with Daddy."

Lest anyone think that children are unaware of what goes on between parents, consider the play a group of Mary Gendler's eight-year-olds presented about a divorce proceeding. It opened with a mother and father in a judge's office, and here is the dialogue the children wrote:

"John, do you take Mary to be your awful divorced wife?" the judge asked.

"I do."

"Mary, do you take John to be your awful divorced husband?"

"I do."

"I now pronounce you divorced man and wife. You may hit the bride."

I recall, too, a point made by Dr. Paul Patterson, a child psychologist in London, Ontario. He said that too often warring parents forget the feelings of the children they are fighting over. Among children of divorced parents, there is always the fear that *nobody* will want them, he said. After all, if one parent can leave, it seems possible for the other parent to leave as well. This deep-seated insecurity can remain for a long, long time. ...

We discussed whether boys or girls coped better with divorce. University of Michigan psychologist Neil Kalter observed that teenage girls have a particularly tough time when their fathers aren't present; as a result, they may go in search of older men to become involved with. But Dr. Fred Seligman, head of the Child and Adolescent Psychiatry Program at the University of Miami, said that girls tend to cope better than boys with the increased responsibility and decreased parental involvement in a lone-parent family because they have a better social support system and discuss their problems more openly among themselves than boys do.

One thing is certain. Children do best after divorce if their absent father or mother keeps in touch with them. "The question I'm most frequently asked by non-custodial parents is how often they should see their kids," said Dr. Seligman. "Seeing one's kids is important, of course, but *interacting* with your kids is much more important. And there are many different ways to interact. For instance, if a parent lives in a different town than the children, telephone calls are probably the most important kinds of regular contact." ...

Human beings are incredibly resilient. It always astounds me that people can survive brutality, starvation and even death camps and resume a "normal" life. We can only guess at the scars beneath the surface. And so life goes on for the survivors of divorce. Because children are adaptable, most kids of divorced parents manage to assume a semblance of normality and stability. But I can't help wondering: at what cost?

—David Suzuki

Blended Families

Divorce continues to rise in Canada (see Exhibit 5-8). The total **divorce rate**—the number of divorces versus the number of marriages—rose 82 percent in 10 years, reaching 365 per 1000 marriages in 1982. Serial monogamy has become more commonplace, as the proportion of re-marriages increases. One reason for the increasing divorce rate is Canada's liberalized laws, which allow couples to divorce quickly and without acrimony over fault and the division of family assets. (Divorce is now granted, regardless of the circumstances, if couples live apart for a period of one year. Family law, which governs the division of property on marriage breakup, varies across provinces, but the trend is toward equal division of all matrimonial property and business assets except for the assets each spouse brings to the marriage.) Other reasons for the rise in divorce include the declining stigma of divorce, the financial and social independence of women, and various psychological factors related to marital and personal expectations.

The growing incidence of **reconstituted or blended families** (one or both spouses bring to the new family children from a previous relationship; the couple may also have children of their own) has prompted researchers to compare family relationships within first and subsequent

Exhibit 5-8
Crude Divorce Rates per General Population and for Canada, 1952–84

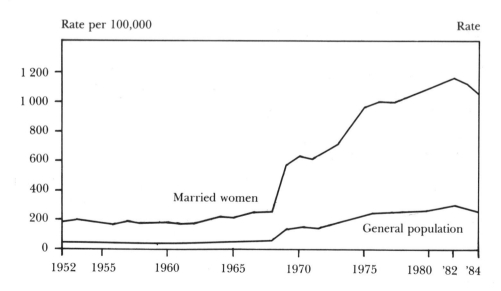

Source: Statistics Canada, *Marriages and Divorces*, vol. 2 of *Vital Statistics 1984*, cat. no. 84-205.

marriages. Not surprisingly, remarried couples rate their current marriages as happier than their first ones. Factors in happiness and sources of conflict differ in first and second marriages. Infidelity, loss of love for each other, and emotional and financial problems afflict first marriages. In second marriages, conflicts revolve around money, emotional problems, sexual problems, and the spouse's former marriage (Eichler 1983, 235). The presence of children has a mixed effect on remarriages, both contributing to the success and adding to the complexity of new family formations.

Research into the effects of remarriage on children's relationships with their new and old parents is beginning to grow (Ambert 1986). Adequate kin terms do not yet exist to describe the new family constellations. Neither are there clear social norms for dealing with stepchildren, ex-spouses, ex-grandparents, and the new set of relatives. Stepparents report problems in disciplining children, in gaining their acceptance, and in adjusting to vague role expectations. Children, in turn, often meet with contradictory parental demands and loyalties. Given that today 20.6 percent of men who marry and 18.8 percent of women who marry, are marrying after divorce, children growing up today are very likely to have experienced personally or through their friends, the problems and delights of blended families.

Homosexual Couples

The term **homosexual** is appropriately used to refer to both men and women whose primary sexual and affectional orientation is toward same-gender partners. Many such people, however, prefer to be called gay (a term that refers to either men or women) or lesbian (for women). Often they distinguish between "homosexual" as a word referring simply to erotic preferences and "gay" as signifying acceptance of oneself and freedom from guilt or shame. Estimates are that 4 to 5 percent of males and 1 to 2 percent of women in the United States would be classified as predominantly homosexual.

Studies of gay relationships reveal interesting findings. Stereotypes to the contrary, most gays are not confused about their gender identity and do not live bizarre lives. In fact they experience the same problems, activities, and conflicts as other North Americans. Although most participants in gay unions do not value sexual exclusivity as highly as most partners in heterosexual unions, gays do desire and value steady love relationships. When interviewed, they consistently rank affection, personal development, and companionship as their most important relationship goals. The popular depiction of gay couples in which one plays the role of husband and the other of wife is inaccurate. Gays tend to reject traditional marital roles and to value their relationships because they are not traditional. Partners usually equitably distribute money, tasks, and responsibilities.

Perhaps because of differential gender socialization, gay men and women differ in the kinds of relationships they tend to form. Gay white men average 100 sexual partners during their lifetimes, while lesbians average 10. The reason for the difference may be that men are raised to view sex instrumentally, as an activity separate from affection, while women tend to view it within a context of love, commitment, and fidelity. The male gay subculture legitimates impersonal sex through the proliferation of gay bars and clubs. Lesbians are not likely to go cruising.

Bell and Weinberg (1978) studied 1000 homosexuals and compared their relationships with those of a comparison group of nearly 500 heterosexuals. They find five homosexual types: (1) close-coupleds: people living in monogamous homosexual relationships similar to heterosexual ones; (2) open-coupleds: people living with a special same-sex partner but also seeking some sexual and emotional satisfaction outside the relationship; (3) functionals: a group comparable to swinging singles; (4) dysfunctionals: troubled people whose lives offer them little gratification; and (5) asexuals: people who are isolated, withdrawn, and uninvolved.

Studies by Bell and Weinberg (1978) of gay men and by Tanner (1978) of gay women emphasize the unique strains on gay unions. In addition to the usual range of interpersonal conflicts over jealousy, money, or friends, gay couples must cope with the lack of social supports for their partnership, the absence of marital role models and scripts, parental disapproval, and problems with housing, insurance, taxes, and inheritance resulting from the lack of legal recognition of their union. Although gay relationships are not as long-lasting as their heterosexual counterparts, they appear to be more egalitarian, emphasizing love within a context of shared commitment.

Older Families

Couples in their fifties and sixties represent a growing proportion of Canadian households. It is estimated that by 2031, the year in which the aging of the population will reach its peak, the median age of couples will be 41.6 years (Nett 1984).

In the early 1900s, spouses tended to live only a short while after the last child left home. Now increasing longevity and the trend toward having fewer children have combined to stretch this period to 20 to 25 years—longer than any other stage in the marital life cycle.

Are these years the happiest or the most stressful of a couple's life together? Stereotypes suggest that aging women suffer from empty-nest syndrome and aging men from mid-life crisis. But evidence does not support these images. Women have new-found independence and energy when their children leave home and they are financially and socially free to pursue their own interests (Hawkins 1978). Women who have worked all their lives have developed multifaceted support networks and enjoy roles other than parenting. The male mid-life crisis appears to be ficti-tious. Farrell and Rosenberg's (1981) study of 300 middle-aged men finds that professional and middle-class executives exhibit neither denial nor identity problems, and reported satisfaction with work, family, and com-munity positions.

It is likely, of course, that couples experience both marital happiness and stress after their children leave home. Income is at its highest, leisure time is abundant, child care is past, and new opportunities arise. These freedoms are offset, however, by newly acquired obligations, including caring for aging parents and financially supporting children in university or newly wed—physical, social, and emotional demands that can depress marital satisfaction. Canadian data (Lupri and Frieders 1981) suggest that couples experience a temporary period of disenchantment with mar-riage at this time, followed by an upswing. Conclusive evidence is sketchy. As the baby boomers age, these questions will undoubtedly receive closer scrutiny.

SUMMARY

The diversity of Canadian family forms and interactions provides soci-ologists with the challenge of capturing family complexities and similar-ities. Recent changes—demographic, economic, social, and legal—have altered family structures. Statistical accounts reveal that although the majority of Canadians marry at least once in their lives, couples marrying today are more likely than in the past to experience divorce and remar-riage, and that they are likely to wait until later in life to marry and likely to produce fewer children. The lowered birth rate and the "greying" of the Canadian population has contributed to the smaller size of families.

Economically, the most dramatic change affecting families has been the entrance of many married women into the labour force. Child care for employed mothers has gained national attention as parents search for accessible, affordable, and high-quality day-care. Although the ma-jority of parents make private arrangements for their children to be cared for in their own homes or in the homes of babysitters, the current income tax laws do not allow all parents to deduct their total child-care expenses. The lack of subsidized day-care may contribute to the fact that day-care centres enrol fewer than one-third of the children under age six whose mothers work outside the home.

The emergence of the dual-worker family has altered the traditional roles of husbands and wives. Family research has focused on the advan-tages, stresses, and consequences of spouses' sharing parenting and wage earning. Feminist rethinking of the family analyzes the slow but inex-orable shift in marital power toward more egalitarian spousal relation-ships. The effects of dual-earner families on the status and role of children remain to be investigated thoroughly.

Little research exists on reconstituted families. The relationships of ex-spouses with each other and with former relatives await study, as does the effect on marital satisfaction of the blending of children from current and previous marriages. Similarly, commuter marriages, homosexual unions, and aging families demand the attention of sociologists.

Modern social changes—including the women's movement, the liberalization of attitudes toward sex, and the human potential movement—have altered traditional definitions of and expectations for intimate relationships. An emphasis on self-actualization, increased personal freedom from cultural and religious traditions, lessening commitments to duty, economic independence for women, and the increased acceptance of divorce have altered present-day attitudes and behaviour. Marriage is no longer viewed as a lifelong commitment or as an essential structure for the production or raising of children. Future improvements in artificial insemination may further alter parenting norms.

The recent liberalization of the federal divorce act, changes in the rights of common-law spouses, and the move to avoid differentiating "legitimate" and "illegitimate" children are institutionalizing marriage and family patterns that had already begun to change. These new laws will structure the form and content of married life for future generations of Canadians.

Canadian families are embedded in a uniquely Canadian society. Unravelling the socioeconomic, ideological, and cultural threads of this relationship continues to fascinate sociologists.

FOR FURTHER READING

Baker, Maureen
1984 *The Family: Changing Trends in Canada.* Toronto: McGraw-Hill Ryerson. This collection of articles is a good introduction to various aspects of family life in Canada.

Canadian Journal of Sociology 6 (3)
1981 The entire issue of this journal examines recent historical, theoretical, and substantive components of Canadian families.

Eichler, Margrit
1983 *Families in Canada Today: Recent Changes and Their Policy Consequences.* Toronto: Gage. This excellent and comprehensive work analyzes the major legal and social policies affecting Canadian families.

Hess, Beth B., and Marvin B. Sussman (eds.)
1984 "Women and the Family: Two Decades of Change." *Marriage and Family Review* 7 (3,4) Fall, Winter. This American collection of articles assesses the impact of recent economic, demographic, and social changes on women's and men's roles in the family.

Ishwaran, K. (ed.)
(In press) *The Modern Family: A Cross-Cultural Introduction.* Toronto: Oxford University Press. This up-to-date collection of articles by sociologists on the family offers a cross-cultural perspective.

Luxton, Meg
  1980 *More Than a Labour of Love: Three Generations of Women's Work in the Home.*
  Toronto: Women's Press.
  Luxton draws penetrating portraits of the lives of working-class families changing
  over three generations in a northern Canadian community.
Wilson, S.J.
  1986 *Women, The Family and the Economy*, 2nd ed. Toronto: McGraw-Hill Ryerson.
  Wilson gives a historical account of the changing role of women in the family,
  work, and public life.

CHAPTER 6

EDUCATION IN THE CANADIAN MOSAIC

Sid N. Gilbert and Ian M. Gomme

THE IMPORTANCE OF EDUCATION IN CANADA

DEVELOPMENT AND GROWTH OF EDUCATION IN CANADA
Beginnings
Recent Developments

SOCIOLOGICAL THEORIES OF EDUCATION
Structural Functionalism
Conflict Theory
The New Sociology of Education

ASPIRATIONS AND ATTAINMENT

THE CURRENT MALAISE IN CONTEXT
Human Capital
Accessibility

Summary
For Further Reading

I love to learn but I do not always enjoy being taught.

Winston Churchill

Get all the education you can: then add the learning.

Jack Miner

The terms learning and education, as Miner's statement suggests, are not perfectly synonymous. Education involves learning, but learning is by no means exclusive to educational activities and contexts. **Learning** is a process, frequently informal and unorganized, through which a person acquires knowledge. Consider the child who burns her fingers playing with matches, the adolescent grounded by his parents for staying out beyond his curfew, and the adult shunned by her fellow labourers because she works too hard. All have learned something. Yet none of these instances would commonly be regarded as examples of education.

Education refers to the transmission of knowledge, skills, and values through formally organized and structured learning processes. Education is typically conducted in institutions such as schools and universities, and involves a series of actors, including administrators, planners, instructors, and students. Learning objectives are conceived and systematically pursued through practices designed for such purposes. Examples of the education process include a teacher's transmission of knowledge about Marco Polo to a Grade 5 social studies class and a lab session providing college students with the skills to program a computer.

Education can be differentiated from learning in yet another way. Educational performance is usually formally evaluated and recorded, and some official certification, such as a degree or diploma, is normally awarded upon successful completion of a program of study. Learning, on the other hand, may go unnoticed (sometimes even by the learner).

THE IMPORTANCE OF EDUCATION IN CANADA

One clue to the salience of education in Canadian society is the number of people involved in this enterprise and the time and money expended upon it. Education is compulsory in Canada: the young are required to attend school until the age of 15 or 16. In addition, a very large proportion of Canadians continue beyond the legal school-leaving age, to finish secondary school, and many go on to secondary institutions. Moreover, the sphere of influence of education is expanding, as increasing numbers of preschoolers are sent to day-care centres and nursery schools, while adult enrolments in graduate, professional, and continuing education programs continue to grow. Also increasingly popular are educational initiatives outside the school system, in sectors such as religion (Sunday school), politics (clubs and voluntary organizations), athletics (swimming and skating lessons), and the arts (piano and ballet lessons). Thus, a great many Canadians are involved in education, though the nature of that experience varies across social groups.

During the years following the Second World War, student enrolment in Canada increased sharply. By the end of the 1970s, education was one of the largest industries in the country, with one-third of all Canadians involved in it as students, teachers, or administrators. Expeditures also skyrocketed. Today education has become the second highest single government expenditure, rising from $8.4 billion in the early 1970s to $33.3 billion in the mid-1980s (Statistics Canada 1985a). Only social security costs more.

Virtually every Canadian now has some direct experience with the education system, as a student, a parent, or both. Taxpayers, whether or not they have children in school, are acutely aware of the enormous costs of a modern education system. Moreover, society now expects education to do more than impart knowledge and skills to the young. Education is commonly touted as a cure for a host of social ills: poverty, unemployment, unwanted pregnancies, delinquency and crime, and so on. Such high expectations make discontent with the system virtually inevitable. The public sees a very costly system that often does not appear to deliver on its promises. Survey data show widespread public dissatisfaction with state-supported education in Canada. The image of teachers is tarnished; the perceived value of university degrees is reduced. Faith in the quality of elementary, secondary, and post-secondary education has also been eroded. When Canadians were asked, "Do you think children today are being better or worse educated than you were?", only 41 percent responded "better." Dissatisfaction was particularly high in Quebec, where only 25 percent of respondents thought that children were receiving a higher quality education than they themselves had acquired (Gallup Poll 1983).

DEVELOPMENT AND GROWTH OF EDUCATION IN CANADA

Canadian concerns about education are best understood in the context of the development of education in Canada. In this section, we present a brief historical overview and highlight current issues.

Beginnings

Education is a relatively recent creation. Before the 19th century, children learned both the social graces and occupational skills primarily at home or, for males, through the apprenticeship process. Boys learned to become farmers or craftsmen like their fathers. Girls were instructed by their mothers in the tasks and duties of a homemaker. Few children, except those of the wealthy, received any formal instruction in schools.

Child-rearing philosophies of the 1800s paid little heed to the inner feelings and emotions of children. Parents were encouraged to value children, not for the joy, affection, and love they could bring into a home, but as miniature workers in the family-owned, small-scale agricultural, manufacturing, and commercial enterprises of the day. The role of parent was a serious and not necessarily pleasant one: to inculcate proper morals and to create desirable work habits.

Throughout the 19th century, urbanization, immigration, and economic development accelerated, resulting in a rapidly changing social order in Canada. In an effort to better provide for social and economic development and for social integration, schools were increasingly promoted by the middle classes. The reformers had hopes of developing human potential, narrowing the gap between the social classes and producing a qualified labour force for the growing industrial sector. The face of education began to change markedly, with several interrelated goals.

Human Development

The school promoters of the 19th century began to stress both the intellectual and moral aspects of human growth. They felt that the baser features of human nature needed to be regulated and kept in check, lest the animalistic side of human beings retard social and economic progress. One result was an increasing view of children as requiring nurture and protection. The school environment, it was believed, should protect the young both from their basic human nature and from corrupting conditions in their rapidly changing social environment. Thus, child-centred reformers stressed making schools more humane—gardens where each child could grow and develop a sense of self. Education was to shape children into "vessels of honour or dishonour—to be made the ornament or disgrace, the benefactors or the plagues, the blessings or curse of their race" (Ryerson 1848, cited in Prentice 1977, 32).

Integration of the Class Structure

Early school reformers felt that society could achieve a harmonious hierarchy by providing equality of educational opportunity to the children of all citizens through universal, free, compulsory education. This is not to suggest that they wanted to dismantle the class structure. Rather, they wanted a **meritocracy**—a hierarchy based not on inheritance but on ability as signalled by educational achievement. Success was to be determined by "the fruit of labour and not the inheritance of descent" (Ryerson 1842, cited in Carlton 1983). An early chief superintendent's report echoes such sentiments: "The children of the rich and poor meeting together . . . commencing the race of life upon equal terms" has positive consequences for the social order by inculcating "feelings of mutual respect and sympathy, which divest poverty of its meanness and its hatreds" (Ryerson 1852, cited in Carlton 1983). In this manner, men such as Egerton Ryerson, Ontario's first school superintendent (from 1844 to 1876) believed that they could minimize class conflict and introduce a more equitable system that would ensure upward mobility for anyone with the requisite ability. In Sennett and Cobb's (1972, 77) terms, education would become a "badge of ability," signifying legitimate achievement won in an impartial competition.

Economic Development

Finally, the school promoters sought to assure economic development through the efficient allocation of individuals to socially important roles. Arbitrary class distinctions, which excluded able lower-class people from effective participation in the labour force, were regarded as impediments to general social advancement and economic progress. Members of all classes were needed to create a new, productive, and prosperous social order.

It was anticipated that all classes would better their condition, as tax-supported state education removed the financial barrier to participation in formal education, and upward mobility became feasible for the poor. All classes would be committed to the new Canadian industrial society, and economic growth would result. "Thus it was the whole society, in the long run, that was to benefit from an integrated and invigorated class of labourers in Upper Canada" (Prentice 1977, 134).

The school promoters planted the seed of another economic theme that was to resurface later. The late 19th century saw the transition from a pre-industrial to an industrial economy. This shift meant a fundamental change in the nature of work, which was reflected in attitudes toward education. Egerton Ryerson was concerned that too many 19th century youths were interested in the learned professions and too few in practical pursuits such as commerce, agriculture, and mechanical arts. To alleviate this problem, he and his staff established new high schools and a new curriculum to emphasize the link between school and work. Practical, technical, and commercial preparation for work careers became increasingly important. Education began to be seen as the foundation for and precondition of national economic growth—"for there is no instance of a people being wealthy and civilized . . . in the absence of education" (Chief Superintendent's report, cited in Carlton 1983).

To these ends, Ryerson engineered a number of school acts, which by 1871 had put in place in Ontario a state-funded, bureaucratically organized elementary school system. This system of free and compulsory education became increasingly centralized and standardized during the early 20th century, and was expanded to include secondary schooling. The Ontario model was subsequently adopted by the other provinces.

Education in Canada has become more and more bureaucratically organized. The British North America Act (recently renamed the Constitution Act, 1867) gave the provinces responsibility for administering the system, although municipalities maintained some input and control through their election of local school boards. Each county, through its school

A one-room schoolhouse of the early 1900s. The move to compulsory, mass education dramatically increased the numbers of students and the degree of specialization of the curriculum, making such schools obsolete.

board, hired its own teachers and later its administrative staff (director, superintendents, consultants, and so on). The certification of personnel and the development and delivery of curricula became increasingly standardized, under the watchful eye of provincial ministers of education. As the publicly supported system steadily expanded over the years, educational funding became an obligation of all three levels of government— federal, provincial and municipal.

Recent Developments

The themes of human development, integration of the class structure, and economic development, although expressed in different terms, have remained central to Canadian education throughout the post–Second World War period of expansion and the more recent period of contraction. The belief that a better-educated populace will sustain and stimulate economic growth remains alive in the form of **human capital theory**. The notion of class integration has come to be articulated as equality of opportunity, or **accessibility**—which came to be considered an end in itself during the 1960s. It is seen as guaranteeing the efficient selection and subsequent allocation of able persons to appropriate educational and occupational roles, resulting in maximum individual and collective economic benefit.

Human Capital Theory

Human capital theory asserts that the level of skill possessed by members of the labour force is the major factor ensuring economic productivity in a given society. Increasingly sophisticated technologies necessitate higher educational levels across existing and newly created occupational groups. Increased expertise is translated into greater and greater industrial efficiency and productivity.

Economists embracing this perspective argue that investment in human capital is more important than investment in fixed assets—technology or physical plant. Economic returns to education are realized at both the individual and collective levels. Individual recompense is ultimately achieved through training and work: education leads to a better job and thus a higher salary and a better standard of living. At the collective level, education has potential economic benefits for Canadian society as a whole. This was underlined by cross-national comparisons of educational levels and economic growth soon after the Second World War. The finding that all prosperous nations had high educational attainment levels did not escape Canadian educational policy-makers. They concluded that if expenditures on education led to prosperity Canada could play that game as well as any developed nation. During the post-war period, there was an immense effort to catch up with education in European countries and the United States.

Thus, after the Second World War, education in Canada showed phenomenal growth. Enrolments increased rapidly (see Exhibit 6-1 and 6-2). During the 1950s, the numbers at the elementary, secondary, community college, and university levels grew by 56, 127, 93, and 103 percent respectively. During the 1960s, expansion in both the elementary and secondary sectors continued, though at a slower rate—12 and 91 percent respectively—while community college enrolment grew by 225 percent and university enrolment by 151 percent. The latter increases were a consequence not only of the baby boom generation's passage through the school system but also of increasingly high participation rates.

Exhibit 6-1
Full-Time School Enrolment in Canada, 1951–84

	Elementary	Secondary	Post-Secondary	
			Non-University	University
	(thousands)			
1951	2146.8	394.5	27.6	63.5
1961	3350.4	895.0	53.4	128.6
1971	3759.7	1706.7	173.8	323.0
1981	3069.2	1568.0	273.4	401.9
1984	3024.2	1547.4	313.4	450.5

Sources: Statistics Canada (1980), *Perspectives Canada III*, table 4.1;
　　　　　Statistics Canada (1985), *Education in Canada 1984*, table 1.

Exhibit 6-2
School Enrolment in Canada, 1867–1977

Elementary and Secondary

(thousands)

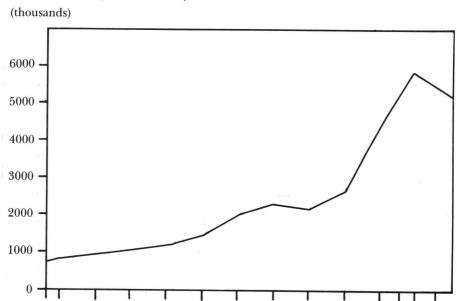

Post-Secondary (Full-Time)

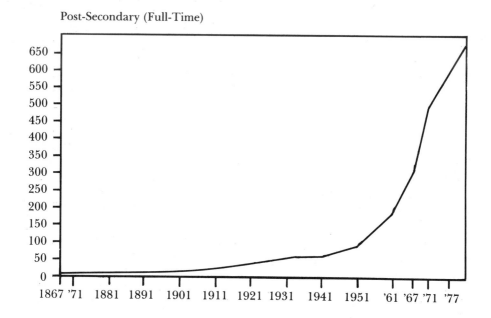

Note: Interpolation between selected years.
Source: Statistics Canada (1978), *Historical Compendium of Educational Statistics*, Chart 1.

An examination of Exhibit 6-3 shows the swift growth and decline in the numbers of 6- to 13- and 14- to 17-year-old Canadians. The former age group peaked in 1971 and the latter around 1977. The population of 18- to 24-year-olds did not start to increase dramatically until after 1962, and began to decline only in the early 1980s. (For more detailed discussion of the baby boom and subsequent baby bust, see Chapter 14.)

It is important to realize, however, that Exhibit 6-3 illustrates demographic change, not enrolments, and that for education the effects of demographic shrinkage have been offset by increased participation rates. For example, in 1976 85.6 percent of 16-year-olds and 59 percent of 17-year-olds were attending school. In only seven years, the participation rates for these age groups rose to 92 and 65 percent respectively (Statistics Canada 1985a). Post-secondary participation climbed sharply. Despite a decline in the population aged 18 to 24, full-time university enrolment grew from 401,900 in 1981 to 450,500 in 1984 (Statistics Canada 1985b).

Expenditures also rose during these decades (see Exhibit 6-4). In 1950, 2.4 percent of Canada's gross national product (GNP) was spent on education. This represented $32 for every man, woman, and child and $116 for every full-time student. By 1970, it was 9 percent of the GNP, amounting to $360 per Canadian and $1207 per full-time student.

During the 1970s, the relative position of education changed. The elementary and secondary levels had begun to decline and post-secondary enrolments to show signs of levelling off (see Exhibit 6-5). Although $956 per Canadian or about $3350 per full-time student was being spent on education by 1980, these inflated dollars represented only 7.5 percent of GNP, a figure that would rise only slightly during the next few years (see Exhibit 6-4). At the end of the 1970s, education was still second only to social welfare as a national expenditure; however, its share of total government expenditures had shrunk to 17 percent, from 22 percent in 1968 (Statistics Canada 1982a; 1982b)—a substantial decline in support.

Accessibility

The educational expansion in the decades following the Second World War was fuelled both by changes in the demographic structure of Canadian society and by faith in the human capital perspective. Another important factor was the pursuit of a more just society, in which everyone would be able to attain the credentials for effective entry into the labour force and the economy.

Any society that espouses education as the major route to social mobility needs to ensure that all groups—religious, ethnic, class, gender, regional, and linguistic—have equal educational opportunity. Only if rich and poor, male and female alike have an equal chance to develop their abilities and human potential can society be assured that the most important jobs go to the most able people.

It is important to realize that the principle of equal access does not mean the production of individuals who have equal training. Equality of

Exhibit 6-3
Selected Age Groups for Canada, 1961–2001

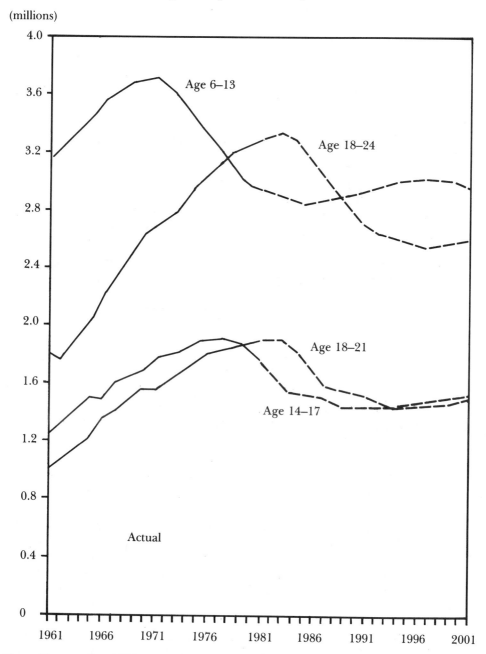

Note: Figures after 1981 are projected, assuming a fertility rate of 1.66 and net annual
migration of 50,000 (see Chapter 14 for an explanation of these terms).

Source: Statistics Canada (1985), *Advance Statistics of Education.*

Exhibit 6-4
Canada's Total Expenditures on Education, 1950–82 (percentage of gross national product)

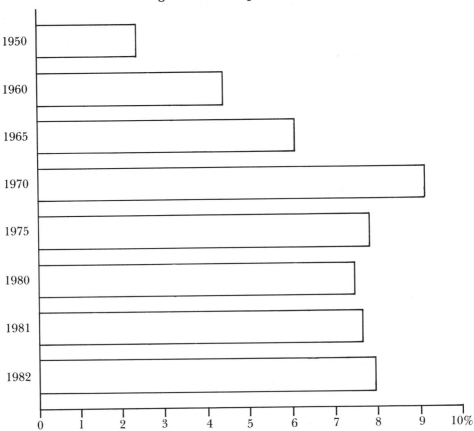

Source: Statistics Canada (1985), *Education in Canada 1984*, chart 12, p. 50.

educational opportunity implies only that all will have an equal chance to succeed at education *"commensurate with their abilities* irrespective of their origins, locality, race or sex" (Pike 1978, 30, emphasis ours). In a system ensuring access to all, inequality of attainment results from differences in talent, interest, and effort, not from unequal access to entry into the competition. Thus, policy-makers felt that if Canadian society was to be characterized by inequalities in wealth, power, and prestige, at least everyone should be given an equal chance to compete for these social rewards. (For a discussion of class and social inequality see Chapter 8.)

The expansion of the educational system in Canada was predicated in part on the extension of opportunities to a broader population base. Not

Exhibit 6-5
School Enrolment in Canada, 1970/1–85/6

Elementary and Secondary Enrolment
(thousands)

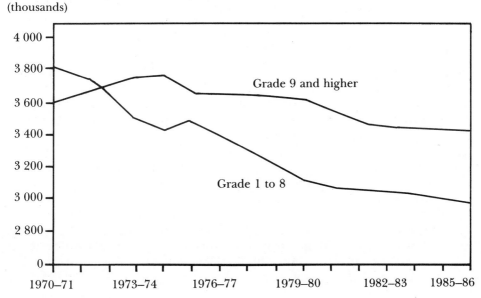

Full-Time Post-Secondary Enrolment
(thousands)

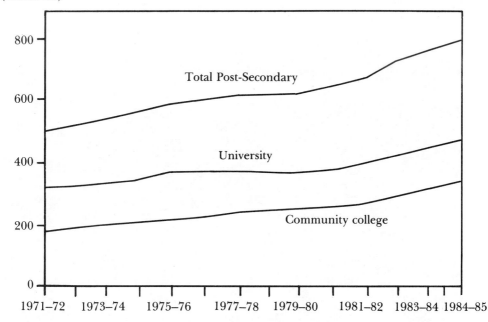

Source: Elementary and secondary: Statistics Canada (1985), *Education in Canada 1984*, chart 3, p. 42; post-secondary: Ibid., chart 3, p. 42.

only was such a system to make individual mobility a more realistic possibility, but society would benefit from a more efficient allocation of talent to positions. Thus, the drive for equality of educational opportunity represented both an appeal for social justice and a concern for efficiency.

Gender and Class Inequalities in Education

Accessibility remains a declared goal of the educational system: whether it has been attained is an empirical question. In a system offering equal opportunity, students possessing similar levels of intelligence and motivation might be expected to perform similarly, despite differences in gender or social class background. Or in other words, the student's opportunity to achieve should not be affected by his or her *ascribed* characteristics (those acquired at birth, such as gender, ethnicity, and family social class) but only by individual aptitude, ability, and effort. Yet do people of both genders and all classes in fact have equal access?

The differences between males and females are small at the lower levels of education. Essentially equal proportions of boys and girls participate through the elementary and early secondary school years (not a surprising finding, given compulsory attendance). Roughly speaking, they are also equally likely to complete secondary school and to enrol there in academic

Vast sums of money were spent on educational expansion in the 1960s; the result was often the creation of cold, impersonal, utilitarian campuses.

Exhibit 6-6
Percentage of Degrees Awarded to Women, 1973 and 1983

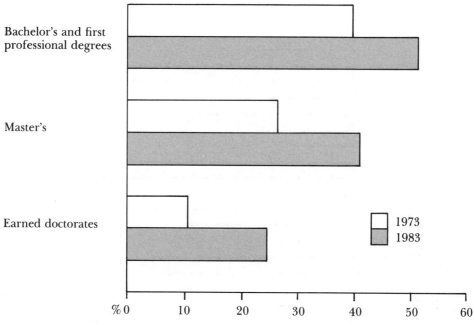

Source: Statistics Canada (1985), *Education in Canada 1984*, chart 21, p. 128.

("university-bound") programs. At these levels, there is, however, evidence that girls outperform boys. Females' oral and written communication and some aspects of their numerical capabilities are superior. Girls fail fewer grades and obtain higher marks than boys. Males are, however, more likely than females both to undertake and to perform proficiently in mathematics and sciences.

An examination of skill-oriented ("terminal") programs and those geared to community college entrance does, however, reveal some disparities. Girls are concentrated in commercial courses, boys in vocational and technical courses (Sadker and Sadker 1982).

Despite equal participation in academically oriented secondary school programs, more men than women traditionally proceeded to university. This gap has, however, shrunk in the past 20 years, particularly at the undergraduate level (see Exhibit 6-6). Slightly more than half of bachelor of arts graduates are now female; however, males account for 60 percent of master of arts and 75 percent of doctor of philosophy degrees (Statistics Canada 1985b). Men are overrepresented in universities' professional training programs, except for those in nursing, teaching, and social work (see Exhibit 6-7). Thus, although male and female participation rates and

Exhibit 6-7
**Percentage of Bachelor's and First Professional Degrees Awarded to
Women, Selected Specializations, 1973 and 1983**

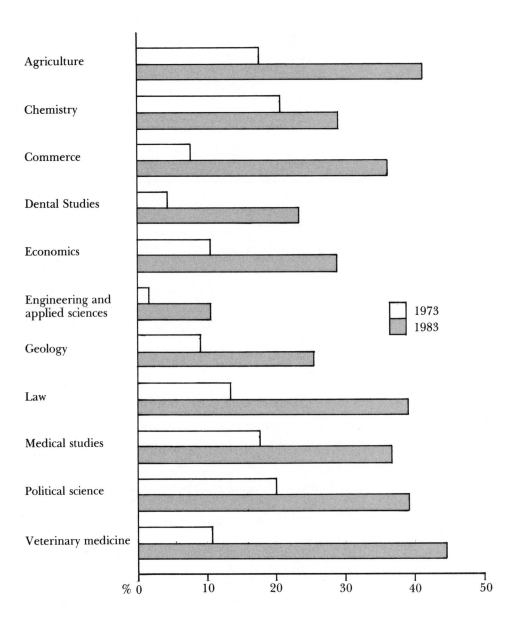

Source: Statistics Canada (1985), *Education in Canada 1984*, chart 22, p. 129.

performance are becoming more similar, differences still exist.

Disparities are greater along class lines. Although the same proportions of lower-class and middle-class students participate in elementary and early secondary school, middle-class students consistently perform better. Even comparisons among students of similar ability and motivation show middle-class students getting higher marks, enrolling more frequently in university-bound programs, and dropping out less often (Porter, Porter, and Blishen 1973). Open access at the elementary and secondary levels has not ensured equal levels of attainment among social classes.

Children from lower-class families are less likely than their middle- and upper-class counterparts to have attended a private school (Clement 1975) or to continue on to post-secondary education (Porter, Porter, and Blishen 1973). Lower-class youths who do continue their education are more apt to go to community colleges while middle-class youths are more likely to enter universities (Porter, Porter, and Blishen, 1973). Middle- or upper-class youths are more likely than lower-class youths to attend professional training or graduate schools. After examining trends over time, Guppy (1984) concludes that recent expansion of the education system has not benefited the lower classes: the class barrier to education is only slightly less formidable now than it was in previous decades (see the box that begins on the next page).

System Rationalization

It is almost impossible to read a newspaper of the mid-1980s without encountering at least one article about under-funding, particularly as it affects post-secondary education. Governments' response to problems of scarce resources has been to attempt to rationalize (make more efficient) educational spending. Governments have sought to achieve cost-effective use of educational facilities by eliminating waste and duplication of programs. The provinces have restricted the money allocated to education ministries. The federal government, feeling that educational programs are not tailored to the needs of the market and that Ottawa receives no credit for transferring funds for education to the provinces, has likewise reduced its support; periodic funding increases once greatly exceeded the inflation rate, but now they are barely above it. (Although education is technically a provincial responsibility, in the past few decades the federal role in financing post-secondary education through transfer funds and technical programs has been substantial.)

Concerns about the allocation of educational funds—more specifically about the relationship between education programs and labour force requirements—were summarized by a federal government inquiry into education and employment, which concluded:

> The overall size of the post-secondary sector is too large and . . . it should be contracted somewhat with resources modestly reallocated from education,

general arts and sciences and social work to engineering, business, economics, and technology. (Task Force on Labour Market Development 1981, 154)

Canadians appear increasingly supportive of this pragmatic approach to higher education. They have come to perceive that post-secondary degrees and diplomas have a reduced economic value when an increasing proportion of the population hold them. With worsening economic conditions, a degree no longer guarantees a job, let alone a good job.

The Quality of Education

The quality of educational instruction and the means of student evaluation have come under fire during the past few decades. As Canadian education expanded during the 1960s and the early 1970s and participation rates increased, the system changed from elite education to mass

INEQUALITIES IN THE OPPORTUNITY STRUCTURE

Although accessibility is presumably more open now, it is unclear exactly how much democratization in higher education has occurred over the course of this century.

One hypothesis, the constant gap hypothesis, predicts that over time, in higher education, the relative proportion of individuals from different class, gender or ethnic backgrounds has remained fixed. While we know that the number of post-secondary students has increased over time, under this hypothesis increases should have come equally from all groups. This hypothesis would be supported by those who believe the educational system has done nothing to ameliorate the attainment chances of individuals from disadvantaged groups.

A second hypothesis, the steadily declining gap hypothesis, predicts that over time there has been a constant narrowing of the gap in participation rates between groups. The increasing numbers of post-secondary students are thought to come disproportionately, relative to some previous point, from one particular group. For example, to achieve a narrrowing of the gap between men and women at the postsecondary level, there must have been a growing proportion of women relative to men in each successive time period, although there may still be more men than women at postsecondary institutions. This hypothesis is supported by those who believe that, with the relative progress of this century, there has been a concomitant increase in the equality of educational opportunity.

A third hypothesis, the accelerating decline hypothesis, also postulates a narrowing of the gap between groups, but considers the rate of this convergence to be accelerating in recent times. This means that, over the years, the proportion of students in higher education from one group increases, relative to a second group, at a *rate* which grows as time passes. For example, the percentage of students from lower class backgrounds, as compared to upper class backgrounds, grows at an exponential rate. Support for this hypothesis comes from those who believe that the rapid post-WW II expansion of the postsecondary system led to a greater democratization of higher education. . . .

The central purpose of this paper has been to examine, using a large national sample, the long-term historical trends in access to higher education. The main findings can be summarized as follows. First, an overall reduction in educational disparities has occurred at the postsecondary level with respect to gender, language group, and socioeconomic background. This is in general accord with the steadily declining gap hypothesis. Second, although disparities have been reduced, they have been eliminated only in terms of differences between men and women in general postsecondary participation rates. Third, with respect to university degree attainment, reductions in disparity have been minimal, with the greatest convergence coming in terms of French-English differences.

These findings raise four important issues: has a dual higher educational system evolved in this country; does the data reveal a trend toward greater accessibility as opposed to an historical anomaly soon to be reversed; what policy relevance stems from inequities in the distribution of opportunity; and finally what does this mean for the place of university education in the contemporary world?

The effects of higher educational expansion in Canada, as this relates to equality of opportunity, would seem to have operated to preserve the place of privilege at the university level. At least for Canadians born in the first half of this century, chances for obtaining a university degree have been consistently better for middle and upper class English-Canadian males. The democratization of postsecondary education, which clearly did occur, resulted mainly from the expansion of opportunities presented by the opening of numerous non-university colleges and institutes. This result is remarkably similar to the dual system of higher education described in both France and the United States . . . and is clearly consistent with Porter's (1970: 329) view that community colleges were "a major postsecondary alternative for lower social and economic strata."

In conclusion, changes in accessibility to higher education operate at two levels. While disparities have been reduced at the non-university level, at the university level democratization has only begun as a slow process. Furthermore, while reductions have occurred, at both levels social attributes remain correlated with both access and attainment.

—NEIL GUPPY

One unanticipated consequence of the ever-increasing demand for educational credentials by employers is that many more people now seek to acquire these credentials. As a result, university degrees, even specialized degrees such as law, have lost their value. Ever greater specialization is demanded, so that the education process is substantially lengthened. Note that the law graduates in this photograph are not all particularly young.

education. It is no longer only a select and fortunate few who advance to post-secondary certification. Although participation rates vary across the country, Statistics Canada (1985b) reports that about 30 percent of Canadians aged 18 to 24 now become involved in post-secondary education (11.6 percent in community colleges and 18.4 percent in universities). In worldwide comparisons, Canada stands second only to the United States in the percentage of the labour force with college diplomas or university degrees.

Concurrently, both instruction and evaluation have become less standardized, and widespread anxiety has arisen that standards and quality have been abandoned in favour of broadened participation. These misgivings underlie concerns about the types of programs offered at the post-secondary level, about the performance of students in university and the employability of graduates, and about their performance in the work force.

Similar concerns are expressed about elementary and secondary schooling. The education ministries of Ontario, British Columbia, and Nova

Scotia are moving to reinstate standardized provincial examinations in response to public perceptions of erosion of quality and standards. The public also frets about a perceived lack of discipline in the public school system. When Canadians were asked in a Gallup poll, "Do you think that discipline in the public schools in this area is too strict or not strict enough?" 58 percent replied "not strict enough," and only 2 percent "too strict" (Gallup Poll 1984).

SOCIOLOGICAL THEORIES OF EDUCATION

Having outlined the origins of education in Canada and highlighted some current issues, we will now examine several of the sociological theories invoked to explain the operation of education in the Canadian social structure.

Structural Functionalism

Functionalist theory presents society as a sizable mechanism composed of various parts. Under normal conditions, these elements or subsystems work together to ensure the continuance of society. In this way, each segment of society is seen as functioning to benefit the whole. (See Chapter 1.)

Structural functionalism applied to education incorporates two related approaches. One examines the ways in which education contributes to the survival of society. The other emphasizes the interrelation of social institutions—including the family, religion, politics, and the economy—that affect, and are affected by, education.

Functionalists believe that the relatively recent development of widespread formal education results from changes in the workplace. The Industrial Revolution, with its increasingly sophisticated technology, meant a growing diversity in the occupational structure—new jobs involving ever more complex skills. To ensure the efficient operation of the economy and the survival of society, a highly skilled workforce was required. A system of role allocation on the basis of ability rather than inheritance was needed if society was to maintain optimal vitality. Education as a formal system developed, according to functionalists, to sort the talented from the inept and to train the former for society's important positions.

The functionalist orientation also views other segments of society as intimately affected by the education system. The economy and its labour force are provided with essential skilled workers. A more informed electorate is furnished for the political system. Some of the childhood training functions once performed by the family and the church are now assumed by formal education.

As noted in Chapter 1, the structural-functionalist tradition commonly specifies two types of functions: manifest and latent. **Manifest functions** are formally articulated and often officially codified; specific outcomes are intended. Education has several manifest functions that are frequently cited.

1. New members of a society need to have transmitted to them their cultural heritage, including history, language, a sense of place, and the norms and values of the group. Through education, the shared non-material products of civilization—ideas, beliefs, customs, and symbols—are passed from one generation to the next, making possible social continuity, survival, and evolutionary progress.
2. Education fosters social and political integration. It helps create a common identity and a sense of belonging to the community. In a pluralistic society such as Canada, ethnic, linguistic, regional, and religious differences are de-emphasized while common shared values and beliefs are stressed, in the interest of a more harmonious and homogeneous society.
3. Education performs a selection and allocation function, assuring that occupational roles are properly filled by screening, selecting, training, and certifying talent. In addition, education fulfils the broader function of allocating social class and status by allowing mobility within the hierarchies of income, power, prestige, and knowledge.
4. Education enhances individual intellectual, emotional, and social development. The ability to think critically and to reason independently are the marks of an enlightened and creative population, able to transcend the achievements of the past by creating new knowledge and new products.

In contrast to a manifest function, a **latent function** has an outcome that is neither formally stated nor officially intended but that nonetheless contributes to the effective operation of society. A major latent function of education is the provision of inexpensive day-care for single parents and two-career families. The education system also operates as a large holding tank, keeping youths occupied and out of an economy that is having difficulty absorbing new graduates. Although it is expensive for governments to support young adults in colleges and universities, it might be even more costly to cope with the problems engendered by a mass of unskilled youths with nothing to do and no perception of a future.

The functional approach to education has been criticized on a number of grounds. Functionalism emphasizes consensus and ignores conflict, say critics. A multiplicity of social groups with various cultures and vested interests meet in the educational arena: is consensus on the purposes and outcomes of education possible? Examples of conflict abound. Teachers and school boards dispute salaries and working conditions. Provincial governments and Ottawa argue over funding formulae. Language and religious groups want public funding to educate their children in their own schools.

A central tenet of functionalism in education is that there is a direct link between the skills required to perform jobs and the development of formal training programs in the sphere of education. This approach does not explain why many employers now call for formal education never used on the job.

Functional theory describes how education functions, rather than explaining why it functions as it does or why it must function that way. More specifically, functional theory speaks as if society were truly a unified system in which everyone works together and ability is always rewarded. It describes the ideal operation of a single normative order, meritocracy, rather than shedding light upon the actual operation of existing societies.

Finally, the functionalist perspective is constrained by its assumption of an integrated system that is in equilibrium. It allows for educational reform only from within the system, neglecting the possibility of fundamental social change. (For more discussion of systems, see Chapter 10.)

ASSESSING THE LIMITS OF EDUCATION: THE SOCIOLOGY OF JOHN PORTER (1921–1979)

John Porter in a typical pose at work. The photograph, taken about a month before his death by Doris Whittaker, was provided to the author by Elizabeth Humphreys.

A major part of John Porter's academic life was devoted to examining the barriers to educational attainment, particularly the barriers created by the existence of social classes. Porter's monumental work *The Vertical Mosaic: An Analysis of Social Class and Power in Canada* was a landmark in Canadian sociology. In addition, a collection of his essays, published as *The Measure of Canadian Society: Education, Equality, and Opportunity* (1979), and a major accessibility study entitled *Stations and Callings: Making It Through The School System* (1982) documented the absence of equality of educational opportunity in Canada. Because these studies were concerned principally with the amount or lack of educational opportunity, rather than with the causes of social inequality in the first place, critics have been quick to brand Porter a functionalist. Indeed Porter did accept the necessity for differences in power in societies and, in fact, in all forms of social organization (1965, 202). Porter also had little patience for the "absurdity of extreme egalitarianism":

> *The simple assertion of extreme egalitarianism, "all humans are equal," is not very helpful since it is both absurd and useless. It is absurd because, over a wide range of characteristics, human beings are obviously not equal; and the statement is useless for analytical purposes if it simply states a circular identity that all human beings are the same as other human beings. It fails to describe any reality, for clearly humans are not equal with respect to strength, naturally endowed intellect, experience from age, physical disabilities, to mention some natural inequalities noted by Rousseau. Thus "all humans are equal" fails as a descriptive statement.*
>
> *As a prescriptive statement that all humans ought to be equal, it encounters many problems of conflicting principles . . . . One does not have to go very far with these questions to see the absurdity of extreme egalitarianism, and so the objective*

becomes one not so much of equality itself as of a choice between different principles of inequality or of distributive justice such as that individuals should be rewarded according to need, according to merit, or according to their contribution to society. (1979, 245–46)

Porter's decision to focus on the role of education in providing opportunity came less from a theoretical commitment than from an assessment of the pragmatic political realities of the times. He simply considered the educational system more amenable to policy manipulation than the system of institutionalized inequality. He opened *The Vertical Mosaic* by attaching great importance to equality of opportunity on both ethical and practical grounds (1965, xii) and concluded that if power and decision-making had to rest with elite groups, at least open recruitment into those elites could exist (1965, 558). Fourteen years later he reiterated:

> *I had always believed that there was no causal link from education to equality of condition, although I had long been an advocate of the view that if we must live with inequality of condition, education has an essential role in equality of opportunity. (1979, 250)*

After a lifetime of empirical research into education and opportunity in Canada, Porter came to believe that the educational system was fairly intractable and actually contributed to perpetuating inequalities of condition rather than breaking them down. In his later reflective essays on education, Porter argued that existing inequalities had to be reduced through other social domains (1979, 260). By this time, research by Coleman (1966) and Jencks (1972) in the United States and by Gilbert and McRoberts (1977) in Canada had demonstrated the importance of the family in the transmission of inequality. Porter felt that these deep-seated and undeserved family advantages needed to be redressed. In other words he believed that reasonable equality of educational opportunity could not be achieved without a reduction in inequality of condition.

Porter, felt however, that the analytic distinction between equality of opportunity and equality of condition, was of questionable utility in the real world, where the two features are inexorably intertwined. Existing inequalities of condition "can nullify the effects of whatever might be introduced to implement equality of opportunity" (1979, 245). Consequently, he believed that neither an emphasis on opportunity alone nor on condition alone would be sufficient to create a just and fair social order.

Whether or not we ought to be satisfied with equality of opportunity and let inequality of condition continue, analyses of both are essential to get the proper measure of any society. (1979, 5)

—Sid N. Gilbert

Conflict Theory

Where functionalism stresses the integration of social institutions, consensus, social stability, and equilibrium, **conflict theory** emphasizes conflict, coercion, and change. Conflict theory argues that the segments of society compete with one another for relatively scarce rewards. Society is composed of various groups that value and believe in different things and that operate under different sets of norms. Change is constant, and stability can be attained only through dominant groups' exercising power over subordinate groups. Groups constantly struggle with rival groups for a greater share of the social rewards of wealth, prestige, and power itself.

Since education represents a major route to social rewards, it serves both as an arena for the struggle and as a mechanism through which powerful competitors further disadvantage the less powerful. Dominant groups attempt to monopolize control of education and thus to bar other groups from this avenue to upward mobility and an improved relative economic position. Conflict theorists scoff at the idea that education overcomes inequality by letting everyone enter a fair contest. They claim that the education system actually preserves inequality.

Two versions of conflict theory are prominent in the sociology of education. The first originates in the work of Max Weber and the second in the work of Karl Marx. Weberian conflict theory sees society as comprising a number of competing status groups, each of which acts in its own interest. Competing groups increase their advantage by acquiring more and more education, which itself becomes a status-verifying device. As a group's level of education rises, so does its chance to acquire wealth, power, and prestige. Thus, a group can maintain its privileged position by denying competitors equal access to education.

Ethnicity, gender, and occupation each represent a **status** (a position in society). Thus, Jews, women, and elementary school teachers are **status groups**. Conflict theorists note that changes in the educational qualifications of these groups have affected their share of social resources. Elementary school teachers, for example, argue that since they must now be university graduates, the increased competence represented by their degrees generates increased confidence from their client groups (students and parents) and entitles them to an increased share of the available social rewards—higher income, more prestige, and a greater measure of control over work conditions.

Conflict sociologists point to the exclusion of certain groups (women, for example) from full participation in the post-secondary education system. They also address the content of schooling and educational decision-making: who decides what gets taught in school? who decides what values schools inculcate in the young? Interest group activity often determines whether or not *Catcher in the Rye* is taught in English classes in St. John's, whether or not the Lord's Prayer is recited in opening exercises in Vancouver, and whether or not evolution continues to be taught in the schools of Tennessee.

The Marxian version of conflict theory stresses conflict between classes rather than between status groups. The education system is seen as a mechanism through which the elite controls subordinate classes. Schools serve the interests of the economic elite by preparing lower- and middle-class students for their roles as labourers in industrial capitalism. The education system steels children to the alienating conditions they will encounter in hierarchical workplaces. Like factory and office workers, students engage in routinized commodity production, learning to "construct" small units in assembly-line fashion without clearly perceiving their relationship to the whole. Students, like workers, have little or no control over their work; they labour under the authority of other people for the extrinsic rewards of grades, which symbolize the money they will work for as adults. Thus, the education system socializes individuals for their future role as workers who are unaware of their exploitation by the capitalist class.

Critics of the conflict approach suggest that the perpetuation of social status through the school system represents an overinterpretation asserted by theoretical fiat. Also, critics argue, educational hierarchies may be influenced as much by organizational and bureaucratic factors or by the division of labour itself, as by control and ownership of the means of production (see Murphy 1979, 135–36). Finally, as Pike (1980, 136) observes, the belief that only a complete restructuring of the entire sociopolitical order can solve problems of inequality leads to a paralyzingly negative view of educational reform.

The New Sociology of Education

Recently, some social scientists have criticized all traditional sociologies of education, structural and conflict-oriented alike, for being macroscopic, atheoretical, pragmatic, largely descriptive, and overly oriented toward policy (Bernstein 1974). They propose a new interpretation that, they argue, remedies many of these deficiencies. These proponents of the New Sociology of Education reject the conventional definitions of problems in education; instead, these diagnoses, by educators, students, and researchers, themselves become things to be accounted for. This approach is based on "the direct observation and description of the processes and content of education in the classroom" (Murphy 1979, 141). Its concerns include:

1. The sociology of the curriculum—the formal and informal content of schooling.
2. The processes of student-teacher interaction in the classroom—particularly how students are socialized (learn to adapt and conform to the ways of society) and what kind of social control operates in the classroom (for a more extensive discussion of socialization, see Chapter 4).
3. The common-sense categories that students and educators use to lend meaning to their behaviour.

Focusing on life in the classroom has revealed the existence of a **hidden curriculum**—an unwritten, informal set of values and norms implicitly transmitted to the student by the school. Children are socialized to be obedient to authority figures, to be quiet and deferential, to be competitive, to defer gratification, and to be materialistic. Success in school is related to the ease with which students embrace these norms. Since these unwritten rules of the game differ from lower-class cultural orientations, it is not surprising that lower-class students do not succeed as easily as middle-class students. Lower-class children, a number of sociologists argue, are distinctly disadvantaged. Even if given equal access to education, they face more obstacles in the actual competition than children of the middle and upper classes.

The work of Bernstein and Bourdieu is particularly instructive in this regard. They demonstrate how language and cultural capital reproduce the class structure through schooling.

Bernstein (1973) links the different attainment levels of lower- and middle-class students to variations in speech codes. He maintains that the language constructions of the lower class are designed to focus upon the immediate in terms of both circumstance and time. Words are basic. Grammar is simple. Sentences are short. The code is restricted. In contrast, the middle and upper classes use an elaborate language code, which is much better suited to the expression, in symbolic form, of complex and abstract ideas. Explicit diction, complicated grammatical constructions, and elongated sentences make this code more suitable for the discussion of the sort of ideas typically explored and evaluated in schools. Thus, lower-class students are at a disadvantage in school in two ways. First, their restricted code makes it more difficult for them to think about and to communicate abstract concepts. Second, since the dominant language of the school is elaborate, it is to a certain extent foreign.

Bourdieu (1973) seeks to demonstrate how broad cultural differences between classes affect the child's school experience. He argues that certain cultural accoutrements are conducive to success and form a type of "capital" that is distributed differently across the social classes. Members of the lower classes tend to possess traits that confer a disadvantage in the race for achievement in school. Lower-class individuals, Bourdieu argues, are more oriented to cooperation than to competition, to material rewards than to symbolic ones, to the present than to the future. They also seem to be less achievement-oriented than people in the middle class. Parents high in the class hierarchy can provide cultural resources for their children that lower-class parents cannot. Thus, the middle-class child enters school already socialized to be competitive, to see the relevance of symbolic compensation such as grades, to work for delayed rewards, and to be ambitious. Middle- and upper-class children inherit the relative advantages enjoyed by their parents; lower-class children inherit their parents' relative disadvantages.

Richer (1982) in his Canadian research discusses in some detail the notion of "equality to benefit." He suggests that equal access to education for all classes is not enough to ensure equality, because the ability of different classes to benefit from the exposure varies significantly. Admitting all contenders to an ice-skating race is laudable perhaps, but those who have seen neither ice nor skates before hardly stand a fair chance of finishing, let alone winning. Richer goes on to argue that an education system that treats all candidates the same way is bound to produce inequality. To reduce social inequality meaningfully, education must compensate those who enter the race handicapped.

This interpretation is not without its critics. They suggest that the "new" sociology is presumptuously named, in that many of its ideas are grounded in conflict theory, and that, like more traditional approaches, this approach is atheoretical, descriptive, and lacking in constructive policy proposals. Links between the classroom and the wider social context are frequently vaguely articulated. Finally, critics point out that the new sociology, while critiquing the traditional approaches, has not put forth many empirically testable propositions of its own.

THE HIDDEN CURRICULUM OF SCHOOLING

First, the child, from the first day of formal schooling, finds himself competing with other children. Differentiation of the children in terms of success or failure is evident in the games played, early printing exercises, proper school comportment and achieving attention from the teacher. Some children do better than others in motor coordination events and are rewarded accordingly. Games such as Simon Says and Cross the River produced a winner—the first, the best in attentiveness and reflex, and the second the best jumper in the class. By the middle of the second month in the classes observed, stars were allotted for especially neat printing, usually accompanied by verbal praise. Show and Tell, a period where children talked briefly about items brought from home, became a period where they sought to impress the teacher with their favorite doll, toy soldier or truck, this inevitably at the expense of their peers. At a more covert level, the children were placed in the position of competing throughout the day for both teacher approval and attention. Regarding the former, children adhering to the teachers' conception of proper school behavior were clearly treated differently from those behaving otherwise. While there were children in the class who rejected this competition for a while and refused to participate,

by the end of the first two months of school all the children were actively seeking the teacher's approval. This was accomplished by the teacher through various types of rewards and punishments.

The institution of Show and Tell, we argue, became a competition along the axis of material possessions. This period, which occurred every day in the classes studied (and in virtually all elementary classes I have observed) was ostensibly established in schools to provide children the opportunity to speak before their peers about an object or objects familiar to them. Confidence in front of others and verbal skills are assumedly enhanced in the process. While these certainly may occur, an unanticipated consequence of Show and Tell would appear to be to reinforce inter-individual competition and simultaneously to inculcate the values of materialism and private property. In a typical session a child stands before the group exhibiting a toy or watch or perhaps a new article of clothing. The teacher usually comments positively on its "niceness" and asks various questions about the object, e.g., "Where did you get this?" "Who gave it to you?" "What is it supposed to do?" and "Does anyone else here have something like this?" For the child who has many toys and games at home this activity becomes an exciting one. He proudly produces possessions day after day. Rewarded for bringing them by teacher as well as peer attention, he cannot help but see the value of material possessions.

The activities for which tangible rewards are allotted provide a clue as to which types of activities are valued in a group. In kindergarten, rewards such as paper stars, animal picture stamps, or colored check marks were distributed only for "3 R" type activities, i.e., letter and number printing and various puzzle work sheets. Play activities, including games and songs, produced occasional praise if well done but no further recognition. In short, those we would term school work activities were associated with tangible rewards, while play activities were not. This, along with the physical centrality of the teacher's desk, the blackboard, and the children's work area, served, I would argue, to convey to the child the primacy of work over play, a primacy to be reinforced from that point on in his life.

—STEPHEN RICHER

ASPIRATIONS AND ATTAINMENT

Not all Canadian students have the same ambitions. Neither, as we have noted, do they experience the same degree of success in school. Both of these variables vary systematically according to region, rural/urban residence, language, ethnicity, religion, and the like. These independent variables are not, however, in themselves powerful predictors of aspiration and attainment. (See Chapter 2 for discussions of dependent and independent variables and of the basis of the regression analysis described below.) There is more variation within than between groups; for example, levels of aspiration within the Maritimes vary more than they do between the Maritimes and Ontario, although the overall levels of aspiration are generally lower in eastern Canada than in central Canada.

To examine the process of aspiration formation, sociologists use multivariate models such as the one illustrated in Exhibit 6-8. This model uses a path diagram to show the causal factors that figure strongly in the formation of educational expectations. The dependent variable (level of education expected) is displayed on the right. Two independent variables, socioeconomic status and mental ability, are presented on the left. The remaining variables are arranged from left to right in the order of their presumed occurrence in time. (These variables are termed **intervening variables** because they intervene between or mediate the independent variables and the dependent variable.) By following the paths from one variable to another, one can examine the process through which each of the independent (causal) variables affects the dependent (effect) variable.

The number above each path indicates its strength. These figures are

Exhibit 6-8
Path Diagram of Academic Stratification and Education Plans

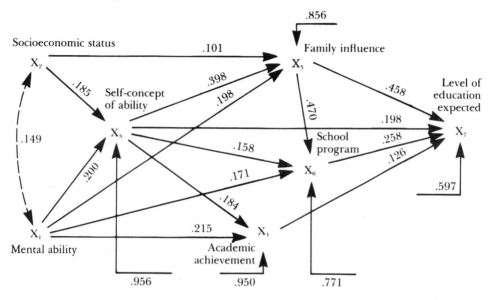

Source: Gilbert and McRoberts (1977, 45).

calculated from the data gathered—in this case, from a sample of students. The procedure used to calculate these numbers is called **multiple regression analysis**. The highest possible value for a path coefficient is +1.0 and the lowest −1.0. Plus signs are customarily omitted from the paths. (All relationships among variables in Exhibit 6-8 are positive.) A positive relationship between two variables in a sequence means that an increase in the first variable brings about an increase in the second variable. Conversely, a negative sign indicates that a negative or inverse relationship exists between the two variables (that is, an increase in the first variable initiates a decrease in the second variable). Paths approaching zero signify that there is no relationship between the variables. Paths approaching zero are normally not displayed in a model; for example, the path from socioeconomic status to school program is omitted from the display, indicating that its impact on this group of students was negligible. (A path diagram may not model every factor believed to be involved in a complicated phenomenon. In Exhibit 6-8, five right-angled arrows indicate exogenous influences—factors that seem to affect the independent or intervening variables but are not measured by the variables in the model. Their coefficients may be high, as they are here.)

Coefficients can be compared in terms of relative strength. Thus it can be said that the independent variable mental ability (path coefficient = 0.200) has a stronger impact on the formation of self-concept than the other independent variable, socioeconomic status (path coefficient = 0.185). Although there is an ongoing debate among researchers about the chronological ordering of the variables in the model (MacKinnon and Anisef 1979; Porter, Porter, and Blishen 1982), the following discussion focuses upon points of substantive agreement.

Research of this type indicates that both ascription (socioeconomic status) and achievement (mental ability) are important in the formation of educational aspirations and in actual educational attainment. (See Chapter 3 for a discussion of ascribed and achieved characteristics.) The influence of performance factors appears to be somewhat greater than the role of ascribed characteristics like socioeconomic status. For example, in the research discussed here, mental ability was measured by a "culture-fair" evaluation, a test that is symbolic, rather than verbal, and hence controls for the class bias inherent in tests based upon language facility alone. Measured in this fashion, mental ability shows only a slight correlation with socioeconomic status (0.149) and has a greater effect than socioeconomic status on the intervening variables in the model. Compare the path coefficients in the links originating from socioeconomic status with those originating from mental ability. It is clear that the overall indirect effects of mental ability (through self-concept of ability, family influence, program, and academic achievement) are generally more powerful than the effects of socioeconomic status through the same variables.

Note that all the intervening variables are important determinants of educational expectations. The effects of both socioeconomic status and mental ability on the level of education expected tend to be indirect—that is, they operate through or are mediated by the intervening variables. (For a path diagram relating individuals' status as reflected in relation to the father's occupation and education, see Exhibit 8-7 in Chapter 8.)

Models like this one offer insight into the relationship between characteristics such as socioeconomic status and mental ability, and outcomes such as aspirations or attainments. They also permit assessment of the relative weights of such factors. Finally, they offer a means of integrating a variety of causes into a theoretical explanation of outcomes. This theoretical model describes how ascribed (socioeconomic status) and achieved (mental ability) characteristics influence structural (choice of school program) and social/psychological (self-concept) traits, which in turn affect aspiration levels. Analysts such as Murphy (1979, 210–11) suggest that such an integration of structural and individual characteristics represents the most promising direction for establishing a sociology of Canadian education.

Results such as those outlined above offer an explanation of the persistent relationship between social class and educational attainment. As discussed earlier in the chapter, this relationship is frequently accounted for by the assertion that education does not offer genuinely equal opportunity for members of each generation to earn their respective places in the social order but, rather, transmits the class structure from one generation to the next. The study diagrammed in Exhibit 6-8 attempts to specify how the middle-class bias of schools or the supposedly meritocratic selection processes affect educational outcomes. In examining the role of school programs, Gilbert and McRoberts conclude:

> The rationale for programs is that they should be an allocation mechanism whereby the more able students get sorted into the more difficult programs and in these programs learn and become prepared for advanced educational careers. As the data above indicate, the family exerts a strong direct influence upon educational expectations and also exerts a very strong indirect influence through its strong influence upon program selection. It appears that the system of differentiated programs in Ontario high schools merely serves to perpetuate the inequalities found in the society in general. The family, through its direct effect upon program selection, serves as a prime mechanism of status transmission. (1977, 45)

Furthermore, according to more radical perspectives, both the hidden and the formal curricula foster in the student the acceptance of hierarchical authority relationships that support the status quo, both in education and in the broader Canadian society. The continuation of an exploitive system of inequality, domination, and suppression is thereby ensured. In short, the liberal emphasis on equal opportunity merely legitimizes a contest between ill-matched competitors; the winners and the losers have already been determined.

Multiple variable causal analyses of educational and occupational attainment shows, however, that any correspondence between class and education is far less than perfect. Some children of working-class parents "make it," and some children of the wealthy and powerful are abysmal failures. Reality appears to be more complex than either the conflict or the functionalist theory would have it. Conflict theorists frequently confuse the persistence of a relationship with the strength of that relationship. Functionalists, speaking of an effective system being produced by the efficient allocation of talent to important positions through perfect equal opportunity, often mistake goal for reality.

THE CURRENT MALAISE IN CONTEXT

Students, educators, parents, politicians, and taxpayers have serious concerns about education in Canada today. There is a widespread feeling that the quality of instruction, standards of evaluation, and discipline are all deteriorating. Declining enrolments at some levels seem to make things worse. People are also worried that education and employment do not seem to mesh well. These issues can best be appreciated in the context of interaction among basic demographic, economic, and ideological factors.

If, as Westhues (1982, 463) argues, students are encouraged to be go-getters but at the same time are given nowhere to go, no one should be surprised at serious questioning of the role of public education. The fact that education could not deliver on the expectations (with regard to employment and incomes) raised by human capital advocates has greatly contributed to the current lack of faith in educational institutions. But the crisis in attitudes toward education has other causes as well. This crisis reflects a deeper social concern—a questioning of the ultimate meaning of education.

Human Capital

Human capital theory is not without its defects. The basic tenet of this perspective is that education leads to greater productivity on the part of both the individual worker and society at large. Recent economic facts have made this assertion more and more dubious. Preparation for the labour market is only one of education's several manifest goals. Moreover, studies of performance in the workplace demonstrate that better-educated employees are not necessarily more productive. Had the economy generated a higher proportion of skilled than unskilled jobs, had the skill requirements of many jobs been upgraded, and had education provided job skills needed, then circumstances might have been different. Unfortunately, the economy has not performed as the human capital perspective predicted. The private sector is not creating many jobs, let alone large numbers of highly skilled vocations. Although employers are demanding increasingly high educational credentials for many jobs, it seems to be more a matter of educational inflation than of skill requirements: applicants are hired on the basis of paper qualifications rather than on their actual ability to perform the tasks required. Is a file clerk with a university degree in English or fine arts more efficient, or merely bored and resentful of the under-utilization of his or her knowledge and skills? Apathy and cynicism are hardly the cornerstones of productivity.

Yet educational policy-makers appear bent on resurrecting human capital theory. Federal and provincial governments alike have diagnosed the current problem as related to the fit between education and employment, and thus to the allocation of educational resources. They have concluded that the post-secondary sector should be shrunk and that disciplines directly linked to labour force requirements should receive greater shares of funding and other resources (Task Force on Labour Market Development 1981). General arts, education, and social work would lose out to engineering, business administration, economics, and technology— areas of anticipated economic growth. In other words, it is now being asserted that productivity is assured not by education in general, but by a certain kind of education—that which provides people with specific labour market skills. Education designed to develop a well-rounded critical knowledge of the world is seen as much less important—perhaps even a luxury we can no longer afford.

To adjust educational systems to productivity goals and material needs is to subordinate education to acquisition and consumption—in other

words, to make it a tool of the market economy. Other equally fundamental purposes of education are neglected. We believe that education
should develop all human intellectual capacities, not just those that lead
to the satisfaction of material desires. Porter, among others, argues that
education should liberate people from strictly worldly pursuits as well as
from other preconceptions:

> Important as these labour force needs are, our model of the just society states
> that the efficiency of the economy does not necessarily have prior claims over
> other desirable ends. . . . In this emerging condition it seems to me that edu-
> cation has a new task not related to economic efficiency nor to humans as
> acquisitive consumers, but rather to their having some measure of control
> over their destinies in the broader sense. (1979, 276)

Finally, one can argue that it makes little sense to fine-tune the educational
system to economic and labour market needs when these needs are shifting and uncertain.

Accessibility

One often hears the complaint that extension of education to a broader
base, while increasing accessibility, has resulted in a reduction of quality
throughout the system. Real equality of opportunity, however, means
equal chances for educational attainment regardless of ascribed or inherited characteristics. It does not mean pushing everyone up the educational ladder with no concern for performance:

> The guiding principle of the Province's policy of financing post-secondary
> education should continue to be universal access to appropriate educational
> services for *all who wish and are able to benefit* from them. (Commission on Post-
> Secondary Education in Ontario 1972, 147, emphasis ours)

Universal access policies, instead of solving the inequality of opportunity
problems, may simply have altered a very important traditional aspect
of education, and in doing so gone astray. In the 1960s, education became
redefined as a purchasable commodity. All that was necessary was that
an individual want an education and the benefits accruing from it. Whether
the individual had the ability to perform became less important. Policies
oriented toward equality of opportunity need not lower either achievement levels or academic standards, but policies oriented toward ensuring
universal access may do so.

Education involves both performance and reward. Education is intended to develop variable human capacities and dissimilar abilities to
perform tasks that require complex knowledge, skill, and reasoning. It
differentiates people along a continuum. In this sense, education is elitist:
only those who can perform ought to advance to the higher levels.

It is surely possible, however, to recognize differences in educational performance without differentiating rewards. The reward aspect of education is the extrinsic, primarily monetary, recompense that is linked to level of education. Although performance and reward are connected in the real world, they are separate aspects of education. One can value education for itself—for the intrinsic satisfaction of learning—rather than for the extrinsic returns that it ultimately provides. The point is that the connection between performance and extrinsic rewards is not carved in stone; it is a norm of our society. If people see a norm as worth changing, it can be changed.

Educational policy and practice in Canada, in emphasizing universal accessibility, may have taken the easy way out. Mobility for all groups has been promised by offering more education for everyone, qualified and unqualified alike. Consequently, the levels of knowledge and skill imparted may have been reduced, and educational attainments devalued in the eyes of the public. But these trends need not continue. Education could be recognized as based on differential performance, but the link to differential rewards could be severed. Such a change would move Canadian society toward true equality of opportunity, while better safeguarding the standards and quality of education.

Interestingly, an increased chance for mobility has also been advocated as the solution to poverty; however, not much attention has been paid to the question of distribution. Giving money to low-income groups was expected to solve the problem of absolute poverty. Similarly, providing more education for all has been expected to resolve inequalities of opportunity. These strategies have not worked. However, Canadians seem extremely reluctant to confront the possibility that giving everyone more education will not solve the problem of unequal opportunity. Before there can be equality of educational opportunity, there probably has to be greater equality in the human condition. Greater equality of condition would ensure that competitors would enter the race on the same starting line, and would finish in order of skill and stamina.

The back-to-the-basics movement, which calls for a return to discipline, standards, and quality, misses the mark. Reinstituting a higher and absolutely uniform set of standards will merely mean that, once again, various groups will have different chances of attaining success because of their initial social advantages or disadvantages. So such action is likely to produce resentment, if not open hostility. Equality is not achieved by exposing all students equally to the same set of high standards, when there are systematic social patterns of inequality. In fact, to do so is to bias the outcome of the competition. Equality of opportunity makes sense only in the context of a fair competition.

A simple raising of standards across the board would serve the vested interests of those who want more elitism, not only elitism of performance but also of status. The correspondence between class and education might thus be strengthened. Indeed, the stable and persistent correspondence between status and education leads some sociologists to conclude that education has come to represent the new basis of inclusion or exclusion from elite groups. Education may simply have replaced the inherited title or the private club as a means of keeping privileged groups closed to unwelcome outsiders (Parkin 1979). Another consequence of universally elevated standards, which some would welcome, would be a reduction in the number of graduates, and thus a lessening of the competition for jobs and an increase in the economic worth of higher education. In short, while discipline, standards, and quality should be ensured, they should not be designed primarily to restrict the supply of graduates (and thus inflate the salaries of those who make it).

In conclusion, the promise for the future appears to lie partly with education as an equalizer of ascribed status differences, partly with education as a means of differentiation that enhances individual abilities and capacities, and partly with education as a liberator that frees people from individual and collective preconceptions and permits them to transcend the structures and ideologies of the past. Perhaps this last promise is the most significant. As Chesterton said, "The chief object of education is not to learn things but to unlearn things."

SUMMARY

Education refers to the transmission of knowledge, skills, and values through formally organized and intentionally structured learning processes. Although almost every Canadian has had some direct experience with the education system, the public sees it as both very costly and often unable to deliver on its promise.

The widespread expansion of the education system that began in the 19th century was designed to develop human potential, narrow the gap between social classes, and produce a qualified labour force for the industrial sector.

Three sociological theories have been used to examine the role of education in society. Structural functionalism examines the ways in which education contributes to the survival of society, and the interrelation of education with other social institutions. Conflict theory holds that since education represents a major route to social rewards it serves both as an arena for struggle and as a mechanism through which powerful competitors further disadvantage the less powerful. The "new" or interpretive sociology of education makes use of direct observation to examine how students are socialized in classrooms and what kinds of social control operate there.

One major concern of contemporary research is the process of aspiration formation and its relationship to educational attainment. Such research remains inconclusive in showing how social class affects educational attainments.

FOR FURTHER READING

Anisef, Paul et al.
  1986 *Accessibility to Postsecondary Education in Canada: a Review of the Literature.*

Catalogue no. S2-161/1985E. Ottawa: Education Support Branch, Secretary of State Canada.
This monograph is an overview of perspectives and current data concerning post-secondary educational accessibility.

Karabel, Jerome, and A.H. Halsey
1977 *Power and Ideology in Education.* New York: Oxford University Press.
This superior reader contains some of the best critical and international pieces, which have become contemporary classics. It also has a fine introduction, "Educational Research: A Review and an Interpretation," and a lively, yet reasoned essay summarizing the state of the art.

Murphy, Raymond
1979 *Sociological Theories of Education.* Toronto: McGraw-Hill Ryerson.
This book illustrates the theoretical ordering of explanatory paradigms in the sociology of education with Canadian studies and contains an excellent assessment. Its breadth of coverage is impressive; it provides food for thought on the future of a sociology of Canadian education.

Porter, John
1979 *The Measure of Canadian Society: Education, Equality and Opportunity.* Toronto: Gage.
This annotated collection has ten of Porter's reflective pieces on inequality of opportunity and inequality of condition in Canada. The final paper, "Education, Equality and the Just Society," is worth the price of the book by itself; it outlines the major contemporary macrosociological issues along with Porter's evaluation of developments in education.

Porter, John, Marion Porter, and Bernard R. Blishen with Maria Barrados, Sid Gilbert, Hugh A. McRoberts, and Susan Russell
1982 *Stations and Callings: Making It Through the School System.* Toronto: Methuen.
This book has the results of an extensive, major accessibility study of 9,000 Ontario students and 3,000 of their parents early in the 1970s with data from follow-up studies in 1973 and 1976. With the excellent data base, a multivariate analysis of the formation of educational aspirations is conducted and implications for inequality of opportunity are drawn up.

Prentice, Alison
1977 *The School Promoters: Education and Social Class and Mid-Nineteenth Century Upper Canada.* Toronto: McClelland and Stewart.
This historical analysis of the mid-nineteenth-century school-reform movement provides a good description of the social and historical context concerning ideological components of the expansion of the Ontario education system.

Statistics Canada
(Annual) *Education in Canada.* Catalogue no. 81-229. Ottawa: Supply and Services Canada.
This annual review of education statistics is a must for keeping abreast of a rapidly changing situation.

Canadian Education Journals

Interchange. This Canadian journal of educational studies is published quarterly by The Ontario Institute for Studies in Education.
The Canadian Journal of Higher Education is a publication of the Canadian Society for the Study of Higher Education.

CHAPTER 7

RELIGION

Stuart Schoenfeld

(singers:)
God is dead, so they say.
He's been dead several days.
Where he's gone no one knows,
But he's dead, I suppose.
He forgave. We forgot
Now he's dead.

(voice off-stage):
  "No, I'm not!"

(Elbling 1973)

We begin with a song and some data that raise sociological questions. For about three hundred years, theologians and philosophers have been proclaiming and interpreting "the death of God." Cultural historians and social scientists have written much about secularization. Nevertheless, religion, as it is conventionally understood, remains part of many people's lives. Religion can be seen playing a role in almost everyone's life if we accept the arguments, discussed later in this chapter, that many activities and ideas that do not at first seem religious actually are.

That Canadians think of themselves as a religious people is shown by the decennial censuses, which include a question about religious affiliation. A time series of results, shown in Exhibit 7-1, gives a statistical profile of denominational self-identification over 110 years. (The "no religion" option was not included in the answers offered on the form before 1971, which may account for the jump in "no religion" responses that year.)

The census data give a very different picture from the one that emerges from counting the number of Canadians actually enrolled as members of various denominations. In 1981, the membership of the Anglican Church was only 23.5 percent of the number of Anglicans reported by the census. The United Church had enrolled only 24 percent of those who identified with that denomination; the Presbyterian Church only 20.6 percent. Even taking into account children, who are counted as part of a religious group in the census but not in church membership data, there is a great discrepancy between census identification and affiliation. Fewer than half the people who are counted as religious by the census are church members, and the gap appears to be widening (Mol 1985, 177, 243).

Another indicator of the importance of religion in people's lives is weekly church attendance. As shown in Exhibit 7-2, which is based on responses to a random survey of the Canadian population, church attendance declined from the 1940s to the late 1970s and then appears to have levelled off.

SOCIOLOGICAL PERSPECTIVES ON RELIGION

Facts do not speak for themselves. Surveys show that many Canadians are church-affiliated and attend services regularly, but that most do neither. Nevertheless, the majority of Canadians continue to identify themselves as Christians. These data raise at least as many questions as they answer. What role does religion play in Canadian society? How does the Canadian pattern of division into various denominations affect Canadian society? Has the role of religion changed with the decline in church attendance and affiliation? Such questions call for a **sociology of religion** in Canada—an explanation or interpretation, based on the systematic gathering and presentation of data, of religious belief and action as a social phenomenon. We will consider several theoretical perspectives on the social dimension of religion before returning to an examination of religion in Canadian society.

Religion and Social Conflict

Sociologists who stress the importance of conflict in social relationships see society as internally divided into groups with different interests. Society is inherently unstable, and changes as different groups constantly compete for advantage. Any social stability is brought about by conditional compromises, temporary alliances, and force.

Exhibit 7-1
**Percentage Distribution of the Major Denominations in
Canada, 1871–1971**

	1871	1891	1911	1931	1951	1971	1981
Anglican	14.1	13.7	14.5	15.8	14.7	11.8	10.1
Baptist	6.8[a]	6.4	5.3	4.3	3.7	3.1	2.9
Congregationalist	0.6	0.6	0.5	—	—	—	—
Greek Orthodox[b]	—	—	1.2	1.0	1.2	1.5	1.5
Jewish	—	0.1	1.0	1.5	1.5	1.3	1.2
Lutheran	1.1	1.4	3.2	3.8	3.2	3.3	2.9
Methodist	16.3	17.8	15.1	—	—	—	—
Pentecostal	—	—	—	0.3	0.7	1.0	1.4
Presbyterian	16.2	15.9	15.6	8.4	5.6	4.0	3.4
Catholic	42.9	41.6	39.4	41.3	44.7	47.3	47.3
United Church	—	—	—	19.5	20.5	17.5	15.6
Other	1.9	2.5	3.7	3.9	3.9	4.9	6.4
No religion	0.1	—	0.4	0.2	0.4	4.3	7.3
Total[c]							
Percentage	100.0	100.0	99.9	100.0	100.1	100.0	100.0
No. (millions)	3 580	4 833	7 207	10 377	14 009	21 568	24 083

[a]Includes Mennonites.
[b]Includes Russian, Ukrainian, and Syrian Orthodox.
[c]Exclusive of Newfoundland before 1951.

Source: Census of Canada, as reported in Mol (1985, 175).

Exhibit 7-2
Church Attendance in Canada, 1946–84

	1946	1956	1965	1970	1975	1980	1984
Catholics	83%	87%	83%	65%	61%	50%	50%
Protestants	60	43	32	28	25	26	29
Total	67	61	55	44	41	35	36

Source: National Institute of Public Opinion (Gallup Poll) data, as reported in
Mol (1985, 179).

The conflict perspective on religion may be traced back to the anti-clericalism of **Enlightenment** social philosophy. The Enlightenment thinkers of the 18th century did not have a uniform opinion on religion, but they shared a uniform respect for freedom of conscience and a corresponding dislike of established churches, which then often used the power of the state to censor views they considered heretical and to punish behaviour they viewed as sinful. Some Enlightenment thinkers proposed varieties of religion that would be consistent with freedom of conscience and with the strict separation of church and state. Others concluded that religion was either a deception or a delusion, a way of distracting the oppressed from their miseries, and a service to those in power for which religious leaders were handsomely rewarded.

In the next century, Marx further developed this critique of religion. Religion, he wrote, "is the self-consciousness and self-feeling of man who has either not yet found himself or has already lost himself again." It is "the sigh of the oppressed creature" expressing and protesting against real distress, but it does not respond to the true source of the distress—the oppression of one class by another. Religion helps to make the pain bearable while leaving the condition untouched. It is thus "the opium of the people" ([1848]1969, 94).) (In Marx's day this metaphor was both novel and apt; the use of narcotics was increasing among affluent Europeans as a byproduct of increased trade with Asia.)

Marx was not the first to argue that religion offers false consolation. But he broke new ground by integrating this view of religion with a theory of economic relationships, inevitable class conflict, and progress. Marx developed the concept of **false consciousness**—an inverted understanding of reality that makes people act against their real interests. Religion is one among many forms of false consciousness that mystify reality. In times of intense social struggle, some religious movements are progressive, in that they justify the resistance of an oppressed class to the oppressors. In general, however, "The ideas of the ruling class are . . . the ruling ideas." Religion is used to justify injustice as the will of God, as a form of false consciousness that legitimates oppressive economic and political structures (Marx [1846] quoted in Bottomore and Rubel 1961, 93).

The feminist movement has also criticized religion for justifying unjust relationships. Male domination of church hierarchies, bias against women in basic scriptures, and biased interpretations of scripture are cited as contributing to the perpetuation of female inferiority. Attention to the religious dimension of male-female conflict has led to studies of female divine imagery and the possibilities of a feminist alternative to traditional religions.

Durkheim: The Functionalist Perspective on Religion

The theory that religion is a necessary part of society was developed by Emile Durkheim, one of the founding fathers of sociology. He saw religion as an activity invented by human beings that serves social purposes. Durkheim's early work ([1893] (1933)) presents a theory of the evolution of social structure to explain the rise of individualism and the corresponding decline of adherence to traditional religious dogma and discipline. Durkheim argues that the basis of social structure gradually shifted from **mechanical solidarity** to **organic solidarity**. Hunting and gathering and agrarian societies, in which status is passed down from one generation to another, have little specialization. Individual villages, even families, are virtually self-sufficient. The cohesion of society is accomplished through common rituals, through shared beliefs, and through living in conformity with shared religious rules and regulations. However, as social structure changes to an industrial economy having a complex division of labour, individuals become more and more specialized and interdependent. Social cohesion develops from their practical, continuous need for each other's specialized skills. There is less need to affirm social cohesion through ritual, common beliefs, and uniform behaviour. Durkheim's research on suicide ([1897] (1951)), as well as demonstrating the possibility of doing scientific work by comparing group characteristics, was important in the development of the sociology of religion. Durkheim points out that there is a long history of self-sacrifice for higher, often religious causes. He attributes the contemporary increase in suicide to excessive individualism (showing that religious groups with a more intensive communal life have lower suicide rates) and to the disruption of social ties. Subsequent work in the sociology of religion picked up these themes of alienation and social disorganization in modern society.

In his last major work, *The Elementary Forms of the Religious Life* ([1912] (1961)), Durkheim develops the argument that a sociological analysis of religion requires understanding it as a group activity. Using Buddhism as an example of a religion in which talk of gods and spirits need not be taken literally, he argues that supernatural belief is not the essence of religion. Rather, the essence of religion is found in beliefs and practices that distinguish the *sacred* from the *profane*. In Durkheim's view, this distinction is a social one, made by the group; there is no inherent sacredness or profaneness in practices or objects. For example, an animal

These volunteers building a Jehovah's Witness Kingdom Hall display the willing self-sacrifice for higher causes that is typical of many members of religious groups.

can be sacred to one group and profane to another. Sacred beliefs, practices, and objects are, in Durkheim's words, "set apart," "profoundly differentiated from," and "radically opposed to" profane beliefs, practices, and objects. The sacred is powerful, mysterious, and ambiguous. It attracts and repels. The sacred strengthens and sustains the members of the religious community, but its mysterious power is also dangerous to them and demands obedience. The distinction between the sacred and the profane is made by groups with shared supernatural beliefs in the definition of religion. Groups without such beliefs can also be considered religious communities if it can be shown that they hold some things sacred and have practices that separate the sacred from the profane.

Durkheim applied and explored the sacred/profane distinction by examining the religious beliefs and practices of a tribe of Australian aborigines. This tribe had a great many detailed religious beliefs and practices, but Durkheim concluded that the totems of the tribe's constituent clans were central and gave meaning to the group's other sacred objects and practices. The totems were a tangible presence of a social experience—the awesome and invigorating experience of group life. In effect, the things held sacred in any society are the things that symbolize the power of the group over the individual. The Cross, the Torah, the Koran, idols, even the belief in God or gods, are all symbolic expressions of the reality and majesty of society.

From this perspective, religion is a **functional necessity**, a social activity essential to the continued survival of society. Sacred rituals and status privileges integrate individuals into the group; myth, theology, and sacred lore interpret their experiences and place their activities within a shared understanding of ultimate meaning. Rules of right and wrong regulate individual behaviour into predictable patterns; sacred objects and activities are a constant reminder of the group's moral authority. Subsequent functionalist studies of religion by anthropologists and sociologists have explored the ways in which sacred beliefs and practices perform these social functions.

Weber: The Search for Meaningful Action

Durkheim's contemporary Max Weber based his studies on the assumption that social action is meaningful—that is, that it involves both subjective intention and orientation to the presumed intentions of others. Religious beliefs are historically among the most important bases of culturally shared systems of meaning that are used to interpret experience. Weber was interested in the connection between religious interpretations of experience and the political and economic structures of society. His studies of the Protestant Reformation, ancient Judaism, Hinduism, Buddhism, and Confucianism explore the relationships among religious beliefs, the societies within which these religions developed and endured, and the social orientations and actions of believers. In these studies and in more abstract work, he developed a vocabulary that has guided much subsequent analysis of the relationship between religion and other social institutions.

Like many conflict and functionalist theorists, Weber sought to develop a theory of social change. He used a distinction between three types of authority—traditional, charismatic, and rational-legal—to argue that the re-interpretation of experience is an important aspect of social change. **Traditional authority** is based upon "the sanctity of immemorial traditions and the legitimacy of the status of those exercising authority under them" ([1925] quoted in Miller 1963, 63). Traditional societies transmit

Most countercultural religious cults tend to focus on a unique, charismatic leader.

their ways of life from one generation to another with only minor modifications.

In periods of crisis—military defeat, economic disaster, failure of political leadership, or the widespread acceptance of new ideas that challenge old ones—traditional authority becomes inadequate. At such times, unique leaders, whose authority rests upon charisma, inspire confidence in their ability to resolve the crises. The term **charisma**, taken from the vocabulary of early Christianity, refers to "a certain quality of an individual personality by virtue of which he is set apart from ordinary men and treated as endowed with supernatural, superhuman, or at least specifically exceptional powers or qualities" (Weber [1925] quoted in Bendix 1960, 88). The message of the charismatic leader follows the formula: "You have been told . . . but I say unto you . . . ." Such a leader, however, cannot be present everywhere to address the many who come seeking guidance, so authority is delegated to appointed disciples. After the leader's death, the disciples record the teachings and interpret and elaborate them into a consistent way of life. The charisma is routinized; old traditions are replaced by new ones. Great religious teachers—Moses, Buddha, Zoroaster, Jesus, Mohammed—are examples of charismatic leaders whose message inspired disciples to preach to a traditional society in crisis. The religions these disciples founded are the outgrowth of the routinization of the charisma of a leader.

Weber's theory is completed by incorporating the role of rational authority in social change. **Rational authority** (also called **rational-legal authority**) rests upon the existence of rules and regulations legally enacted as the means to a socially agreed-upon end. Problems are solved, not by appeals to tradition or divine inspiration, but by analysis and the implementation of new rationally devised techniques. Modern Western society is historically unique in the extent to which it has accepted rational approaches. Systematic philosophy, science, written music, representative democracy, bureaucracy, and factory manufacturing all indicate the rationalistic tendency within Western culture. (For more discussion of Weber's view of authority, especially rational-legal authority, see Chapter 10.) As rational authority pushes back the claims of tradition and charisma, the world becomes increasingly *disenchanted*.

In medieval Europe, Catholicism had been so entrenched in the culture that the Church was able to suppress heretical movements, endure corrupt clergy, and incorporate reforms and innovations successfully. However, during the same centuries in which Europe's feudal economy had been transformed into a capitalist one, the Protestant Reformation had led many people out of Catholicism. As scholars began to consider this phenomenon, many who were influenced by the Marxist emphasis on the fundamental importance of economic change interpreted the Reformation as one consequence of the transition from feudalism to capitalism. Weber also examined the relationship between religious and economic change, paying close attention to the implications of certain Protestant teachings for economic behaviour and developing the argument that religious and economic institutions have a reciprocal influence on each other.

In his studies of religion, Weber looked at how religious explanations of the meaning of suffering—what he calls the problem of theodicy—are connected to social structure. Each religion offers a concept of "salvation"—the victory of the spirit over the brutal facts of life. In Eastern religions, for example, the material world is conceived of as a veil that conceals a higher spiritual reality. Physical suffering, like other physical sensations, is an illusion. It is the highest religious act to renounce worldly pleasure and pain and to withdraw into other-worldly asceticism, an austere, self-denying life that simplifies the pursuit of spiritual insight.

In Catholic teaching, salvation is achieved through confession of sin and repentance. The priests of the Catholic Church are the contemporary recipients of Jesus's instruction to his disciples to preach the good news and offer salvation to all. Some Christians may choose a life of intense religious devotion and renunciation of worldly things. Catholicism honours these religious ascetics and accommodates them in its monastic orders, but asceticism is not a requirement of salvation.

Protestantism originated in part as a protest against what its leaders saw as the Catholic Church's overly indulgent attitude toward the sinful lives of its adherents. But rather than enjoining people to withdraw from the world, Protestant theology urged them to fulfil their worldly obligations in an ascetic spirit. Weber traces the development of worldly asceticism by discussing the psychological implications of certain Protestant teachings. The first step was Martin Luther's teaching that the individual's status in society is not a matter of indifference to God. God calls each person to a particular vocation; in work in society, just as in specifically religious activities, the individual is the instrument of God's will. It is virtuous to fulfil the obligations of one's worldly calling; it is sinful to neglect them.

Weber then develops in detail the argument that a life of dedicated, conscientious work acquired moral urgency as a consequence of the Calvinist doctrines, especially the doctrine of predestination. Calvin taught that God created the world for his own reasons, which are beyond human understanding, and from eternity, ordained that only a limited number of souls were to be admitted to heaven. Human beings can know, through revelation, what God views as virtuous conduct and what he views as sin, but there is absolutely no way of knowing who is among the elect. These doctrines undermine the possibility of reassuring the believer. The deity of Calvinism is so utterly transcendent that instead of a theodicy there is only mystery.

Calvinist theologians responded to the resultant anxiety with pastoral teachings that helped adherents to develop confidence in their own salvation. Each person was duty-bound to consider himself or herself among the elect and to reject doubt as a temptation of the devil. Self-confidence could be developed by committing oneself to doing one's best in one's worldly vocation. Success in work—accomplished for the greater glory of God—was not a way of achieving salvation, but it might be a sign of God's favour; successful people were more likely to be among the elect. Added to this doctrine was the simpler one of avoidance of sin. Sin, like doubt, was a sign of not being among the elect, and there was no priest to grant absolution for past sins. A host of temptations had to be avoided scrupulously. Income in excess of that needed for an ascetic life was an obvious temptation to luxury and self-indulgence, which could be avoided by investing surplus capital in works for the greater glory of God.

Protestant sects that did not espouse the doctrine of predestination also taught that the road to salvation lay through hard work, self-discipline, and scrupulous personal conduct. Some sects offered emotional confirmation of being saved through conversion experiences in which an old identity as an undisciplined, impulsive sinner was discarded and a new identity as a worldly ascetic publicly assumed.

Weber argued that people who accepted these pastoral teachings of devotion to the greater glory of God through dedication to a calling and the avoidance of sin were psychologically prepared to participate in an economic system based on individual competition, self-discipline, economic class inequality, and the re-investment of profit in economic expansion. Contrary to some popular misunderstanding, he did not claim that Protestantism caused capitalism, but only that Protestantism and capitalism were, in early modern history, mutually supportive. The theological injunction to live an orderly, self-disciplined, rationally controlled life parallelled the widespread, rationally planned reorganization of the economy.

Protestant theologians have since led many denominations away from an emphasis on worldly asceticism to other means of achieving salvation. Worldly asceticism, however, is still very much with us.

Weber's studies of the relationship between religion and social structure have been influential within sociology. The issues he raised continue to be addressed in modern literature dealing with charismatic leadership, the routinization of charisma, the problem of theodicy, "the Protestant work ethic," the distinction between churches and sects, the disenchantment of the world, the process of rationalization, and the role of religion in social change.

Secularization and Religion

The theoretical perspectives discussed so far were developed as attempts to explain the changes in social relationships that accompanied the transformation of agricultural, rural Europe into an urban, industrial society. Over a few centuries, Europe developed the world's first industrial economy, inaugurated representative democratic government, turned the pursuit of science and technology into a major societal priority, and exported these social patterns throughout the world, by colonization.

At the same time, Western religion was also changing. The Protestant Reformation and the Catholic Counter-Reformation led to the permanent division of Christian authority. Scientists from Galileo to Darwin challenged religious explanations of the natural order. Religious tolerance was extended to philosophical scepticism. Religious beliefs and practices became a matter of private choice. Sociologists summarize these changes with the concept of **secularization**, which has been defined as "the process by which sectors of society and culture are removed from the domination of religious institutions and symbols" (Berger 1967, 107).

Does secularization lead to the gradual extinction of religion? To many theorists influenced by Marx, the demystification of religion is part of the progress of humanity. The functionalist perspective suggests that the increasing complexity and differentiation of modern society have made societal integration less dependent on common beliefs and rituals. For those influenced by Weber, the increasing role of rationalism as a basis of social relationships and undermining traditional norms (accepted rules of behaviour), is part of the process of disenchantment.

Not all sociologists agree, however, that the end of religion is at hand.

Greeley (1972; 1982), for example, argues that even as dramatic a social trend as secularization is the product of a particular historical era, and that religious beliefs and institutions remain important in the present and will continue to be important in the future. Within the functionalist perspective it is possible to argue that modern, apparently secular societies have sacred beliefs and rituals that, although lacking a supernatural theology, are the functional equivalent of traditional religion. Some scholars who accept the Weberian perspective, with its emphasis on the problem of meaning, believe that religion will endure because purely rational, scientific thinking cannot give value to human activity. Mol (1976), adapting ideas from both the functionalist and the Weberian perspectives, emphasizes a process of **sacralization**, which stabilizes personal identity and social structure by giving them qualities of untouchability and awe.

Two examples from the extensive literature on secularization illustrate how this debate stimulates research. Stark and Bainbridge (1985) examine data on the social distribution of various modern religious groups and conclude that even while established religions atrophy new religions are born. Martin (1978) examines secularization in historically Christian countries and finds that the process has been experienced differently in different places, leading to varied types and degrees of secularization. For example, in the Soviet Union and other countries with secular, revolutionary ideologies, religion, although somewhat tolerated in private life, has become negatively valued in the dominant cultural institutions; in traditionally Catholic countries, such as France, religion, instead of remaining a common bond, has become a matter of continuous political contention between left and right; in the United States, as in Canada, continuing and widespread positive valuation of religion in general is found along with a decline in commitment to the beliefs and practices of the religions with which North Americans identify.

The debate over secularization often hinges on disagreements over the proper sociological definition of **religion**. A *substantive definition* considers as religions only those sets of beliefs and practices that make reference to a supernatural reality. A *functional definition*, on the other hand, accepts Durkheim's argument that any set of beliefs and practices that a group uses to give meaning to life may be considered a religion. To avoid confusion with everyday language, these beliefs and practices are usually referred to as **functional equivalents** of religion. Functionalists have a broader scope in their sociology of religion; since they include in their studies functional equivalents that others exclude, they are more likely to find evidence of the continuance of religion.

RELIGIOUS GROUPS IN CANADIAN SOCIETY

Let us now return to the Canadian situation. We will first use the substantive definition of religion—the one that has been most commonly used by Canadian sociologists—to examine religious groups in this country. We will then use the broader functionalist definition to look briefly at two hypotheses about modern systems of sacred belief and practice: the hypothesis that national societies are considered sacred and the hypothesis that the self within each individual is considered sacred.

Some of the most prominent features of organized religion in Canada are the division between Protestants and Catholics, the divisions within Protestantism, the relationship between ethnic identity and religion, and the recent rise of new religious movements. Another topic of considerable study is what religious identification means to Canadians.

The Catholic-Protestant Division

The division between Protestants and Catholics reflects Canada's history of colonization, conquest, settlement, and immigration. The Canadian federation was created from colonies that differed in religion as well as in language and culture. During the French colonial period, Quebec was homogeneously Catholic. The Church, through the establishment of parishes, played the major role in organizing the scattered agricultural settlers into local communities (Falardeau [1949] 1976). When the British conquered Quebec, the religious privileges of the Church were left largely intact, as a matter of law and of policy. Subsequent colonization brought Protestant settlers to British North America, as a minority in Quebec and as a majority elsewhere. The British North America Act (now renamed the Constitution Act, 1867) protected the established rights of the Protestant minority in Quebec and of the Catholic minority in the other provinces to public support for denominational schools.

Many studies indicate the importance of the division between Catholics and Protestants in the Canadian social structure. As Guindon notes in Chapter 18, from the Conquest until the Quiet Revolution of the 1960s, the educational and social welfare institutions of Quebec society—schools, universities, hospitals, charities—were largely initiated, staffed, and managed by the Catholic Church. These Catholic institutions for the majority were parallelled to some extent by the development of Protestant and Jewish institutions. **Institutional secularization**—the transfer of responsibility for these institutions from religious groups to the provincial government—occurred rapidly in Quebec in the 1960s. At the same time, Quebec shared in a North American, indeed worldwide, phenomenon among Roman Catholics: many priests and nuns left their religious orders, and weekly church attendance dropped.

Elsewhere in Canada, where religious pluralism was an early part of the social structure, Protestant and Catholic groups contributed to the development of educational and social welfare institutions in several ways. In some cases, church groups sought provincial support for religious institutions (as in the case of many early universities and separate school systems in some provinces), for non-denominational institutions that served a Christian purpose (as in the case of Protestant lobbying for public schools to teach the literacy needed to read the Bible and for religious instruction as part of the curriculum) and for new services (as in the case of various charities and settlement houses, which pioneered elements of the modern welfare state). Today the federal and provincial governments continue to provide substantial financial support to the activities of religious groups in the areas of education, social work, low-cost housing, and services for the elderly.

The Catholic-Protestant distinction was found to be a major source of social division in Lucas's study (1971) of small, one-industry towns. These communities, isolated and scattered across the country, are, Lucas argues, a distinctive feature of Canadian society and have contributed to the formation of the Canadian national character. Communities of this type typically had a dual system of Catholic schools and schools that were either officially Protestant or Protestant by default. Since almost all organized social and recreational activities for adults and children were under church sponsorship, friendships and cliques developed along denominational lines. Romances across religious lines were known, and deplored; intermarriage was rare and socially difficult. The people Lucas interviewed frequently made derogatory remarks about religious groups other than their own, sometimes using negative stereotypes and conspiracy theories. People also voted along religious lines, potentially alienating the religious minority from the local government. In communities with particularly large religious minorities, parties put up token minority candidates or even carefully balanced slates. Religious differences were often accentuated by parallel ethnic-cultural differences.

In the 19th and early 20th centuries, major cities such as Montreal, Toronto, and Winnipeg had patterns of religious division similar to those found in single-industry communities in the 1960s. However, religiously neutral settings for educational, recreational, and other activities have now become common in Canada's cities. Many people still live within religiously homogeneous social networks, but many others choose not to. It would be interesting to find out whether single-industry communities are still as sharply divided as they were in the 1960s.

Religion has been important for Catholics as well as Protestants, throughout Canadian history. Contemporary interpretations of the Fenian raids and the Riel Rebellion cast these events in terms of Catholic-Protestant struggles, and the Métis's Catholicism certainly had a part in shaping their culture—and Riel's vision. For a long time, the militantly anti-Catholic Orange Order was a major force in Ontario politics. In Alberta during the Depression, William Aberhart, a radio evangelist, turned politician and led the Social Credit Party from obscurity to power. The rise of the Co-operative Commonwealth Federation (later the New Democratic Party) in Saskatchewan and Manitoba was assisted by its early links to the Protestant Social Gospel movement and the presence of ordained Protestant ministers in its leadership. Studies of voting preferences (summarized in Mol 1985, 285-88) show that, although individual voters shift their support from one party to another, voting patterns at all levels of government constantly tend to follow religious lines. At the federal level, voters identifying as Catholic have tended to support the Liberals, while those identifying as Protestant have tended to vote Conservative. The statistically identifiable effect of religion is a stronger factor in voting preference than either social class or ethnic group.

The division between Catholics and Protestants most recently became a public issue in Ontario in 1985 when the provincial government extended full public funding to grades 11 through 13 of separate (Catholic) schools. (They were already receiving funding through grade 10.) Teachers who opposed the policy (on both philosophical and pragmatic grounds) were joined in opposition by the Anglican and United Churches. In addition, supporters of private schools—many of them under Protestant or Jewish sponsorship—responded by increased lobbying for provincial support for the education they offer, which currently receives no state funding in Ontario.

The strong emotions that can still be evoked by the Catholic-Protestant division are suggested by this poster, prepared by the Ontario Secondary School Teachers' Federation and displayed, among other places, in the window of the national headquarters of the United Church. The diversity in unity of non-denominational public education is illustrated by students dressed in red and white grouped together to form a Canadian maple leaf. The poster implies that those who support non-denominational public schools are loyal Canadians. What inference are we expected to make about those who support Catholic separate schools?

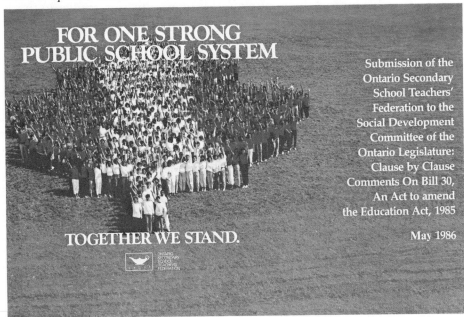

Divisions within Canadian Protestantism

The colonists of British North America belonged to various Protestant groups. Despite areas of cooperation, and the union of Methodists, Congregationalists, and Presbyterians as the United Church of Canada in 1925, Canadian Protestantism remains divided.

In discussing divisions between Protestant groups, it is common to distinguish between church and sect. This distinction appears in Weber's studies of the Christian groups that rejected important features of the Roman Catholic Church during the Reformation. In Weber's terms, a **church** is established—initially it is the only religion permitted by the state—and as religious tolerance is extended, it continues to receive special favour and support. While respecting and promoting intense religious devotion, a church is tolerant of varying degrees of commitment and conformity. Members are born into a church, just as they are born into a society. During the Reformation, the Anglican and Lutheran Churches developed as national rivals of the Roman Catholic Church. The religious dominance of churches was challenged by **sects**—exclusive congregations with doctrines and practices distinct from those of the surrounding society (Weber [1922] 1963, 65). Members of sects join voluntarily as adults, strongly identify with each other as a special group, and are critical of the surrounding society. The church/sect distinction, as developed further by Niebuhr (1929) and Troeltsch (1931), is shown in Exhibit 7-3. In contrasting these two different types of religious organizations, it is important to remember that the definitions were devised to analyze religious change, not a static situation.

Clark (1948) studied sectarian movements in Canadian Protestantism, ranging from the Newlight movement in colonial Nova Scotia to turn-of-the-century urban revival movements such as the Salvation Army. He concluded that sectarian movements were characteristic of unstable frontier conditions in the colonies, the West, and later the growing cities. Former soldiers, refugees, poorer people from settled areas, and European immigrants all sought success in a new setting. Conditions of life were harsh. Poverty, drunkenness, and gambling were common. Demoralized settlers on the frontier found little comfort in established denominations with formal rituals conducted by seminary-trained clergy. Instead they sought emotional release from a powerful sense of sin and failure through the preaching of charismatic individuals, who themselves had struggled against sin under harsh frontier conditions and who taught that it was possible to be saved from sin and restored to God's grace. Religious revivals and evangelistic movements helped people to regain their faith in themselves, to be "born again" into a new respectability. As these movements became successful in re-integrating their adherents into society, the movements began to change, becoming less sectarian in their characteristics.

These findings indicate how the church/sect distinction can be used to interpret movements in Canadian Protestantism. They also recall Weber's

Exhibit 7-3
Characteristics of Sects and Churches
as Delineated by Troeltsch and Niebuhr

The Sect	The Church
1. Volitional membership (emphasis on adult conversion and commitment).	1. Membership largely on the basis of birth (emphasis on religious education of children).
2. Exclusive membership policy—closely guarded.	2. Inclusive membership—may coincide with national citizenship or geographic boundaries.
3. Particularism—judgmental attitude toward those who do not accept the one true path; self-image that of the "faithful remnant" or the "elect."	3. Universalism—acceptance of diversity and emphasis on the brotherhood and sisterhood of all humanity.
4. Small faithful group.	4. Large, bureaucratic organization.
5. Salvation achieved through moral purity, including ethical austerity or asceticism.	5. Salvation granted by the grace of God—as administered by church sacrament and church hierarchy.
6. Priesthood of all believers; clergy de-emphasized or non-existent; lay participation high.	6. Leadership and control by highly trained professional clergy.
7. Hostile or indifferent to secular society and to the state.	7. Tendency to adjust to, compromise with, and support existing social values and social structures.
8. Fundamentalistic theology—only the original revelation is an authentic expression of the faith.	8. Either orthodox or modernist theology—formulations and interpretation of the faith in later periods of history are legitimate in their own right.
9. Predominantly a group of lower-class persons or those otherwise socially disenfranchised. (Worldly prestige is eschewed and spiritual or charismatic qualities become the basis for internal stratification.)	9. Membership comprises upper- and middle-class people, but with professional classes controlling most leadership positions. (Stratification of the society is reflected within the church.)
[a]10. Informal, spontaneous worship.	[a]10. Formal, orderly worship.
[a]11. Radical social ethic—emphasizing the equality of all persons and the necessity of economic equality.	[a]11. Conservative social ethic—justifying the current socioeconomic relationships.

[a]Stressed by Niebuhr but not by Troeltsch.

discussion of charismatic leaders' appearing to groups in crisis and his analysis of the contribution of sectarian religion to self-discipline and social mobility. Subsequent studies of the Social Credit movement (Mann 1955), the temperance and sabbatarian movements (Burnet 1961), and far-left political groups (O'Toole 1977) have found in such groups the enthusiasm, austerity, and self-righteousness of sectarian movements.

Although some scholars continue to use the conceptual contrast between church and sect, others criticize it on several grounds (Wilson 1982, 88-120). It is often not accurate to speak of a particular religious group as simply a church or a sect. A group may have some characteristics of each. The charismatic movements within the Roman Catholic, Anglican, and United Churches in Canada, for example, have sectarian characteristics. Religions that are churches in their native countries may develop sectarian characteristics when brought to a new country by immigrants (Millet 1969). Groups that originate as sectarian movements may develop into churches in as short a time as one generation. Greeley (1972a) points out that the church/sect distinction was developed in societies in which the political system supported an established church; religious groups outside the church were dissenting sects. This relationship between the political system and religious groups does not exist in present-day North America. Religious groups—some of them rooted in European churches, some in European sects, and some in other origins—are all voluntary associations dependent on the free affiliation of members. Sociologically, religious groups that are structured as voluntary associations in a pluralistic society are **denominations**. The United States has a purer form of the denominational pattern of religious organization than does Canada, where some vestiges of the established church pattern remain.

Most scholars of Canadian Christianity replace the church/sect dichotomy with a rough distinction based on size. The Catholic, Anglican, and United Churches, with which about 75 percent of Canadians identify, are considered the major or main-line denominations. These denominations have primarily churchlike characteristics, while many smaller denominations, such as the Pentecostals and Missionary Alliance Churches, retain such sectlike characteristics as fundamentalist theology (theology based on a literal interpretation of scripture), emotional worship, and entry through conversion. The large denominations, however, contain sectarian groups, and some denominations that began as sects, such as the Baptists, have been split by arguments about internal development toward more churchlike characteristics. Many small denominations think of themselves as sharing a conservative or "evangelical" Christianity (Sawatsky 1985). Others, like the Mormons and Jehovah's Witnesses, have highly distinctive beliefs, and still others, like the various Orthodox Churches, are small and churchlike.

Since the late 1960s, it has been argued that "conservative" sectarian denominations are growing in North America. Conservative Christian movements have always had a much larger following in the United States than in Canada, and in recent years some of these groups have become highly visible in American mass media and national politics. Census data show no such growth in Canada, however. Although the percentage of the population identifying with the United, Anglican, Presbyterian, and Lutheran Churches has fallen, it is not because people are flocking to the conservative Protestant denominations. Rather, the portion of the population identifying with these denominations has held steady throughout the century at about 6 percent; although the Jehovah's Witnesses and Mormons have grown, their adherents still number fewer than 1 percent of the population (Bibby 1985, 289).

Ethnic Identity and Religious Denomination

Religious and ethnic traditions are often intertwined, but their relationship is more complex than it may first seem. While it is common to talk about English Protestants and French Catholics, the actual pattern of religious-ethnic identity in Canada is much more varied. Canadian Catholics include descendents of early colonists from the British Isles, especially Ireland, and many Catholics who emigrated from southern Europe at the turn of the century and after the Second World War. Thus, religious tradition is an important bridge between Catholics of French descent and the almost equal number of Catholics of non-French descent.

Religious groups have been quick to adopt the mass media to spread a message of self-growth, development and fulfilment through religion in a more personal way than can be done within the confines of a church.

Nor are all Canadian Protestants British in origin; they include descendants of immigrants from northern Europe, the United States, and recent immigrants from a wide variety of countries. But sometimes religion, instead of being a bridge between ethnic groups, creates internal divisions. Canadians of German descent, for example, are divided into Catholics and Lutherans. Canadians of British descent are found in many Canadian denominations.

Canada is also home to groups whose religious traditions are aspects of distinctive ways of life. Driedger's (1980) comparison of the experience of three such groups in the Prairie provinces—the Plains Indians, the Hutterites, and the Jews—shows how religious issues can become intertwined with minority ethnic identity. In making his comparison, Driedger uses Berger's (1967) concept of "the sacred canopy"—the idea, following the Weberian and phenomenological approaches to sociology, that the human craving for meaning leads to the social construction of symbolic systems that interpret experience. These symbolic systems are shields against the terror of meaninglessness. Religion is the human activity that establishes meaning in the universe as a whole, by treating some aspects of it as sacred. As in Durkheim, "sacred" is defined as "a quality of mysterious and awesome power, other than man and yet related to him, which is believed to reside in certain objects of experience" (Berger 1967, 25). Religion thus acts as a sacred canopy, a shelter against the terror of meaninglessness.

Driedger extends the metaphor of the canopy by asking about what holds it up. The traditional sacred canopy of each of the groups in his study was supported by four "stakes"—religion, ethnic community, ethnic culture, and the group's land or territory.

The Blackfoot

The Blackfoot, like other Plains Indians, lived in nomadic communities on the open prairie for thousands of years. The hunting of buffalo, which provided food, clothing, and utensils, was central to their culture. Through distinctive myths, sacred objects, and rituals, their religion integrated land, community, and culture into a meaningful interpretation of life. The coming of the Europeans destroyed all these supports of their sacred canopy. Beginning in 1871, treaties restricted them to reserves: the Blackfoot were expected to become farmers or ranchers instead of nomads. The buffalo were hunted to virtual extinction. Missionaries, backed by white authorities, suppressed traditional beliefs and practices and substituted Christian ones. The sacred canopy of the Blackfoot was rapidly destroyed.

Other scholars (Shimpo 1976; Bock 1976; Vallee 1976; Warburton 1976) have written about traditional Indian and Inuit religion and about the mixed effects of institutionalized Christianity on the lives of native peoples. The Canadian experience has followed a pattern common in colonial and third world settings. Established churches—in Canada, the Catholic and Anglican churches—took the lead in converting the natives. Traditional religious beliefs were looked upon as savage superstitions to be eliminated. Heroic martyrs and dedicated missionaries lived and died for the faith they preached. Colonial authorities supported missionary work as a means of controlling the indigenous people; thus there were many nominal and reluctant conversions. More recently, the churches have been criticized for their role in undermining the self-reliance and self-respect of indigenous peoples. Some Indians and Inuit have revived aspects of traditional religion—rituals, myths, and beliefs. Small but intense religious groups, such as Pentecostal movements, have challenged the local monopolies of the large denominations. In response to internal and external criticism, many major denominations have developed new approaches to better ally themselves with the indigenous congregations they serve.

The Hutterites

Hutterite colonies are found in Manitoba, Saskatchewan, and Alberta, as well as in the adjacent American states. Hutterites came to North America in 1874, almost three hundred years after their society was founded during the Protestant Reformation. Their interpretation of Christianity teaches pacifism and communal ownership of property. They established communal settlements in Europe but were periodically persecuted in and expelled from several countries. In Canada, they have established more than 150 agricultural colonies of one hundred or more members. Within such a colony, all aspects of life are expressions of their religion. Even dress is prescribed by religion. Hutterites preserve 16th-century German styles: the women wear long dresses, shawls, and polka dot kerchiefs over hair parted in the middle and braided; the men wear suspenders and distinctive hats and hair styles. The preacher, who is elected, is the leader of the colony, with the farm boss second in authority. To minimize the intrusion of outside values, the group prohibits television, radio, and record players. The Hutterites have, however, adopted modern farming techniques. The combination of simple living, collective work, and modern techniques has made Hutterite colonies economically stable. This distinctive group has successfully transferred its canopy supports—land, community, culture, and religion—from Europe to North America (Driedger 1980, 346-47).

The Jews

Since the Roman destruction of Jerusalem almost two thousand years ago, Jews have resisted absorption into pagan, Muslim, and Christian societies. Their religious separatism required some territorial and cultural

CHRISTIANITY AND CANADIAN INDIANS: A CRITICAL VIEW

The speaker is an elderly Cree.

I personally think religion is a good thing. Man should be humble before the gods. But we cannot understand what the missionaries are trying to do. . . .

According to our grandparents, our ancestors knew that other Indians worshipped different gods from ours, but they never declared that they should not worship these gods. And men of other tribes never criticized our god and asked us to worship their god. In the past, Indians sometimes fought among each other, but they did not interfere with others' religions. . . .

The Bible tells us, "All men are brothers and sisters," "God is love and men are all sinners," and so on. . . . It follows that men should love each other instead of judging each other. We quite agree with the teaching.

But look at what the missionaries are doing. What they tell us to do is different from what they are actually doing. On this reserve, the Anglican Church has been the only church. According to the missionaries, all other churches but Anglican are wrong. If you go to the neighbouring reserve, the Roman Catholic missionaries will tell you the same thing, claiming that the Roman Catholic Church is the only right one. Under these circumstances, can you believe the missionaries from different churches love each other as their brothers? It seems to me they hate each other as if others are a bunch of devils. . . .

We feel particularly bitter when the missionaries say all men are created equal. Do whites really believe Indians are equally created by the Christian God? Some whites criticize us that we do not have good education: this is true. As some other whites say, we do not farm as well as the white farmers do. We are more frequently drunken than the whites are. But a number of whites are like some of us. And, even the ignorant, poor, and drunken whites despise us because we are Indians. They look at us as if we Indians are a kind of animal. . .

You may not know this, but our religion is quite close to Christianity. This is why I like Christianity. But I do not like what the whites do. By this I include missionaries. It seems to me that missionaries are concerned with their achievement only, and that they regard the number of Indian converts as the criterion of their achievement. In brief, they use us as a means of their personal success. If this is the case, why should we not use missionaries for our purpose as well? Indeed, we do. When the missionaries promise some gifts, we go to church to get it. When they do not offer anything, we do not go.

—MITSURU SHIMPO

cohesion. For example, dietary laws, the prohibition of travel on holy days, the requirement of communal prayer in Hebrew, and the high value placed on group study of sacred texts throughout life meant that the requirements of Judaism could be met properly only in a neighbourhood that included other Jewish families and was organized to meet their special religious needs. Persecution—in pagan countries for their stubborn monotheism and in Christian and Muslim countries for their refusal to acknowledge these new revelations—forced Jews into segregated residential districts and fostered cultural distinctiveness. The secular Jewish languages of Yiddish in Central and Eastern Europe and Ladino (Judeo-Spanish) in the Iberian peninsula and North Africa developed alongside the holy language of Hebrew, which was restricted to religious uses. But Jews were not insulated from cultural developments in the surrounding society. Modern intellectual and political thought profoundly affected Jewish life. Zionism transformed the ancient prayers for the restoration of a Jewish homeland into a secular nationalist movement. Scepticism and tolerance led to the division of modern Judaism into the three branches of Reform, Conservative, and Orthodox, and to Jewish participation in revolutionary movements that promised a radically new society based on non-religious values.

Jews on the Canadian Prairies are mainly descendants of turn-of-the-century immigrants from Eastern Europe. Some, however, are more recent survivors of the Holocaust[1] or refugees from North Africa or the Soviet Union. The transformation of their sacred canopy, which began in Europe, has continued. Religion, community, culture, and land all continue to support it in Canada, but in a modified form. Relatively few people attend synagogue regularly or observe the dietary laws or most other ritual practices. The use of Yiddish has virtually, though not entirely, disappeared. On the other hand, synagogue affiliation is conventional; religious educational standards have improved; the Holocaust is remembered as a collective disaster; the sense of shared fate with the Jews in Israel and elsewhere is very strong; there are numerous active and efficient communal and cultural organizations; in-group marriage and in-group friendship rates remain comparatively high. While most Jews live in neighbourhoods less distinctively Jewish than the immigrant ghettos of earlier generations, they still concentrate in Canada's largest cities. The traditionally strong separation between Jews and non-Jews has been replaced by a variety of choices, including secular Zionism and various branches of Judaism, which allow different adaptations to Canadian society. Within Canada, as elsewhere, the Jewish sacred canopy has been partitioned into sections in which experience is interpreted in different ways, but it is still possible to move from one area of the canopy to another.[2]

The three groups discussed above are examples of how sacred canopies can change. The Plains Indians had theirs destroyed, and are faced with the task of reconstruction. The Hutterites transferred theirs to a new agricultural enclave. The Jews transformed and adapted theirs (Driedger 1980, 343).

New Religious Movements

In recent years, groups collectively called either cults or new religions have received a great deal of publicity. (The word cult is often used in a pejorative sense; yet many so-called cult groups want to be considered religions with the same status in society as Christian denominations.)

Beginning in the early 1970s, a group of researchers studied a wide range of new movements in Montreal. The researchers called these groups "religious and para-religious" because, while all "utilize to some degree ritual practices or techniques which have been integral to one or more of the great religious traditions," some presented themselves as religions, some did not, and some gave ambiguous messages (Bird 1977, 448; Bird and Reimer 1976).

Bird and Reimer (1982) divide these movements into four categories. The first includes Charismatics, Jesus groups, and the Lubavitcher Chassidim, who all practise new or unusual forms of worship but hold to the prevailing beliefs of some denominational religion. Groups in the second category, which the analysts call countercultural, engage in worship based on imported or unconventional beliefs; this category includes Baha'is, Spiritualists, and various groups based on Buddhist, Hindu, or Muslim teachings. The third category consists of groups such as EST, ARICA, Silva Mind Control, and Psychosynthesis, which teach apprentices how to reach sources of power and well-being that lie within themselves. Apprenticeship groups use ideas and practices related to transcendentalism, occult wisdom, gnosticism, and transpersonal psychology. Groups in the fourth category, which include Yoga groups, T'ai Chi groups, Vedanta meditation groups, and Zen centres, base their teachings on Eastern religions and aim at developing the disciple's self-mastery and harmony of mind and body. The groups in the first two categories present themselves as religions. While the groups in the third and fourth categories use ideas and practices from religious traditions, they are not worship groups, but settings for personal development.

In 1975, 1607 adults who had registered, mainly for evening classes, at Concordia University in Montreal completed a questionnaire about participation in a given list of groups of the types discussed above. Almost 32 percent replied that they had participated in one or more of these groups. Taking into account the special characteristics of their sample, Bird and Reimer estimated that about 20 percent of the general Montreal population had participated in such groups, a figure suggesting that new religions hold considerable appeal.

The lowest rates of participation were, however, in groups in the countercultural category, which are the only groups that explicitly present themselves as alternative religions. The highest rates of participation were in the apprenticeship and discipleship groups, which do not present themselves as religions. More than 75 percent of those surveyed reported that they no longer participated. This high drop-out rate might be expected of groups that emphasize skill acquisition, but it also applied to those presenting themselves as religions.

The tentative commitment of most participants to new religious and para-religious movements is indicated in the responses of nine groups surveyed in 1980 (Bird and Reimer 1982). The responses, given in Exhibit 7-4, show a small inner core and a much higher number of various types of affiliates—students, clients, initiates, occasional attenders, and even passive audiences. Within these nine groups, those with the largest core of members were a charismatic Christian group and two skill development groups—Sivananda Yoga and Transcendental Meditation. The alternative religions of Krishna Consciousness, the Spiritual Healing Church, and the followers of Sri Chinmoy were much smaller.

Westley (1983) examined in detail six groups—Psychosynthesis, ARICA, EST, Shakti, Silva Mind Control, and Scientology—which Bird and Reimer (1982) include in their category of "apprenticeship group." These groups have distinctive organizational principles and beliefs. Individuals participate by paying fees for courses, which are by nature transient structures. The groups believe that they are using scientific techniques to purify the

Exhibit 7-4
Participation in a Selection of New Religions and Para-Religious Movements, Montreal, 1980

	Numbers of Affiliates	Numbers of Members	Type of Members
Krishna Consciousness	800	66	Householders, Celibates
Spiritual Healing Church	200	36	Regulars
LaJourdain (Charismatic)	1 500	310	Staff plus an estimate of those most directly involved
National Research Institute for Self-Understanding (Palmistry)	3 950	50	Staff, mediators, members
International Meditation Institute	200	90	Core, regulars
Transcendental Meditation (those ever initiated)	14 725	275	Instructors, Siddhis
Integral Yoga Institute	300	56	Premonastics, monastics, close members
Sivanada Yoga (on mailing list)	7 000	204	Staff, regulars
Sri Chinmoy Followers	70	25	Initiated

Note: Participation data as reported by groups themselves. The high drop rate from these movements means that the actual number of persons who still consider themselves to be affiliates is probably less than half the number of those reported by the group themselves.

self and to properly relate the self, through internal psychological processes, to others.

Westley sees a connection between these groups and Durkheim's prediction of a "cult of man" emerging in complex societies. Durkheim argued that, as society becomes more differentiated and specialized, and people come to feel that they have little in common besides their sheer humanity, the sacred symbols of group unity would become more abstract. In the religion that would emerge, the human individual would be idealized, worshipped, and held sacred. In the "cult of man," humanity would be "invested with that mysterious property which creates an empty space around holy objects which keeps them away from profane contacts and draws them from ordinary life" (Durkheim quoted in Westley 1983,6).

The groups studied by Westley clearly locate the sacred within the human individual. This sacred self, which has considerable powers if properly reached, is distinct from the machine-like profane self imposed by society. Some of the rituals of "cult of man" groups purify the sacred self from the contamination caused by the fragmented, unsystematic social roles imposed by a "mechanized, rationalized, artificial, inanimate" (Westley 1983, 133) profane world. Other rituals develop the ability of the sacred self to manipulate the machine-like self in social life, or enact the transformation of the person into someone whose sacred self has mastered and transcended the segmented, inconsistent experience of life.

Describing these groups as "cults of man" implies that they are alternative religions, in competition with established religions. This may be true for their small cores of members, but it does not appear to be the experience of most participants. In the Bird and Reimer survey, most of those who reported participating in apprenticeship and discipleship movements continued to identify themselves as Christians. More than 25 percent reported participating in more than one group. Most participants in "cult of man" groups did not commit themselves to a comprehensive system of meaning or to the discipline of continuing group life. Rather, participation was a compartmentalized experience, a fragment of the individual's biography.

Secularized Religion

The Canadian denominational pattern seems to be quite stable. Most people identify with the religion of their parents. Of those who say they have no religion, many are young adults who are likely to identify with a conventional religion later in life, often after marrying (Bibby and Weaver 1985, 454). Seekers after religion who change their lives by joining sectarian movements or new religions are statistically rare. The most notable statistical change has been the growing proportion of the Canadian population (almost half) that identifies with the Roman Catholic Church, but this change is explained by immigration and birth rates.

CHURCHES PRACTISING TOO MUCH INSTITUTIONAL COERCION

Blackmail is not a nice word. But a number of clergy and churches now use a kind of emotional blackmail on people who don't attend yet want some service or rite.

For example, the non–church-going couple who request a traditional wedding are often made to feel they are religious lepers.

They have to attend classes, services—the works—to get what they really are after. If they can accept or jump through the required hoops, they still end up paying more for the actual wedding than those who are a visible part of the flock.

A little of this may be understandable. As the book says, "Marriage is not to be taken in hand unadvisedly, lightly, or wantonly. . . . " And somebody has to pay for the building to be there the rest of the time; somebody has to sweep up the confetti.

Still, there is far too much institutional coercion going on. People regarded as "outsiders" are being forced to conform. They do so only because their life situation or need makes them vulnerable to manipulation.

For any priest or minister knowingly, or even unconsciously, to exploit this vulnerability is wrong. It's a tempting, but faulty, use of power.

The blackmail is yet more obvious and un-Christian when it comes to having babies baptized or christened.

Thousands of parents and families are being compelled to take lengthy instruction sessions and to promise to attend and support the church in question.

Otherwise, the request for the child's baptism is turned down flatly. I know from readers and my many contacts that frequently the denial is blunt, almost to the point of rudeness.

Formal religion, powerless in virtually every other way to make society do its bidding, knows it can still make this particular whip crack.

I suppose it might be great if everybody wanted to go to church.

Parents ought to find out ahead of time what it is they profess to be doing when they make baptismal vows on behalf of their offspring.

I can comprehend the irritation of clergy who at times feel they are being used by people to get little Johnny "done" so that they can have a big family party and finally satisfy the grandparents.

The heirloom christening robe is brought out of mothballs once again.

I well remember having to bite my tongue occasionally when I had a parish myself. In the middle of a hectic schedule you would get a call from somebody you had never seen or heard of literally demanding to have the baby done. Once or twice they had already set a date!

There was a strong impulse to say facetiously: "Yes, and how would you like the little nipper done—well, medium or rare?"

But, in those days, we never refused anybody. The service itself quotes Jesus' saying: "Let the young children come unto me."

In fact, I baptized so many babies some Sundays at my suburban church that a few of the more staid, old-time members used to object loudly at every annual meeting.

I continued to get my way, but there were some baptismal services where I was careful not to meet their critical eyes.

That was a while ago. Today, the churches are taking a much stricter line. Some of them defend it as tough love or "taking our theology more seriously."

Whatever the justification, it is a mistake. To turn people away or take a power trip at their expense is a missed opportunity to serve.

The church was never meant to be some kind of exclusive elitist club. Its true nature is to be the one institution or community that exists for the sake of those who don't belong.

—TOM HARPUR

It should be noted, however, that stability in religious identification conceals low levels of involvement.

Nation-wide surveys, conducted by Bibby in 1975 and 1980, explored religious commitment in Canada. The findings on church affiliation and attendance are consistent with those given at the beginning of this chapter: although more than 90 percent of Canadians identify themselves as Christian, fewer than half belong to local churches and fewer than a third attend on a regular weekly basis (Bibby 1983, 2). The surveys also found that less than half the population, including many who are church-affiliated, hold such traditional Christian beliefs as the existence of God, the divinity of Jesus, and life after death (Bibby 1983, 7). In part, this finding reflects the influence on liberal Protestantism of theology that places ethics, rather than supernatural belief, at the core of Christianity, but it also indicates a gap between official church teaching and the actual beliefs of adherents. In addition, many of those surveyed reported that they never or only occasionally thought about questions of ultimate meaning and purpose in life. And when respondents were asked whether they had found the answer to life's meaning, almost half chose the response, "I don't think there's an answer" (Bibby 1983, 10).

These data lead Bibby to conclude that Canadian Christians fall into two broad categories. Some are the highly committed minority, who are likely to be members of a congregation, who attend church regularly, and for whom Christianity provides an authoritative meaning system. The other category consists of a growing number who "draw upon Christian belief, practice and organizational fragments" (Bibby and Weaver

1985, 457). This piecemeal appropriation of Christianity is parallelled by the use of fragments of astrology, psychic phenomena (ESP, precognition, telepathy), and magic, without a commitment to beliefs and practices that place these supernatural phenomena into a meaningful system.

This pattern of fragmented, eclectic, and tentative religiosity substantially qualifies the statistical stability of Canadian religious identification. For many Canadians, religion, rather than giving meaning to all of life, is one aspect of identity, relevant in limited situations, such as the life-cycle transitions of birth, marriage, and death. Personal identity does not rest on identification with a community that shares sacred values and practices, but on the systematic pursuit of such individual goals as well-being and affluence. In this sense, Canadians may be said to have become more secular, without having given up religion.

THE RELEVANT CHURCH: DENOMINATIONS AND SOCIAL ISSUES

Throughout Canadian history, individual denominations and religious coalitions have taken stands—sometimes conservative, sometimes reformist, sometimes radical—on social issues. Although researchers have studied past denominational involvement in social issues, the modern sources and consequences of religious social activism in Canada remain largely unexplored.

With a large percentage of the population now participating only peripherally in religious activities, the significance of church involvement in social issues may be changing. It has been argued that the real religious issues of our time are issues not of doctrine or ritual but of personal and social ethics. If this is true, the argument continues, religious denominations must speak publicly to these issues. Their success is to be judged not by their ability to fill up their churches on Sunday mornings but by their contribution to the morality of public policy.

In many parts of the world, religious groups are deeply involved in political and social issues. Groups seeking the establishment of political systems based on Islamic law are found in the wide arc from Afghanistan to North Africa. In Israel, political parties representing the Orthodox minority have used their parliamentary balance of power to win concessions from the secular majority. The Catholic Church in Poland plays an important role in the resistance to Soviet authority. In the Philippines, Catholic Church support was crucial to the transfer of power to Corazon Aquino. In Latin America, the theology of liberation serves to ally many members of the Catholic clergy with political movements that are striving to transform oligarchical, capitalist societies into egalitarian, socialist ones. In many countries, minority groups seeking independence or autonomy appeal for support on the dual basis of ethnicity and religion. Closer to home, the "moral majority" in the United States actively campaigns for

To many religious groups, the social issues of the day are of more immediate concern than doctrinal issues.

conservative domestic and foreign policies, while the National Council of Churches has a history of support for liberal ones.

Religion, social activism, and sociology have long been linked. Much of the early sociology in North America developed from the interest of religious groups in social issues, and today many religious writers use sociological theories and findings. Religious writers committed to social action, including the Canadian priest and sociologist Gregory Baum (1975), have called for a sociology directly critical of social injustice and alienation.

THE WIDENING SCOPE OF THE SOCIOLOGY OF RELIGION

For those who use a functionalist definition of religion, the sociology of religion extends beyond the study of groups that call themselves religions. In the following section, we examine the hypothesis that beliefs and practices about the nation and the self may be considered functional equivalents of religion, operating in combination with denominational religions or in explicit or implicit opposition to them.

The Sacred Country: Civil Religion and Political Religion

Traditionally, religion and the state viewed each other as natural allies, parallel instruments of God's (or the gods') will. Religion legitimated the social order, giving it moral authority, and the state granted privileges and support to religion, often in the form of an established church.

Most historically Christian countries have now separated church and state and treat religious conviction as a matter of private conscience. In other countries, the political regime works toward the elimination of religion. It seems, then, that religion is no longer fulfilling its function of unifying society. Some social scientists argue, however, that, in a religiously pluralistic society, a functional equivalent of religion may transcend differences and unite the people in a common sacred task; in an officially atheistic society, social unity may be expressed and dramatized through a political religion.

Civil Religion in the United States

In a religiously heterogeneous society, no one religion can serve as the symbol of societal unity. Bellah (1970, 1975) argues that the United States has developed a "civil religion" to fulfil this function. American civil religion has its sacred texts (the Declaration of Independence, the Constitution), its sacred history of moral purification (the War of Independence, the Civil War), its rituals (pledging allegiance to the flag), its holidays (Independence Day, Memorial Day), its saints (Washington and Jefferson), its martyrs (Kennedy and King), its shrines (Arlington Cemetery, the Gettysburg battlefield) and a central belief: that America stands for ennobling ideals and has a sacred mission to live by these ideals and to spread them.

The American civil religion does not challenge conventional religiosity. Its documents and leaders acknowledge God and the obligation of America to do God's will. It assumes that in their private lives Americans will continue to differ in their conceptions of God, but that all Americans, regardless of formal religious identification, can share an understanding of their national society as a meaningful, moral entity.

Political Religion in the USSR

The government of the Soviet Union, while tolerating the stubborn commitment of some of its population to traditional religions, has developed its own alternative beliefs, objects, and rituals around the sacredness of the state. Its beliefs are based on communist ideology, as found in canonical texts and commentaries. Just as students at Catholic universities used to take compulsory courses in theology and dogma, students at Soviet universities must study Marxism-Leninism. The lives of the Soviet Union's saints and martyrs—above all Lenin—and its struggle for survival are the elements of a sacred history. Red banners (and stars and kerchiefs), the hammer and sickle, portraits of Lenin, and the eternal flames of war memorials are among its concrete symbols. There are Soviet rituals for life-cycle events, for initiating people into social and political groups, for honouring group labour and individual workers, for observing seasons of the year, and for celebrating military and patriotic occasions. May Day and October celebrations, commemorating international proletarian solidarity and the Communist revolution, respectively, involve mass public rituals (Lane, 1981).

A SAINT AND HIS SHRINE IN THE SOVIET UNION

Every visitor to the Soviet Union is aware of the fact that the visual image and the words of Lenin accompany Soviet citizens from the cradle to the grave and that one cannot move about in public places without noticing the omnipresence of Lenin. On mass political holidays . . . it's impossible to look up into the sky without being confronted with Lenin's name in blazing letters. . . . A slightly more active relation to Lenin is encouraged by the existence of countless Lenin museums, Lenin statues and Lenin memorials. . . . They are visited by groups and by individuals all through the year and have become the focus of mass pilgrimage on anniversaries of Lenin's birthday (22 April) when they are submerged in flowers.

Lenin's mausoleum in Red Square . . . is the symbolic centre, the "holy shrine". . . . To this ritual centre both individual persons and society (in the form of its representative groups) come to draw moral strength at crisis points, to give an account of important missions accomplished, to display and rejoice in successes or just to give homage . . . In 1941 soldiers went there before leaving for the front, and after the war was won the most heroic soldiers from all over the Soviet Union returned there for a victory parade, a triumphant presentation to Lenin of enemy flags. Yuri Gagarin, the first Soviet cosmonaut, is reported to have gone to the mausoleum before his flight to make a symbolic report. School leavers come here on their last day of school and fall into reverent silence during the changing of the guard. New officers from a Moscow elite training institute receive their diplomas here from Lenin, their Honorary Commander. Pioneers are initiated "in the presence of Lenin" . . . and newly married couples come to offer thanks after their wedding. All the important mass political holidays have their culmination in Red Square in front of the mausoleum. There, greetings, reports and displays of economic, cultural or military achievement are not only directed at the living political leaders on the platform erected over the mausoleum but also at the dead leader inside it. The whole nation participates via the television screen. On ordinary days there is a constant queue of patiently waiting pilgrims from all corners of the Soviet Union, as well as from other countries.

—Christel Lane

Religion and the State in Canada

It is not surprising to find that in Canada—a regionally diverse and culturally pluralistic country created by a federation of former colonies—the relationship of religion to national integration has been approached in various ways. An alliance between church and state, a non-denominational civil religion, and a political religion can all be found.

From the time of colonization to the Quiet Revolution of the 1960s, the Catholic Church was a partner of government—sometimes the dominant partner—in the shaping of Quebec society. At Confederation, Protestants became the national majority, although Catholicism, centred in Quebec, remained the single largest denomination.

The missionary goal of building a Christian nation, which appears early in Canadian history within both Catholicism and various Protestant denominations, peaked in the 19th century (Grant 1977, 13). Catholic priests and Quebec nationalists together affirmed the sacred mission of Quebec: to resist assimilation into English Canada and to defend the rights of French Catholic minorities outside Quebec. Many Protestant groups, on the other hand, shared a broad consensus that public life should be shaped by a vision of Canada as "His Dominion"—a homogeneously Anglo-Saxon, Protestant society. The broad coalition supporting this vision influenced public policy on education, Sabbath Day observance, Prohibition, immigration restriction, and social welfare (Clifford 1977).

How could these competing Catholic and Protestant national visions be merged into a united Canadian vision? One source of common ground is a shared commitment to the goals, specified in the British North America Act (now called the Constitution Act, 1867), of "peace, order, and good government." This vision of Canadian society allows religious denominations to continue to play a major role in shaping national destiny, through direct connections with government at the provincial level and as voluntary associations encouraging religious commitment on the part of the citizenry. Social diversity and political compromise also created the conditions for the gradual emergence of a civil religion, in which the sacred mission of the Canadian confederation is the establishment of a pluralistic society based on toleration, compromise, and common sense. The BNA Act and Constitution are texts of this religion; federal/provincial power-sharing and structures of representative democracy at all levels of government are its institutions, and political ceremonies are its rituals.

The repatriation of Canada's Constitution in 1981 was marked with a ritual event featuring the signatures of Queen Elizabeth and Canadian political leaders.

WILFRID LAURIER ON RELIGION AND TOLERANCE

"So long as I have a seat in the House, so long as I occupy the position I do now, whenever it shall become my duty to take a stand upon any question whatever, that stand I will take not upon grounds of Roman Catholicism, not upon grounds of Protestantism, but upon ground which can appeal to the consciences of men, irrespective of their particular faith, upon grounds which can be occupied by all men who love justice, freedom and toleration."

Other elements that once had sacred status in Canadian society—the British connection in English Canada, the Catholic Church in French Canada, traditional religious beliefs and practices in all parts of Canada— no longer command the same degree of loyalty. Similarly, the symbols, beliefs, and practices of Canadian civil religion have been revised (Mol 1985, 249-65). The 1960s were a particularly active time of national reconsecration. The adoption of the maple leaf flag and official choice of *O Canada* as the national anthem were symbolic of a national sense of destiny no longer dependent on the British Empire. The many celebrations of the hundredth year of Confederation in 1967, especially Expo 67 in Montreal, evoked images of Canadians, united as never before, with a faith in their future together. The enthusiasm culminated in "Trudeau-mania" in 1968, when Pierre Trudeau was seen by many as a charismatic leader embodying a new national vision that would sweep away the historic legacy of regional distrust. The high expectations of the 1960s have ebbed with the country's economy, but the reformed civil religion remains. Although many would argue that Canadians do not connect their religious and their political beliefs, God was (after some debate) written into the new Canadian Constitution and into the revised English version of *O Canada*.

Just as Canada has elements of a church-state alliance and a civil religion, the Canadian nationalist movement shows some characteristics of a political religion. Although there is much diversity among Canadian nationalists, it is probably safe to say that they all view Canada as sacred because they believe it can make a unique contribution to humanity. This means more than keeping Canada from becoming an economic, political, and cultural colony of the United States. It also means granting sacred status to Canada's right to develop its own economic and social welfare strategy, to the principle of an independent foreign policy, and to the best products of the country's art and literature. Nationalists thus expand the sphere of what is considered sacred about Canadian society. Although relatively few in number, they influence the climate of opinion.

The Sacred Self: Invisible Religion

Developing Durkheim's broad approach to religion, with its emphasis on the distinction between the sacred and the profane and on the functional necessity of religion, Luckman (1967) related modernization and secularization to the growth of an "**invisible religion**." In modern society, denominational religion no longer fulfils one of its traditional functions—the integration of all aspects of life into a socially shared system of ultimate meaning. With religious pluralism and toleration of non-belief, religious belief and practice are no longer considered public matters. They have become private—something for each individual to decide. This shift is an indication that the public conception of what is sacred has changed. The sacred object, which is affirmed with the acceptance of pluralism and toleration, is the autonomous personality.

Traditional religions are replaced with an invisible modern religion based on the belief that each person has the right to be himself or herself. Because its basic principle makes each individual responsible for constructing a personal system of ultimate meaning, this religion is invisible; it does, however, have identifiable themes. Self-realization and self-expression are held to give transcendent meaning to life; family, sex, and work relationships are adjusted accordingly. Perhaps this is why performers, traditionally people of very low status, have become objects of veneration. In 1938, Hughes rightly perceived that one of the signs of secularization in the small industrial city he studied was the popularity of Shirley Temple (Hughes 1938, 201).

Although this thesis is controversial, it does open up the possibility of examining the religious dimensions of many aspects of society. For example, the invisible religion rejects the Protestant understanding of work as a "calling" in which one can serve God. Instead, work is valued because it provides not only a living but also what economists call disposable income—income in excess of basic needs. Disposable income can be used to pursue self-expression and self-realization in leisure time through the purchase and use of consumer goods.

Ideally, work also provides intrinsic opportunities for personal growth, for "self-actualization," in the phrase of the widely read Abraham Maslow (1970). Maslow is the best known of a group of organizational psychologists who stress the importance of designing work to be interesting and to enhance technical and personal skills. Their writings may be considered the invisible religion's theology of work, a vision of salvation in this world through self-fulfilling labour. The most valued work in this view offers self-gratification and self-expression *off* the job, by providing high disposable income, and self-actualization *on* the job, by allowing individual autonomy and the opportunities to develop new skills. The sacred ideal in the invisible religion is not a calling, but a career. (For more discussion of modern views of work, see Chapter 11.)

The *Crestwood Heights* study of an affluent Toronto suburb in the 1950s (Seeley et al. 1956) found a way of life remarkably consistent with what Luckman later called invisible religion. The high-level managers and professionals who lived there were not typically from wealthy back-grounds. Their childhood memories were of the Depression. Competitive and talented, they had risen in their chosen careers in the booming economy of the 1950s. The personal goals that gave meaning to their lives were health, happiness, and success. These goals were to be achieved through dedication to a career. Home life was organized around the perpetuation of a successful career; school life, around preparation for a career. The Christians and Jews of Crestwood Heights did not abandon conventional religion. They belonged to churches and synagogues and occasionally attended, viewing denominational adherence as "a socially useful practice rather than a source of spiritual solace" (Seeley et al. 1956, 214).

There were stresses, of course, in Crestwood Heights. Competition involves losing as well as winning. Academic and social competition at school was intense. Women struggled to reconcile the ideal of self-actualization with their roles as junior partners in their husbands' careers.

Some children raised in settings like Crestwood Heights did, for a time in the 1960s and early 1970s, question the emphasis on a career. They espoused countercultural variations of the invisible religion, which preached self-fulfilment through love, radical politics, communal experiments, drugs, and exotic religious experiences. Today, most of the women raised in settings such as Crestwood Heights have since built careers of their own, but they remain ambivalent about their roles in home and family (see Chapter 9). Some men have also questioned the personal costs of excessive career commitment. These shifts in emphasis have not, however, changed the transcendent goals of self-fulfilment, self-actualization, self-realiza-tion, and self-expression.

We have seen the invisible religion before in this chapter, but we haven't stopped to notice it. The findings on participation in new religions and para-religions in Montreal indicate that people become involved with them as consumers of self-help techniques. Most people don't make a commitment to these groups as permanent religious communities but rather use the experience as part of an idiosyncratic project of personal growth. The findings about the relationship of many Canadians to con-ventional religion indicate much the same pattern. Many Canadians who are not personally committed to the beliefs and practices of a religious community continue to identify themselves with one because it offers resources on which they can draw to help reach their goals of self-real-ization and self-expression.

Two examples from the world of sports suggest the sort of analysis that can be done if one accepts the concept of the invisible religion.

Consider ice hockey and the formal characteristics of a religious group. As Sinclair-Faulkner (1977) points out, hockey has a distinct system of meaning, shaped and maintained by a well-defined doctrine (formal rules and widely shared understandings about the game), a full-time priesthood (referees and coaches), its own authority system (officials, the NHL Board of Governors), and a body of committed adherents (fans). Moreover, by examining changes in the sport, one can find a movement from a 19th-century Calvinist understanding of the game as training for success in life through dedication and rational self-control to a late 20th-century understanding of it as a televised career for athletically talented entertainers (Badertscher 1977).

Freedman (1983) analyzes wrestling as a morality play dramatizing the conflict between right and wrong. The special emotional quality of wrestling comes from the fact that the "good guys," who are presented in the fan magazines as nice people who "fight fair," usually lose to the villains, who say they don't have friends, fight for money, and cheat. The referees, who are supposed to see that the rules are observed, often don't notice gross infractions. The fans become angry and abusive when these predictable injustices occur, and have been known to assault the villainous winners. Most fans are low-income earners, at the opposite end of the economic spectrum from the residents of Crestwood Heights. In a competitive economic system, the match dramatizes their failure and renders it meaningful. The official line—that one can get ahead by hard work and honesty—is a lie; the cheaters win, and those responsible for fairness look the other way. This meaning system offers a kind of salvation to the fans. The losers of the world who don't give up and don't become corrupt are the truly good people. Sometimes they win, but when they lose, which is most of the time, they are permitted to feel anger as righteous indignation.

SUMMARY

The sociological study of religion in Canada has mostly dealt with denominational religion. Findings suggest that religion is declining in significance in the lives of Canadians. But they also suggest that it would be premature to consign religion to the periphery of Canadian society. For a sizable minority, religion remains a major focus of life, a source of ultimate meaning, and a guide to living properly in the company of other people. Religious identification persists because the distinctive cultural traditions of the Canadian mosaic usually have a religious dimension. The denominations themselves retain a high-profile commitment to the moral improvement of society. Outside of denominational religion, much remains to be explored. The discussion of models of sacred nationhood developed for other countries is just beginning to affect our understanding of Canada. The idea that the self is held sacred in modern individualistic societies opens the way to recognizing and studying the religious aspects of many social settings.

NOTES

1. See Abella and Troper (1982) on Canadian resistance to Jewish immigration during the Holocaust.
2. See Shaffir (1974) for a study of a Jewish group that retained firm boundaries between its sacred society and the outside world.

FOR FURTHER READING

There are numerous textbooks and general discussions on the sociology of religion. Browsing through the library shelves (the call no. is BL 60) or asking your professor are the best ways of finding these general reference books. Important theoretical works have been mentioned in the chapter and are listed in the references at the back of the text, along with the studies mentioned in the chapter.

The suggestions given below indicate the range and depth of what has been written by sociologists about religion in Canada. The suggestions are limited to Canadian materials because, with the much greater volume of American and British publications, the Canadian materials are sometimes hard to find.

Baum, Gregory
1975 *Religion and Alienation*: *A Theological Reading of Sociology*. New York: Paulist Press.
A synthesis of theology and sociology, Baum's analysis focuses on religion as a response to the human condition and the movement of religion from the legitimation of social institutions to criticism of them.
Bibby, Reginald W.
1983 "Religionless Christianity: A Profile of Religion in Canada in the 80s." *Social Indicators Research* 13(1): 1-16.
This is one of several articles interpreting Canadian data from surveys done in 1975 and in 1980; variations in religious commitment receive particular attention.
Bird, Frederick, and William Reimer
1982 "Participation Rates in New Religious Movements." *Journal for the Scientific Study of Religion* 21:1-14.
This overview and typology of new religious groups in Montreal in the late 1970s provides data on types of participation.
Crysdale, Stewart, and Les Wheatcroft, eds.
1976 *Religion in Canadian Society*. Toronto: Macmillan.
The only collection of its type, this excellent reader includes important readings on religion in Canada.
Fallding, Harold
1974 *The Sociology of Religion*. Toronto: McGraw-Hill Ryerson.
This introduction to the sociology of religion, developing a perspective based on Durkheim, emphasizes the meaning of religious identification and experience to the adherent.
Freedman, Jim
1983 "Will the Sheik Use His Blinding Fireball?" Pp. 67-79 in Frank E. Manning, ed., *The Celebration of Society*: *Perspectives on Contemporary Cultural Performance*. London, Ontario: Congress of Social and Humanistic Societies, University of Western Ontario.

Freedman's analysis gives a provocative example of how the structure of a sport dramatizes issues in the lives of the spectators and provides a meaningful framework for their lives.

Mol, Hans

1976 *Identity and the Sacred: A Sketch for a New Social-scientific Theory of Religion.* Oxford: Basil Blackwell.

This book reviews the major theories of religion and presents a synthesis. The concept of sacralization is presented as the theoretical opposite of secularization.

1985 *Faith and Fragility: Religion and Identity in Canada.* Burlington, Ont.: Trinity Press.

Mol organizes and interprets, implicitly using the theory developed in *Identity and the Sacred*, most of the sociological literature on religion in Canada. The book is full of information.

Seeley, John R., R. Alexander Sim, and Elizabeth W. Loosley

1956 *Crestwood Heights: A Study of the Culture of Suburban Life.* Toronto: University of Toronto Press.

This Canadian classic shows how dedication to success in a career acts as the foundation of all aspects of the lifestyle in a particular suburb. The analysis includes school, family life, and the use of psychological experts as a new priesthood.

Westley, Frances

1983 *The Complex Forms of the Religious Life.* Chico, Calif.: Scholars Press.

Westley explores Durkheim's concept of the emergence of a "cult of man," using data from the Montreal study of new religious movements that locate the sacred within the self.

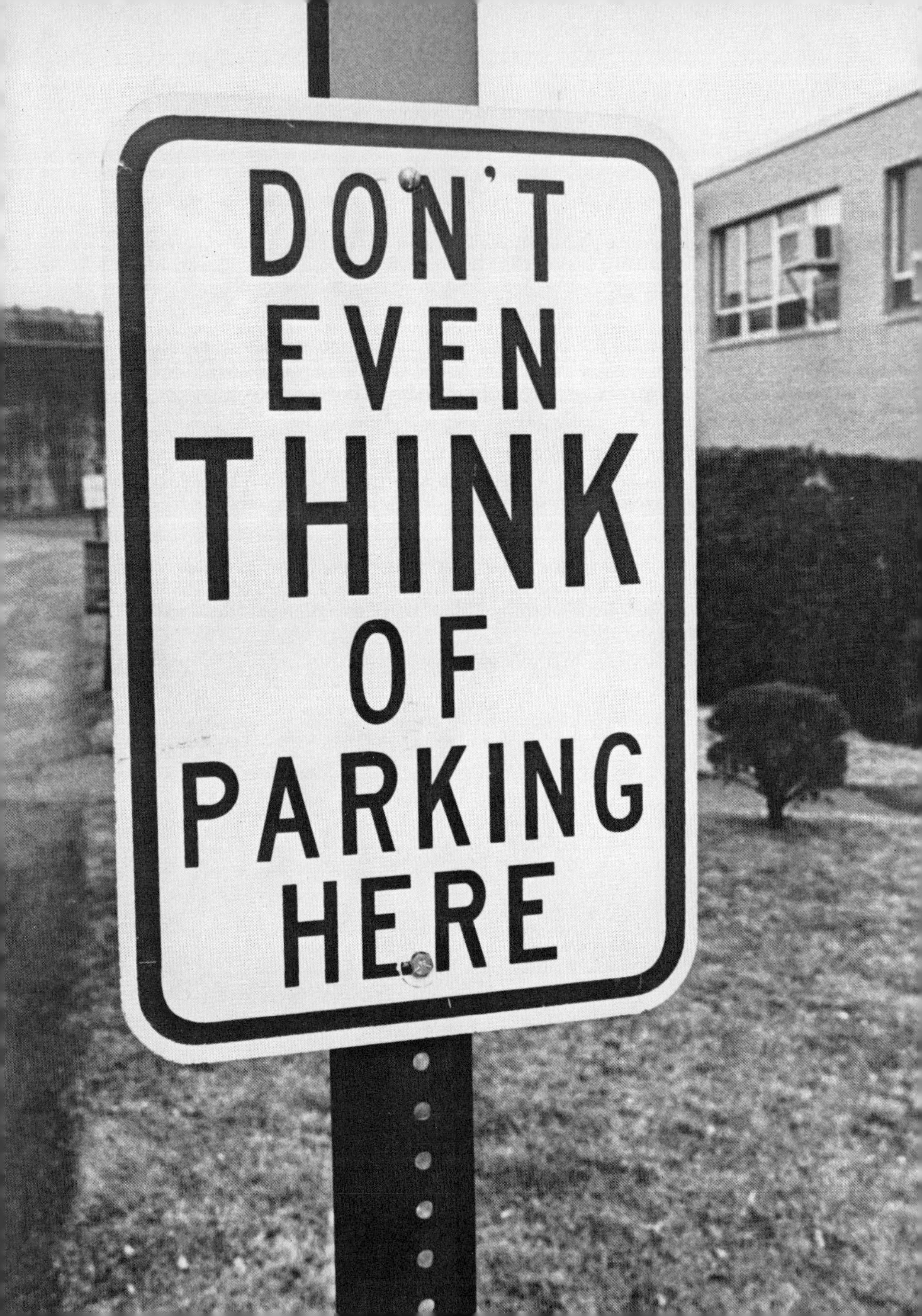
DON'T
EVEN
THINK
OF
PARKING
HERE

PART III

THE STRUCTURE OF DOMINATION

"Man is born free, and he is everywhere in chains." With these words the 18th-century French social philosopher Jean-Jacques Rousseau underscored his harsh view of the effects of society on the liberty and self-expression of individuals. Rousseau, influenced by conditions in pre-revolutionary France, saw domination and coercion as the central features of social order. It was society that actively created inequalities and systematically crushed the human spirit.

Domination, inequality, and stratification are major themes for today's sociologists. Some, identified as conflict theorists and influenced by people such as Rousseau, Karl Marx, and Max Weber, see society as an arena of conflict. Others share the assumptions of John Locke, for whom society was a "social contract," that is, a voluntary agreement of individuals and groups to a certain hierarchical structure in order to prevent anarchy and perpetual conflict and to produce a stable, ordered community that could ultimately benefit all its members. Today's functionalist sociology, with its emphasis on consensus and the social benefits of stratification, builds on this assumption.

No matter which set of assumptions one starts from, there is no question that social stratification and inequality are facts of life in Canada. Individuals differ in the amounts (and kinds) of power, prestige, and money they have. Family background continues to play a large role in determining the life chances of Canadians. Although many complain about the "system," they feel powerless to change it.

Sociologists who study the stratification system in Canada are concerned—and legitimately so—not only with understanding how it operates but also with evaluating it on the basis of moral criteria reflecting their notions of a just and fair society. In Chapter 8, Peter Pineo gives an overview of the issues involved in social stratification and their implications for understanding Canadian society.

Domination is not limited to the macrostructural processes of political or class structure; it is a pervasive feature of everyday life for most Canadians. In Chapter 9, R.A. Sydie shows the myriad ways in which the structure of gender roles in North American society is a structure of domination. Similarly, anyone who has worked in a large organization, on a production line, or in the lower ranks of a bureaucracy is aware of the myriad constraints, rules, and regulations that define the limits of acceptable behaviour and stifle individual efforts, creativity, or motivation. The question of how people organize themselves to get things done in everyday life has fateful significance for everyone; Frank Jones discusses this aspect of modern life in Chapter 10 on bureaucracy. Michael Smith focuses more specifically on work in Chapter 11, examining how effectively such notions as domination and alienation account for the workers' experience of themselves and their activities.

Of course, if social control is present everywhere, most people have become so accustomed to it as not to see it. Only in the case of deviance does social control become blatant and openly coercive. Even though modern society exalts the new ethic of "doing your own thing," most people agree that there are definite and enforceable limits on what one can do. The response to individuals or groups who challenge social conventions can vary from bemused curiosity to extreme hostility. Robert A. Stebbins outlines Canadian responses to deviance in Chapter 12.

As mentioned above, a moral stance has inspired much of the Canadian work on stratification, particularly that in the tradition of political economy, an interdisciplinary approach that stresses the link between the political system, the economic system, and the class structure. Canadian practitioners have a specific interest in the pattern of continental exploitation of the country's wealth by dominant American interests. Wallace Clement describes this approach in Chapter 13.

As a Western liberal democracy, Canada compares very well with other nations in its blend of equality of opportunity and personal freedom provided for its citizens. Yet this virtue must not blind Canadians to the reality of poverty and inequality or to the tenuous nature of their civil rights.

CHAPTER 8

SOCIAL STRATIFICATION AND SOCIAL CLASS

Peter C. Pineo

INEQUALITY IN CANADIAN SOCIETY

Sociologists studying social stratification are concerned with the nature of inequality in society and the reasons for its existence. That inequality exists is evident to anyone living in Canada. Within this country today are families that enjoy a house, a summer cottage, a condominium in Florida, three cars, all household appliances known to humankind, and imported wine with dinner. At the same time, it is easy to find families crowded into half of a converted small house, with the stove the source of winter heat and a permanent odour coming from the rotting wood in the walls and the deteriorating floor covering.

Such extremes show that inequality exists; the study of it requires much more careful examination. Precise measurement is required to monitor any trends in the amount of inequality. Continuing research is required to observe its distribution. Are the rural areas of Canada less or more prosperous than the cities? Is poverty more common among the old or the young? How much does unemployment or marital breakdown affect one's standard of living? Are there differences across major categories within Canadian society, such as ethnic groups or religious denominations? Why are some people better off than others? What are the consequences of differing degrees of achievement: are those at the bottom bitter? do those at the top feel particularly pleased with Canada and with life?

Cases can be found that represent the extremes of wealth and poverty in Canada today, but this is not the whole story. Exhibit 8-1 shows the results of a Canadian sociological survey that asked for the earned income, in 1980, of the head of the household. The range is obvious. A few report incomes of less than $2,000, and one must wonder how they survive. (Perhaps income from other family members or social assistance ekes out the household's income.) Many households are getting by on very moderate incomes, as 12.5 percent report that the head earns less than $8,000. A handful report enormous incomes in excess of $100,000.

The table shows that Canadians are far from equal in annual income. It also immediately suggests a series of questions. How different are rural and small-town Canada? Is the distribution different in the various regions of Canada? Did the heads of household include women, and does this make a difference? Would a survey of family income produce a picture different from the one produced by asking about the income of household heads? These are the sorts of questions pursued by sociologists and others; some answers are provided later in this chapter.

Equity and Equality

Even without further data, some logical questions can be raised about any evidence of inequality within a society. Perhaps most basic is the distinction caught in the concepts of "equality of opportunity" and "equality of condition" (Gilbert and McRoberts 1975, 115) or, in more recent terms, between equity and equality (Daymont 1980). The theoretical question of **equality (equality of condition)** concerns how much variation there must be in a society in the distribution of some valued good such as income. Could a society exist in which every family earned exactly the same amount? For the small, pre-literate societies studied by anthropologists, the question is not easy to answer. Before Western influence produced major changes, many such societies did not have money, so income would have to be determined by careful consideration of the value of various goods and services received. Thus, the degree of inequality would be hard to determine and was presumably often obscure even to the members of the society. But after careful consideration of the evidence, a prominent anthropologist reports that, except for a few totally impoverished groups, some degree of variation in economic wealth can be found in every society (Herskovits 1960, 413).

Exhibit 8-1
Income from Jobs or Business of Household Heads, 1980

Income Category	Respondent Households	
	Number	Percentage
< $2000	42	2.0%
$2 000–3 999	63	3.0
$4 000–5 999	66	3.2
$6 000–7 999	89	4.3
$8 000–9 999	101	4.8
$10 000–11 999	124	5.9
$12 000–13 999	158	7.6
$14 000–15 999	182	8.7
$16 000–17 999	161	7.7
$18 000–19 999	219	10.5
$20 000–24 999	345	16.5
$25 000–29 999	215	10.3
$30 000–39 999	177	8.5
$40 000–49 999	68	3.2
$50 000–74 999	47	2.3
$75 000–99 999	17	0.8
≧ $100 000	12	0.6
Total	2086[a]	100

[a]Sample size was 2947. Of these, 861 cases reported no income from job or business in 1980, or gave no answer.
Source: York University, Institute of Behavioural Research, Quality of Life Survey, 1980.

Farming modest plots of land is still the principle means of survival in much of the world. Such agrarian societies are characterized by much greater extremes of inequality than are industrial societies such as Canada.

In reviewing the same evidence, which was taken from many societies and from different historical periods, sociologist Gerhard Lenski (1966) observes that the degree of inequality found in societies varies and the variation follows certain orderly principles. Lenski reports that inequality appears to be at its maximum in larger societies with economies based almost exclusively on farming. These societies, which are often classified as **agrarian,** include the ancient civilizations of the Middle East, India, and China, and typically display a degree of inequality greater than that found today in industrialized societies such as Canada.

No case of a society with perfect equality in economic wealth exists, so the question of whether such a society could exist remains a subject for speculation and indirect study. Since reducing inequality to exactly zero would be a painful business requiring great effort, the more reasonable question to ask is how little inequality could exist in a society that was trying, but not trying obsessively, to keep it to a minimum? Could today's Canada be near that minimum? While no society seems completely free of inequality, the degree of inequality varies; thus, it is possible, by comparing different systems, to investigate factors that might increase or decrease inequality of condition. Lenski's work is concerned with this kind of analysis.

The question of **equity (equality of opportunity)** is different, though again largely a matter of common sense. Given that there is inequality in a society, is it distributed fairly? Does the handful of Canadians earning more than $100,000 a year really deserve that much? Or is it luck, unfair advantage, or even exploitation?

For the average Canadian, the question of whether a completely equalitarian society is possible is probably too remote to be of any importance, but the question of how fair the system is in allocating advantages is of some immediate concern. For young people just starting out, the question of whether effort will be fairly rewarded affects their motivation to persist in school, to save their money, and so forth. In the midst of the separatist crisis of the 1960s (see Chapter 18), a sociological study showed that English-Canadian youth saw the Canadian system as much fairer than did French-Canadian youth. Johnstone asked a national sample of young Canadians what it takes "to get ahead" in Canada. An overwhelming number of English Canadians endorsed activities such as working hard, getting good grades, and the like (1969, 8). French Canadians tended to refer to contacts and to coming from the right family as the sources of success. More recent work (Lambert and Curtis 1979) suggests that French Canadians still have less confidence than English Canadians in institutions such as schools and government.

Which group, the English or the French, was nearer the mark in describing how fair the Canadian system is? Again the answer is not yet available, but study of the issue is one of the basic questions of social science. Sociologists have long distinguished between two kinds of characteristics—ascribed and achieved. **Ascribed characteristics** are fixed, usually at birth; they include sex, racial origin, ethnicity, and—although it continuously changes—age. **Achieved characteristics** come later and reflect some activity by the individual. Educational level is the most obvious achievement, but subtler skills can also be achieved, as can the advantages of geographic location and the like. The more that inequalities seem to be allocated according to ascription rather than achievement, the less fair the system of stratification appears to be. A recent Canadian study, described more fully later in the chapter, addresses this question at considerable length (Boyd et al. 1985)

Poverty and Relative Deprivation

The opening of this chapter mentioned the poverty-stricken Canadian family living in half a house, amid odours. Clearly such people deserve sympathy, but it should be noted immediately that 90 percent of the population of, say, China or India would change places with them in a minute. The definition of what it is to be really poor, or really rich, is elusive. Considering the world as a whole and the span of human history, most Canadians live like aristocrats. All enjoy virtually free medical care and free schooling for their children. Poor or not, all live in a rich society, so there is good clean running water, police and fire protection, and adequate roads. Canada's welfare state offers a safety net of basic entitlements, such as unemployment insurance and welfare. The safety net may break if too many people land on it at once, but in a normal year it can be counted on.

From this perspective, one might expect enlightened opinion within Canada to push for a major flow of Canadian money to India, China, and other poor countries. Yet there is no such flow—only a trickle of money leaves Canada each year in foreign aid and assistance—and there is not much pressure to increase the flow. Rather, government policy is concerned about poverty within Canada, partly for the very good reason that the Canadian poor have a vote in Canadian elections, while those in India and China do not.

Is there such a thing as real poverty? Is say, $7,000 a year enough to live on nowadays in Canada and less than that too little? If real poverty exists, the problem of inequality has a special character. Up to a certain level, it is a matter of life and death; beyond that point it is less serious.

Is there such a level? Many people think so, and calculations are made of **poverty lines,** which are estimates of the amount of money needed for households of various sizes. One set of levels proposed recently for

Some Canadians rely on food banks to ease the burdens of poverty.

Canada included: $7,571 a year for a single person in a rural area, $11,961 for two in a small city, $26,500 a year for six in one of the largest cities, and so on (National Council of Welfare 1985). Below these lines, say their authors, a household is poor and needs help; above them, a household is providing adequately for itself. From the point of view of most of the people now alive, of course, these "basic" levels would seem incredibly lavish.

Can such lines be justified? To some degree, yes. Canadians do need more money than many people elsewhere in the world. A car and a telephone are regarded as necessities these days. It is the law that one must provide one's children with schooling rather than have them out earning money at the age of 10. One feels obliged to dress one's children well enough that they will not be pariahs at school. But if these are selfless imperatives, beyond them is another level of needs that might more accurately be called expectations. Canadians must have meat quite often; smokers must have some funds for their habit; no one can go through life without a little expensive fun. One can imagine some absolute measure of poverty: a level of living so low as to seriously shorten one's life-span. Poverty is this severe for much of the world, but it is no longer so for the vast majority of the Canadian population. Official poverty lines have nothing to do with so serious a contingency as shortening the life-span. Rather they represent another level of need: an expectation not just of survival but of good health and a degree of comfort.

If it is difficult to decide what constitutes poverty, it is also difficult to determine what it means to be rich. Is there some point in the distribution of Exhibit 8-1 beyond which the amount of money ceases to have any real meaning? If so, money can easily be taken from those above that level to raise the income of the rest. But it does not seem to be so. Those earning $100,000 a year manage to spend it and yearn each year for a "decent raise." In fact, wealth seems to operate like an addiction, with larger amounts required to achieve the same psychological effect. Thus pay raises in our society are typically calculated in percentages. A person earning $10,000 is rewarded by a 10 percent raise of $1,000; one earning $100,000 is given $10,000 to achieve the equivalent reward.

This kind of evidence suggests that wealth must be viewed in a relative rather than an absolute sense. People want as much money as others have, not merely enough to achieve some concrete goal. There is no release from the pressures of comparison at any income level. Thus, sociologists realize that poverty must be seen as relative deprivation, rather than as an absolute (see Whyte 1965), but that it is nonetheless very real in its consequences. A Canadian executive earning $300,000 a year will undoubtedly tell you that is a paltry sum compared to what his counterpart in the United States earns. And the family living in half a house is in certain ways truly poor—having much less than others in the same society means a kind of exclusion, even stigmatization, which can have ramifications.

Other Axes of Stratification: Education and Occupational Status

Income earned from a job is not the only axis of stratification in a society like Canada. Inherited wealth, income from investments, and, to an ever-larger extent, funds received for some reason or another from the government (transfer payments) mean that earned income is part of what is more generally called wealth, and sociologists study this whole phenomenon (for instance, Hunter 1986). Other standards are also used to assess stratification. Sociologists studying industrialized nations, such as the United States, Great Britain, and Canada, emphasize stratification by education and by occupation.

Canadians differ appreciably in the amount of education they have attained. As shown in Exhibit 8-2, again from the national survey of Canada, some people have almost none and a handful have degrees beyond the bachelor's level. The differences are particularly great today because of the rapid growth of the school system during the past few decades. Old and young Canadians differ more today in their average levels of education than they ever have in the past and perhaps more than they will in the future.

Educational levels play a complex role in the stratification system. Education is partly a means to an end—one gets education in order to achieve a better job and greater income. In this sense, the effects of education show up in other dimensions of the stratification system and are not of immediate importance. But, to some degree, education is also a factor in itself. (See Chapter 6 for more discussion of education as a cause and an effect of stratification.) A Canadian interacting with another who is much better educated typically shows a complex set of actions and attitudes,

Exhibit 8-2
Educational Attainment of Canadian Adults

	Males	Females
No schooling or did not complete grade school	8.5%	9.8%
Primary school (with graduation certificate)	11.7	9.8
High school (no graduation certificate)	26.2	25.7
High school (with graduation certificate)	17.6	21.3
Technical training beyond secondary school	9.4	9.4
Some college or university	13.4	16.3
Bachelor's degree	8.6	6.3
Master's degree	2.4	.9
Professional degree or doctorate	2.3	.4
Number of cases (weighted)	1443	1500

Source: York University, Institute of Behavioural Research, Quality of Life Survey, 1980.

including some deference, often mixed with hostility and envy. The interaction is frequently difficult for both individuals involved. It is no accident that most marriages occur between two people of roughly equivalent levels of education. Many friendship choices are also influenced by educational level. Education can also create some degree of obligation or duty; thus, one often reads of a judge telling a well-educated offender, "A person with your advantages—with your excellent education—cannot be excused and I am going to sentence you most severely. . . ." The situation in which high status confers special obligations as well as privileges is best captured in the French phrase *noblesse oblige*. This concept recurs in stratification systems—although perhaps rather little in modern Canada.

Sociologists also see occupational status as an important aspect of stratification, perhaps more important than either education or income. It is common sense that some jobs are "good jobs" and others are not. Researchers find that Canadians—like people in most other societies that are industrialized to some degree—can, when asked to do so, rank occupations in a way representing their "social standing," although some qualifications are needed (see, for example, Guppy 1982). Exhibit 8-3 shows the ratings, often called **occupational prestige,** given to some typical occupations by the Canadian public (Pineo and Porter 1967).

Exhibit 8-3
Ratings Given to a Selection of Occupations,
on a Scale from 0 to 100

Provincial premier	89.9%	Owner of a food store	47.8%
Physician	87.2	Receptionist	38.7
College professor	84.6	Railroad brakeman	37.1
Journalist	60.9	Trailer truck driver	32.8
TV announcer	57.6	Filling station attendant	23.3
Advertising executive	56.5	Farm labourer	21.5

Source: Pineo and Porter (1967).

There is a strong consensus about the status of jobs. Armed with this information, some sociologists have created scoring systems for occupations (Blishen 1967; Blishen and McRoberts 1976), and others have grouped occupations in classifications that more or less parallel the public rankings (Pineo, Porter, and McRoberts 1977; Pineo and Porter 1985a). Exhibit 8-4 presents the distribution of the Canadian labour force according to one such classification. As with education and income, occupation, as shown in the table, has a considerable range: from a handful of people in the top professional and managerial jobs through to substantial percentages in the unskilled and semiskilled categories.

Exhibit 8-4
The Labour Force by Socioeconomic Category, 1981

	Males	Females
Self-employed professionals	1.2%	0.3%
Employed professionals	7.3	7.3
High-level management	3.0	1.0
Semi-professionals	3.9	8.6
Technicians	2.1	1.5
Middle managers	7.2	3.7
Supervisors	3.1	3.3
Foremen and forewomen	5.0	0.4
Skilled clerical/sales/service workers	4.4	18.7
Skilled crafts and trade workers	17.1	1.4
Farmers	3.0	0.4
Semiskilled clerical/sales/service workers	8.3	27.0
Semiskilled manual workers	13.3	7.5
Unskilled clerical/sales/service workers	2.3	9.1
Unskilled manual labourers	16.6	8.0
Farm labourers	2.2	1.7
No.	6 845 325	4 622 095

Sources: Computed from *1981 Census of Canada*, vol. 2, cat. no. 92-917, table 1, Labour Force 15 years and over by detailed occupation and sex, for Canada and Provinces, 1981.

Although one might expect the same individuals to rank high in education, occupation, and income, there are actually many exceptions. High income can be earned through business success, for example, even if one is not well educated. Some occupations of high rank, such as high elected office, have no specific educational requirements. Certain honoured occupations, such as minister or rabbi, may not be well paid. Thus, all three dimensions must be considered in studying stratification in a society like Canada. Of the three, most sociologists have treated occupation as the most important, although this matter is open to debate. Education is, as noted, to some degree a means to an end, so it is secondary to the other two. Occupation can, of course, also be seen as a means to the end of earning an income. Perhaps sociologists have so emphasized occupation partly because it is the most public of the three. It is in better taste to ask people what jobs they have than to ask them how well educated they are or how much they earn. Occupation may also be considered a more reliable indicator of status than income because it is more enduring. Income figures, if solicited in the usual way of asking how much was earned in the preceding year, are subject to ups and downs because of unemployment, illness, windfalls, and the like. Occupation may be not only important in its own right but also a good clue to what a person's normal income would be.

Non-Economic Stratification Systems

In emphasizing economic matters—particularly occupation, education, and income—sociologists studying the stratification system of Canada and similar countries, are reacting to what they think is of greatest importance to the people in these societies. Stratification systems can, however, be based on other factors. A society could be more concerned with who is or is not excelling in, say, religious devoutness or purity than in economic matters. Such a preoccupation with religious matters may have characterized medieval Europe and seems to be part of the traditional caste system of India.

Even an emphasis on material possessions need not take the exact form it does today in Canada. The native Indians of Canada's west coast, before Westernization, were concerned with material goods, but with giving them away rather than with acquiring them. In large ceremonies we know as the potlatch, a host and his kindred would give his guests presents—in later years, most often blankets made by the Hudson's Bay Company—and in doing so would earn social honour. The system of the Kwakiutl Indians, who lived in the area north of Comox on Vancouver Island, the mainland, and the smaller islands in between, has been particularly well

The Kwakiutl Indian copper plate is typical of the material goods given away at the potlatch ceremony. It was the giving away of wealth, rather than its possession, that indicated high status in the Kwakiutl stratification system.

described (Codere 1950). People's names in this society were like the aristocratic titles of England, explicitly carrying status, so that it was possible to talk of a particular name as being the sixth highest in the whole society. The status of these names was maintained by the giving of gifts. Status was not, however, fixed; the system included provision for social mobility through excelling in gift-giving.

The stratification system of the Kwakiutl was, in some ways, the opposite of our current system, emphasizing giving away material goods rather than consuming them. But in other ways it was curiously similar; it was, after all, based on material goods, which had to be acquired before they could be distributed.

Other systems are based on non-economic criteria. The subculture that develops in the high school is an example of a partly non-economic stratification system. As described by Coleman (1961), students in a high school are rated on several criteria. The school system itself awards academic grades, which form a set of distinctions among the students. (Distinctions based on grades are not economic, although they have some bearing on the students' ultimate economic success). Society's broader system of stratification also impinges on the school as students show and respond to signs of parental affluence; those from the more affluent families wear better or more fashionable clothes and have easier access to automobiles, thereby creating another criterion for distinction. Especially among boys, success at sports forms another basis for ranking, one that is wholly independent of economic matters. Finally, students ranked one another on the complicated criterion of "popularity," a phenomenon that feeds on itself, as popularity breeds popularity. Since Coleman conducted his research, other criteria, such as musical skill or commitment to politics, may have become important. To the middle-aged, this system seems a trivial game played by children, but to those involved, losing badly in the system is undoubtedly a source of intense personal discomfort.

High-school students are particularly trapped in the subsystem of stratification that builds up in the schools. But other small, non-economic systems develop recurrently in society. Suburban gardeners, for example, carefully inspect each other's lawns, and the question "Who has the best lawn in this neighbourhood?" is both meaningful and answerable. Those very complex rankings called "office politics" can become obsessive and hurtful. But in most instances these smaller systems are less important than the national, economic stratification system, and many are more a source of humour than of anguish.

SOCIOLOGICAL DISCOVERY
OF THE NORTH AMERICAN STRATIFICATION SYSTEM

It is a curious intellectual fact that sociologists in North America, particularly in the United States, had to discover that a social stratification system existed. In Europe, the presence of a hereditary aristocracy in countries such as Great Britain and the remnants of aristocracy elsewhere prevented sociologists from neglecting the stratification system. North American sociologists were, of course, aware that economic inequalities existed. In describing the structure of the North American city as early as 1925, E.W. Burgess noted that neighbourhoods within the city differed in socioeconomic level. He used the term workingman, for example, where a more recent sociologist would use working class or blue collar, but otherwise his terminology seems modern. Most important, he used the term class freely, in a manner suggesting he expected to be readily understood by his readers. Nevertheless, Burgess was one of the first North Americans to use class. (Today the word has a variety of meanings. We will look at several in this chapter.)

North American sociologists' perceptions of class differences were altered in the late 1940s and 1950s by a series of books called the Yankee City Series, written by W. Lloyd Warner and various associates (for example, Warner et al. 1963). The series was a detailed description of a single, small New England city, including its stratification system. Warner, an anthropologist by training, used that messy but effective method of collecting data known as participant observation, as well as any other procedure he could think of, and produced a set of works that not only significantly influenced sociological thought but was also a bestseller. Warner was certainly not the first to see that inequality existed in North America, so his importance must lie elsewhere. For one thing, he argued that status differences are not just economic. **Social status** is more than inequality in income, in education, or in occupation or even in any simple combination of these three. Rather, social status is a more profound facet of the social system; differences in education, in income, and the like are only reflections of social position. Money alone could lead to acceptance into Warner's "upper-upper" class, nor would poverty immediately force one into the "lower-lower" class. (His other four classes are upper-lower, lower-middle, upper-middle, and lower-upper.) Family background, style of life, including use of leisure time, and above all acceptance by others already within the class are the real determinants of where one belongs in the system. Warner's classification system was based on Yankee City residents' perceptions of what existed.

Warner emphasized the idea that social stratification is a core organizing principle of society. His earlier work had been a study of the kinship system of Australian aborigines; now he argued that, just as kinship was the core of the aboriginal social system, so social status was the core of American society. This was a new view of how North Americans lived. The people Warner described seemed to base their whole lives around their position in the social stratification system. Members of different social classes had profoundly different lifestyles: they drank different beverages, read different magazines, ate different food, raised their children differently, went to different churches, and felt differently about religion. It was not only that Warner's "lower middles" had more of the good things of life than the "upper lowers." They were different.

Canadian sociologists studied Warner's books, of course, and considered them generally applicable to Canada. One full-scale community study of a Toronto neighbourhood, called *Crestwood Heights* (see Seeley et al. 1956), was written somewhat in the Warner mode, although it never reached major success. The real Canadian counterpart to Warner's work came almost 20 years later. John Porter's major book, *The Vertical Mosaic: An Analysis of Social Class and Power in Canada,* was published in 1965. It enjoyed the same kind of success in Canada that Warner had achieved in the United States. Not only sociologists, but everyone with intellectual interests read it, or at least said they did. Porter's work was quite different from Warner's in that it was based not on community study, but on analysis of government statistics and library information, such as entries in *Who's Who.* But, like Warner's work, it carried the basic message that social stratification did exist and was important. Social stratification had been discovered in Canada too.

Small Towns and Cities

When Warner's work appeared, it was faulted for being based on the study of a single city. That the city he chose was relatively small, located in New England, and suffering an economic decline may have influenced what he found. Perhaps people in such cities cling to the honour of old family names more than people do elsewhere. And perhaps the picture

The large mansions of Shaughnessy and Westmount locate pockets of the extremely wealthy in Canada.

he painted of a system of social classes in which everyone knows his or her place and also that of everyone else can develop only in a relatively small city with a stable population.

Other aspects of Warner's description may hold even for the largest cities, however. He noted that living in a particular neighbourhood could symbolize an individual's social class, and of course every Canadian city has at least some neighbourhoods—such as Rockcliffe Park in Ottawa, Westmount in Montreal, and British Properties in Vancouver—that represent relatively high levels of social status, and others, such as Winnipeg's North End or Montreal's St. Henri, that represent lower status. Real-estate agents report that the status of the neighbourhood is of importance to homebuyers, and in urban Canada seeing "good" and "bad" neighbourhoods must be one of the first indications to children of the existence of inequality in society.

Links with Ethnicity

Why did North American sociologists take so long to discover the importance of social stratification? One reason may be simply that other issues were of greater importance in earlier periods. It is hard to imagine today how important rural-urban differences were to Canada until well into this century. As recently as the 1940s, for example, the "farm vote" was crucial in deciding federal elections. Perhaps the most important work in Canadian sociology before *The Vertical Mosaic* was Everett Hughes's prophetic *French Canada in Transition* [1945] (1963), which focused on rural-urban differences, rather than socioeconomic inequalities.

In both Canada and the United States, the issue of social inequality was further obscured by the related phenomena of ethnic diversity and immigration.

For Americans viewing their society early in this century, the obvious evidence of economic inequality could be explained by a process most clearly articulated in Sibley (1942). Toward the bottom of the ladder were immigrants, paying the price for having caught a late ship to the United States, but doubtless better off than they would have been in the Old World. No injustice was being done. (This theory did not, of course, explain the poverty of blacks, southern sharecroppers, or native people, but perhaps each of those could be seen as a special case.) In Canada, the theory did not fit as well, since immigrants were encouraged to go west and take up farming, rather than to take on the bottom jobs in urban factories. The perceived tendency of the French or other groups to cling to Old World patterns could, nonetheless, be offered to explain their relative lack of economic success. Canada and the United States differ from most European nations in having a great diversity of ethnic groups and in having continual changes in the mix because of immigration. It seems likely that, if North Americans did not see the stratification system as clearly as did Europeans, it was partly because ethnicity and immigration were blurring their perception and also quite probably truly affecting the system.

Ethnicity and social inequality continued to be seen as fused phenomena in John Porter's work. Hence its title *The Vertical Mosaic*. Later work, some of it by Porter himself (for example, Pineo and Porter, 1985b) suggest *The Vertical Mosaic* inadvertently exaggerated the link between ethnicity and stratification, which probably peaks after each major wave of immigration and then subsides. (For further discussion of this link, see Chapter 15.)

Lifestyles and Consumer Behaviour

One theme in Warner's work—the idea that social status was linked to a broad set of attitudes and behaviours—received confirmation, almost instantly, from a very different research tradition. About the time Warner was writing, modern techniques of public-opinion polling, which came to be called "survey research," were being perfected. These techniques— a careful random sampling of households by planned, structured interviews—were much more rigorous than Warner's techniques, but they freed the researcher from having to concentrate on a single community with the attendant risks of bias. Paul Lazarsfeld of Columbia University's Bureau of Applied Social Research was a particularly skilful and innovative user of these techniques (see Lazarsfeld et al. 1948, for example). He and others found in their data considerable confirmation of Warner's conclusions. Social status, measured by some combination of education, occupation, and income, was related to a great variety of social practices and attitudes. For example, U.S. residents of higher status favoured Republican candidates, and those of lower status preferred Democrats. This relationship immediately interested politicians, of course, although it must be noted that, contrary to what Warner would have expected, religious affiliation was a more important factor than was social status in influencing voting patterns.

Has Canada Real Social Classes?

Yankee City, as Warner describes it, displays what is often called a "class" system. Real grouping existed, according to Warner, and he estimated what percentage of the population fell into each. The groups differed from one another in social rank and in style of life. People knew what group they belonged to and where others belonged. Many social scientists would question the use of "class" to describe such a system, since the word has a strong and specific meaning in Marxist theory, as we note elsewhere in this chapter. But setting aside the question of wording, one can ask about how accurately Warner's model describes today's Canada. Do all Canadians fall into one or another of a small number of distinct social groupings?

SURVEY RESEARCH AND SOCIAL STATUS

The survey research developed in the middle of this century showed sociologists that a whole host of problems they considered important had some relationship to social status. Almost every topic in this book—from socialization, the family, education, and deviance through to urbanism, ethnicity, and regionalism—bears some relationship to social status.

Much of what American sociologists were doing from about 1950 to the mid-1960s involved exploring the relationship of social status to other aspects of social life. Some of this work was a search for evidence of compensation. Did people of lower status enjoy some benefits, such as a friendlier family life or more relaxed child-training practices? The results of this search were negative; to be of lower status is to experience greater discomfort in almost every imaginable way in our society. On the other hand, the survey researchers found that, although Warner was correct in saying status intrudes into almost every aspect of social life, he seems to have exaggerated its strength. Social status is ubiquitous in its influence but rarely the most important causal factor.

Survey research also indicated that social status influences another area of behaviour: consumer behaviour. It is not surprising that people who buy Cadillacs are better off than those who buy Chevrolets. But sociologists in the 1950s and 1960s discovered that even identically priced products had an image that influenced purchasing. Bank managers lit up Du Mauriers, while factory hands puffed Export As. Thus, sales managers and advertising executives learned about the segment of the market their products had acquired and how to market a product as upscale or downscale. Marketing developed as a field unto itself. For the first time, sociologists became useful to business.

In other societies and at other times, this question could be answered readily. In some social systems, groupings are perfectly distinct. Several different terms are used, rather loosely, to classify these systems, and Lenski (1966) endeavours to organize the terminology more carefully. Systems in which stratification is actually a part of law, with distinct rights and duties assigned to each group, are called **estate systems.** Systems in which intergroup marriage and other forms of shifting membership are forbidden are called **caste systems.** In contrast, Yankee City, as Warner describes it, was a **class system** because movement between the status groups was both legal and accepted. Even if few people managed to move into a higher class during their lives, the possibility was there, making the system relatively open and operating as a safety valve.

Maintaining a traditional and highly valued lifestyle, as these East Coast fishermen are attempting to do, is difficult in a modern industrial society.

Clearly the "class system" comes closer to describing Canada than "estate system" or "caste system," but many would question the appropriateness of the first term. Does the idea of some six distinct groupings, however open to in-movement they are, accurately portray the system? Or should one think of each family being, as it were, a class of its own, occupying a unique position in the social hierarchy slightly different from the position of any other? No one has yet come up with exactly the right term for such a system. The latest attempt, suggested by Tyree (Tyree et al. 1979), is the word glissando, but it does not seem to be catching on. (The word is used in music to refer to that one passage everyone can play on the piano, running one's finger rapidly up or down the keyboard and playing each note with equal duration and stress.) Instead, most sociologists use the term **social stratification** and oppose it to **social class** (this is the source of the double title of this chapter). The term is used even if the metaphor does not apply perfectly. Stratification, in geology, refers to a land formation in which distinct, observable layers have been formed; the comparable social formation would be the class system.

Is Canada more like a class system or a glissando? There is no simple answer. Neither the question nor the problem of definition is unique to Canada.

Most sociologists would agree that, in terms of social organization, Canada closely resembles the United States and is not very different from any of the European nations, so the problem is broadly shared by sociologists. In pursuing the issue, they have carefully weighed the distinction between office work ("white collar") and factory work ("blue collar"). Is there a real gap between the two types of work that would make the glissando rather more like a two-class system? Although today the wages paid for the two kinds of work show considerable overlap, researchers note that even the lowest white-collar workers have real advantages in job security and in fringe benefits. The debate is unsettled. Many sociologists use the terms blue collar and white collar without actually meaning that, in their view, Canada has two distinct classes. Rather they use the terms as convenient shorthand to refer to the lower and upper part of the glissando.

THEORIES OF SOCIAL STRATIFICATION

Sociologists have reached no consensus on why inequalities are always found in human societies. Rather, they have a variety of theoretical perspectives, often sharply contrasting with one another. Some theories deal with the reasons for inequality. Others describe what kind of systems are likely to exist. Some of the major perspectives currently used for studying stratification are briefly outlined here.

Functionalism and Parsons

Functionalism, often called structural-functionalism (see Chapter 1), was originally and most fully developed by anthropologists. Although Radcliffe-Brown ([1952] 1956), Durkheim ([1893] 1964), and others used the term in the 19th century, a particularly vivid and concrete exposition of the idea came from Malinowski (1944).

Like many other anthropologists, Malinowski studied a small, nonliterate society. In endeavouring to understand its customs he gradually came to the conclusion that historical explanations were of little use. Without a written language, the people he studied had no accurate history to tell him. So he attempted to explain the customs solely in terms of the contemporary situation. He found this shift in emphasis rewarding. For example, he noted that Trobriand Island fishermen used magic extensively only when they were in dangerous ocean waters; when fishing in tranquil inland waters they did not bother with magic. Malinowski concluded that magic performed a psychological and social function in allaying anxiety. He became convinced that one can find a contemporary function for every custom. From this belief grew a view of human societies as exquisitely fine-tuned machines, with no wasted parts. As each organ performs a function within the human body, so each social custom performs some crucial and useful function that contributes to the survival of the whole society.

A functionalist looking at Canadian society asks what positive function is contributed by each social custom. What is the function, for example, of the cult of sports prowess among males in high school? Perhaps sports are informal training for manual jobs requiring physical strength and skill. Or perhaps team sports help develop cooperative skills useful in work settings. Functionalism turned social scientists away from seeking historical explanations. Functionalists do not, for instance, believe that a battle won or lost on the Plains of Abraham more than 200 years ago is the source of the separatist movement in modern Quebec. Rather, they insist instead that one look for the source in present-day irritants.

The best-known attempt at a functionalist explanation of social stratification was made by Davis and Moore (1945). Writing mainly of the United States, but in a way that is relevant to Canada, Davis and Moore note that jobs differ in the talent they require, in the training they require, in their difficulty, and in their importance to society. Because of these differences, the rewards offered for various jobs must differ. More income and prestige are given to some occupations than to others in order to recruit the most able individuals to the occupations and to motivate them to perform the jobs well. From these differences, inequalities inevitably arise, which ultimately form a system of stratification. Published first in 1945, this seemingly obvious piece of reasoning created a controversy within sociology that has not yet died down. Many sociologists were appalled at the theory, seeing it as a defence of privilege and exploitation. Tumin (1953) raised a particularly strong criticism. He argued, for example, that criminals, too, get rich in modern society, and that in the United States of the time, discrimination made it impossible for any black, however talented or useful, to receive the rewards available to a white.

Too frequently this skirmish between Davis and Moore and their critics is taken to be a test of the value of functional theory in its entirety. Davis and Moore were not important figures within the functionalist school, and their work should not be considered the school's best effort. A much more significant theorist within the tradition, Talcott Parsons, also discussed the nature of stratification in a series of three papers (1940; 1953; 1970) and more generally in his last works (for instance, 1977). Parsons's discussion differs extensively from that of Davis and Moore, and yet it cannot be considered the definitive statement on stratification, since Parsons's many revisions suggest dissatisfaction with it. Perhaps one should see the whole incident as unfortunate in having pre-empted the chance for the functionalists to make an effective statement about their position on the issue of social stratification.

Marx and Weber

One reason for the sharp criticism of the Davis-Moore theory was that many sociologists were already committed to a different theory explaining the reasons for social inequality. Karl Marx, they felt, had already provided an adequate explanation of why there was social stratification (for example, Marx [1867] 1956). Each historical period is characterized by a distinctive economic base or **mode of production.** In the Middle Ages, production was agricultural; in modern times, it is industrial. In each historical period a minority controls the means of production. In the Middle Ages, the landowners controlled the society and the peasants did the work. In the present era, a few powerful people control the means of production by owning the factories. In the Middle Ages, the few powerful landowners exploited the many peasants; today the few powerful owners, the **bourgeoisie,** exploit the many workers, the **proletariat.** The bourgeoisie, or capitalists, seized power from the landowners in a series of violent rebellions, particularly in the early 1800s. Another series of violent revolutions, according to Marx, will eventually occur as the proletariat seize power from the capitalists. Meanwhile, inequality in industrialized societies is to be explained as a system of exploitation by the capitalists, coupled with differential rewards given out to those who show varying degrees of support for them. (See Chapter 1.) The theory must be taken seriously, if only because it is the official ideology of many governments today, including the Soviet Union and China. It is also followed by a number of sociologists studying stratification in Canada today (for example, Cuneo 1978a).

The term class is important to Marxist theory, where it has a somewhat different meaning from Warner's. His six divisions would not be considered real social classes by the Marxists. Warner, they say, had found some rather trivial differences. To Marxists, only a status group based on a distinctive relationship to the mode of economic production is a **social class.** Owners form one class and workers another, whether they realize it or not. One can see the utility of this concept of class. The farmers within Canada form an economic class in this sense, and whether they realize it or not, government decisions or world events can affect each of them more or less equally. Thus, it would seem reasonable for them to develop some consciousness of kind and to take action to protect themselves as a group. This sequence of events—a group sharing economic interests gradually developing a consciousness of this common interest and then going on to direct political action—was to Marx the main process by which social change occurred. Marxist theory suggests that social stratification is the most important subfield of sociology.

Marx's work has earned much criticism and much praise. Soon after he wrote, a major criticism of his work was made by Max Weber. Weber particularly questioned Marx's idea that economic interests formed the only important axis of stratification. He proposed instead a view of society in which hierarchies are found not only in class but also in what he called status and party ([1930] 1958). In identifying "class" as one component of stratification, Weber conceded the importance of economic elements, although he emphasized orientation to the market rather than to modes of production. But beyond this Weber suggested that rankings could be based on non-economic criteria, and he used the term **status** for that kind of hierarchy, based only on "honour." Possibly the clearest example of a status system in Weber's own time was the continuing deference given to the remnants of aristocracy throughout Europe; today we might think of celebrity, as displayed on late-night TV talk shows, as an example of high status not necessarily associated with wealth. Finally, in referring to **party,** Weber was drawing attention to the role played by politically based collectivities and the role of sheer power in the structure of societies.

By suggesting a three-way classification on the basis of class, status, and party, Weber was not minimizing the importance of economic considerations. Class was clearly dominant, with status only rarely operating independently. But in drawing attention to the role of power and authority, Weber foreshadowed work such as that of John Porter, which has become of considerable importance within Canada.

Elite Theory: John Porter's View of Canada

In *The Vertical Mosaic* (1965), John Porter presented evidence about the existence of inequality in Canadian society and about the manner in which such inequalities intertwined with ethnicity. As already discussed, this book changed Canadians' awareness of social stratification. It also did more, because in the second half of the book, Porter went on to examine the distribution of power in Canada with a discussion of elites. Underlying this discussion was a theory of society that was only partially stated. In Porter's view, a modern society like Canada is formed by large, important institutions—the business firms, the government, the schools and universities, and the labour unions are the most significant today in Canada. (In the United States, the military would also be of importance, one would suppose, and in earlier times one could not have omitted the church.) Each of these large structures is organized and administered by a small group at the top, and these people, collectively, form the **elite.** A small elite—some two or three thousand people—runs Canada. To Porter, it could not be otherwise. Large structures require powerful central leaders, so an elite is inevitable.

Porter did not criticize the existence of an elite. Rather, he was concerned about whether every Canadian had an equal chance to enter it, and he concluded that everyone did not. To enter this inner circle, it seemed, one must be a male of British origin, come from a prosperous family, and have attended the "right" schools. To Porter these requirements were both unfair and unwise. Everyone should have a chance, and to omit certain groups meant that people of real talent and ability were probably not being properly used. More recent studies have followed Porter's lead (Clement 1975; Olsen 1980), while others have suggested problems to be found in his work (Hunter 1976; Ogmundson 1982).

Many other writers have seen the inevitability of elite rule (for example, Pareto 1935; Michels 1959). Such theories do not see perfect equality as a realizable goal but often argue for the development of procedures to ensure that the most talented and able are given the powerful and privileged positions. Such a system has been called a **meritocracy** (Young 1958).

Developmental Perspective

The theories of social stratification that we have described differ extensively from one another and have generated much debate and conflict among Canadian sociologists. Yet as each theory has been adapted to fit the Canadian case, a common theme has grown. All sociologists studying stratification within Canada, regardless of their theoretical orientation, seem to share to some degree an unspoken consensus: that Canada is a developing country, on its way to some better, more prosperous future. They thus share what could be called a developmental perspective. The Marxists see Canada's development as slowed by the bourgeoisie, because they are foreign in origin or at least too oriented toward other nations, particularly the United States. Others are concerned that the Canadian elite, chosen without truly extensive competition, lacks the skill or legitimacy to guide the country's development. When functionalist terminology is used (as it was frequently by Porter), it is used not to describe what Canada presently is but rather to present a vision of a more rational and fair Canada that could be developed. The experience of living next to a much more powerful and more affluent country may dominate Canadian thought, producing a basic consensus with the effects, both positive and negative, that such consensus can produce.

INEQUALITY OF OPPORTUNITY IN CANADA

Since quite considerable differences in socioeconomic status exist within Canada and will persist into the foreseeable future, it is important to study who gets the better jobs and the higher income. Studies of this issue are called studies of social mobility or of status attainment, and they are a separate subfield within the general area of social stratification. The differences detected in such work are often quite subtle, so the research must use precise statistical procedures. "Social mobility" and "status attainment" do not refer to different processes but to differing methodological approaches to the common problem.

Classic Approaches: The Mobility Tables

Social mobility, the older of the two approaches, concentrates on the analysis of what are called intergenerational occupational mobility tables. The use of this method within sociology was begun independently but in a similar manner in the United States by Rogoff (1953) and in England by Glass (1954). Exhibits 8-5 and 8-6 present the data for such tables for Canada, based on a national study conducted in 1972. The tables show

Exhibit 8-5
Intergenerational Occupational Mobility of Canadian Males (aged 25–64)

	Father's Occupation							
Son's Occupation	Professional, upper manager	Semiprofessional, technician	Middle manager, supervisor	Clerical, sales worker	Foreman, skilled craftsman	Semiskilled worker	Unskilled labourer	Farm owner, operator, labourer
Professional, upper manager	251 40.9	53 22.0	240 24.5	225 18.5	320 11.6	133 8.9	119 8.3	196 5.7	1535 12.6
Semiprofessional, technician	75 12.3	49 20.3	73 7.5	108 8.9	179 6.5	80 5.3	70 4.9	113 3.3	747 6.1
Middle manager, supervisor	102 16.6	29 12.2	216 22.1	207 17.0	352 12.7	163 10.9	160 11.2	243 7.0	1471 12.1
Clerical, sales worker	71 11.7	34 14.1	148 15.2	230 18.9	389 14.0	177 11.8	192 13.5	289 8.4	1530 12.6
Foreman, skilled craftsman	71 11.7	41 17.2	168 17.2	231 19.0	917 33.1	436 29.1	382 26.9	879 25.5	3126 25.6
Semiskilled worker	18 3.0	10 4.0	49 5.0	86 7.1	254 9.2	251 16.8	191 13.4	460 13.3	1319 10.8
Unskilled labourer	20 3.2	18 7.3	72 7.4	116 9.6	326 11.8	232 15.5	287 20.2	579 16.8	1650 13.5
Farm owner, operator, labourer	4 .7	7 2.9	11 1.2	13 1.0	35 11.2	27 1.8	21 1.5	694 20.1	811 6.7
	612 5.0	240 2.0	977 8.0	1216 10.0	2772 22.7	1499 12.3	1422 11.7	3453 28.3	12190 100.0

the responses of an adult sample (called sons and daughters in the exhibits) to questions about their current occupation and that held by the father when the respondent was 16 years of age. The information about occupation is coded into a system that represents socioeconomic status (in this case, an adaptation of the classification shown in Exhibit 8-4). The numbers in the body of the table are percentages representing the frequency with which various patterns of intergenerational occupation change occurred. Thus, the top left cell of the first table shows that of the men in the sample whose fathers held professional or managerial jobs, 40.9 percent reported that they also held a job falling into that category.

Exhibit 8-6
Intergenerational Occupational Mobility of Canadian Females (aged 25–64)

Daughter's Occupation	Father's Occupation								
	Professional, upper manager	Semiprofessional, technician	Middle manager, supervisor	Clerical, sales worker	Foreman, skilled craftsman	Semiskilled worker	Unskilled labourer	Farm owner, operator, labourer	
Professional, upper manager	106 / 25.7	22 / 13.2	71 / 11.1	88 / 9.2	113 / 6.8	40 / 4.5	40 / 4.5	139 / 8.6	620 / 8.6
Semiprofessional, technician	102 / 24.6	37 / 22.2	99 / 15.6	122 / 12.7	168 / 10.2	76 / 8.7	84 / 9.3	179 / 11.0	867 / 12.0
Middle manager, supervisor	29 / 7.0	12 / 6.9	55 / 8.7	77 / 8.1	137 / 8.3	58 / 6.6	63 / 7.0	107 / 6.5	537 / 7.4
Clerical, sales worker	161 / 38.9	85 / 50.9	329 / 51.6	551 / 57.4	978 / 59.1	485 / 55.4	521 / 57.5	685 / 42.1	3795 / 52.4
Forewoman, skilled craftswoman	2 / .4	4 / 2.2	22 / 3.4	15 / 1.5	40 / 2.4	29 / 3.3	20 / 2.2	28 / 1.7	159 / 2.2
Semiskilled worker	12 / 2.9	1 / .7	40 / 6.3	64 / 6.7	130 / 7.9	112 / 12.8	86 / 9.5	237 / 14.6	683 / 9.4
Unskilled labourer	2 / .5	6 / 3.7	19 / 3.0	39 / 4.0	79 / 4.8	73 / 8.3	87 / 9.6	190 / 11.7	495 / 6.8
Farm owner, operator, labourer	0 / 0	0 / .2	2 / .3	3 / .3	10 / .6	2 / .2	5 / .5	64 / 3.9	85 / 1.2
	414 / 5.7	168 / 2.3	636 / 8.8	959 / 13.2	1653 / 22.8	875 / 12.1	906 / 12.5	1630 / 22.5	7241 / 100.0

Studying the tables reveals the basic patterns. Beginning with Exhibit 8-5, which shows the results for the males, one can note that almost anything that can happen does happen. Thus, there are quite a few cases of the sons of farmers or farm labourers making it to the very top of the rank, ending up in professional or managerial occupations. There are also a few cases of sons born into highly successful families ending up at the bottom. The second pattern that can be noted is that many sons do follow more or less in their fathers' footsteps. The cells falling on the diagonal, which is marked off by the slanting shaded areas, represent those cases in which the son closely followed the father. There are always sizable numbers in these cells, so some occupational inheritance does occur—but it is never the majority. The most common pattern is for the son to end up in a category relatively near the father's—in one of the cells adjacent to the diagonal—but not in exactly the same category. Clearly this is a long way from a caste or estate system, in which each son would have to end up exactly where his father was, but it is not a totally open system either, since there is some tendency for sons to follow fathers. Comparing a table such as this one with those produced from many European nations and Australia shows that the tendencies within Canada are remarkably like those found elsewhere. The differences among the various industrialized nations are in fact so slight that very careful and detailed statistical analysis is needed to detect them.

The table constructed for the women in the sample is necessarily somewhat different from that for men. Vast numbers of women flow into the clerical-sales category of jobs and into the semiprofessional occupations, such as teaching and nursing—the traditional jobs for women. Since we are comparing women to their fathers rather than to their mothers, less correspondence is to be expected. (So few of the mothers worked when the daughters were 16 years of age that a comparison with them is impractical.)

Despite these differences, the overall patterns are not totally dissimilar. Again it can be said that almost everything happens at least a few times. And there is, again, a tendency for cases to cluster toward the diagonal cells, representing occupational inheritance. Those not on the diagonal tend again to be close to it. Tables like this made for women are not yet common around the world, so it is less possible to talk about how closely Canada resembles other nations, but what information there is to date suggests that once again Canada is not unusual.

Further study of the tables can show other patterns. Comparing only the row and column totals and ignoring the main bodies of the tables is informative. Looking at Exhibit 8-5, one can see, for example, how much smaller a component of the labour force farmers are among the sons than they were among the fathers. Although 28.3 percent of the fathers reported they were farm owners, operators, or labourers, only 6.7 percent of the sons reported this kind of job. Another difference is that many more sons than fathers hold white-collar jobs in the professional, clerical, and sales occupations, as this part of the labour force has shown the greatest growth in employment in recent decades.

These kinds of shifts influence the patterns within the table. The cells falling above and to the right of the diagonal represent cases in which the son has a better job than his father did—called **upward social mobility.** Those below the diagonal represent **downward social mobility.** As the components of the labour force have varied in size, with higher status jobs becoming more common, the number of sons who are upwardly mobile exceeds the number who are downwardly mobile, so there are more cases on the diagonal than below (57.5 percent compared to 18.8, the rest being on the diagonal). More are winning than losing at this game in Canada. Such a pattern can persist only so long as the trend toward creating more high status jobs and phasing out those with lower status continues; thus one can see how the commitment to economic development in Canada has real consequences for individuals.

The patterns for women are similar. Clerical and sales occupations are considered to have relatively high status, so they rank more highly than most jobs held by the fathers. Again, there is a tendency for there to be more winners than losers (68.2 percent compared to 17.2).

Status Attainment: Educational and Occupational Attainment

While the mobility tables portray the extent to which occupations are inherited, other questions—particularly those about the extent to which educational attainment is involved in the process—are not examined. The **status attainment** approach considers the other factors as well, although at the expense of simplicity. Exhibit 8-7 shows the way in which the status attainment approach handles the same problem. The exhibit presents what is called a **path diagram,** a statistical presentation of results that is used in other areas of sociology and in other disciplines. This path diagram organizes the information from the same 1972 national survey into a pattern, with the arrows in the diagram signifying presumed causal relationships. Thus, the diagram assumes that both the education and the occupational level of the father influence the respondent's educational attainment. It also assumes that the respondent's educational attainment, as well as the father's occupation, influence the respondent's job upon entry into the labour force. This job, education, and the father's occupation are, in turn, assumed to have a direct relationship to the respondent's occupational level at the time of the interview. This way of presenting the data was pioneered by Blau and Duncan (1967) in the United States and is felt to give a deeper understanding of the whole process of status achievement than the mobility tables alone. (For a path diagram on the formation of educational aspirations, see Chapter 6.)

The numbers given beside each line in the diagram are **path coefficients.** They can range from 0.00 to 1.00 and under special circumstances can be negative numbers. They measure the strength of the presumed causal relationships discussed above. A coefficient of 0.00 would mean the assumption is untrue and no causal influence exists. A perfect relationship of 1.00, in which one factor *always* leads to another, is never expected in real data. So the question is where the coefficients lie between 0.00 and 1.00. This diagram shows strong effects of the respondent's education on occupational status. It shows that the father's level of education is important in influencing the educational attainments of both males and females. The manner in which the father's occupational level influences the son or daughter is shown to be mostly indirect, through education and through the status of the respondent's first job. Only a very small coefficient (0.107 for males and 0.047 for females) lies on the path from the father's occupation to the respondent's, suggesting little direct causal effect.

Exhibit 8-7
Path Diagram of Occupational Status Attainment, Canada: The Basic Model

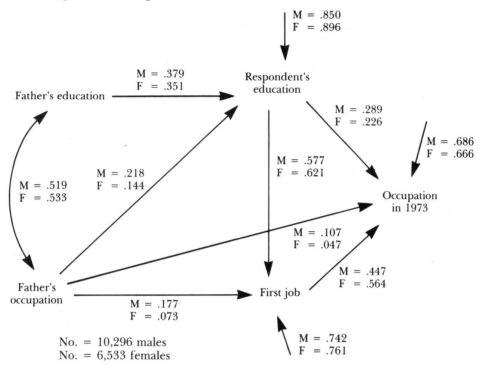

No. = 10,296 males
No. = 6,533 females

The coefficients in the diagram are quite similar for males and females, suggesting that the differences between males and females shown in the mobility tables must be qualified. Although daughters do not follow their father's footsteps quite the way sons do, an examination of levels of occupational status (rather than of the precise categories into which the jobs fall) shows that what happens to the daughters seems very much like what happens to the sons.

Comparable path diagrams have been prepared for a number of nations. The Canadian results are remarkably like those from the United States (for example, see Blau and Duncan 1967, 170.) Getting ahead in Canada is much the same process as in the United States, and there is no evidence to suggest that barriers to getting ahead are greater here than abroad.

The diagrams can be altered and extended to test for the influence of other factors that influence status attainment, such as ethnicity, province of birth, and size of family of origin. An analysis of these influences has been done for Canada (Boyd et al. 1982; 1985). Major differences between men and women appear when one considers the determinants of income, rather than occupational status (Goyder 1981).

SOCIAL CHANGE AND SOCIAL STRATIFICATION

Canada's stratification system has continuously changed through recent years and will doubtless continue to do so in the future. In recent years the major change to the system stems from a general process of economic development and growth that has characterized Canada throughout the past few decades. The changes affect income levels, education, and occupational status. Some are changes of level across the board; in other cases the growth has been uneven in different sections of the society.

Changes in Level of Income

Economic development has led to a real increase in income and wealth within Canada throughout this century. Inflation has been a factor obscuring the trend, particularly in recent years, but the growth in affluence is nonetheless unmistakable. Questions routinely included in the Canadian censuses of 1941 and 1951 asked whether the household had running water, a flush toilet, and electricity. Today a question concerning the number of telephones would be more apt.

The overall wealth of each nation has come to be measured by a single figure, the **gross national product** (GNP), the total dollar value of goods and services produced in a given year. This statistic is now so universally recognized that newspapers regularly report its value and each year's percentage change. The **per capita** GNP, which is simply the GNP divided by the number of people in the society, corrects for the size of the nation and gives a figure that roughly measures average individual affluence. Canada's per capita GNP has grown continuously but in fits and starts through this century, with a bad setback only during the Depression of the 1930s. By mid-1985 it had reached $17,700 (Statistics Canada 1985d; 1985e). The individual, on average, does not see this much money, of course; much of it disappears in various ways in taxes, reinvestment, and the like. But as the GNP increases, individuals on average get more affluent and are able to live at a higher standard of living.

The growth in income has not been even across all sectors of the society. It appears that workers in industries with particularly well-developed unions have improved wages the most. Until recently these industries were those that had large manufacturing enterprises—automotive, for example. This uneven growth has had real consequences. The gap in pay between the factory workers in this type of industry and the office workers in other sectors has narrowed or vanished, and the distinction between white-collar and blue-collar occupations has come into question. Since such industries have tended to employ more men than women there have been implications for gender differences in rates of pay. More recently unionization has developed in other sectors, such as education and the civil service (Hunter 1986), which may result in further shifts in average incomes by sector.

The three-bedroom middle-class house ties up much of the wealth of the average Canadian.

The real growth in average income for all—plus the narrowing gap between the incomes earned by blue-collar and white-collar workers—has raised the question of whether some of the class differences in lifestyle will also disappear. In particular, Marxist-oriented sociologists have been interested in whether higher incomes will lead the traditional working class to become more like the middle class, a process they call *embourgeoisement*. This matter has been extensively studied in England (see Goldthorpe and Lockwood 1969) and the answer seems to be that lifestyles in general are changing so rapidly that, although there is some convergence, it is not toward the old middle-class way of life but toward some emergent third style, a particularly home-oriented and family way of life that they have called privatization.

Prolonged Schooling

Until quite recently, Canada was a country in which a "real boy" dropped out of school as soon as he legally could. Girls and sissies went on to become high-school graduates, and they could count on fairly easy jobs as teachers or in offices as a reward. This is a caricature, of course; many young men dropped out of school because their families desperately needed extra income, but the idea that many years should be spent in schooling is for the majority quite recent.

Much controversy surrounds the issue of how much schooling is needed or wise. In the 1960s, governments and intellectuals believed that ensuring more schooling for the workforce would result automatically in faster economic growth. This perspective, called **human capital theory**, had a period of dominance that led to generous government support of high schools and post-secondary institutions. Now the pendulum has swung again, and concern is expressed that the society may be becoming overeducated. (For more on educational methods and priorities, see Chapter 6 of this book.) The heart of the concern is the belief that employers simply upgrade the requirements for an occupation if a supply of highly educated people exists.

Will a B.A. be required of an office secretary if B.A.s are plentiful? In support of this viewpoint, note that no one today expects high-school graduation to be the key to open any doors, although it may have had such properties not long ago when university degrees were scarce. But counter-arguments are possible. A secretary with a B.A. may indeed be a better secretary, able to handle more responsibility, and worth more pay. While it is hard to imagine a Canada in which most of the labour force has education beyond high school and jobs that match, before the 1950s it must have been equally hard to imagine the Canada that has developed now, in which some high-school training is almost universal. Somewhere in the Canadian newspapers of 1920, one can surely find dire predictions about the foolhardiness of making high-school training available too readily; with a few changes in wording, such statements would look much like the dire predictions of today.

The Changing Occupational Structure

Comparing the row and column totals of Exhibits 8-5 and 8-6 gives some flavour of the changes that have been occurring in occupations within this century, but the comparison is imperfect because the father's generation in the table is only a rough indication of the earlier state of the society. Some men have no children and are thus omitted from the table. Since immigrants are included in the table, some of the fathers probably worked in the country of origin, not in Canada. However, other data on occupational changes are available (see Ostry 1967), and they confirm the basic patterns.

Farmers and farm labourers have sunk from a dominant part of the male labour force to an almost trivial proportion (5.2 percent in 1981). This change, which means a movement from experiencing some degree of independence to holding a wage-earning job, has been met with ambivalence. In a 1965 survey, English Canadians reported that a return to farming was the occupation they would most prefer beyond whatever they then held (from my unpublished data). French Canadians, perhaps remembering the job of the farmer more accurately, did not share this attitude. A less regretted change must be the disappearance of what could

THE CONSEQUENCES OF AFFLUENCE

After the Second World War, the whole industrialized world, led by North America, underwent an enormous growth in income and wealth, which John Kenneth Galbraith (1978) christened *affluence*. It brought with it many surprises. We did not simply move forward in lock step to a time in which very wealthy stockbrokers had their shoes shined by moderately wealthy bootblacks. Rather, affluence has led to a complex set of transformations. The kinds of work we have learned to call *labour intensive* became inordinately expensive. A new pop-up toaster became cheap; getting it repaired when it broke became unthinkable. Do-it-yourself repair work by suburban husbands, a butt of many jokes, was a realistic reaction to the observation that their own weekend time was now worth less than that of most repairmen. Domestic service became rare.

The full story of why certain kinds of occupations disappeared rather than just becoming better paid still needs to be told. It may be that long-held aversions to certain kinds of work—such as domestic service—could at last be expressed. A consequence for social stratification was that symbolizing wealth through the immediate employment of others became more rare. Gentlemen learned to soil their hands, and certainly carried their own luggage. This produced at least a superficial levelling of lifestyles.

be called brute labour—jobs involving lifting, carrying, digging, and so on, in which the worker was hired for physical strength and endurance and was expected to sweat through the eight hours or more of each workday. Either machines have replaced the men who did this work, as a mechanical backhoe is brought in to dig even the tiniest ditch, or the work is simply no longer done. Also more rare today are the jobs implied in the term sweat shops, such as the huge rooms full of sewing machines with female operators—often working on piece-work wages—that underlay Montreal's textile industry. These jobs have not disappeared, but many of the employers have moved the work to places with lower wage rates, such as Hong Kong, Korea, or, more recently, Indonesia. The most modern of technical devices, the silicon chip, was invented in the United States, but the chips are assembled in Indonesia and Taiwan.

Few people regret the loss of brute-labour jobs, which have been replaced most often by semiskilled work: the sort of factory job, tending a machine, that a worker can learn in the plant in three months or less. The kind of skilled work that was done by craftspeople, such as cabinet makers or skilled machinists, is also disappearing to some degree in a process that has been called de-skilling. (For more on de-skilling, see Chapter 11.) Braverman (1974) argues that the process of de-skilling is now dominant; others would note that the development of extremely challenging jobs in computer programming and the like is occurring at the same time and may be the stronger tendency.

Other changes that are met with some regret include the disappearance of many small businesses, as the small grocery store either becomes part of a chain or is franchised. Independent professionals are also more rare. Doctors have almost become government employees, and many lawyers, engineers, and so on, now work for salaries rather than fees.

Marx argued that many of the changes in the nature of work that came along with industrialization reduced the involvement of the worker in the product; he used the term **alienation** to refer to this process. Marx's position continues to be considered of relevance and importance.

SUMMARY

The study of social stratification is so fundamental to sociology that it appears throughout this book. Questions of stratification are intrinsic to basic sociological theoretical perspectives. Social stratification is an issue in the discussion of gender, ethnicity, the family, deviance, and regionalism.

It has been suggested in this chapter that where the available evidence makes comparison possible, the Canadian stratification system resembles that of other industrialized societies. When inequality and stratification influence other parts of the social system, the effects in Canada are much like those in other countries. Canada falls into a group of societies that share the characteristics of relative affluence, a high degree of industrialization, and a predominantly urban, rather than rural, population. These industrialized societies have each developed stratification systems that are highly similar and that differ from the systems of less industrialized countries. The degree of similarity appears greater than popular opinion would expect and also greater than might be expected given the somewhat different government policies and institutional arrangements of the various nations. As sociological research proceeds, it becomes evident that powerful forces, as yet only partly perceived, produce within each industrialized society almost identical systems of social stratification.

FOR FURTHER READING

Boyd, Monica, John Goyder, F.E. Jones, H.A. McRoberts, P.C. Pineo, and J. Porter
1981 "Status Attainment in Canada: Findings of the Canadian Mobility Study." *Canadian Review of Sociology and Anthropology* 18: 657-73.
A summary presentation of the basic results of the Canadian mobility survey, this article requires some statistical background of the reader. It presents the most recent information on barriers to mobility within Canada, and could be read in conjunction with Peter M. Blau and Otis Dudley Duncan, *The American Occupational Structure* (New York: John Wiley and Sons, 1967).

Curtis, James E., and William G. Scott
1979 *Social Stratification: Canada.* Toronto: Prentice-Hall.
This work is a collection of research papers by sociologists dealing with social stratification. The basic dimensions of stratification are discussed, and selected papers deal with the correlates of class, power, and status differences. An extensive, extremely useful bibliography of Canadian works on stratification is included.

Hunter, Alfred A.
1986 *Class Tells: On Social Inequality in Canada,* 2nd ed. Toronto: Butterworths.
An upper-year textbook on social stratification in Canada. The work includes a review of major theories, description of the present-day distributions of rewards, and special sections on social stratification and sex roles and ethnicity.

Porter, John
1965 *The Vertical Mosaic: An Analysis of Social Class and Power in Canada.* Toronto: University of Toronto Press.
This book was the first major work on social stratification to receive acclaim among both sociologists and the broader reading public. It remains of importance, although parts of it are now dated, because the work strongly influenced the development of Canadian sociology. More recent works in the same tradition include Wallace Clement, *The Canadian Corporate Elite,* and Denis Olsen, *The State Elite.*

Marx, Karl
1956 *Selected Writings in Sociology and Social Philosophy.* T.B. Bottomore, trans. London: C.A. Watts.
This is one of many sources for basic writings of Karl Marx.

Weber, Max
1958 "Class, Status and Party." In H.H. Gerth and C.W. Mills, eds. *Max Weber: Essays in Sociology.* New York: Oxford University Press.
The classic paper on stratification by Weber, which is to some degree a reply to Marx, is translated and presented in this collection. Other useful work by Weber can be found in the same collection.

CHAPTER 9

SOCIOLOGY AND GENDER

R.A. Sydie

315

Man for the field and woman for the hearth;
Man for the sword, and for the needle she;
Man with the head, and woman with the heart;
Man to command, and woman to obey. . . .

Tennyson, *The Princess*

Each society has a set of assumptions about the nature of masculinity and femininity. The most basic such assumption, common to nearly all societies, is that men and women are unequal in some sociocultural way. Assumptions about relations between men and women seem to change very slowly, and Tennyson's 19th-century sentiments are not entirely misplaced in Canadian society today. Legal reforms and social constraints may point to increasing equality between the sexes, but widespread beliefs and attitudes persistently undermine abstract legal or political changes. The laughter with which many male members of Parliament greeted a report on wife-battering in the House of Commons in May 1982 provided a clear and public demonstration of this cultural resistance to change in relations between the sexes.

GENDER ROLES

From birth, each individual is labelled male or female in terms of biological sex.[1] The **sex** of the individual is determined by chromosomal, hormonal, anatomical, and physiological characteristics. Sex is a **status**— a place in society with culturally defined obligations and rights—that is ascribed; in other words, it is a fixed quality over which one has no control. In contrast, gender is an achieved status. **Gender** refers to the social, cultural, and psychological characteristics assumed appropriate to a particular sex status. Gender is, therefore, learned behaviour that individuals internalize more or less successfully. Learning appropriate **gender roles**— the expected patterns of behaviour for males and females—involves learning rules that are both proscriptive and prescriptive. For example, in our society boys are explicitly instructed not to be like girls but to be independent and tough, while girls are told not to be pushy (aggressive) but to be sweet (docile).[2] What they are learning is gender norms—collections of beliefs and behavioural expectations about what society considers appropriate gender behaviour and attitudes and what penalties are imposed for non-compliance.

Cross-culturally, gender roles vary considerably. Margaret Mead's well-known study (1949) of several South Pacific peoples illustrates the range of differences in what societies label appropriate male and female behaviour. The Arapesh, she found, were a gentle mountain people concerned with growing things, including children. The relations within the group were generally cooperative, and for both sexes there was an emphasis on the parenting role. The Mundugumor also exhibited similar traits for both sexes, but, in contrast to the Arapesh, they were a hostile, aggressive people. The society was characterized by institutionalized hostility that affected all relationships irrespective of kin or lineage ties, and both sexes disliked the parental role. The Tchambuli were a further contrast. Essentially they reversed the gender expectations of our own society: the women undertook the group's major social and economic tasks, leaving the men to artistic pursuits, adornment of themselves, and gossip with other men.

Within a single society, the social norms for gender roles may vary over time and with circumstances. For example, the expectations applied to the pre-teen role in our society are different from those applied to the role of young adult, even though the same individual fills both at slightly different times. The role of wife or husband alters with a range of possibilities, such as the production of children, the number and age differences of the children, and marital dissolution (separation, divorce, or death). Expectations are also modified by other social attributes, such as class position, ethnicity, race, and religion. For example, the Manchester factory hands of the 1860s would have had great difficulty recognizing Tennyson's verse as a description of their own daily reality.

Women's Idealized Gender Role

The domesticity, emotionality, and passivity of woman in the Tennyson verse represented an ideal, but an ideal with a great deal of influence. An illustration comes from a lecture, titled "The Proper Sphere and Influence of Women in Christian Society," delivered to the Young Men's Christian Association in Halifax in 1856. After demonstrating that the home was woman's proper sphere, Reverend Robert Sedgewick asked, "How is she to be adjusted to her place?" His answer was education, and although he admitted the three Rs and perhaps some music or languages, the most important part of her studies was to consist of the essential "ologies":

> washology and its sister bakeology. There is drainology and scrubology. There is mendology, and cookology . . . a science this the more profoundly it is studied it becomes the more palatable, and the more skilfully its principles are applied its professors acquire the greater popularity. (Quoted in Cook and Mitchinson 1976, 20, 21.)

The ideal of Tennyson, the Reverend Sedgewick, and many, many others was, however, at odds with the conditions that many women confronted in both the industrial cities of Europe and the wilderness of Canada. Susanna Moodie, Catharine Parr Traill, and Anne Langton would have agreed that their proper sphere was the home. However, the nature of the homes they came to in Canada and the realities of their daily lives made nonsense of the behavioural and even attitudinal expectations of the ideal. As Anne Langton confessed in her journals, the feminine virtues and manners were of little use in the bush, and at times she found herself "wishing a long-forgotten wish that I had been born of the rougher sex." Indeed, the angel in the home idealized by Langton's male counterparts was transformed in her view to a "bit of a slave" in the Canadian wilderness (Langton 1964, 60, 95).

The ideal of the Western world has, however, survived despite its obvious unreality for the majority of women over the years. One reason for its tenacity has been its adoption in early socialization, so that even intellectuals supposedly concerned with the objective description and explanation of the social world have not proved immune. Of course, not all male thinkers have been unaware of the disadvantages Western gender relations pose for the female; John Stuart Mill is an example of one who was not "sex blind." And many intellectuals have seen the endorsement of the domestic role of women as supporting what women themselves desired. Nonetheless, the pervasive ideal has meant that scientists, and specifically sociologists, have often produced descriptions of the social world that were essentially descriptions of a man's world in which women, when they made any appearance, were present only as wives and mothers or—the other side of the ideal—as fallen women.

In some cases, social scientists have taken pains to demonstrate the appropriate (traditional) female roles in society in the face of what they regarded as disturbing trends, such as the increasing participation of women in the paid labour force. In the late 1940s, Ferdinand Lundberg, a sociologist, and Marynia Farnham, a psychiatrist, collaborated on a book called *Modern Woman: The Lost Sex* in which they asserted:

> Women are the pivot around which much of the unhappiness of our day revolves, like a captive planet. To a significant extent they are responsible for it. . . . Our contention is that women as a whole (with exceptions) are maladjusted, much more so than men. For men have appropriate means to social adjustment: economic and political power, scientific power and athletic prowess. (1947, 24)

This maladjustment, they claimed, resulted from women's abandonment of their traditional roles as wives and mothers and their attempts to compete with men in the world of paid labour. The general unhappiness of society could be blamed, in large measure, on the "repeated verbal fouling of their nests by a long line of disordered female theorists" who had attached "disproportionate odium" to household work. The solution advanced by the authors was for the majority of women to "recapture those functions in which they have demonstrated superior capacity," which were, of course, "the nurturing functions centering around the home" (1947, 368).

Lundberg and Farnham were somewhat extreme but, in general, sociology has not seriously questioned the assumption that the proper place for women is in the home. In most cases, sociologists have not engaged in a nefarious chauvinist plot but have worked from the perspective they brought to the understanding of the social world. In general, that perspective has dichotomized the roles of the sexes in society as irreconcilable but natural opposites.

Sociological models of "man" imply generic use of the term, but most are actually predicated on a world in which male and female are opposites or complements. In these models, as de Beauvoir ([1949] 1974, xvii)

Gail Cummings's determination to play hockey with the boys made the public aware that separating athletes on the basis of gender, rather than skill, denied girls the opportunity to display or develop those skills and made them into second-class citizens.

points out, masculine and feminine are symmetrical "only as a matter of form"; in reality, masculine represents the positive and neutral "as indicated by the common use of *man* to designate human beings in general," and woman represents the negative.[3] The consequences of this equation for sociology are illustrated by the early studies on leisure. They concentrated on the work-leisure contrast as a problem essentially of males, assuming that women, as housewives at least, had leisure already. This assumption is only possible when beliefs about gender roles have been so internalized that reality is obscured. Housewives can be seen to have leisure only to the extent that housework is not seen to be work. As Gla r and Waehrer (1977, 6) indicate, the problem for the housewife is more likely to be too little leisure.

The dichotomized view of gender relations is not surprising when we consider that sociology is concerned with the regularities of behaviour and assumes some discoverable order in the world of human interaction. At the same time, sociological investigation is conducted within the very world that is the focus of inquiry. Consequently, given the relatively small number of female sociologists and the nature of sociological training, it comes as no surprise that the frameworks used to understand the social world have reflected the experiences and expectations of males. In the case of North American sociology, the frameworks have been particularly circumscribed, confined to reflecting the expectations and experiences of white middle-class males.[4]

DICHOTOMIZED FRAMEWORKS IN WESTERN HISTORY

The dichotomized perspective has provided a blueprint for the examination of the relationship of the sexes. The ideal of femininity—and its opposite, the evil temptress—provides the ideological basis for the application of distinct spheres in everyday life. In this section we will examine the interaction of the ideology and its manifestations in social arrangements historically.

The idea that women and men should occupy separate spheres and, therefore, play different roles in society as a result of their biological endowments has been and continues to be an important organizing principle for our society, one that is endorsed by many sociologists who see the harmony and well-being of society as dependent upon appropriate role-playing by the sexes. The ideology is translated into structural arrangements for the sexes in society in the manner indicated in Exhibit 9-1.

Strict division between the **social locations** of the sexes (the complex of status and roles assigned to and/or achieved by individuals of each sex) is, of course, an ideal. Although the industrialized capitalist countries of the West endorse this ideal and attempt to ensure its reality, in fact the female side of the equation is increasingly reality for only a minority of women. More generally, the dichotomized locations—as both ideal and reality—are historically and culturally limited. In many societies the basic division between home and work, or production and consumption, was and is simply not applicable.

The Middle Ages

The dichotomies are often assumed to have had some meaning in the feudal past of the West but, in fact, the divisions make little sense for those times.[5] Work and home, public and private were combined in feudal society in the most direct physical sense. For example, medieval domestic architecture indicates that the main hall, the major room, was the place in which all the business of living and working was conducted and to which all members of the household had free access. Sleeping quarters set off from the hall were rare, even in quite wealthy households. From the great estate to the peasant dwelling, daily life was public life for both women and men. Similarly, the production/consumption division was not clear-cut, as the household generally consumed most of what it could produce. Finally, tasks were not differentiated on the basis of real work (the work of men) and housework (the work of women).

This is not to suggest that feudal society had no clear role distinctions between the sexes. On the contrary, the Catholic Church, the source of much contemporary ideology, made a strong distinction in terms of biological sex, to the detriment of the female. Eve's temptation and the Fall were regarded as sufficient justification for women's subjection to men. As punishment to Eve, God had commanded, "I will greatly multiply thy sorrow and thy conception; in sorrow thou shalt bring forth children; and thy desire shall be to thy husband, and he shall rule over thee" (Genesis 3:16). The pronouncement combined nicely with the church fathers' belief that, because Eve was fashioned from Adam's rib, women were defective forms of men and therefore inferior matter. The whole ideology defined women's "natural" subordination to men.

Woman's inferiority was most clearly demonstrated, in the eyes of the Church, in her capacity for reproduction, which seemed to place her in closer touch with nature and, as a result, to make her more susceptible to the lures of the devil. Her sexuality in general also made her dangerous since women's sexual desires were thought to be greater and more uncontrollable than men's. Given these ideas it is understandable the Church taught that celibacy was the best state for both women and men. Since not everyone was strong enough to resist sexual temptation, marriage was regarded as the next best alternative, but people were cautioned against too great or too frequent enjoyment of sexual acts, even within the conjugal bond.

This medieval view of woman as the eternal temptress leading men into sin was not the only contemporary ideal. Rather, it was countered by the

> image of the wife who is also a companion and a helpmate to her husband; the adored mistress of the courtly romances, for love of whom men were

moved to goodness and beauty; the virtuous woman of the Book of Proverbs; or, now and then, the devoted mother. (Shahar 1983, 280)

The positive images were, however, often overshadowed by the negative ones. For example, an 11th-century bishop of Rennes suggested that, of all the devil's snares, "the worst . . . is woman, sad stem, evil root, vicious fount . . . honey and poison" (quoted in Geis and Geis 1980, 38).

As a result, the absence of a clear division of labour between the sexes did not mean equality. The general patriarchial principle of the rule of men over women prevailed and was given solid ideological justification in the teachings and practices of the Church. (The principle and methods of patriarchy are discussed in more detail later in the chapter.) The actual power of any patriarch varies, however, according to the social arrangements that support his position and the willingness of subordinates to obey his wishes. In feudal society, the power of the patriarch was demonstrated in the general rules governing inheritance of property and the maintenance of privileged position for high-status groups, but for the vast majority of men and women in feudal society—the peasants, the small traders and merchants, the artisans—that power was likely to be curtailed by the necessity for the joint labour of husband and wife in the common enterprise of obtaining a living on a daily basis.

The Rise of Capitalist Society

When did the dichotomized framework become appropriate for describing social reality? Several authors (Hamilton 1978; Hartmann 1976; Eisenstein 1979) indicate that the framework takes on meaning in the transition to a capitalist society. In feudal society the household formed the central, most significant part of the world for any individual, irrespective of sex; under capitalism the household shrank, in some cases restricting its female members to the domestic realm, in others throwing them out of the domestic sphere into paid labour.

A feudal economy is based on property ownership and a complex web of relationships of personal dependency, in which all members of society have both rights and obligations. In Western Europe, the rights and privileges of the great lord were balanced by his obligations to his vassals, and they had complementary patterns of rights and obligations with respect to their lord. With the introduction of capitalist forms of economic organization, the traditional ties were gradually broken, and money, rather than land, became the important unit of exchange and measure of status. Over time, the feudal status divisions based on lifestyle and claims to status honour were replaced by class divisions based on the ownership or non-ownership of the means of production. These changes in social organization affected the relationship between the sexes, the organization of the home and workplace, and the division of labour. The dichotomies illustrated in Exhibit 9-1 began to have some meaning for some social classes.

Exhibit 9-1
Dichotomized Gender Locations

Male	Female
Work	Home
Production	Consumption
Public	Private

In medieval times, all women, from the lady of the manor to the peasant's wife, had been involved in productive activities alongside their men. With capitalism , upper- and middle-class women were gradually removed from direct participation in the productive process:

> As the division of labour became more complex and specialised the richer yeoman's wives tended to withdraw from agricultural labour, though the responsibility for the dairy and catering for the farm servants who lived in and ate off their board meant that they were still very busy. In the towns, as the units of production became larger, the amount of capital a small master needed to start off on his own became greater, and so fewer journeymen could hope to become employers of labour. This affected the organisation of the guilds and the regulation of trade. Separate organisations developed to protect the masters, and the terms of entry became formalised. It was consequently more difficult for journeymen's wives to be involved in the workshop, or for the master's wife to supervise the apprentices, and less customary for widows to take over from their husbands. (Rowbotham 1973, 1)

The productive process gradually moved out of the domestic area, and the division of tasks between the sexes relegated some women to the private domestic sphere, reserving the public world of work for men. Although domestic work still entailed a considerable amount of labour, the expanded employment of servants, especially among the newly rich middle classes, meant that the wife's direct domestic duties decreased somewhat and her supervisory role increased. Indications of these changes are found in the increasing number of complaints from the late 16th century on, about idle wives interested only in gossiping and spending money (see Hamilton 1978, 42).

Capitalism may have provided upper-class and middle-class women with greater leisure time and an easier material life, but for peasant women it was a threat to the stability of the family unit. As wage labour gradually replaced subsistence agriculture, marriage was no longer a mutually beneficial arrangement for male and female peasants. Wages were earned by individuals, not families, so marriage could be regarded as a liability for men, especially in times of depressed wages; women, on the other hand, received wages a half to a third less than those of men

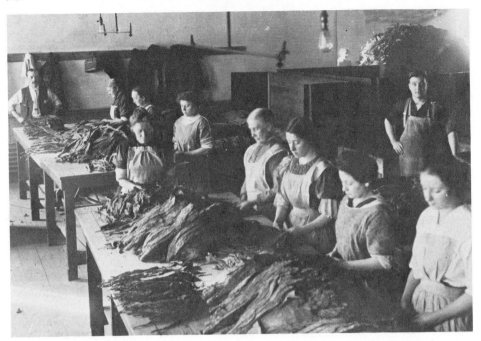

The distinction between classes of women became more defined with the rise of capitalism.

and so became increasingly dependent on marriage. One indication of this situation can be found in the records of the poor law administrations and charity organizations, which make it clear that the problem of destitution was often a problem of the abandoned woman and her children.

In brief, the advent of capitalism produced two groups of women: those of the privileged upper and middle class (the **bourgeoisie**), who were relegated to the private sphere of the home and whose primary function was consumption, and those of the working class (the **proletariat**) whose sphere, like that of their male counterparts, was often the public world of wage work and whose domestic life was precarious. These groupings continue today, and it is worth noting that, although the two share subordinate status as women in relation to men, they have opposed interests when examined in terms of the dichotomies.[6]

The changes in the household and in production set in motion by capitalism were parallelled by changes in ideology with regard to the nature of the female. As noted, the pre-Reformation Catholic Church held that woman's nature was an essentially lesser form and that celibacy was the ideal state, a protection for women as well as men. Marriage was distinctly a second-best state, and the Church had so little interest in it that it never developed inflexible rules about the ideal marital relationship. Protestantism took a different view of the situation. It taught that all of an individual's life should be conducted in a godly manner, and since most people lived their lives in families, the family became the location of the individual's dedication to the godly life. Obviously that life would be in jeopardy if one partner were the evil temptress of the medieval Catholic view. For Protestants, then, the ideal relationship between husband and wife was a close, even loving companionship in which the industrious wife was guided by the husband's benevolent authority.

This Protestant reformulation, coupled with the relegation of women to the home, reversed the former judgments regarding the nature of the sexes. Now the woman was to be the moral and religious centre of the family, uncontaminated by worldly temptations. Her task was to act as a moral touchstone for her husband, whose constant commerce with the world left his soul in peril. The idea spread, and soon the Roman Catholic Church revised its view of women, paying greater attention to the nature of conjugal relations and the regulation of female sexuality in marriage. In both the Protestant and the Catholic paradigm, the ideal woman became the wife/mother whose spirituality, although somewhat inferior to the male's, was nevertheless critical to maintaining both the purity of the home and the soul of her husband.

Despite these structural and ideological changes, a constant feature of Western gender relations was the persistence of patriarchy. **Patriarchy** can be defined as the control of women by men. It is accomplished by (1) controlling the labour power of women by preventing them from participating in some tasks or activities and thus making them dependent on men; (2) controlling women's sexuality by making heterosexuality the norm and regulating their biological reproduction; and (3) controlling women through the male ownership of children.

The particular ways in which the controls are exercised vary between cultures and historically within any culture, but the general subordination of women to men is found and ideologically reinforced in most, but not all, societies. As Hartmann (1976) points out, a patriarchal system in which men control women and in which there is solidarity among men (despite hierarchical relations between them) was found in many pre-capitalist as well as capitalist societies. The specific addition of capitalism was the ideology that celebrates the family and the domestic role of the female and makes the male head of the family that group's representative in the public world. It is another way by which some women can be controlled.

THE GENDER DICHOTOMIES TODAY

The preceding summary of changing historical trends as they have affected gender relations in Western societies provides a foundation for the examination of gender relations in our own society. Today the dichotomized assumptions retain their importance and are acted upon as "natural"—meaning unalterable. In particular, social scientists have assumed that the dichotomies characteristic of capitalist society are "natural." Not until the late 1960s was the appropriateness or usefulness of the dichotomized perspective seriously questioned. Even then, the impetus for re-assessment of sociological frameworks and assumptions came largely from feminists outside the discipline of sociology.

We now turn to an examination of the use of the dichotomized perspective in sociology and the consequences for the analysis of gender roles and relationships. In general, the public world of men is contrasted with the private world of women, and this contrast affects the conception of male/female roles and natures and the locations of the sexes in the public productive world of work and the presumed private sphere of the home as the sphere of consumption. In later sections, we will review the modern feminist movement and the emergence of feminist sociology.

MALE/FEMALE

Clearly the sexes do differ in certain biological characteristics, and these differences provide the basis for different roles for men and women in all societies. The difference that is critical in any assessment of gender roles is a woman's reproductive capacity. The production of a child is a biological act, but the behavior and attitudes that precede and follow the birth are socially produced. Most significantly, the motherhood role after the birth is socially defined, as changes over time indicate. For example, middle- and upper-class women no longer send their infants to be wet-nursed; we no longer assume that restricting the movement of babies by tight swaddling is good post-natal care; we expect parents to celebrate the birth of a healthy baby of either sex more or less equally; and we assume that the major tasks of a mother are both physical and emotional care that will continue for a long time, perhaps even throughout the whole overlapping lifespans of mother and child.

In the examination of gender roles, social scientists have usually tied together the reproductive function and the nurturing role. Nurturing has been assumed to be a mothering role on the grounds that it is biologically natural as the act of reproduction. The usual response to criticisms of this assumption is to turn to pre-history reconstructions to support the "biology is destiny" position, contrasting the status of Man the Hunter with that of Woman the Gatherer and Mother.

As Ambert (1975) indicates, the reproductive function of the female and the relatively long period of dependence of the human offspring do suggest that biology generated a sexual division of labour for our early human ancestors. But that division did not necessarily reflect "traditional" differential evaluation of the sexes. On the contrary, in a world ruled by myth, where procreation was likely to be poorly understood, women's reproductive ability probably gave them status. The excavations of the neolithic site of Catal Huyuk in the Middle East indicate a matrilineal society; the goddess was the principle deity, and the depictions focus on her fertility and procreative power. Moreover, the assumption that the production and care of infants restricted women's activities and thus their status in early societies is speculative at best. Even if women did most of the foraging for plants and roots while men did most of the hunting, there is nothing to suggest that the different roles were exclusive or that they were evaluated as more important or less important to the survival of the group. Hubbard (1983, 63) suggests:

> It makes sense that the gatherers would have known how to hunt the animals they came across; that the hunters gathered when there was nothing to catch, and that men and women did some of each, though both of them probably did a great deal more gathering than hunting. After all, the important thing was to get the day's food, not to define sex roles.

In addition, the helplessness of the human infant has "not necessitated a sedentary way of life among nomadic peoples right to the present."

Whatever the nature of prehistorical gender roles, the "naturalness" of the motherhood, nurturing role is socially defined. As many authors (Flandrin 1975; Foucault 1978; Rubin 1975) indicate, the significance and practice of both motherhood and sexual relations have varied greatly throughout history, even within the same society.

Reproduction and nurturing as "natural" functions are usually contrasted with the "man-made" world of culture that supports the public/private dichotomy in our society. But the social mediates the natural, especially in the issue of paternity. The inherent uncertainty of paternity can be solved only through socially constructed practices. One of the ways in which men attempt to achieve certainty is through the control of women's sexuality. If, as is usual, a primary goal of patriarchy is the transmission of property to legitimate (male) offspring, women's reproduction has to be controlled so the patriarch can be certain about which are his children.

With some exceptions, sociologists have left the question of reproduction unexamined, simply stressing the inherently "natural" connection of women's reproduction and the subsequent biological urge to nurture. This maternal "instinct" has been used to justify another presumably unchangeable "natural" law—the superior-subordinate relationship of the sexes. For example, when Emile Durkheim wrote his sociological classic *Suicide,* reporting his findings that the institution of marriage had the general effect of protecting men against suicidal impulses but encouraging the suicidal impulses of women, he suggested that the only solution to the problem was to modify the marital relationship in order to make women more satisfied with their lot in life. Thus, he said, perhaps as men become "more and more absorbed by functions of utility," they could leave the aesthetic functions of social life to women; the different but complementary functions of the sexes in marriage would thus provide for a more companionate relationship and, he hoped, more contented married women ([1897] 1951, 385).

Durkheim's assumption of different but ideally complementary roles for men and women in the marital and family situation and, by extension, in the world of paid labour has been important to more recent sociologists,

SEXUALITY

The normative regulation of sexual behaviour is tied to and has an effect on the social practices of the society. All societies regulate sexual behaviour in some manner—for example, in terms of appropriate sex objects, the nature of sexual contacts, the appropriate occasions for sexual expression, and even the appropriate frequency of sexual relations.

In our society a major source of regulation has been the Judeo-Christian heritage, which regards sexual expression as problematic (sinful) unless practised in the forms dictated by the religious institution. In general the religious dictates indicate that sexual behaviour should be (1) heterosexual, (2) for the purposes of procreation, (3) within the sanction of marriage, and (4) controlled by the male. Variations are condemned with varying degrees of opprobrium as, for example, the history of the treatment of prostitution and homosexuality illustrates. Many of the practices condemned in our society are allowable sexual expression in other societies. For example, Ford and Beach (1951) indicate that nearly two-thirds of the cultures they studied approved of homosexuality for some of their members.

The regulation of sexual behaviour is necessary to the extent that it is tied to the structure of power relations in the society. Examining the four dictates indicated above for our society illustrates the connections of sexuality and its control to the exercise of power:

1. *Heterosexual behaviour.*
All women are subordinate to men. (Some women, through their connections with men, are superior to some particular men, nevertheless, as females, they are sexually subordinate to males in general.) One result is that the connections between men must be carefully regulated. Sexual connection between males can be tolerated only if it is confined to a small, exclusive group who have command over other males—slaves, plebians, or peasants. When the nature of power is obscured through the token participation of all men— and even women—in the political process, then homosexuality is potentially disruptive and must be controlled. (The bonding of men implied by homosexuality could potentially alter the hierarchical, competitive structure of the male world of power.) Homosexuality can be effectively controlled through normative pressure and formal prohibition. As women are of less significance, the sexual connections between women are of less import and may even be tolerated or simply not recognized, as long as the relationships do not threaten patriarchal power. (As long as women's status is dependent on connection with males, the threat will be minimal since women themselves will act to preserve that power in their sexual preferences.)

2. *Procreative purpose.*

The increasing world population has had a somewhat negative effect upon this dictate, but the basic problem underlying the injunction remains. In the Judeo-Christian code sexuality is related to a human being's animal nature and thus represents a threat to the rationality of men. More particularly, women's animality, a consequence of their closer connection with nature, is expressed in their insatiable sexual desires, which must be restricted by men. According to Thomas Aquinas, "Every act of intercourse was a sin unless performed with a reproductive intent." The idea of the excessive sexual appetite of the female and its attendant dangers to the male is the background to such practices as clitoridectomy and infibulation as well as the assumption of the greater guilt of the prostitute who "lures" the male into temptation and persuades him to forego, for temporary pleasures, his rational self. (This presumption also provides a rationalization for rape, father-daughter incest, and sex between a male adult and a female child: "she led him on" or " 'no' means 'yes'.")

3. *Marital sanction.*

Confining sexual relations to the marital relationship is most important for those societies or groups within society that require the chastity of the female for the legitimate inheritance of property. Although the economic function is insignificant for all but a few in our society, the patriarchal power expressed in the function remains. Only fathers legitimate children.

In addition, the playboy version of a sexual revolution or the feminist recognition of women's right to control their own bodies has done little to alter the force of the marital sanction for the sexual behaviour of women. As Firestone (1971, 130) points out, "Women cannot afford the luxury of spontaneous love. It is much too dangerous. The love and approval of men is all-important. To love thoughtlessly, before one has ensured return commitment, would endanger that approval."

4. *Male control.*

The assumption of male control over sexual relations is critical to the maintenance of patriarchy. As Person (1980, 605) points out, "The double standard, the cult of virginity, and the requirement that female sexuality find expression solely within monogamous heterosexual marriages" are conventions that support male dominance. Rich suggests that compulsory heterosexuality directed at all women is the means to ensure men sexual access to women (Rich 1980). The need to ensure such access, Person (1980, 619) suggests, has to do with the significance of genital sexual activity for the "maintenance of masculine gender while it is a variable feature in feminine gender." In our society, the definition of masculine gender is almost rigidly tied to heterosexual relations; consequently, homosexuality represents a particularly threatening practice both for identity formation and for the preservation of the hierarchical relations of power among men.

especially his intellectual heirs, the proponents of structural-functionalist theory. In the work of one of the most prominent exponents of this theory, Talcott Parsons, the model of man is that of a rational, goal-oriented individual who is concerned with the maintenance of order and harmony in society. That order is maintained, in part, by the distinction between task or goal-oriented actions (the **instrumental dimension**) and social-emotional or integrative actions (the **expressive dimension**). When this framework is applied to gender relations, the usual assumption is that the expressive dimension describes female functions and the instrumental dimension describes male functions in North American society, and that the "normal" context of the female role is the nuclear family. As Collier, Rosaldo, and Yanagaisako point out, the structural-functionalist "Victorian assumptions about gender and the relationship between competitive male markets and peace-loving female homes," as well as the concern "to understand all human social forms in terms of biological 'needs'," strengthened "earlier beliefs associating action, change, and interest with the deeds of men" because these sociologists "thought of kinship in terms of biologically given ties, of 'families' as units geared to reproductive needs, and finally, of women as mere 'reproducers' whose contribution to society [is] essentially defined by the requirements of their homes" (1982, 32).

Unexamined assumptions about "natural" proclivities of men and women produce a partial understanding of the social world. This partiality is demonstrated further in the work/home and production/consumption dichotomies.

WORK/HOME

In Western capitalist society, the stress on occupational position as a major indicator of power and status is parallelled by the number and seriousness of sociological investigations into the instrumental world of paid labour. Sociologists have treated it as an inexhaustible research topic—and one that might be amenable to social engineering.[7] The domestic world of unpaid labour, on the other hand, has received little attention, with interest restricted to the decline of domestic service as an occupation and the problem of housework that has resulted from the movement of women, especially middle-class women, into the paid labour force.

This relative neglect has both resulted from and highlighted a number of assumptions about women's paid labour that emerge from and reinforce the dichotomized framework. For example, it has been assumed that women enter paid labour as a choice, not a necessity, and that because married women's primary responsibility remains the home, they make unreliable workers. Women's presumed unreliability, supposedly expressed in their sporadic relationship to paid labour, has meant that they have not been an important variable in analyses of labour-force characteristics. For example, Blau and Duncan's "systematic analysis of the

American occupational structure" (1967, 1) was, in fact, an analysis of the male occupational structure in which women appeared either as "good matches" contributing to their husbands' occupational mobility, or, by implication in the comments on the broken family, as impediments to male mobility and success.

Women have also been more or less absent from examinations of what many sociologists see as one of the important aspects of paid labour: the question of its alienating characteristics. Most occupations in an industrial-capitalist society have some alienating features (see Chapter 11). Sociological analyses of their impact have generally not, however, considered possible effects on the home and family. Where any consideration has been given to the relationship, it has been usually to demonstrate the necessity of keeping the home as a "haven in a heartless world" (Lasch 1977) to which the work-alienated man returns each day to be stroked and refreshed by the ministrations of his wife in preparation for the next day's labour. The analytical division of the world into home and work ignores the fact that men and women are not so neatly divided and that the characteristics of paid labour spill over into the private sphere of the home and have consequences for the preservation of that privacy.[8]

In our examination of the work/home dichotomy that has informed much sociological analysis of the world of paid labour we will first look at some male occupational characteristics. It is clear that for men in our society investment in occupational success can be an alienating activity in itself. In our examination of female labour force participation and the largely female world of domestic labour, it will become clear that alienation can result from both paid labour and the unpaid labour of housework.

Masculinity and Paid Labour

Our society assumes that when a man completes his education he will enter the paid labour force and remain there more or less continuously (barring disabling accidents or economic recessions) until old age. It is also assumed that paid labour will be a fulfilling experience that validates the individual's sense of self-worth. (Again, see Chapter 11.) Work is the means to the desired rewards of power, prestige, and wealth, and the degree to which a man achieves them is often taken to be a measure of his masculinity, both in his own estimation and that of others, including women. It is because of the investment of self in work and the need to "succeed" at it that unemployment is such a devastating and alienating experience for many men.

Brenton (1976) suggests that the four major dimensions of **alienation**—powerlessness, meaninglessness, isolation, and self-estrangement—are the defining features of the work world at all but the highest levels. That is, the ability to make significant decisions and feel in control of events is the prerogative of very few men; the sense of being a cog in some impersonal machine is a more common complaint. The fragmentation of tasks means that workers are unable to relate to others outside their immediate specialty, and the creative jobs that can generate a sense of accomplishment and autonomy are very few.

Although the alienating characteristics of the work world are present whether the employee is a man or a woman, some social scientists now suggest that the centrality of occupational status for the definition of masculinity makes the adult male role in our society, in Jourard's (1974) word, "lethal." Men on the average die earlier than women, and Jourard suggests one reason may be male "dispiritation." That is, when the meaning and value of a man's continued existence is questioned or eliminated, dispiritation—low morale, decreased immunity to disease, and even suicidal tendencies—increases. If the male role is predicated on the narrow bases of gainful employment, sexual potency, and high prestige, the possibility of male dispiritation is high:

> It is a well-documented observation that men in our society, following retirement, will frequently disintegrate and die not long after they assume their new life of leisure. . . . [In contrast, women seem to] find meaning and raison d'être long after men feel useless and unneeded. (Jourard 1974, 27-28)

No occupation level or type is immune; indeed, the corporate executive may suffer from retirement more than the blue-collar worker because the net loss of prestige and power is greater.

Certainly the world of work is the location of valued rewards in our society, but work is structured so that only a few can achieve them. Men who do not reach the top in the occupational arena may find compensation in leisure time associations and clubs, where status can be acquired for being the best at something, despite occupational status. These organizations provide another arena for the assertion of masculinity, one that can be critically important if a man's paid labour is in a low-status and poorly remunerated occupation.

In practical terms, the men who do succeed in the upper reaches of the occupational world are most frequently those whose wives are participants in a **"two-person career"** (Kanter 1977). That is, the success of the husband depends upon the joint efforts of himself and his wife. With the entry of many middle-class women into paid labour, however, the two-person career has come under fire. When the wife is off doing her own thing, the ambitious corporate man may be checked by the absence of her input into his career. Thus, a wife's career can provide an "explanation" for her husband's lack of success—he has "chosen" to sacrifice part of his career to ensure that she has one too. This sort of rationalization is very useful for any corporate organization. The fiction of success through individual effort is maintained while the real occupational structure of a few winners and a lot of losers is obscured. In addition, given the nature of most women's jobs and the wages they can command, the primary identification of men with the productive sphere remains untouched.[9]

Because the occupational structure is an hierarchical structure of a few top dogs and a lot of supporting workers, the two-person career pattern of the upper middle class applies to a minority in our society. Much more frequent is the two-job pattern in which both husband and wife are in the paid labour force because the wife's wage is critical to raising the family's standard of living above the poverty line.

Femininity and Paid Labour

In the world of paid labour that assumes the continuous presence of adult men until retirement or death, male unemployment is a problem. In contrast, married women's employment has been considered a problem both at work and in the home for three reasons. First, it is assumed that her employment can lead to the neglect of her children, possibly encouraging juvenile delinquency. Second, her paid labour is seen as a direct threat to her husband's role as the major breadwinner; it may reflect negatively upon his masculinity and thus contribute to the problems of separation or divorce. Third, her talents, attitudes, and behaviour on the job can make her a problem employee.

The three problematic aspects of women's employment are interrelated and combine to present a picture of women's paid labour as inappropriate and the home as her appropriate place. That is, society sees married women as working either as a consequence of emergency need or, more commonly, by choice and for pin money. It is assumed that a woman's central concern remains the home and her children and that this makes her an unreliable worker. In addition, it is assumed that her unreliability is compounded by the fact that her husband's occupation will always take precedence over the needs of her employment. And since most women marry, the work world and past sociological analyses of that world have assumed that the problems anticipated for married women on the job can be extended to all women in paid labour. The result has been a general conviction that women will have higher absenteeism and job turnover rates and be less committed to their work than men.

Consequently, runs conventional wisdom, there is no point in giving women much job training or jobs with promotion potential; women will simply leave to get married, so the employer is not likely to get a good return on his investment. Furthermore, since a job is simply a means of filling in time until marriage and of making pin money thereafter, why should any company try to retain female workers by surpassing the legally required wage and benefit package? It is not only employers whose logic proceeds in this fashion. Trade union executives, who are mostly men, have followed the same reasoning and thus, until recently, have made few serious efforts to organize women. The result for the majority of women in paid labour has been the formation of low-status, low-paying job ghettos, and the conventional wisdom about the women in them has become a series of self-fulfilling prophecies. For example, the observation

Computers and office automation may have changed the office, but not who does the office work. Women continue to predominate in the routine jobs of typing, filing, envelope stuffing, etc.

that women have high turnover rates is transformed into "a property of women and not of the jobs which they occupy" (Barron and Norris 1976, 49).

For the few women in professional, managerial, or executive positions, the conventional assumptions and their consequences are somewhat different but no less limiting. For example, there is no male equivalent for the corporate wife, and studies of dual careers do not indicate any radical shifts in the relationship of the sexes to housework and child care.[10] The hierarchical organization of the work world also operates negatively for women. They are not routinely trained for supervisory or management positions, and when one does achieve such a position, her sex status becomes a complication, an inhibitor, to her occupational status. The sponsor system that is a critical part of any individual's mobility in an organization is also a problem for women. Men are less likely to sponsor women as their successors, and if they do, the relationship is likely to be misinterpreted by others. The interpersonal relationships that inhibit sponsorship also inhibit the informal, after-hours socializing that can be so critical to an individual's promotion. Finally, the scarcity of women in these occupational positions means that no equivalent to the old boys' network exists to smooth the path of female achievers.

Samuelson summarizes the contradictory beliefs about women in paid employment that act as deterrents to their equal participation:

> Men will not work under a woman. Man-to-man talk will be inhibited by the presence of women. Even women prefer a male physician to a female one.

Women lack imagination and creativity. If you mix men and women on the job, they will carry on to the detriment of efficiency and good morals. By the time you have trained a woman, she'll get married and leave you; or have a baby; or alternatively, you won't be able ever to get rid of a woman once you've hired her. If a woman does turn out to be a superlative economic performer, she's not feminine, she's harsh and aggressive with a chip on her shoulder against men and the world (and she's killing her chances of getting married). Women workers, seeking pin money, take bread from the mouths of family breadwinners. (1976, 790)

The conclusion is that the world of paid labour should be a male club. Masculine bonding is a "coalition of equals against inferiors for the maintenance of power" (Walum 1977, 161) and it is made possible by the emotional support provided by the inferior, subservient women.

The significance of these relationships is illuminated by the situation of the male homosexual. Rituals of reassurance of masculine identity are vitally important to men, and any deviation from the norm, be it sexual preference or sex status, may be seen as a threat to that identity. In other words, anyone who deviates from the male norm presents our society with a problem, especially in situations that carry some significant power, prestige, or wealth. Consequently women, gay men, and members of racial and ethnic minority groups are likely to become social problems to the extent that they move out of their place as subordinates in society at large and as low-status employees in the world of work. Women especially may be tolerated in the higher ranks of the occupational sphere as long as their jobs both avoid competition with men's jobs and reflect the nurturant, domestic roles of femininity.

Labour Force Participation—A Canadian Profile

The realities of the work world both mirror and distort the assumptions made about the appropriate gender relationships to paid labour. As the employment patterns and legal changes of the past two decades illustrate, the reality upon which some of the traditional assumptions rest has changed significantly, and gradually some sociologists are challenging the assumptions themselves.

Any general description of Canadian women in paid labour indicates that they are concentrated in low-status, low-paying jobs with poor pension and other benefit arrangements. Moreover, they are concentrated in a few occupations, such as clerical work and nursing, and they generally receive less pay than men.

These characteristics of women's paid labour are common to all Western industrial societies, as is the rapid increase since the late 1950s of women entering it in significant numbers. In Canada in 1951, women were 24.1 percent of the total labour force; by 1983 the figure had risen to 42 percent (Statistics Canada 1985f, 49). The statistics for the United States are comparable: 27.9 percent in 1950 and 43 percent in 1980

(Lengermann and Wallace 1985, 188). In both cases the increases were largely the result of an influx of *married* women, including mothers, into the labour force. By 1983 more than half (51.5 percent) of Canadian women who had a husband and children of preschool age at home were in the labour force (Statistics Canada 1985f, 49). The percentages for women with school-aged children and for mothers without a husband at home were even higher.

Although the percentage of women in the labour force has increased sharply, women remain concentrated in a few sex-typed occupations. As of 1983, clerical, sales, service, health, and teaching occupations led the list in Canada, accounting for 77 percent of all working women, compared to 34 percent of men. Within these five occupational categories, women were not evenly distributed. For example, 83.2 percent of all employed women were in the service sector in 1983, but they were primarily in community, business, or personal industries. For example, they were 60 percent of employees in finance, insurance, and real estate but "under-represented in the other service industries: they made up only 43% of those in trade, 37% in public administration and just 24% in transportation, communications and other utilities" (Statistics Canada 1985f, 43). Some changes have been observed over the years; for example, women managers increased from 3.4 percent of the 1975 total to 6.1 percent in 1983.

The segregated nature of the labour force generally depresses the wages received by women. Overall, women earn less than men even when education and skill are the same. In 1982, the average earnings of full-time employed women were 64 percent of those of full-time employed males. Equal-pay legislation has not had a significant impact on the wage gap between men and women because such laws are generally irrelevant. Wilson suggests;

> When the law requires equal pay for equal work, it is a simple matter to technically differentiate the jobs men do from the jobs women do. But the segregated labour force makes even this technicality generally unnecessary. In essence, equal-pay legislation may serve to reinforce occupational segregation. (1986, 107)

Armstrong and Armstrong (1975, 378) concur, observing that employers "may simply hire women only and pay them all the same low rate" rather than raise wages to match those of men. Equal pay for work of equal value might prove a more relevant principle for the vast majority of women in the labour force.

This broad picture, which differs only in detail in most of the Western industrialized countries, reveals the misleading nature of recent media hype about the influx of women into paid labour. The pervasive image is the cool, chic business woman (who, incidently, buys whatever expensive consumer product is being advertised). In fact, the number of women in highly paid, prestige occupations is very small, and even within these occupations women generally receive less income than their male counterparts. Statistics Canada (1985f, 26) reports that women in professional occupations in 1983 "still only had earnings of 68% of those of male professionals." This discrepancy reflects the sex-typing of occupations within the professions and semiprofessions:

> More than three-quarters of the dental hygenists, librarians, physiotherapists, and dieticians were women. At the same time, more than three-quarters of the university teachers, doctors, pharmacists, lawyers, industrial engineers, and dentists were men. (Armstrong and Armstrong 1975, 376)

The claim that women have come a long way is spurious as far as their actual labour-force experiences are concerned. What the media image points to is corporate capitalism's real gains in the promotion of expensive, conspicuous consumption items. It also suggests that domesticity is not real work and certainly not the "real you"!

Women and Work—Explanations from Mainstream Social Science

Sociology has not ignored the increased presence of women in paid labour, and several theories have been advanced to explain the differences between women's and men's positions and remuneration in the labour force. Two of them, the status attainment theory and the dual labour-market theory, attempt to provide explanations that fit women into the traditional analyses of the labour force. These theories purport to give an objective explanation of gender and occupational positions and relations but instead, as we will see, end up blaming the victims—that is, women—for their low status, low pay, and ghettoized jobs.

The Status Attainment Theory

The **status attainment theory** focuses on the importance for occupational success of educational achievement, a factor regarded as gender-neutral since it is common to both sexes. The assumption is that "if women could only get the same education (quantity and quality) as men, they would achieve the same occupational *statuses*—although not necessarily the same *rewards*" (Sokoloff 1979, 73).[11]

Women's participation in higher education has indeed risen significantly over the past decade. Statistics Canada (1985f) reports that in 1971 women received 38 percent of undergraduate degrees awarded, 22 percent of the master's degrees and 9 percent of the doctorates; the comparable figures for 1982 were 51 percent, 40 percent, and 25 percent.

Although more women are entering non-traditional occupations, our surprise at seeing them there indicates that our stereotypes concerning the appropriate kind of work for women remain very much alive.

Moreover, women have made important gains in the professional faculties: for example, 13 percent of the M.D.s were awarded to women in 1971, compared to 36 percent in 1982. (Nevertheless, some areas of higher education—particularly engineering, mathematics, and the physical sciences—remain relatively unaffected by the increased participation of women.)

Many studies show that the more education an individual has, the greater the likelihood of that person's being in the labour force and the less likely that that person will be unemployed. (For more details—and some *caveats*—see Chapter 6.) This general picture holds for both men and women. Moreover, the more education, the greater the earning power. Nevertheless, various studies of men and women in highly ranked occupations indicate that a woman must be twice as good as a man to hold the same occupational status and, as a general rule, she will earn less than a male counterpart. On average,

> women with a university education who work full-time have earnings which are only 67% of male university graduates . . . [and] are only $1,600 a year more than the earnings of men with only high school experience. (Statistics Canada 1985f, 27)

Thus, although the status attainment theory accommodates women in its framework, it misses factors that confound the effect of education on paid-labour participation and rewards. The theory ignores the critical variable of women's responsibility for the home and child care, which affects their paid labour performance, and it has overtones of blaming the victim by suggesting that if only women were more aggressive and worked harder they would achieve equality in the marketplace.

The Dual Labour-Market Theory

Dual labour-market theory argues that Western economies have two labour markets, primary and secondary. **Primary market jobs** are relatively stable, with high wages, good benefits, and provisions for job security; **secondary sector jobs** are characterized by low wages, poor working conditions, instability, and few opportunities for advancement. It is generally males who are recruited into primary sector jobs, while women and disadvantaged, minority males are found largely in secondary sector jobs. (See Chapter 11 for a further discussion of this theory.)

Given the nature of jobs in the secondary sector, individuals holding them tend to have lower levels of commitment and higher turnover rates than workers in the primary sector. But these employment characteristics, which are a consequence of the nature of the job, are mistakenly attributed to the individual in the job. Witness the observation that women have high turnover rates and are "unreliable." As Kanter (1977, 161) points out, men in occupations that also offer little opportunity or incentive "look more like the stereotype of women in their orientation toward work."

Dual labour-market theory identifies the division between male and female paid labour, but it does not explain the differences between men and women in primary sector jobs or why the labour market is segregated in the first place. In addition, like the status attainment theory, it takes no account of women's domestic work as a significant factor in the labour-force participation of women.

The Reserve Army of Labour Theory

Another theoretical framework used to explain women's labour-force participation is the Marxist concept of the **reserve army of labour.** The argument is that capitalism, especially monopoly capitalism, requires a pool of reserve labour that can be activated cheaply when the need arises. The reserve is made up largely of women, who can be used when needed and sent back into the home when demand ceases. Although this theory identifies an important feature of the operation of a capitalist economy and deals explicitly with the marginal and problematic position of women in paid labour, nevertheless, as many Marxist-feminists and socialist-feminists point out, "neither Marx nor Monopoly Capital theories focuses *directly* on women" (Sokoloff 1979, 74),[12] because their domestic labour is not part of the account.

Critiques of the Theories

Any explanation of the nature of women's paid labour is a partial explanation as long as it ignores the interaction with their domestic labour. This failure tends to show up quickly in practice. For example, the traditional Marxist assumption that women's entry into paid labour was the initial, essential development for the equality of the sexes that would be accomplished under socialism is refuted by the experiences of women in present-day socialist states. As Burstyn puts it, the oppression of women is similar "for women in the U.S.S.R. and Eastern Europe and China" and for women in the West. Women in the socialist countries have a somewhat higher rate of participation in the labour force, but in all cases "women are ghettoised into jobs where their work tends to reflect their roles as sustainer and drudge . . . [and] women's central condition is that of the double day of labour" (1985, 66-67).

Mainstream sociology has also produced some questionable assumptions about the relationship of women's paid labour and their subordinate status. For example, it has been assumed that women's entering the labour force would give them more power in the marriage relationship and thus produce egalitarian couples. What this theory ignores is the pay differentials between the sexes. Since the wife's earnings are nearly always less than the husband's, his wage remains the major one upon which the family depends and, in the last analysis, the difference ensures the husband's superior status in the family and, therefore, his power. The theory also assumes that the wife is able to retain control over the spending of her wage, an assumption that is not necessarily justified. Finally, the effects of the wife's wage are understood in terms of the meaning that money has in the male occupational world. The male equation of money and power does not necessarily apply to the married woman's wage.[13]

Housework

As already suggested, any consideration of gender relations and paid labour must take into account the unpaid labour of women in the home. This work is a critical support for a market economy, but until recently sociological analysis has ignored **domestic labour** as work, and considered it a "natural" extension of women's biological role. (Indeed, initial examinations of housework as work activity were often regarded as being trivial subjects for research.) In general, the daily work of the vast majority of women has been invisible to sociological experts, a situation that is understandable as long as housework is seen as a private, personal service performed by women for men. But understanding the reason for the neglect is not a justification for the partiality of sociological explanations.

In 1954 Caplow suggested that housework was the only occupation that has no qualifications, such as specific aptitudes or intelligence, and consequently the dissatisfaction of housewives could be partially explained by the fact that "the same job requirements are imposed on morons and on women of superior intelligence" (1954, 261). Housework does, however, require some specific talents—the prime one being the ability to coordinate a variety of discrete, often contradictory instrumental tasks with the personal needs of the individual family members so as to produce a smooth-running household. This is a managerial talent that rivals anything demanded of the male corporate executive. Caplow's remarks, therefore, can be explained only as the result of masculine myopia about the nature of housework. In fact, since the occupational world is supposedly a masculine world and housework is not regarded as real work, it is not surprising that society does not stress specific requirements for the task. (The exception occurs when the task is undertaken for money; the requirements for domestic service are likely to be explicitly formulated.) All wives are assumed to be houseworkers, and all women to have unique, innate abilities for the job.

The assumption of women's unique capacity for housework is an extension of the previously discussed distinction between the male instrumental world of paid labour and the female expressive, integrative world

Public male reactions such as this to the spread of the women's movement are instructive precisely because they are so rare. Does this indicate that most men have accommodated quickly to women's demands for equality and greater opportunity — or that they have not had to?

of domesticity and the family. The sharp distinction obscures the nature of housework as work. As Oakley (1974, 28) points out, for the house-wife/wife/mother to be "constantly person-oriented and conciliatory" she could not be occupied with such instrumental tasks as house-cleaning, laundry, shopping, and cooking. Oakley's study of housewives and their work indicates that housewives themselves are aware that the instrumental-expressive role analysis provides a poor explanation of their actual activities. Her respondents tended to describe housework as monotonous, fragmented and excessively paced—in other words, as similar to instrumental work on a factory assembly-line. They often contrasted it with the expressive, emotional satisfaction of child care; the need to balance the roles of houseworker and mother was experienced, at times, as contradictory and frustrating.

For most women, the acquisition of the status of wife marks a critical transition point in the relationship to housework. As Lopata (1971) points out, single adult homemakers, male or female, set housework standards in terms of their own personal requirements (and perhaps their mothers' past training). The housewife, however, is subject to the expectations of at least one other person, who evaluates her service daily. The husband may introduce other, external evaluations of her efforts. As Smith indicates, the wife of a corporate manager has her standards of home care and child care defined in terms of the needs of the corporation and she must perform them with regard to the appropriate corporate image of the "ideal home and family." For example, "it is not sufficient that the clothes and bedding be clean, they must be seen to be clean. What constitutes cleanliness is determined by the advertisements for detergents, whiteners, etc." (Smith 1973, 35).

Whatever the constraints, external or interfamilial, upon housework, it remains a woman's major responsibility. Most men do not share the work or want to share it, and, as Hamilton (1978, 83) puts it, women "feel guilty if they do suggest" that men participate. Lopata (1971) reports that 47 percent of her housewife respondents indicated that their husbands never help with the housework: 39 percent said they receive some help, but only 11 percent indicated that it is a "regular feature," while 18 percent named it an "emergency pattern." Both Lopata and Oakley (1974) find that a husband's assistance is greatest with child care, but that helping with the children is seen as a "favour to the wife," usually freeing her to perform other household tasks. In addition, his help is most frequently with the more expressive and enjoyable tasks, rather than the routine chores of feeding, bathing, and changing diapers. Today, after another decade or so of "liberation," the picture is little changed.

Housework remains the wife's primary responsibility even when she enters the paid labour force. Meissner et al. find two noticeable effects as women's hours of paid labour increase:

Their hours of regular housework decline without being made up for because the husbands' housework remains virtually at the same low level of some four or five hours a week; and . . . despite the successively more compressed hours of housework, the wives' total workload increases a great deal while the husbands' *declines slightly.* (1974, 429)

Luxton also finds that generally husbands do not increase the amount of time spent on domestic labour when their wives take on paid labour. Middle-class husbands especially decrease their domestic labour.

These men seemed to feel that no matter what else she was doing, domestic labour was the woman's responsibility. They also implied that if the woman had enough "free time" to take on paid work then she could obviously handle her domestic labour as well. (1981, 18-19).

These researchers and others find that employed housewives tend to spend less time on housework than full-time housewives, not because they are suddenly more efficient, but because, in Vanek's (1978, 402) phrase, they "cut corners." In addition, many find that since the house is empty and the children are elsewhere for much of the day, there is less to do.

Whatever amount of help the husband provides with housework and child care, the management of the tasks, as opposed to their actual performance, is the wife's responsibility. As a male sociologist confesses:

I help in many ways and feel responsible that she have time to work on her professional interests. But I do partial, limiting things to free her to do her work. I don't do the basic thinking about the planning of meals and house-keeping or the situation of the children. I will often do the shopping, cook, make beds, "share" the burden of most household tasks; but that is not the same thing as direct and primary responsibility for planning and managing a household and meeting the day-to-day needs of children. (Miller 1972, 249)

Miller's insight into society's gender restriction on the managerial component of domestic work points directly to the poverty of the instrumental/expressive dichotomy.

PRODUCTION/CONSUMPTION

A consideration of differences in the production/consumption role rounds out our view of the poverty of the dichotomized model of gender relationships and underlines the inherent interdependence of these relations. As we have seen, a central role for adult males in our society is their occupational role—in family terms, their breadwinner role. Men are expected to take on the primary responsibility for production, and their remuneration from this activity is supposed to enable women to fulfil their primary role as consumers. The 19th-century angel-of-the-home was made possible by the direct exploitation of the labour of other women. Similarly, both the career woman and the leisured suburbanite of the 20th century depend upon the exploited labour of other women. In addition, a considerable amount of production undertaken in the home was, and still is, a necessary underpinning to paid labour. Although various commercial innovations have diminished the amount of domestic production, the work that women perform in the home as producers and as reproducers of future workers remains a critical and substantial base for the world of paid labour. Given estimates of the monetary worth of household productive labour—for example, Proulx (1978, 4) sets the average value of housework to each Canadian household as $13,346 annually in terms of 1971 wages—it is ironic that such labour may not be regarded as "real" work.

In our society's view, real work is production for a wage or salary. Housework is work that is not worth money; on the contrary, housewives spend money. The **production/consumption division** applied to the sexes is a particular feature of capitalist development. As we saw earlier, the initial transformation of the household from a unified production-and-consumption unit, in which all members made a contribution, varied according to class position. In general, the greater efficiency and productivity of capitalist industrial organization meant that more people, especially women and children, could be taken out of the paid labour market and allotted the role of consumption. This division, of course, stimulated the production of household goods, which in turn supported capitalist expansion. Thus the houseworker as consumer does not simply provide personal services for her family in the privacy of the home; she also works "for the maintenance of capitalism"—that is, for the economy as a whole (Glazer-Malbin 1976, 919).

Because the consumption of the household is tied to the world of paid production, all housewives cannot be simply consumers at all times. Women have been drawn into and pushed out of paid labour according to a number of factors, whose implications may differ with the family's class position. As Fox (1980) indicates, many of the married women who began to enter the labour force in the 1950s and 1960s were middle-class, and their move was largely the result of their growing inability to meet basic family needs through household labour. Changes in the standard of living, generated by technological innovations in consumer household items, meant an increasing number of desirable consumer items for which there were no homemade substitutes. Store-bought items became preferable to homemade ones, and as more and more household goods became commodities, more and more women went out to earn wages. In the 1970s the promotion of the wife's career as an integral part of the middle-class lifestyle also contributed to the influx of women into the paid labour force.

For working-class households (and more recently, for some middle-class ones) the difference between a woman's productivity in the household and in paid employment made the latter economical—even taking into account low female wages and the added costs a family incurs when the wife/mother works outside the home. As Armstrong and Armstrong

(1975, 383) indicate, a married woman's earnings are increasingly necessary to supplement the husband's wage if the family is simply to maintain its economic position. In fact, they suggest, the "increasing participation of married women in the labour force obscures the growing disparity in income distribution in Canada." For many families, the wife's wage makes the critical difference between poverty and a modicum of comfort.

This interdependence of production/consumption patterns makes nonsense of the idealized dichotomies of gender relations:

> As the standard of living in Canada rises, married women whose husbands earn low incomes must work outside the home to maintain their relative standard of living. . . . To stay at home and try and stretch their husband's wage is no longer a viable alternative. To maintain what is now considered a reasonable standard of living, families must purchase a growing number of goods and services which are rapidly becoming indispensable. . . . The existence of these goods and services is a prerequisite for women taking outside employment. At the same time it is the production of these goods and services that women themselves once produced in the home which has led to the expansion of "female" occupations. (Connelly 1978,33)

Further problems with dichotomized framework of gender relations are evident when one considers that it presumes a norm of the nuclear family—a heterosexual couple and their legitimate offspring. When the male breadwinner disappears, problems arise both from the assumption that the home is the appropriate place for women and from the assumption that women in paid labour do not need the same wages as men. In many Western societies, the proportion of single-parent households headed by women has increased steadily. Marital dissolution increased dramatically in Canada after the 1968 revision of the divorce laws, and by 1981, one family in ten was headed by a single female parent. About two-thirds of these women were either divorced or separated.

The impact of marriage breakdown is dramatic for women, whether they have children or not. In households headed by men, the average income for 1983 was $36,000, but for households headed by women it was $18,400. Not surprisingly, it was estimated that in 1983 45 percent of female-headed households fell below the poverty line, compared to 10 percent of male-headed households. Divorced or separated women are most likely to seek paid employment, irrespective of the ages and numbers of their children, but when they do so they confront the "phenomena of sex segregation and low incomes which characterizes the entire female labour force" (Boyd 1977, 58). The idealized consumption role is a joke for most once-married female heads of households.

Even in situations in which the dichotomized framework seems to apply—those in which the wife concentrates on domestic and child-care activities and the husband on paid labour—the framework proves inadequate. The work in the household is often tied directly to the work of the husband in paid labour and may be critical to the family's social mobility. Papanek (1979, 775) indicates that some domestic work is undertaken to "maintain and enhance the family's social standing" (though not necessarily the wife's standing in the family). The nature of this **status-production work** varies across cultures and between social classes, but it is largely women's work located in the household. In our society it takes the form of conspicuous consumption and the delicate tasks of gauging social contacts and friendships and participating in the correct leisure activities—all in the interest of advancing the husband's career. This is the particular task of middle-class wives, but it is not confined to women of the middle classes.

Papanek (1979, 775) suggests that status-production work is undertaken when the household is able to live "according to its aspirations on

INSTITUTIONAL SEXISM

The United Nations Universal Declaration of Human Rights was adopted by Canada in 1948. The adoption meant that Canada endorsed an ideology of equality involving individual autonomy, freedom of choice, equality of opportunity, and equality before the law. In many respects the ideological commitment has not been matched by practical action, as illustrated by the fact that equal-pay provisions were not incorporated into the Canadian Labour Code until 1971. In addition, attempts to legislate change are circumscribed because they can apply only to the public sector; as well, they effect only broad structural change, leaving the detailed implementation and the critical attitudinal underpinning untouched. For example, equal-pay-for-work-of-equal-value legislation has a positive impact on only a small proportion of the female

labour force. A range of structural and ideological barriers remain that work adversely for women in paid labour.

Equal pay for work of equal value assumes that the sexes do comparable work throughout the world of paid labour. As the majority of women in paid labour are located in female job ghettos, few comparisons with men's jobs are possible and no changes are likely in the rates or remuneration, fringe benefits, or working conditions. In cases in which men and women do perform the same or comparable tasks and there is some evidence of discrimination in favour of males, the onus for change is frequently on the complainants—the women. Yet recall that women are not unionized to the same extent as men, and where unions exist, they are often not willing to work very hard on behalf of their female constituents—

particularly if such actions may have an impact on the position of their male constituents. Without the assistance of experts such as union personnel, collecting evidence to support the complaint may be difficult if not impossible, quite apart from the on-the-job harassment her complaint may occasion.

Finally, the legislation assumes that a means for the evaluation of "equal worth" of various jobs already exists. Job evaluation is not a neutral process. The process of job evaluation is conducted by management and, even if independent consultants perform the actual assessment, it is undertaken largely by males. (In fact, evaluations may be used to consolidate the status quo through the "discovery" that the women's jobs were different all the time.) As long as women are not involved in the process, little change may be expected from any legislation on this issue.

The implementation of the ideal of equality in the marketplace is severely circumscribed by the general assumption that the world of paid labour is the world of men. The critical consequence of this assumption is that the world of paid labour is organized in terms of male needs—and ideally the needs of the male as sole, or at least major, breadwinner for the family group of wife and offspring. Discrimination—exemplified in women's having low wages, few benefits, and limited or no access to training and upgrading schemes, lacking mentors or sponsors for a career, and facing the assumption (particularly for married women) that a woman is not committed

to the job or a career—emerges out of the above attitude and subsequent structural arrangements.

The assumption that paid labour is male labour is particularly important in regard to the dual responsibility assumed by the majority of adult women in Canada. The major responsibility for the home and child care remains that of the woman, and the construction of the world of paid labour does not take account of this dual responsibility. (In fact, it cannot. To incorporate the work of women as reproducers of labour power into the public sphere would be impossible, because such a move would mean the total transformation of the system so that public/private dichotomies would be meaningless.) The physical as well as psychological damage to many women that the dual burden imposes is rarely compensated by the remuneration and/or the prestige that many males obtain from stressful or physically debilitating jobs.

Discriminatory practices in the work world are the visible illustrations of a pervasive sexism that is built into the social structure and carried through language that asserts "he is aggressive, she is pushy" when questions of individual autonomy and freedom are addressed. Indeed, when the liberal ideology of equality, outlined at the outset, is put into practice, it produces the "crisis of liberalism." That is, a capitalist, patriarchal society cannot in the long run deliver on its promises of equality or even equal rights to women or other disadvantaged groups, without radically changing the system.

the resources produced by *fewer than all* its members." That is, status-production activities are possible only when one of the members, usually the wife, is not in paid labour. But even when the wife is employed, her role in status-production activities is usually expected to continue. For example, Luxton (1981, 19) discusses the case of wives of professional and business men who are expected to maintain "an appropriately furnished home," to produce "acceptable social events such as dinner parties," and to accompany their husbands "to social occasions organized by others, whatever the wives may be doing elsewhere." In addition, the status-production functions of the wife may extend to her paid labour. For an upper-income man, the wife's occupation may become another status item for the household and thus for himself—so long as her work brings less income and status than his and so long as it can be regarded as glamorous or socially rewarding or morally uplifting.

SUMMARY OF THE DICHOTOMIZED FRAMEWORK

The dichotomies used for the analysis of gender relations prove inadequate as an explanatory framework. They also reveal their origins in specific class and gender perspectives;[14] the idea that the domestic sphere is somehow an arena of non-work is a conclusion possible only to someone shielded from the day-to-day activities of the housewife/mother. The use of a dichotomized framework also obscures the realities of male-female interactions, as well as those of male-male and female-female connections.

The dichotomized framework used in sociology is rooted in the philosophical conception of Man's nature as dual—natural, and socially transcendent of the natural—but it does not extend the concept to Woman, whose oneness with nature is regarded as inescapable. It is this dualism that underlies the dichotomies:

> [The] private realm is the realm of man's animality, the public realm that of his humanity. The first is governed by necessity and is where Woman lives. The second is created in freedom, and is the realm in which man's first nature is transcended by his second. (O'Brien 1981, 147-48)

Both men and women probably recognized that the practical expression of this separation between public and private is circumscribed by social class, that it has "as little meaning to the man on the assembly line as it did for the ordinary medieval serf." But the abstract conception of the separation, especially when applied to gender relations, is important "for the ordinary man, for whom it is unreal but consoling and for all women, for whom it is unreal but exploitive" (O'Brien 1981, 148). Many men whose wives are also in paid labour find it important to their sense of masculinity that they remain the major breadwinners and that they not be expected to take on domestic tasks. Many a woman who takes up paid labour excuses her work as something temporary until the family gets on its feet or as something she enjoys and that enables the family to afford a few luxuries, even when the economic reality of the family situation seems to contradict her statement (Luxton 1981).

Feminist sociologists have attempted to provide critiques of the mainstream dichotomized frameworks. The major focus of the work has been attempts to connect the personal world of everyday life with the abstract world of institutional arrangements. The intention is to develop a means of transcending the dichotomies that alienate all human beings from themselves and others. As we will see in the next section, feminist sociology is not an abstraction but a "mode of analysis, a method of approaching life and politics, a way of asking questions and searching for answers, rather than a set of political conclusions about the oppression of women" (Hartsock 1979, 58). The feminist perspective is necessary because the traditional sociological models of reality have proved limited as viable descriptions of social systems and as paradigms for future action. Janeway (1980, 574) points out that when paradigms begin to fail as exemplars, when the data no longer fit the theoretical model, they "cease to be recipes for managing processes and getting on comfortably with one's life. Instead they are preached as ideals to which life should be dedicated." The dichotomized framework as a model for sociological analysis has taken on the status of an ideal that is being preached by sociobiology. But this model's lack of reality is apparent.

THE WOMEN'S MOVEMENT

In the development of alternative perspectives, feminist sociology has a close connection with the practice of social change as advocated by the feminist movement. Although the women's movement has existed in Western society at least since the time of the 19th-century suffragettes, it was espoused by only a minority of women until the mid-1960s and rarely had the public impact of more recent years. A brief examination of this resurgence of the women's movement is in order before we consider the question of feminist sociology.

In 1970 the Royal Commission on the Status of Women documented gender inequalities in Canada. The commission and its report were part of a general resurgence of the women's movement in Western societies. The United States' Commission on the Status of Women had issued its report in 1963. The same year Betty Friedan published *The Feminine Mystique,* showing that the "happy housewives," whose lives seemed to be exactly what the dichotomized framework suggested was natural, were in fact profoundly dissatisfied.

> Experts told them how to catch a man and keep him, how to breastfeed children and handle their toilet training, how to cope with sibling rivalry and adolescent rebellion; how to buy a dishwasher, bake bread, cook gourmet snails, and build a swimming pool with their own hands; how to dress, look,

and act more feminine and make marriage more exciting; how to keep their husbands from dying young and their sons from growing into delinquents. They were taught to pity the neurotic, unfeminine, unhappy women who wanted to be poets or physicists or presidents. They learned that truly feminine women do not want careers, higher education, political rights—the independence and the opportunities that the old-fashioned feminists fought for. (Friedan 1963, 11)

And yet they were unhappy, struggling with what the author called "the problem that has no name."

The dissatisfaction that Friedan documented was parallelled by the disillusionment of many women who were involved in various left-wing political organizations of the 1960s. As an American describes what happened, women found that their situation within the movements

> unavoidably conflicted with the ideologies of "participatory democracy," "freedom," and "justice" that they were expressing. They were faced with the self-evident contradiction of working in a 'freedom movement' but not being very free. (Freeman 1975, 57)

Canadian women had similar experiences and voiced similar protests. Four women from the Student Union for Peace Action stated in 1967:

> It is our contention that until the male chauvinists of the movement understand the concept of liberation in relation to women, the most exploited members of *any* society, they will be voicing political lies. (quoted in Bernstein et al. 1972, 39)

They put the men of the movement on notice that women would no longer be "the typers of letters and distributors of leaflets (hewers of wood and drawers of water)" (Bernstein et al. 1972, 39). In brief, the climate was ripe for the resurgence of a feminist movement, and it began to grow throughout the Western world.

Some of the first activities went almost unnoticed by society in general. Small groups of women disillusioned with the male-dominated New Left political groups began to meet to voice their dissatisfaction and in doing so discovered their common condition. So did other informal groups of women, many of them centred on university and college campuses. What they invented came to be called **consciousness-raising,** a means by which women gradually came to understand their common oppression as women. The process expanded in an unstructured fashion through many localized community groups.

More organized, structured groups also began to be formed in most parts of the Western world. In Canada, Laura Sabia, national president of the Canadian Federation of University Women, organized a meeting of representatives from all Canadian women's organizations to discuss women's issues and concerns. Delegates from 32 organizations met in

Toronto in May 1966 and set up a steering committee. One of its mandates was to pressure the government into conducting a serious investigation of the status of women in Canada. A royal commission was appointed in 1967, and the wide variety of research and briefs presented to it gave women's concerns formal, legitimate status as social problems.

The commission tabled its report in 1970. One of the 167 recommendations, that a federal advisory council on the status of women be established, was in place by 1973. Many of the other recommendations were, however, ignored or changed, and much of the subsequent lobbying for their implementation and for solutions to newly identified women's problems in Canada has come from outside the Council. An important lobby group and watchdog has been the National Action Committee, which came out of the initial steering committee set up by Sabia.[15]

It was the National Action Committee that organized the protest against the application of the override clause to Section 28 of the Charter of Rights and Freedoms when it was being written in 1982. Although Section 15 of the Charter prohibits discrimination on the basis of race, national or ethnic origin, colour, religion, sex, age, or mental or physical disability, it is Section 28 that acts as a trump card, stating that "notwithstanding anything in this Charter, the rights and freedoms referred to in it are guaranteed equally to male and female persons." In the bargaining on the Constitution among the provinces and the federal government, the politicians seemed to be ignoring the significance to women of permitting the override (a clause embodied in Section 33 that allows a provincial or federal government to discriminate as long as the intention to do so is clearly stated in law) to touch matters of sexual equality. Only after they received massive protests from women's groups did they make Section 28 not subject to the override.

Although Canadian women have, by virtue of Section 28, the equivalent of the Equal Rights Amendment that women in the United States have sought but still lack, it is still important that the Charter be tested in the courts. The interpretations in regard to specific cases will determine the degree to which its promise of equality translates into practice.

Moreover, the Charter cannot be a final cure for gender inequality in Canada. There are many areas of social life that the law simply cannot touch. And although the law can be used to implement social change, it cannot instigate change. Doerr points out:

> Many of our laws reflect social values and establish social arrangements which have been designed primarily to protect the dependent married woman who engages in no paid work. . . . [Also] the overlay of constitutionally entrenched rights respecting equal status for women on a system of laws which continues, in large measure, to uphold the traditional role of women is bound to have a number of unintended, as well as intended, consequences. (1984, 44)

One result is that the fit between the Charter's equality provisions and social and economic realities may be imperfect. Another is that local

Sexism in advertising, with response.

feminist organizations dealing with specific issues, such as day-care, abortion rights, wife-battering, rape, sexual harassment, and so on, remain important in the day-to-day advancement of women's issues and concerns. So do the many grassroots women's organizations that are not confined to single issues but are also concerned with more general problems, such as nuclear disarmament and environmental concerns.

The Problems of Today's Feminist Groups

The multiplicity of women's groups that emerged in the late 1960s and early 1970s in North America and around the world makes it difficult to catalogue their characteristics or problems in the terms traditionally used for social movements. Many of the groups were short-lived, many of them were deliberately outrageous in their initial protests, and many experienced a rapidly fluctuating membership as some women became more or less radicalized than others and left to regroup or to join other organizations. The fluid nature of the grassroots movement is illustrated by the difficulty the contemporary mass media experienced in identifying leaders. Today, although the earlier anti-leadership ethic has given way to demands for structure (generated in part by the organization of opposition to women's interests), the deliberately collective actions of feminist groups and the frequent coalitions formed for specific actions still point to the feminist commitment to act in a more egalitarian manner than do most organized structures in our society.

The multiplicity of groups, their often loose structures, and their variety of purposes and goals also make it difficult to generalize about their problems. A few common difficulties are, however, easily discerned.

Money

One of the problems faced by all women's groups, including the National Action Committee and the Advisory Council on the Status of Women, is the lack of funding for women's concerns. At all levels of government, the interest in women's issues is sporadic and usually rises only in politically opportune circumstances. The private sources of funds for women's issues are scarce as the proverbial hen's teeth—not a surprising situation given the fact that women control a minute fraction of the wealth in Canada.

Anti-feminism

Feminist groups have not been without opposition from women themselves. *The Feminine Mystique* was an indictment of the idea that a woman's sole happiness consisted in her role as wife and mother. Two years later, in 1965, another book, *Fascinating Womanhood,* appeared that gave precise instructions as to how women could find total happiness and fulfilment in marriage. The book claimed to:

> teach *the art of winning a man's complete love and adoration.* It is not necessary for the man to know or to do anything about the matter. This is not to say that men do not make mistakes or need to improve their behaviour. But when women correct their own mistakes, they can bring about a wonderful loving response in a man. (Andelin 1965, 3)

Fascinating Womanhood and a rival, *Total Woman,* emphasize the submissive, subordinate, and purely domestic role of women, justified on the basis of nature and divine decree. The books offer an explanation of gender relations as well as advice on how a woman can maintain her marriage by using a variety of manipulative techniques on her husband. Both books have proved enormously popular, as have courses based on them.

This success in seeming defiance of the facts—such as women's increasing participation in the labour force—can be partly accounted for by recognizing that, for many women, divorce or marital breakdown is a threatening possibility that could leave them in dire circumstances. Consequently, anything that promises marital harmony is worth their attention.

These books are also part of an anti-feminist backlash, whose organization has been particularly important in stopping the passing of the

Equal Rights Amendment in the United States. Many of the leaders, such as Phyllis Schlafly, regularly portray feminists as whining, straggly-haired women who degrade and betray their sex in their search to become just like men. Freeman (1984, 576-77) suggests that this sort of opposition to feminism can be seen as status politics. That is, the support for modern anti-feminism comes from lower-class, unemployed women, and "perhaps the attraction of this ideology lies in its defense of the traditional middle-class family with male as provider and female as homemaker, long a symbol of upward mobility in the United States." In this context, the idea that the idealized gender roles are obsolete seems to "threaten the male breadwinner role and force wives into the labour force to support families," a threat with "a powerful class appeal."

Co-option

Another problem for feminism as a movement for the liberation of *all* men and women has been the potential for the deflection of aims and for co-option—a potential provided by the very multiplicity of special interest groups and the multifaceted nature of feminist theory. For example, Shulman (1980, 603) notes that the radical feminist critiques of sexuality and sexual repression, factors that the writers saw as "aspects, or examples, of a much larger male domination of women," became diverted in many instances into "concern with mere sexual technique or increased activity." The resulting co-option and tokenism have often made it "easier for people to deny that anything is still drastically wrong between the sexes."

Part of the co-option process in the view of Shulman and others has been the manner in which academic feminists have related to the movement. People who claim expertise on women's issues and problems have often been the very people responsible for the deflection and co-option of the issues. For example, to suggest that women must be ever ready to protest against every instance of sex discrimination or sexual harassment on the job, even when that minimal-pay and minimal-status job represents the thin line between subsistence and welfare, is to be insensitive to the real existence of such women. Yet sensitivity is claimed as the cornerstone of attempts to formulate feminist theory and practice.

FEMINISTS AND SOCIOLOGY

Understanding the experience of the everyday world as described by women is critical to developing an alternative, feminist perspective. That understanding must extend to the position of women in the generation of knowledge. For many women in academia, the consciousness of their status as women, rather than as academics, is made clear in the organization and timing of their training, both undergraduate and graduate, and their subsequent work experiences. Academia, like the world of paid labour in general, is organized on the male model, with the expectation of a continuous presence in the paid labour force and minimal responsibilities for domestic labour and child care.

More subtle than the organizational constraints imposed by the male model is the devaluation of women's knowledge and expertise. In academia the central goal is the production and teaching of new ideas. This production is largely in the hands of males, since women are "excluded from full participation in creating the forms of thought which constitute the social consciousness of a society" (Smith 1975, 365). The most visible demonstration of Smith's contention is the distribution of the sexes throughout the educational system. Women are most often found at the lower levels, as elementary school teachers, rather than at the higher levels, as university professors. Consequently, women are primarily involved in the transmission and conservation of existing knowledge, rather than in the production of new knowledge. It is men who are in the disciplines that are concerned with the production of new ideas, as well as in those positions that "prepare people for positions in the managerial and governing structure" of the country (Smith 1975, 361).

The production of knowledge is accomplished in the absence not only of women but also of others, such as members of either sex from the working class and ethnic and racial minorities. This exclusion is also a means to justify who should be excluded. Robinson points out how this self-fulfilling prophecy works in regard to high culture.

> To be conscious of race, class, or sex with respect to high culture is to be conscious, first of all, of exclusion. The black, the woman, the worker, and the peasant are all forced to acknowledge the existence of a mainstream, self-proclaimed as the whole of "culture" in which they do not—or do not fully—participate. (1978, 29)

Such groups do not participate fully because they are less well educated, an explanation that reverses the "real causes and effects" and generates the conclusion that "certain people do not have access to culture because they are uncultured" (Robinson 1978, 29)

Women and Science

Of all the areas from which women are excluded, science ranks highest. Although some scientists have been, and are, women, and although open assertions that women do not have sufficiently logical minds to cope with science are now rare (although not unknown), science as an enterprise is still seen as a masculine endeavour. Its characteristics are regarded as male: hardness, impersonality and objectivity. Women are soft, emotional, and subjective. As a result:

> The presumption is that science, by its very nature, is inherently masculine, and that women can apprehend it only by an extreme effort of overcoming

their own nature which is inherently contradictory to science. They must, therefore, either forego science or cease to be women. The inaccessibility of science to women is thus not due to the difficulty of the subject matter, nor to the lack of education and opportunity afforded to women; but rather to the incongruity or the lack of fit between "science" and the "female mind." (Hein 1981, 370)

The problem is not simply one of the relative absence of women in science or of the relative absence of their contributions to the scientific endeavour. A more fundamental issue concerns the cornerstone of the scientific enterprise—objectivity. The absence of values—of "bias"—is supposed to

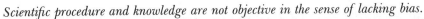

Scientific procedure and knowledge are not objective in the sense of lacking bias.

govern the problems investigated, the methods used, and the results judged in the production of "factual" knowledge. Scientific procedure and scientific knowledge are not, however, objective in the sense of lacking bias, because of the gender relationships between men and women and because of the object of science, which is nature. The control and domination of the forces of nature has been, since Roger Bacon wrote in the 13th century, the object of scientific knowledge and manipulation. It is men who are contrasted with, and opposed to, nature, and women who are identified with nature.

> Man's attitude toward nature is colored by his attitude toward woman, his attitude toward woman by his attitude toward nature. Both function as the *Other* against which he endeavors to establish his *Self*—Conscious, free, essential, transcendent. Man the scientist/engineer is no exception to this rule. (Schweickert 1983, 202)

In recognizing the problem, the critique developed by feminist scientists does not imply the abandonment of the scientific intention.

> The radical feminist critique of science and objectivity, . . . needs to be developed in ways that will allow us to identify those aspects of scientific activity and ideology which need to be questioned and rejected, without at the same time abandoning the ideal that we can come to an ever more complete understanding of the natural world through a collective and disciplined process of investigation and discovery. (Fee 1983, 16)

Feminist Sociology

Sociology has attempted to emulate the physical sciences, and the discipline has not been immune to the siren call of numbers to give it a superficial resemblance to a physical science. The machismo element in sociology accords prestige to quantitative methods that produce "hard" data, in contrast to qualitative techniques said to produce "soft" data. This division of method and data, however, has proved particularly problematic for producing any coherent, holistic description of society or for producing explanations with predictive power.[16] The emphasis on quantitative measures designed to produce predictive theory has resulted, as Acker puts it, in carving up the "living, moving actuality of human experience" into discrete, manageable pieces that can be dealt with in sterile, abstract categories and thus most easily mastered and controlled. Percentages and graphs can be very good for summarizing data, she says, but that approach has been a "spectacular failure at anticipating social change . . . for example, no sociologists predicted the reemergence of the women's movement" (1978, 138). More significantly, the hard data of statistical relationships produces an impoverished description of social reality, giving rise to sociological theory that cannot conceptualize society with both sexes as significant participants.

Sociology has had its share of "founding mothers," who have occasionally challenged the prevailing male orientation. In the past, many female sociologists and anthropologists did research on women, but most of them, according to Luxton, wrote "without intending to challenge the existing frameworks of their discipline." A few, who would become "the founding mothers for the latest generation of feminist scholars could be heard muttering, mainly to themselves, in the pages of the occasional journal or book," but it was with the resurgence of the women's movement that "the muttering emerged as a Greek chorus of women, usually students, booing heartily whenever the principles on the state spoke of 'mankind,' crying out at every opportunity 'what about women?'" (Luxton 1981, 71).

The recognition of the poverty of past sociological explanations, does not, however, mean that simply "adding women in" will solve the problem. Neither does the recognition of the sterility of the quantitative method mean that it should be replaced entirely with qualitative methods. On the contrary. The recognition of the problems of sociology means that we need a total revolution in the manner in which we discover social reality, a "re-orientation of research which would equal the re-orientation that had to take place when scholars realised that the sun does not revolve around the world but the world around the sun" (Eichler 1984, 34).

With such a revolution, the dichotomized frameworks examined earlier in this chapter would have to be discarded as descriptions of social reality and gender relations. This is not to say that the dichotomies cannot be used to illustrate the fallacy of the position that regards humans as males, and females as existing in relation to, and therefore being less than, males. Indeed, a feminist sociology must recognize that in the dichotomized perspective, to be female was to be understood as having no autonomy, to be conceptualized as *Other*—the object to the male subject (de Beauvoir [1949] 1974). With that recognition, a feminist sociology takes women as the subject of concern in order to approach an understanding of a social universe of women and men. That is, women's own descriptions of their lives, women's own reality, are taken seriously and the attempt is made to construct a "sociology *for* women rather than *of* women" (Smith 1975, 367).

In brief, feminist sociology does not simply include women, or, just as simplistically, include only women, but it understands that women are active subjects in the production of knowledge. Feminist sociology also maintains that the distinction drawn between the production and the use of knowledge is an artificial one, as is the distinction between objectivity and subjectivity. Feminist research takes seriously the slogan of the consciousness-raising groups, the "personal is political." As Stanley and Wise point out:

The social sciences claim to provide us with objective knowledge independent of the personal situation of the social scientist. But, of course, women's perspective, women's knowledge, and women's experience, provide an irrefutable critique of such claims. Within such products of social science research women's lives are omitted, distorted, misunderstood, and in doing this men's lives too are similarly distorted. (1983, 165)

How can a feminist sociology be done? A key factor is scepticism about received wisdom dealing with sexually differentiated behaviour and relationships as either natural or historically entrenched. (The latter usually means, for sociology, that no one has re-tested the original study that discovered the differences.) An example of some preliminary research in this vein is found in the studies reported in *Women and the Public Sphere* (Siltanen and Stanworth 1984). They focus on the presumed differences in men's and women's orientation to organized political parties and their participation in and attitudes toward trade union activities. In general, the editors note, in "electoral politics and work-based politics, the characterization of women's political life as marginal, shallow or conservative" is pervasive and is the "product of male-stream analysis—that is, it derives from traditions of thought which are, in both their theoretical and empirical dimensions, rooted in masculine experience" (1984, 14). For example, Bourque and Grossholtz examined the findings of political sociology and political science regarding gender differences. They first thought that the treatment of women in political research could be accounted for by the assumption that men and women accept "certain divisions within the society (of labour, status, behaviour) along sex lines and these have been translated into politics." But in their examination of the literature and the data presented there, they discovered:

If politics was to be man's realm, then at levels that political scientists measured political involvement, women were not getting the message. Women turned out to vote at about the same rate as men . . . they had about the same level of interest and involvement in politics as most men. (1984, 121)

The authors find that a substantial number of the conclusions drawn in the past about the different political orientations of the sexes "were created by the political scientists out of their own notions of what should be the case" (1984, 121).

Scepticism can also be useful in re-examining the assumed characteristics of female-female relationships. The idea that a woman will always reject a female friend in favour of a male, in contrast to the solidarity of the male buddy system, has been shown as a myth somewhat peculiar to Western, and even North American, society. But despite the evidence of the paucity and shallowness of adult male friendships and of the enduring nature of many female friendships, the myth dies hard, as the mass media presentations of male buddies illustrate. The myth is particularly significant in that it obscures a source of female strength even in periods in which patriarchal power appears to be particularly strong. For example, Cott, in an analysis of New England women in 1750 to 1835, illustrates the development of sisterhood among women's church groups. These groups provided women with support on a day-to-day basis as well as a means for them to exercise some influence (power) in the community. Women's associations such as these were able to use the ideology of the "women's sphere" to their advantage by arguing that only women could understand the needs of women and then pressing for some reform of benefit for women. The "bonds of womanhood" were bonds among equals, and the "internal dynamics of women's sphere, by encouraging women to claim a social role according to their sex and to share both social and sexual solidarity, provoked a minority of women to see and protest those boundaries" (Cott 1977, 204). From the "women's sphere" sprang the 19th-century women's protest. Cott's study, like those in *Women in the Public Sphere,* indicates both the manner in which the received wisdom can be approached critically and the rich store of knowledge to be regained as a consequence of looking at the "facts" with new eyes.

Feminist sociology means more than simply uncovering the distortions of past assumptions about gender relations. Any research that is feminist must take the people involved into the process as both determiners of what the world is to them and appraisers of the results of the research. Research is in search of answers and can confer power, because knowledge is power. Consequently, says Malmo, "if researchers have knowledge about the subjects of their research and this knowledge is either purposely or inadvertently withheld, then the subjects are being exploited and the status quo is maintained." The aim of feminist research is to find ways "to bridge the gap between researchers and the people being researched, so that the power of knowledge can be shared by all" (1984, 129-30).

Finally, feminist sociology emphasizes the experiences of women, the uncovering of hidden realities, because there can be no sociological generalizations about human beings as long as a large number of such beings are systematically excluded or ignored. This means that feminist sociology is political in the sense that it reveals the manner in which past sociologists have provided intellectual justifications for the persistence of gender inequalities that have had negative consequences for the whole human race.

CONCLUSION

Despite the spread of feminism and the fundamental changes to society brought about by the repositioning of women in the labour force, idealized gender roles persist as the dominant assumptions about the nature of masculinity and femininity. Such assumptions continue to affirm a significant difference between men and women and to assign to each a unique and distinctive role in society.

Feminist sociology has been instrumental in opening up a variety of methodological and theoretical approaches to the question of human relationships. The scholarship has been frequently of an exciting inter-disciplinary nature that has proved extremely fruitful in opening up previously unexplored or murky corners of the human experience. In North America, the experiences and the expectations of white, middle-class males that provided the past benchmarks for sociological frameworks have been discredited. As feminist research examines and re-makes the ways we understand the everyday lives of women and men, the challenge it faces is not simply to uncover but also to point to ways for change. In this, women and men are inseparably connected:

> The public and the private worlds are inseparably connected; that the tyrannies and servilities of the one are the tyrannies and servilities of the other. . . . A common interest unites . . . us; it is one world, one life. How essential it is that we should realize that unity the dead bodies, the ruined houses prove. For such will be our ruin if you, in the immensity of your public abstractions forget the private figure, or if we in the intensity of our private emotions forget the public world. Both houses will be ruined, the public and the private, the material and the spiritual, for they are inseparably connected. (Woolf [1938] 1977, 162)

NOTES

1. For research on individuals with the sex characteristics of both sexes, see Money and Ehrhardt (1974).
2. The prescriptions and proscriptions are not absolutes. Girls in their pre-teen years are tolerated as tomboys. The latitude for boys appears to be less than that for girls, however; any feminine behaviour on the part of boys is not tolerated to the same extent as some masculine behaviour in girls.
3. See also Acker (1978) and Smith (1975).
4. See Glazer and Waehrer (1977); Bernard (1981); Smith (1975); and Eichler (1975).
5. See Power (1975); McNamara and Wemple (1977); and Leacock (1983).
6. This division and commonality are problematic for the feminist movement both theoretically and at the level of practical action. The issue is not new, as the history of women's suffrage protest and subsequent activities indicates (see Rothman 1978 and Spender 1983). Today one of the movement's greatest problems is the middle-class status of many feminist women and the co-option of movement action by academics pursuing their own career interests (see Leffler, Gillespie, and Ratner 1973).
7. The trials and tribulations of employees and employers have proved a rich resource for applied sociology. From the scientific management of Frederic Winslow Taylor at the turn of the century, through the human relations approach of Elton Mayo and others after the Second World War, to the current interests in tripartism, rectifying the productive sphere has been of critical importance for sociology. Like crime and deviance, the world of work provides an area in which (male) sociologists can prove they are one of the boys, as opposed to effete intellectuals.

8. See Smith (1973); Komarovsky (1976); and Delphy (1984).
9. I am indebted to Dr. Dallas Cullen for these insights.
10. See Fogarty, Rapoport and Rapoport 1971; Holmstrom 1973; Vanek 1978; Meissner 1976.
11. Emphasis in the original.
12. Emphasis in the original.
13. This critique does not ignore the fact that many women regard their wages as giving them some independence, especially over those items that are somewhat peripheral to the household's immediate daily needs. But most women are conscious of the limited power of their wages in comparison to that of their husbands' through the simple fact that the money earned does not eliminate their domestic labour or place them on a par with their husbands.
14. The founding fathers of sociology were drawn, largely, from a restricted social background. As Luxton (1984, 66) illustrates, in the theorizing on the nature of the family and gender relations, the founding fathers "saw the family forms idealized by their own class as the end product of the evolution of society from savagery to civilization. . . . These men considered Victorian culture and its sexual relations as representing the pinnacle of human evolution."
15. Other developments in the 1970s included a number of status of women reports from Canadian universities, as well as some government departments.
16. Rosaldo and Lamphere (1974) indicate that anthropologists too who have asked women about their lives, rather than taking the word of male respondents, have often uncovered very different accounts of what occurs in the society.

FOR FURTHER READING

David, D.S., and R. Brannon, eds.
1976 *The Forty-Nine Percent Majority*. Menlo Park, Calif.: Addison-Wesley. The focus of this book is largely American, but some of the articles are still the best available on the question of the male role in our society.

Finn, Geraldine, and Angela Miles, eds.
1982 *Feminism in Canada: From Pressure to Politics*. Montreal: Black Rose Books. This important Canadian book concentrates on feminist developments in scholarship and political action during the past two decades.

Fox, B., ed.
1980 *Hidden in the Household*. Toronto: Women's Press. A Canadian book, this collection has an excellent series of articles on the question of household labour.

Hamilton, R.
1978 *The Liberation of Women*. London: George Allen and Unwin. This study offers a good discussion of the historical position of women in Western countries as well as coverage of the debate between Marxist and feminist frameworks as explanation of gender relations. Hamilton attempts to transcend the debate and provide a means of reconciling the explanations.

Vickers, Jill Mccalla
1984 *Taking Sex into Account: The Policy Consequences of Sexist Research.* Ottawa: Carleton University Press.
This book comprises a series of discussions dealing with the practical consequences for gender equality of sexist research theory and methods. The focus is basically Canadian.

Journals

Two journals must be mentioned as most significant and should be monitored by students interested in pursuing any of the topics covered in this chapter:

Resources for Feminist Research is a Canadian publication and, in addition to commentary on current issues and events, carries bibliographies, notices of meetings, addresses of other journals (international listing), and information on current research and the current interests of Canadian researchers.
Signs: Journal of Women in Culture and Society is published in the United States but has an international authorship of articles. It has carried research that has been and continues to be on the "leading edge" of feminist issues.

CHAPTER 10

BUREAUCRACY AND WORK ORGANIZATION

Frank E. Jones

Organizations are a dominant feature of societies such as Canada. Indeed, one observer, Robert Presthus (1978) views organizations as such an important feature that he uses the label organizational society to describe today's industrialized world,[1] conveying their pervasiveness and the magnitude of their growth.

In Presthus's view, organizations are omnipresent in most aspects of present-day living. A Canadian is likely to be born in a hospital, educated in a school and possibly in a university, employed by a corporation or a government agency, and enrolled in a union or other work association. Leisure-time activities are provided in great measure by the large enterprises that dominate film production, radio and television, vacation travel and accommodation, and organized sports. Hospitals come back into the picture as the dominant context for the treatment of illness—and death is likely to involve a large insurance company. Presthus emphasizes not only the pervasiveness of organizations but also their tendency to increase in size and complexity. During this century, business firms have grown through mergers and takeovers into giants, such as ITT, IBM, and EXXON.

One frequently noted feature of a bureaucracy is that the individual is subordinate to his or her position, rather than the other way around. An organizational chart shows a set of positions, rather than the people who occupy them. Promotion to a position often means taking on the values, lifestyle, and attitudes of others in a similar position.

Unions too have become large, centrally directed organizations. The large hospital and the large high school and university dominate health care and education.

Some observers argue that the proliferation of large organizations is undesirable, saying, for example, that they stifle individuality and produce conforming robots. Thus Whyte (1956) describes the transformation of executives and managerial employees of large organizations into "organization men," beings characterized by uniform speech patterns, dress, and family lifestyles. Bowles and Gintis (1976) argue that schooling in the United States conditions students to the conformity and submissiveness required of organizational employees. Galbraith (1967) perceives a danger to democracy in the power that the technical experts employed by large public and private organizations exert over the important decisions taken in modern societies. All these charges focus on the tendencies of organizations to create a mass society and to develop strong bases inimical to the development and persistence of democracy.

Other observers regard large organizations in a more favourable light. They point out that large organizations, through economies of scale, are able to produce and widely distribute a rich variety of goods and services. Large-scale manufacturing makes automobiles, electronic equipment, and sophisticated consumer items available to people with a wide range of incomes. Large schools and large hospitals make more resources available for education and health care than do their smaller counterparts.

However one judges the social consequences of organizations, it is apparent that they provide an important environmental content throughout the life cycle in Canada and other modern societies. Obviously, if it is important for human beings to understand their social environment, it is important to study organizations.

WHAT IS AN ORGANIZATION?

A main concern of this chapter will be the nature of organizations—that is, what is meant by the term "organization." In particular, we will discuss both the prevailing popular conception and the major sociological conceptions of bureaucracy, the most important form of modern organization. This discussion will consider some advantages and disadvantages of bureaucracy, especially the tension between bureaucratic and democratic structures.

Although sociologists do not completely agree on a definition of the **organization,** there does seem to be broad agreement that it differs from other forms of social groups, such as the family. A person normally belongs to a family by virtue of birth or marriage, and the division of labour among family members is relatively loosely defined. By contrast, membership in organizations is normally a matter of choice (although this choice may be constrained by economic and other considerations). Obviously, relationships between members of an organization are based on ties other than those of family and kinship. Again, the division of labour tends to be defined more precisely in organizations than in kin-based groups. Many sociological definitions of the organization emphasize the idea that organizations, unlike other kinds of social groups, or **collectivities,** are formed to achieve explicit goals (see, for example, Hall 1982, 29, 33; Parsons 1960, 17). Schools, hospitals, and business firms are deliberately created as means for educating people, treating illness, and pursuing economic activities; they do not "just happen," as families and kinship groups do.

While this emphasis on the unique nature of organizations is useful and consistent with common sense (the relationships between the members of a family *are* different from those between employees of a factory), it is important to bear in mind that from a sociological perspective all collectivities share certain features. For example, sociological analysis treats social relationships as the basic units of analysis of all collectivities, whether they are organizations, families, street gangs, or other social groupings. **Social relationships** are the mutual involvements of the people who belong to a collectivity and may be differentiated in terms of task distribution, power and authority, and emotional commitment. From the perspective of sociology, the distribution of tasks, power, and authority among the members of a collectivity and the intensity of the members' emotional relationships are important for describing the collectivity and, if recurrent consequences can be related to the way tasks are distributed and so on, for explaining how the collectivity "works." Thus, although families may be distinguished from organizations by their less complex task distribution, simpler structures of authority, and higher intensity of emotional commitment, the same units—social relationships—are the basis for analysis of both families and organizations.

BUREAUCRACY

Most people identify most organizations—especially large-scale organizations—in modern societies as bureaucracies. As this chapter will demonstrate, the popular meaning of the term bureaucracy is different from its meaning in sociology. In everyday language, "bureaucracy" sometimes refers only to government departments and agencies, sometimes to all organizations or all large organizations indiscriminately. The popular image of bureaucracy is often negative: it is equated with "red tape," an overemphasis on procedures and regulations. Thus, a person urgently in need of money for food and rent may perceive as unnecessary the time-consuming procedures that a welfare agency uses to determine if the applicant qualifies for help. Hospital admission procedures may require a prospective patient to complete an application form and provide personal information—a requirement that the patient sees as a nuisance.

Many critics see red tape as a way of slowing down or denying the provision of services. Others regard it as a means of increasing the number of organizational employees beyond the number required to perform necessary services. For these critics, red tape is synonymous with inefficiency.

If the popular conception of bureaucracy is accurate, it seems necessary to believe that most large-scale organizations, public or private, deliberately seek to be obstructive or inefficient, since they tend to be highly bureaucratic. However, the fact that bureaucracy is characteristic of private-sector organizations, which, more perhaps than public-sector organizations, must be concerned with efficiency in order to survive, suggests that bureaucratization would not occur if organizations did not expect it to be efficient. Contrary to the popular image, then, bureaucracy can work well, some of the time at least.

As these conflicting views of bureaucracy are not easy to reconcile, it is time, perhaps, to examine what the sociologists have discovered.

WEBER'S MODEL

The study of bureaucracy is most closely associated with the German sociologist Max Weber (1864-1920), who made lasting contributions to the development of sociology. Weber's interest in bureaucracy derived from his interest in understanding why human beings are responsive or obedient to the directions of others. Although he recognized that human beings can be coerced—that is, forced by fear of punishment or injury into following another's wishes—he argued, in *The Theory of Social and Economic Organization* ([1922] 1947), that not all obedience or compliance can be regarded as coercion. Rather, if the exercise of power is regarded as legitimate, compliance is the appropriate response from those whose shared beliefs confer the legitimation. Weber called the legitimate exercise of power **authority** and described three types:

1. **Charismatic authority,** in which the exercise of power by an individual is legitimated by a shared belief that the person possesses unique gifts or characteristics. The classic example is the acceptance of Christ's authority by his followers because they believed him to be the Son of God.
2. **Traditional authority,** in which an individual's exercise of power is legitimated by longstanding custom, as in the case of a sovereign or a chief who is chosen from a particular family or larger kinship group.
3. **Rational-legal authority,** in which the exercise of power is legitimated by **rationality**—that is, by the demonstrable relevance of directions and orders to the achievement of a group's shared goals or values—and by a shared belief in the "legality of patterns of normative rules" that establish the rights and responsibilities of the members of a collectivity, including the right to issue directions and orders.

Weber linked his idea of rational-legal authority to the use of a bureaucratic administrative staff,[2] arguing that such authority can effectively issue commands relevant to the attainment of the collectivity's goals only if the organization has certain kinds of procedural and structural elements. These procedures and structures are the components of **bureaucracy,** and the basis of their use is their greater efficiency, relative to alternative measures in attaining the collectivity's goals. The result, in Weber's view, is the most efficient form of organization that human beings have invented.

Maintaining his emphasis on efficiency, Weber identified the basic elements of bureaucracy. We shall discuss four structural elements and one procedural element.[3]

1. A highly structured division of labour.
2. Appointment on the basis of technical competence.
3. A hierarchical authority structure.
4. Impersonal relationships.
5. The use of rules.

Task Specialization

In Weber's model, the various tasks and responsibilities required to achieve the bureaucracy's goals are carefully allocated among the incumbents of its various **offices** (positions) so that they have different but well-defined **jurisdictions** (sets of responsibilities). In other words, the first characteristic of the bureaucracy that Weber identified is **task specialization** or a highly complex **division of labour:** the overall task of the organization is divided and subdivided into subtasks that are then assigned to various members of the organization. For example, a company may divide managerial responsibilities among several vice-presidents on the basis of function—vice-president of sales, vice-president of production, and so on. The principle of division can be carried out at all levels of the organization. Weber separated his comments on the distribution of tasks and responsibilities among the offices of the bureaucracy from his comments on the distribution of authority, although both are aspects of the division of labour. As indicated above, Weber held that bureaucratic authority is rational-legal; that is, legitimacy is established by a framework of rules that is seen to have the force of law and that defines the scope of authority, as well as by the possession of the technical competence relevant to attaining the bureaucracy's objectives.

Thus, a critical feature of the bureaucracy in Weber's model is its **hierarchical structure:** some officials have more authority than others, and an official at a lower level is subordinate to one at a higher level. For example, the manager of the meat section of a supermarket is subordinate to the store manager. Nevertheless, an official at a given level has a prescribed sphere of competence and the authority to make decisions at that level. Thus, although an official can be overruled by an official at a higher level and although ultimate authority rests at the highest levels

The extensive task specialization that is characteristic of bureaucracies makes communication essential to the coordination of activities. Thus there is an emphasis on meetings. Often it is only at such meetings that employees find out what others are doing and why. Many organizations become dependent upon holding meetings before making any decisions, so that meetings may often delay rather than accelerate decision-making.

(usually in one office, such as that of deputy minister or general manager), authority is essentially delegated and decentralized. A hierarchical authority structure contributes to efficiency by allowing decisions to be made at each level by an official with the required technical competence; through this decentralization, decisions can be implemented without undue delay.

Since the incumbents of the bureaucratic office are human beings, the nature of their commitments to each other is critically important. Weber distinguished relations in the bureaucracy—especially between people of greater or lesser authority—from those in other kinds of social organizations. In feudal organizations, for example, retainers might have a positive emotional commitment to the lord, expressed as respect, loyalty, or love. Bureaucracies, however, are characterized by **impersonal relationships**; feelings between officials are expected to be neutral. Neither strong feelings, such as love and hate, nor mild feelings, such as affection or disdain, should determine responsiveness to the orders of a superior or rewards or punishment for subordinates. Presumably, Weber saw the relation of impersonality to efficiency as being indirect. The exercise of favouritism could lead to the neglect of technical competence in decisions concerning task allocation or promotion. Weber probably also assumed that free emotional expression would undermine the rationality that characterizes a bureaucracy.

The Significance of Rules in the Bureaucracy

Finally, Weber noted that, in the bureaucracy, decisions and directives tend to be written and are accumulated in files (that is, records are kept of them). These decisions, arrived at rationally and tested by experience, form the bases of rules that regulate the future actions of bureaucratic officials. For example, instead of deciding each case of tardiness on an individual basis, the officials of a bureaucracy can formulate a rule specifying sanctions and apply it to everyone who arrives late for work. Although rules can be passed on orally, the written form they take in the bureaucracy facilitates their application to recurrent events or situations. Thus, if someone arrives late for work, the appropriate response to the offence can be found in the company manual. Rules contribute to efficiency by using past experience to solve recurrent problems, thereby minimizing the use of time and energy.

Rules, whether formally recorded or informally understood, are vital to any collectivity. Their purpose is to control the behaviour of its members and, in consequence, to generate predictability. In social groups whose members have homogeneous interests or characteristics—say, they are all golfers or all of the same age, sex, or ethnicity—informal, unwritten rules may be sufficient to control behaviour, ensure predictability, and thus protect the collective interest. In a bureaucracy, however, where heterogeneity of individual characteristics is the likely condition[4] and the division of labour creates division of interests, control and prediction of behaviour are more problematical. Informal understandings must give way to explicitly stated rules, which, to be effective, must have the force of law.[5] Thus, for the bureaucracy seen as an instrument of rational social action, the explicit, quasi-legal character of rules is essential.

Finally, rules promote impersonality by reducing the discretion of officials. A manager may not give a lighter punishment to a friend and a heavier punishment to someone he or she dislikes but must punish everyone as required by the rules. A manager may decide not to implement the rule in some cases but, in doing so, risks punishment from his or her own superior.

The Significance of Weberian Theory

It is not difficult to find examples of organizations thought to be bureaucratic that do not conform to Weber's formulation of bureaucracy.

For example, some organizations may favour the employment of males over females or people with one ethnic affiliation over another without demonstrating that gender or ethnicity affects technical competence.[6] Superiors have been known to usurp the authority of subordinates—or even the authority of their own superiors.

Weber did not, however, assume that actual organizations could do more than resemble, in some degree, his ideal bureaucracy. In other words, he was describing an **ideal type**—a general prototype or model. If the model is an accurate one, it is correct to state that the more closely an organization resembles Weber's ideal, the more efficiency it will achieve. For example, if two organizations are involved in the same activity, the one that has the more complex division of labour will, assuming the correctness of Weber's reasoning, achieve the greater efficiency. Similar conditional statements can be made about the other structural and procedural elements of Weber's model. So in assessing that model, the question is not whether it describes reality but whether it correctly identifies the critical features of bureaucracy. An affirmative answer to this question requires evidence that the structural and procedural features of Weber's bureaucracy actually do contribute to efficiency.

Evidence presently available to assess the efficiency resulting from Weber's bureaucratic model is ambiguous. On the positive side is the widespread adoption of bureaucratic features, especially by organizations whose prime criterion is "the bottom line." However, research from organizations suggests that efficiency is not an outcome to be taken for granted in all circumstances. Such research calls attention not only to inefficiencies resulting from failure to adhere to the model but also either to some consequences of bureaucratic features that Weber did not anticipate or to specific bureaucratic features' inappropriateness to particular conditions. For example, efficiency presumably depends on cooperation among the members of an organization, yet some bureaucratic features, such as the division of labour, generate potential conflicts of interest that may reduce cooperation. Similarly, the bureaucratic emphasis on impersonality may inhibit the development of cohesion, consequently inhibiting cooperation and thereby reducing efficiency. In the next section we shall examine several organizational features that seem to depart from the bureaucratic model yet also seem to contribute to organizational efficiency.

STRUCTURAL VARIATIONS IN ORGANIZATIONS

Mechanistic and Organic Organizations

In a study of electronics manufacturing firms in Great Britain, Burns and Stalker (1961) find that although some resemble Weber's bureaucratic model others appear to be almost an inversion of bureaucracy. The researchers label the latter the organic system of management. Instead of conforming to a strict division of labour, employees of **organic organizations** tend to accept whatever tasks and responsibilities, relevant to their expertise, are necessary to solve a problem. Interaction between the employees tends to be lateral rather than vertical; communication takes the form of "information and advice rather than instructions and decisions" (Burns and Stalker 1961, 121). It turns out that this structure does not emerge in organizations whose management is unconcerned about efficiency or lax in imposing sanctions for failure to conform to bureaucratic regulations; rather, it is associated with an environment marked by rapid technological change in the products demanded by clients. Because organic organizations appear to be more capable than bureaucratic organizations of responding to such change, Burns and Stalker's findings suggest that the efficiency of an organizational structure depends on the nature of its activities and of its environment. Bureaucratic structure, which they called **mechanistic,** functions efficiently in a stable environment, but an organic model is more efficient in an unstable environment.

The analysis by Burns and Stalker marked an important step in thinking about organizations, for they conclude that organic organizations are not just deviations from Weber's bureaucratic model but represent a different and conceptually valid model of organizations. In addition, they suggest that organizational efficiency depends on the relationship between the features of an organization and its environment, whereas Weber's analysis implies (at least by omission) that the bureaucratic mode of organization will maximize efficiency in any environment.

Bureaucracy and Status Groups

Burns and Stalker are not the only sociologists who have started from a Weberian tradition but found it necessary to modify Weber's model as a consequence of what they observed in actual organizations. Gouldner (1954a) studied a firm engaged in mining gypsum and manufacturing wallboard. His findings lead him to conclude that the structure of bureaucracy is variable, not fixed as it is in Weber's model. Gouldner regards rules as the fundamental feature of bureaucracy, necessary for regulating relationships between the various status groups that compose an organization. In his analysis of rules, he argues that the structure of a bureaucracy depends in part on which status groups participate in formulating the rules, which status groups' values legitimate the rules, which status groups are the target of the rules, how infringements of the rules are seen to be motivated, and how the different status groups are advantaged or disadvantaged by implementation of the rules. Although the details of Gouldner's arguments need not concern us here, it is important to recognize his contribution to the concept of variation in organizations.

The Application of Bureaucratic Rules

In a study of government agencies in the United States, Blau ([1955]1963) finds that Weber's bureaucratic features are indeed present in these agencies. He concludes, however, that organizations cannot be satisfactorily described in terms of Weber's static model. Instead, they must be thought of as constantly undergoing change that results from the actions of their members in relation both to each other and to external demand. Thus, he observes that employees conform to certain rules but ignore others that are formally regarded as essential or fundamental.

For example, Blau found that in a government employment agency he studied, counsellors ignored a set of formal rules that were consistent with the agency's objective of providing employment counselling aimed at fitting clients' qualifications to those required by available jobs. Instead, the counsellors focused their efforts on job placement—that is, on finding their clients employment and filling job vacancies. The counsellors were apparently responding both to a labour market that provided little demand for variations in employment skills and to pressures to find employment and fill jobs for the agency's clients, who were job seekers *and* employers. Another agency's task was to monitor regulations imposed on business organizations. Blau observed that the staff invariably ignored several rules regarded as essential to the agency's functioning. For example, although staff members were forbidden to consult each other about their cases, Blau observed that they regularly did consult each other

The cold impersonality promoted by bureaucratic organizational structures has created its own aesthetics. Notice that the reflective surfaces of these buildings evoke impenetrability.

on a variety of matters, such as the application of a particular government regulation. He concludes that supervisors overlooked the non-compliance because the negative effects of ignoring the consultation rule were outweighed by the positive effects of allowing staff members to pool their experience and thus to achieve more effective enforcement of the government's regulations.

Systematic Observation of Organizations

The work of Gouldner and Blau, like that of Burns and Stalker, is important because it is based on systematic observation of actual organizations rather than on hearsay or conventional beliefs about bureaucracy. These researchers sought to understand the extent to which Weber's account of bureaucracy actually conforms to what occurs in operating organizations. Their findings, with those of other researchers, drew attention to gaps in Weber's model. Thus, in addition to Weber's emphasis on formal status differentiation (the division of labour and the hierarchization of authority), Blau drew attention to the considerable importance of status differences that evolve in the daily interaction of employees on the job. In addition and in contrast to Weber's emphasis on impersonality, Blau observed that interpersonal commitments among employees were quite prominent in both of the agencies he studied. In Blau's view, the level of **social cohesion,** as he terms the product of these interpersonal commitments, was very closely related to the efficient functioning of the agencies.

Other researchers, some working in traditions other than the Weberian, have also called attention to inadequacies in Weber's model of bureaucracy. In the famous Western Electric research project (see for example Roethlisberger and Dickson 1939), which was undertaken before Blau or Gouldner began their studies, the investigators observed that the behaviour of employees engaged in making parts of telephone equipment included more than the activities required for their jobs.

One of the studies involved a work group of five female employees that proved to have a consistently high record of production. The women initially had little knowledge of each other, but they were observed to develop friendships; they talked about and did things together that had no bearing on their work or on any formal relations required by that work. In the absence of findings to support the proposition that fatigue or monotony accounted for variations in productivity, the investigators included this social activity among the possible reasons for the sustained high productivity of the five workers. In a later study designed to observe systematically the social interaction of a group of male workers, the investigators concluded that the social ties between workers were directly related to productivity. Thus, the Western Electric research drew attention to the importance of social cohesion through their observation of the way productivity and employee motivation are influenced by informal relationships among employees—in contrast to Weber's formal relationships.

A consequence of these studies is a widespread conclusion that Weber's model of bureaucracy does not capture the actual structure of the processes of bureaucracy satisfactorily. Indeed, as Perrow (1979) notes, the weight of research findings has led to a view that bureaucracy hinders rapid, effective decision-making, alienates employees and clients, and is therefore—contrary to Weber's conclusions—inefficient. Perrow argues, however, that this view is ill considered. He believes that the bureaucratic elements identified by Weber contribute to efficiency, but that the extent of the contribution is modified by other conditions, a position he shares with Burns and Stalker.

The Variability of Organizations

The work of Blau, Burns and Stalker, Gouldner, Perrow, and many others has led to a rethinking of the concept of bureaucracy as descriptive of organizations. Generally, the work of these researchers suggests that it is more useful to regard the elements identified by Weber as variable aspects of organizations rather than to think of bureaucracy as a distinct type of organization.

For example, when Burns and Stalker describe their two models, the mechanistic and the organic, as the extreme forms that organizations can take, they imply that organizations should be described in terms not of absolute types but of variations on a set of dimensions, such as the complexity of the division of labour, the emphasis on routine procedures, and the emphasis on hierarchical control. Rather than focusing on types of organizations, an approach that calls attention only to gross variations,[7] it is more useful to think in terms of the fine differences among organizations. Some pay greater attention to rules and procedures than others; some have a more complex division of labour than others; some emphasize hierarchical communication and decision-making, while others emphasize lateral and horizontal communication. A recognition that these variations are more than lapses from bureaucracy not only provides a better description of organizations but also enhances the possibility of explaining why the variations exist. Rather than being simply indications of a failure to implement bureaucratic structures and procedures, variations in bureaucratization can be related to conditions such as the size of the organization, the type of activity that it pursues, and the market conditions that it faces. Variations in organizational features may also be related to outcomes, such as productivity and employee satisfaction.

Moreover, to think of organizations as conforming to or deviating from a bureaucratic model, rather than as varying in terms of a set of organizational dimensions, is to run the danger of concluding that there is a unique organizational structure appropriate to all activities and all environments. For example, although today's Canadian universities apply bureaucratic procedures to a wide range of activities, many of these procedures became appropriate only at a certain stage in each school's development. Most universities have always used some bureaucratic procedures in dealing with matters such as admission, registration, curriculum, and the review of grades, but the number and range of these rules tended to be quite small when a university had a small number of students and faculty. Their use increased as the organization increased in size and became increasingly diversified in its course and program offerings. Moreover, universities may use bureaucratic procedures for some activities but not for others; budgeting and registration procedures are more easily bureaucratized than are the research activities of faculty.

Although bureaucratization does occur as an organization grows and as it diversifies its activities or services, it is not clear that bureaucracy is inevitable. The prevalence of bureaucracy does suggest inevitability, but it is possible that it simply reflects the prevalence of certain values, such as efficiency, among people who have the authority to determine organizational structure.

In fact, although highly bureaucratized organizations can achieve high levels of efficiency, they can also be inefficient. Again, an organizational structure, if it is to be efficient, must be appropriate to its environment, and a high level of bureaucratization is not appropriate to every organizational environment.

Moreover, like all social structures, bureaucracies contain the seeds of their own destruction. Merton (1949), for example, argues that bureaucratic rules, which may contribute to efficiency, may also encourage officials to overconformity, expressed as rigid interpretation of the rules and perceived by clients of the bureaucracy as red tape. Similarly, the division of labour and the hierarchical structure that may result in efficiency also results in status distinctions that may generate conflict. Intraorganizational conflict can encourage efficiency, but it can also reduce it (Blau [1955] 1963; Dalton 1959). Moreover, the use of rules to resolve or constrain intraorganizational conflict may result in the rigidities already described.

INNOVATIONS IN ORGANIZATIONAL STRUCTURE

Efficiency is not the only motive for organizational innovation. For example, the members of organizations often resent the impersonality that results from the application of organizational rules and procedures, which they feel are dehumanizing or degrading. People resist being put into categories.

The most prominent motive for organizational change, however, derives from commitment to democratic values. In societies in which such values are widely held, employees resist inequalities of status and authority structures that allow them no say in their work. Thus there is a tendency in many organizations to reduce status distinctions by emphasizing informality (say, by using first names and abandoning the patterns of deference), by facilitating interaction among people holding different positions or statuses in the organization, and, in varying degrees, by providing opportunities for employees to participate in organizational decisions.

In democratic societies, there is an inconsistency between the expectation that all adult residents will participate, if only indirectly, in community decisions and the procedures in bureaucratic organizations, where rules and decisions are made only by those in positions of formal authority. Thus over the past 40 years or so and increasingly in the past 10 or 15 years, there has been considerable interest in modifying organizational structures to make them more responsive to democratic concerns. These modifications address concerns that arise from the autocratic formulation of organizational rules and from the restriction of decision-making to those in authority—especially the higher positions of authority. These modifications are anti-bureaucratic: they represent attempts to **debureaucratize.** Although we cannot discuss in detail the wide variety of modifications that have been implemented or proposed, we can provide a brief overview of the major efforts in this direction.

Of the innovations we will discuss, **the Quality of Working Life approach** is the least radical—that is, it represents the smallest departure from the structures of bureaucracy. The changes in this case are made at the level of the workplace. The division of labour is modified to increase the number and variety of tasks that workers are to perform, and workers are permitted to engage in collective decision-making about matters relating to the immediate productive process. For example, Volvo, the Swedish automobile firm, has established an automobile assembly plant that has no conventional assembly line. Instead, the workers control movement of the automobiles through the operational areas and, in a given operational area, all workers are able to perform all the required tasks and are permitted to decide who will do what and for how long. Tasks are usually rotated, and workers may decide to work in teams of varying size. Decisions concerning the operation are made by the work teams, rather than by a supervisor or foreman. This approach is a clear attempt to modify two essential dimensions of bureaucracy—the division of labour and the lower levels of the hierarchical authority structure—although it does not change the larger hierarchical structures of the organization.

A different response to democratic concerns, adopted widely in Europe, involves the appointment or election of workers to the organization's board of directors, known usually as the supervisory board, and the establishment of a **workers' council** that receives certain core decision-making rights and consultative powers and the right of access to information about the organization.[8] In most West German firms, for example, worker and non-worker directors share the responsibility for making policy decisions for the firm and for supervising top management.

The workers' councils share with managers the power to make decisions about matters such as wage-payment procedures and working conditions. They are usually consulted about matters such as vocational training and receive, by right, information about organizational changes such as mergers, plant transfers, and closedowns.

A more radical participatory scheme, called **workers' control** or self-management, has developed in Yugoslavia. It provides a complex form of participation for all employees in all decisions concerning the organization. There are separate participatory structures at different levels of the organization, culminating in a company-wide structure. Adizes (1971) describes the structure of two Yugoslav textile firms. The governing body of each is the workers' council, composed of representatives of all employees; it meets regularly to decide on a wide range of policy issues, including such important matters as investment in new machinery or the construction of a new plant, production and marketing plans, and the distribution of any surplus earnings over costs. Units similar to the workers' council make decisions or recommendations to higher committees about issues that arise in organizational divisions of the firm, called economic units, that have specific functions, such as weaving, dyeing, and accounting. In this way, workers participate in decisions at the level of their immediate jobs or work units and at the plant and company levels.

A final type of participatory organization is the **cooperative.** Cooperative organizations vary considerably, but a widely observed principle requires each participant to purchase a share in the cooperative and to have a vote on all matters requiring decision. Where this principle is applied, the cooperative consists of worker-owners who share all the policy decisions of the enterprise. Many countries have cooperatives; some are successful, some are not. Among the most successful are those in Spain, where such organizations provide an array of goods and services (Oakeshott 1978), and those in the plywood industry of the western United States (Bernstein 1980).

The success of these various experiments in industrial democracy or debureaucratization is ambiguous. Most studies indicate that employee satisfaction is high (Blumberg 1968, 123). Evidence concerning productivity is less firm (Stokes 1978, 33); some reports reveal an increase, but others report no significant change, or a decline. Although participatory structures, especially workers' control and cooperative structures, may reduce management-worker conflict by weakening or eliminating the line between managers and managed, strikes and other forms of conflict have occurred in organizations of this type (Abrahamsson 1977, 218; Bernstein 1980, 20).

Despite the inconclusiveness of the evidence on how well participatory structures work, the weakness associated with bureaucratization and a widespread commitment to democratic values continue to support a strong interest in developing organizational structures that reduce bureaucratization.

INDUSTRIAL DEMOCRACY IN ACTION

Adizes studied workers' control, a participatory organizational structure, in two textile firms in Yugoslavia. Although the formal structures are identical, he found differences in management style that greatly influence the decision-making process. This excerpt describes a meeting of each firm's governing body, the workers' council.

Workers' Council, Company XYZ
The meeting is opened by the President. The Secretary of the Council takes attendance. Everyone is present—a situation which does not always occur, but this meeting seems to be of importance; no one is even late. The time is 2:15 P.M. and, since those present finished working at 2 o'clock, no one has eaten lunch. At the head table are the President and the Secretary of the Council, the Production Manager of XYZ, and the Finance Manager. The Director is somewhere among the Accountant and several heads of shifts at one of the corners of the U-shaped tables. I am sitting by the Director of TC, who remarks:

"You can see how many meetings we have—the Trade Union, Party, *Collegium,* Collective, and now this." He really looks exhausted.

"You don't have to come," I comment.

"If they send you an invitation, *you come,*" he says. "They have questions; we have to answer."

The Production Manager of XYZ is stating the problem. Because of the need to produce products different from those planned, people have to be transferred from one Unit to another. Weaving Unit No. 1 will have to give up thirty people. The Unit is refusing to do so because, with thirty fewer people, they will not be able to fulfill their group norm and, thus, will lose their potential bonus for surpassing the plan. The Production Manager is asking permission to transfer workers and to pay the bonus to the weaving department even though the unit's plan will not be fulfilled. . . .

The Finance Manager disagrees. He thinks the present planning process is ridiculous. Instead, the company should start from the financial conditions and proceed into the production plans rather than vice versa. On this specific issue, he suggests transferring the people without altering the plan and without giving bonuses to the dispatching unit.

General disagreement occurs in the Council. I cannot hear the words, but I can detect the tone. The Finance Manager has to speak more strongly in order to overcome the voices of disagreement: "But we hardly have money to pay the basic salaries. The inventories are piling up and you want to distribute bonuses. The spinning department has been losing bonuses for years because it did not surpass the plan and it did not surpass the plan because of uncontrollable factors like the one we are discussing."

He is quieted by voices of disagreement. Apparently, the dissenters feel that simply because an anomaly has existed in the past does not mean that it should continue in the future.

The Production Manager of RN tries to explain the issue, and he supports XYZ's Production Manager. Voices are heard: "Yes, that is right." The Finance Manager withdraws and does not participate further in the discussion.

What seems to be the pattern in this specific case is that some individuals discuss the alternatives, while others provide the background noises. It is the workers, though, who will make the final decision by voting. Those who do not fully understand the issues are looking for clues which will guide them in their voting. The voices of agreement or disagreement in the crowd serve as one such clue. Furthermore, the background voices serve as a clue to the executive as to whether his idea is acceptable or not, and his voice accordingly becomes stronger or softer. Thus, even though the participation of many workers may not be structured, words and phrases like, "Yes," or "That is right," or "What do you mean?" or "But this is not so" have an effect on the course of the discussion and eventually on the voting.

Workers are taking the floor. They criticize the executives for day-to-day planning: "fire extinguishing," rather than "fire prevention." The executives defend themselves by saying that they cannot offer plans which will not change, since the market is changing so rapidly. It is apparent that some members want the same certainty in plans which they had previously in the stable environment—a situation which cannot be achieved under the conditions of uncertainty now prevalent.

At the meeting, it is already 5:30. People seem exhausted. Voices can be heard asking the President to conclude. A suggestion is accepted to transfer the problem for study to the Governing Board, which would then make recommendations to the Council. Thus, the Production Manager's request for power to transfer workers and allocate bonuses to the dispatching Economic Unit is defeated, either because of lack of trust in the executives which results in reluctance to hand them a "blank check," or because the Council has not felt that a consensus has been achieved.

Thus, the problem is transferred to a smaller group, which presumably will discuss it in greater depth and possibly reach a consensus, after which the proposal can be offered to the Council for a vote. However, what might happen— and has happened in other cases where a deeper conflict exists— is that the smaller group also fails to achieve a consensus. Its recommendation to the Council is based on the group's points of agreement without specifying points of disagreement, and it is hoped that this omission will be detected and clarified in the larger group. "There are more people in the Council; they know more than we do" is a common reaction. In the meantime, no one group really debates the crucial points which are in dispute because to do so might be too explosive.

However, since time pressure exists to force a decision, the big group apparently prefers to trust that the small group's recommendations are the most prudent, and the small group, in turn, believes it is the responsibility of the larger one to test these recommendations. The end result is that the proposal, even though not fully debated, is accepted in a general, abstract, and thus accepted-by-all form. The points of disagreement remain unresolved and will reappear repeatedly until the situation itself dictates the solution, i.e., "the law of the situation" resolves the conflict rather than do the participants in it. . . .

Workers' Council, Company ABC
From the following short description of the meetings of the Council at ABC, it can be noted that they differ significantly from those of XYZ. The Director and the President of the Council decide on the items to appear on the agenda. ("I don't let them talk about whatever comes to their minds. I argue and try to indicate to them what I believe is crucial.") The meeting is held after working hours, and lunch is served. Tables set in a U-shape are covered with white cloths; flowers are everywhere, and there is a feeling of festivity. At the head table sit the President of the Council, the Director, and all the top executives; at the rest of the tables sit the general membership. The President, Director, and those around him are served coffee out of special, gold-rimmed cups. A tape recorder is provided to record what is said. Invariably, the President opens the meeting and then recognizes the Director,

who speaks for thirty minutes to an hour about the main topic on the agenda. If a discussion develops, it occurs in a very orderly manner. If people disagree, they murmur softly or repress their feelings; unlike the discussions at XYZ, there are no vocal, disorganized interruptions.

For the Council's meeting on modernization, the Director, a prolific writer, has written a pamphlet about fifty pages long. It deals with the business policy of the company: what is needed, why it is needed, and how it can be achieved. It is distributed to all the members of the Council and the Governing Board. There is no opposition to or comments on his exposé, and it is accepted (decided) unanimously.

—I. ADIZES

BUREAUCRATIZATION: ADVANTAGES AND DISADVANTAGES

Nevertheless, there are reasons for maintaining bureaucratic elements in organizations. As we noted earlier, the widespread adoption of conventional bureaucratic elements suggests that bureaucratizaton results in more efficiency than inefficiency. It is also noteworthy that organizations with participatory structures often use conventional bureaucratic procedures to carry on day-to-day operations. Presumably, effective decision-making and effective coordination are more readily achieved in routine matters through a hierarchical authority structure than through a participatory structure. Clear status distinctions and related rights and responsibilities facilitate rapid decision-making and the rapid exercise of authority, whereas participatory decision-making, which requires the setting aside of status distinctions and the achievement of compromises, can be time-consuming.

Similarly, some degree of division of labour appears to be necessary to the efficient operation of organizations. An organization may be able to tolerate a measure of flexibility in the boundaries between roles, but the complex tasks involved in most organizational activities do require specialized skills. Rules and procedures that routinize responses to recurrent situations can increase efficiency by permitting a more immediate response than would be possible if each situation had to be analyzed before a decision could be reached. Although it is important to remember that the efficiency of bureaucratic features may vary with the organizational environment, the widespread adoption of bureaucratic features—by various kinds of organizations in various sociopolitical systems—suggests that they are compatible with a wide range of environmental conditions.

Organizations sometimes find it necessary to choose between incompatible purposes or to assign priority to one of several purposes. For example, a symphony orchestra may have to decide between maintaining a sizable audience and introducing contemporary music; a business firm may have to choose between undertaking a high-risk but potentially high-profit venture and maintaining a certain level of financial stability. Similarly, an organization that operates in a sphere that is experiencing rapid technological change or rapid changes in demand must be able to adapt its procedures and techniques quickly if it is to keep its markets. It may be easier to reach decisions about organizational priorities of purpose in a conventional authority structure, which restricts decision-making to people likely to be homogeneous in interests and opinions, than in a participatory structure, in which decisions likely involve people who differ considerably in their interests and opinions. Similarly, decisions about operating procedures and techniques are more likely to be appropriate to a changing environment if decision-making is restricted to those with the relevant technical knowledge, than if such decisions are made by the representatives of various interests within the organization.

Whatever the purposes of an organization, they cannot be achieved unless enough people are sufficiently motivated to perform the necessary tasks. **Motivation**—people's willingness to conform to organizational norms and organizational role expectations—is a key concern for organizations. The importance of motivation has been clearly recognized by those in positions of authority. For example, Bendix (1974) identifies the formulation of distinct **managerial ideologies** in the historical development of industrial societies. These ideologies, intended to justify the authority of owners and managers over non-managerial employees, include a concept of the basic nature of the employee and of the rewards and punishments that will induce conformity. Thus, in the early stages of industrialization in Great Britain, owners and managers saw workers as irresponsible children who had to be disciplined, controlled, and coerced into conformity. Later, however, managers saw workers as beings with personal and social needs that the workplace had to satisfy if workers were to be sufficiently motivated to achieve the purposes of the firm. In other words, they recognized that the structures and procedures of an organization may influence the motivation of its members.

As we said earlier, workers' dissatisfaction with bureaucratic features arises in large part from perceived inconsistencies between democratic values and the structure and exercise of authority in bureaucraticized organizations. If employees have a strong commitment to democratic values, hierarchical authority structures can reduce their motivation. People committed to democratic values do not necessarily reject status distinctions in organizations, but an orientation toward equality may generate resistance to large distinctions or to an emphasis on status. Thus, democratically oriented workers can be expected to resist hierarchical authority and non-participatory decision-making; they may therefore be

"*Of course, it hasn't started to earn its keep yet, but it does have a very businesslike hum when it's doing whatever it does.*"

less likely to comply with consequent decisions and rules. However, decisions that concern the entire organization seem to be less likely to stimulate resistance among rank-and-file employees than decisions that directly affect the workplace (see, for example, Blumberg 1968, chapter 5).

As we noted earlier, research findings indicate that organizational effectiveness may depend on the development and maintenance of some measure of social solidarity or affective commitment among organizational participants. However, because solidarity is more easily achieved among status equals than among status unequals, the status distinctions associated with a hierarchical authority structure may constrain the development of solidarity (Blau [1955] 1963; Patterson 1955). Consequently, organizations must modify this aspect of bureaucracy if they are to develop and maintain appropriate levels of solidarity. Other bureaucratic elements can also have negative consequences for both solidarity and motivation. For example, in societies, such as Canada, that place great value on the uniqueness of the individual, people may resent bureaucratic rules and routine procedures that tend to treat everyone alike (a consequence compatible with autocracy *and* democracy).

It appears, then, that there is a tension in the organizations between the demands of efficiency and the conditions that promote motivation and social solidarity. The demands of efficiency push organizations toward bureaucracy; the need to ensure employee satisfaction pushes them toward democracy. Presumably, all organizations arrive at some sort of compromise between these rival demands. However, the outcome, as a solution to these conflicting pressures, may depend more on conditions external to the organization than on the decisions of the organization's participants.

SUMMARY

This chapter has focused on the nature of organizations. In effect, our emphasis has been on the appropriate way to describe an organization. We began by recognizing that modern organizations are characterized by a number of features called bureaucratic. We showed that a considerable debt is owed to Max Weber, who, by describing a model of bureaucracy, identified several critical features of the bureaucratized organization. As the study of organizations developed and took the form of empirical research, sociologists found that Weber's model did not always fit the observed structures of actual organizations, even though the features he identified were important. These observations led to a recognition that there are valid organizational forms in addition to the bureaucratic model described by Weber. It is now also recognized that the structures and procedures of organizations are subject to pressures from both within and without—pressures that arise from the actions and relationships of the members of the organization, and pressures that arise from the conditions of the organizational environment, including market conditions and societal values.

Because organizations are such a prominent feature of modern society, all educated citizens need an understanding of the nature and consequences of organizations. As collectivities or structures of human social action, organizations are an important focus of study in sociology. Although sociology has contributed a great deal to the understanding of organizations, many problems remain to be explored.

NOTES

1. Presthus competes with others' attempts to summarize in one adjective the essential characteristic of contemporary societies. Thus we have the *technological* society (Ellul 1964), the *post-industrial* society (Bell 1973), the *affluent* society (Galbraith 1978), the *active* society (Etzioni 1968).
2. Weber's discussion of the organizational counterpart of traditional authority need not concern us here. Pure charismatic authority, since it inheres in the individual, cannot have an organizational counterpart.
3. Although Weber identified other elements of bureaucracy, only those most relevant to our discussion are presented here. Notice that his formulation of the bureaucratic model refers only to the organization of administrative staff or officials. However, his ideas can—and have been—employed to analyze all levels of organization.
4. Adherence to the technical competence criterion increases the likelihood of heterogeneity of age, sex, ethnicity, social origin, and other characteristics in an organization that draws its employees from a labour force that is likewise heterogeneous.
5. Rules are, in fact, often a means of resolving conflicts of interest.
6. Explanations or rationalizations for such employment decisions may, of course, be given: preferences based on gender may be explained in terms of the superiority of males or females with respect to specified abilities; preferences based on *ethnicity* may be explained in terms of, say, the greater emotional stability of one ethnic group relative to another. Such explanations, or rather rationalizations, are based on prejudice and not, as required by the criterion of technical competence, on demonstrated superiority in the performance of the relevant tasks.
7. This is similar to referring to human beings as tall or short as compared to making finer distinctions on a measurement scale.
8. *Co-determination,* as this system is called in the literature, varies in detail from one country to another. The sketch given here is of the system introduced in West Germany (see, for example, Adams and Rummel 1977).

FOR FURTHER READING

Adizes, I.
1971 *Industrial Democracy: Yugoslav Style.* New York: The Free Press.
Although the formal workers' control structures in two textile firms in Yugoslavia are identical, Adizes finds that differences in managerial style account for marked differences in the decision-making process in the two factories.

Blau, Peter M.
1963 *The Dynamics of Bureaucracy,* rev. ed. Chicago: University of Chicago Press.
In two case histories of government agencies, Blau finds that employee behaviour may conform to or deviate from what is required by bureaucratic structure and processes. Blau's observation that some recurrent, rule-breaking behaviour went unpunished leads him to suggest that such behaviour is part of a continuous process of change by which bureaucracies adapt to their environment and thus that bureaucratic structure, rather than being static, is continually changing.

Blauner, Robert
1964 *Alienation and Freedom.* Chicago: University of Chicago Press.
On the basis of survey data for rank-and-file workers employed in plants distinguished by different kinds of production technology, Blauner concludes that workers' attitudes to work and their jobs vary systematically with technology.

Crozier, Michel
1964 *The Bureaucratic Phenomenon.* Chicago: University of Chicago Press.
In this work, based on research in two bureaucracies in France, the author offers a general theory of organizations. Along the way, he provides rich descriptions and challenging interpretations of bureaucratic behaviour, including rule-making and intraorganizational conflicts.

Dore, Ronald
1973 *British Factory-Japanese Factory.* Berkeley: University of California Press.
A comparison of the industrial-relation systems, as observed in selected electronics factories in Great Britain and Japan, leads the author to suggest that Japan may be in the vanguard of developments in the relations between management and workers.

Gerth, Hans, and C. Wright Mills
1946 *From Max Weber.* Oxford: Oxford University Press.
This book provides a readable translation of some of Max Weber's work, including his seminal statement on bureaucracy.

Gouldner, Alvin W.
1954 *Patterns of Industrial Bureaucracy.* New York: The Free Press.
In this landmark study, the author identifies the conditions that help or impede the bureaucratization of a plant engaged in gypsum mining and plasterboard manufacturing.

Perrow, Charles
1979 *Complex Organizations,* 2nd ed. Glenview, Ill.: Scott, Foresman.
This established text on organizations argues the case for bureaucracy.

Roethlisberger, Felix J., and W.J. Dickson
1947 *Management and the Worker.* Cambridge, Mass.: Harvard University Press.
If you want to know what the Western Electric Researches were all about, read this classic example of the "human relations" approach to organizations.

Scott, W. Richard

1981 *Organizations: Rational, Natural and Open Systems*. Englewood Cliffs, N.J.: Prentice-Hall.

This advanced text presents the dominant approaches to the study of organizations along with some thoughtful discussion of related issues of concern.

Woodward, Joan

1980 *Industrial Organization: Theory and Practice*, 2nd ed. Oxford: Oxford University Press.

In this pioneer study of a large number of manufacturing firms, the author argues that technology is the main determinant of organizational structure.

Zey-Ferrell, Mary, and Michael Aikin, eds.

1981 *Complex Organizations: Critical Perspectives*. Glenview, Ill.: Scott, Foresman. This collection of important articles challenges the "dominant perspectives" in the study of organizations.

CHAPTER 11

WORK

Michael R. Smith

People **work** to produce goods and services. Throughout human history save for the past few centuries, the bulk of what has been produced has been directly consumed by the same individuals engaged in its production, a situation that still exists in quite a lot of the world today. In contrast, in industrial societies such as Canada, work has a quite different character. It involves the production of goods and services that will be sold to someone else; in exchange for what they do, people receive an income. (In this chapter I am setting aside the unpaid work involved in housework, which is extremely important but is dealt with in Chapters 5 and 9 of this volume.)

Furthermore, in such a society, most people hold a job that involves the performance of a limited range of tasks. They may spend all their working time selling copying machines or spray-painting the fenders on automobiles or writing romantic fiction, or whatever. Some **division of labour**—specialization of tasks—is found in all human groups. The point is that the phenomenon is extensive in industrial societies and is a central and salient aspect of them. It is also a major concern of writings on the sociology of work.

With people spending their time in more or less specialized jobs, some mechanism is necessary for coordinating their activities. The two mechanisms found in industrial societies are hierarchies and markets. One worker cannot spray-paint fenders unless someone else has taken steel sheets and stamped the fenders out of them and yet another person has attached them to the rest of the car body. In all industrial societies, capitalist or socialist, divided labour of this kind is coordinated by **bureaucratic hierarchies**. A pyramid of authority is established within a plant to ensure that work is done in an appropriate sequence, to appropriate standards, and in appropriate amounts. (I will come back later to what "appropriate" means. For further discussion of the division of labour and bureaucratic hierarchies, see Chapter 10.)

The alternative to hierarchy as a device for coordinating work is markets, which, in their centrality and pervasiveness, are the distinguishing feature of capitalist societies.[1] A **market** in this sense is not a place but a set of social arrangements whereby supply and demand determine price and thus the allocation of an economy's resources and the distribution of the goods and services it produces.

This concept deserves a bit more consideration. People earn an income because the goods or services they help to produce (if they are employed) or produce directly themselves (if they are self-employed) are sold—for the most part in competition with other producers. Goods and services, in other words, are traded in **product markets**. This trading is another kind of coordination of work. A producer decides to buy components, raw materials, or services from other producers when these goods seem to be needed and when they are of the appropriate quality and price and are reliably supplied; final consumers make the same kind of decisions. Thus, it is market signals—the decision to purchase or not purchase or

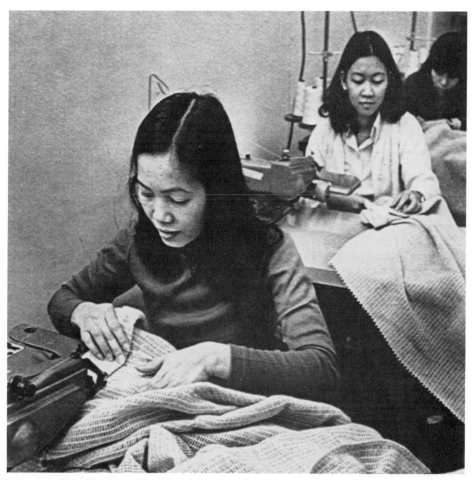

The semi-skilled, low-paying jobs of the manufacturing sector are often the only ones available to recent immigrants.

to supply or not supply—that lead supplier and purchaser to mutual adjustment of their activities. In parallel with this process, people compete with each other to get jobs that have varying degrees of desirability in terms of income and working conditions and employers compete to get more or less skilled and conscientious workers. In other words, the distribution of goods and revenue through the product market is complemented by the distribution of people among jobs through the **labour market**.

A central feature of markets is that any participant is in principle replaceable. In fact, a market provides positive incentives for people or businesses to try to replace other people or businesses. If firms wish to increase their profits, they have to do so by taking business away from other firms; if individuals wish to get more desirable jobs, they have to compete against other individuals to get them. The effect of all this competition is to impose constraints on what people do. Getting more business or keeping the business they already have requires that employers keep their costs of production—including labour costs—as low as possible. To the extent that the operation of the market is not itself constrained (by, for example, a trade union or a body of labour law), getting and keeping a more desirable job requires that a worker accumulate traits—such as skills, education, and a stable work history—that employers find desirable. Workers who fail to do so tend not to get desirable jobs, just as employers who let their labour costs get out of control tend to lose business and eventually go bankrupt.

TWO SOCIOLOGICAL APPROACHES TO WORK

The analysis of the properties of markets is, of course, the special domain of economists. But markets are also a central concern in writing on the sociology of work; much of it is concerned with the ways in which the operation of labour markets is institutionally restrained. The bulk of this chapter discusses the forms of institutional restraint that emerge in modern labour markets. Before doing that, however, I will outline what I take to be the two most common and influential general interpretations of work in modern sociology: those in the alienation tradition and those in the orientations-to-work tradition. These clearly contradictory approaches provide different interpretations of the same facts on these institutional restraints.

The Alienation Tradition

The alienation approach to interpreting work in modern society comes directly from Karl Marx's view of that society, specifically his critique of capitalism. It starts something like this. Although self-employment remains important in capitalist economies, most people are employed by others. Consequently, they usually have no control over what they produce and negligible control over how they do it. These things are decided by their employers, whose decisions are designed to maximize profits, not to cater to the needs or interests of their workers. The goal of maximizing profits means that the interests of workers and employers conflict fundamentally. The less an employer spends on wages, the more profit there is. So the fact of working forces workers into an antagonistic social relationship with their employer. It also forces them into an antagonistic relationship with other workers, with whom they must compete to secure a job and to maintain it.

Now, Marxist philosophy asserts that the essential attributes of human beings include both the capacity to work creatively and an inescapable need for gratifying social relations (Ollman 1971, 97-113). What happens to such capacities and needs under capitalism? It is difficult to be creative if one's work activities—what one produces and how one produces it—are narrowly prescribed by someone else. It is hard to enter into gratifying social relations with an employer and other workers with whom one is forced to conflict. All of this is to argue that, in capitalist societies, fundamental human needs go unmet. **Alienation**, then, is this "state of human existence" (Ollman 1971, 132) in which the fundamental needs to work creatively and to maintain gratifying social relations go unmet.

Assertion Based on Definition

The general thrust of writings inspired by the Marxist notion of alienation is that workers are seriously and negatively affected in various ways by the deprivations of work. How do we know that this is so? Writings in the alienation tradition diverge at this point. In one approach, best exemplified in the work of the political philosopher Bertell Ollman, it is all a matter of definition. Thus: "Strictly speaking, all Marx's laws are tautologies" (1971, 19). Capitalism involves an employer-employee relationship and competitive product and labour markets. These institutions subject the bulk of the population (employees) to discipline imposed by others (employers) and insert all of the population into a system of antagonistic social relations. Since creativity at work and gratifying social relations are the essence of being human, capitalism is inconsistent with human needs. And because people—both workers and capitalists—are alienated (see Ollman 1971, 152-56), they act in ways that healthy, unalienated humans would not. For instance, because people have negligible opportunity to act creatively at work, they assert themselves, to a pathological degree, in consumption. The shopping centre becomes the locus of self-assertion for alienated people (see Gorz 1965, 348).

I do not draw attention to this approach because I regard it as useful. Quite the contrary. Ollman's writing is simply a set of claims. If we are to conclude confidently that workers (or capitalists) are somehow marked by deprivations built into their lives by capitalism, we need to go beyond claims; we need some independent evidence of the deprivations and their effects. I draw attention to Ollman's work simply because some Marxists tend to combine the sort of philosophical approach found in Ollman with an empirical—and this, in principle, acceptable—treatment of alienation. When you read writings on work, you should try to sort out which parts are presented as if they are true by definition and which parts rest on some evidence adduced in support of the claims being made.

The Empirical Approach to Alienation

The empirical approach to alienation depends on two kinds of evidence. First, it is argued, jobs vary in the degree to which they are alienating. Work on assembly lines in automobile plants is typically treated as the embodiment of alienating labour: there is the usual obligation to follow

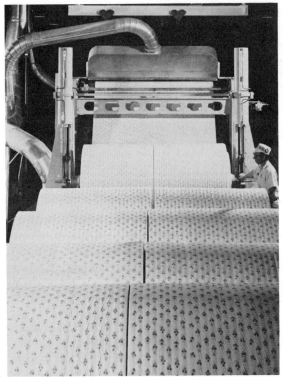

Although the solitary worker operating some monstrous machine is often seen as an example of alienation, such an interpretation may not be appropriate. Workers who have acquired the skills necessary to run such machines may often have high wages, and thus may view their working conditions quite favourably.

instructions and submit to supervision that goes with being an employee, but in an extreme form; the job itself involves a repetitive and limited task; and the periodicity of effort is regulated by the speed of the line. Moreover, because the demand for automobiles is sensitive to the fluctuations of the business cycle, the job itself is insecure. Thus, autoworkers feel even less in control of their own destiny. At the other extreme, some craft jobs allow workers to use a variety of skills that they have learned, to plumb their capacities in solving a series of technical problems associated with a job and, within limits, to choose their own pace of work. Given that the degree of alienation varies across jobs, one should find corresponding variations in how people are affected by and respond to their jobs. Much is made, for instance, of Kornhauser's (1965) finding that for the workers he studied, the incidence of stress-related symptoms (sweaty palms, difficulty sleeping, lack of reported self-esteem, and so on) was higher among unskilled workers than skilled ones and highest of all among unskilled workers doing repetitive work. Other studies attempt, in one way or another, to make the same sort of point, and a number (Blauner 1964; Marchak 1983, 392-3; Sheppard and Herrick 1973) report that less-skilled workers are less satisfied with their jobs. There is, furthermore, a general claim to the effect that the most extremely alienating work (of which the automobile assembly line is the prototype) generates the most antagonism toward employers (this point is implicit in Garson 1975, 86-98; and Glaberman 1975, 9-14).

Second, the extent to which work is alienating in a particular society is likely to vary over time. The government, for example, may become more supportive of employers in their attempts to extract more effort from their workers. It has been widely reported that this is what happened during the mid-1960s in France, and Seeman (1972) attempts to explain the disorders of the spring of 1968 in that country as a response to the increased level of alienation that resulted. Or the work of a particular group of workers may become more alienating because employers create an increasingly subdivided set of working arrangements—that is, increasingly divided labour. (I will come back shortly to the reason employers might do this.) There is some evidence that this division of tasks has happened in office work; alienation theory would lead one to expect that the change will lead to greater militancy on the part of white-collar workers and that, in some places, it has already done so (see Rinehart 1975, 88-89, 109-21).

Clearly, the empirical alienation tradition stands or falls on its capacity to show that the effects of work in capitalist societies are, for the most part, both negative and pervasive, and that, other things being equal, people with the most alienating jobs display the most evidence of psychological damage and are the most inclined to protest at their conditions. Several times in this chapter I will consider whether empirical studies support this hypothesis.

Orientations-to-Work Tradition

Now consider the alternative approach to the sociology of work. The starting point here is that, within markets, people can make choices. Only rarely is anyone forced to produce any particular good or service.[2] In principle, an individual has the option of taking or not taking any particular job. Consequently, it is argued, the jobs people hold reflect their choices. Not, to be sure, choices from an infinite array. I certainly cannot choose to play hockey for the Montreal Canadiens. Neither can I choose to be the chief executive officer of CP Enterprises. And if I lived in some parts of Canada I might have hardly any opportunity for a job at all, let alone a choice among several. Nevertheless, at one time or another, almost everybody is in a position to make job-related choices: whether or not to complete high school, to go to university, to complete an apprenticeship, to migrate to where the opportunities are best. And most people have the option of choosing between jobs at some point in their careers (most frequently in the early years).

If people can make choices, what criteria guide their decisions? The first part of finding an answer to this question is to find out what people want. Hamilton and Wright (1986, 109-19) have looked at the question carefully. In a national survey in the United States, people were asked to rank their priorities in life. The highest personal priorities listed were marriage and family. The most frequently cited second priorities were health and religion. Only 7 percent of respondents ranked interesting work as their first priority and 2 percent ranked it second. For most people, work is not their central life interest.

If work is not the central interest for most people, what affects their choices with respect to jobs? It is reasonable to assume that they regard earning the highest possible wage as the best way of taking care of their families. Consequently, they approach their jobs as vehicles for supporting their standard of living outside work. For the most part they do not expect their jobs to be interesting or gratifying. They expect only that their jobs will pay them an acceptable wage. If, however, some workers do particularly want interesting jobs, the diversity in the labour markets allows them that option too. They can forego income for a number of years while they complete the education or apprenticeship that more skilled and interesting jobs require. If they value less bureaucratic relations with their employers and less narrowly defined jobs, they can seek employment in small firms, where employment with these characteristics is most frequently found but typically at lower-than-average wages. If they live where the climate makes working out of doors a reasonable preference (say, in parts of Western Europe or the southern United States), they can seek outside work, often at lower wages. And so on.

Notice, too, that the orientations-to-work approach involves no attempt to deny that some jobs are tedious and unpleasant and experienced as such. Quite the contrary. A variety of analysts (for example, Goldthorpe et al. 1968, 10-37) find quite clear evidence that people who do work that one would expect them to find dull are, indeed, more likely to report that it is dull. What is asserted is that, because most people are looking for something that they can get from their jobs (a fairly reliable income) and are not looking for something that they mostly cannot get (interesting work), one would expect workers to be much more satisfied with their work than the alienation writers would lead one to believe. And, indeed, the most striking result from surveys that ask people how satisfied they are with their employment (see, for example, Exhibit 11-1) is the high levels of satisfaction reported.

> In spite of such differences in technique, time and coverage, there is a certain consistency in the response patterns: few people call themselves extremely satisfied with their jobs, but still fewer report extreme dissatisfaction. The model response is on the positive side of neutrality—"pretty satisfied." The proportion dissatisfied ranges from 10 to 21%. (Kahn 1972, 169)

Finally, notice that the orientations-to-work approach leads one *not* to expect that workers will respond to varying working conditions in the way that alienation writings suggest. Although workers who do dull or unpleasant jobs will recognize them as such, it does not follow that workers

Exhibit 11-1
Job Satisfaction of Canadian Workers
(No. = 1067)

All in all, how satisfied would you say you are with your job?	Very satisfied	46%
	Somewhat satisfied	42
	Not too satisfied	9
	Not at all satisfied	2
Knowing what you know now, if you had to decide all over again whether to take the job you now have, what would you decide?	Take same job without hesitation	61%
	Have some second thoughts	33
	Definitely not take job	6
If a good friend of yours told you he/she was interested in working in a job like yours for your employer, what would you tell him/her?	Strongly recommend it	59%
	Have doubts about recommending it	34
	Advise against it	7
If you were free to go into any type of job you wanted, what would your choice be?	Same as now	50%
	Would want to retire and not work	8
	Take some other job	31
	Don't know	10
In general, how well would you say that your job measures up to the sort of job you wanted when you took it?	Very much like	47%
	Somewhat like	39
	Not very much like	14

Source: Burnstein et al. (1975).

in the dullest or most unpleasant jobs will be more hostile to their employers or dissatisfied with their jobs than workers in more intrinsically gratifying jobs. If both kinds of worker use wages to measure their jobs, the best predictor of job satisfaction should be wages (and the job security, which is a promise that the wages will keep coming). There is quite a lot of evidence that that is so (see, for example, Goldthorpe et al. 1968; and Berg, Freedman, and Freeman 1978, 64-67).

The Two Approaches: A Preliminary Assessment

On the whole, research focusing on responses to questions about job satisfaction tends to support the orientations-to-work interpretation. From the point of view of alienation theory, the high levels of job satisfaction reported within capitalist societies, in which workers do not control what they produce or how they produce it and in which they have to struggle against their employers for improvements in wages and work conditions, are a bit of a problem. So is the lack of priority given to work when

JOB SATISFACTION OF CANADIAN WORKERS

If Canadian workers were predominantly alienated, would 88 percent of them report that they were somewhat or very satisfied with their jobs? Would 61 percent report that they would take the same job again without hesitation? Or 59 percent strongly recommend their job to a friend? And so on (see Exhibit 11-1). Yes, according to writers such as Rinehart (1978, 7-9). Workers report that they are satisfied with their jobs, so the argument goes, because they have been forced by the harsh reality of the labour market to reduce their aspirations to such an extent that people are happy to have practically any job and because to be satisfied with one's job is the conventional response. The argument is that attitude surveys do not tap the real character of working-class discontent because respondents interpret the questions in such a restricted frame of reference. To really get at workers' discontent, it is claimed, one must look at the record of strikes, of output restriction, of sabotage, of insubordination—in short, of "the war at the workplace."

Is this argument persuasive? Well, perhaps. There is no doubt that considerable sources of discontent are built into people's jobs. Many are monotonous. Many have no prospects. Many constitute health threats. There is also no shortage of evidence of discontent with aspects of jobs in precisely the forms that Rinehart mentions. But it *is* a little surprising that so many workers can be persuaded that they have satisfactory jobs if those jobs are, in fact, overwhelmingly oppressive. Furthermore, if workers are truly ground down by the harsh reality of the labour market, one might expect younger workers, who have less experience of its oppressive realities, to express much more interest in work that allows autonomy and discretion than do their disabused elders. In fact, there is no adequate evidence that that is so and some to the contrary. As you can see, survey data on job satisfaction poses some serious problems for the alienation interpretation.

people are asked to rank their central life concerns. And so is the fact that some careful studies (such as Goldthorpe et al. 1968) do not find that the most dissatisfied workers are those in the most ostensibly alienating jobs. On the other hand, the association between job satisfaction and income is exactly what the orientations-to-work account would predict.

The alienation theorists have an obvious response; they argue that survey research on job satisfaction does not get at workers' real responses to their jobs. The box on this page deals with this line of argument, and

Since people spend most of the day at work, the work setting becomes important for friendships, personal satisfactions, and self-esteem. A group of fellow workers may form a company softball or bowling team, organize a picnic, or, as in this photograph, celebrate a co-worker's birthday. These are all forms of job satisfaction that have nothing to do directly with tasks or salaries.

I will return to it at the end of this chapter. Before continuing to consider the alternative approaches to work, I will review some of the major areas of research in the sociology of work, because the findings from them have some bearing on the problem of appraisal.

THE LABOUR MARKET

First, consider the organization and operation of the labour market. In orthodox economics texts, the model of the labour market runs roughly as follows. At any given time the division of labour produces a range of jobs that vary in the skills and aptitudes they require and in their attractiveness (how dull or interesting, how dirty or dangerous, and so on). At the same time, the working-age population has a range of skills, aptitudes, and preferences. Some people are smarter than others. Some people have at one time or another been willing to forego income while they acquired skills in schools or in training programs. Some people do not mind dirty work as much as others. And so on. The operation of the labour market channels individuals with particular skills and preferences into appropriate jobs. It is variations in the incomes attached to jobs that ensures appropriate matches. Jobs, such as doctor or lawyer, that require their incumbents to have endured seemingly endless years in educational institutions pay more than jobs that people can occupy immediately after the legal minimum of years in school. People willing to work in dangerous situations are in short supply and so get paid more than most people. To the extent that the market is allowed to work unhindered by government regulations (such as minimum wage laws) or other restraints (such as trade unions), the resulting income distribution is purely a function of the demand for and the supply of workers of each kind. If the supply of some kind of worker—say, welders—suddenly increases for some reason, one would expect employers to reduce the wages of the welders they employ (perhaps over a period of time), and if the supply decreases, to raise their wages.

The Theory of Segmented Labour Markets

Now, as I observed earlier, much writing in the sociology of work is concerned with institutional restraints on the operation of markets. Segmented labour-market theory, which is specifically concerned with such restraints, originated in the work of some economists but has been enthusiastically taken up in recent years by a number of sociologists. For the sake of simplicity, I will outline the dual labour-market version of the segmentation theory; there are more complicated formulations.

The thrust of **dual labour-market** arguments is that the job choices of many individuals are grossly constrained, and that the labour market for working-class occupations (blue-collar and lower white-collar jobs) is divided into two substantially non-competing groups. Some industries, it is argued, are made up of firms that use sophisticated technology, constantly innovate to increase productivity, and have labour costs that are a small proportion of the total costs of production. Often these industries are dominated by a small number of large producers so competition is not fierce. Because competition is not too fierce and labour costs are a small proportion of total costs, firms in these industries (such as basic metals, aerospace, and petroleum refining) can afford to pay high wages, which, furthermore, grow steadily as productivity increases. Moreover, the jobs in these industries tend to require the acquisition of skills specific to the firm (familiarity with a particular kind of machine and product), so employers have an incentive to dissuade their workers from quitting. Firms provide such dissuasion by organizing jobs in a hierarchy of desirability and allowing workers to move up the resulting **internal job ladder** as they accumulate seniority. The firms providing such jobs are said to be located in the **primary sector**.

In contrast, other industries (such as apparel, textiles, and some assembly industries) are made up of large numbers of considerably less technically dynamic firms with labour costs constituting a high proportion of total costs. These firms cannot afford to pay high wages. Nor do their jobs typically require firm-specific skills. Consequently, these employers have no incentive to elaborate an internal job ladder in order to deter workers from quitting. These firms are said to be located in the **secondary sector**. (Be careful not to confuse the primary/secondary distinction of dual labour-market theory with the terms used to designate sectors of the economy according to different kinds of production. (See the box on pages 404-405.)

Clearly, jobs in the primary sector are more desirable than those in the secondary sector. That jobs should vary in their desirability is no surprise at all. However, the dual labour-market argument goes further than this. It claims that only white males of prime age (say, 20 to 40) with some minimum level of education and a stable work history are likely to get primary-sector jobs. Women, immigrants, young people, and high-school dropouts, according to this argument, are systematically excluded and forced into the secondary sector and its inferior work conditions. Worse still, the undesirable working conditions in that sector and the absence of the inducement not to quit provided by the job ladder lead workers in the sector to change jobs frequently; consequently, many of them develop precisely the kind of unstable work history that disqualifies them from ever getting into the primary sector. Hence, there is an effective and discriminatory barrier to mobility from the secondary to the primary sector, but not vice versa. (For a feminist view of dual labour-market theory, see Chapter 9.)

Empirical Testing of Segmentation Theory

The theory of labour-market segmentation has evoked a great deal of research in recent years. Studies such as those of Oster (1979) and Apostle, Clairmont, and Osberg (1985) tend to show that one can classify industries or establishments by the characteristics given in segmentation theory (using various permutations more complicated than those described here). Thus, industries or establishments with above-average wages tend to have above-average levels of market concentration, growth rates of productivity, levels of education, and percentages of male employees, and below-average quit rates. In short, they tend to display the cluster of attributes that the theory leads one to expect to find in the primary sector. Industries with lower-than-average wages tend to have the opposite properties. The economy seems to offer not a continuous array of jobs with various combinations of desirable and undesirable traits and skills and aptitudes demanded; rather, segmentation research suggests, it is subdivided into sectors with generally good jobs on the one hand and generally bad jobs on the other, with females concentrated in the latter (see Marchak 1983, 246).

The findings of segmentation research do, however, present some serious difficulties. First, the segments uncovered tend to vary from study

SECTORAL SHIFTS

Whatever choices or alienating conditions workers may confront are tied to the jobs for which a demand exists. That structure of demand is embodied, in the first instance, in the industrial structure. This structure has been undergoing an important change, as reflected in the table in this box.

It is customary to classify industries into the broad categories *primary* (extractive), *secondary* (transformative), and *tertiary* (services) used in the table, in which the tertiary sector is further broken down into the four subcategories. This system, in which the basis of classification is the kind of product, should not be confused with the dual labour-market theorists' classification of the economy into primary and secondary sectors, which is essentially, a distinction between good jobs and bad jobs. Good jobs and bad jobs, however, can be found in each of the three broad industrial categories.

The table shows that the major shift in Canada's industrial structure during this century has been a decline in employment in primary industry (principally, agriculture) and a rise in employment in tertiary or service industry. Primary industry accounted for somewhat more than a third of employment in 1921, but barely more than 7 percent in 1981; over the same period, employment in all services rose from about a third of total employment to more than two-thirds. The share of the secondary sector was about a quarter at the beginning and the end of the 60-year period, although it had risen somewhat in the interim, peaking at a third in 1951.

Do these shifts lead one to any conclusions about the balance of jobs with desirable and undesirable traits available to Canadian workers? Unfortunately, no. The decline in employment in agriculture results from the technological transformation of that industry; the character of work in that industry today cannot, therefore, be generalized to 1921. (Certainly, one should avoid romanticizing the agricultural labour of the early part of this century.) Neither can the increase in employment in services be easily characterized. You can see from the table that one of the largest increases has been in social services and government, which include health and education. This sector includes occupations such as teaching, nursing, policing, and some other service jobs that pay quite well and offer good conditions of employment. But the service sector also includes many clerks, sales workers, security guards, and cleaners who typically are poorly paid and have insecure employment.

The balance of these opposite trends is not at all clear, and social scientists do not agree on their interpretation (compare Singelmann 1978, 136 with Rinehart 1975, 88-89).

Distribution of Employment by Industrial Sectors						
	1921	1931	1941	1951	1961	1971	1981
Primary Extractive (agriculture, forestry, mining)	36.9%	34.4%	31.7%	21.6%	14.7%	9.1%	7.1%
Secondary Transformative (manufacture, construction, utilities)	26.1	24.7	28.2	33.7	31.2	30.0	26.7
Tertiary Distributive services (transportation, communication, trade)	19.2	18.4	17.6	21.7	23.9	23.0	23.8
Producer services (banking, insurance, real estate, etc.)	3.7	3.3	2.8	4.0	5.3	7.3	10.2
Social services and government (health, education, public administration, etc.)	7.5	8.9	9.4	11.3	15.3	21.1	22.9
Personal services (amusement and recreation, hotel accommodation, laundries, entertainment, etc.)	6.7	10.3	10.3	7.8	9.6	9.5	9.1
	100.1	100.0	100.0	100.1	100.0	100.0	99.8

Note: Because of rounding, some columns do not total 100 percent.
Sources: 1921–71: Singelmann (1978, 146-7); 1981: Census of Canada 1981 vol. 1 (92-920).

to study, depending on the units of analysis and the statistical procedures used. Thus, all these studies have not yet produced anything that one could regard as a reliable map of the structure of the Canadian economy—or any other one, for that matter. Second, there is little evidence of the kind of immobility across segments that the theory assumes (see Cain 1976, 1231). Third, there is no adequate evidence of the learned irresponsibility that is supposed to accompany secondary-sector employment.

Nevertheless, there is no doubt that jobs vary in their desirability and that a number of mechanisms channel people by personal characteristics other than skill or aptitude but including gender into those jobs in different proportions (see Chapters 8, 9, and 15). And the existence of the job ladder does seem to shield some primary-sector workers from conditions in the labour market. If jobs at the upper end of a firm's ladder are accessible only to people on the lower rungs of the same ladder, variations in the supply of people with appropriate skills in the labour market as a whole become largely irrelevant.

WORKERS' RESPONSES

The job ladder is an institutional restraint on the operation of the labour market that is employer-initiated (though most trade unions actually support its introduction). Workers also have options available.

Consider that, in law, paid work has a contractual character. An employer provides the worker with a wage and a package of fringe benefits (paid holidays and vacations, a pension plan, insurance, and so on) in exchange for his or her willingness to accept some degree of employer authority—to follow orders, in other words. What can workers do if they do not like the contract they have been given?

Quitting

People who do not like their jobs can quit. Doing so normally imposes some costs on their employers. There is the cost of any formal job-specific training (involving classroom instruction or the time of an experienced worker allocated to supervise the trainee). Even if the job involves no formal training but is instead learned through practice, there is the cost of the new employee's learning period, when he or she operates at less than peak efficiency. And in all cases there are the costs of recruiting that replacement. Although Canada Employment Centres do not charge for their services, advertising and private agencies cost money, as does the time of the people responsible for recruitment. These two kinds of costs can add to a substantial sum, constituting a significant sanction for some employers whose workers quit in large numbers. (That this is so is evinced by the tendency of employers, under some circumstances, to **hoard labour**—to keep on workers during business downturns even though there are not enough orders to keep them busy. Employers who do this estimate that the costs of replacing the workers during the next upturn would exceed the costs of the wages paid during the idle period.)

There is considerable evidence that workers do respond to undesirable conditions by quitting. Industries with unhealthy and unsafe working conditions have relatively high quit rates (Viscusi 1983), as do those that involve remotely located work, such as mining and forestry (Economic Council of Canada 1976, 92-3). Low-wage industries such as leather goods and furniture manufacture have high quit rates—(Berg, Freedman, and Freeman 1978, 187)—as dual labour-market theory leads one to expect. To the extent that high quit rates impose a cost on employers, they constitute an inducement for them to improve the wages and conditions of work they offer and to establish a job ladder, tying wages, fringe benefits, and access to more desirable jobs to seniority, thereby giving employees an incentive not to quit.

Nonetheless, quitting has limited effectiveness as a sanction. First, workers may not see quitting as a feasible choice where and when the rate of unemployment is high.[3] Second, it is an effective sanction only if the worker involved has some skills, for only in that case does the employer incur any significant costs in finding and training a replacement. Many employers have no difficulty functioning with very high rates of turnover of obviously easily replaceable labour.[4]

Since quitting—which is the quintessential *market* response to jobs workers do not like—is not a feasible or desirable response in many circumstances and is ineffective in others, it is not surprising that workers often turn to other ways of modifying their contract. These include theft that is tacitly accepted by the employer, output restriction, unionization, and the strike (which is usually but not necessarily combined with unionization). All put the labour market under some institutional restraint (recall that sociologists define an institution as a reciprocal set of patterned social relationships).

Theft

One way in which workers modify their contract is by stealing from their employer. This is quite common. The cab drivers studied by Vaz in the 1950s (1984) held back a portion of the fares they collected; Dalton (1959) found that managers cheated on their expense accounts; and so on. What is interesting about theft is that it sometimes becomes tacitly accepted. In the gypsum mine and plant studied by Gouldner, workers could, within limits, take home "glass, tin, screws, wood," borrow equipment, and get their furniture repaired without charge by the company maintenance department (1954a, 51). The contract of employment did not incorporate these benefits; they were simply agreed to by the foreman and ignored by the plant manager. The acceptability of some jobs is increased by the opportunities they provide for this kind of theft, which becomes part of the workers' compensation package.

The opportunity to appropriate company property is, however, a fragile "fringe benefit." There is always the possibility that a cost-cutting manager will move against the practice, as happened in the case Gouldner studied. A new manager brought in to improve the productivity of the operations fired a miner for taking a case of dynamite, which, the miner claimed, he had been authorized to do by his foreman (1954a, 59-61—Gouldner does not tell us why the miner wanted the dynamite). This and other attempts to tighten up the operation resulted in a deterioration of work relations and ultimately a wildcat strike (Gouldner 1954b).

Gouldner's story illustrates how the formal contract of work—a specified compensation package in exchange for the willingness to follow orders—is often modified in practice and, furthermore, is always open to renegotiation. Why do lower-level managers tolerate theft (or some amount of goofing off or tardiness)? Although the formal contract requires that workers follow orders in exchange for their compensation package and the hierarchy provides supervisors responsible for ensuring that workers do so, in practice it is usually difficult (or impossibly expensive) to supervise employees closely and continuously. For most jobs, getting a good day's work out of a worker requires some degree of cooperation on the worker's part. Lower management can get that cooperation by allowing workers some latitude with respect to some of the rules—in other words, the work/reward tradeoff is modified in the workers' favour.

Output Restriction

In the chapter opening, I referred to the fact that one function of hierarchies is to ensure that work gets done in appropriate amounts. But how much is appropriate? Workers and employers often disagree on this point, particularly if the job in question is dull or otherwise unpleasant. The work/reward tradeoff is subject to continuous renegotiation, and the result at any given time is what Baldamus (1961) calls the "effort bargain." To enhance their control over this bargain, employers often introduce piece-rate systems under which the workers' pay is tied, by some formula, to the amount ("pieces") of work done. Typically, these systems involve some sort of base hourly rate and increments for the work done above some specified minimum.

In principle, such a system directly ties what workers get paid to how hard they work and allows each worker to establish his or her own effort bargain—to choose whether to put out more effort for more money or less effort for less money. In practice, there is a serious tactical problem: the rate paid for additional pieces is not set in stone. Employers have an interest in minimizing total wage costs. If it turns out that at some particular piece rate most workers can take home very high total wages, the employer may decide that the effort bargain is inappropriate—that the existing rate embodies too small a demand on the workers' efforts.

Groups of workers can, however, protect themselves from this threat by restricting their output. In this phenomenon, which is quite common (it is documented by, for example, Roethlisberger and Dickson 1939; Burawoy 1979; Roy 1967), an acceptable work rate becomes established among a group of workers, and those who violate the rate are subject to sarcasm, ridicule, and perhaps ostracism. In this way, a work group can protect a particular effort bargain and perhaps the jobs of some of their members. Certainly, the switchboard wirers Roethlisberger and Dickson studied at General Electric thought that if they did not restrict output in this way, some of them would become redundant. This kind of informal restriction of effort is not unique to piece workers.

There are three observations worth making about output restriction of this kind. First, it clearly constitutes an institutional limitation on the operation of the market, in that it substitutes a collectively determined effort bargain for the series of individual bargains that would be struck in an unrestrained market. Second, the phenomenon is by no means universal, even among piece workers. Some workers seem to embrace piece work with enthusiasm and to produce to maximize their weekly income. Third, implementation requires a substantial degree of group solidarity. Protecting rates by refusing to work to one's maximum is not a strategy that an individual worker can pursue successfully. Such group solidarity is always problematic, as we will see in the next sub-section.

Unionization

About 39 percent of Canada's non-agricultural workers belong to trade unions. Trade unions are deliberately constructed and designed to protect and advance the interests of workers by reducing or eliminating competition for jobs. There is some evidence that unions often succeed in advancing their members' interests; on average, unionized Canadian workers are paid 15 to 25 percent more than non-union workers (Starr 1973; Kumar 1972; Maki and Christensen 1980; MacDonald and Evans 1981), and there is some evidence from the United States that unionized workers' fringe benefits give them an even greater advantage over non-union workers (Freeman 1978; Ichniowski 1980).

These averages conceal a wide range of union wages and conditions of work. Nonetheless, there is obviously much to be said for joining a trade union and bargaining collectively to improve conditions. But most Canadian workers do not belong to trade unions, and establishing unions in this country has been a long and often arduous process. If unions are so useful to workers, why has this been so?

Bain and Elsheikh (1976) and Bain (1978, 25-7) find that union growth in Canada has historically been associated with the following conditions: inflation, low unemployment, the growth of union membership in the United States, and the introduction of legislation expressly recognizing the right of workers to organize and bargain collectively and enjoining employers from unfair labour practices (for example, intimidation to discourage workers from joining a union).[5] How can one account for this pattern? The association with inflation probably reflects the fact that workers see rising prices as a threat to their living standards. When inflation accelerates, they look to join those organizations that might be expected to protect them.

To understand what underlies the association between the other factors and unionization, first consider a general and serious problem that confronts all unions: that of **free riders**. If I am a worker in a non-unionized factory and think that unionization would get me better wages, the strategy that best serves my economic interests is to let all my fellow workers go on strike to force our common employer to recognize our union while I dutifully turn up for work and collect my paycheque. After all, I can tell myself, the actions of one individual are not going to make any difference to the success or failure of the organizing drive. Clearly, if it is rational for me to act in this way, it is just as rational for any one of my co-workers to act in an identical fashion. But if all of us try to be free riders, the union will never get formed! Indeed, the development of the modern labour movement has been a long and painful business precisely because, given resistance from employers (which imposes costs on individual workers), the tendency for people to act as free riders has frequently undermined the capacity of a group of workers to force union recognition.[6]

In the light of these considerations, think again about the predictors of union growth. When unemployment is low, workers striking for union recognition can find part-time or temporary work. Thus, if the strikers fail and the employer manages to dismiss them there is the possibility of another job. Dismissing workers during a dispute is now legally difficult but possible if the employer can come up with some grounds for dismissal other than the strike itself. And, during most of the period when the labour movement was growing, there was no legal obstacle to dismissal. More fundamentally, the federal and provincial legislation that now imposes legal limits to employers' opposition of union organizing drives has reduced the costs that employers can impose on their unionizing workers. Thus, low unemployment and labour laws have reduced the salience of the free-rider problem by reducing the personal costs involved in securing union recognition. But both factors turn up in any historical examination of the growth of unions and both still exist to some extent.

What is the historical link between union growth in Canada and union growth in the United States? About 36 percent of Canada's union members belong to **international unions**—that is, unions whose headquarters are located in the United States. American-based unions had an interest in organizing Canadian workers since they worked for firms that competed with U.S. firms. It was in the interests of U.S. unions to ensure that grossly lower Canadian wages did not put U.S. employers at a competitive (and thus job-threatening) disadvantage. Consequently, U.S. unions were willing to help organize Canadian workers by providing resources, such as experienced organizers and, sometimes, strike funds that reduced the personal costs incurred by Canadian workers when they attempted to form trade unions. The magnitude of the assistance from the United States should not, however, be exaggerated, and its importance has undoubtedly varied from one period to another.

Today a variety of factors, some of them fairly new, are affecting the Canadian labour market, making it possible that future growth will be in non-traditional directions. (See the box on this page.) Whatever the changes, however, Canadian unions seem likely to constrain labour markets on behalf of some workers for a long time to come.

CLC SET FOR WHITE-COLLAR DRIVE

OTTAWA

After spending a lifetime in the tough, frequently smoke-filled world of industrial unionism, Canadian Labour Congress President Dennis McDermott steps down next week from labor's top job to begin a new career as Canada's ambassador to Ireland.

The 63-year-old union leader leaves behind him a labor movement that has changed fundamentally and irrevocably during his eight-year presidency. At the beginning of his tenure in April, 1978, the country's unions were aggressively militant, concentrated in industry, overwhelmingly male-dominated and still tied, in good measure, to head offices in the U.S.

Today, the union movement is still quiescent even after four years of business recovery, industrial unions are a declining force, women are a significant 35% of total union members and the U.S. links are eroding.

These realities go a long way to explain why next week's CLC convention will be electing CLC Secretary-Treasurer Shirley Carr to succeed McDermott. Carr, a government union leader who used to work for the city of Niagara Falls, Ont., is replacing a former head of the United Auto Workers and onetime assembly line worker.

The transfer of power is more than a vivid symbol of the enormous changes that have shaken the 2.1-million-member congress during McDermott's tenure. It could—if Carr plays her cards right—mark the beginning of a new phase of consolidation and organizing for the labor movement itself. . . .

As the congress's first white-collar president, Carr is in a much better position than any of her predecessors to appeal to the four million-plus white-collar office workers who have stubbornly resisted the blandishments of union organizers. . . .

The key may prove to be whether non-union workers begin to perceive in the CLC and its affiliated unions a labor movement that has their interests at heart.

Carr's ability to bring some unity to a highly fragmented labor movement—there are no fewer than five competing union centrals—is likewise thought to be helped by her appeal to women unionists. For example, close to one-quarter of the country's 3.7 million union members belong to unions that remain independent of any labor central such as the CLC. Many of these are teachers' and nurses' organizations that, again, consist largely of women.

In the past, they have resisted overtures to join the CLC because they consider themselves professionals first, unionists second. But this reluctance also has a lot to do with their perception that the congress is a male-dominated bastion of industrial unionists. That may have been true during the early McDermott years. It is no longer.

Here are some of the more dramatic changes that have occurred within the union movement during McDermott's tenure from 1978 to present. In many ways, they make it look as though the Carr presidency was inevitable:

● Women in Unions. In 1978, roughly 28% of Canada's unionists were women. This year, that proportion is estimated to be 35%—about 1.3 million. This represents an annual growth rate of 5% vs less than 2% for men—a pattern that owes a lot to the fast growth of government unions, which tend to have equal numbers of men and women.

So far, women have not been landing top union jobs in anywhere near the same proportion as their membership. Only two of the country's 25 largest unions (which, combined, account for 60% of total union membership) have women presidents. Labor centrals like the CLC and Ontario Federation of Labour have recently amended their constitutions to reserve a minimum number of executive seats for women. (In the CLC's case, it's six of 38). But these are labor federations that cannot promote women's issues where it really counts—at the bargaining table.

● Nationalism. Last year's flight of the United Auto Workers from its Detroit-based headquarters was simply the tip of the iceberg. With the notable exception of unions like the United Steelworkers and United Food & Commercial Workers, Canadian unions are increasingly contemptuous of their U.S. counterparts' general conservatism. This applies not only to the greater U.S. willingness to accept wage and benefit concessions during bargaining, but also the relative inability of American labor to organize new members. Last year, fewer than 18% of employed U.S. wage and salary earners carried union cards, less than half the proportion in Canada.

In 1978, nearly half of Canada's union members belonged to a union with headquarters in the U.S. Now, only about 36% remain

Dennis McDermott, Shirley Carr

faithful to "international" union-ism—a proportion that's expected to fall gradually over the next few years.

Within the CLC, the shift has been even more dramatic. When McDermott first assumed the presidency, the congress was home to more than 1.3 million union members with ties to the U.S. Less than 600,000 remain—partly because 10 construction unions left the CLC in 1982, but also because of the general loss of jobs in manufacturing and building trades, where most international unions are concentrated.

• New Organizing. Although recent drives to sign up bank workers and retail employees have been stalling, the Canadian labor movement has held its own during the McDermott years. Eight years ago, 3.3 million union members made up 39% of the work force. The unionized work force remains about the same proportionately, but the total numbers have edged up to 3.7 million, a 12% jump.

The pattern naturally varies widely by union. Of the five unions experiencing the most growth, four draw their membership mainly from government and services. The Canadian Union of Public Employees, with an increase of 65,000 members, led the list, while the two biggest construction unions—Carpenters and Laborers—had big net declines over the same period. . . .

— JAMES BAGNALL

Strikes

Unionization increases workers' bargaining power in a number of ways. It usually raises the technical skill they bring to negotiations. It introduces some protection against victimization for those workers who are active in the bargaining process. Perhaps most important, it increases the capacity of a group of workers to mount a strike. In theory, any group of workers, large or small, unionized or not, can mount a strike in an effort to extract a better work/reward tradeoff from an employer. In practice, unions provide the organizational framework without which an effective strike is hard to sustain. They can, for example, keep track of free riders and impose discipline on them, reinforce the morale of strikers, and provide strike pay. Where unions have been illegal, organizational substitutes in the form of various mutual aid and self-help societies seem to have been necessary in the mounting of effective strikes.

Workers strike to improve their pay and working conditions and sometimes to challenge the authority of their managers (the latter goal is much stressed by writers in the alienation tradition). Most unions bargain on behalf of workers who have a range of skills and levels of experience. How do they balance the interests of their higher-paid members against those of their lower-paid members? There is considerable evidence (some summarized in Wood 1978, 180-4) that, on balance, unions seek to equalize their members' pay—that is, they tend to seek settlements that reduce pay differentials for skill and experience levels. But those differentials are precisely the ones likely to reflect market forces. In the model market of an economics text, tool and die makers, for instance, expect to be paid more than welders because the supply of tool and die makers is reduced by the fact that, as Meltz (1982, 5-9) points out, acquiring the requisite skills takes a number of years of training when pay is likely to be very poor indeed. The threat or act of striking, then, sometimes enables unions to raise wages and does so in a generally egalitarian fashion, which inhibits the operation of the market.

However, an examination of strike propensity as distributed among industries suggests that access to the strike as a device for levering better wages and working conditions from employers is not universally available, even among union members. Within the manufacturing industry, days lost per union member is generally relatively high in industries that pay relatively high wages. This correlation does not mean that a particular strike wave temporarily shifts an industry into the high-wage category. The rankings of industries by both wages and work days lost are relatively stable. (Rubber, transportation equipment, and electrical equipment firms, for example, have consistently relatively high average wages and workdays-lost rates over time. Food and beverages, leather goods, and knitting mills, on the other hand, have consistently low average wages and work days lost.) Rather, there are good grounds for thinking that this pattern reflects differences in the opportunity for striking effectively. Industries such as clothing manufacture are made up of a large number of intensely competitive firms for which labour constitutes a substantial part of the total production costs. Rather than make a concession to striking workers, employers in these industries often prefer to shut down a plant or move it to a location with a more congenial labour-relations climate. In contrast, the manufacture of transportation equipment (which includes automobiles) is concentrated in the hands of a small number of producers for whom labour costs are a relatively smaller proportion of total costs.[7] In such industries employers may be willing to concede a wage increase in order to end a strike.

In short, striking can be expected to pay off in some industries but not others. The former industries are the better paying, concentrated industries ("primary" in the terms of dual labour-market theory) and the latter are the poorly paying, more competitive ("secondary") industries. There is an element of irony in all this. In industries of the latter type, where wages and working conditions are most wretched, a major tactic for improving conditions is considerably less effective.

But despite the existence of sectors that have limited opportunities to strike effectively and consequently have low strike rates, Canada is located close to the top of the international strike league. The incidence of industrial conflict is often measured by days lost per thousand paid workers. By this measure, Canada is second only to Italy among rich capitalist countries (see Exhibit 11-2). One can, however, look beyond this overall measure of industrial conflict to the frequency, duration, and size of

Exhibit 11-2
The Pattern of Industrial Conflict,
Selected Countries, 1979–83

	Volume (days lost per thousand workers)	Frequency (number of strikes per million workers)	Duration (days lost per worker on strike)	Size (workers involved per strike)
Australia	521.5	382.5	2.9	487.7
Austria	2.0[a]	2.2[a]	1.6	1147.0
Belgium	114.6[b]	47.8[b]	8.5[b]	259.0[b]
Canada	710.2	88.0	18.0	471.9
France	114.6[a]	154.8[a]	4.2[b]	207.8[a]
Italy	978.5	109.3	1.6	5680.4
Netherlands	34.1	5.0	5.8	1994.0
Norway	47.9	9.4	6.4	645.4
Sweden	228.6	31.4	2.4	1081.0
United Kingdom	530.8[a]	66.4[a]	6.5	1154.6
West Germany	6.0	—	2.0	—

[a] 1979–82 only
[b] 1979–80 only

Source: International Labour Office (1984).

strikes. As Exhibit 11-2 shows, Canada has neither especially frequent nor especially large strikes. Its days-lost rate is so high because strikes go on here for rather longer than they do elsewhere. In this respect, the pattern of strikes in Canada is similar to that found in the United States (although recent changes in that country's method of data presentation make it impossible to show this point for the time period covered by Exhibit 11-2). In both countries, the product of collective bargaining is a signed contract that binds both signatories for a term of as long as three years, and the level of industrial disputes is strongly marked by this fact.

During this term, workers do not normally have the right to strike. The contract tends to cover a wide range of issues, including not only wages but also fringe benefits, such as medical insurance. Grievances tend to build up over the lifetime of the contract, and when time to renegotiate comes, the bargaining process is complicated and fraught with contentious issues. Nevertheless, most contracts are renegotiated without a strike. But when union and management fail to agree, the resulting strike is a test of strength designed to influence the terms of the contract that will determine labour costs and the conditions of work for the next one to three years. A great deal rides on its outcome.

Notice, furthermore, that the effect of these contracts is to slow down the adjustment of wages to market forces. The firm must pay the regular increments that the contract provides for over its term, whether business goes up or down. In the market of the economics textbook, in contrast, when business goes down, so does the demand for labour and thus the wage rate.

EMPLOYERS' RESPONSES

The hierarchy of the firm is designed to keep the effort of its workers as close as possible to the standards it defines as acceptable. Piece rates directly tie effort to reward. Job ladders deter quits. When attempts to unionize challenge the authority of employers, their most common reaction has been to fight back as aggressively as possible: to refuse to bargain, to dismiss identifiable "troublemakers," to reassert forcibly the "right to manage" (Harris 1982; Smucker 1980, 163-4). There is another tactic that can, at least in principle, assist in the process of supervision, make piece rates more feasible, reduce the need to resort to the relatively costly device of a job ladder, and even weaken unions. Harry Braverman outlined this tactic in his brilliant, though flawed, *Labor and Monopoly Capital* (1974). The reasoning goes as follows. Other things being equal, skilled workers are always in a stronger bargaining position than unskilled workers. If skilled workers quit or go on strike, they are, by definition, less readily replaceable than their unskilled counterparts. If they restrict output, managers find it difficult to enforce a different norm; these workers are quite likely to know more about their jobs and what is possible for them to do than those who give them orders. The relatively high average wages that skilled workers receive embody these facts. Given all this, it is in the interests of employers, wherever possible, to substitute less skilled workers for more skilled ones.

Employers can accomplish this shift by redesigning the work process. When suitably analyzed, jobs that require diffuse knowledge and skills (such as, say, tool and die making) can sometimes be broken down into separate, simplified operations, many of which can be designed into a machine. Consider what happens with this increase in the division of labour. First, in the process of analyzing the jobs, employers (or the industrial engineers they hire) break the skilled workers' monopoly of knowledge over the production process and reduce the extent to which they can freely determine output norms. Work becomes easier to supervise. Employers are, as a result, better equipped to establish and enforce what is to constitute the appropriate sequence of work, the appropriate standard, and the appropriate amount. Second, the supply of potential workers is enlarged. Almost anyone can do semiskilled or unskilled work. Consequently, employers no longer have to be concerned about the problem of replacing workers. Quits are simply less of a problem, the job ladder is less necessary, and strikes are less of a threat. Sooner or later the wage premium for skill is eroded. Third, the fragmentation of the

In 1946 these Westinghouse workers in Hamilton, Ontario, were striking for a 25-cent-an-hour raise and a 44-hour work week. The strike remains a major union bargaining tool today.

work and management's increase in understanding of the work process makes piece-rate systems more feasible. In short, employers can weaken the bargaining position of workers, unionized or not, by redesigning the work process.

For all the brilliance of this analysis and its immense popularity with sociologists of work, de-skilling has not been nearly as important a process as Braverman maintains. His analysis suggests there was a period in the 19th century when most jobs required a range of skills that took considerable time to acquire. But *most* jobs never required a great deal of skill or a prolonged learning period, and almost all jobs today require literacy—a skill that was quite rare in the 19th century. Nonetheless, there are periods in the history of some occupations that do seem consistent with Braverman's model, and it is important to bear in mind that de-skilling remains a tactical option open to employers.

PROFESSIONALIZATION

So far, I have focused on the employer/employee relationship. There is, however, a set of occupations that may not involve an employer/employee relation but that has greatly interested a number of sociologists of work. These are the **professions**, whose distinctive characteristic is that their practitioners have succeeded in laying claim to a monopoly over a specialized body of knowledge related to the work they do. Associated with this monopoly is a more or less prolonged training period and a substantial degree of autonomy. Doctors, for example, are privy to a body of knowledge on medical practice that is not shared by people who have not had prolonged medical school training. Thus, doctors can plausibly claim that lay people are not capable of controlling them sensibly, that, on the contrary, only doctors can make decisions about medical training and professional conduct. Associated with this claim to autonomy from extraprofessional control is, typically, a claim that the profession's members are inculcated with a sense of community service and obligation. Because of their specialized knowledge and the dedication to community service that they claim, members of the profession make the case that they should be self-regulating, that representative bodies of established practitioners should decide who can be admitted to practice. Claims to self-regulation are very difficult to enforce, however, without the assistance of the government. Effective professional control over who qualifies to practise is difficult to assert, unless there is a law forbidding people to practise without having been licensed by the relevant professional body. **Occupational licensure** is the common aspiration of would-be professions, and its much preferred form is licensure backed by legal authority.

It is quite clear that the specialist knowledge involved in the practice of, say, medicine and law does raise difficulties for lay control. It is also clear, however, that securing the autonomy that goes with professionalization confers considerable advantages on the members of the occupation involved. First, professional occupations tend to be prestigious. Second, effective occupational licensure limits the operation of the market for professional services in a way that serves the interests of practitioners; they can lengthen training requirements, limiting the supply of entrants into the occupation and thus maintaining fees at a rate higher than would otherwise be the case. Self-regulation also allows the establishment of codes of conduct that can protect professional incomes. For example, prohibiting practitioners from advertising—a quite common professional rule—reduces effective competition among them. There is no doubt that many professional associations have made decisions on eligibility to prac- tise and other matters that, although cloaked in the rhetoric of community service, have in reality been based on their economic interests (see, for example, Friedman 1962; Johnson 1972).

This pattern of occupational privileges, called **professionalization**, is clearly a desirable state for an occupation. Consequently, the central feature of the history of many occupations has been the struggle to secure professional recognition, complete with vesting of the legal authority to license with the relevant professional association. Doctors and lawyers spring to mind as having had such battles, but barbers, social workers, funeral directors, and members of many other occupations have engaged in analogous struggles to achieve equivalent authority (with varying de- grees of success).

One result is that professionalization reflects not only the inherent technical complexity of the work involved but also the political skills and opportunities of the occupations involved. Professionalization is not a natural state; it is something that has to be struggled for. And because the principal motivation for professional status comes from the interests of the members of the occupation, successful professionalization is not by any means an unalloyed blessing for clients.

Recent years have seen increasing pressure on established professional privileges, and the climate for securing such privileges is less propitious than it has been in the past. As I noted, effective professional self-regulation depends on the sanction for it provided by legally authorized occupational licensure. That is, one is much less likely to practise medicine without a licence if doing so leads to a heavy fine or imprisonment. One is less likely to violate a professional code that, for example, prohibits adver- tising if the result is likely to be disbarment and therefore loss of liveli- hood. However, what the government gives in the form of legal sanction, it can also take away. For many years in Canada the professions were specifically exempted from competition law. They could restrain trade (by, say, prohibiting advertising) in ways that ordinary businesses could not. Between 1974 and 1976, however, Canadian competition law was amended to extend its application to the professions and other service industries from which it had previously been excluded (Ostry 1984, 456-57). Nonetheless, some professions continue to enjoy special legal protection from competition (to varying degrees in different jurisdic-

High-status, high-income professionals such as physicians are typically seen to have the most favourable working conditions and to be in the best position to control their working activities. These professionals may feel intolerably imposed upon when their control is limited, even in a minor way. The dramatic and emotional protests by physicians against the Ontario government's restriction of extra-billing in 1986 is an example of how relative deprivation is felt by those at the top of the occupational ladder.

tions). More recently, the struggle over extra-billing between medical practitioners and both levels of government has provided another example of increasing attenuation of professional autonomy. The reasons for this tendency are not entirely clear but certainly include the current financial difficulties of the federal and provincial governments, which pay most of the cost of the services of medical professionals and part of the cost of the services of legal professionals (for example, legal aid lawyers, government lawyers). Moreover, deregulation of everything from airlines to professions is now intellectually fashionable.[8] More struggles over professional autonomy are a certainty for the near future.

CONCLUSION

At the beginning of this chapter I outlined two alternative approaches to the interpretation of work: the alienation tradition and the orientations-to-work tradition.

Which of these alternative interpretations is correct? I have already observed that job-satisfaction research tends to support the orientations-to-work tradition. If the desire of workers to be creative and to have amicable relations with other people is so uniformly thwarted by their work experiences, why do so many of them report satisfaction with their jobs? And if the division of labour makes so much difference to people, why have the more careful studies of job satisfaction found no tendency for workers in jobs involving fragmented and repetitive tasks (and thus likely to be alienating) to report high levels of job dissatisfaction? (Those studies that do report such differences have either rather poor measures of technology—that is, alienating conditions—or do not control for income.)

As suggested in the box on page 400, writers in the alienation tradition have an answer to these points. They say that people report they are satisfied with their jobs because the question they are being asked is abstract. Workers can answer it without thinking about its implications and do so according to what they have learned is appropriate conduct—that is, to be satisfied with their job. The likelihood of this response is reinforced by the fact that workers have had to come to terms with the negligible range of choice of jobs available to them. What is the point of being dissatisfied with one's work if all the alternative jobs are just about as bad? The evidence that this interpretation is correct lies, it is claimed, in what people do rather than what they say, in "slow downs and sit ins, restriction of output, wildcat strikes, working to rule, absenteeism and tardiness, personnel turnover, insubordination, and sabotage" (Rinehart 1978, 10).

Now, it is certainly reasonable to argue that research on the sociology of work should go beyond standardized questionnaires. Strikes, output restriction, quits, and so on, are all important areas for research. But most workers in Canada never strike; there is no evidence that most of them restrict output; evidence on sabotage is negligible, and what there is—largely newspaper accounts—suggests that it occurs mostly as a pressure tactic during industrial disputes rather than as a *cri de coeur* in response to oppressive working conditions. Thus, one must question the extent of the protests that the alienation tradition stresses.

Furthermore, protest is not inconsistent with the orientations-to-work approach. If most people view work primarily as a means of getting income and if they are not satisfied with the income they receive, they have every reason to strike or quit. If they think that working hard under a piece-rate system will lead to a rate cut or threaten their jobs, they have every reason to restrict their output. To provide support for the alienation account, advocates would have to show that the various forms of protest are principally directed at the organization of work. Some of them certainly are, but the extent and importance of the issue is a contentious matter. Examples of strikes that are cited as having been concerned with the organization of work prove, on closer examination, to be concerned with wages (see Smith 1979, 600-601). Neither is the evidence of psychological damage from repetitive work very good. The much cited study by Kornhauser (1965) suffers from serious methodological defects, including use of a very small sample and a research design that does not allow one to distinguish whether the sweaty palms and other symptoms of the unskilled workers were a product of their experiences at work or simply reflected a pre-existing state that had prevented them from getting into better paid, skilled jobs. At present I believe that, on balance, the evidence tends to support the orientations-to-work-interpretation.

Writers in the alienation tradition do, however, raise two issues to which the orientations writers have no satisfactory answer. One is the origins of workers' preferences. Orientations writers stress that work is not a central priority in most people's lives, that people are more concerned with a number of other things—in particular, their families. But writers such as Goldthorpe et al. (1968, 182-4) treat the origins of these priorities as entirely unproblematic. They make no attempt to explain how it is possible for people to treat with indifference such a large part of their lives. Alienation writers offer an answer. They say that people do not pay much attention to how interesting their jobs are or how gratifying their relations with their fellow workers are because choice in the matter is negligible. Almost all jobs in capitalist societies, they claim, are dull: "Workers opt for jobs with relatively high wages in exchange for what can only be minor losses in intrinsic satisfaction" (Rinehart 1978, 7). This answer may or may not be satisfactory, but the alienation writers at least raise the issue. The orientations writers simply set it aside.

The second and related issue is the extent of job choice available to people. Some orientations-to-work writers tend to assume that one of the reasons for findings of such high levels of job satisfaction is that corresponding to the array of workers' preferences (for dull, well-paid work versus interesting, poorly paid work, and so on) there is an array of jobs with different characteristics, so that most people can find what they want (Blackburn and Mann 1979, 8). Alienation writers argue that in fact, the range of choices is narrow. Very few studies actually attempt to specify the range of jobs in the economy, although this issue is partly what segmented labour writings are about. If the range of choice is narrow, the plausibility of the orientations-to-work interpretation is correspondingly reduced.

The current state of research, then, leads me to put more credence in the orientations-to-work interpretation than in its alienation counterpart but not because the evidence for the former is overwhelmingly persuasive. The fact is that alienation writers have yet to make a serious attempt at marshalling the kind of evidence that would adequately test their vision of the way the world works. We need more original research and more careful reviews of the existing research on the range of choice in jobs and the origins of preferences. Showing that some workers sometimes strike and sometimes restrict output does not really address the issue because these actions are entirely consistent with the orientations interpretation. But highly limited job choices and preferences formed in response to the existence of limited choices are not consistent with it. It is to those issues that future research should be more carefully directed.

To summarize, the alienation tradition, rooted in the writings of Marx, sees work as a source of alienation. Work is organized in capitalist societies, it is argued, so that people's basic needs for creative expression and non-antagonistic social relations are frustrated. The only choice is between more or less alienating jobs. As a result, people experience varying amounts of psychological damage, and some of their behaviour at work takes the form of protests against the conditions that alienate them.

The orientations-to-work approach stresses the choices implicit in the capitalistic labour market. Followers of this interpretation believe that most people are more centrally concerned with their lives outside work than with work itself; they approach their jobs as vehicles for generating an income that will support that life, rather than as an end in itself. Consequently they often choose jobs that are downright dull in order to get the higher wage that, other things being equal, is likely to go with unpleasant work. Because there is a deliberate exchange involved, most people are relatively contented with their jobs overall (though if the jobs in question are dull, they certainly do not delude themselves that the contrary is true).

NOTES

1. For a general and brilliant treatment of the conditions under which business people choose to coordinate work through the market or through hierarchy, see Williamson (1975).

2. There are occasional exceptions. For example, the Canadian Transport Commission compelled Canadian Pacific to provide passenger rail service long after the company would have preferred to abandon it.

3. The availability of unemployment insurance on relatively generous terms is likely to reduce a high unemployment rate's disincentive effect on quitting. For a review of the literature on this issue, see Hum (1981).

4. The existence of non-vested, non-transferable pension plans is another curb on the feasibility of quitting.

5. The relative effects of these variables on growth in union membership in Canada were assessed using multiple regression analysis, the analysis of more than two variables by the regression technique discussed in Chapter 2.

6. Olson (1965) also shows how a number of other characteristics of the history of trade unions can be explained in terms of the free-rider problem. Take, for example, the fact that intimidation of and violence toward strike-breakers have been features of labour history. How else could striking workers modify the incentives of their free-riding peers? Similarly, unions have sometimes facilitated growth by offering benefits that accrued only to members, excluding free riders. For example, the early railway unions offered life insurance, which was not adequately available to these workers from private companies and which was extremely important to them because of the high accident rates attached to their jobs at the time.

7. This argument, it should be stressed, should not be pushed too far since in many industries international competition is every bit as important as domestic competition (but only the latter is measured by the concentration ratios customarily used as indicators of the extent to which production is concentrated in a small number of firms).

8. It should be clear that access to a body of knowledge not shared by the lay public and significant amounts of training are traits that the professions share with some of the skilled manual trades. And, indeed, the guilds into which skilled trades were once organized served functions quite similar to those of the self-regulatory bodies of the modern profession. The decline of the guilds may be interesting not only on historical grounds but also because the process *may* give some clues to future developments in some of the professions.

FOR FURTHER READING

Anderson, John, and Morley Gunderson, eds.
   1982 *Union-Management Relations in Canada.* Don Mills, Ont.: Addison-Wesley. This comprehensive textbook, which includes an outline of Canadian labour law, is a useful and convenient source of evidence on industrial relations in Canada.
Hamilton, Richard F., and James D. Wright
   1986 *The State of the Masses.* New York: Aldine. This analysis includes an appropriately scathing critique of much of the evidence cited by alienation theorists and a clear statement of the orientations approach.
Littler, Craig
   1982 *The Development of the Labour Process in Capitalist Societies.* London: Heinemann.
   A very sensible treatment of Braverman's de-skilling thesis, Littler's book deals largely with Great Britain but includes useful coverage of the United States and Japan too.
Olson, Mancur
   1965 *The Logic of Collective Action: Public Goods and the Theory of Groups.* Cambridge, Mass.: Harvard University Press.
   Chapter 3 of this book contains an immensely valuable theoretic treatment of trade unions.
Rinehart, James W.
   1975 *The Tyranny of Work.* Don Mills, Ont.: Longmans Canada.
   Rinehart gives a clear and succinct statement of the alienation approach to the sociology of work.

CHAPTER 12

DEVIANCE AND SOCIAL CONTROL

Robert A. Stebbins

WHAT IS DEVIANCE?

At first thought, it seems reasonable to define deviance as a breach of moral rules. Certainly there are people who violate the generally accepted rules. Some worship the devil. Others cavort naked at nudist camps. Still others cheat on their income taxes, sell bootleg liquor, rob, steal, or act as prostitutes. The list of infractions is long.

Most people think of deviance—often referred to as criminal behaviour, delinquency, immorality, perversion, or any number of other pejorative terms—as something inherently bad or immoral. Although sociologists have long realized that standards of behaviour vary somewhat from one society to another, until the latter part of this century they worked, for the most part, from an absolutist definition of deviance. It had the merits of simplicity and apparent objectivity. The social scientists' classification of a certain action as deviant was accepted as valid, since it usually squared with what "everybody knows" about morality. Less attention was paid to the definition of deviance than to predicting or categorizing deviants. And that facilitated **social control**, which—then as well as now—seeks to eliminate or at least to control deviant behaviour.

In day-to-day usage, most people still treat deviance as an absolute, depending on common sense to define it. Not so for social science. Sociologists in particular realize that common sense embodies unquestioned assumptions. As in other areas of life, identifying and reacting to deviance hinges on one person's interpretation of another person's deeds, and deviance is identified by using a moral measuring stick.

Deviance is more than a set of acts; it is also a socially constructed reality. The word deviance literally means departing from the road. But there are many roads. To understand how deviance is seen, one must understand how societies set standards of acceptable behaviour. Every group has values and beliefs about how society functions, even if these are rarely formally expressed. Based on these values are **norms**, or rules as to how people should behave: some are codified into formal **laws**, others (called **mores**) are informal but very important, and many are less important, more flexible rules, such as rules of etiquette or custom, called **folkways**. (For more discussion of social values and rules, see Chapter 3.) Violating important norms is **deviance**.

Because values and norms vary from one culture to another, the definition of deviance also changes. For example, in Canada, where liberty and the security of the person are important values, unlawful confinement and assault are serious offences. But there have been societies in which the chief good was maintenance of the social hierarchy; therefore owning slaves was considered normal, and beating or even killing them was acceptable.

In a society that values the right to own property, theft is deviant. In traditional Inuit society, where property was not an important concept and communal sharing was, the deviant was not the hunter who took from another's cache but the hunter who hoarded food without sharing. The medieval duellist or the Wild West gunslinger would be deviant in 20th-century Canada. A deliberately childless couple, fairly common in Canada today, would be seriously deviant in many cultures.

In fact, even within a given society at a given time, certain behaviour may be deviant in some groups but not in others or in one situation but not in another. For example, drinking alcohol is deviant in certain church groups, but refusing to drink it may be considered mildly deviant in some social circles.

Today, when it comes to defining deviance, most sociologists are relativists. They realize that human action is not inherently deviant or non-deviant. To eat pork is deviant for an Orthodox Jew or Muslim, but not for others. Marriage between cousins is defined as incest in some societies, tolerated in others, and an ideal arrangement in still others. One relativist puts his case this way: *"Deviance, like beauty, is in the eyes of the beholder . . .* almost every conceivable human characteristic or activity is pariah in somebody's eyes" (Simmons 1969, 4).

As communities define deviance, some people (the deviants) become differentiated from the rest (the non-deviants):

> "Deviance matters" deal with the process of differentiation, how people become differentiated, and what moral significance is attached to their differences. The center of concern is moral ideas, their rise and fall, their invocation and application either as informal social designations or as administrative categories by agencies of social control. (Lemert 1982, 238)

Deviants may be rejected, isolated, punished in one of many ways, or considered sick and treated or rehabilitated. Deviants experience **stigma**— a mark of discredit or unworthiness, the opposite of a status symbol. In the original Greek, the word stigma meant a physical mark warning others to keep away from a person considered bad or unclean. Athough people are no longer physically branded or marked, deviants are still metaphorically marked and set aside from society. Sometimes a deviant act is considered to be an isolated occurrence, not seriously affecting a person's standing in society. In other cases, a person is given the permanent status of deviant. He or she is no longer seen primarily as, say, a teacher, a parent, or a chess champion, but as a killer or a schizophrenic.

TYPES OF DEVIANCE

Sociologists classify deviance according to three standards: legality, victimization and tolerableness.

Legality

In terms of its legality, deviance can be criminal, non-criminal, or legitimate. Criminal deviance is commonly referred to as **crime** or violation

Armed and masked farmers guard against attempts by bankers to repossess their farms for failure to make mortgage payments. Ordinary citizens may often be driven to take violent action they would otherwise consider deviant, when their own interests are at stake.

of the criminal law. The strongest case for an absolutist definition of deviance can be made here. If any precision is possible in defining deviance, surely a legal code should differentiate deviant from non-deviant actions. Because legal or formal norms are usually carefully worked out and repeatedly tested through application, they certainly add a degree of clarity to the handling of social offences. But laws incorporate subjective values. They are also susceptible to varying interpretations. Indeed, the study of deviance shows how personal interpretations sneak into the formal social-control process, to the chagrin of those who claim impartiality and absolutism in their handling of deviants (Antony 1980; Haas and Shaffir 1974, chap. 7-11). For example, psychiatrists, often unwittingly, may use a common-sense concept of mental disorder to identify mental patients.

Most deviants are not criminal, for they have violated no criminal laws. They are nevertheless cast in a deviant role because they have acted in a morally reprehensible way, as defined by an influential segment of the community. In Canada, murder, sexual assault, public drunkenness, theft, breaking and entering, forgery, assault, living off the avails of prostitution, embezzlement, and fraud are defined as criminal acts. Some forms of drug use and gambling are also illegal.

Other deviant roles fall beyond the purview of law (non-criminal) and may even be guaranteed by it (legitimate). These categories include nudists, compulsive gamblers, alcoholics and heavy drinkers, people with mental disorders, homosexuals, mate swappers, striptease dancers, transvestites, occultists, transsexuals, drug addicts, and political and religious deviants. It is noteworthy that addiction to alcohol, drugs, or gambling is not unlawful in itself, even though the acts it leads to may be.

As if to confuse matters more, people tolerate certain kinds of criminal deviance while scorning or actively opposing certain non-criminal and legitimate types. For instance, alcoholism, compulsive gambling, and severe mental disorder are presently regarded as more serious breaches of community standards than are casual marijuana use, illicit off-track betting, or perhaps even prostitution. Hence, no facile claim can be made that crime is always more serious than non-criminal deviance.

Victimization

Deviance (especially crime) can also be categorized on the basis of whether it victimizes anyone.

> This . . . conception of "victimless crime" is applied to all those situations in which the proscribed offense consists of a "consensual transaction," a willing exchange of goods or services that does not often generate a directly involved complaining "victim" who initiates enforcement activity. These are, then—to use a less controversial term— "complainantless" crimes. (Schur 1974, 183)

Victimless crimes include the sale of illicit drugs, illegal gambling, and prostitution and other legally proscribed sexual behaviour. The people involved in these crimes see themselves as something other than victims. In comparison, people who have been robbed, raped, assaulted, defrauded, and the like see themselves and are seen by others as victims.

In a pluralistic society such as Canada, which allows some leeway in what is considered personal moral choice, victimization is becoming a standard for tolerability; many people say that as long as an action hurts no one, it should not be penalized—even if they personally disapprove of it. The distinction is not, however, always clear. Many people would include abortion (when illegally performed) and the distribution of pornography among victimless crimes. But opponents of abortion consider the fetus to be a person, and thus a victim. Opponents of pornography claim that it makes victims of women, especially the models.

Tolerableness

It is often difficult to categorize deviance according to standards of legality and victimization. Tolerableness is always a matter of empirical assessment. For example, Canadian society is generally tolerant of alcohol use, but specific groups strongly oppose it. Moreover, public sentiment changes. Opinions about marijuana use, prostitution and homosexuality appear

CHICKENS SLAUGHTERED TO EASE KIN'S SPIRITS

BRAMPTON Ont. (CP)—Two brothers who were caught slaughtering chickens over five freshly dug graves in a Mississauga, Ont., cemetery told a spellbound courtroom why they did it.

The men told Provincial Court Judge Gerald Young they meant no disrespect and were trying to release the spirits of relatives whom they believed had died violently at the hands of the army in their native Uganda.

Young gave the men an absolute discharge after they agreed to pay cemetery officials $100 for the cost of the cleanup.

The men, who have refugee status in Canada, belong to a Ugandan tribe which was politically active and is now being persecuted by the present government. The elder brother, aged 32, testified that during the spring, he was having dreams in which his father was shot and his mother and sister were "raped and killed by the army."

Those visions, with the lack of communication from the family and news of continuing "genocide" in their native land, led the man to believe his family had died violently, he said.

The elder brother, who had learned tribal customs from his grandparents, said he believed he had to find fresh graves and shed blood over them "for the spirits (of his family) to rest in peace and harmony."

to be in a state of flux at present; other forms of deviance will certainly be redefined in the future. Moreover, it is sometimes difficult to establish who (if anyone) has been victimized and how. Rape trials often turn on just this question. Should alcoholics or compulsive gamblers be considered victims of their own actions or victims of a system that allows people to develop such habits?

EXPLANATIONS OF DEVIANCE

Neither sociology nor any of the other social sciences can fully explain why some people take up deviant lifestyles or become identified as deviant. But sociology does offer several theoretical frameworks to explain aspects of deviance. Here we present four such explanations: differential association, anomie and opportunity, labelling and societal reaction, and conflict.

Differential Association

Edwin H. Sutherland first presented his differential association theory of crime in the 1939 edition of *Principles of Criminology*. That statement differs little from the modern version written by Sutherland and Cressey (1978, 80-82). The theory consists of nine propositions:

1. People learn how to engage in crime.
2. This learning takes place through interaction with others who have already learned criminal ways.
3. The learning of crime occurs in small, face-to-face groups.
4. The learning covers criminal techniques (for instance, how to open a safe), motives, attitudes, and rationalizations.
5. Among criminals, an important learned attitude is a disregard for the community's legal code.
6. One acquires this attitude by associating with those who hold it, and by failing to associate with those who do not. This pattern of interaction is called **differential association**.
7. Differential associations with criminals and non-criminals vary in frequency, duration, importance, and intensity.
8. Learning criminal behaviour through differential association follows the same processes as learning any other kind of behaviour; the learning can be analyzed in the same way as any other learning.
9. Criminal behaviour is a response to the same cultural needs and values as non-criminal behaviour. For instance, one man steals to acquire money for a new suit of clothes, while another works as a carpenter to reach the same goal. Consequently, tying societal needs and values to crime fails to explain crime.

Sutherland's theory seems to offer a valuable, albeit partial, explanation of theft, burglary, marijuana use, and prostitution. And differential association often precedes drug and alcohol addiction and the pursuit of homosexual relations. It may even contribute to some mental disorders. But few would believe that a person becomes addicted, homosexual, or mentally ill through association alone; other explanations are necessary.

Anomie and Opportunity

The common English translation of the French word **anomie** is "normlessness." Emile Durkheim used the term to describe the situation of people whose social order is changing so rapidly that old communal values are eroded before new ones can develop to take their place. People are adrift, with no clear sense of meaningful rules or norms. Durkheim gave fullest expression to this idea in 1897 in his landmark study of suicide. Anomic suicide, one of the three types he examined, "results from man's activity's lacking regulation and his consequent sufferings" ([1897] 1951, 258).

More than 40 years later, in 1938, Robert K. Merton recast Durkheim's ideas in a general theory of deviance. (The following discussion is based on his own revision of the theory, published in 1957.) Deviance, Merton says, results from the malintegration of success goals and the institutionalized means of reaching them, particularly the job. He calls this failure to mesh culture and social structure anomie, giving the term a meaning somewhat different from Durkheim's. Members of an anomic society try to adapt to their unsettled condition in various ways.

Merton developed a typology of five adaptive modes, four of which are deviant. (See Exhibit 12-1.) The first mode is conformity, with both the prescribed goals of society and the usual means of achieving them. Innovation (Mode II) occurs when people accept society's success goals but reject its means for reaching them. Sutherland's ninth proposition makes the same point. So does the following fantasy of a gambler who hopes to be a financial success without suffering through the grind of a nine-to-five job:

> My wife asked me to quit gambling, but I told her I was working on a system to beat the races that would get all of my money back plus enough to buy a large home with swimming pool, two pink Cadillacs, beautiful clothes, and a trip around the world. (Livingston 1974, 28)

In ritualism (Mode III), individuals scale down their personal success goals, thereby rejecting those normally pursued by people like themselves, but continue to strive for these reduced goals via socially acceptable means. An example is the middle-aged bureaucrat who gives up the thoughts of advancement entertained by his colleagues and falls into a ritualized pattern of working strictly by the rules to try to avoid a feared demotion. Retreatist deviants (Mode IV) reject both goals and means; today, people often do so through alcohol, drugs, life on skid row, or devotion to a deviant religion such as a millenarian cult. Finally, one may adapt to anomie by rebelling (Mode V), choosing both new goals and new means.

Exhibit 12-1
A Typology of Modes of Individual Adaptation

Modes of Adaptation	Cultural Goals	Institutionalized Means
I. Conformity	+	+
II. Innovation	+	−
III. Ritualism	−	+
IV. Retreatism	−	−
V. Rebellion	±	±

+ = acceptance
− = rejection
± = rejection followed by acceptance of new goals and means

Source: Adapted from Merton (1957, 140).

Communalists who settle in the wilderness to form a new society exemplify this mode, as do revolutionaries who want to replace the present government with a "better" one of their own.

Merton's theory sparked a tremendous amount of research and theorizing on deviant behaviour, which helped to extend, revise, and refine the original statement. For example, Richard Cloward (1959) noted that Merton wrote only about legitimate, institutionalized means. But to engage in deviance, one needs access to illegitimate means, which Cloward says are of two types: **learning structures** and **opportunity structures**. Building on differential association theory, he argues that tomorrow's deviants must first make contact with practising deviants, from whom they learn anti-social techniques. Moreover, they must find opportunities to express what they have learned. Novice burglars, for example, must not only learn the techniques of breaking and entering from experts; they must also find out what buildings are worth burglarizing and establish a network of contacts who can fence the stolen goods.

Labelling and Societal Reaction

The previous two theories assume that deviance can be explained by factors located within the deviants themselves: their learning, motivation, attitude, adaptation, or choice of goals and means. But a number of 20th-century theorists—the best known are Edwin Lemert and Howard S. Becker—challenge this assumption. They assert that deviance is created by society:

> Social groups create deviance by making the rules whose infraction constitutes deviance, and by applying those rules to particular people and **labelling** them as outsiders. . . . The deviant is one to whom that label has successfully been applied; deviant behavior is behavior that people so label. (Becker 1963, 9, emphasis added)

Since the rules (norms) are applied to some people and not to others, and since the application process may be biased, some people remain at large as "secret" deviants, while others go through life "falsely accused" of unsavoury acts they did not commit. To discover why only certain groups of people are labelled deviant, one must study those who make the rules and how they apply them.

Once publicly labelled, deviants are typically subjected to some sort of community or societal reaction to their misdeeds (Lemert 1951). Depending on the nature of the deviance and of the society that labels them, they may be imprisoned, ostracized, fined, tortured, kept under surveillance, or ridiculed. All labelled deviants soon discover that they must also cope with stigma, the invisible mark that sets them outside the community.

Partly because of the force of societal reaction, a deviant may develop a *career* in the deviant role. The stigma of the deviance itself, made worse if the deviant has been subjected to other kinds of reaction (such as

It is often difficult for us to grasp that people whose norms are different from our own consider their behaviour to be perfectly — normal.

imprisonment), makes it difficult to interact with agents of social control and non-deviant members of the community. For example, many employers are reluctant to hire a known homosexual or an ex-convict. Some people cool toward a friend discovered to be mentally disordered or alcoholic. A deviant may have difficulty finding a spouse or sustaining a marriage. In short, the deviant career interferes with family, work, and leisure. Excluded from conventional careers, the deviant may become committed to or trapped in the deviant career.

Conflict Perspective

Over the years, several criminologists have tried to adapt to the area of crime parts of the general **conflict perspective**, which sees society as a collection of groups struggling for power. One of the most successful of these theoretical efforts is that of Vold and Bernard:

> Thus the whole process of lawmaking, lawbreaking, and law enforcement directly reflects deep-seated and fundamental conflicts between group interests and the more general struggles among groups for control of the police power of the state. To that extent, criminal behavior is the behavior of *minority power groups*, in that these groups do not have sufficient power to promote and defend their interests and purposes in the legislative process. (1986, 274)

This statement is obviously compatible with the labelling and societal-reaction explanation; both direct attention to those who make the rules, rather than to the deviants. The conflict model underscores one of the points of labelling theory: to make rules and to identify rule-breakers is inherently arbitrary.

Richard Quinney (1970) has fashioned a conflict theory of crime based on the principle of social reality. His theory has six propositions:

1. Certain human actions are defined as crime by **societal agents** [people whom society has] authorized to make such judgments.
2. Agent definitions describe behaviour conflicting with the interests of groups who have the power to make laws.
3. These groups are also powerful enough to apply the laws protecting their interests which they do through law enforcement and administration of justice.
4. The various segments of complex industrial societies develop distinctive patterns of behaviour. The segments that develop and apply definitions of crime are less likely to have their actions defined as crimes than the segments whose behaviour patterns are not well represented—if at all—in the developing and applying of those definitions of crime.
5. The definitions of crime are communicated in many ways to the different segments of society. In other words, cultural conceptions of crime emerge from portrayals in the mass media and from interpersonal relations.
6. The definitions of crime, their applications, the criminal behaviour patterns, and the communicated conceptions of crime, together, constitute the *social reality of crime*. This reality is fluid; it is subject to constant change. It "is constantly being constructed in society" (Quinney 1970, 25, emphasis added to point 1)

The social reality of crime portrayed by the mass media is by no means the same as the official reality of police crime data. Conklin (1986, 80-82) notes, for example, that in the United States, violent crime is 12 times as common on television as in real life, with murder 100 times as common on television. Not surprisingly, people who watch television frequently have a more violent view of the world than infrequent watchers.

CRIME

Each month Statistics Canada uses the Uniform Crime Reports submitted by Canadian police departments to compile official **crime rates** (the number of offences of a particular kind as a proportion of the population, as recorded by the police). Exhibit 12-2 shows some examples. But statistics are slippery. These rates are not an accurate measure of criminality.

Exhibit 12-2
Selected Crime Rates in Canada
(per 100 000 population)

	Robbery	Murder	Theft	Breaking and Entering
1966	28.5	1.1	1331	510
1970	54.6	2.0	2013	834
1974	75.5	2.4	2401	1040
1978	83.7	2.6	2672	1186
1984	93.0	3.0	3611	1421

Source: Statistics Canada (1975–1984), *Crime and Traffic Enforcement Statistics*, cat. no. 85-205.

Some crimes are never reported, and some police officers fail to record reported crimes. Criminologists estimate that only 20 percent of all crimes in Canada, on average, are reported to the authorities, although the reporting rate varies considerably by type of crime (Statistics Canada 1980a, 151). Black and Reiss (1970) calculate that 35 percent of all crimes reported to American police go unrecorded. And, of course, some crime is never even detected and hence would be impossible to record. Donald Black (1970, 733) writes, "It has long been taken for granted that official statistics are not an accurate measure of all legally defined crime in the community." Recently, surveys of victims in selected cities have begun to provide an alternative picture of crime rates. The Uniform Crime Reports are, however, still the only source of regularly collected, national crime data.

Accuracy of crime reporting is only one issue in the generation of criminal statistics. Another is the interpretation of the police and other **social control agents**. What cues are used by police and by the citizens whose complaints they answer to determine that an action witnessed is a crime? Here come into play such varied factors as appearance (clothing, cleanliness, grooming), location of the act (slum, bar, home, suburb, park), sex and age of the suspected person, apparent socioeconomic status (occupation, education, income), and accessories (gun, knife, car). What did these witnesses or complainants really see or experience? Is the accused already known to or suspected by the police or other agents for deviant activities? If so, does this mental set predispose them to see behaviour as deviant and, perhaps, therefore criminal?

For example, if a man is known to be a member of a motorcycle gang (which is a deviant, but not a criminal, activity) will the police expect him to be a drug dealer as well? An arrest is only the beginning. Control agents must convince a court that there is enough evidence to justify the interpretation of an action as criminal deviance. Here again, judgment

CRACK'S DEADLY CYCLE

With their flashy clothes and hair arranged in dreadlocks, the six dealers stood out among the soberly dressed young executives on Vietnam Veterans' Plaza in Manhattan's financial district last week. They showed signs of nervousness as they moved back and forth between the plaza's benches and overflowing trash cans. Throughout the morning the dealers had been turning away customers—Wall Street messenger boys and unemployed kids—looking for crack, known locally as "jumps." Gesturing toward several policemen swinging their billy clubs in one corner of the park, one dealer said: "No jumps here, man. Bad for business."

[. . .] With frightening rapidity, crack had become the drug of choice throughout New York City. And public outrage is reaching feverish levels. Mayor Ed Koch, for one, has suggested that anyone convicted of large-scale drug deals should receive the death penalty. One recent poll showed that Americans considered the crack epidemic as one of the most serious problems in the United States.

But the same poll showed that many citizens question the motives of politicians engaged in the current crack crusade. Fully 60 percent of the 1,210 respondents said that they believed that most of the demands for so-called "crackdown" campaigns and for drug testing were merely publicity-seeking statements by elected officials.

But despite the rhetoric, the horrifying results of crack addiction are clearly visible—particularly in the poor, black inner-city areas of New York, Los Angeles and Miami. A survey of 576 U.S. hospitals reports that almost 15 percent of people admitted with cocaine-related health problems between January and March, 1986, had smoked crack. And crack-related crime in such predominantly black New York neighborhoods as Washington Heights in Manhattan and Bedford-Stuyvesant in Brooklyn has contributed to an alarming 23.5-percent rise in murders and a 12.2-percent rise in robberies in New York between January and June of this year and the same period last year. In addition, New York schools chancellor Nathan Quinones noted that police were making up to 20 percent of their recent arrests near elementary schools. Said Quinones: "Pushers know that here they have potential customers at their most vulnerable age."

Hunched over a kitchen table in a squalid apartment on Barclay Avenue in Montreal's Côte-des-Neiges district, Wayne, a lanky young man from Trinidad, carefully rotated the flaming heads of two match sticks around the base of a small, heat-resistant vial. Behind him, a cockroach skittered up the yellowing wall, but Wayne's gaze remained fixed on the vial's contents—a solution of water, baking soda and cocaine. By 7 a.m.

that day, Wayne and André, a Haitian-born procurer in his late 20s, had been using cocaine for four hours, first "cooking" the powder in a purifying solution, then smoking the "rocks" of crack that formed when he dipped the heated vial into a glass of cool water. The utensils they used in a technique known as a free-basing—including a glass pipe and a propane torch—were supplied by Junior, a Jamaican-born cocaine dealer who lives in the apartment.

[. . .] Some cocaine users call them "base houses," while others prefer the term "white houses"—and in Montreal the locations change as quickly as the terminology. One Montreal narcotics agent told *Maclean's* that he has heard of about 16 base houses in different parts of the city. Many are found in poor neighborhoods like Barclay Avenue, a run-down residential strip of red-brick apartment blocks. There, last April a man stabbed and killed another cocaine user in an early-morning quarrel at one of the local base houses. The police investigation curtailed local free-basing activities temporarily, but residents say that operations have now resumed. Said a 24-year-old Nova Scotian black who has lived on Barclay for 10 years: "Nobody sniffs coke anymore, they smoke. My uncle owned a record store and drove a BMW. He got into the pipe and now he has nothing."

Despite such cautionary tales, the free-basing houses continue to do business. At Junior's place, visitors came and went all day and night last week. After smoking his last hit of crack at 8 a.m.,

Wayne remained at the kitchen table, staring at the linoleum-tiled floor in search of a stray pebble of cocaine. Then two women and a regular customer known as "Bigfoot" came into the kitchen. Formerly a husky man, Bigfoot appeared drawn and thin under his blue tracksuit, and his friends attributed his weight loss to a diet of free-basing. As the three waited, apparently hoping that André would invite them to get high with him, a neighborhood marijuana dealer entered and announced that he had quit free-basing. Said the dealer: "There comes a point when you either turn around or let the pipe take you way down. I got to turn it around."

[. . .] But Wayne and André smoke each day until their money is gone. One day last week Wayne smoked until mid-afternoon. Then, edgy and ill-humored, he left the apartment, returning two hours later to purchase a gram of cocaine for about $120. When asked where he got the money, he replied that he had broken into a house and sold stereo equipment he found there for enough money to buy the cocaine. Wayne acknowledged that he is caught in a vicious circle: 15 minutes of euphoria followed by a crash into depression and a search for more cocaine. It is also chillingly clear that he and growing numbers of users have no wish to escape that bondage—and the brief moments of euphoria it provides.

may be affected by all the factors described above. A judge or jury must decide whom to believe, how seriously to weigh an allegation, how severely to judge an act (Brannigan 1979). Can even the most impartial judge separate fact from impression? Who is more likely to be considered deviant, and likely to be guilty of crime: a young woman in a business suit or one wearing a short leather skirt and studded belt? How much do such factors affect the examination of deviance? There is no clear agreement.

FORMS OF DEVIANCE

Deviance takes a bewildering array of forms. It could almost be asserted that any standard a society could form would be violated by some group. Perhaps each form of deviance has a different cause and each group a different characteristic. But the examination of any deviant individual or group, its lifestyle, and the response of society as a whole can reveal something about the nature of deviance and social control.

We could look at violent crime, such as murder and armed robbery (the incidence of which is increasing in Canada, although it is still lower than in the United States or many other Western countries); at crimes of property, such as theft or breaking and entering; or at subtler types of crime, such as fraud, embezzlement, and income tax evasion—so-called white-collar crime.

The use of illegal drugs is a particular type of deviance, different in some ways from other criminal deviance. The effects on a person's status may relate not just to the effects of the drug itself on health, behaviour, or lifestyle but also to the user's relationship with the deviant group using the drug and to social attitudes toward the drug and the group using it. For example, someone using marijuana or cocaine may become secretive in his or her habits (to avoid detection) and may become alienated from non-users. However, attitudes may shift a great deal; marijuana, once condemned as evil and dangerous, became so widely accepted and used during the 1970s that one might question whether using it was deviant at all. Today the push to decriminalize it seems to have lost steam, as new research suggests more health risks and as society becomes in some ways more conservative. While marijuana is still the most widely used illegal drug, use of cocaine is growing rapidly. The deviant users include both street kids and upper-class partygoers.

Neither the use of alcohol nor addiction to it is illegal (though public drunkenness is), but it is deviant to be alcoholic. Compulsive gambling is also deviant. In the extreme, compulsive overeating or compulsive self-starvation (anorexia nervosa) become forms of deviance, setting a person off from society.

Membership in certain groups or subcultures—motorcycle gangs, for example, or punks—marks one as deviant, as does membership in a conspicuous and not widely accepted religious group or a political group considered extremist.

There are many forms of sexual deviance, some more tolerated than others. Of course, the rapist or the molester of children is considered criminal (although the definitions of both categories have varied over time). The line separating acceptable from deviant sexual behaviour has, however, become blurry. Prostitutes are still deviant, although their legal status is unclear. But are the clients of prostitutes deviant?

The study of homosexuality is particularly interesting because of shifting attitudes among both homosexuals and society at large. Although homosexual acts have not been illegal in Canada since 1968, homosexuals are still subject to society's disapproval. But during the past 20 years or so, they have organized themselves into interest groups, political lobbies, churches, counselling agencies, and so on, constituting a social movement (Humphreys 1972). Many homosexuals have come out of the closet; in cities such as San Francisco, Toronto, and Vancouver, one can find entire gay circles of leisure, work, religion, and family. At what point should sociologists no longer consider homosexuality deviant? Some might argue that this point has arrived; after all, general acceptance has increased to the point at which the City of Toronto school board has discussed establishing a committee to protect the interests of gay high-school students. Although activists have not succeeded in having discrimination on the grounds of sexual orientation formally encoded in the Canadian Charter of Rights and Freedoms, many lawyers consider such discrimination to be in violation of the general terms of the Charter. However, widespread fear about acquired immune deficiency syndrome (AIDS), which came to public knowledge in the 1980s, may stem the tide of acceptance.

Gays have actively campaigned to assert their right to their own kind of difference.

WHY THE BOSS STEALS

It was a gamble that captivated the imagination of the Canadian public. On April 26, 1982, Brian Molony, assistant manager of a downtown Toronto branch of the Canadian Imperial Bank of Commerce, lost $1.4 million in six hours at an Atlantic city casino. The next day, he was arrested for speeding while driving downtown from Toronto's international airport. Police discovered $30,000 in American cash in the car. Then they began to suspect that the pudgy 27-year-old executive had defrauded the Bank of Commerce of $10.2 million through a series of false loans. During a later fraud trial, evidence showed that Molony—who only a few weeks before his arrest had been described as a man of "good judgment and proven ability to make decisions" by one of his superiors—had used the money to finance a two-year gambling spree. Molony was released after serving under two years of a six-year jail sentence. He had traded his corporate identity for membership in an exclusive club of businessmen: Canada's fraternity of white-collar criminals.

[. . .] Over the past decades, an increasing number of company presidents, politicians, doctors, lawyers, stockbrokers and many other well-educated Canadians have turned white-collar crime into big business. Smarter than most, prompted by greed, treated more gently by the justice system than the average thief, the typical white-collar criminal has until recently largely evaded punishment. Borders pose no obstacles to his activities, and police forces have just begun to catch up with his paper trail of illegalities. Indeed, experts say that the economic impact of white-collar crime easily outstrips that of bank robberies, violent thefts, burglary and other common types of property crime. White-collar crime is usually an "inside job," and the practitioner someone with a position of trust. Said prominent Toronto criminal lawyer Edward Greenspan: "We have gone from crime in the streets to crimes in the suites."

The evidence that the boss is pilfering on a grand scale mounts every week. In the past several years more and more professionals—some of them well-known and highly regarded—have paid fines or gone to jail for an increasingly wide range of crimes.

Documenting the impact of white-collar crime is difficult. Canada lacks research and statistics on economic crime. But in the United States, government estimates put the cost at as much as $44 billion a year. Canadian law enforcement officials say there is little reason to believe that there is proportionately less white-collar crime here. If that is so, the cost domestically would be more than $4 billion annually. By comparison, $2.8 million was lost in Canadian bank robberies last year.

There are other clues to the extent of white-collar criminal activity. In 1984 the RCMP's commercial crime division investigated

8,400 offences involving $336 million—about $100 million more than the previous year. A recent paper in the *Canadian Journal of Criminology* estimated that doctors were defrauding medical plans of as much as $400 million a year through practices such as billing for services never performed. And according to Statistics Canada, police reports on frauds—the most common of many white-collar crimes—increased by 42 per cent from 1976 to 1984. But experts say that statistics understate the problem. Declared University of Toronto criminologist Philip Stenning: "It is quite unreliable to rely on official police estimates; police just are not told of all the crimes."

[. . .] Government regulators and police officials include fraud, stock manipulation, money laundering, franchise frauds, cheating on government contracts and kickbacks in a wide variety of illegal activities in the business world. And in the United States, white-collar crime is expanding to include decisions taken by managers that result in injury or death. Some recent high-profile crimes include:

• Canada's largest cheque-kiting scheme, in which Toronto lawyer Steven Bookman was sentenced to 2½ years. Bookman had siphoned about $668,000 from the banking system over several weeks in 1982 by writing a series of phony cheques.

• A $7.2-million conspiracy in which two Ontario men, Louis Nadalin and Terence Alty, were sentenced to four years in prison in 1984 for defrauding 500 people who were promised large profits if they invested in vending machine operations.

• An $8-million Kitchener, Ont., real estate operation in which scores of investors were defrauded over a period of 15 years. Financier Gustav Ruder was sentenced to three years in 1985 after he sold farmland at inflated prices to investors who were led to believe that it would be developed.

• The 1981 $273,000 collapse of Atlantic Securities Ltd. of Halifax. Principals in the firm were convicted of fraud and theft and one of the company's founders was sentenced to four years in prison. Company executives had misrepresented Atlantic's financial situation to regulatory authorities.

In Canada, despite evidence of a growing problem, there have been few studies focusing on the new-style criminal. One of them was prepared for the federal solicitor general's office by the Toronto-based consulting firm Abt Associates of Canada in 1982. It noted, "Reliable information is clearly lacking." Added University of Calgary sociology professor and white-collar crime specialist Charles Reasons: "The United States is far ahead of us in terms of study and research—and in getting tough."

[. . .] As a criminal, the white-collar thief is a member of the elite. Usually an expert in the company he is preying upon, he often has a solid reputation in his community. Explained Dr. Selwyn Smith, psychiatrist-in-chief at the Royal Ottawa Hospital and president of the American Academy of Psychiatry and the Law: "The individuals in my experience have had excellent work records, come from very good backgrounds and have been high achievers. They are viewed by colleagues and friends alike as people who are highly successful and have attributes that are to be admired in general by society."

The white-collar criminal usually has a single motivation for breaking the law. Said Smith: "The bottom line is usually one of greed." Often, they do not set out to commit crimes. Instead, they seize an opportunity when it presents itself. Experts such as Smith say that such criminals often engage in questionable practices in an attempt to meet company objectives or in a last-ditch effort to rescue a failing business. Robert Fomon, chairman of New York-based stockbroking firm E.F. Hutton, which was fined $2 million last year for an elaborate cheque-kiting operation, said that it was a result of managers who "crossed the line" looking for a way to increase profits.

John R. Phillips, co-director of the Los Angeles-based Centre for Law in the Public Interest, suggests that cheating—such as the practice of inflating costs—starts not at the top of a company but among mid-level managers who are promoted on the basis of how well they run their departments. Often, he said, such managers rationalize their dishonest or illegal behavior as corporate loyalty.

Mental Disorder

One in eight Canadians can expect to be hospitalized for a mental disorder at least once during his or her lifetime (Statistics Canada 1981a). On the basis of self-report surveys, researchers have concluded that about one-quarter of the North American population is impaired by various types of psychological disorder (Hagan 1984, 53).

An examination of mental disorder reveals some of the controversies that plague discussions of deviance. What is mental, or psychiatric, disorder? Why are we considering it here as a form of deviance? A common-sense definition of deviance might exclude mental illness. Surely an illness cannot be considered in the same light as a pattern of behaviour chosen by a person or a label attached by society to certain behaviour? But it is clear that people considered mentally ill are treated as deviant: ridiculed, barred from certain positions and relationships, and generally stigmatized. At one time, when religious definitions held more sway than medical ones, mental disorder was considered to be caused by demonic possession.

Defining mental disorder in theory, much less applying this definition to actual cases, is still more an art than a science. Psychiatrists assume that mental patients present symptoms, as other medical patients do, and that these symptoms enable the trained professional to diagnose certain psychological disorders. They assume, that is, that mental disorders are objective phenomena.

Some psychiatrists see most mental illness as the result of traumatic experiences, especially during childhood. Others place more importance on physical causes, such as chemical imbalances in the brain. (Although it would be impossible to give in this chapter even the most general outline of current psychiatric theories, it should be noted that there is lively debate among psychiatrists as to the cause, classification, and treatment of mental disorder.)

Several sociologists and psychologists argue that the identification of mental disorder is even more complicated than psychiatrists are willing to admit. In a field experiment, Rosenhan demonstrated that psychiatric diagnoses incorporate symptoms that "are in the minds of the observers and not valid summaries of characteristics displayed by the observed" (1973, 251). Thomas Szasz, himself a psychiatrist, suggests that "to understand Institutional Psychiatry (or the mental health movement) we must study psychiatrists, not mental patients" (1970, 98).[1] After reviewing several studies, Scheff (1975) concludes that psychiatrists responsible for admitting patients to mental hospitals rely heavily on family and community definitions of an individual as psychologically unsound. He argues that friends, relatives, and co-workers use the concept of mental illness as a sort of vague catch-all to explain any actions that they consider unacceptable but that are not subsumed under the conventional categories of deviance.

> If people reacting to an offense exhaust the conventional categories that might define it (e.g., theft, prostitution, and drunkenness), yet are certain that an offense has been committed, they may resort to this residual category. In earlier societies, the residual category was witchcraft, spirit possession, or possession by the devil; today, it is mental illness. The symptoms of mental illness are, therefore, violations of residual rules. (Scheff 1975, 7)

Mental disorder as a violation of residual rules is a common-sense definition of this kind of deviance. People judge their behaviour and that of others by these rules.

The deviant career of mental patients has attracted considerable sociological attention. Cameron (1974), among others, notes that in the "pre-patient phase" of this career close friends and relatives often collude with psychiatric and legal agents to persuade such people to submit to a psychological examination—the first step in the process of being committed to a mental hospital or other treatment facility. This benign pressure ("it's for your own good") is necessary because few people voluntarily seek such treatment. Once institutionalized, mental patients soon discover that they are expected to act as if they belong there (Bursten and D'Esopo 1965; Rosenhan 1973). In other words, they are expected to manifest the stereotyped symptoms of their deviance, such as strange movements, incoherent talk, irrational thoughts and actions, or delusions about identity ("I'm Jesus Christ"). So which actions arise from a mental disorder and which are response to expectations? For that matter, what are the symptoms of mental illness? Which behaviour patterns are truly abnormal and which are within the range of normal human behaviour? The answers depend both on personal interpretation and on the medical, psychological, and sociological theory accepted.

Once released from the mental hospital, the ex-patient quickly learns that associates have not forgotten that he or she was once treated for psychological problems. Friends, relatives, and co-workers act, in many subtle ways, as if the ex-patient were still sick (Scheff 1984, 66-67; Nunnally 1961). For example, when such a person does something a family member thinks is strange, however reasonably the ex-patient may explain the act, the tendency is to view the behaviour as a manifestation of the remittent mental illness. "She let the roast burn? You see, her concentration is still off." "He got angry? Well, his equilibrium is pretty fragile; you can't be too careful what you say to him." Carlton Brown (1974) describes how the stigma of having been a mental patient contributed to the deterioration of some of his social and professional relationships in the community.

CONTROLLING DEVIANCE

When a form of deviance becomes intolerable, non-deviants seek ways to control it. Social control is an area of great concern to sociological **functionalists**, whose primary interest lies in the study of the achievement and maintenance of social order and stability. Here we will outline the principal elements of the mainstream functionalist control theories of Parsons (1951) and LaPiere (1954), among others, and the related theories of social scientists such as Reiss (1951) and Hirschi (1969). The common theme is the attribution of deviance to the failure of socialization, internalization, and commitment to conventional values and roles. All these theorists see deviance as the violation of norms owing to the misbehaving individual's inadequate control (Meier 1982, 46).

Phases of Control

The process of deviance and control begins with the value placed by society as a whole (or an influential or powerful segment of it) on a certain pattern of action and its harmonious fit with other patterns. This value is inherently conservative: those who uphold it want either no change or smooth, gradual change.

In the second phase of control, a variety of means are used to establish or preserve the desired pattern. For example, Whitehurst (1975, 433) argues that most Canadians value the monogamous marriage so much that some of them define as intolerable such alternatives as group marriage. Gossip, ridicule, and ostracism are among the ways in which they try to combat this threat.

Approaches to Control

People are offended or threatened by deviance in others. Consequently, society attempts to ensure conformity by positive or negative means.

Positive control is achieved through **internalization**, a process by which individual members of the society are socialized to play respectable roles. They come to identify so strongly with the values and norms of these roles that they willingly regulate their own actions, behaving in ways acceptable to their fellows (for more on this process of socialization, see Chapter 4.) When socialized individuals meet with an opportunity to deviate, their strong commitment to the established order leads them to snub the opportunity.

Positive social control achieves conformity to norms (laws, rules, and customs) through various rewards, such as praise, acclaim, ritual recognition (receiving an award or diploma), privilege, and money. (See Exhibit 12-3). These rewards, aside from their possible material benefits, symbolize society's approbation, which can also be conveyed in subtler ways.

Exhibit 12-3
Approaches to Social Control

| Phases | Approaches | |
	Positive	Negative
Value	Internalization	Compliance
Means	Praise	Fines
	Ritual	Imprisonment
	Acclaim	Death
	Privilege	Torture
	Money	Demotion
	Gifts	Scolding
	Promotion	Gossip
		Ridicule
		Satire
		Ostracism
		Firing

Such approbation is rewarding in itself and therefore likely to reinforce the individual's pattern of acceptable behaviour. Thus, the "good corporate employee," who has internalized the rule of "thou shalt not steal," not only rejects the opportunity to embezzle company funds but shrinks from the very thought. Such conformity brings the reward of pride in one's image as a trustworthy, responsible, devoted worker.

But some individuals and groups prefer certain behaviour to the ways of the majority. Potential deviants are defined by the dominant segment as in need of external control, since self-regulation is apparently lacking: coercive methods must be used to force their compliance with established values. These would-be deviants are compelled to live by moral standards they would reject were it not for the high cost of doing so. To keep

Deviance provokes some level of enforcement on the part of authorities. The ultimate form of enforcement in Canada is imprisonment.

potential deviants in line, those who accept the status quo threaten or actually use **negative social control**—means such as scolding, gossip, ridicule, satire, ostracism, firing or demotion, fines, imprisonment, torture, and death.

Types of Control

Means of social control may be formal or informal. Formal means are codified, scheduled, organized, or regulated in some way. They include positive means, such as ritual recognition, monetary payment, promotion, public satire, and mass media acclaim, and negative means such as firing, demotion, fines and imprisonment. Informal means of control, on the other hand, are casual, unwritten, sometimes spontaneous. They include positive means, such as gifts, casual praise, and smiles, and negative means, such as ridicule, gossip, ostracism, torture, and scolding. A single deviant action may be managed by both types of control. For instance, a man fired because of homosexual activities has probably also been ostracized and ridiculed; the firing itself leads to further ostracism. Exhibit 12-4 shows a cross-tabulation of the means of social control by approach and type.

Exhibit 12-4
Means of Social Control

Approach	Type	
	Formal	Informal
Positive	Ritual Money Privilege Promotion Mass media acclaim	Casual praise Gifts
Negative	Imprisonment Fines Public execution Demotion Satire Firing	Ridicule Ostracism Gossip Torture Scolding

Every society presumably uses all four means of control, for no society enjoys total acceptance of its social order by its members nor suffers total rejection of it. But the ratio of formal to informal and positive to negative means varies considerably from one culture to another. Totalitarian countries seem to rely more heavily on negative means than do democratic countries. Certainly, Canada falls closer to the positive pole than, say, present-day Iran or El Salvador. But negative means *are* used in this country to achieve and maintain an order defined as desirable by those in control. The existence of courts and prisons attests to the fact that some Canadians have, in Merton's terms (see Exhibit 12-1), innovated, retreated, or rebelled, and have been sanctioned for this wayward behaviour.

SUMMARY

Against the dictates of common sense, most sociologists take a relativist view of deviance. Human activity is not inherently deviant or non-deviant; rather, it is relative to the norms set by a particular society.

There are several theoretical explanations of deviance. Differential association explains deviance as a response to needs, learned by associating with committed deviants. Drawing on Durkheim's concept of anomie (normlessness), theorists such as Merton posit that deviance results from a malintegration of success goals and institutionalized means of reaching them. Other sociologists concentrate on the rule-makers rather than the rule-breakers, describing the process by which certain individuals are labelled as deviants. Conflict theorists take this idea further; they see rules as a reflection of the interests of dominant groups.

Deviance may be punishable by law, ignored by the law, or even protected by it. Some forms of deviance have an obvious victim, while others seem to affect only willing participants. In present-day Canada, deviance that does not victimize anyone seems to be more readily tolerated than victimizing deviance.

All societies develop means to control deviance. An examination of what is deviant and of how this deviance is controlled tells us much about the values and the structure of a particular society.

NOTE

1. Institutional psychiatry refers to psychiatric invervention imposed on people by others to the point that patients lose control over their relationship with the health professional.

FOR FURTHER READING

Bahr, H.M.
  1973 *Skid Row: An Introduction to Disaffiliation.* New York: Oxford University Press.
  This somewhat dated but still excellent review of the theories of and research about skid row concentrates largely on American skid rows but has occasional references to those in Canada.
Foster, M., and K. Murray
  1972 *A Not So Gay World.* Toronto: McClelland and Stewart.
  Two journalists travel from Vancouver to St. John's to gain, through observation and selected interviews, a sense of the lifestyles of Canadian homosexuals.
Goffman, E.
  1961 *Asylums.* Garden City, N.Y.: Doubleday.
  In this participant-observer study of an American mental hospital, life in the institution is seen through the eyes of the inmates.
  1963 *Stigma.* Englewood Cliffs, N.J.: Prentice-Hall.
  This book is an essay on the nature and effects of stigma, or spoiled identity, among the physically and mentally abnormal and the morally deviant.
Lemert, E.M.
  1982 "Issues in the study of deviance." Pp. 233-57 in M.M. Rosenberg, R.A. Stebbins, and A. Turowetz, eds., *The Sociology of Deviance.* New York: St. Martins.
  One of the most respected scholars of deviance comments on some of the main theoretical issues presently facing the sociological study of deviance including the definition of deviance, the nature of the deviant act, and the critiques of the deviance research by radical criminologists.
Prus, R., and C.R.D. Sharper
  1977 *Road Hustler: The Career Contingencies of Professional Card and Dice Hustlers.* Lexington, Mass.: D.C. Heath.
  A sociologist and a full-time road hustler conducted this participant-observer and unstructured-interview study of Canadian and American professional gamblers.
Prus, R., and S. Irini
  1980 *Hookers, Rounders, and Desk Clerks.* Toronto: Gage.
  This book is a study of social organization and deviance in the hotel community in a rundown area of a major Canadian city.

Quinney, R.

1970 *The Social Reality of Crime*. Boston: Little, Brown.

One of the first statements of the new criminology, this work is still one of the most influential theoretical studies.

Rosenhan, D.L.

1973 "On Being Sane in Insane Places." *Science* 179: 250-58.

Rosenhan, a psychologist, and several other sane people are admitted as pseudopatients to twelve different mental hospitals, where they experience at first hand how inmates are treated there.

Tripp, C.A.

1975 *The Homosexual Matrix*. New York: McGraw-Hill.

A thorough and scientifically impeccable account of the nature, origin, and consequences of being homosexual in modern industrial society. This work is also very readable.

CHAPTER 13

CANADIAN POLITICAL ECONOMY

Wallace Clement

The first issue of the Canadian journal *Studies in Political Economy* defined **political economy** in its broadest sense as an "interdisciplinary blend of the history of economics, political *and* cultural relations" (1979, v-vi).[1] In Canada the term refers to a specific tradition of scholarship, ranging in its assumptions from liberal to Marxist, which has experienced a revitalization since the mid-1970s. Canadian sociology has both contributed to political economy during this period and been reshaped and redefined by it. It can be said without overstating the case that Canadian sociology has had its most dynamic and innovative movements when it has intersected with political economy. The classic work of S.D. Clark originally flourished alongside liberal political economy; later John Porter wrote in debate with Marxist political economy; today many sociologists are working within a Marxist tradition of political economy.

Fundamentally, political economy is a holistic approach to the understanding of society from a materialistic perspective. Many of the classic works within sociology are based in this approach; those by Karl Marx are paramount. Originally the social sciences—history, economics, psychology, philosophy, political science, sociology, and anthropology—were all understood to be contained within political economy. As specialization became the hallmark of these various disciplines, the broad strokes painted by political economists began to be submerged. Sociology, the most eclectic of the modern disciplines, tended, however, to remain in touch with its political-economy traditions, even though its major subfields became specialties in their own right.

In the 1970s, many Canadian sociologists joined with economists, political scientists, historians, and anthropologists to address common concerns and issues. With the re-emergence of Canadian political economy, sociology has proved its significant place in this interdisciplinary arena.

THE MEANING OF POLITICAL ECONOMY

If sociology is understood as the study of relationships between people, then a **political-economy perspective on sociology** means understanding these relationships as the development of economic, political, and cultural/ideological phenomena combined. Political economy is the study of this totality, a totality understood in a particular way. First and foremost, the focus is materialist, which means that the relationships between people are fundamentally understood in terms of the way a society reproduces itself, that is, how its people make a living—as subsistence producers, producers of goods for sale (simple commodity producers), or wage earners—and are able to continue as social beings.

It is at the point of production that the understanding of human relationships begins for a materialist analysis, but it does not end there. The analysis is also historical and dynamic since it seeks to understand the motion of society and the forces of change as production and reproduction become transformed. Thus, political economy seeks out the tensions within a society—those forces producing struggle and resistance to the prevailing order. Finally, as will be discussed shortly, it incorporates an understanding of the cultural/ideological moments of society.

A Materialist Approach

Saying that political economy takes a **materialist approach** to examining society means that the starting point of analysis is the way a society meets its basic economic needs—that is, the way the production of goods and services is organized. Materialists recognize that production is an inherently social and political phenomenon shaped by the way people are organized to relate to one another. Every system of production needs to be justified, and people participating in it must be convinced that it is generally right, just, and proper. (Usually this conviction takes the form of a popular belief that the way production is currently organized is somewhat natural. Without some such belief, people must be coerced into participating, and coercion can be sustained for only limited periods of time.)

An **idealist approach** to the organization of society—which is the opposite to a materialist one—begins with the values, beliefs, or attitudes of people and from these explains society's workings. From a materialist perspective, the subjective characteristics are what require explanation; they do not, on their own, explain anything. They are, however, integral to the reproduction of society, to what is often referred to as the ideological or cultural levels rooted in an economic base. An idealist argues, for example, that people in liberal democracies, such as Canada, hold, as a core value, equality of opportunity for each individual; hence, they organize their society to correspond to this ideal. A materialist, on the other hand, contends that the ideology of equality of opportunity is a justification for the structural inequalities of the capitalist mode of production, which requires that a few people accumulate capital while many are dispossessed from the means of realizing their own labour (working for themselves) and thus must sell their labour power to others (work for wages). The ideology serves to justify inequalities inherent in such a system and places blame for failure squarely on the shoulders of the individuals who fail to succeed. In other words, capitalist relations of production require the general belief that everyone has an equal chance to succeed (as measured by the ability to accumulate capital) and that those who fail deserve to fail because of their own lack of abilities, skills, or luck. These are fundamental assumptions of liberalism—all individuals can determine their own fates, and individual actions in aggregate make society. A materialist analysis is less concerned with the individual than with the social relations that follow from the way a society is organized into classes, but it does recognize that conscious, active people are located within these class relations and have the capacity to change them.

The Historical Dimension

Another important aspect of the materialist approach is the recognition of process and change; hence it insists on the historical dimension of society. The way society is currently organized depends on the past. The organization of society is the working out of patterns and relationships that result from the way production and reproduction are organized. Thus, materialism is never static. It never regards capitalism or any other mode of production as a uniform and timeless way to organize society. Production takes different forms at various periods and in various places. Central to a materialist understanding is the unfolding of both the social and the technical class changes contained within capitalism. A great deal of Canadian political economy has focused on these processes within Canada and on the ways they have been influenced by relations with the great imperial powers of the United Kingdom and the United States.

The Political and Cultural/Ideological Dimensions

The best of political economy (including, one hopes, that which is now being created in Canada) has sought to avoid **economism** (economic-determinist arguments), which contends that everything in Western society follows naturally from the laws of motion of capitalism. It has sought to impregnate materialism with what is known as **human agency** (the importance of the actions of people in affecting the course of history). This is why political economy at its best incorporates the political and cultural/ideological within a materialist understanding. While the economic provides the context, it is the political and the cultural/ideological that write the text of history, the particularities of each nation, and the possibilities for the future. The script is one in which human actors have significant freedom of action.

Politics here means not simply the government, but all power relations, whether they involve nations, workers, or family members. The term contains the notion of contradictory or conflicting relations and the idea of struggle or resistance as a dynamic. What occurs within the workplace, within unions, or between the sexes is as political as elections. It is a struggle for social control. Such a notion of what is political fundamentally alters the idea of democracy, stretching it from a mere kind of government to the way people are organized, coordinated, and controlled in all aspects of their lives.

Culture/ideology is the meaning people attach to their lives—the way they understand and justify what they do and who they are, and the guidelines they use for their behaviour. Culture/ideology is both inherited and created; each person is subject to the socialization of the dominant assumptions of his or her society, but each person also has the capacity to challenge those assumptions and to develop new ones. Included within culture/ideology are religion, cultural traditions, sexism, and class-consciousness—the values, attitudes, interests, and ideals people hold. In political economy these factors are not seen as autonomous. They arise out of and help shape people's material existence. They are in a dynamic, integral relation to the political and economic realities.

POLITICAL ECONOMY IN CANADA

Political economy is by no means confined to Canada, but examining its European roots would take us too far afield. Neither will I outline the various traditions of political economy that have arisen in Canada, since this has been done elsewhere (see Drache 1979; Drache and Clement 1985). My focus will be on Canada's New Political Economy tradition, which tends to be critical and founded on the classic writings of Pentland, Macpherson, and Ryerson, often in debate with the contribution of Innis.

H. Clare Pentland

H. Clare Pentland

H. Clare Pentland has had a profound impact on the revitalized Canadian political-economy tradition, even though his major works were unpublished during his lifetime.[2] He is noted less for his theoretical contribution than for his example of careful, detailed scholarship.

Pentland investigated the process of capital accumulation and making of a working class in Canada, posing two basic questions: "How are workers induced to flow into the labour market pool? And how are they prevented from flowing out again?" (1959, 450). Using these questions as his guide, Pentland forged the most thorough analysis within Canadian political economy to date. He argued that the development of a capitalist labour market flowed from three factors: the steady demand for labour resulting from extensive transportation, construction, and creation of a home market for manufactured goods; the limited access to the land, which forced immigrants to work for wages; and the way immigration policy focused on groups prepared to remain in wage labour. The capitalistic labour market did not develop suddenly or without resistance, however, and its impact was uneven throughout the country. Pentland's analysis of changes in the mode of production, in the demand for labour (both in quantity and skill), and in state policies governing immigration and industrial relations, like his understanding of industrial and resource workers as well as the petite bourgeoisie, all located within specific regional contexts, was profound not only because of its scope but also because of the way he integrated his studies with the central issues of Canadian political economy.

Although Pentland's analysis was fundamentally materialist (being centred on the way society organizes production), he was sensitive to the political and cultural/ideological activities of the population. Clearly he did not exhaust the possibilities for research, but he initiated a valuable line of enquiry that has become central to the recent revival of Canadian political economy.

C.B. Macpherson

C.B. Macpherson's impact has been dramatically different from Pentland's. Macpherson began with the path-breaking *Democracy in Alberta* ([1955] 1968), an innovative analysis of class struggle by the agrarian petite bourgeoisie in the face of national and international forces. It is an analysis of ideology, class politics, and the dynamic of resistance as experienced in the Canadian West during the 1930s. His major contribution, however, has been the developing of theories of liberal democracy, property, and possessive individualism (Macpherson 1962; 1977; 1978; 1985).

Unfortunately, Macpherson's impact was stronger in Europe than in Canada until the revival of Canadian political economy, for much of which his work has served as a theoretical guide. The clarity of his thinking and the innovations he brought to Marxist analysis (particularly his understanding of the state) have provided intellectual direction to those seeking to explain Canadian society in materialist terms. Although Macpherson's theoretical writings may not speak specifically to Canada, the issues he addresses and the insights he provides are of direct relevance. More than any other writer, Macpherson has set the theoretical

C.B. Macpherson   *Stanley B. Ryerson*

foundation for political economy in Canada; the closer it adheres to his insights, the stronger will be the analytical base of the revival.

Stanley B. Ryerson

In a way resembling Pentland more closely than Macpherson, Stanley B. Ryerson has also had a major impact on Canadian political economy. Many students have found his two major substantive works, *The Founding of Canada* (1960) and *Unequal Union* (1968), valuable points of entry into the revival of political economy. Based less on original research than on a re-interpretation of history, these works have helped political economists better understand the formation of the Canadian state, its flaws and contradictions, and the importance of class forces in history.

Ryerson's most important role in his two major studies and elsewhere (for example, 1972) has probably been interpreting Quebec for an English-speaking audience. A controversial figure whose views have often been challenged, Ryerson has nevertheless made an important contribution to the revival of political economy. He provided an alternative to Innis's interpretation (see the following subsection) giving centrality to class forces in Canadian history and showing sensitivity to the struggles of the Quebec people.

Harold Adams Innis

Harold Adams Innis

Harold Adams Innis was a little earlier than the other scholars in this list, but his work, in the classic liberal tradition, was the background for much of the revival of the 1970s. Perhaps most important was his famous **staples thesis**: that Canada, as a white settler society, was developed in order to exploit a series of raw materials for advanced metropolitan nations. Each staple had its own peculiarities and left its mark on Canada's pattern of development. Common to them all, however, was a dependence on export markets beyond the control of producers, which led to underdevelopment of the manufacturing capacity within Canada. The early staples of fish, fur, and timber, destined for European markets, were organized by commercial capitalists oriented to those markets. The later industrial staples of pulp and paper, minerals, and energy, destined for the United States, were organized directly by its capitalists to meet their requirements. Each staple imposed specific requirements on Canada. Of particular importance was the development of a transportation infrastructure for exporting bulky products—thus, the extensive investments in ports, roads, railways, canals, and pipelines, to the relative neglect of an industrial capacity. Innis examined various staples in terms of their "linkages" to other developments: backward linkages, such as the development of the instruments of production necessary to exploit the resource (for example, mining equipment); forward linkages involved in the processing of the resource (for example, the milling, smelting, refining, and manufacturing of mineral products); and demand linkages created by the economic activities associated with servicing the society (for example, consumer goods). Canada failed, Innis argued, to capture adequately the benefits of these various linkages because of its inferior power relationship with the major metropolitan centres. Because of this failure, Canada moved from "colony to nation to colony" and was locked into a spiral of dependence and subject to severe fluctuations in the world economy (Innis [1930] 1956a; [1930] 1956b; 1936; [1940] 1978).[3]

Overview of the New Political Economy

Clearly, Canadian political economy is a hybrid of several intellectual traditions. Its classical mode was dominated by a liberal tradition best exemplified in the work of Innis; its revival has been strongly influenced by Marxist thought. Yet this historical split is by no means absolute. John Richards and Larry Pratt's important recent study, *Prairie Capitalism: Power in the New West* (1979), for example, is not Marxist, while the classic works of Ryerson, Macpherson, and Pentland were influenced by Marxist assumptions.

Perhaps it is best to say simply that Pentland, Macpherson, Ryerson, and Innis provided the intellectual fodder for the revival of Canadian political economy. As much distinguishes them as draws them together, but the basic positions they set continue to be the major lines of debate. Possibly because of these diverse roots, Canadian political economy not only tolerates but also invites critical thinking about its core concepts. No one of the stature of these founders has emerged to set the tone for investigation, and it is not likely that anyone will; the enterprise has become such a diverse community of scholars that it cannot have one heart (or head). The revival has been more a cooperative effort than the result of any dominant influence.

Some of the earliest of the "new" political economists—Kari Levitt, Mel Watkins, Tom Naylor, and Wallace Clement—tended to focus on the development of particular types of capital in Canada in relation to external capital (initially from the United Kingdom, then from the United States), to the relative neglect of class foundation within Canada. No one within the political-economy tradition would argue that the international context is less than central, but making it the sole focus leads to a tendency to analyze factions of the capitalist class in isolation from other classes. The same type of criticism can be levelled at those—such as the early Macpherson, Greg Kealey, and Bryan Palmer—who have concentrated on either the working class or petite bourgeoisie without locating their development in relation to capital. The essence of a class analysis is the social relations involved, but the political-economy tradition in Canada has been guilty of the relative neglect of this central tenet, and is only

Mel Watkins

recently overcoming this flaw. (I argue that it is a flaw because the struggles and resistance of dominated classes have a direct bearing on the nature of capital formation and patterns of development. So to omit the relationship between classes is to admit a limited dynamic, thus restricting the ability to understand social change.)

Particularly in contrast to Pentland and Ryerson, Innis has been criticized for failing to integrate a class dynamic into his analysis of staples. David McNally concludes that "Innis's staple theory has no common ground with Marx's historical materialism" because it is founded on "commodity fetishism" and on a "technicist conception of production" that considers "the creation of material things but not as the reproduction of social relations" (McNally 1981, 56-57). Yet Daniel Drache (1982) and Mel Watkins (1982) continue to build on the Innis tradition and to argue for the continued vitality and richness of his insights, stressing the inherent value of an evolving, indigenous political-economy tradition.

Debate over labour has been equally profuse, turning to some extent on the same issues as the debate over Innis, except this time the key point is the importance of culture/ideology versus economic structures. (See, for example, Kealey 1981; Bercuson 1981; Morley 1979; and Palmer 1979a.)

However brief this overview, it should be clear that Canadian political economy is not a uniform discipline and does not represent a specific political or ideological position. Rather, it is a somewhat amorphous collection of various perspectives, approaches, and subjects. There is no universally accepted methodology or theory. Virtually all its writers provide limited examinations of specific topics and time periods—although their works do fit, in a loose way, into an overall picture of what Canada is and how it developed. On the whole, the contributors to Canadian political economy take into account the work of others and frequently disagree with their interpretations. Its short history has included many debates—a sign of its vibrance—both within the tradition and between those within political economy and those in established disciplines. Most practitioners continue to be based in these disciplines: for example, Greg Kealey and Brian Palmer within history; Tom Naylor and Mel Watkins in economics; Leo Panitch and Larry Pratt in political science; Patricia Marchak and R. James Sacouman in sociology. Although active within their respective disciplines, they share the assumption that the confines of specializations contain their understanding of society, while political economy expands their horizons, knowledge, and ability to make convincing arguments.

SOME FINDINGS IN CANADIAN POLITICAL ECONOMY

It is evident that the New Political Economy in Canada is undergoing a period of consolidation and rethinking, questioning its roots and re-evaluating its arguments. Moreover, the work has not developed to the point at which one can say it offers a systematic set of propositions arrived at by careful research. Rather, it is in a blooming stage: basic features of the society have been identified. The following list shows 15 of these features. They are not distinct—each overlaps with and affects the others—but each has been identified as an important aspect of Canadian political economy, and serves as the focal point for specific arguments. Taken together, they indicate something of the totality of Canadian political economy and the issues it is addressing.[4]

1. The importance of external relations for Canada's internal development, particularly its colonial ties with France and the United Kingdom and its more recent dependence on the United States. This feature has been common throughout the Canadian political-economy tradition from the early writings of Innis ([1930] 1956) and Creighton ([1937] 1956) to more recent writings, such as those by Levitt (1970), Naylor (1975), and Clement (1975). External dependence has been the subject of important government inquiries, most notably the Watkins Report (Task Force on the Structure of Canadian Industry 1970), the Gray Report (Task Force on Foreign Direct Investment in Canada 1972), and the studies of the Science Council of Canada.

2. Canada's origin in a staples economy, its movement into commercial and financial specialization, and its continued reliance on resource extraction—a factor directly related to the previous one.[5] Innis ([1930] 1956; 1936; [1940] 1978) has been the most prominent proponent of the staples thesis. Recent Science Council of Canada studies have documented the continued reliance on raw materials with limited processing for export (Bourgault 1972; Britton and Gilmour 1978). Several studies have examined the "successful" staples of wheat in Upper Canada (McCallum 1980) and energy in western Canada (Richards and Pratt 1979), thus challenging the original staples thesis. Even though Canada has become an industrial society, there is little question that it continues to rely on resource development, such as megaprojects in gas and oil and hydropower development, while major regions of the country depend heavily on exports of forest products, minerals, grains, and fish production.

3. Canada's dependence on external markets, both as outlets for raw materials (which make the domestic economy vulnerable to world conditions) and as capital resources (which ultimately drain investment capital).[6]

4. The effect of technology and its ownership, especially patent rights, in shaping the economy and labour force.[7] Canada continues to import the science and labour-intensive machinery used in resource extraction, while it exports raw materials with limited processing. Its industrial base tends to be dominated by branch-plant industries, such as the automotive industry, which are vulnerable to de-industrialization during periods of recession. Another result is limited research and development within Canada; therefore, there are few jobs within this activity, and Canada is dependent on foreign-generated and foreign-owned technology.

5. Canada's role as a go-between in the world system, acting as an intermediary, especially in finance, for many U.S.-based multinational corporations operating out of Canada, and also as a base for Canada's own multinationals.[8] Canada is the location of important multinational corporations, such as the dominant banks and life-insurance companies that are powerful in the world economy. It has also been used by foreign companies to penetrate other markets. For example, in order to take advantage of preferential tariffs, the Ford Motor Company uses its Canadian subsidiary to control operations in Australia, New Zealand, Singapore, and South Africa. Thus, Canada has an ambiguous position within the world system, being both host to many branch plants and base for multinational operations in other countries.

6. The implications of being such a large country with expansive, sparsely populated areas next door to the largest industrial giant in the world. Traditional staples arguments stress the constraints imposed by ge-

ography, especially the rapids of the St. Lawrence River, the Laurentian Shield, the Rockies, and the North.[9]

7. The tremendous cost of transportation networks, from early roads, canals, ports, seaways, and railways to modern pipelines for gas and oil, and the role of these networks in creating a national and continental economy. This factor is related to the previous one, as well as to the need to exploit the country's resource riches and to transport them for export. The costs of developing transport systems have been a particularly heavy burden on the Canadian state and have stimulated the government to be particularly interventionist in supporting economic development.

Canadian workers have become aware of the extent to which they are dependent on foreign-based multinational corporations.

8. The continued active role in the economy of the Canadian state with its fragmented federal-provincial structure, aggravated by resource dependence and foreign investments. This fragmentation results from a constitutional split: federal responsibility for major transportation systems to secure and export resources and provincial jurisdiction over the extraction of these resources.[10] The Canadian state has also been particularly interventionist in labour relations, another area in which the split in jurisdictions has an impact.[11]

9. The persistence of enormous regional differences within the country. The under-development of the Atlantic region and of the northern sections of the central and western provinces are expressions of uneven development.[12] Political economists analyze regionalism as a social relationship involving class struggle, not simply as federal-provincial government relations, as is often the case with political scientists.

10. The role of immigration in filling the West during the early stages of development (1879 to 1914) and the urban centres of today (especially Montreal, Toronto, and Vancouver). This factor has been important in building an indigenous labour force and domestic market and in creating an ethnically diverse society that is stratified by class.[13]

11. The persistence of the petite bourgeoisie class (largely farmers) as the most powerful class outside the capitalists until the Second World War. While Canada was largely rural with an agrarian/resource base, this large "third class," standing between capital and labour, had an important impact on the way class struggles emerged, particularly the way the state was used as a forum for class conflict.[14]

12. The continued existence of a large resource-based proletariat situated in isolated, single-industry communities built around mining, minerals, timber, pulp and paper, fishing, and hydroelectric power.[15] The resource proletariat in Canada has been particularly militant but also somewhat apart from the industrial struggles of the urban working class.

13. The relatively slow development of an urban industrial working class, the product of large-scale industrialization, which did not become a dominant force in Canada until well into the 20th century, and which continues today to be rivalled in importance by the service sector of the labour force, especially state workers, adding to an already overdeveloped commercial sector. Palmer (1979) and Kealey (1980) have produced excellent studies of Hamilton and Toronto industrial workers, but industrial labour outside this manufacturing heartland is less developed. Recently the state sector has become particularly well developed; in fact, much class conflict since the 1970s has focused on state employees' struggles for recognition and against cutbacks.[16]

In Canada, a large proletariat is situated in single-industry communities built around a resource such as timber.

14. The United States' cultural dominance of English-speaking Canada through the arts, education, and the media; in parallel is the reaction to this dominance, in the form of variants of nationalism.[17]

15. Finally, the continued survival of two nations—the conquering English and the conquered French—within a single state and the demise of the native people, along with the reactions of the repressed minorities.[18] Canada's duality is mirrored within its political-economy tradition. English-speaking political economists have not given the position of Quebec the attention it merits, but within Quebec has emerged a sophisticated, French-speaking political-economy tradition.

Women's Studies

The study of women in Canadian political economy, as in most areas of intellectual inquiry, has been relatively neglected, although a flurry of studies have appeared since the late 1970s. A handful of examples here can suggest some recent research in this area.

Pat and Hugh Armstrong's *The Double Ghetto* (1978) uses labour-force data to examine the occupational segregation of women, demonstrating that female labour-force participation has involved women in a segregated work world that functions as a form of low-pay, low-skill, low-authority, and dead-end career ghetto. The same authors' *A Working Majority* (1983) and Pat Armstrong's *Labour Pains* (1984) are major studies of women's work located in the context of the effects of the economic crisis.

Women's work in the paid labour force in Canada is, for the most part, a source of low-cost and expandable labour reserve, while domestic labour continues to consume much of women's energies. Patricia Connelly's *Last Hired, First Fired* (1978) examines the historically developing relationship between domestic and wage work for women in Canada. Using Marx's concept of a reserve army of labour in the context of capitalist development as her starting point, Connelly demonstrates that changes in the demand for labour in Canada determine women's participation in both domestic and wage labour. Charlene Gannagé links paid work in the garment industry with women's domestic labour in *Double Day, Double Bind* (1986).

Domestic labour is the focus of the collection *Hidden in the Household* (Fox 1980), a sophisticated theoretical treatment of reproduction under capitalism. Meg Luxton's *More Than a Labour of Love* (1980) is a case study of domestic labour in the mining community of Flin Flon, Manitoba. She convincingly argues the importance of women's work in the home for the reproduction of capitalism, treating domestic labour as a labour process subject to significant changes as capitalism itself transforms. An important extension of this analysis is contained in Luxton and Rosenberg's *Through the Kitchen Window* (1986).

Each of these studies is a valuable contribution to Canadian political economy, but the tradition will not reach maturity until women are an integral part of *all* investigations and do not require separate, special studies.

DOING POLITICAL ECONOMY

Questions and Data

For sources of data, political economists tend to rely heavily on archival documents from political, business, and labour organizations,[19] on government census and labour-force data (which are not without their problems, since the state tends to gather its statistics for the purpose of understanding features of the labour market rather than for class analysis), and on interviews with business, state, and labour leaders and with workers. Survey data are less frequently used, mainly because of the expense. However, several national surveys of class (conducted at York University and Carleton University) have been undertaken recently to provide systematic data on class formation, class structure, class consciousness, and the labour process (see Black and Myles 1986).

The way data are gathered has less importance than the way they are

DOING POLITICAL ECONOMY: AN ILLUSTRATION

In an attempt to better understand class structure and dynamics in Canada, I am engaged in a series of projects designed to disaggregate and recombine patterns of class relations. In addition to the part described here, the study will comprise examinations of the political and ideological expressions of class formations within the fishing industry and a national survey of class structure and the labour process. When the series of case studies is combined with the survey data, I expect the result to be a more thorough understanding of class than has hitherto been possible.

The first case study has been published as *Hardrock Mining*. I selected this area for study because it includes both resource and industrial production in its underground and surface operations. The study begins by tracing the class structure of Canadian mining. Initially, Canadian mining (such as placer gold mining in the Klondike) was organized by independent commodity producers; it came under the control of capitalists through their control of mining properties (formal subordination of labour) and eventually through the introduction of large dredges, and thus their control of the labour power of miners themselves (real subordination of labour). After tracing these developments, mostly using secondary sources such as Innis's "Settlement in the Mining Frontier" (1936), I concentrated on changes in the social relations under capitalist production, using the example of the International Nickel Company of Canada.

The most obvious change in mining since the Second World War involved the companies' introduction of technology to reduce reliance on labour. Mining companies were induced to mechanize underground operations and automate surface plants in part by the traditional militancy of Canadian miners and by problems in obtaining skilled workers. To research these developments, I began by examining industry publications, such as the *Canadian Mining Journal*, to understand developments in technology; company annual reports and histories (such as Thompson and Beasley's *For the Years to Come: A Story of International Nickel of Canada* [1960]) to find out about company practices; and union publications (such as *Miners' Voice*) to find workers' response. Armed with this backgound and a familiarity with the language of mining, I contacted the company and union locals involved and arranged to interview key officials and tour the mines and plants, selecting sites so I could observe both traditional and modern operations. From among Inco's mines I chose both traditional mines (such as Crean Hill), which had not been highly mechanized, and those which were highly mechanized (such as Levack

West); from among the surface operations I selected both modern and traditional mills, smelters, and refineries. I travelled to Sudbury and Port Colborne, Ontario, and to Thompson, Manitoba, as well as to the Sheridan Park Research Laboratory, to see the actual labour processes and to talk to miners, supervisors, and managers. Many of these interviews were recorded and used in the latter analysis.

Once the information was gathered, it was placed within the context of the political economy of mining to explain the developments I had discovered. The international context was important to understand the booms and busts experienced by the miners, mainly as layoffs and labour shortages. The political context was important to understand state policies concerning royalties, concessions, markets (such as the building of Thompson), and health and safety issues. (For the last, background submissions and testimony at the Royal Commission on the Health and Safety of Workers in Mines were useful.) The structure of unions and political struggles between them (particularly the conflict between the Mine, Mill and Smelter Workers' Union and the Union Steel Workers of America) revealed something about the militancy of miners and their ideologies. Also important to understanding developments was the geographical isolation of the single-industry town, such as Thompson, and dependency on a single resource, such as occurs in Sudbury.

The primary theme that emerged from the study was the dynamic between managerial strategies and workers' resistance. This focused on the introduction of technology and training practices designed to reduce the number and skills of workers. Related to this was the 1978–79 strike at Inco, which was the largest strike in Canadian history and has taken on particular cultural and ideological significance for the Canadian working class.

While this study in and of itself uses a political-economy approach in both the kinds of questions asked and explanations offered, its full value will not be evident until it is compared to a variety of other case studies and placed within the context of the national class structure.

For additional information see Clement (1981; 1980).

analyzed—that is, what informs the data, the categories used, the questions posed, and so on. Evidence is data of any sort that objectively informs and is informed by logical argument. Thus, the sources of data for political economy range from figures on capital formation to informal discussions with workers. There are no barriers between the political-economy tradition and the type of information that is potential evidence. What is important is the type of question posed to inform, organize, and present the data.

Analysis

Political economy operates at several levels of analysis, from highly abstract (for example, the laws of motion of capitalism) to very concrete (the experiences and activities of individuals). The best or most complete form of analysis is one that can operate at several levels, using abstractions to inform and guide research—thus increasing the explanatory power of the investigation—but also using the specifics of the concrete to evaluate, reinforce, and develop the abstract.

A description of two papers from the same issue of *Studies in Political Economy* can illustrate the different levels of analysis within the political-economy tradition. Michael Lebowitz's "The General and the Specific of Marx's Theory of Crisis" (1982) is an example of an abstract analysis. As the title indicates, Lebowitz examines the crisis of capitalism with respect to general and specific barriers to its expansion. Throughout, the paper remains at a high level of abstraction concerning the laws of motion in capitalism, but the author introduces the importance of political considerations to the development of capitalism and, particularly relevant for Canada, the implications of natural-resource development for the productivity of capitalism. Contained within the paper are analytical tools directly relevant for the enrichment of Canadian political economy.

Carl Cuneo's "The Politics of Surplus Labour in the Collapse of Canada's Dependence on Britain 1840–49" (1982) is a concrete analysis. Using detailed archival research, the author argues that class relations in Canada and Britain (including their respective internal class relations) explain the crisis in capitalism that led to Canada's movement out of the British sphere of influence and into one dominated by the United States. In this analysis Cuneo considers not only the economic factors underlying the crisis but also the political and ideological struggles waged. At the core of his argument is the struggle in Canada over gaining surplus value internally and internationally and the ensuing crisis that resulted, in part, from resistance by dominated classes. His analysis of political struggles and state policies is located within the material conditions of the various classes and class fractions involved.

These two articles, each at a different level of abstraction, offer powerful explanations of Canada's pattern of development. One is based exclusively on a theory of crisis, while the other is a concrete examination of the factors involved in a specific crisis. Each provides considerable insight into Canadian political economy.

SUMMARY

Canadian political economy acknowledges that Canadians have conditions in common with all people, particularly with all people in advanced capitalist societies. Yet it also recognizes the peculiarities of each social formation and the need to understand the conditions unique to Canada.

Political economy is a diverse tradition that is drawn together by one overriding concept: the totality of the cultural/ideological, the political, and the economic. Each is a part of a larger whole, a whole that is founded on a materialist understanding of society. Each dimension has its history and place within the totality.

The lesson of political economy is that divisions between disciplines have served as blinders. As windows on the world, the social disciplines have failed to reveal the panorama that includes the breadth of the horizon and the dynamic of history. The society, culture, economy, and polity of a nation are a totality, having a common history, present, and future. To abstract one of these elements without being aware of its broader context is to isolate and stifle it. This is to say not that everything must be related to everything else all the time, but that each facet can be illuminated by its context and location. The tradition of political economy is attempting to facilitate this broader vision so that Canadians can better understand the conditions they have inherited and make their future in light of that understanding.

NOTES

1. *Studies in Political Economy*, a scholarly journal, was the result of several years of work by political economists. Earlier publishing outlets were mainly disciplinary journals, such as the *Canadian Review of Sociology and Anthropology*, the *Canadian Journal of Political Science*, the *Canadian Journal of Economics*, and the *Canadian Historical Review*. Other, more specialized interdisciplinary journals such as the *Journal of Canadian Studies*, *Labour/Le Travailleur*, and the *Canadian Journal of Social and Political Theory*, also include work within political economy. The revival of Canadian political economy can be dated in institutional terms from the first annual political economy sessions held at the Learned Societies Conference in Quebec City in 1976 and the *Political Economy Network Newsletter*, organized by Daniel Drache, that followed.

2. *Labour and Capital in Canada, 1650–1860*, which was Pentland's doctoral thesis, defended in 1961 at the University of Toronto, was finally published in 1981, edited and with an introduction by Paul Phillips. Pentland's other major work, *A Study of the Social, Economic and Political Background of the Candian System of Industrial Relations* was prepared for the Task Force on Labour Relations in 1968 but circulated only to a few libraries. Both documents have, however, been widely circulated among political economists.

3. Innis is never an easy read; the most accessible work is *Essays in Canadian Economic History* ([1930] 1956b).
4. These features are drawn from my preface to Clement and Drache (1979).
5. For an overview of the staples thesis, see Watkins (1977).
6. For an overview, see Clement (1978a).
7. For a historical examination, see Naylor (1975); for a modern account, see Bourgault (1972) and Britton and Gilmour (1978).
8. Case studies include Deverell (1975); and Swift (1977).
9. On the North, see Berger (1977).
10. See Richards and Pratt (1979); Mathias (1971); Kierans (1973); Pratt (1976); and Nelles (1974).
11. On labour relations and the Canadian state, see Craven (1980); on the effects of split jurisdiction and other factors, see Pentland (1968).
12. For an overview, see Clement (1978b); Campbell (1978); Cuneo (1978) and Matthews (1978b). Also see Bercuson (1977); Phillips (1978); Pratt and Stevenson (1981); Brym and Sacouman (1979); and Sacouman (1981).
13. See Hughes and Kallen (1974); Porter (1965); Pentland (1959); and Avery (1979).
14. See Macpherson ([1955] 1968); Sacouman (1981); Craven and Traves (1979); and Schmidt (1981).
15. See Marchak (1979); Clement (1981); Williams (1979); and Lucas (1972).
16. See Deaton (1972); and Armstrong (1977).
17. See Atwood (1972); Cappon (1978); Crean (1976); Godfrey and Watkins (1970); Grant (1967); Hardin (1974); Laxer and Laxer (1977); Lumsden (1970); and Resnick (1977).
18. See Hughes and Kallen (1974); Berger (1977); and Watkins (ed.) (1977). On Quebec, see Bergeron (1971); Drache (1972); Lévesque (1968); Milner and Milner (1973); Milner (1978); McRoberts and Rosgate (1976); Rioux (1978); Ryerson (1968); Vallières (1971); Niosi (1979); Bourque (1979); and Fournier (1980).
19. Some useful guides for researchers include Hann, Kealey, Kealey, and Warrian (1973); Knight (1975); Roberts (1978); and *Labour Notes*, a periodical published by the Labour Studies Research Group, Carleton University (Ottawa).

FOR FURTHER READING

Brym, Robert, and James Sacouman, eds.
  1979 *Underdevelopment and Social Movements in Atlantic Canada*. Toronto: Hogtown Press.
  This collection of historical and modern articles on the politics of class on Canada's East coast unlocks the analytical and substantive dynamics of what is often referred to as a quiet region of the country.
Clement, Wallace
  1983 *Class, Power and Property: Essays on Canadian Society*. Toronto: Methuen.
  This collection of ten essays includes studies of elites, classes, and property relations in Canada.

Drache, Daniel, and Wallace Clement
    1985 *The New Practical Guide to Canadian Political Economy*. Toronto: Lorimer.
    This compilation of 25 sections plus an introduction and listing of "the staples"
    provides a comprehensive bibliography and guide to the field of political
    economy in Canada.

Grant, George
    1967 *Lament for a Nation: The Defeat of Canadian Nationalism*. Toronto: McClelland
    and Stewart.
    The classic conservative nationalist statement on the Americanization of Can-
    ada—including its culture, politics, and economy—this book has had a wide-
    spread impact on the way Canadians think about themselves.

Innis, Harold
    1956 *Essays in Canadian Economic History*, rev. ed. Toronto: University of To-
    ronto Press (original 1930).
    This book is the most comprehensive collection of Innis' wide-ranging writings
    and the clearest statement of his staples thesis.

Kealey, Gregory S.
    1980 *Toronto Workers Respond to Industrial Capitalism 1867–1892*. Toronto: Uni-
    versity of Toronto Press.
    An important example of the revival of social history focusing on labour, this
    detailed study documents the impact of industrialization on Toronto workers
    and their struggles to form working class institutions.

Levitt, Kari
    1970 *Silent Surrender: The Multinational Corporation in Canada*. Toronto:
    Macmillan.
    One of the first major statements on foreign investment in Canada, this study
    documents the impact and implications of U.S. ownership on Canadian man-
    ufacturing and resource industries.

Macpherson, C.B.
    1968 *Democracy in Alberta: Social Credit and the Party System*, 2nd ed. Toronto:
    University of Toronto Press (original 1955).
    The social and economic basis of the class politics of the petite bourgeoisie in
    Canada's West are examined in this classic study.

Naylor, Tom
    1975 *The History of Canadian Business, 1867–1914*, 2 vols. Toronto: Lorimer.
    By examining the formative stages of Canadian capitalism, this study docu-
    ments the financial domination of Canadian manufacturing and the impact
    of foreign ownership.

Palmer, Bryan D.
    1979 *A Culture of Conflict: Skilled Workers and Industrial Capitalism in Hamilton,
    Ontario, 1860–1914*. Montreal: McGill-Queen's University Press.
    Written in the tradition of E.P. Thompson, this study of class concentrates
    on the social and cultural dynamics underlying the formation of Canada's
    industrial proletariat.

Panitch, Leo, ed.
    1977 *The Canadian State: Political Power and Political Economy*. Toronto: Uni-
    versity of Toronto Press.
    This collection is the most comprehensive set of articles on the Canadian state
    written from a political-economy perspective.

Pentland, H. Clare
1981 *Labour and Capital in Canada 1650–1860*. Edited with an Introduction by Paul Phillips. Toronto: Lorimer.
Originally written in 1961, this work is the classic study of the development of class in Canada before Confederation.

Richards, John, and Larry Pratt
1979 *Prairie Capitalism: Power in the New West*. Toronto: McClelland and Stewart.
Focusing on resource development in Alberta and Saskatchewan, this study challenges both the staples tradition and Macpherson, while providing a detailed investigation of class politics.

Rioux, Marcel
1978 *Quebec in Question*, 2nd ed. Toronto: Lorimer (original 1969).
A classic analysis of the social history of Quebec, this book examines the dynamics of class and nation as they have emerged in the struggle for independence.

Ryerson, Stanley B.
1968 *Unequal Union: Confederation and the Roots of Conflict in the Canadas, 1815–1873*. Toronto: Progress Books.
Located within a class analysis, this book examines the struggles and interests involved in Canada's Confederation, focusing on the domination of Quebec.

Teeple, Gary, ed.
1972 *Capitalism and the National Question in Canada*. Toronto: University of Toronto Press.
This collection was the first to bring the concepts of class and nation to the fore in analyzing Canadian society.

PART IV

Social Variation in the Canadian Mosaic

Canada's population is far from homogeneous. Perhaps the major challenge facing the Canadian polity is to govern effectively a population that is so differentiated. Indeed, as many newspaper headlines remind us, it often seems as if the very political unity of the country is at risk.

Few people are aware of the role that population characteristics play in creating the context for a variety of social behaviours. Demographic variables—specifically the age-sex structure of a population and the rate of growth—provide the data to illuminate major social issues confronting Canadian society as we enter the 21st century. Many sociological questions can often be answered in whole or in part by reference to such variables and projected changes in them. In Chapter 14, Wayne W. McVey, Jr., introduces this aspect and presents the Canadian statistics.

Canadians are by origin a microcosm of this extraordinarily diverse planet; in Chapter 15, M. Michael Rosenberg and Morton Weinfeld examine how, as an immigrant society, Canada has had to deal—and continues to deal—with the problems arising out of this ethnic diversity. Thus, Canada is a kind of laboratory for the sociologist interested in ethnicity. The official Canadian position, one we would share, is that, despite the problems, ethnic diversity in Canada is a source of strength and cultural enrichment. There is no denying the many stains on Canada's record regarding minority treatment in the past, notably of the native peoples. But there is also no denying that in the post-war period Canada has begun attempting—often haltingly and incompletely—to right those wrongs. That process, reflected in the new Constitution, is continuing but is by no means complete.

At one time the rural/urban dimension was another source of diversity. Today we live in a largely urban society in which rural areas come to be ever further removed from the centres of power and culture. Life in an urban setting is more than just a change of scene from the rural. It produces a new kind of mentality, a new way of experiencing the world and of understanding one's own place within it. And it also creates a new form of diversity, one in which geographical or ecological features—slums, red-light districts, suburbs—are constant visual reminders of social differences. A walk along a few city streets is a powerful lesson in the diversity and variety of lifestyles and life chances in Canada. Lawrence Felt in Chapter 16 describes the evolution and current state of the city.

One of the other sources of diversity that has recently become prominent in Canada is regional differences; today they divide Canada more than ever. Despite the dramatic improvements in transportation and communication that have overcome the geographical barriers, Canada remains a nation dominated by regional interests and identities. Chapter 17, by David V.J. Bell, on regionalism shows that in part this fragmentation is the unintended consequence of Canada's political structure; in part it is the outcome of social, economic, and cultural factors. In Canada the question of regionalism is of more than intellectual curiosity; many of the key policy decisions made in parliament and in the courts involve the relationships between regions or between regions and the federal government.

Canadians who have been particularly aware of and interested in demographic factors are the Québécois. Demography has played a large role in the debate over minority versus majority language and cultural rights that has gone on in Quebec over the past decade. Quebec, as most other Canadians now realize, is not simply a province like any other. For the Québécois it is a national territorial base and the focus of their cultural, linguistic, economic, and political aspirations. Quebec's history and array of social and political institutions are in many ways without parallel in the rest of Canada. Chapter 18, by Hubert Guindon, describes and analyzes Quebec's development over the past few decades and indicates the unique course that development has taken.

CHAPTER 14

THE STUDY OF POPULATION

Wayne W. McVey, Jr.

479

The Canadian public is continually exposed to varied treatment of population-related issues in newspapers, magazines, and television. This proliferation of issues publicizes the importance of population and keeps the discipline of demography prominently in public view. **Demography** is the "study of population size and distribution, as well as the composition of the population, changes therein, and the components of such changes, which may be identified as natality, mortality, territorial movement, and social mobility" (Hauser and Duncan 1959, 31). Essentially, it addresses questions concerning the magnitude, compositional character, and structure of populations; their implications for social organization in society; and the determinants, as well as the consequences, of their growth and change (Matras 1977, 14). Thus, demography is not concerned simply with the "population explosion," as is often believed, but with a whole array of variables that aid in the understanding of population change and its implications for society.

Knowledge of population achieved through demography touches upon each Canadian through the variety of policies, programs, and planning activated at every governmental level. Illustrative of this relationship are many familiar questions:

1. Is Canada's birth rate at an all-time low?
2. Will a rising cost of living make more potential parents decide against children?
3. When I retire 25 years from now, who's going to be paying for my pension?
4. Who will fill the jobs vacated by the retiring population in twenty years?
5. Should Canada place a ceiling on the number of immigrants allowed into the country?
6. Is the higher-risk lifestyle of the younger population contributing to increasing death rates?
7. Are existing health programs successful in reducing cancer mortality?
8. Should there be a controlled growth policy for the larger metropolitan areas?
9. Can adolescents' premarital sexual behaviour be curbed to decrease the high teenage birth rates?
10. When will Canadian universities again witness increasing enrolments?

It is readily evident that the dimensions of population are intertwined with an ever-expanding range of human behaviour and activities. The size and character of the single population influences marriage patterns. Changes in the size of the widowed population influence policies governing social assistance and housing. Fluctuations in the number of births have repercussions for school system planning. The housing industry seeks to align its markets with changes in the composition of the population. Shortages in the labour force may require increased dependence on immigration for a supply of workers. Resource communities endeavour to monitor the number and character of the migrants they attract. Health services and programs must measure their success against changes in mortality. All these issues are related to population change. An understanding of these relationships improves the chances that policy design and implementation will be aligned appropriately with future population changes and needs.

Demographic research has answered many questions germane to the foregoing issues—and raised many others. There are two primary approaches. **Demographic analysis** deals exclusively with **demographic variables**—the components of population change and variation, such as fertility, mortality, migration, population composition and characteristics, and population size and distribution (all of these terms are defined or explained in this chapter). Demographic variables are used in turn to explain changes in other demographic variables. For example, study of declines in infant mortality may provide insight into changes in the survivorship of the population (that is, how many children will survive to what age). Techniques of population analysis, the tools of this approach, then enable the demographer to project age and sex distribution of the population to future dates. Thus, the causal variable of infant mortality and the effect variable of future population age structure are both demographic facts.

A **population study**, on the other hand, incorporates non-demographic variables in the analytical equation and uses them to explain and predict variation in the demographic variables. Changes in the demographic elements can be explained by variables derived from many disciplines, such as sociology, economics, medicine, geography, public health, and psychology. For example, the researcher may wish to explain declines in infant mortality (demographic variable) by analyzing the effects of improvements in post-natal care and obstetrics and the increased use of hospitals for child delivery (non-demographic variables). Conversely, a demographic variable may be used to explain variations in non-demographic elements. For example, declining birth rates and resulting alterations in the age composition of the population may influence marketing strategies and product diversification. This may partially explain the successful marketing of electronic games with adult appeal and the promotion of some brands of baby shampoo and powder to the adult consumer market, rather than solely for infants. Exhibit 14-1 illustrates some other relationships within these analytical frameworks.

Early Chinese writings on population indicate a strong interest in the effects of changes in population size and composition. These people showed a clear understanding of population dynamics with the emergence of the **optimum population concept**. In order for the land to be

Exhibit 14-1
Analytical Approaches: Demographic Analysis and Population Study

Analytical Approaches	Independent Variable	Dependent Variable
Demographic analysis	*Demographic* Birth rate Age composition	*Demographic* Changes in the age composition Changes in the birth rate
Population study, type I	*Non-Demographic* Social class (sociological)	*Demographic* Birth rate
	Attitude toward maternal role (psychological)	Number of births
	Mass-media portrayal of lifestyle alternatives (sociological)	Number of marriages
	Economic opportunity (economic)	New migration
	Government health programs	Death rate
Population study, type II	*Demographic* Age composition	*Non-Demographic* Voting behaviour (political)
	New migration	Social disorganization (sociological)
	Decline in births	Changes in immigration policy (political)

Source: Adapted from Kammeyer (1971, 4).

utilized properly, to yield maximum productivity, it must have the right number of people—no more, no less. Having more than the optimum number of people, they said, meant overworking the land, and thus famine would result, while less than the optimum number would yield less tax money and great hardship because of lower crop production. During the Han dynasty (207 BC–AD 220), a poll tax was instituted on infants from birth. The consequence of this act was an increase in infanticide, which eventually resulted in the termination of the tax.

Before the development of scientific inquiry in the Western world, much of the understanding of population was based on folklore, misconceptions, and rumour. During the great plague years in Europe, people perceived that the urban centres of that time were merely graveyards and that there were more males than females in the rural areas. The casual observer of the day could be easily deceived since working men in the fields were more visible than the farm women, whose activities centred on the home. Similarly, contagious diseases were of greater incidence in the highly congested cities, where, of course, the numbers of victims were highly visible in the compact urban cemeteries.

The connection between population and consequences, explained partially by fact and partially by fiction, became the basis for the development of two main perspectives on population growth: (1) that population growth is good regardless of social costs; and (2) that the welfare of the individual takes precedence—a stance that supports restricting population growth. These positions have survived to the present day and can be found, often co-existing, at every level within society. For example, it is not unusual to find one political candidate supporting continued population growth for the economic well-being of the community, while the opponent proposes controlled population growth to ensure the maintenance of the constituents' quality of life.

POPULATION GROWTH

Population is considered a **dynamic variable**—one that is in a state of continual change. Every second, infants are born, people are dying, and people are moving from city to city and from country to country. These key events or transitions in life constantly create new equilibriums in population.

Modern societies have two primary means of monitoring these life events. The **population census** is a periodic national survey of the residents of a country. Canada conducts one every five years,[1] collecting data on its residents' age, sex, marital status, ethnicity, religion, income, occupation, cumulative fertility, migration and immigration status, current residence, housing, and household and family arrangements. These data are recorded on mail questionnaires for each household member, and the analysis of these responses provides a very important social accounting of the status of population and its character for a specified moment in time.

The second monitoring device is the **vital registration system**. This is the day-to-day recording of vital events or transitions in the life course that involve personal changes in status. When the life course is initiated through birth or terminated through death, the event is certified and duly recorded with the provincial registrar. Other changes in personal status, such as divorce, annulment, abortion, and adoption, are also registered. The certificates also contain allied information concerning these events, such as age at marriage, divorce, or death, residence, cause of death, marital status of deceased, order of birth, and the like.

Personal status changes are recorded through certification in the vital registration system as soon as possible after they occur. Editing and computer processing of both vital-event and census data commences shortly after they are received at Statistics Canada in Ottawa. Nevertheless, it is impossible to achieve a current accounting of Canada's population because of the time lag involved between the collecting and processing of data and the release of data publications.[2] Despite this real problem of datedness in information, Canada's monitoring systems rank among the best in the world.

COMPONENTS OF POPULATION CHANGE

Population change has three basic components: births, which add to the population; deaths, which subtract from it; and migration, which may add to or subtract from it. **Natural increase** refers to the net balance between births and deaths, which can be either a loss or a gain. **Net migration** is the difference between the number of people who move away from a particular area and the number of people who move into it.

With these two components, one can assess population change for any given area and time period. When the amounts of an area's natural increase and net migration for the specified time referent are added to its total population at the beginning of that time period, one has a measure of the total population at the end of the period. This relationship can be expressed as

$$P_2 = P_1 + (\text{births} - \text{deaths}) + (\text{in-migration} - \text{out-migration}),$$

or

$$P_2 = P_1 + (\text{natural increase}) + (\text{net migration}),$$

where

P_2 = population at the end of the time referent, and
P_1 = population at the beginning of the time referent.

Thus, the three basic population variables linked together form the **demographic equation**, which is the fundamental conceptual equation in population study. Although the concept is simple to understand, arriving at accurate measures of these key variables is difficult. Vital registration can provide birth and death data; the migration component, however, must be estimated.

The three basic and dynamic factors—fertility, mortality, and migration—influence the magnitude, growth, and distribution of the population. Understanding the interaction of these basic variables is essential, as they determine the size of the population, the rate of population growth, and variations in distribution and density (Thomlinson 1976, 6). Other key variables, of interest to demographers and non-demographers alike, include age, sex, marital status, ethnic origin, religious affiliation, occupation, educational level, employment status, nativity, period of immigration, and language. The rest of this chapter will emphasize the way these variables influence and are influenced by the three basic variables of population change. This two-way street of influence can be illustrated by considering how the population's age distribution can affect reproductive behaviour and, conversely, how changing fertility can shape the age distribution. For instance, higher fertility is expected if the population has a high proportion of females in the childbearing ages of 15 to 44 years, and a period of high fertility alters the age distribution through the introduction of larger numbers in the birth cohorts. (**Cohort** refers to a group of people who share common life experiences by entering the key transition points in the life cycle at the same time, such as a 1932 birth cohort or a 1975 marriage cohort.)

Consideration of auxiliary characteristics, such as marital status and level of education, further refines the analysis. Most childbearing takes place within marriage; hence, a high proportion of married females of childbearing age could have a great influence on the level of fertility. Since the reproductive level tends to decrease as education increases, the number of births is likely to decline if a high proportion of married women in the childbearing years are university trained. In turn, the offspring of these low-fertility females are likely to be socialized toward similar parenting values and, therefore, are likely to generate relatively small birth cohorts themselves. Correspondingly, the age and sex distribution is shaped by fertility.

In summary, the primary interaction of births, deaths, and migration and the shaping influences of the auxiliary demographic variables on this interaction provide the essential ingredients for understanding population changes.

UNDERSTANDINGS OF POPULATION GROWTH

Before the 20th century, population theories were essentially concerned with the consequences of population growth. Whether excessive population growth would prove a hardship on the individual in terms of the quality of life, food supply, disease conditions, housing, productivity, and poverty were concerns of early writers. The noted population theorist Robert Thomas Malthus (1766–1834) espoused the position that the power of population growth was so great that, if unchecked, population would soon exceed food supply, resulting in malnutrition, starvation, poverty, and increased vulnerability to disease. Malthus's second essay outlined the means by which he believed population growth could be held in check—that is, in balance with food supply. Since population increases through births and decreases through death, he conceptualized two kinds of checks that maintain this balance. **Positive checks**, which increase deaths, include war, pestilence, disease, poor work conditions, starvation, and any other condition that is hazardous to the population. Conversely, **preventive checks** include behaviour that effectively reduces births, such as moral restraint, celibacy, and postponement of marriage. If the population does not exercise the preventive checks effectively enough to control growth, the positive checks will operate.

With this major theoretical contribution, Malthus was acclaimed the father of demography, and for more than a century population theories

TOWARD A WORLD OF TEN BILLION PEOPLE

Even if the continents are not going to sink one day under the sheer weight of human bodies, the problem of over-population in some countries is going to make people wish they had never been born. "Some countries" is the key point to notice, though—and not a great many, either.

The present cycle of population expansion is already slowing down, and birth rates may drop to replacement level in most of the world in the next 25 years. It could take another 70 years before world population stops growing, because almost half the population in Third World countries is now under 21. A century from now, however, the world's population will probably have stabilized at somewhere between eight and 11 billion people.

That is *not* a horrifying figure. It would put an intolerable strain on today's world resources of food and raw materials, but we cannot even envisage what will be the important raw materials for 2075-style technology. Ten billion people implies an average density of population throughout the world about half that of Italy (New York state, Vietnam, Burundi) now.

You would hardly notice in most places that such a world was fuller than the present (just as it did not seem empty in 1925, when it held half the present number). But there will be specific countries for which overpopulation will be an utter disaster.

Overpopulation is a misleading term, if you take it to signify poverty, hunger and hopelessness. England is not "overpopulated" with more than 350 people per square kilometre; India is said to be "overpopulated" with fewer than 200 people per square kilometre. Poverty, in other words, is not caused by two many people; it is the result of too little money.

Most Third World countries have not developed their resources and their people are not trained to exploit them properly. Most of their people, therefore, are poor. But the fact that their populations are growing rapidly is not the cause of their poverty.

Apart from the Indian subcontinent, China, and a few islands in the Caribbean and Indian Oceans, Third World countries have very low population densities. Their only problem with population growth is the need to make their economies grow faster, so as to raise living standards. To a greater or less extent most of them are succeeding.

Only if they fail consistently do they start running into the classic Malthusian symptoms of overpopulation: famine, disease, and chronic violence. It can happen at any population density—the question is not how many people there are, but how much food and other resources are being produced to support them.

The classic case in the modern era was Ireland. Like the rest of the British Isles, its population began to grow rapidly around 1600. It doubled in the seventeenth century, and more than doubled in the eighteenth; by 1850, at its existing growth rate, it would have reached 10 million. But it never got there.

Ireland had exactly the same population density as England at the time, but in Ireland there was no industrial revolution going on; the extra population had to find a living on the land. By 1845 a quarter of the population had no work and were virtually starving in the winters.

In 1846 the Irish potato crop failed. In the next five years a tenth of the population starved to death, and a million fled to England and America. The emigration never ceased after that, and during the 19th century more than five million people left Ireland. The population fell from the 1845 peak of 8.5 million to 4.5 million in 1900. Ireland is the classic modern example of demographic disaster.

This sort of catastrophe now lies in wait for Bangladesh or the Indonesian island of Java. Each has over 90 million people, almost all still on the land, at a density of around 600 per square kilometre.

Already the incidence of disease is rising in Java, and the average food intake is falling; the physical size of the Javanese is actually decreasing. And when Malthus arrives this time, scythe in hand, there will be no escape through emigration.

Fortunately, there are very few places like that in the world. A more typical pattern is that of Mexico or Brazil, where the population is exploding—three per cent growth a year—but where the economy is expanding even faster, new lands are being opened up, and the population growth is going into the cities. (Mexico City, Sao Paulo, and Rio will be first, third, and sixth in size among the world's cities in 2000.)

This kind of growth is so fast it's frightening, and as always the experiences of first-generation city dwellers straight off the land are grim. But it actually resembles the experience of the United States between 1850 and 1900, when the population more than tripled and New York became the world's biggest city.

The present cycle of world population growth will create a few horribly mutilated casualties in the Third World, just as it did in Europe in the last century. Most countries, however, will come through it without a disaster.

—GWYNNE DYER

were largely variations of his position. Not until the 20th century did the theoretical focus shift from the consequences to the determinants of population growth.

The Demographic Transition

Eventually demographers, economists, and philosophers began to pay serious attention to the primary components of population change—births, deaths, and migration. By the mid-1940s, demographers concluded that societies proceed through three demographic stages in the transition from agrarian to urban-industrial economies. In each stage of societal development, the interaction of fertility and mortality determines population growth, assuming that intersocietal migration is controlled. This transformation of vital events derived from historical data in Western Europe is the basis for the theoretical model portrayed in Exhibit 14-2.

Low population growth characterizes societies in the pre-industrialized period (Stage 1 in Exhibit 14-2). Death rates are high and fluctuating but exceeded by somewhat higher fertility. Societal norms supporting high fertility are essential for family survival because of the high incidences of stillbirth, maternal death, and death of children from communicable diseases. The agrarian family is tied to the land and requires children to contribute economically to the productive system at very early ages, thus increasing agricultural efficiency and ensuring survival. It is also important to have some children who live to adulthood to provide care for the elderly, since the family is the sole source of support—a primitive form of social insurance. Sons are particularly valued because of their usefulness on the farm and the support they can provide to the elderly. (The singular importance of farmers' sons was demonstrated in Canadian censuses of the late 1800s, where this status was tabulated as a separate occupational category.) In brief, successful reproduction and survivorship are paramount to survival, ensuring that the family can defeat the many visits of death. The unpredictable death rate determines population growth, and high fertility, supported by marriage norms and social custom, ensures that the effects of mortality are sufficiently offset to provide a few surviving children.

During the transition stage in the development of societies (Stage 2 in Exhibit 14-2), mortality rates begin to decline as a consequence of technological and social changes. The health of the population improves on exposure to a variety of developments, including better public and personal sanitation, widespread personal hygiene practices, increased crop yields and nutritional improvements, refrigeration, pasteurization, humidity and temperature control, improvements in housing and in transportation and communication technology, the mass production of goods and services, and the introduction of social reforms and work safety standards, not to mention medical advances such as new surgical skills,

Exhibit 14-2
The Demographic Transition

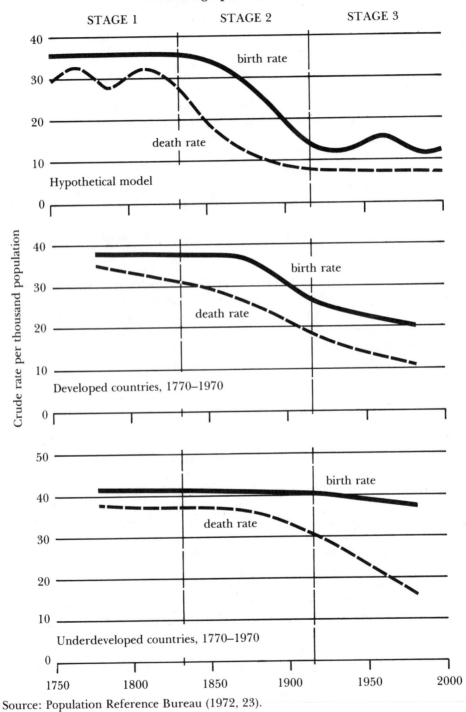

Source: Population Reference Bureau (1972, 23).

sterilization procedures, and the development of antiseptic treatment and immunology. With increased control over communicable diseases, which had primarily accounted for the high levels of childhood mortality, the survivorship of infants and children to adulthood increases. The level of fertility, however, does not decline. This widening gap between birth and death rates results in a large population increase. Fertility remains high because changing reproductive patterns is contingent on changing the strong cultural and family fertility norms established in Stage 1 to preserve the family. The necessity for continued cultural support of high fertility norms must be challenged in order for structural changes in the family to emerge.

As more and more children live, it becomes increasingly clear that a family need not produce large numbers of children for a few to survive. In fact, large numbers of surviving sons seriously threaten culturally supported inheritance rules, whereby land holdings are passed down to the eldest sons to provide support for their families. If there is not enough land to support all surviving sons, the family structure is at the threshold of change since the youngest sons are left out of any inheritance. The excess children from the farms tend to migrate to the growing industrial centres, where they are welcomed as cheap sources of labour. Lower fertility norms begin to emerge as children increasingly become viewed as economic liabilities for the urban family. The smaller, nuclear family emerges as a form more amenable to a highly competitive industrialized economy in which mobility is a prerequisite of survival. Fertility begins to decline to lower levels.

When a society reaches an advanced industrialized state (Stage 3 in Exhibit 14-2), the mortality rate has fallen to a very low level, but the fertility rate has also declined, resulting in low population growth similar

As this photo of a 1909 baby contest shows, the values attached to having children were once quite different from those of today.

to that experienced in Stage 1. The society experiencing secular declines in both birth and death rates has an aging population that is predominantly female. The modernizing country experiences accelerating urbanization and a shift from extractive and agrarian occupations to industrial, commercial, and service ones. The nuclear family, which de-emphasizes kinship ties, becomes the dominant family form.

The demographic transition framework, although extremely useful for understanding population change and modernization, is subject to several criticisms. Since the model is based on what has happened in the past in European countries, one can argue that it describes only historical events and has little application to today's developing countries, where different precipitating conditions prevail. Rapid technological advancement in recent years has stimulated relatively faster declines in the death rate; many developing countries trigger rapid improvements in mortality conditions by "borrowing" developments in medicine, preventive health care, and agriculture made earlier in the developed countries. It has been argued that if such external factors can be borrowed to effect declines in mortality, it is also appropriate to apply external agents to stimulate corresponding declines in fertility, such as family planning programs. In addition, many of the developing countries have birth rate levels considerably higher than those that typified European countries in Stage 1 of the demographic transition. Not all countries follow similar patterns in the modernization process, in that the fertility levels may vary from country to country in their timing and rate of decline, as well as in the ultimate lows that they reach. In sum, it may be said that a variety of internal and external factors that were non-existent or very weak in the demographic transition of European countries may produce different patterns of transition for countries that are developing in the second half of the 20th century.

Although all countries in the world may eventually complete the transition from high birth and death rates to low birth and death rates, there is no guarantee that they will follow similar patterns. Nevertheless, the focus of the demographic transition framework is upon the determinants of population growth patterns—that is, the interactive effects of birth and death rates.

The World Population Situation

Since the Second World War, the less developed countries of the world have received a great deal of agricultural, financial, health care, and general economic assistance. The improvements in mortality that followed, coupled with sustained high birth rates, moved them rapidly to the transition stage of accelerating, often explosive population growth. Many have annual population growth rates in excess of 2.0 percent, which will generate a doubling of population in less than 35 years or about one generation. In contrast, the more industrialized countries now in the controlled-growth stage of the demographic transition model are experiencing much lower rates of population growth. By the 1960s, the European countries had growth rates of less than 1.0 percent, which yield doubling times in excess of two generations. (See Exhibit 14-3).

Progress has produced this unanticipated rapid population growth in the very countries that can least afford it. Excessive population growth magnifies the strain on governments in the areas of urbanization, industrialization, public hygiene, health care services, education, employment, housing, welfare services, and public works. The pressures of population growth may contribute to an increase in social disorganization and political instability in the short term, causing the downfall of governments and infectious political unrest.

Most of the countries listed in Exhibit 14-3 have experienced declines in both birth and death rates since the early 1950s; however, the less developed countries show more marked declines in death rates than the developed countries. Of considerable importance is the fact that many of the developing countries have lowered their death rates to levels comparable to, or lower than, those found in the more industrialized countries. For the most part, the less developed countries have emerged into the transition stage.

In contrast, the more developed countries are firmly entrenched in the incipient decline stage of population growth. In fact, a few of the Western European countries now face a no-growth situation in which births are often offset by deaths. If fertility remains at the same level or declines, the death rate will increase as a consequence of aging of the population, resulting in negative growth such as that experienced recently by West Germany. Thus, there is a real possibility of a fourth stage of the demographic transition model, in which the death rate exceeds the birth rate for a period of time. Obviously, a country would not endure an extended population decline before introducing measures either to encourage fertility increases or to induce population rejuvenation through immigration.

Both Canada and the United States are in the incipient decline stage. Birth rates of 15 and 16 and death rates of 7 and 9, respectively, yield a rate of natural increase of 0.8 for Canada and 0.7 for the United States. Assuming no change, these rates of natural increase will generate a doubling of the population in about a century. Continuing declines in the birth rates, coupled with stabilizing death rates, will produce an aging population and corresponding increases in the doubling time for both countries.

These vital event trends have influenced the regional distribution of the world's population. The less developed regions—Africa, Asia, and Latin America—already have the largest share, with more than 78 percent in 1985. It is estimated that they will contain about 85 percent by the year 2020, if current vital rates continue, and the developed regions will decline accordingly from 21.8 to 15.9 percent. The most significant pop-

Exhibit 14-3
Birth, Death, and Natural Increase Trends for Selected Less Developed and More Developed Countries, 1950–85

	Crude Death Rate				Crude Birth Rate				Crude Rate of Natural Increase				Years to Double Population
	1950–55	1960–65	1970–75	1985	1950–55	1960–65	1970–75	1985	1950–55	1960–65	1970–75	1985	
Less Developed Countries													
Mexico	15.1	10.8	8.8	6	46.9	44.6	41.8	32	31.8	33.8	33.0	26	27
Chile	13.6	11.9	8.4	6	35.2	35.7	26.0	24	21.6	23.8	17.6	18	39
Venezuela	14.9	10.1	6.8	6	47.3	45.2	37.5	33	32.4	35.2	30.7	27	25
Singapore	10.6	7.1	5.1	5	44.4	34.0	21.2	16	33.8	26.9	16.1	11	64
Sri Lanka	11.5	8.5	6.3	6	38.5	34.7	28.6	27	27.0	26.2	22.3	21	33
Costa Rica	12.3	9.1	5.8	4	47.6	45.3	31.0	31	35.3	36.2	25.2	27	26
Honduras	21.8	17.7	13.7	10	51.3	50.9	48.6	44	29.5	33.2	34.9	34	20
Brazil	15.1	12.4	10.1	8	44.2	42.1	35.8	31	29.0	29.7	25.8	23	30
Developed Countries													
United Kingdom	11.7	11.8	11.7	12	15.9	18.2	16.1	13	4.2	6.4	4.4	1	630
Austria	12.3	12.5	12.2	12	15.0	18.5	14.7	12	2.7	6.0	2.5	0	—
Belgium	12.2	12.1	11.2	11	16.7	17.1	14.8	12	4.5	5.0	3.6	1	1 155
France	12.8	11.2	10.6	10	19.5	18.0	17.0	14	6.7	6.8	7.4	4	198
Netherlands	7.5	7.8	8.7	8	22.1	20.9	16.8	12	14.6	13.1	8.1	4	192
Switzerland	10.1	9.5	10.0	9	17.3	18.5	14.7	11	7.2	9.0	4.7	2	330
Sweden	9.8	10.0	10.5	11	15.5	14.5	14.2	11	5.7	4.5	3.7	0	6 930
West Germany	10.8	11.4	12.1	11	15.8	18.0	12.0	10	5.0	6.6	-0.1	-2	—
East Germany	11.9	13.3	13.2	13	16.6	17.4	14.0	14	4.7	4.1	0.8	1	990
Canada	8.7	7.7	7.7	7	27.8	25.3	18.6	15	19.1	17.6	10.9	8	90
United States	8.5	9.4	9.4	9	24.8	22.6	16.2	16	15.3	13.2	6.8	7	100

Note: A crude rate, which is the simplest measure used in the study of population, relates the number of a particular kind of event (births, for example) that occurs in a calendar year to the mid-year estimate of the total population. The advantages and disadvantages of using various kinds of crude rates are discussed in later sections of this chapter.

Sources: Death rates and birth rates, 1950–75: *UN Population Studies *78*, table A-9, medium variants; 1985 figures: 1985 Population Data Sheet, Washington, D.C.: Population Reference Bureau.

ulation increases are likely to occur in Africa, where the population is expected to almost triple in size from 551 to 1433 million, representing an annual growth of 4.6 percent. Somewhat less dramatic changes are projected for Asia and Latin America with a 1.5 and 2.4 percent annual growth rate, respectively. China accounts for more than one-third of the population in Asia. (The 1982 census of China, a historic enumeration of more than one billion people, was the focus of considerable interest as it was the first complete population count for that country since 1964.)

Throughout the countries of the world, the student of population can discover varying historical patterns of growth, as well as different societal reactions to population change. As Matras (1977) notes, population pressures as a consequence of the interaction of fertility and mortality produce changes in the strategies of adaptation. In addition to the social norms already mentioned, policies encouraging family planning, immigration restrictions, preventive health programs, marriage and divorce laws, family assistance legislation, and "baby bonus" schemes are illustrative of mechanisms employed by governments sensitive to population growth.

THE MOVEMENT OF PEOPLE

Of the three elements in the demographic equation, migration is the most difficult component to assess. In Canada, migration data are limited to a single census question concerning previous residence and immigrant records containing a few basic characteristics. There is a paucity of data concerning individual migration histories, the frequency and determinants of migration, and the adjustment problems migrants encounter. Moreover, moving within a country constitutes a status change that is not recorded by any continuous registration system.

For demographers, **migration** is geographical movement across a specified boundary involving a change of residence. The migrant changes residence from the place of origin or sending area to the place of destination or receiving area. Demography classifies migrants according to the type of move that they have made. **International migration** is the movement of people across national boundaries. From the Canadian viewpoint, the international migrant moving to Canada from Sri Lanka is an **immigrant**; however, Sri Lankan authorities view this same migrant as an **emigrant**.

The second major type, **internal migration**, involves movement within a country's borders, whether it be between cities or from rural to urban areas (or vice versa). Accordingly, the **internal migrant** is a person who crosses a county line, no matter how short the distance, and the **mover** is one who changes residence within the county. For example, the Edmonton resident who moves from apartment to apartment within the city is classified as a mover; however, the person who moves from Edmonton to the contiguous community of St. Albert is classified as an internal migrant.

Historically, Canada's population size, distribution, and composition have been influenced by immigration; in recent times, internal migration has been even more important. Freedom of movement within the country's boundaries has contributed to a volume of internal migrants far exceeding the number of immigrants admitted annually. Because of the importance of internal migration, as well as immigration, in the shaping of the population, it is relevant to review the major migration patterns and their contribution to the growth of Canada.

The Influence of Immigration on Canada's Growth

While European countries were moving into the industrial age, Canada was developing the agricultural economy that prevailed into the 20th century. In contrast to European development, defensive or fortified settlements were established before the clearing of land for agricultural use because they provided the protection necessary for the early Canadian farmer. Timber cleared from the land became the leading export commodity in the early 1800s, allowing the new colony to participate in the infant international markets.

By 1850, wheat and flour rivalled timber as export commodities, a shift made possible by agricultural expansion into the interior. Increased trade necessitated the establishment of more settlements, the majority of which were ports along the waterways of Quebec and Ontario. At Confederation, the population was predominantly rural, however, with only 16 percent residing in such urban centres as Halifax, Saint John, Quebec City, Montreal, and Toronto.

From the time of initial exploration, immigration and emigration fluctuated, responding to changing and uncertain economic conditions. Following Confederation, the new nation directed efforts toward establishing a firm position in world trade, as well as developing an internal market. Tariff expansion, the development of a transportation and communication network linking new settlements with the vast undeveloped lands of the interior, and a minor surge in technological innovation in the sphere of manufacturing increased the competition for economic opportunities. These changes provided further impetus to the development of internal markets and the growth of urban communities. Industrial development was limited to sites located near energy sources; thus Hamilton and Windsor made their appearance on the urban scene.

During the 1880s, about 100,000 immigrants were arriving annually in Canada; however, large numbers of people, foreign born and native born, were leaving to settle in the United States, where the availability of free land and access to it were attractive incentives. For many immigrants, Canada served only as a temporary stopover before they continued their movement. Emigration was of sufficient magnitude between 1871 and 1891 to depress the rate of population growth in Canada, and positive net immigration did not occur until about the turn of the century.

Until that time population growth was the result of natural increase, and Canadians were accustomed to maintaining higher fertility to offset the effects of mortality.

Towards the end of the century, the government began to establish immigration policies that would help it realize its goals. During the construction of the Canadian Pacific Railway, an immigration policy was implemented to permit the recruitment of large numbers of Asians to satisfy labour requirements. When they were no longer needed, the Chinese Immigration Act of 1885 was passed to stop further immigration. The completion of the railway facilitated the settlement of the western provinces. The country's greatest influx of immigrants—more than three million between 1896 and 1914—contributed to the settlement of the prairie provinces. Incentives in the form of free ship passage, rail transport, and homesteading rights were made available to new immigrants who were willing to face the hardship of developing new agricultural lands. In addition to the establishing of a wheat economy and a mosaic of service communities in the interior provinces, this mass immigration altered the character of the population. The ratio of immigrants to emigrants increased, and immigration became the significant contributor to population growth. In the decade of 1901 to 1911 alone, the population of Canada increased by one-third, from 5,592,000 to 7,449,000.

Immigration was necessarily curtailed during the First World War years (1914 to 1918), dropping to an all-time low of 20,000 annually. The urgency of the war effort, however, sparked a demand for manufactured products. Employment opportunities increased in the urban centres as the industrial sectors of the economy expanded. With immigration blocked as a source of labour, further urban development was contingent upon the internal migration of population from the rural areas. People were free to meet this need since the agricultural sector of the economy was reaping the benefits of technological change: it yielded more efficient productivity and, correspondingly, decreased the demand for farm labour. The recourse for this surplus farm labour was migration to the urban areas of greater opportunity. Following the war, this movement continued, though the rapid pace of population growth was not regained. Despite a slight upsurge in immigration in the post-war years, the economic depression of the 1930s served to lower both immigration and natural increase, resulting in a low population growth until the beginning of the Second World War.

During the post-war period of the 1940s, both natural increase and immigration stimulated population recovery. Canadian fertility began to increase during the war years and continued into the 1950s, contributing to the post-war "baby boom." Net migration accounted for 30 percent of the total growth in Canada between 1951 and 1956. In the same period, industrial concerns further diversified and explored for new resources. When resources were discovered, further stimulation of urban growth occurred as a consequence of new employment opportunities. Predominantly rural agricultural areas, such as the Prairie provinces, registered significant increases in urban populations during the 1941–51 decade. Oil and gas exploration and development, along with the establishment of resource communities and allied industries, created labour demand for a new wave of immigrants. Migrants responding to these needs came from the industrial and commerce centres of Europe with construction, manufacturing, and kindred skills—in sharp contrast to the immigrants of the turn of the century, most of whom were farmers from predominantly rural areas of the East European countries.

Immigration Today

It is evident that immigrants have performed an essential role in the economic history of the nation. Immigration levels can be manipulated through the enactment of policies to meet the country's requirements for workers in specific numbers and with specific skills. For a number of years until 1978, the Immigration Act simply imposed a ceiling on the number of immigrants admitted into Canada each year—specifically, 1 percent of the total population.

With the decline in fertility since 1959 and the worsening economic situation in Canada, policy-makers have recently taken the view that immigration may be the key component in future population growth. The Immigration Act of 1978 permits greater control of immigration in terms of total volume, ethnic balance, and the destination of immigrants. The total volume of immigrants to be admitted is determined annually, affording the government an opportunity to adjust it according to labour force needs as well as to natural increase. Control of ethnic composition provides the mechanism by which an equitable linguistic balance can be maintained. The desire to control destination is in response to the concerns expressed about the post-war concentration of new immigrants in the three major cities (Vancouver, Montreal, and Toronto); more than half the new arrivals indicate one of these three cities as their destination. The intent is to provide incentives to attract immigrants to other localities.

Although the act provides these various mechanisms for controlling immigration, applying them equitably is quite problematic.

The Determinants of Migration

Many factors can contribute to the complex decision to migrate, as well as the choice of destination. The chief reason for moving is to better one's economic position. This can involve searching for a job, improving one's salary, making a career move, or relocating to an area that has better employment opportunities.

In addition, people move for health reasons. For example, people with respiratory disorders may move to areas with dryer climates. Recent cases of families' moving because of hazardous pollution illustrate the importance of the health factor in the migration process. Dissatisfaction with climatic conditions, as well as other environmental hazards such as tornadoes and earthquakes, can also influence a migration decision.

An increasing number of older people opt for relocation following retirement. Age-segregated communities are attracting retired couples to areas of more temperate climate, such as British Columbia. Some people may relocate to take advantage of more favourable tax structures or welfare laws. Others move because of dissatisfaction with local municipal services or concern about urban congestion, pollution, spiralling crime rates, and transportation problems.

At various times, people have been forced to move as a consequence of war or political or religious persecution. This is involuntary migration; the migrants have little or no choice but to relocate. At the outset of the Second World War, Canadians of Japanese descent, who were concentrated on the west coast, were forced into camps in the interior of British Columbia, in Saskatchewan, and even in Ontario. In more recent times, Canada has made special allowances for the admission of refugees, such as Hungarians, Czechoslovakians, Vietnamese, and Cambodians who have been impelled to move because of deteriorating conditions in their home countries.

The propensity to move often increases at major transitional stages in the life cycle. Short-distance moves are likely to occur when people marry, increase the number of children in their family, seek specialized education or face the departure of children from the family or the death of a spouse. In contrast, the long-distance move, which involves more severe breaks with social ties in the community of origin and perhaps more difficult adjustments in the community of destination, is usually precipitated by an economic factor.

Historically, the migrant has tended to be a young man; however, since the Second World War, young women have increasingly participated in migratory movements in Canada. It is interesting to note that it is young adults who usually encounter many of the key life cycle transition points that may determine migration, such as first marriage, initial job entry, entrance into university, and early family formation. Correspondingly, people in the later maturity stage of the life cycle—ages 45 to 64—tend to be non-migrants as they are likely to be more established in an occupation, have become homeowners, and be more firmly tied to the community.

The Consequences of Migration

The consequences of migration for the areas of both destination and origin are demographic, economic, and social. The social significance of the consequences often depends on the number of migrants relative to the size of the population in the sending and receiving areas. A large number of migrants has the greatest effect on a small receiving area in terms of needs for services, hospital and health care, education, employment, and housing. Because of the age- and sex-selectivity of migration,

CANADA'S POPULATION WILL FALL GREATLY WITHOUT MORE IMMIGRANTS—TORY

TORONTO (CP) — Canada's population will fall dramatically by the year 2000 unless the immigration process is improved, says a federal Tory.

Andrew Witer, member of Parliament for Parkdale-High Park in Toronto, told a weekend conference on immigration and family reunification that immigrants are vital to the growth and development of the Canadian economy. More people must be allowed to settle in Canada to boost population, he said.

"There is a myth that immigrants take jobs away from Canadians, and they are a burden on the Canadian economy," said Witer, a member of a federal standing committee on labor, employment and immigration.

"Our research has shown us that immigrants bring good economic times to this country because an influx of immigrants leads to instant consumerism."

Witer said that with Canada's traditionally high rate of emigration and the present birth rate of less than two children per family, the population could fall to 20 million by the end of the century from the current 25 million.

New Democrat MP Dan Heap, also a member of the standing committee on immigration, said the country's immigration policy favors people with money and brains.

Between April 1, 1985, and March 31 this year, 232 foreign entrepreneurs immigrated to Ontario alone.

Heap, who represents Toronto's Spadina riding, also said sponsorship fees introduced this year serve to "subsidize" the cost of processing wealthy businessmen. Government should focus on training and educating Canadians, rather than "scooping the educated of the Third World."

A 47-page report by the six-member committee, tabled in the House of Commons in June, . . . made almost 60 recommendations. . . , many aimed at expediting the immigration process. It called for more overseas immigration centres, more selective use of in-depth security checks for prospective immigrants and broader eligibility to allow people to sponsor distant relatives.

the proportion of young adults in their early childbearing years increases in the receiving area. One result is greater potential population growth in the receiving area. Resource communities that have a high influx of young migrants often reflect higher-than-average birth rates, a phenomenon that contributes to continued pressure for health and educational services.

The sending area's population is no less affected by the departure of young adults. Its composition reflects losses in those particular age and sex groups. The community of origin may experience shortages in people of labour-force ages, and these shortages jeopardize its economic viability. With proportionately fewer young adults, the sending area's population becomes older. When a disproportionate share of the young males of a community migrates, the pool of eligibles for marriage is reduced, with possible implications for future population growth.

Symptoms of social disorganization may increase as a consequence of rapid in-migration to a community, as more strain is placed upon the infrastructure. Economic opportunity may attract more young male migrants than can be accommodated, resulting in a rise in unemployment, welfare case loads, crime, and housing demand. These social consequences characterize areas subject to seasonal migration. Young families who migrate may similarly be affected. Although migration of younger, higher educated professionals may rejuvenate receiving areas with aging populations, there may also be negative consequences in the form of pressures for new kinds of services, high competition with the resident population for existing jobs, and political rivalry between the two distinct age segments for the greatest voice in the community decision-making process.

Urbanization and Metropolitanization

In an historical process that continues today, population mobility, the transition from agrarian to industrial economy, and population increase have interconnected and resulted in urban concentrations of magnitudes never before attained. Generally, **urbanization** is defined as a process involving three interrelated trends: the multiplication of points of concentration, the growth of these concentrations, and the increasing proportion of the total population living in these concentrations (Eldridge 1942). Further elaboration of the urbanization concept includes the movement from rural communities or areas to communities primarily centred on government, service, and allied urban activities. One effect of this movement to the city has been rural depopulation. Agriculture uses land as an instrument of production, encouraging the dispersion of population. Manufacturing, industry, and commerce, on the other hand, use land only as a site, stimulating the concentration of both population and economic activities, since non-agricultural activities can locate in close proximity to one another.

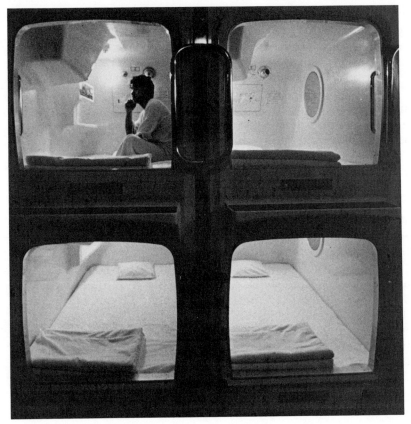

*The Capsule Hotel in Osaka, Japan, has 368 "rooms" containing the
necessities of life — a bed and a TV. Is this really, as the owners suggest,
how we'll have to live in the future?*

Statistical evidence points toward an increasingly urbanized nation.
Despite Canada's large land mass, about three-fourths of the population
reside in urban areas that occupy less than one one-hundredth of the
total land area (Economic Council of Canada 1967, 173). Since the beginning of this century, Canada has witnessed a dramatic increase in
urban population. In 1901, about 35 percent of the nation's population
were classified as urban, as defined by the census.[3] By the beginning of
the Depression period, mass immigration and the consequences of improved agricultural technology had shifted the balance for the first time;
almost 53 percent were living in urban areas by 1931. More than three-
fourths of Canadians resided in urban areas in 1981, and only 4.5 percent
were classified as rural farm residents principally engaged in agricultural
activities. (The remaining 20 percent were rural non-farm residents—
people who resided in rural places but were not farmers; a person who
lives on a rural land holding but commutes to the city to earn a livelihood
is so classified.)

The distribution of urban population in Canada reveals marked regional variations. Ontario has more than 80 percent of its total population classified as urban, and Prince Edward Island only 36 percent. The entire Maritime region, which comprises provinces engaged in primary industries, still manifests low proportions of urban populations, while the Prairie provinces, Quebec, and British Columbia are close to the national average.

In an effort to derive viable statistical units that would contain the ever-expanding urban population, analysts formulated the metropolitan area concept. Essentially, a metropolitan area is a group of urban communities that are in close economic, geographic, and social relationship. The **Census Metropolitan Area (CMA)**, introduced in the 1941 census, consists of a central city and its area of influence, which encompasses adjacent incorporated and unincorporated settlements.

The growth of metropolitan areas illustrates the increasing importance of the large urban complex in today's Canada. The proportion of Canada's population residing in metropolitan areas has increased from 30.3 percent in 1931 to 56.1 percent in 1981. In the same period of time, the number of metropolitan areas has more than doubled, from 10 to 24.

Although the increasing concentration of population in metropolitan areas has been impressive, the growth in major Canadian cities has weakened in recent years. The central cities of the larger CMAs have experienced declines, while the smaller and younger CMAs, expecially in the West, have sustained growth. The central cities that have lost population have reached their threshold of growth; they have become saturated with people and have no room for expansion. The suburban components of metropolitan areas have overtaken the central cities in terms of population growth. In 1981, 52.8 percent of the CMA population lived in the suburbs and 47.2 percent in the central cities. This shift in population balance results partly from the trend to decentralize the central city, coupled with residential development beyond its municipal limits. For example, Canada's largest central cities of Montreal and Toronto are surrounded by other municipalities that prevent further expansion. It is expected that these cities will continue to show population declines in future censuses.

(For a detailed examination of these and other aspects of urbanization, see Chapter 16.)

MORTALITY IN CANADA

One of the hallmarks of recorded history has been the continual struggle for survival. Human progress has been frequently dampened by catastrophe, famine, disease, war, and pestilence. Exposure to these harbingers of mortality has been duly recorded in family bibles, diaries, letters, personal testimonies, and grave markers.

Societal concern for the causes of death is reflected in the early development of vital-event record-keeping. During the 14th to the 17th centuries, Europe frequently suffered extensive epidemics. Until the Industrial Revolution, outbreaks of smallpox, cholera, typhus, and the notorious bubonic plague, or black death, were common, and killed proportionately more children than adults. These episodic conditions of high mortality served to depress population growth in the Western European societies, where mortality levels were high at the best of times.

Given the primitive communications of the day and the lack of any form of death certification, relatives often did not learn of the death of kinfolk, particularly if the latter lived in the congested urban centres where living conditions were particularly hazardous. It was not unusual for an urban newcomer to die from disease and simply be ignored or avoided by other city residents, especially during an epidemic. Early in the 16th century, this situation prompted the establishment of the first rudimentary system of vital registration.

London parishes initiated a primitive registry whereby corpses were collected and identified, and the cause of death diagnosed. This information was then circulated weekly so that subscribers and parish members could establish the status of missing friends and relatives. These records, which were identified as Bills of Mortality, were first printed in 1629. A generation later, analysis of these records by John Graunt, a draper by trade, provided documentation of the leading causes of death before the Industrial Revolution.[4] He noted that the three ranking causes were "chrisomes and infants" (diseases of infancy), consumption (tuberculosis), and fever—all parasitic infectious diseases.

In the industrialized world of today, these diseases are largely under control. All infectious diseases, including tuberculosis, diphtheria, whooping cough, smallpox, measles, and polio, accounted for less than 1 percent of all deaths in Canada in 1985 (Statistics Canada 1986, table 1). In contrast, the leading causes of death are degenerative diseases, which strike the elderly more often than the young.

Mortality Measures

One of society's foremost concerns is the health of its members. Any nation is at a serious disadvantage in the world community and politically vulnerable from within if it cannot ensure the maintenance of a healthy population. **Mortality** refers to death or termination of the life cycle, and **morbidity** to sickness, disease, and disability. The measures of both are considered symptomatic of a society's state of well-being. Data regarding mortality and morbidity in Canada are derived from vital statistics registration and life tables.

In demography, a **crude rate** of some occurrence relates the number of times that event occurs during a calendar year to the mid-year estimate of the total population. Thus, the **crude death rate** relates the number of deaths occurring in a specified calendar year to the population exposed to the risk of death. Since everyone is exposed to the risk of death during the life cycle, it is relatively simple to calculate a crude death rate. For example, the number of deaths that occurred in 1985 are divided by the country's mid-year population and the resulting figure is multiplied by 1000.[5] To say that the 1985 Canadian death rate was 7.2 means that there were 7.2 deaths per 1000 population in that specific calendar year.

Crude rates require a basic caution in interpretation. Variations in the proportionate size of age groups with particularly high or low mortality risks can produce distortions in the crude death rate, even if the actual mortality remains constant for the age groups in question. For example, the establishment of a large terminal-care nursing home in a city may dramatically increase the proportion of the population over 65 years of age, raising the crude death rate to a level higher than it would have been otherwise. In other words, the city's crude death rate conceals the influence of disportionate presence of "high mortality risk" age groups. The crude rate averages and hence attenuates the effects of high- or low-risk groups. More refined mortality measures are used to isolate such age effects. (This is not to deny the usefulness of crude mortality rates. They are easy to understand, are symptomatic of general levels of mortality, and are often the only measures available for less developed countries with limited population data.)

Exhibit 14-4 portrays for Canada the more precise **age-sex-specific mortality rates**, which take into account the fact that mortality is affected by the age and sex structure of the population. Whenever possible, separate mortality rates are calculated for each age category by sex, thus isolating the influence of high and low mortality risks, such as the very old and young males and females.

Contributors to Mortality Declines

Various social, economic, and technological advances over the years have influenced the state of health in the world today. Thomlinson (1976, 97-99) identifies ten leading contributors to the decline in mortality and improvement in morbidity witnessed by the developed countries over the past two centuries. The precipitating factors were improvements in agricultural technology. Such innovations as crop rotation techniques, improved fertilizers, farm machinery, and weed control served to raise the quantity and quality of the food produced. Then the Industrial Revolution developed the factory system, which eventually permitted the mass production of a vast variety of products to assist the population in fending off death—from thermopane windows, humidifiers, and winter clothing to refrigerators for the preservation of food. Transportation improvements over time facilitated the distribution of these products to more and more people. Social reforms reduced the occupational hazards in various lines of work by requiring the use of safety devices and estab-

Exhibit 14-4
Age-Sex-Specific Death Rates, Canada, 1921 and 1985

	Males		Females	
	1921	1985	1921	1985
	Rate per 1000 population			
All Ages	10.9	8.0	10.2	6.0
< 1 yr.	98.2	8.7	77.4	7.1
1–4	7.9	0.5	6.9	0.4
5–9	3.1	0.3	2.7	0.2
10–14	2.1	0.3	1.9	0.2
15–19	3.1	1.0	2.7	0.4
20–24	3.7	1.4	3.7	0.4
25–29	4.0	1.3	4.1	0.4
30–34	3.8	1.4	4.5	0.6
35–39	4.7	1.6	5.5	0.8
40–44	5.6	2.4	5.9	1.4
45–49	7.3	3.9	7.1	2.4
50–54	9.8	6.9	10.2	3.8
55–59	15.2	11.3	13.5	5.9
60–64	21.9	18.0	19.7	9.1
65–69	33.4	28.9	33.2	14.6
70–74	56.9	44.7	52.8	22.9
75–79	89.4	67.6	80.9	38.7
80–84	133.8	106.0	122.4	63.7
85 +	228.2	205.5	224.9	145.7

Sources: Statistics Canada, *Vital Statistics, Vol. III, Deaths, 1971*, table 14; Statistics Canada, *Vital Statistics, Vol. IV, Causes of Death, 1985*, table 1.

lishing more healthful work guidelines, such as minimum working ages, maximum working hours, the provision of work-site health services, and designated rest and exercise periods. The vast improvements in public sanitation and the health regulations that govern the quality of food and water supply have also had considerable influence on the population's health. Changes in personal hygiene and preventive health practices—brushing the teeth, bathing regularly, using soap, having periodic medical examinations, and using cosmetics carefully—have also improved health. The seriousness and incidence of respiratory disorders have been attenuated through the capability to control temperature and humidity in homes and workplaces. In the medical arena, advances in biochemical applications, such as sterilization techiques, the use of surgical masks, aseptic and antiseptic surgery, sulfa and antibiotics, and the development of immunology, have led to the increased survival of the injured or diseased.

The net effect of these factors has been a long-term fall in mortality. The death rate for Canada has declined fairly continuously, from 11.6 in 1921 to 8.2 in 1954 and 7.2 in 1985. This levelling off is simply the consequence of a lack of any recent innovation with major implications for either mortality or morbidity. To be sure, there have been improvements, but nothing has approached the magnitude of the foregoing contributors. This increasing ability to control mortality, as well as morbidity, has resulted in improved survival chances. Communicable diseases, the child-killers of previous times, have been brought under control through immunology and the establishment of preventive health programs. The consequence of this singular change in mortality has been an improvement in life expectancy and the relatively new health concern with the degenerative diseases of old age.

Causes of Death

The remarkable shift from high to relatively low mortality in Canada, which is typical of industrialized countries, is well evidenced by comparing cause-of-death data from 1921 with 1985 mortality data. (See Exhibit 14-5.) The leading causes of death in 1985 were diseases of the circulatory system (43.3 percent of all causes) and neoplasms—cancers (25.8 percent). Together they represented 70 percent of all causes, while in 1921 they accounted for almost 21 percent. Over the 60-year period, death from infectious and parasitic diseases declined from an incidence of 106.7 to less than one per 100,000 population. Corresponding declines occurred for diseases of the respiratory and digestive systems and perinatal diseases.

As the incidence of death from infectious, parasitic, respiratory, and perinatal diseases declines, the survivorship of the younger population improves. The nation's mortality concerns are now directed toward the degenerative diseases, which take their toll among the older segments of the population.

Exhibit 14-6 shows the ten leading causes of death by sex in 1985. Diseases of the circulatory system were most common, cancer was in second place, and diseases of the respiratory system were third. To consider specific causes, rather than general categories, ischaemic heart disease accounted for 60.4 percent of all diseases of the circulatory system,— 26.1 percent of all deaths—in 1985. This type of heart disease caused the most deaths among both males and females.

In recent years, the government's health system has made strong efforts to increase public awareness of personal health care, diagnosis, and treatment with respect to such causes of death as heart disease, breast cancer

Exhibit 14-5
Percentage Distribution of Causes of Death, Canada, 1921 and 1985

Cause of Death	1921[a] (No. = 67 722)	1985 (No. = 181 323)
Infectious and parasitic diseases	13.8	0.6
Diseases of circulatory system	13.5	43.3
Diseases of respiratory system	12.8	7.8
Diseases of digestive system	10.1	3.7
Perinatal	9.0	0.7
Malignant neoplasms	7.4	25.8
External causes	6.2	7.4
All causes of death	100.0	100.0

[a]Data exclude Newfoundland.
Sources: Statistics Canada, *Vital Statistics, 1921*, table 19; Statistics Canada, *Vital Statistics, Vol. IV, Causes of Death, 1985*, table 1.

Exhibit 14-6
Death Rates for the Ten Leading Causes of Mortality, Canada, 1985

Cause of Death	Both Sexes	Males	Females
	Rate per 100 000 population		
All circulatory system diseases	309.4	333.8	285.6
Ischaemic heart disease	186.8	219.4	154.9
All malignant neoplasms	184.4	205.1	164.2
All respiratory diseases	55.4	68.3	42.8
Cerebrovascular disease	54.7	47.2	62.0
All accidents	52.9	74.9	31.3
Lung cancer	45.1	65.9	24.7
Pneumonia	22.3	23.0	21.5
Breast cancer	16.7	0.3	32.8
Motor vehicle accidents	16.2	22.9	9.6

Source: Statistics Canada, *Vital Statistics, Vol. IV, Causes of Death, 1985*, table 1.

Exhibit 14-7
Death Rates for Selected Causes of Mortality, Canada, 1970 and 1985

Cause of Death	Both Sexes		Males		Females	
	1970	1985	1970	1985	1970	1985
	Rate per 100 000 population					
Ischaemic heart disease	230.1	186.8	283.6	219.4	176.4	154.9
Breast cancer	13.0	16.7	0.3	0.3	25.8	32.8
Lung cancer	23.7	45.1	40.3	65.9	7.0	24.7

Source: Statistics Canada, *Vital Statistics, Vol. IV, Causes of Death, 1985*, table 1.

among females, and lung cancer. If the public is responding to these information and educational programs, their health behaviour should improve. For example, women should be able to notice the danger signals of breast cancer in time for proper medical treatment; both men and women should recognize the connection between smoking and lung cancer, and both respond to the symptoms of heart disorder and be aware of the appropriate emergency treatment. These positive changes in health behaviour at the individual level should be reflected in declines in the incidence of these causes of death.

Exhibit 14-7 reveals that, of the mortality rates for these causes of death, only that for ischaemic heart disease declined from 1970 to 1985. In fact, deaths from breast cancer in women and from lung cancer increased over the 15 years. It may be too early, however, for these mortality rates to register the benefits of some campaigns, particularly the anti-smoking efforts directed toward the teenage population. It is also interesting to note that deaths from ischaemic heart disease declined more among men than women. This phenomenon may be the result of the general notion prevailing in Canada that heart disease is more common among men than women; hence, more preventive attention is directed toward men.

Death Rate Trends in Canada

Since 1921, Canada has experienced a decline in mortality for the population as a whole, as well as for each sex. One notable pattern is that the male mortality rates have been consistently higher than those for females for every age group. The female mortality rates have declined more rapidly than those for males over the 65-year period.

This mortality differential between males and females has been attributed to the effects of several factors. One is that the sex ratio is high at birth. The **sex ratio** measures the relationship of males to females; to say that the sex ratio at birth is 105 signifies that 105 male infants are born for every 100 female infants. This fact, coupled with significantly higher fetal and infant mortality rates for males, suggests that males are biologically more vulnerable to the risks of mortality in the initial period of the life cycle. Sex-specific factors in adult life, such as military deaths in wars and specific hazards in occupations that have been restricted to or dominated by men, obviously contribute to this mortality differential. It has also been argued that the greater exposure of men to tension in their occupations has contributed to their relatively greater risk of certain stress-related diseases, such as heart failure, ulcers, and strokes. Another claim is that women have inherent biological superiority; it is disputed, but there is some medical evidence of the greater hardiness of females. A sociological factor of considerable importance is that women are more health-conscious than males, in that they are socialized to respond more quickly than men to symptoms and therefore make greater use of health

Demographers have found that population changes reflect changes in the death rate more than in the birth rate. The numbers of occupants in the hospital morgue, rather than in the baby nursery, determine a population's characteristics.

services.[6] Finally, some of the causes of death to which women were most susceptible in the past have been brought under control. It is difficult to assess the relative impact of each of the foregoing factors upon the sex mortality differential; however, the net effect has been dramatically in favour of women.

For both males and females, it is evident that mortality declines markedly after the first year of life has been successfully completed. The human infant is a quite defenceless and dependent organism and is thus exposed to high mortality risk. It is not surprising that infant mortality is extremely high in societies that lack proper nutritional levels, medical care, hospital facilities, and emphasis on pre-natal and post-natal care. Within Canada, relatively high **infant mortality rates** (mortality rates for the first 12 months of life)[7] are likely found in health-disadvantaged areas, such as Indian reserves, rural farm areas, and smaller rural settlements. The level of infant mortality is often used as a symptomatic indicator of a society's well-being.

After the first year of life, the death rates decline until the 10-to-14 age range. After this point, the rates increasingly advance with age, and the differences in mortality between the sexes begin to get larger in the middle years of life.

Mortality by Marital Status

As already noted, death rates are relatively high at the outset and toward the end of the life cycle because of great vulnerability to death at birth and the accelerating risk later in life resulting from the degeneration process. At various stages of the life cycle, however, other factors—including environmental conditions, economic activity, lifestyles, travel, leisure pursuits, and marital status—may influence age patterns in mortality. The marital role is a positive influence, in that married people enjoy more favourable mortality rates than the divorced, widowed, or single people.

One cause of this variation is the mate selection process, because healthy mates tend to select one another. In addition, marriage provides a health support network in which the spouses detect symptoms in each other, encourage treatment, and ensure a good health environment. Conversely, non-married individuals are not likely to have this type of network, may be exposed to a more risky lifestyle, and may get less adequate nutrition and hence be more vulnerable to mortality. Divorced and separated people also likely experience health consequences of the fact that the marital status change is stressful; they may engage in "stress-release" behaviour and are likely to suffer the most from acute conditions, such as respiratory, digestive, and infective illnesses, as well as injuries (Verbrugge 1979, 272). Widowhood is similarly disruptive but may not require as severe an alteration of domestic routine as that likely to be experienced by the divorced and separated. Widows who fall ill are, however, likely candidates for institutional care to replace the home care that they have lost.

All of these factors operate to create varying risks for mortality among people with different marital statuses. In addition to age, sex, and marital status, demographers have found other significant mortality differentials, such as place of residence (urban or rural), occupation, race, education, ethnicity, and religion.

Implications of Mortality Changes

As mortality levels decline, the obvious implication is that increasing numbers of Canadians will enjoy more years of life than ever before in history. Other implications are less apparent but equally significant. Declining mortality in the 20th century has produced several social changes that have influenced the Canadian way of life. The increased survival chances of infants have undoubtedly encouraged stronger emotional bonding between parent and child. The improvement of survivorship within the early and late maturity age ranges (20 to 50 years) has reduced orphanhood,[8] which was not uncommon at the turn of the century. The decline in mortality has also reduced the proportion of children who experience the death of a member of the immediate family; in earlier times it was common for a parent or sibling to die or a stillbirth to occur within the family.

The family of earlier times is often thought of as the extended type in which several generations of blood kin reside in a single household. Modern times have produced a more demographically ideal situation for extended families than ever before, in that survival rates have increased the number of living grandparents. This factor alone has compounded the difficulties encountered by the more advanced societies, which are characterized by the nuclear family. The problems such a society has in coping with the needs of larger numbers of elderly are given vivid testimony in the recent controversies over pension planning and benefits, institutionalized care facilities, hospice strategies, housing for the elderly, and leisure programs, to name a few. On the other hand, there are positive social benefits from a child's relationship with grandparents who survive well beyond the initial socialization stage in the life cycle.

Improvements in mortality have negative as well as positive consequences within a society. For example, an increasing proportion of elderly depend upon their children for survival since existing (and projected) societal services do not meet the demand. The "children" here are themselves middle-aged and faced with a social problem for which there are no guidelines at present. It is evident that improved longevity also increases the number of years that marriages survive; however, the number of years that marriages are exposed to the risk of divorce is correspondingly increased. This change has undoubtedly influenced the increase in the divorce and separation rates experienced in recent years. In other words, although children may not be exposed to the disruptive aspects of death in the immediate family, they face an increased probability of family disorganization through divorce and separation.

The fact that women have a distinct mortality edge over men has resulted in a lengthening of their exposure to the status of widowhood. This may eventually have implications for the remarriage pattern of older females. As discussed later in this chapter, women in our society tend to marry men somewhat older than themselves. The mortality differential does not operate in favour of the widow because there are relatively fewer eligible men in the older age categories. It is conceivable that if a widow wishes to remarry, she may be forced to select a mate from a pool of younger men—a deviation from the traditional mating-age norm.

The prevailing emphasis today is, of course, upon the degenerative diseases and the means of coping with the terminally ill, infirm, and essentially dependent-aged population. But the "dependent age" may no longer begin at 50 or 65; nearer 80 may be more realistic. The implication is not only that the older population is going to be healthy and active for a longer period of time, but that a significant number will want to remain active in working careers. This will obviously increase the pool of eligibles for part-time and even full-time employment, as well as for leisure activities. A related implication is that there will be an increasing proportion of **contracted families**, or "empty nests," where the children have all matured and left home, leaving reduced families that consist of just the surviving spouses.

In brief, it is essential to be cognizant of the many implications of increasing longevity. Retirement consciousness and the necessity of viable pension programs, the contracted family form, the potential for changes in the marriage and divorce patterns of the elderly, late career shifts, an older work force, an emphasis on degenerative disease control and research, and the fact that older age groups will enjoy a more healthy and active life in their later years will generate a new set of values for and attitudes toward the elderly in Canada.

NUPTIALITY AND LIVING ARRANGEMENTS IN CANADA

Traditionally, the family has served to provide societal continuity from one generation to the next through reproduction and socialization of its members. The family life cycle is initiated by the act of marriage, which provides the legitimate status for childbearing within Western society. The study of **nuptiality** refers to this marital status, its rate of occurrence within society, and the characteristics of the marital partners, as well as marital dissolution. **Marital dissolution**, accordingly, refers to the dissolving of marital unions through divorce, separation, and death. The monitoring of marriage and divorce is of considerable importance in order to assess the nature of the risk population for future fertility within a society.

Although separation is also a status that reduces the pool of women eligible for childbearing, it is not monitored as a vital event in Canada because it is not always officially recorded. Marital partners may informally agree to maintain separate households and not seek a documented, legal separation through the courts. Thus, measuring only legal separations could seriously underestimate the actual occurrence of separation, which is an important component of the population's marital status. In an analysis of self-reported marital statuses from the 1976 census of Canada, McVey and Robinson (1981) find that the number of separations is significantly higher than that of divorces in every age group.

Marriage

Several factors influence the dynamics of the marriage process. Clearly, the ratio between males and females in the relevant age groups influence marriage opportunities. The relevant age groups in this instance are in accordance with the prevailing **mating gradient**, which is the normatively supported age difference between the sexes at the time of marriage. Our culture has norms that support and reinforce marriage between younger females and older males. The age difference is customarily two to three years; for example, a twenty-year-old female is likely to seek a marital partner two to three years older. The socialization process prepares girls for dating and mate selection at an earlier age than it does boys. Continuing social pressures discourage our twenty-year-old female from seeking a mate whose age diverges much in either direction from the prevailing marriage age norms. Veevers (1977a, 34) notes in addition that the husband's position of dominance is enhanced by a maturity in age.

When the relevant age groups are in imbalance—that is, when the numbers of either males or females are deficient—the frequency of marriage is likely to alter. For example, a woman caught in such a **marriage squeeze** must marry a man somewhat older or younger than prescribed by the mating gradient norms, or postpone marriage. If the social pressures to marry at a certain age are very strong, the female (or male) may have to deviate considerably from the mating gradient in order to conform. Canadian women were confronted with a marriage squeeze in the mid-1960s, the consequence of the maturing of female babies born just after the Second World War. When these large female birth cohorts reached marriageable age, the eligible male cohorts were smaller as a consequence of the lower pre-war birth rates. In general, the women decided to deviate from the mating gradient and marry men of their own age.

Societal pressures concerning the appropriate length of the period of formal education can also influence the norm for the age at marriage. It was customarily the practice to wait until completion of formal schooling before taking on the responsibility of marriage; hence, if the length of formal schooling was of some duration, the age at marriage was relatively late, reducing the number of marriages. It is of interest to note that this marriage norm formerly extended to university training. Veterans returning to campuses following the Second World War provided new role models for younger university students, and the schools began to respond to married students' needs by providing housing, day-care services, and financial assistance. The younger students learned that classroom and marriage could co-exist, and there was a precedent for an emerging norm of not deferring marriage until after completion of a university degree.

Another factor influencing the incidence and age of marriage is the level of economic activity in the country. Times of favourable economic conditions encourage marriage, in that jobs and other opportunities are plentiful, unemployment is low, and income potential seems likely to be realized. Thus promising economic indicators offer considerable encouragement to the young person who is entertaining marriage. Correspondingly, in times of economic recession these indicators discourage marriage. Limited job opportunities increase competition for available employment, and the uncertainty of job security is threatening. The economic, legal, and social responsibilities of marriage may seem too much of an additional burden during times of stress.

Restrictive or liberal divorce legislation also influences marriage rates by affecting the number of remarriages occurring in a society. Liberalizing the grounds for divorce can stimulate an increase in the incidence of remarriage, as was the case in Canada following the enactment of the Divorce Act of 1968. Since then remarriages have accounted for a significant portion of the annual number of marriages.

Finally, the optional lifestyles and living arrangements presented by the various mass media influence the incidence and age of marriage, in that they offer alternatives to the traditional forms of marriage and family. The televised portrayal of economically independent career women, the divorced and the widowed coping with stress, financial hardship, and a variety of cohabitation combinations indicate increasing societal acceptance of these living arrangement options. The mass media not only convey the prevailing values of the public, they precipitate change in marriage and parenting values.

Trends in Marriage and Divorce

The effects of the foregoing factors are clearly revealed in the historical trends of marriage and divorce. Although the absolute numbers of marriages have increased from the 71,254 recorded in 1921 to 184,096 in 1985, it is interesting to note that the marriage rates were about the same for these two time periods (7.9 and 7.3 respectively). The **marriage rate** is defined as the number of marriages per 1000 population in a given calendar year.

Low marriage rates were recorded during the economic Depression of the early 1930s—the lowest ever recorded in Canada was 5.9 for 1932—reflecting the hesitancy of the eligible population to take on the additional responsibilities of marriage. These collective decisions, of course, resulted in lower birth rates during these years, and when these relatively smaller cohorts of Depression babies reached marriageable age in the early to mid-1950s, the supply of eligibles was reduced, partially contributing to relatively lower marriage rates from 1956 to 1961.

Higher marriage rates in the early to mid-1940s were stimulated by social and economic influences. Canada entered the Second World War in 1939, precipitating an economic revival from the Depression period. Employment levels increased, contributing a measure of stability and prosperity that lasted into the post-war period. Marriages that had been postponed because of the Depression or wartime absences helped to stimulate a peak rate of 10.9 per thousand in both 1942 and 1946. This period of high marriage rates generated large cohorts of women for childbearing. One consequence of the resultant baby boom appeared about 20 years later in the form of high marriage rates, commencing in the early to mid-1970s.

Since reaching a high of 9.2 in 1972, the Canadian marriage rates have continued to decline. Shrinking cohorts of eligibles (produced by the

lower birth rates of the 1960s), coupled with increasing economic uncertainty, job competition, and changing values relating to marriage, seem
likely to sustain declines in marriage rates. It is interesting to note in
Exhibit 14-8 that, of all the provinces, Alberta evidences the highest
marriage rates. This is not surprising since the economic prosperity and
employment opportunities that the province enjoyed served to attract
young migrants, as well as to retain young Albertans, in the prime marriage ages.

Exhibit 14-8
Marriages and Divorces, Canada and Provinces, 1985

	Marriages		Divorces	
	Number	Rate	Number	Rate
Canada	184 096	7.3	61 980	244.4
Newfoundland	3 220	5.5	561	96.6
Prince Edward Island	956	7.5	213	167.6
Nova Scotia	6 807	7.7	2 337	265.4
New Brunswick	5 312	7.4	1 360	189.1
Quebec	37 026	5.6	15 814	240.3
Ontario	72 891	8.0	20 854	230.0
Manitoba	8 296	7.8	2 314	216.3
Saskatchewan	7 132	7.0	1 927	189.0
Alberta	19 750	8.4	8 102	344.9
British Columbia	22 292	7.7	8 330	288.0
Yukon	185	8.1	96	421.0
Northwest Territories	229	4.4	72	141.4

Note: Marriage rate is per 1000 population; divorce rate is per
        100 000 population.
Source: Statistics Canada, *Vital Statistics, Vol. II, Marriages and Divorces,
        1985*, table 1.

The **divorce rate**—the number of recorded divorces per 100,000 population in a calendar year—increased dramatically from 6.4 in 1921 to
244.4 in 1985. Significant increases in marriages tend to generate high
numbers of divorces a few years later. The first peak divorce years of
1946 and 1947, with rates of 63.1 and 65.4, respectively, reflected the
marital disruption experienced by the large marriage cohorts of the Second World War period. A second notable upswing in divorce began in
1969 with a rate of 124.2, demonstrating the effect of the 1968 divorce
legislation.
Marital stability is publicly questioned in light of the high divorce rates
in recent years, and many people quickly conclude that the outlook is

dismal for marriage and the family in Canada. It is important to recognize, however, that the high rates since 1969 likely reflect the final dissolution of many marriages that have been disrupted for some time. The liberalization of divorce grounds permitted separated couples and partners maintaining "empty shell" marriages to resolve their marital discord. Although it is likely that the Canadian divorce rate will long remain higher than it was before 1969, the yearly increases will probably not be as dramatic as they were between 1966 and 1976. Higher rates of divorce will be sustained in future years because of the relative ease in obtaining divorce as a means of resolving marital discord, the increasing economic independence of women, the viable lifestyle options to marriage conveyed through the mass media, and even the declining birth rate, which is linked with less complicated divorces.[9]

Remarriage

It is obvious that with the increase in divorces over the past two decades, the supply of marriage eligibles has grown, resulting in several interesting changes for nuptiality. An examination of the marital status of brides and bridegrooms at the time of marriage reveals that people who had been married at least once before—that is, the widowed and divorced—account for an increasing share of the total marriages, from 8.7 in 1961 to 21 percent in 1985.

Another measure of this phenomenon is in terms of marriages in which at least one partner has had previous marriage experience. There are eight possible combinations, ranging from a single man marrying a divorced woman to the marriage of two widowed people. Remarriage has become a significant element in the total marriage scene. Schlesinger (1970) notes that, between 1954 and and 1964, remarriages averaged only 13.1 percent of all marriages. By 1985, however, this proportion increased to about one-third of all marriages (29.7 percent). The most common combinations in remarriage are, in order, two previously divorced partners, a divorced man and a single woman, and a single man and a divorced woman. These three accounted for 85.2 percent of all remarriages in 1985.

It is likely that the notion of marrying "until death do us part" will give way to "until divorce do us part." The past twenty years alone have seen a significant shift in the previous marital status of remarriage partners. In 1961, the widowed made up 55.2 percent of all remarriage partners; by 1985, the divorced were 86.2 percent.

The relaxation of the grounds for divorce, the increased tolerance toward divorce and alternative living arrangements, and increased longevity raise the probability of a Canadian's experiencing more than one marriage over his or her lifetime. Serial (sequential) marriage has become one of the common nuptiality patterns in Canada. Selecting a single mate for a lifetime is no longer the only option in a marital career.

Remarriage after being widowed or divorced late in life is, however, more likely for men than for women in Canada because of the differential in mortality and the mating gradient. Widowers who elect to remarry have an ample supply of eligibles to select from, but widows find eligible men in shorter supply. This explains, in part, the tendency for widows not to remarry over the remaining years of their lifespan and the like-lihood of widowers to remarry. This is consistent with the tendency for the older population who separate to remain in this status, rather than to divorce and then remarry (McVey and Robinson 1981). It is suggested that the older population are very much aware of the shortcomings in the marriage market.

Age at Marriage

Changes in Canadian society's view of the appropriate age to marry are less dramatic but equally important. Women who marry at an early age are exposed to the risk of childbirth, planned or unplanned, for a longer period of time than women who postpone marriage until later in their life. A societal norm of early marriage is thus likely to generate a higher fertility than occurs in societies with later marriage-age norms.

Measuring this phenomenon is, however, more complex than appears at first glance. The obvious measure, average age at marriage, is affected by the incidence of remarriage, which, of course, involves partners who are older. The more sensitive measure is the average age at first marriage. It controls for the distorting influence of remarriage and, therefore, better reflects the prevailing attitude toward appropriate first-time mar-riage age, as well as the effects of economic pressures.

Between 1941 and 1966, the average age at both marriage and first marriage steadily declined for brides and bridegrooms, indicating an increasing societal tolerance for younger marriages. The urgencies of the war period, as well as the immediate post-war economic prosperity, likely contributed to this tendency. The distorting influence of remarriage was minimal because of its low incidence at this time. Age at first marriage declined until 1971, when brides married at an average of 22.6 years and grooms at 24.9 years. The marriage squeeze likely contributed to this continued decline.

Over the past decade, both measures reveal an increase in marriage age. The increase in remarriages undoubtedly affected the average age at marriage; the increases in age at first marriage are more complicated to explain. Societal prohibitions may dictate a lower age at first marriage that becomes a social limit, thereby discouraging further declines for either males or females. It is not likely that this threshold had been reached in 1971—in fact, other evidence suggests there has been greater social acceptability of younger marriages in Canada—yet the average age at first marriage has increased steadily since then. One social trend that contributed to this rise in first marriage age is the increased popularity of cohabitation among young people, as an alternative to marriage. The exclusion of cohabiting young people from the official records would effectively bias the age at first marriage toward the somewhat older young people who do marry.

One of the notable points revealed by the age-at-marriage measures is the changing age difference between brides and bridegrooms. Since 1941, it has narrowed from more than three years to 2.2 years for first marriages and 2.6 years for all marriages. In other words, the marriage gradient has changed significantly over the 40-year period. This phenomenon may reflect other changes occurring in modern marriage, such as more equitable division of labour within marriage, a reduction in differences between bride and groom in education and experience, and shifts in power and authority structures that have given women more equitable influence in decision-making within the household and strengthened their position within marriage.

Another subject to consider is teenage marriages, which have been of considerable concern over the past decade to high school administrators, family planning agencies, and religious and municipal counselling professionals. In fact, teenage marriages have not increased. Such a rise would have lowered the age at first marriage, and, as already noted, this has not been the case in recent years. A more detailed examination reveals that the marriage rates have declined for young people of both sexes between 15 and 19 years of age. Between 1977 and 1985, the marriage rates for teenage females dropped from 36.0 to 16.6 per 1000 and from 9.4 to 3.1 for teenage males. (Because of the mating gradient, female teenagers always have higher rates than males.) This decline may be an illusion, since little is known about the extent of cohabitation among teenagers.

Early marriage or cohabitation increases the number of years that young couples are exposed to the risks of childbearing and marital disruptions. In addition, married or cohabitating teenagers are handicapped in terms of educational attainment, financial resources, and opportunities for personal growth and development. Early marriage coupled with childbearing immeasurably increases the young people's burden of dependency and intensifies the emotional strain within the marriage itself. These social, psychological, and economic strains increase the probability of marital failure at an early age. Studies indicate that the rate of marital dissolution is highest for young men between the ages of 15 and 19 years (Carter and Glick 1976, 236). The younger the marriage age, the higher the risk of separation and divorce.

The Emergence of New Living Arrangements

The husband-wife family is the most common living arrangement in Canada, where it represents 88.7 percent of all families recorded in 1981. The **lone-parent family** accounted for the remaining 11.3 percent, an almost 50 percent increase in the decade following 1971. This rise came entirely from the dramatic increase of lone-parent families headed by women. Wargon (1979) points out the increasing probability that children will experience living in a single-parent family at some point in their lifetime. The continuing increase in divorce and separation will sustain the lone-parent form as a significant non-traditional family living arrangement.

Of all the other categories of living arrangements, the non-family household has become singularly important in Canada. The **non-family household** is essentially an economic living arrangement in which one person lives alone or a group of unrelated persons share a dwelling. In contrast, a **family household** is a social unit that must include at least one family. Using this framework, one can study living arrangements as one-family and two-family households plus one-person and multiple-person non-family households.

Between 1961 and 1981, non-family households increased by 238.4 percent, from 605,801 to more than 2 million. Improved longevity and mortality differentials have led to a dramatic increase in the number of widows and widowers who opt to live independently in one-person non-family households. In addition, increasing numbers of young people are electing to live by themselves at earlier ages than before. Many divorced and separated people also choose such a living arrangement. There has been a remarkable rise in the number of people living alone in Canada over the past 25 years, from 425,000 in 1956 to more than 1.6 million in 1981. In fact, the one-person household is the fastest growing of any household size in Canada. Living alone accounted for more than one-fifth of all households in 1981, and 82 percent of all non-family households.

This trend will likely continue throughout the 1980s, with an increasing impact on various social services, transportation systems, housing markets, recreational facilities, and health services. Small living groups create a substantial demand for apartment and townhouse accommodation. The housing industry and government subsidy programs are called on to cater to the varying needs of the specialized populations who make up the non-family household. Many lone-parent families, as well as single, divorced, separated, and widowed individuals—all growing populations—continue to opt for independent living arrangements. Although these groups require less space than traditional families, their lifestyles are more financially vulnerable. In addition, elderly people who attempt to maintain independence and privacy require more low-cost, specialized housing and services as their health begins to decline with age (Fletcher and Stone 1982). The locational preferences of these groups will increase demand for housing in inner cities close to cultural, health, recreational, and other urban amenities.

The continued growth of the lone-parent family and the single person non-family household is contingent, in large part, on a reasonably viable economic situation in Canada. In a deteriorating economy, the high costs of housing and mortgage interest rates may force shared living arrangements in what is called the **doubling process**. Single people may live with their parents longer, the divorced, the separated, and lone parents may either share accommodations or return to their parental families, and the elderly may have to rely on kin network.

(For more discussion of non-traditional living arrangements, including cohabitation, see Chapter 5).

FERTILITY: THE CRUCIAL FACTOR

Of the three basic components of population change, fertility has played the crucial role in population growth and the consequent alteration of the age structure. With mortality and migration levels relatively controlled, the changes in the fertility of the Canadian population during the past 40 years have had profound effects upon the age composition.

The **fertility**, or actual reproductive behaviour, of women has been of general concern in Canada for several decades. Fertility levels are of specific concern to government leaders, medical professionals, educators, policy-makers, and the private sector for varying reasons. The growth of Canadian society is measured by natural increase and thus is contingent on Canadian women's fertility behaviour. Generally speaking, fertility behaviour is social behaviour—an outcome of the prevailing values and attitudes concerning parenting and family size, and, as already noted, values and attitudes are subject to modification in response to many economic and cultural factors.

Declining Family Size

Canadian society has witnessed declining family size since the turn of the century, and this decrease accelerated after the Second World War as a consequence of several key economic and social factors. The average family size for Canada in 1800 was 5.7 (with both parents present); it has now declined to 3.3, according to the 1981 census.

In the early 19th century, birth rates exceeding 50 per 1000 had to be maintained to offset equally high mortality rates (Henripin 1972). The lower birth rates of the 1970s and 1980s in part reflect the progress made in health care and medical technology.

These low birth rates also reflect many of the socioeconomic factors discussed earlier as common to the Western industrialized countries. As Canada changed from an agricultural economy to an urban-industrial nation, children were increasingly viewed as liabilities rather than assets to the family. Any increases in the length of formal education required for children extends the period of time that the child is dependent upon parents. Another push toward declining family size has come from the increasing number of lifestyles available to Canadians. There are alternative ways of spending family income, and the increasing cost of raising children is balanced against the acquisition of consumer products, such as a newer home, a new or second car, or an annual vacation. The child is being equated with consumer durables as part of a preferred lifestyle package. As well, the increasing acceptance of women in the labour force over the past 40 years has had implications for family size. The family may become dependent upon the income that the wife's employment provides, and she may develop a lifestyle that she prefers over the domestic role of raising children.

Another factor is that Canadian society has become characterized by occupational mobility as a means to occupational success. The young couple may feel that children will hinder their freedom to take advantage of occupational opportunities elsewhere. In addition, modern entertainment, in all its forms, promotes the "good life" associated with small families, and the diffusion of the mass media to rural parts of the country has exposed formerly isolated populations to urban values and attitudes toward family size.

The family of the post-war era usually resides in a smaller house or city apartment, which makes an additional child an expensive and bothersome undertaking for some couples. Currently, high housing prices, mortgage financing, and maintenance costs impose further economic

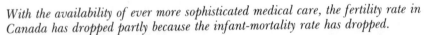

With the availability of ever more sophisticated medical care, the fertility rate in Canada has dropped partly because the infant-mortality rate has dropped.

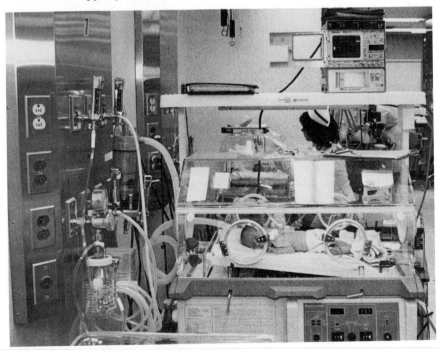

constraints, and the young Canadian couple is less likely to be able to purchase a home. Young married people may be forced to reside in small, rental accommodations or with their parents for a relatively long period of time.

All these social and economic constraints serve to discourage early family formation and result in a lowering of the average family size.

Shifts in the Age Structure

Canada's birth rate increased from a low of 20.3 births per 1000 population during the Depression years to slightly more than 28 in 1947 and 1958. This deceptively modest increase produced successively larger birth cohorts from the 1940s into the 1950s, generating what is now popularly known as the baby boom.

Canada's fertility behaviour was responding to the post-war period of prosperity. Couples who had deferred having children during the Depression and war years now began to have them. Fertility levels specific to young adult cohorts (1951 to 1961) increased substantially. Young married couples commenced childbearing soon after marriage and became leading contributors to the nation's fertility level. Other factors influencing this post-war phenomenon were the return of the military from overseas, a continuing increase in the marriage rates, and a decline in the age at first marriage. The net effect of all of these factors together contributed to this unprecedented increase in Canada's birth rate.

Exhibit 14-9 portrays the age and sex distribution of the Canadian population from 1951 to 1981. The larger birth cohorts introduced in 1951 produced a "shoulder effect" that continues to influence the shape of the age structure in succeeding years.

Many sectors of our society were caught unaware as these increasingly larger birth cohorts were introduced into Canada's age structure. Demands for age-specific products, expertise, facilities, and services were immediate; maternity ward space was in short supply; and existing child care professionals experienced strain, as did obstetricians, gynecologists, nursing staffs, and support personnel. As these birth cohorts aged, there were corresponding needs for a broad assortment of products and services, ranging from pull toys, baby oil, soft foods, and diaper delivery to playgrounds and endowment plans.

Different age-specific needs and consequences emerged as these cohorts matured into the adolescent and teenage years. Increasing elementary and secondary school enrolments during the mid-1950s and 1960s served notice to the provincial governments for more school facilities, teachers, nurses and counsellors, and equipment and supplies. The innovative school portable unit was testimony to the difficulty encountered in meeting the demand for space. The private sector soon realized that the teenage population of Canada was both large and affluent. Various industries responded quickly to this growing consumer

Exhibit 14-9
Age Structure, Canadian Population, 1951–81

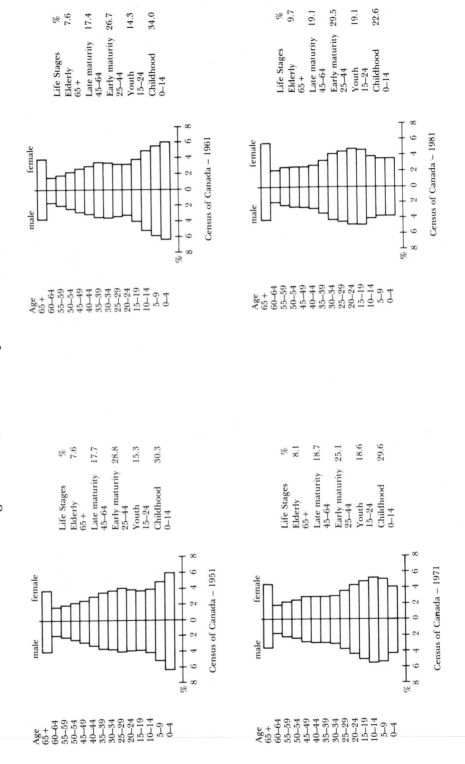

Life Stages	%
Elderly 65+	7.6
Late maturity 45–64	17.7
Early maturity 25–44	28.8
Youth 15–24	15.3
Childhood 0–14	30.3

Life Stages	%
Elderly 65+	7.6
Late maturity 45–64	17.4
Early maturity 25–44	26.7
Youth 15–24	14.3
Childhood 0–14	34.0

Life Stages	%
Elderly 65+	8.1
Late maturity 45–64	18.7
Early maturity 25–44	25.1
Youth 15–24	18.6
Childhood 0–14	29.6

Life Stages	%
Elderly 65+	9.7
Late maturity 45–64	19.1
Early maturity 25–44	29.5
Youth 15–24	19.1
Childhood 0–14	22.6

Census of Canada – 1951

Census of Canada – 1961

Census of Canada – 1971

Census of Canada – 1981

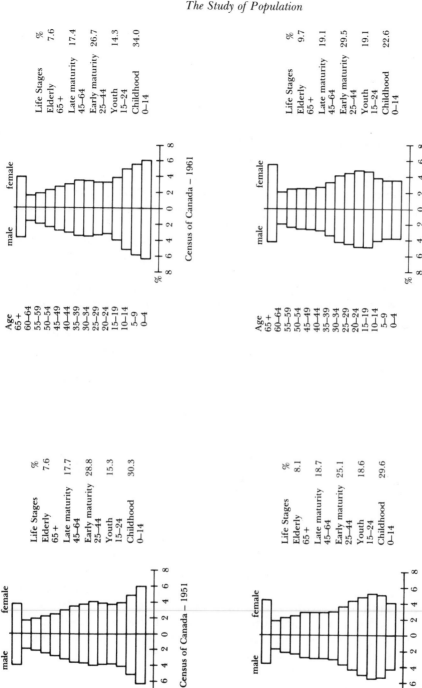

Source: Census of Canada (1971 b), Census of Canada News Release (1982 c).

market with such age-specific products as ointments for acne, teen magazines and fashions, vitamin pills, dry breakfast foods, sporting goods, and rock 'n' roll records.

The late 1960s and 1970s heralded yet another shock to the educational system as the baby boom birth cohorts entered colleges and universities. University capital expenditures and faculties increased accordingly to ease the strain. Concerns began to appear about the premarital sexuality of the youthful population—their younger marriages, alternative living arrangements, and use of contraceptives and drugs. The housing industry began producing proportionately more apartments than single-family housing. The entertainment industry emphasized films and music catering to the tastes and ideals of youth. Government initiated age-graded programs, such as the Company of Young Canadians, the Student Temporary Employment Program, and the Part-time Employment Programs, to serve the needs of the youthful population. Competition for jobs became severe, unemployment rates started to increase, and occupational choice was limited. Economic opportunity was not as promising for these birth cohorts as it had been at their age for the smaller birth cohorts of the 1930s and 1940s.

Following the baby boom cohorts came the cohorts of the baby bust years. With few exceptions, the 1960s and 1970s witnessed the downturn in Canadian fertility. The consequences of shrinking birth cohorts are no less important to the public and private sectors than are those of the earlier larger birth cohorts. It is important to recognize that both birth cohort groups will leave their respective imprints on Canadian society as they progress through the age and sex structure.

The dramatic decline in Canadian fertility to a low of 14.8 births per 1000 in 1985 has resulted in the slowing of population growth. Although the number of women in the childbearing years (15 to 44) has continued to increase since 1961—by more than two million, or 58.1 percent—measures of their fertility indicate unabated declines in reproduction. The general fertility rate, which is a more sensitive measure of fertility behaviour than the crude birth rate, relates births to the more appropriate "at risk" population of women in their childbearing years (ages 15 to 44). Between 1961 and 1985, the general fertility rate declined from 111.5 to 55.1. This decline in fertility is even more remarkable when one realizes that at the same time, younger women (ages 15 to 34), who are in the prime childbearing years and thus the chief contributers to national fertility, increased by almost 75 percent. The expected repeat performance of the post-war baby boom has not been forthcoming.

Examination of historical trends in age-specific fertility rates (see Exhibit 14-10) indicates that since 1961 fertility has steadily declined for each of the childbearing age groups. It is of particular interest that at the beginning of the 1980s, the 1945–55 baby boom birth cohort was in the 25 to 35 age range. During each year of this decade, an increasing number of women reach age 35, which is often viewed as the last chance

Exhibit 14-10
Age-Specific Fertility Rates, Canada, 1921–85

	Age Group						
	15–19	20–24	25–29	30–34	35–39	40–44	45–49
	Live births per 1000 women						
1921	38.0	165.4	186.0	154.6	110.0	46.7	6.6
1931	29.9	137.1	175.1	145.3	103.1	44.0	5.5
1941	30.7	138.4	159.8	122.3	80.0	31.6	3.7
1951	48.1	188.7	198.8	144.5	86.5	30.9	3.1
1961	58.2	233.6	219.2	144.9	81.1	28.5	2.4
1971	40.1	134.4	142.0	77.3	33.6	9.4	0.6
1981	26.4	96.7	126.9	68.0	19.4	3.2	0.2
1982	26.5	95.4	124.7	68.6	20.2	3.1	0.2
1983	24.9	92.4	124.6	70.5	20.5	3.0	0.2
1984	24.4	88.8	126.0	73.3	21.5	3.0	0.1
1985	23.7	85.3	125.3	74.6	21.8	3.0	0.1

Sources: Statistics Canada, *Vital Statistics, Vol. I, Births, 1976*, table 6;
Statistics Canada, *Vital Statistics, Vol. I, Births and Deaths, 1982,
1983, 1984, 1985*, table 5.

for childbearing. In 1981, age-specific fertility rates for older females aged 30 to 39 started to increase, largely attributable to a rise in the number of first and second births among women in this age group. This marginal upswing is the effect of the trend toward delayed marriage and childbearing among Canadian women (Dumas 1985). Even stronger increases in the fertility of older women will not reverse the general fertility decline. Slowing the decline of Canadian fertility will be contingent upon the fertility behaviour of the women in the younger childbearing ages.

Explanations put forth for this unprecedented decline in fertility involve not only the increased acceptance and diffusion of effective contraception, but more importantly, changing attitudes toward childbearing. Carl Grindstaff (1975) notes that the norms and values toward parenting changed dramatically over this decline period, and will likely play a significant role in contributing to further decreases in the birth rates. Also instrumental to this shift in attitudes have been, as already discussed, Canadian women's participation in the labour force and the corollary trend to social and occupational roles becoming the primary focus of family life. The working wife is likely to avoid or reduce the risk of conception by efficiently practising birth control.

The first national fertility study conducted in Canada in 1984 provides further evidence supporting this fertility decline. Balakrishnan, Krotki, and Lapierre-Adamcyk (1985) found high percentages of women practising contraception—73 percent of the currently married, 69 percent of the previously married, and 57 percent of single women. Sterilization is

The development of reliable contraceptives such as the birth control pill has fundamentally altered demographic patterns around the world.

the method most widely used by both married and previously married men and women, while the oral contraceptive pill is the most popular method among younger single women.

For the foreseeable future, the public and private sectors will have to be flexible enough to accommodate the changing requirements of the older and larger cohorts in the age structure, as well as the younger, diminishing birth cohorts entering the age structure. The impact of the baby bust is already being felt as elementary schools are confronted with declining enrolments, resulting in less demand for teachers and classroom space. Declining demand for infant- and child-related goods and services has been partially offset by the demand for instant foods by the baby boomers, who have swelled the labour force with considerable consequences for continuing unemployment rates, occupational demand, union membership, and job counselling.

FERTILITY AND THE FUTURE

The sensitivity that is so necessary in today's rapidly changing society begins with an understanding of the basic elements of demographic change and the implications of their interaction for Canadian society.

Future **population projections** are based on what is likely to occur with respect to the three basic components of change: fertility, mortality, and migration. The accuracy of these projections is conditional on certain itemized assumptions' holding true—specifically, if births, deaths, and migration hold constant or change in specified ways (Thomlinson 1976). Accurate projections provide planners and policy-makers with detailed data on the future size of the population, its age and sex structure, and its distribution by province for future dates.

The mortality assumption is less critical to population projections, since it has been quite low for some time and future reductions are likely to be moderate. Although migration is determined by various legislative, political, and economic considerations, it is the least significant component numerically. The most crucial variable in determining future population growth is fertility, because it is influenced by national policies, contraceptive technology, and individual preferences.

As noted earlier, decreases in almost all age-specific fertility rates, most importantly those of the younger women, have resulted in the dramatic decline of Canadian fertility since 1959. The **total fertility rate**, an estimate of the averge number of children that would be born alive to a woman during her lifetime, assumes that she successfully completes her childbearing years and experiences the current age-specific fertility rates. Shortly after the downturn in crude birth rates, the total fertility rate reached its peak of 3.9 live births per woman in 1960 and has since declined to its all-time low level of under 1.7 births in 1985. It is likely that Canadian fertility will continue its downward trend, resulting in a total fertility rate closer to a one-child average.

Exhibit 14-11
Population, Canada, 1981 and Projections for 2001

| Age Group | 1981 Census | | 2001 Projections | | | |
| | | | High Growth | | Low Growth | |
	No. (thousands)	%	No. (thousands)	%	No. (thousands)	%
0–14	5 481.1	22.5	6 577.2	21.7	4 632.2	16.7
15–24	4 658.7	19.1	3 847.8	12.7	3 725.9	13.4
25–44	7 184.3	29.6	9 035.8	29.9	8 662.7	31.1
45–64	4 658.1	19.1	6 937.5	22.9	6 912.1	24.8
≧65	2 361.0	9.7	3 862.0	12.8	3 883.5	14.0
Total	24 343.2	100.0	30 260.3	100.0	27 816.4	100.0

Source: Statistics Canada (1985), *Population Projections for Canada, Provinces and Territories: 1984–2006*, cat. no. 91-520.

Recent Statistics Canada population projections (cat. no. 91-520) confirm the likely prospect of continuing slow growth for Canada. Following the 1981 census, several series of revised projections were prepared, taking into account the continuing decline in Canadian fertility. Exhibit 14-11 shows a summary of two of them. The low projection (Series 1), considered the most likely population scenario for Canada in the near future, is based on assumptions that reflect the continuation of current trends. On the other hand, the high projection (Series 5) represents the maximum growth scenario.

The high projection assumes that a total fertility rate of 2.2 births per woman will be reached by the year 1996, generating a total population of 30.2 million by 2001.[10] This projection yields an elderly population of more than 3.8 million, which constitutes 12.8 percent of the total population. Series 1, the lowest projection series, assumes that a total fertility rate of 1.4 by 1996 will produce a population of 27.8 million by the turn of the century, of which 14.0 percent will be 65 years of age or more.[11]

The most significant implication of both the high and low growth scenarios is the continued aging of the Canadian population and the corresponding decline in emphasis on youth and youth-related products and services over the next 15 years. If the high projection is realized in 2001, the late-maturity age group (ages 45 to 64) will have increased by almost 50 percent since 1981 and the age 65 and over population by 63.6 percent. The low projection yields increases of 48.4 and 64.5 percent, respectively, for these age groups. The consequences of such growth patterns will be reflected in a more mature and experienced work force. The increase in the elderly population will severely test the private and public sector's capability to accommodate the distinctive needs of the aged. An older population will strain traditional pension and retirement schemes. Public health-care facilities will have to expand. The housing requirements of the elderly will range from small, multiple-dwelling structures for the independent to quite age-specific designs for the partially impaired. A greater number of nursing homes and intensive-care facilities, as well as geriatric professionals, will also be required.

The entertainment, leisure, and tourism sectors of the economy will be affected by an increase in the older age groups. Films, magazines, and television programming will cater to the age-specific tastes of the elderly. Since older people are heavy consumers of mass transportation, health services, and the cultural amenities of the inner city, there will be an intensification of movement toward the central areas of the city, as well as support for programs that will enhance these amenities. The private sector has already responded with greater emphasis on such product lines as soft foods for the elderly, specialty products for the disabled and handicapped, perhaps fashions in a relatively conservative vein, cosmetic surgery, health spas, age-graded retirement communities, and aids for the partially deaf and blind. The public sector will continue to respond with age-specific programs and policies in health care, adult education, leisure and personal development programs, housing for the aged, research in degenerative diseases, transportation, social services, and financial-support schemes.

With mortality levels already low and not likely to manifest any significant further decline in the future and with fertility continuing in its downward direction, it is conceivable that in the 21st century Canada will achieve a **stationary population**—one in which fertility and mortality are in balance, resulting in zero natural increase. This would mean that neither the total population size nor the number of people in each age group would ever change. Whether or not Canada confronts this situation is contingent upon a continuing decline in the fertility rate.

The question that is uppermost in the minds of demographers and policy-makers alike is whether the fertility decline will slow down or even reverse itself as a consequence of late childbearing by the baby boom generation. One of the difficulties in projecting future fertility is that there is uncertainty about whether women are delaying births or simply not having children at all.

Future fertility levels in Canada and the United States are not, of course, entirely dependent on the reproductive behaviour of the baby boom generation. In fact, the smaller baby bust birth cohorts now probably hold the key to the future of Canadian fertility. The important question may thus be: how are the behaviour and attitudes of the baby boom generation influencing the fertility of their successors—the baby bust generation?

Richard Easterlin's **relative income hypothesis** (1978) states that the large baby boom cohorts will be relatively disadvantaged and, hence, produce smaller birth cohorts, which, in turn, will become relatively advantaged, as competition for employment, income, and the necessities of life becomes less severe. As these smaller cohorts of potential mothers reach maturity, they, in turn, will develop a more favourable outlook on marriage and family formation, and hence these relatively advantaged baby bust cohorts will themselves produce larger numbers of births. The suggestion is that Canada will experience future cycles of boom and bust fertility. This hypothesis is predicated on the assumption that the baby boom generation is unique in that their attitudes toward marriage, family, and reproductive behaviour are not being passed on to the following generations. Nevertheless, if Easterlin's hypothesis proves correct, Canada will experience another baby boom cycle in this decade.

The counter-argument to the Easterlin hypothesis emphasizes the lasting influence of several major social and economic trends prevailing in North America. Not only has Canada experienced a de-emphasis of parenting values, but marriage itself is no longer defined as the sole legitimate status for women. The increases in age at first marriage since 1971 suggest that young people are finding cohabitation a viable option to marriage, which may continue to influence the postponement of childbearing until later years—and perhaps indefinitely. With longevity improvements, the traditional notion of "one partner forever" is being severely tested. The improvement in equality between the sexes is also having far-reaching effects. The increasing number of women in their prime childbearing years actively engaged in the labour force has reduced the "risk" years for parenting. As Westoff (1978) states, women will not choose to return and actively pursue a familiar role, particularly if society reaches a level of full equality that would make the female even more economically independent of marriage.

Considering that the total fertility rate, already below the replacement level of 2.1 children per woman, has resumed its downward trend, and taking this into account with the other social and economic changes in today's Canada, one must entertain the possibility of lower total fertility rates in future years and consequently of a much slower growth rate. Even if the total fertility rate levels off at 1.6, Canada will have to manipulate the immigration component of the demographic equation in order to prevent decline in the population. Thus the interaction of mortality, fertility, and migration will force society to respond with population-related policies at both the macro and micro levels to help produce a demographic equation in line with the future goals of Canada.

NOTES

1. The Canadian census was conducted for the first time in 1851 and every ten years thereafter until 1956, when the quinquennial census was introduced.
2. Annual vital statistics reports require at least a year's preparation before public release. Basic census counts are made available to the public about four to six months after questionnaires are received in Ottawa, while more detailed analyses of data may take one to five years before release.

3. At the turn of the century, the urban population included those people who lived in incorporated municipalities regardless of size. By 1971, however, only a concentration of 1000 inhabitants or more with a minimum density of 400 people per square kilometre, regardless of its legal status, was considered urban. (See Chapter 16 for more discussion of the meaning of "urban.")

4. John Graunt's monograph, entitled *Natural and Political Observations Made Upon the Bills of Mortality* and published in 1662, is considered the first scientific study to stimulate public awareness of the importance of vital-event registration and the conclusions that can be drawn from their study. These Bills of Mortality evolved to include the recording of christenings (births), marriages, burials (deaths), and casualties (causes of death), thus providing the basic components for population studies.

5. For years when censuses are not conducted, the mid-year population figure is derived through estimation techniques. Because population is usually growing or declining, it is more appropriate to use a mid-year population figure than the 1 January or 31 December figures.

6. This does not refer to the regular use of health and medical services pertinent to the woman's unique childbearing function.

7. This refined rate is calculated by dividing the number of infant deaths (age 0 to 12 months) in a specific year by the risk population, which in this case would be the number of live births.

8. It is interesting to note that orphanhood has become so uncommon in modern times that the Canadian census schedule no longer collects information regarding this status.

9. Jean Veevers (1977b) indicates the increasing numbers of couples choosing not to have children in Canada, a choice that would theoretically reduce the complexity and financial negotiations in divorce actions involving children.

10. Series 5 projections: total fertility rate = 2.2 by 1996; annual net immigration = 100,000

11. Series 1 projections: total fertility rate = 1.4 by 1996, net annual immigration = 50,000

FOR FURTHER READING

Hauser, Philip M., and Duncan, Dudley Otis, eds.
1951 *The Study of Population: An Inventory and Appraisal.* Chicago: University of Chicago Press.
This classic is a collection of writings by leading population experts reviewing the entire discipline. Demography as a science, its interdisciplinary nature, and its substantive components are treated in considerable detail. Extensive reference listings are provided at the conclusion of each contribution.

Jones, Landon Y.
1980 *Great Expectations: America and the Baby Boom Generation.* New York: Coward, McCann & Geoghegan.
A readable general treatment of the baby boom phenomenon and its implications for the United States, this work incorporates many illustrative examples.

Kalbach, Warren E., and McVey, Wayne W., Jr.

1979 *The Demographic Bases of Canadian Society*, 2nd. ed. Toronto: McGraw-Hill Ryerson.

This first comprehensive demography text written for the university market in Canada includes chapters dealing with the labour force, marital status and family, housing, religious affiliation, educational attainment, ethnicity, foreign-born population, as well as the major components of population change.

Romaniuc, Anatol

1984 *Fertility in Canada: From Baby-Boom to Baby-Bust*. Cat. no. 91-524E. Ottawa: Statistics Canada.

This excellent treatment of the Canadian fertility experience covers the period from the Second World War to the present.

Shyrock, Henry, and Siegel, Jacob S.

1975 *The Methods and Materials of Demography* (2 vols.), 3rd ed. Washington, D.C.: U.S. Government Printing Office.

The most comprehensive handbook on demographic measurement available, this book is an absolute must for the demographer involved in research. It covers the major population variables, population composition and characteristics, and estimation and projection techniques.

Wargon, Sylvia T.

1979 *Canadian Households and Families: Recent Demographic Trends*. Statistics Canada. Cat. no. 99-753E. Ottawa: Minister of Supply and Services.

In this detailed analysis of household and family patterns in Canada, the author uses historical census data and explores the linkages between these patterns and the broader social and economic trends that have stimulated changes in the living arrangements of the Canadian population.

United Nations Publications

1978 *The Determinants and Consequences of Population Trends: New Summary of Findings on the Interaction of Demographic, Economic and Social Factors*. Population Studies, no. 50, vols. I & II. New York.

1980 *World Population Trends and Policies: 1979 Monitoring Report*. Population Studies, no. 70, vols. I & II. New York.

These United Nations references represent the wide range of demographic materials published by this organization. Its extremely comprehensive publications provide a thoroughly documented world perspective on population trends, population policy, and mortality.

Demographic Periodicals

American Demographics. Ithaca, New York: American Demographics, Inc.

Canadian Studies in Population. Edmonton: Population Research Laboratory, Department of Sociology, University of Alberta and The Canadian Population Society.

Demography. Washington, D.C.: Population of America.

Family Planning Perspectives. New York: Planned Parenthood Federation of America, Inc.

Population Bulletin. Washington, D.C.: Population Reference Bureau, Inc.

Population Index. Princeton: Office of Population Research, Princeton University and Population Association of America.

CHAPTER 15

ETHNICITY AND PUBLIC POLICY

M. Michael Rosenberg
Morton Weinfeld

MOVIES FROM INDIA

KALA
KENDAR
SAREES · FABRICS · HANDICRAFTS

LICENSED
DINING LO

PIZZA

ASHDALE AV.
268

PEDESTRIAN
X
STOP FOR
PEDESTRIANS

STOP

DS
461 4432

Ethnicity, like religion and politics—to both of which it is intimately tied—pervades Canadian history and Canadian society. Modern Canadian society owes its structure largely to the union of two distinct ethnic groups, the British and the French. While ethnicity is no longer so central a factor in Canada, it remains a significant one. Many Canadians consider their ethnicity an important part of the answer to the question "Who am I?".

An **ethnic group** may be defined as a collectivity with most of the following characteristics:

1. It is largely descent-based or biologically self-reproducing.
2. Members have similar cultural traits, including language.
3. There is a significant degree of social interaction among group members.
4. Members are conscious of and accept this group identity.
5. Others perceive the collectivity as a definable group, on the basis of visible (physiological) or other traits.

A feeling of membership in an ethnic group—an **ethnic identity**—is one of many components in how people define themselves and are defined by others. **Ethnicity** refers to a person's "background," excluding the parents' socioeconomic status. It is usually an ascribed status, inherited or transmitted by kinship; it is difficult, though not impossible, to achieve or change an ethnic identity. Because ethnicity embodies both subjective and objective components it is particularly hard to define; moreover, the basis of an ethnic group can be one or a combination of many group characteristics or **markers**: race, religion, ethnic or national origin, and language. Thus, it is not always possible to identify clearly the ethnic origin of a person, nor is ethnicity equally meaningful for everyone. In a modern society, ethnicity is only one component of identity, along with gender, sexual orientation, occupation, place of residence, marital or family status, and political leaning.

Some people's ethnicity pervades their personal lives. This is often the case with immigrants, for whom ethnic identity may be a psychic shelter easing the trauma of immigration; with ethnic groups or subgroups defined largely by religion, such as Hutterites or Doukhobors; and with groups whose race or dress makes them conspicuous. Other people's ethnicity is a minor component of their identity, important only at ethnic festivals or family celebrations, or when they cheer their homeland's sports victories or fear for it in time of war. And there are people for whom ethnicity is completely irrelevant.

Because of the complex components of ethnic identity and the many ways in which it can interact with other components of identity, sociologists have found it helpful to examine ethnic groups in terms of **boundaries** that set one group apart from another, and help groups survive as distinct entities; a neighbourhood, a language or accent, a style of dress, or some other custom may act as a boundary.

Ethnic groups can be regarded as voluntary or involuntary. When an ethnic group has developed organizations to accomplish members' shared objectives and when the members feel, in Kurt Lewins's words, a certain "interdependence of fate," as well as a collective conscience (Emile Durkheim's phrase, connoting a shared way of acting, thinking, and feeling), that group can be thought of as an **ethnic community**. Such communities provide for many people a sense of belonging that protects them against the alienation common in modern societies. People who belong to two ethnic groups or feel estranged from their own ethnic group may be termed **marginal** to the group. As ethnic boundaries become weak, the number of marginal people will increase, and some people may "pass" from one identity to another. Some light-skinned blacks, for example, prefer not to identify themselves as blacks. People marginal to their ethnic group usually seek identity elsewhere, perhaps through an occupation or hobby.

THE SOCIOLOGY OF ETHNICITY: EVOLUTION

Although the founding fathers of sociology—Karl Marx, Emile Durkheim, and Max Weber—frequently mentioned ethnic groups in their writings, they failed to identify ethnicity as a significant social factor. Perhaps this was because ethnicity was taken for granted in the nationalistic and imperialistic era during which modern sociology was formed. Weber's discussion of the Polish peasants of turn-of-the-century East Prussia, for example, is essentially a political analysis, and he apparently saw ethnic groups merely as status groups competing for social honour (Weber [1925] 1946). Despite their many theoretical differences, the works of Weber, Marx, and Durkheim all seemed to imply that the industrial world would gradually reduce the significance of ethnicity in comparison to other social identifiers. This theoretical position has been reaffirmed more recently by Talcott Parsons (1971).

The origins of the present-day sociology of ethnic group relations can be traced to the interest of American scholars in the problems of the adjustment of European migrants to the New World at the turn of the century. Unlike Europe, where ethnic differences were entrenched in a long history and were taken for granted, the United States was a nation being formed of a multitude of ethnically distinct individuals who did not share a common language, culture, religion, political background, or occupational skills. The challenge facing the United States in the early 1900s—or so it seemed to the sociologists—lay in transforming this seething cultural mass into "Americans." Robert Park (1950), drawing on his observations of immigrants' lives in Chicago, argued that **assimilation** of the cultural minority group into the majority culture was both inevitable and desirable. The horrors associated with prejudice against immigrants and blacks in the United States and with Nazi anti-Semitism further contributed to a longstanding assimilationist perspective in the field. But the "ethnic revival" of the 1960s and the search for "roots" of the 1970s, which suggested that ethnicity and ethnic groups were gaining, rather than losing strength, sparked the development of an alternative paradigm. Glazer and Moynihan (1970, 1975) developed a **survivalist perspective**, in which ethnicity is seen as a fundamental basis on which political, economic, and cultural interest groups organize. From this perspective, ethnicity rivals or even supersedes class as a major unit of social structure. (Other current theoretical approaches to ethnicity are outlined in other sections of this chapter.)

COMPONENTS OF ETHNICITY

Nationality

The roots of what are now called ethnic groups are often found in nations and related national groups; many Canadian ethnic groups have European origins. Regardless of the advice of the Canadian census (see the note in Exhibit 15-1), many Canadians feel their ethnicity is synonymous with their nationality—Chinese, French, Italian, Greek, Polish or whatever. At any rate, national ties or ethnic group origins are taken seriously by many Canadians, as shown by the large number of ethnic organizations and ethnic periodicals that serve these groups. (How effective these organizations and periodicals are is quite another matter.)

National identity can be a powerful force, associated with the feelings of patriotism (and, at worst, chauvinism) that have marked European history since the proliferation of nation states in the 19th century. The phenomenon of nationalism is a precursor for what is now called ethnic identity, a composite of political, cultural, and social allegiances. It is important to note that Old World national origins are not always transplanted exactly to the New World. For example, many early immigrants arrived here with a sense of linkage to small regions, rather than to a nation per se; the classic example is turn-of-the-century Italian migrants, who would have identified themselves as Sicilian or Bolognese or even as residents of a particular village, but not as "Italian," as they have in North America. A similar pattern applied to many early Chinese immigrants. Thus, a national ethnic identity was created in the New World.

Territory

Attachment to a homeland—literal or figurative—is another component of ethnic identification. Such an attachment may be maintained through links with kin or friends still residing in the homeland or through a pattern of frequent visits. It is also reinforced by preoccupation with political and other events in the homeland (elections, coups, wars, natural disasters).

For most groups, a homeland refers to a state (say, Italy, Poland, or

Exhibit 15-1
1981 Census Questions on Ethnic Origin or Background

Major Question

26. To which ethnic or cultural group did you or your ancestors belong on first coming to this continent?
(See Guide for further information)

25 ☐ French	Native Peoples
26 ☐ English	37 ☐ Inuit
27 ☐ Irish	38 ☐ Status or registered Indian
28 ☐ Scottish	39 ☐ Non-status Indian
29 ☐ German	40 ☐ Métis
30 ☐ Italian	
31 ☐ Ukrainian	
32 ☐ Dutch (Netherlands)	
33 ☐ Polish	
34 ☐ Jewish	
35 ☐ Chinese	
36 ☐ Other (specify)	

Other Questions

6. What is the language you *first learned* in childhood and *still* understand?

23. Where were you born?

27. What is your religion?

28. What language do you *yourself* speak at home now?

Question 26, the census instructions note: Ethnic or cultural group refers to the "roots" of the population, and should not be confused with citizenship or nationality. Canadians belong to many ethnic or cultural groups—English, French, Irish, Scottish, Ukrainian, Native Indian, Chinese, Japanese, Dutch, etc.

If applicable in your case, a guide to your ethnic origin may be the language which you or your ancestors used on first coming to this continent, e.g., Dutch, Japanese. Note, however, that in cases where a language is used by more than one ethnic group, you should report the specific ethnic group, e.g., Austrian rather than German.

For Native Peoples, the phrase "on first coming to this continent" should be ignored.

Métis are descendants of people of mixed Indian and European ancestry who formed a distinct sociocultural entity in the nineteenth century. The Métis have gone on to absorb the mixed offspring of Native Indian people and groups from all over the world.

Source: Statistics Canada (1981), 1981 Census, cat. no. 95-903.

Greece), a province (Quebec), or an autonomous region (the Ukraine). In some cases, the homeland may incorporate a religious-symbolic value, as Israel does for Jews. In other cases, the homeland refers to a non-existent political entity to which an ethnic group retains political loyalty (Armenia). A territory with its landscapes, geographic features, or typical plant life may be evoked by paintings, poems, and songs that sustain ethnic identification. This is captured for Canadian francophones in the ode to Quebec written by Gilles Vigneault, which has become an anthem of Québécois nationalism:

> Mon pays ce n'est pas un pays,
> C'est l'hiver;
> Mon jardin ce n'est pas un jardin,
> C'est la plaine;
> Mon chemin ce n'est pas un chemin,
> C'est la neige;
> Mon pays ce n'est pas un pays,
> C'est l'hiver.

Language

Language is an important component of identity for many ethnic groups, though it plays somewhat different roles for different groups. For French-Canadians, language, religion, and ethnic/national origin are strongly linked. Some analysts (for example, Reitz 1974) argue that the retention of an ethnic language is perhaps the most important factor in preserving a culture. Some people speak the ethnic language at home, others remember it as the mother tongue—the language they first learned and still remember—while a few others decide as adults to learn the ethnic language out of curiosity or a desire to get in touch with their roots.

Many minority groups make strong efforts to retain their ethnic language. Poles and Ukrainians, for example, tend to place a particularly strong value on their respective languages because for so many years both these languages and cultures were restricted or controlled by foreign authorities (Polish by Czarist Russia in the 19th century and Ukrainian, in less clear-cut ways, by Soviet Russia in the 20th).

Language is clearly an effective group boundary, since, unless members are bilingual, communication between groups is restricted. It should be stressed that language may sustain an ethnic identity even if it is used not as a comprehensive system of communication but primarily as a symbol system in emotionally charged settings, such as family festivals and holidays, or in songs, curses, and jokes. Even a dialect or accent can serve as a group boundary.

Race

For our purposes, we can consider race as an element of ethnic distinctiveness; evident physical differences act as strong markers in setting

UNDERSTANDING ETHNICITY THROUGH THE CANADIAN CENSUS

One of the major tools of ethnic research in Canada is the Canadian census. The basic question used to determine the ethnic origin of Canadians in the 1981 census was question 26, shown in Exhibit 15-1. Be sure to read the explanatory notes quoted there; with them the 1981 census guide aimed at clarifying questions for Canadians.

Several things should be noted about the question and responses to it.

1. There is a sharp attempt to discourage anyone from claiming a "New World" Canadian or American ethnicity. Thus, the question is clearly about ethnic origin or ancestry, not about ethnicity as a currently meaningful social attribute. We know from survey research that many Canadians are quite ready to select "Canadian" as their ethnic identity (Weinfeld 1981a). A fifth-generation Canadian of German ancestry is designated a German Canadian, of whom there were more than 1.1 million according to the 1981 census. Yet only 516,000 Canadians claimed German as their mother tongue. The census instructs respondents not to confuse ethnic origin with nationality or citizenship, which are presumed to be Canadian.

2. Race is not treated as a separate category. (As recently as 1941, the Canadian census asked about "racial," rather than ethnic, origin,

treating European nationalities as races. The horrors of the Second World War may have led to the substitution of the term "ethnic" for "racial.") One consequence of this may be an undercount of black Canadians. The 1971 census reported roughly 34,000 "Negroes" in Canada and the 1981 census had no category at all equivalent to "Black."

The Canadian procedure is the opposite of that used in the American census, which collects extensive information on race, but next to nothing on ethnicity or religion. The reason in the American case derives in part from that country's constitutional separation of church and state.

3. Many Canadians have mixed ancestry. As recently as the 1971 census, the instructions were for respondents to trace back their ancestors on the *paternal* side. The reason was probably that children inherited the name of their father, which would serve as an indicator of ethnic origin, at least as perceived by outsiders. The problem was that in many families the mother was most active in socializing the child. In the 1981 census, respondents were permitted to select a multiple ethnic origin, and 1.8 million Canadians did so. One effect was to make comparisons between 1971 and 1981 far more difficult.

4. Many Canadians do not really know their ancestry. The census

suggests using a language criterion (assuming that is known).

5. Several other census questions relate to what we define as ethnic identity (they are also listed in Exhibit 15-1). For some people, the categories reflected in these questions may be a more important measure of identity than the ethnic categories of question 25.

Certainly, these intersecting categories lead to some "interesting" designations. For example, the 1981 census included 7,100 Ukrainian Unitarians, and 1,400 Jewish Roman Catholics. These combinations are not actually as unlikely as they sound. They indicate that ethnic origin is relatively easy to shed, and they caution us to be careful when dealing with census figures on ethnic groups since the data collected on ethnic origin are historical, while other indicators, such as religion and language of home use, are aimed at obtaining current information. Thus a person may have had Jewish ancestors who converted at some point to Christianity, or be of British origin but since converted to Greek Orthodoxy. In an ethnically plural society, a census can be a politically charged instrument. In Lebanon, the ruling Maronite Christians for decades forbade a census, knowing that the rapid population growth of the Muslim Lebanese would change the distribution of political power. In the United States, blacks and Hispanics have regularly criticized census procedures as leading to undercounts, with repercussions in the distributions of seats in legislatures and in the percentages used to design affirmative-action programs for minorities. In Canada,

the census is a major factor in the ongoing English-French debate, with francophones using census trends on the assimilation of French outside Quebec and within it (notably in Montreal) to bolster the case for outright separation, more autonomy, or more language protection. In a different vein, international events have also affected Canadian census results; the German ethnic group in Canada mysteriously shrank from 474,000 to 465,000 between 1931 and 1941. A similar drop had occurred between 1911 and 1921.

There is no perfect census system when it comes to providing data for ethnic research. Many of the problems listed above are a result of the complexity of ethnic identity itself and not the fault of poor census procedures. Indeed, Canadian sociologists interested in ethnic research are fortunate in having an instrument such as the Canadian census available. At the very least, the ethnic-origin figures can be used as a maximum baseline from which to measure the subsequent assimilation suggested by other census indicators or sample surveys. Remember, census data do not tap the subjective dimensions of ethnicity—namely, how respondents feel about their ethnic origin or how important it is to them.

group boundaries. The precise definition of races has preoccupied scientists (and pseudoscientists) for quite some time. One categorizaton, Ashley Montagu's taxonomy of the human species, is presented in part in Exhibit 15-2; as can be seen, the three major groups (he avoids the term race) are Caucasoid, Negroid, and Mongoloid. These divisions are not absolute; substantial genetic mixing has occurred across groups, and no individual is likely to be racially "pure"; thus, the notion of distinct races is largely unfounded.

Exhibit 15-2
Major Racial Groups

NEGROID	MONGOLOID
African Negroes	Classical Mongoloids
Oceanic Negroids	Arctic Mongoloids
African Pygmies or Negrillos	Paleoasiatics
Asiatic Pygmies or Negritos	Neoasiatics
Oceanic Pygmies or Negritos	American Indians
	Indo-Malay

CAUCASOID
Subdivision: Australoid or Archaic Caucasoid

Source: Montagu (1960, 470-71).

In any case, sociologists are interested primarily in the social, rather than the physical, significance of race. The problem of determining the biological components of race can be left to geneticists, physiologists, and physical anthropologists. Some sociologists, such as van de Berghe (1981), have attempted to link the study of ethnicity to the emerging field of sociobiology, which explores the biological bases of social behaviour. Nevertheless, sociologists treat race as a symbolic marker used by individuals to categorize themselves and others.

Facets of ethnic identity similar to race are body language and physiognomy. Voice inflections, accents, pronunciation, hand gestures, and facial expressions are all possible indicators. Although people's notions of the characteristics of other groups are often stereotypical, in many cases these indicators do reliably show ethnic group membership. Some people claim they can identify other people's ethnic origin by looking at them and hearing them speak.

Religion

While religion represents a voluntary allegiance to a set of beliefs or rituals, it is also an ascribed characteristic, handed down by parents and usually retained for life. Religious groups behave like any social group; their beliefs and customs can be as effective as visible differences in setting up group boundaries. Historically, religion has provided the basis for particularly violent intergroup conflict; some present-day manifestations are Protestant-Catholic tensions in Northern Ireland, Muslim-Christian tensions in Lebanon, intra-Muslim rivalries between the Shia and the Sunni, and Sikh-Hindu conflicts in India.

A religious identification often intersects with other axes of ethnic differentiation. Thus, francophones in Quebec are predominantly Catholic, while anglophones are—or have been—predominantly Protestant. In some cases, group identity is seen as both ethnic and religious; the Canadian census considers Jews both a religious and an ethnic group. The Hutterites are a similar example. In some groups, such as the Italians and Poles, religious tradition is an important element of a total identity; although one can theoretically be a non-Catholic Italian, the mainstream Italian culture includes a Roman Catholic component.

Culture

The culture of an ethnic group can mean many things. On one level is high culture, works of art that represent the highest achievements of

This group studying the Torah exemplifies how nationality, religion, and language intersect.

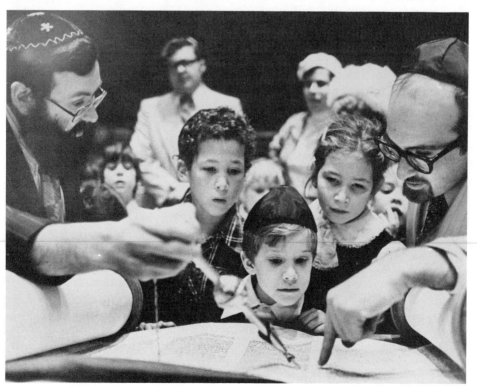

scholars and artists working in certain traditions (say, Verdi and Dante for Italians). At a second level is popular or folk culture, comprising the many facets of life that underlie daily existence: fundamental values, customs, mores, cuisine, dress, social and sexual relations.

In a modern society such as Canada, both levels play a role in maintaining ethnic identity. High culture gives people the pride of knowing that their group has produced works that can compete with the best of the Canadian host society; however, access to and appreciation of the ethnic high culture is often limited to an intellectual elite. Both forms of ethnic culture can play a major role in defining or buttressing an ethnic identity.

In his study of ethnicity, *Idols of the Tribe* (1975), Harold Isaacs points out that basic group identity is also conveyed through extremely subtle symbols. First names and surnames provide not only clues to ethnic identity (until they are anglicized) but also links with family history or ancestral origin. Moreover, since names identify people to the outside world, they often signal ethnic origin even when the substantive commitment is no longer present.

THE EVOLUTION OF THE CANADIAN MOSAIC

An **ethnically plural** or heterogeneous **society**, such as Canada, has distinct ethnic groups living within one sociopolitical unit. It has become something of a cliché to describe Canada as an "ethnic mosaic." Nevertheless, this phrase captures something essential about Canada. Canada is a nation composed of peoples of many different national origins, languages, religions, and races (see Exhibit 15-3), all of whom participate in and contribute to Canadian society. The essential pluralism of Canadian society has in large part determined Canada's past and much of its present-day social and political concerns.

Canada's diversity is the product of hundreds of years of colonization and immigration. The native peoples were the first to arrive, although the period of their arrival and their place of origin are still uncertain. Once European colonization of the New World began, the French, British, Dutch, Spanish, and Portuguese scrambled to establish their claims. First to colonize Canada were the French; the English also had some early settlements in what would become Atlantic Canada. Following defeat on the Plains of Abraham by the British in 1759, France ceded its Canadian possessions to Great Britain. Immigrants stopped coming from France, but they were soon replaced by Loyalists fleeing revolutionary America and then by British migrants. By the end of the 19th century, large-scale immigration to Canada from continental Europe had begun. Since 1945, Canada has also attracted non-white immigrants from developing nations.

Because Canada has so many ethnic groups, sociologists find it convenient to group them into categories sharing certain important characteristics. There are three such categories: the "charter" groups, the

Exhibit 15-3
Numbers of Canadians Claiming Selected Ethnic Origins, Mother Tongue, and Home Language, 1981

Ethnic Origin Group by Language[a]	Population (000s)	Number with Mother Tongue (000s)	Number with Ethnic House Language (000s)
British (English)	9 674	14 750	14 518
French	6 439	6 176	5 748
Other European:			
German	1 142	516	153
Italian	747	531	337
Ukrainian	530	285	88
Dutch	408	146	23
Scandinavian	283	66	7
Jewish[b]	264	39	11
Polish	254	127	51
Portuguese	188	165	122
Greek	154	123	88
Hungarian	116	83	32
Spanish	53	70	46
Asian/African			
Chinese	289	224	172
Indo-Pakistani	196	117	77
Philippino	73	47	25
Japanese	41	20	10
Other East Asian[c]	77	59	39
African[d]	45	—	—
Caribbean[d]	82	—	—
Native Peoples[e]	413	122	83

[a]These figures represent only those respondents who claimed a single ethnic origin. More than 1.8 million Canadians claimed a multiple ethnic origin. Thus, to a certain extent, the ethnic origin figures here underestimate the size of ethnic groups, using the definitions of earlier census enumerations.
[b]Yiddish and Hebrew.
[c]Includes Burmese, Cambodian, Korean, Laotian, Malay, Thai and Korean ethnic origins. Languages are Cambodian, Korean, and Vietnamese.
[d]There are no reliable census estimates of the black population in Canada since African and Caribbean ethnic origins are claimed by whites as well as blacks. But these figures do give a certain order of magnitude.
[e]Amerindian languages.
Source: Statistics Canada (1981), 1981 Census, *Ethnic Origin and Population*, cat. no. 92-911; 92-910.

"other" groups, and the native peoples. So although the English and French are separate ethnic communities, sociologists class them together as **charter groups**—politically and culturally dominant groups whose claim to special privilege is based on their status as the self-proclaimed earliest arrivals or founding races. Roughly one-quarter of Canada's population is of neither British nor French descent, and the many people in these "other" ethnic groups are beginning to have a significant impact on Canadian society. The native peoples have for so long been kept out of the mainstream of Canadian society that their problems and concerns are unknown and misunderstood by most Canadians.

The Charter Groups

The British and the French have a special place in Canada, one entrenched in the Canadian constitution. These groups have special language rights and privileges—in the legislature, the courts, and the schools— denied to other groups. As a nation, Canada is understood by most Canadians as a union of the British- and French-Canadian ethnic groups. However, it has been not the unity but the separation of these two groups that has given Canada its special character. Despite the legislative fiction of Canada as one country, it is 200 years of rigid separation that have engendered the rights so prized by each group. The result has been, in Hugh MacLennan's famous phrase, a Canada composed of "two solitudes."

Structurally, this separation has taken the form of **institutional self-segregation**. French and British Canadians have lived different lives in separate institutions—separate schools, churches, residential districts, clubs, and, in the case of Quebec, even separate banks and trade unions—and, most important, separate languages. If Canada has in many ways failed to gel fully as a nation, it is the persisting pattern of ethnic institutional self-segregation that is most responsible. In the 20th century, this segregation has led to a real feeling by many Québécois that Canada is not their nation and that Quebec must separate from the rest of Canada. Although the Quebec separatist movement has been stymied for the moment with the 1985 electoral defeat of the Parti Québécois, the long-term consequences for all Canadians are still very much uncertain. The very ethnic diversity that Canada was created to protect may yet prove its undoing.

Interestingly, Porter (1965) suggests that the desire to maintain separate institutions first emerged, not in British-French relations (where such separation was at first seen as "natural" and requiring no special rights), but in the relations between Scottish and English colonists, who wanted to maintain their distance both socially and institutionally. Since colonization tends to promote a great awareness of social honour and to establish a hierarchical system of status, the English and Scottish went to great pains to emphasize their differences. It was only when they were flooded by large numbers of other immigrants whom they both defined as inferiors, such as the Irish, that they joined forces to protect their privileges. Today, the English, Scottish, and Irish in Canada are considered one ethnic group—the British.

The relations between the British and the French have been determined by the pattern of domination and subordination that developed between them. The inequality experienced by the French, especially in the division of labour along ethnic lines in Quebec, has bred a sense of injustice and antagonism toward the British that has increased the separation between the groups and reinforced French nationalism.

Membership in a charter group is both institutionally and psychologically quite different from membership in the other ethnic groups. Italians, Poles, Pakistanis, and others realized when they came to Canada that this new land would be culturally, linguistically, and politically different from their homeland. Thus they accepted that the onus would be on them to adapt. Members of the charter groups, however—many of whom are descended from colonists who first came to Canada more than 300 years ago—see Canada as a nation created in their image and adjusted to their specifications. If the charter group members feel more at home in Canada than do many members of other ethnic groups, they also feel more threatened by change and by what they perceive to be threats to their established positions.

The "Other" Ethnic Groups

How did Canada come to have such an ethnically diverse population? Despite the widely held notion of Canada as an open society that welcomes anyone wishing to live here, without reference to race, language, or religion, this has never really been the case. At the time of Confederation, more than 90 percent of Canadians were of British or French origin; many of them opposed the admission of other ethnic groups. Nevertheless, Canada was clearly suffering from a severe population shortage, which posed a threat to its viability as a nation: immigrants were needed. Even so, immigration was never a "natural" process in which anyone who wished to come was admitted. Rather, from the very beginning, Canada's pattern of immigration has reflected the interests and concerns of dominant groups, which have sought to control immigration.

Canadian attitudes present a sharp contrast to the **melting pot ideology** of the United States, in which every ethnic group is expected to merge into the general American society. The ethnic immigrants who came to Canada were neither absorbed nor particularly welcomed by the two charter groups. The newcomers therefore tended to imitate the model of institutional self-segregation they found in place and to develop and preserve their own cultural, social, and economic institutions.

In the past, most Canadians viewed immigration as a source of human raw materials. The immigrants were traditionally the unskilled labourers who filled the factories and worked at low wages or the farmers who cultivated the land in remote areas. Such immigrants were seen mainly as fulfilling an economic function and were acceptable only as long as they were considered neither cultural nor economic threats. Government policies sought to mediate between those who demanded more and cheaper labour and those who opposed any immigration whatsoever. The result was an inconsistent approach to immigration, alternating between periods of relatively free access and periods when the doors slammed shut.

The sign on the wall between the two flags says "Welcome to Canada," but the immigration process is still intimidating and disorienting.

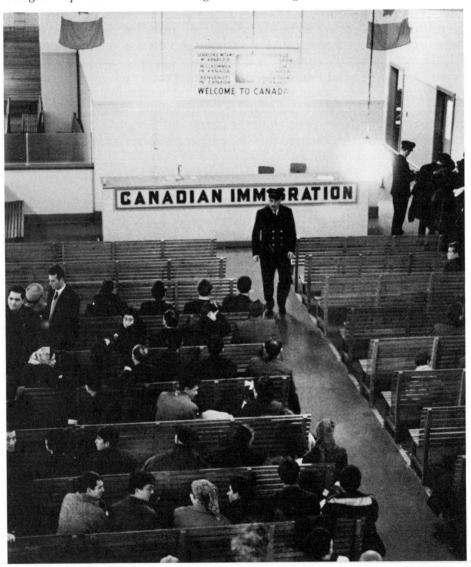

The Canadian mosaic, then, has evolved under the control of government policies determining who could and could not enter Canada. To understand the ethnic mosaic one must examine its gradual evolution in relationship to the political, social, and economic structure of Canada.

The influence of government policy on immigration has been evident from the very beginning of European colonization in North America. New France was restricted by French colonial policy to those immigrants who were of "French and Catholic stock" (Rosenberg 1970, 18). This restriction prevented such groups as the Huguenots (French Protestants) from coming to North America, and effectively closed the colony even to the British-American merchants from the south.

The French policy was in marked contrast to that of the British, who allowed and even encouraged the immigration of religious minorities, political dissidents, and "criminal" elements to the New World. While the French were concerned with ensuring a homogeneous and manageable population in the colony (a goal they largely achieved), the British ended up with an unruly set of colonies, some of which eventually declared independence. Following the conquest of New France in 1763, the British authorities at first discouraged any further migration to their new colony, fearing an influx of Americans and other disruptive elements. Only after the American Revolution, during which thousands of United Empire Loyalists fled the new states, did migration to Canada resume. The colonial authorities were, however, relatively indulgent toward the francophone society they now ruled; the Quebec Act of 1774—which permitted Roman Catholics to hold public office, established the titles of the Catholic Church in Quebec, and re-established the privileges of the seigneurs (large landholders)—started the Canadian tradition of enshrining special rights to ethnic groups.

After Confederation, a concerted effort to encourage European immigration was undertaken, with offers of free land and financial support for immigrants. The government founded the North Atlantic Trading Company in 1889 to foster immigration—but only by the "right" kind of people—that is, those of British or "Nordic" background. Southern Europeans were considered undesirable, unable to integrate culturally into Canada's British and French heritage, and too lazy to undertake the hard work of building up the nation.

Even in the 1880s, a few immigrants not of Northern European origin were allowed, but for the most part they were special cases. The Chinese, for example, were brought to Canada specifically to work on the railroad and were to be returned to China when the work was done. The scope of immigration gradually broadened, not because of any change of heart on the part of either the government or the general public, but because of the continuous demand for cheap labour.

Indeed, many people in Canada remained opposed to allowing extensive immigration until after the Second World War. The two charter groups differed somewhat in their reasons for this opposition. Many

English Canadians saw immigration as a threat to Canada's British cultural heritage and to the viability of British social and political institutions. While many people supported more immigration from Britain, the labour movement generally opposed any immigration, fearing that it would lead to high unemployment and lower wages. In times of general economic depression, most people agreed.

Canadians of French descent considered themselves already threatened culturally by the economic and social dominance of the British. In their view, any further immigration, whether from Britain or elsewhere, would contribute to the numerical decline of the French and worsen their subordination. Since French rights were constitutionally protected, it was to the political institutions that the French looked for protection; in a system of representative democracy such as Canada's, a large influx of immigrants would weaken the political influence of the French and thus threaten their special status. One tragic consequence of this hostility to immigration, in combination with prejudice, was Canada's disgraceful policy of restricting the immigration of German Jewish refugees fleeing Nazi persecution in the 1930s.

Today Canada's immigration policy is still fundamentally oriented to an economic perception of immigration. The criteria for selecting suitable

The arrival in 1986 of a boatload of Tamil refugees reawakened the debate in Canada over our immigration policy and criteria for accepting refugees.

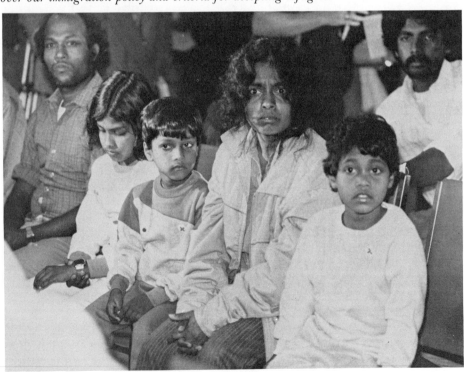

DESPERATE VOYAGE

The four Newfoundland fishermen aboard the Atlantic Reaper were hauling in nets heavy with cod early last week when eerie sights and sounds emerged from the dense fog. Less than half a kilometre away two fibreglass lifeboats, powerless and lashed together, bobbed on the light ocean swell. A throng of dark-skinned people shouted and waved for help. Skipper Gus Dalton and his crew abandoned eight nets—along with most of their catch—and raced to the rescue. They found 155 people—145 men, four women and six children ranging in age from 10 months to 10 years—floating less than 10 km from the jagged shore of St. Mary's Bay on the southeast coast of Newfoundland. The fishermen lashed the boats to the sides of their long-liner and helped aboard the women, the children and the most seasick of the men. Recounted crewman John McEvoy, 22: "They wanted to know, right away, 'was it Canada?'" But as the castaways clambered onto the Atlantic Reaper, they brought with them a deeper issue for Canadians even as the government tries to decide how welcoming Canada should be to the world's homeless.

[. . .] The new arrivals were Hindu Tamils from the troubled island nation of Sri Lanka . . . (their) unorthodox arrival caused problems for the government of Prime Minister Brian Mulroney. As [Junior Minister for Immigration] Weiner pointed out, the government wants to ensure that "our shores can be available to those that are legitimate refugees with legitimate claims." It would be legally difficult to deport the Tamils since Canada's ruling in September, 1983, that it would not return Tamils to strife-torn Sri Lanka. And even though the Tamils came through West Germany, they could still fulfil the legal definition of a refugee: any person with a "well-founded fear of persecution for reasons of race, religion, nationality, membership in a particular social group or political opinion."

But Ottawa was also concerned that the warm reception could encourage other refugees to smuggle themselves into the country— and perhaps lie about their voyage. At least five Conservative MPs reported that their constituents were furious about the decision to let the Tamils live and work in Canada. Declared powerful Tory MP Donald Blenkarn, who represents the suburban Toronto riding of Mississauga South: "I sense very strong objections to allowing people in who cheat the system and break the law." Some media commentary was equally critical. *The Vancouver Sun* noted, "There is a difference between being compassionate and being a sucker." After a day-long cabinet meeting, [Immigration Minister] Bouchard warned that Canada will review its refugee policy if other groups follow the Tamils' example. "We have a tradition of hospitality in Canada, but at the same time Canadians are getting to be perhaps a little more prudent, and they want politicians to see exactly what is the involvement of such an adventure," he said . . .

Life is better for the up to 16,000 Tamils in Canada, the majority of whom are in Montreal and Toronto. Since Sri Lanka became a refugee-producing nation in 1983, Canada has not deported Tamils—even if it refuses to grant refugee status to them. Last year more than 1,500 Sri Lankans asked for that status—and 48 per cent of those requests have already been granted. In the meantime, the refugees can live—and work— in Canada. . . .

Last May, former minister of state for immigration Walter McLean introduced changes to clear up the backlog of 20,000 cases— and to speed up the refugee determination process (. . .). He also introduced proposals for changes to the Immigration Act under which immigration officials would be able to short-circuit a claim if the prospective refugee already has the right to enter another country and receive refugee status. Although immigration officials sent fingerprints and photographs of the Tamil refugees to West German police, Immigration Minister Bouchard ruled out the possibility that they would be sent back to Germany if they had refugee status there. He added, "I would really hope that we could let them live their own life in Montreal and Toronto."

. . . But as some Tory MPs declared last week, many constituents were also angry that the Tamil smugglers selected Canada because they were certain of a warm welcome. Declared Calgary East MP Alex Kindy: "Many legitimate applicants [are] getting hassled while these people are allowed into Canada right away—people say that system is unfair." Clearly, the controversy surrounding the Tamils will color the debate in Ottawa as politicians try to balance the painfully conflicting demands of fairness and humanity in Canada's immigration policy.

—MARY JANIGAN with CHRIS WOOD, BRUCE WALLACE and PAT ROCHE in St. John's, ANN FINLAYSON in Toronto, ROSS LAVER in Hamburg, BRIGID JANSSEN in Paris and HILARY MACKENZIE and DAVID LORD in Ottawa

immigrants have changed, however. The government no longer assumes that certain races or people are intrinsically lazy or unsuitable to become Canadians. The current selection system is more objective (although, like all systems, open to occasional abuse) and more functional. Potential immigrants receive points for meeting criteria such as level of education and experience or training in jobs considered economically useful. People may also be sponsored by relatives already residing in Canada. Even this system allows a certain degree of latitude in the assignment of points, and immigration procedures are tightened or loosened depending on economic conditions and public opinion.

Immigration has been a major force in shaping Canadian society and will probably remain significant for years to come. In 1971, Kalbach (1978) notes, fully 33 percent of Canada's population consisted of either first- or second-generation Canadians. (A first-generation Canadian is a person who immigrated to Canada at any age; a second-generation Canadian is an immigrant's child born in this country.)

The Native Peoples

Treated as wards of the Canadian government, unable to determine their own fate and shunted onto reservations or remote areas, Canada's native people have been kept from playing a full and active role in Canadian society. Indeed, Valentine (1980, 47) goes so far as to assert that "native societies, rather than forming an integral part of Canadian society, exist as a cluster of satellites." This is in no way comparable to the voluntary pattern of ethnic self-segregation that characterizes most ethnic-group relations in Canada. Instead it has produced a state of dependence: the autonomy of the native peoples has been systematically eroded, and some cultures completely destroyed.

In recent years, Canada's native people have become concerned with resurrecting their cultural past; as they have explored their roots, other Canadians have also come to learn of the richness and diversity of native lifestyles. Before European colonization, Canada's native people had far more complex social organizations and far more developed cultures than most Canadians supposed. Brought up on the Hollywood stereotype of Indians as savages, alternately ignorant and wily, childlike and violent, other Canadians are only now beginning to realize the significant contributions of Canada's native people to Canadian society and culture. Yet, despite the gradual development of new attitudes toward the native people, they still "have the lowest incomes, the poorest health, and the highest rates of unemployment of any single group in the country" (Valentine 1980, 47).

One instance of the neglect of native people is the conflicting maze of regulations and documents governing the definition of who is or is not considered native. Valentine (1980, 65) lists thirteen terms in official use: Native Indian, Status Indian, Non-status Indian, Treaty Indian, Non-treaty Indian, Registered Indian, Reservation Indian, Treaty Half-Breed, Enfranchised Indian, Métis, Half-Breed, Inuit, and Eskimo. Such a list indicates that Canadians neither know nor care who the native is. It also illustrates the degree to which natives have been subordinated to the whims of government bureaucracies.

These terms have real consequences in the lives of the native people. For example, a Status Indian is one who has recognized status under the Indian Act of 1876 and is registered on band lists with the Department of Indian and Northern Affairs. Until recently, non-status Indians included not only all Métis but also native women who lost their status by marrying non-native men and the descendants of such a marriage. This sexist distinction broke up families and added to the alienation of native peoples. With the recent passage of Bill C-31, native women married to non-native men are eligible to regain their status, but their previously born children are not.

By and large, the native peoples do not see themselves as a minority group of Canadians whose collective interests will be served by government programs designed to nurture and preserve aspects of their cultural heritage. Instead, they seek the establishment of some form of self-government that would guarantee their permanent influence as a people, as well as economic self-development with the benefits accruing to themselves.

This family portrait was taken on an Indian reservation near Sept-Iles, Quebec, in 1959. It would be nice to report that conditions have improved dramatically since then, but unfortunately they have not. This photograph remains an adequate depiction of life on many reservations.

A CANADIAN TRAGEDY

Just outside the Cree Indian settlement of Peerless Lake, Alta., there are five graves side by side on the flank of a grassy knoll. Beyond the graves, higher up, is a thin rank of tall poplars, and beyond the poplars the lake is still and smooth and blue in the northern sun. Each grave is sheltered by a little plywood house, and there are wild flowers on the sloping roofs. Two of the huts are painted yellow and three are blue—yellow for females, blue for males. The females in the graves were Patricia Houle, 16, and Eliza Netawastenum, 30. The males were Robert Cardinal, 27, and two of Eliza Netawastenum's brothers, William, 25, and Raymond, 27.

During the evening of March 10, at a party in Eliza's unpainted frame shack, all five drank duplicating machine fluid from a one-gallon plastic jug marked "Poison," and shortly after midnight they were all dead. A sixth victim, Hubert Bellam, 34, is buried near his home in Slave Lake, 200 km to the south. There were more than a dozen people at the party; the lives of two were eventually saved by the dialysis machines and doctors at University Hospital in Edmonton, 350 km south of Peerless Lake. The deaths were bizarre, and in the days that followed reporters from all over flew in chartered planes to the marshy airstrip at Trout Lake, and then drove 30 km along a dirt road to Peerless Lake to cover the funerals and ask the 350 inhabitants—without

success—how people could want to get drunk so badly that they would drink duplicating machine fluid. . . .

The national statistics are plentiful and alarming. The federal health department says the alcoholism rate among native people is 13 times the rate among whites. The number of Indians on welfare ranges from 60 to 90 per cent in communities across the country. The federal department of Indian affairs and northern development says that the juvenile crime rate among Indians is three times the national average. . . . So are deaths from accidents, violence and poisonings. And the Indian suicide rate is six times the national figure. Diane Syer-Solursh, a clinical psychologist and former director of the crisis intervention centre at Toronto East General Hospital, said Canadian Indians probably have one of the highest suicide rates in the world. All of the ills, commented the Edmonton-based native weekly newspaper *Windspeaker* on March 14, "threaten to destroy Indians as a people." . . .

John Cardinal, gesturing, now and again punching the table with a finger, recalled the night of Eliza Netawastenum's fateful party when somebody woke him up and told him there was trouble. . . .

[. . .] For John Cardinal, Eliza Netawastenum's party was not the end of the nightmare. One night about a month after the drinking party, his 17-year-old stepson, Roderick, left a talent show at the community centre and went home and shot himself to death. "He was a nice boy," recalled his stepfather, "and we never realized what was going on with him. We sat down with the RCMP afterward and tried to figure it out. He hadn't been drinking, and so I think it must have been frustration." Cardinal paused periodically. Each time, Gordon Auger, seated at the end of the table, repeated what he had said in Cree for those around the table who spoke no English. They listened impassively and said nothing.

But Auger did: "People read about Indians drinking duplicating fluid, and they say, 'There's just another bunch of drunken Indians.' Our people go out to urban centres, and they see somebody drinking some stuff, and so they think they can drink it too. It might say 'poison' or 'danger,' but maybe they drank stuff that said that before, and it was okay. You know, we're a hundred years behind the South, but Indian leaders have tried to avoid this problem by saying, OK, we need special counselling for alcohol, special counselling for education, counselling for employment.' But nobody listens. Then the tragedy happens, and all of a sudden there's all kinds of programs available." . . .

Across the village, Roe Graham brewed tea in an electric coffee-maker in the kitchen of his house trailer, which has a freezer with bear, white-tail deer meat and Parkay margarine. . . .

"I sometimes think the white man will never understand how the Indian mind works," he said. "Here is an example. Indians share what they have with each other. If I come home to make a meal and find I have no fish, I will go to my neighbor's house, even though he is not there, and I will take a fish, no more than I need. Then one day, he will find that he has no potatoes so he will come to my house and take some potatoes. That is how we live. If a man shoots a moose, he will take what he needs for his family and give the rest to his neighbors. Once, one of the men of the village came home from hunting and needed to take a shower. So he went to the home of a white schoolteacher and had a shower. The teacher called the police. To this day, the man does not understand why what he did was wrong."

A few blocks from the Edmonton Municipal Airport is a two-storey building that houses a credit union and the Alberta Métis Association. In a big office on the second floor, association president Samuel Sinclair sat uncomfortably behind a desk. It is a long way from Lesser Slave Lake, where he grew up as a Cree hunting moose and running a trapline. In the weeks following the deaths at Peerless Lake, Sinclair said unemployment lay at the root of the tragedy, and he assailed the Alberta government for not doing more to find jobs for Indians. Now, he looked out the window and said: "They had better start looking at us as human beings who have solutions in approaching this real dog-fight we have in just surviving. They say there's life after death. How about some life after birth?"

Rae Corelli in *Peerless Lake*

ETHNIC COMMUNITIES: A TYPOLOGY

Despite the acknowledged pluralism of Canadian society, many Canadians have ambivalent feelings about its diverse ethnic groups. Multiculturalism has become an official policy of the federal government, which provides financial aid and other services to groups seeking to preserve their cultural heritage. But Canadians seem to assume that such cultural heritages consist of little more than exotic customs, folk dances, and costumes brought over from the old country, all peripheral to the real life of ordinary Canadians. Although the federal government considers all Canadians to be ethnics (as seen by the census), many Canadians are indifferent to the cultural heritage of any group including their own and know very little about the ethnicity of any other group (Brotz 1980; Weinfeld 1981a).

Even the federal government, despite its rhetoric of multiculturalism, seems unsure of just what ethnicity means and of what role it plays in Canadian society. This is shown in the comments found in the Report of the Royal Commission on Bilingualism and Biculturalism, which, unable to specify any particular concrete role for the "other" ethnic groups in Canada, turned to the picturesque: "Thus, streams empty into a river and their waters mix and swell the river's flow" (vol. 4:11)—a pretty but insubstantial metaphor.

This report rejected any independent political role for the "other" ethnic groups, focusing instead on their cultural "contribution" to Canadian society, which the Commission understood to consist of the two charter groups; thus the other ethnic groups have contributed to Canadian society "particularly if they have brought enrichment to one of the two dominant cultures and continue to flourish and benefit through their integration with one of the two societies" (vol. 4:11).

If we are to understand the phenomenon of ethnicity in Canadian society, we must begin by examining how people view their own and other people's ethnicity. It is important to understand that ethnicity is not something brought from the homeland (although important elements may be). The ethnicity of any group in Canada is created in the Canadian context and is a response to the Canadian setting.

Since there are so many ethnic groups in Canada, we cannot begin to understand them by simply cataloguing the essential elements of each group's ethnicity. Instead, we will develop a typology of styles of participation in ethnic communities. One way to set up such a typology is to find some simple dimensions of contrast. For example, is the ethnic group **isolationist**—that is, does it close itself off from other groups in an effort to retain its traditions and institutions—or is it **integrationist**—that is, determined to participate as fully as possible in Canadian society. A second dimension of contrast is between what Anderson and Frideres (1981, 50) call primary and secondary groups. A **primary ethnic group** has retained intimate and warm relationships among its members through close contacts with family and friends. **Secondary ethnic groups** result from the migration of isolated individuals whose ties to fellow group members are mainly limited to participation in common institutions.

Exhibit 15-4
Ethnic Typology

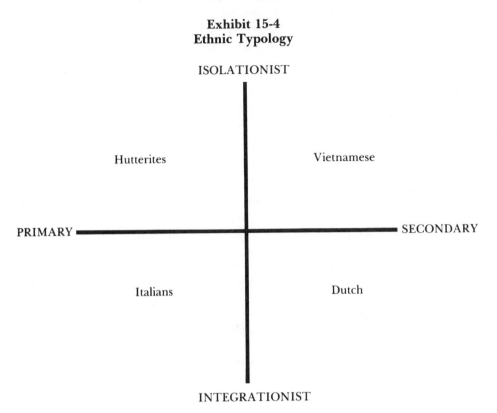

Exhibit 15-4 shows the simple typology set up by using these two distinctions. It yields four types of ethnic groups: primary isolationist, secondary isolationist, primary integrationist, and secondary integrationist. The diagram gives one example of each type. While any typology is somewhat simplistic and this one probably ignores many other ways in which ethnic groups differ, it is a first step toward a systematic comparison of Canadian ethnic communities. We will examine each type briefly.

Primary Isolationist

Primary isolationist ethnic groups tend to differentiate themselves from the surrounding community in order to maintain a highly specific set of beliefs (usually religious) and a traditional way of life. The Hutterites, Doukhobors, Mennonites, and Hassidim are examples of such groups. The members of these groups purposely emphasize their difference: they wear traditional clothes, rather than modern dress, and avoid many modern practices that the rest of society may view as conveniences.

Two groups that have shown a remarkable ability to adapt to the modern world without giving up their traditional values and beliefs are the Hutterites and the Hassidim. The Hutterites, who live in rural collectives, have adopted some modern machinery, for example, but tend to use mechanization only for agriculture and collective activities, rather than for personal comfort. "Automatic thermostats were used in hog barns before they were used in dwelling houses. Floor coverings first appeared in the communal kitchen before they were allowed in family apartments" (Hoestetler 1974, 299). Although the Hutterite way of life does undergo inevitable, if slow, change, the community acts "as if change were not taking place" (Hoestetler 1974, 297), insisting that the use of modern machinery is consistent with the traditional goal of agricultural productivity.

The Hassidim, an ultraorthodox Jewish sect (actually a set of small sects) maintain a rigorously traditional style of life in the very centre of Canada's major cities. Again, this group has adapted to its surroundings by defining them as an alien world. The activities and secular lifestyle of the city are then seen not as seductive but as proof of how different this alien world really is (Shaffir 1974). Like the Hutterites, the Hassidim emphasize their difference as a marker of group identity.

Secondary Isolationist

The Vietnamese community of Canada, which probably includes somewhat more than 100,000 members, is an example of a secondary isolationist ethnic group. Refugees who have been torn away from their family and friends, the Vietnamese have not had an easy time adjusting to life in Canada. Most have settled in the cities, where they have tended, whenever possible, to group together and to try to maintain their traditional style of life. This has not been easy. Most Vietnamese are Buddhists, but Canada has few Buddhists and there are not enough to support extensive religious institutions. Many of the Vietnamese have dropped sharply in social class, having been middle-class in Vietnam but forced to take work as dishwashers or factory workers in Canada. Women, traditionally expected to stay home, have had to take jobs to help maintain the family but are still expected to cook, clean, and provide all the other services of housewives. The result for many of the Vietnamese has been confusion, even anguish, and a fierce determination to re-establish their lives as they would wish. Before they can concern themselves with making a cultural contribution to the dominant society, they must concern themselves with economic survival and psychological adjustment (Bong 1980). However, if the number of Vietnamese businesses sprouting on Toronto streets is any indication, this group may be finding a foothold in Canadian society and possibly starting down the city streets to integration.

Primary Integrationist

At one time Canada's Italian immigrants faced problems similar to those of the Vietnamese, but today they form a well-established and dynamic community. The Italians form a primary ethnic group: they usually define their ethnicity in terms of their relationship to their family and friends. Typical Italian Canadians identify strongly with the region or village in Italy from which they or their parents came, and often live close to others who are also from this region. They visit other family members frequently and remain highly committed to using their native language in the home. The Italian community is characterized by a high degree of what Breton (1968) called **institutional completeness**—that is, the community provides a full range of services to its members. Italians have their own social assistance organizations, clubs, newspapers and magazines, and even television programs. They also have an active and clearly identified set of leaders.

At the same time, the Italian community does not isolate itself from the rest of Canadian society but seeks to participate as fully as possible. Being integrationist does not mean, however, that the Italians wish to simply merge into the Canadian population and renounce their ethnic identity. Italians are proud of their heritage and wish to preserve their close ties to one another. They see no conflict in being both Italian and Canadian. The institutions they have developed, while designed to preserve their ethnic identity, are Canadian institutions with a Canadian form and organizational style. The same is true of the majority of Canada's ethnic groups: the Ukrainians, Jews, Poles, Portuguese, and the many others that can be categorized as primary integrationist ethnic groups.

Secondary Integrationist

The Dutch provide a model of still another type of ethnic group. Although the rural community of Holland Marsh in Ontario forms a definite and distinctive community, most of the Dutch in Canada, who are mainly urban, do not form an ethnic community in any real sense and have developed few ethnic institutions. The Dutch seem not to define their ethnicity as a bond with fellow Dutch in Canada, although they do remain strongly attached to the Netherlands, tend to retain their Dutch citizenship, and on average visit the Netherlands every few years. Perhaps because they retain such close links with their homeland, they feel little need to form an ethnic community in Canada. Whatever the reason, the Dutch consider being Dutch a purely personal matter, not a basis for establishing friendships or institutions. To all intents and purposes, outwardly at least, the Dutch have merged into the general Canadian population.

Persistence and Change

Our typology has several major shortcomings. Not all ethnic groups can choose to be isolationist or integrationist. Prejudice and discrimination bar many Canadians, particularly those of non-European ethnic origin, from full participation in Canadian institutions and isolate them, unwillingly, in their own communities. Indeed, given that the broader Canadian society is itself split into British- and French-Canadian communities, any integration is inevitably partial.

A second weakness, one characteristic of all typologies, is the static depiction of the ethnic groups. Ethnic groups are, in fact, dynamic entities that undergo change and adapt to meet new conditions. The Vietnamese, overwhelmed by the difficulties of adjustment to a new environment, may be isolationist now, but they will likely become more integrationist as the crisis of adjustment eases. The Italians, who retain strong ties to their family, may lose them in one or two generations as they become more and more integrated into the institutions of Canadian society. The Hutterites may ultimately find that modernity in the form of technology breeds secularization and may one day disappear as a viable religioethnic group. Conversely, some regional groups, such as the inhabitants of Newfoundland, are developing strong regionally based identities and may come more and more to take on the characteristics of ethnic groups over the next few generations. To recognize that ethnic groups are not static but dynamic, ever-changing sets of people whose interests, identities, and forms of organization are transformed over time is to hold an **emergent view of ethnicity**.

Until a few years ago it was generally taken for granted that ethnic groups were cultural survivals and would disappear in time by merging into the broader society of which they were a part. This **melting-pot theory** of ethnicity, popular in the United States, assumed that the ethnic group would gradually undergo a process of assimilation. Ethnic groups would lose both their distinctive characteristics and their ties to the homeland and become indistinguishable from any other segment of the society.

The melting-pot theory assumed that ethnicity was mainly a cultural phenomenon, but as we have seen it has many other aspects. As Milton Gordon (1964) points out in his multidimensional analysis of assimilation, even if cultural assimilation were to occur, ethnic group members could retain their own institutions and a fierce sense of loyalty to a collective past. In other words, **structural assimilation** does not necessarily follow **cultural assimilation** or vice versa. Indeed, the existence of an independent ethnic institutional structure may be more significant than cultural factors.

Residential segregation, whereby ethnic group members tend to live close together, is an obvious indicator of the importance of ethnicity in our society. The causes of this pattern are both voluntary (group preference) and involuntary (housing discrimination). Although decreasing slightly, ethnic residential segregation is still common in Canadian cities.

An ethnic group may lose its native language, customs, and most of its festivals and rituals, yet still define itself in terms of the institutions it has created. Furthermore, these institutions may themselves generate new cultural symbols and new cultural differences from the broader society.

While few Italian Americans can speak fluent Italian or feel a strong affinity for Italy, they feel a sense of pride and identification with other Italian Americans on Columbus Day. (In fact, Columbus Day is unknown in Italy itself, for it is the day on which Italian Americans celebrate their contributions to American society.)

Of course, assimilation is not an either/or affair, and there are many degrees of participation in the broader community. Smith (1981) outlines six strategies by which ethnic communities relate to the broader society:

1. **Isolation**, which we discussed in the case of the Hutterites and Hassidim, is a strategy of separation and non-involvement in the broader society.

2. **Accommodation** refers to some degree of integration into the broader society and the fullest possible participation in its institutional life.

3. **Communalism** is a strategy of local control in which a group that may be a minority in the society but is a majority in a particular region asserts its right to control local institutions. Demands by blacks in the United States for community control of schools in inner cities are an example of such a strategy.

4. **Autonomism** has become relatively common in Europe in states that can be seen as federations of regional ethnic groups, such as Yugoslavia, Switzerland, and most recently France, where Corsica has been granted a measure of political autonomy. It also describes recent demands by Canada's native peoples. A version of autonomism was seen in the sovereignty-association advocated by the Parti Québécois in the Quebec referendum of 1980; it would have had Quebec and Canada sharing certain economic structures and a common currency but would have allowed them to act independently of each other in most matters.

5. **Separatism** refers to "ethno-national self-determination" (Smith 1981, 16), in which the goal is to remove the group from the society in which it is an ethnic minority and to create a new state in which it is a national majority. This strategy is favoured by many Quebec nationalists and by such groups as Black Muslims in the United States.

6. **Irredentism** is a strategy whereby an ethnic community "whose members are divided or fragmented in separate states, seeks reunification and the recovery of the 'lost' or 'unredeemed' territories occupied by its members" (Smith 1981, 17). There is also a cultural irredentism in which people scattered over a broad territory are taught a new understanding and pride of their cultural past, as is the case with the Chicanos in the southwest United States. Many Chicanos have begun to refer to this region as "Aztlan" as a reminder that this land was once theirs.

ETHNIC STRATIFICATION

Ethnicity has its greatest impact on people's lives through its effect on their socioeconomic status. In his extraordinarily astute analysis of Canadian society, John Porter (1965) described Canada as a **vertical mosaic**—that is, as a nation in which ethnicity is inextricably intertwined with stratification. A glance at some of the sociodemographic characteristics of Canada's ethnic groups readily confirms Porter's description. The ethnic groups differ markedly in income, level of education, typical occupation, and rate of unemployment.

Recent evidence suggests strongly, however, that ethnic stratification—and the resulting inequalities—may not be as severe as sociologists once thought. For example, Exhibit 15-5 indicates that many visible minorities have high levels of educational attainment, compared to the British group. (This data may overstate the case, however, since many of the foreign credentials of immigrant workers may be undervalued by the Canadian labour market.) As discussed in Chapter 6, educational achievement, income, and status are closely related.

Exhibit 15-5
Distribution of Educational Achievement of Males 15 Years and Over, 1981

	Less Than Gr. 9	Gr. 9–13 but No Certificate or Diploma	High School Certificate or Diploma	Trade Certificate or Other Diploma Community College or Some University	University Degree
British Isles	15.6%	34.4%	17.0%	22.7%	10.3%
French	25.9	23.6	20.1	23.0	7.4
Other European	23.7	27.6	14.9	24.0	9.8
Indo-Pakistani	8.9	21.3	16.2	24.0	29.7
Indo-Chinese	16.0	28.9	20.3	17.2	17.6
Japanese	10.8	24.6	20.5	23.8	20.4
Korean	4.0	22.5	21.8	16.8	34.8
Chinese	16.7	26.5	18.6	17.1	21.1
Pacific Islands	13.4	31.9	17.2	27.6	9.9
Philippinos	6.9	16.7	18.9	24.6	33.0
Black	9.7	28.7	16.5	31.4	13.7
Native People	42.2	35.8	7.7	12.7	1.6
Central South American	12.7	27.5	20.1	25.0	14.7

Note: Data are for people reporting single ethnic origin only. Because of rounding totals may not equal 100 percent.
Source: Statistics Canada. Unpublished data. 1981 Census, in Abella (1984, 143).

Charter Groups and Entrance Status

We noted earlier that the pattern of ethnic self-segregation between the British and French groups in Canada served as an example for other ethnic groups. The charter groups defined the rules of the game, so to speak, and others must play by these rules.

From the very beginning, British-French relations were characterized by a pattern of domination and subordination. After the British conquest of New France, the French were defined by their conquerors as culturally, economically, and politically inferior. Although the British did protect the French right to remain a separate and distinctive group, this generosity had the consequence of raising the British status vis-à-vis the French.

Over the next two centuries, the British maintained their dominance by, in effect, closing off the channels of social mobility to all but a very few of the French. Canada's economic elite, for example, was almost exclusively of British descent. As recently as the 1950s, Porter found Canada's economic elite to be 92 percent British. The one major exception to this pattern has been in the area of politics: the French have been accepted into the political elite and have so far provided three prime ministers.

Channels of social mobility were also closed to the other ethnic groups as they began to arrive. The result was that, by and large, most groups retained their **entrance status** for at least two or three generations (Porter 1965). Recently, evidence suggests that this pattern is beginning to change. Clement (1975), in replicating Porter's study of the economic elite, found a somewhat higher level of participation by members of non-charter ethnic groups (although the numbers remain low). Certainly, other elite sectors have been successfully penetrated by non-charter group members. Symbolic examples of these changing conditions are former Governor-General Edward Schreyer, Supreme Court Chief Justice Bora Laskin, Ontario Lieutenant Governor Lincoln Alexander and Prince Edward Island Premier Joe Ghiz.

New, methodologically sophisticated research also suggests that ethnic origin is becoming less and less important in determining status attainment for Canadians (Darroch 1979; Ornstein 1981). For example, second- and third-generation Irish and Italians have moved up from their largely working-class entrance status into the middle class. Japanese Canadians, severely victimized during the Second World War, now have incomes well above average.

Most Canadian sociologists have emphasized the economic inequalities facing visible minorities. Exhibit 15-6 presents data that suggest the reality is a good deal more complex. The incomes of some visible minorities are above the Canadian average, while others are below. The income differential may affect men and women of a group differently. For example, Chinese males earn less than the Canadian average for men, but Chinese females earn more than the average for Canadian women. Racism clearly exists in Canada, but it may be losing its effect as a barrier to upward mobility.

Perhaps the most dramatic changes in Canada's pattern of ethnic stratification have occurred in Quebec. Provincial government legislation concerning the language of work and the "francization" of businesses has forcibly opened the channels of social mobility to the French, who are rapidly moving into managerial and executive positions. Other ethnic groups in the province, however, claim that these policies work to their disadvantage, and some feel that Quebec may no longer have as many opportunities for them.

Changes in Canadian stratification patterns do not necessarily mean that ethnicity will soon become completely irrelevant. The influence of some factors, such as prejudice and intragroup conflicts, may be hard to overcome.

Prejudice and Discrimination

Prejudice refers to an attitude in which individuals are pre-judged on the basis of characteristics assumed to be common to all members of a group. To believe that a person who is a Scot is a miser is prejudice based on acceptance of the stereotype that all or most Scots are misers. One person's stinginess is another person's thrift. Prejudice describes an attitude, which may or may not determine behaviour. **Discrimination** refers to the action of treating a person differently, usually unfairly, because of his or her membership in a particular group. Racial or ethnic discrimination may be embodied in law (**de jure**) as in South African apartheid, or may be illegal but present (**de facto**) as a result of people's aggregate behaviour. Institutional or **structural discrimination** is similar to de facto discrimination and refers to discrimination that results not necessarily from racist motivations or from specific acts, but from traditions or forces built into the social system that are hard to eliminate. For example, requiring a university degree or a college diploma for a relatively unskilled job penalizes poorer minority groups whose members are less likely than others to have post-secondary education.

Strong and distinctive attitudes toward different ethnic groups persist in Canada. It is not surprising, given that the majority of Canadians are of British or French origin, that these two groups are seen most favourably by most Canadians. It is only natural for people to believe that their own group is the best, and that people like themselves are the most decent, friendly, trustworthy, or even clean. It is somewhat more surprising that members of other ethnic groups tend to agree with the charter groups. The typical Italian Canadian agrees that the charter groups have these positive attributes but insists that Italians do too. Similarly, the typical Ukrainian Canadian believes that the charter groups have these attributes, but that Ukrainians do too (Berry et al. 1977). This is an excellent

Exhibit 15-6
Average Income of Individuals, Age 15 and Over, from Selected Ethnic Groups, 1981

	Blacks[a]	Chinese	Philippinos	Japanese	Indo-Pakistanis[b]	Indo-Chinese[c]	All Canadians
Males	14.9	15.1	15.1	18.7	17.6	10.5	16.9
Females	9.2	9.0	11.6	9.4	8.6	7.0	8.4

[a]Includes Caribbean.
[b]Includes persons who reported an origin from the Indian subcontinent such as Indian, Pakistani, Bengali, Gujarati, Punjabi, Tamil, Singhalese, Sri Lankan, or Bangladeshi.
[c]Includes persons reporting Thai, Vietnamese, Kampuchean/Cambodian, Laotian, Malay, or Burmese origin (more than 70 percent of the immigrants from these groups in Canada in 1981 had come within the previous three years).
Source: Multiculturalism Canada (1986).

Exhibit 15-7
Prestige of 14 Ethnic Groups Judged by Torontonians

	Rank	Mean Score	Don't Know/ No Response[a]
English	1	3.94	5.8%
Scottish	2	3.66	11.8
Irish	3	3.59	14.2
Jewish	4	3.45	10.0
Germans	5	3.26	12.8
Ukrainians	5	3.23	20.4
Italians	7	2.13	6.0
French	8	2.98	12.9
Greeks	9	2.89	15.7
Chinese	9	2.87	11.8
Portuguese	11	2.58	14.8
West Indians	12	2.01	13.2
Canadian Indians	13	1.87	18.7
Pakistanis	14	1.71	13.9

Notes: The sample (No. = 2338) rated social standing on the following scale: Excellent = 5, Very Good = 4, Good = 3, Fair = 2, Poor = 1.
[a]Parentage of respondents who said they did not know a group's prestige or who did not respond.
Source: Goldstein (1985, 188).

indication of the degree to which the charter groups are defined by all Canadians as the exemplars of the "real" Canadian. Exhibit 15-7 presents a Toronto sample's perceptions of the prestige of 14 ethnic groups. Significantly, this prestige ranking corresponds closely with the occupational or income rankings of these groups.

Racism can be described as a belief that racial differences reflect not only physical traits but also a wide variety of personality characteristics (intelligence, diligence, sobriety) and that these differences have—or ought to have—social consequences. "Scientific racism" emerged in the 19th century and helped rationalize European nationalism, colonialism, and imperialism by claiming to establish scientifically the various inabilities of the "inferior races" (which often included southern European nations).

In Canada, racist thinking was reinforced by the theory of climatic determinism. Specifically, many people believed that, because of the difficult Canadian winters, only the fittest, Northern races—such as the Anglo-Saxons, Celts, Normans, Scandinavians, and Germans—could survive in Canada. To Canadian racists, the image of the North, with its associated values of sobriety, diligence, and self-reliance, contrasted with the image of the South (the United States) where, they believed, the warmer climate nurtured laziness, impulsiveness, and anarchy. Because of the difficulty of disentangling simple, visible racial differences from notions of racial hierarchies, and because these differences make labelling easy, racial conflicts are among the most intractable ethnic tensions.

Although most Canadians recognize that there is some degree of prejudice in their society, they like to think of Canada as a land free of discrimination. This is simply not so. The pattern of institutional self-segregation of ethnic groups makes institutional discrimination part of the very fabric of Canadian life. Many Canadians prefer to live their lives in a web of institutions where they deal with people just like themselves. They prefer a doctor, lawyer, bank manager, politician, or police officer from their own ethnic group or one they perceive as similar. A case in point: in Montreal, a taxi company fired more than 20 Haitian cab drivers in 1982. The company noted that they were fired not because they didn't do their job properly but because the public simply didn't want to take cabs driven by Haitians. According to the company, the public complained that the Haitians didn't know their way around the city and so got lost; that their cabs were dirty and smelled; and that they were rude and spoke an incomprehensible French. Although the drivers were re-hired after extensive media coverage, the incident made public the degree of prejudice and discrimination general in Montreal. Even when de facto discrimination is not intended as such but is merely the consequence of ethnic group members preferring to do business with their own kind, the result is that newcomers, outsiders, or people who are visibly or markedly different do not have the same opportunity to get jobs or the trust of the established group.

Discrimination has little or nothing to do with any objective features of the group discriminated against. Because of the point system in current use, recent immigrants to Canada tend to be well-educated and relatively highly skilled. Yet often they cannot find work in the occupation for which they are trained and must instead take menial or low-status jobs. Thus, an East Indian engineer may have to work in a factory as a clerk.

In pursuit of equality and as a result of pressure from minority groups, particularly women, the federal government has supported **affirmative action programs**, or what is termed "equality of result." Thus, the government has encouraged the civil service and crown corporations to hire women, French Canadians, native peoples, visible minorities, and the disabled, in numbers approximating their percentage of the population (Abella 1984; Weinfeld 1981b). While successive provincial governments in Quebec have announced their interest in hiring non-French civil servants, little has been done; well over 90 percent of Quebec's civil service remains French in origin.

Most social scientists who evaluate the record of Canadian treatment of immigrants tend to accentuate the negative. Perhaps this represents an internalization of Porter's image of the vertical mosaic. As we have seen, there indeed has been—and remains—substantial prejudice and inequality. On balance, however, we argue that most immigrants, who compare Canada with their country of origin, are glad that they came here. Their own experience and their common sense tell them that Canada offers them—and certainly their children—economic opportunity and political freedom undreamed of in most of the world.

Conflicts within Ethnic Groups

Although ethnic groups may give the appearance from the outside of being a single, unified entity, members are well aware that each group is really a sort of alliance—often an uneasy alliance—of distinctive subgroups. As an example, Italian Canadians, while acting together on certain issues and sharing many similar concerns, identify more closely with a particular regional group. Such ethnic subgroups are often in sharp disagreement over issues they consider vital and may share only a few institutions. Moreover, even a relatively homogeneous ethnic group, such as the Haitians of Montreal, may break up into a number of subgroups on the basis of different lifestyles and patterns of participation in their new environment. Haitians have begun to split up into three subgroups: one that identifies itself as distinctively Haitian, and retains an interest in the problems besetting Haiti; another that identifies itself along linguistic lines as a francophone Québécois group and seeks to integrate into the broader Québécois community; and a third that identifies itself as a black group and seeks to integrate into the North American (anglophone) black community.

Class conflict besets many ethnic communities. Workers are often employed by people with the same ethnic identity but fundamentally different class interests and lifestyles. Since the economic elite often speaks for the larger group, the leadership of ethnic groups may not represent or respond to the majority of the group's members.

ETHNICITY AND PUBLIC POLICY

In an ethnically plural nation like Canada, the sociological study of ethnicity is far more than a theoretical exercise. Ethnic issues intersect with Canada's political agenda in a variety of ways. The Canadian government is publicly dedicated to achieving two goals: (1) ensuring equal opportunity and, where possible, equality of condition regardless of ethnic background or origin; and (2) ensuring the continued survival of Canadian ethnic groups and their cultures. These are the usual objectives of cultural pluralism, as practised in liberal-democratic societies. Public policies are adopted to further one or the other of the goals.

Ethnicity also affects policy-making in areas not clearly recognized as falling within ethnic spheres of interest. For example, most Québécois are relatively unaffected by fisheries policy, and Italian Canadians might be relatively unconcerned—as Italian Canadians—by Canadian energy policy. But the Québécois as a group might be concerned with foreign

Although Canada's immigration policies in the 1880s were racist, Chinese labourers were allowed into the country to work on railway construction. This was done, however, on the assumption that they would be shipped back to China when the work was completed.

policy or transportation policy, while Italian Canadians might be concerned with immigration policy, if such policies are perceived to affect the welfare of the group. Similarly, some policies designed in an ethnically neutral manner may actually affect different ethnic populations differently, producing tensions. Wildlife conservation laws, for example, may harm native peoples more than non-native sports hunters or fishermen.

In liberal-democratic states, where minority groups are free to organize voluntary associations, ethnic groups often assume the character of interest or pressure groups—at times even organizing lobbies to attempt to influence governments. Examples of such organizations in Canada are the Ukrainian Canadian Committee and the Assembly of First Nations. Social scientists are divided about the effect of such interest groups on political life. Some argue that these groups undermine the power of individual citizens and corrupt the political process, that policy-makers are overly influenced by the views of powerful group interests, to the detriment of the national interest in any policy issue (Mills 1956). Interest groups may thus become veto groups, limiting the possibilities for major social or economic change. Other analysts depend on political pluralism, seeing the proliferation of interest groups as a way to maximize the political leverage of citizens through associations of mutual interest; the groups provide an orderly way to channel input into the political process while maintaining a basic stability in the society (Lipset 1960; Dahl 1976).

However one views interest groups and their role in social and political life, it seems useful to study ethnic groups and their organizations as a **polity**—a political mini-system with selected leaders, constituencies, and decision-making and representative functions. Ethnic polities, in turn, act as interest or pressure groups vis-à-vis the larger society in areas of direct or indirect concern to the perceived interests of ethnic group members—economic, cultural, or social.

Exhibit 15-8 provides data from seven ethnico-racial groups in Toronto. Respondents were asked to describe their involvement with their ethnic polity, and to evaluate ethnic organizations and leadership.

Thinking about other ethnic groups as self-contained political communities may seem strange to Canadians who are members of one of the two charter groups, but, after all, Canada *is* understood as a political union of the British- and French-Canadian polities. It should not be surprising, then, that members of other ethnic groups feel it is in their interest to act in this manner. Still, what members of dominant groups take as their due, they see as presumption on the part of minorities. In the past, attachment on the part of some minority group members to an ethnic polity was viewed with disdain as evidence of a kind of dual loyalty that undermined commitments to the Canadian state. Today, however, attachment to ethnic organizations and involvement with communal leaders are recognized as part and parcel of Canadian multiculturalism, and treated as an exercise of the right to freedom of association as defined in Section 2 of the Canadian Charter of Rights and Freedoms.

Exhibit 15-8
Ethnic Group Members' View of Their Own Polity

	Chinese %	German %	Italian %	Jewish %	Portuguese %	Ukrainian %	West Indian %
1. Know of any organizations or associations in the community	38	36	49	89	32	57	61
2. Was or is now a member of one or more ethnic organizations or associations	7	10	24	67	20	51	19
3. Perceived degree of closeness to the centre of activities in ethnic community							
– Close	2	5	38	19	22	18	30
– Intermediate	14	1	20	29	24	23	9
– Distant	85	94	42	52	54	59	61
4. Express views about community affairs							
– Sometimes	5	6	28	42	9	40	35
– Never	95	94	72	57	91	60	65
5. Know leaders in the community							
– Personally	5	1	26	49	10	34	19
– Not personally	23(28)	4(5)	43(69)	27(76)	27(37)	14(48)	27(46)
– Not at all	72	95	31	24	63	52	54
6. Frequency of contacts with leaders							
– Frequently & occasionally	2	1	11	31	20	25	15
– Seldom or never	26	4	53	40	17	22	31
– Do not know leader and no answer	72	95	36	28	63	53	54
7. Informed about activities of leaders							
– Very much and somewhat	3	2	31	45	10	27	24
– Not too well or not at all	25	3	36	29	27	20	22
– Do not know leaders and no answer	72	95	33	26	63	53	54
Number weighted	(57)	(178)	(431)	(168)	(67)	(89)	(118)
Number of interviews	(152)	(321)	(351)	(344)	(163)	(345)	(150)

Source: Breton (1981, 38, 41, 44, 45).

Language Policy

In some ways language is to Canada what race has been to the United States—an axis of division that threatens the very unity of the nation. Clearly, language per se is not the issue. Rather, it symbolizes the deep divisions—religious, cultural, and political, as well as linguistic—among the people who came together to form the Canadian state. Put differently, it is *who speaks* the language that is really at issue. This has been seen most clearly in recent years in the debates over language in the provinces of Quebec and Manitoba. Nevertheless, precisely because language is symbolic of these divisions, the commitment to bilingualism initiated in the late 1960s indicated new attitudes and a new vision of Canada.

Bilingual policy in Canada emerged initially as a response to the stirrings of Québécois nationalism. In the 1970s it became the Liberal government's solution to the fundamental dualism of Canada. Efforts to strengthen the French language in Canada have followed two different directions. On the one hand, the federal government and certain provinces (to varying degrees) have sponsored efforts to develop bilingualism. On the other hand, both the Liberal and Parti Québécois provincial governments have promoted French unilingualism in Quebec.

Federal bilingualism policy, as entrenched in the new Canadian constitution, consists of four basic provisions:

1. A guarantee for French-speaking minorities to French-language public education wherever numbers warrant it.
2. The right to communicate with the central office of any federal government institution in French, and with branch offices where there is significant demand.
3. The requirement that federal parliamentary statutes and records be printed in both official languages.
4. The right to use French in any federal court. (The same right applies in the provincial courts of New Brunswick, the only officially bilingual province.)

In addition, a series of sometimes controversial steps have been taken in the federal public service to increase the use of French as a language of work and to encourage the employment and promotion of francophones.

Social science has helped fuel both initiatives, by documenting the assimilation of French Canadians outside Quebec (Joy 1972; 1978), the economic inequalities facing francophones in the civil service (Beattie 1975), and the income disparities between anglophones and francophones, particularly in Quebec (Raynauld et al. 1967; Porter 1965; Vaillancourt 1978). Sociological evidence is used in ongoing debates on such questions as whether the French language is still in danger of erosion in Quebec. Sociodemographic analyses of the effects of the declining French birth rate and the integration by immigrants into the anglophone community have sensitized the Québécois to this danger.

Policies of direct support for the French language have engendered controversy. Anglophones worry about the possibility that **reverse discrimination** in the civil service might make it difficult for the once-dominant group to get jobs or promotions; others stress the costs involved in making the machinery of federal government bilingual or claim that government programs are ineffective in increasing the use of French in government or in advancing the careers of francophones. These issues continue to be hotly debated.

Language policy rears its head in unexpected places. An example is the debate begun in the mid-1970s over the use of French as a language of air-traffic control in Canada, which had been conducted exclusively in English (Borins 1981). Unilingual French pilots were at a disadvantage, and francophone controllers argued that they ought to have the right to communicate with francophone pilots in French. Anglophone pilots and controllers said the use of two languages could lead to errors in communication and thus would lower the level of air safety. Supporters of bilingualism alleged that opponents were bigots who wanted to preserve the job security of unilingual air-traffic controllers. The example shows how a seemingly non-ethnic issue may become ethnically politicized. It also illustrates the close relationship among ethnic, political, and economic factors. Indeed, it has been asserted (see Chapter 18) that the air-traffic controllers' affair contributed to the 1976 election victory of the Parti Québécois.

Multiculturalism

Canada is both bilingual and multicultural. In recognition of these facts, the Canadian government supports minority ethnic cultures by providing funds to groups for various educational, social, or cultural projects via the Multiculturalism Directorate of the Secretary of State. Similar programs or subministries exist in all the Canadian provinces. The importance of multiculturalism has also been enshrined in Section 27 of the Constitution, which states: "This Charter shall be interpreted in a manner consistent with the preservation and enhancement of the multicultural heritage of Canadians." (No one knows what effect, if any, such a vague provision will have on judicial interpretations.)

One of the problems with the current policy of multiculturalism is that it adopts a restrictive view of culture—as something transmitted through the arts, whether highbrow or popular. Thus, grants are given to support dance groups, theatres, libraries, community centres, and the like. Yet it is not clear to what extent Canadian society can really accommodate different cultures or values as they affect people in their daily, private lives. As an example, in many traditional societies, the father and brothers of a girl who has been sexually compromised are required, by a code of honour, to take direct physical action against the girl, the man involved, or both. Yet Canadian law clearly prohibits the carrying out of this important cultural norm. More generally, the traditional values and practices of many cultures discriminate against women, which is culturally and legally unacceptable in modern Canadian society. John Porter (1975) went so far as to decry the whole notion of multiculturalism as making no sense in a modern post-industrial society, which he saw as having one dominant culture, that of science and technology.

Some people question whether a policy of multiculturalism is meaningful without a corresponding multilingual policy. Thus, many ethnic leaders urge that, in addition to English and French, third-language instruction be available from public school boards where demand is sufficient and where numbers warrant it. As these people ask, why are French minorities deserving of more state support for language training than Ukrainians in Alberta or Italians in Toronto? In fact, in the mid-1980s school boards in Toronto introduced a heritage language program, which offered classes for elementary school students in the language and culture of any ethnic group if requested by a certain number of parents. The program became a political hot potato. Some parents, some politicians,

The exuberant display of ethnic pride by Italian Canadians when Italy won the 1982 World Cup in soccer is an illustration of how strong the ties with the homeland and ethnic group remain even after emigration.

and the teachers' union opposed it, on the grounds that, as implemented, it increased teachers' workload and fragmented classes into potentially divisive ethnic groups. Supporters of the program, who claimed it gave children a new sense of belonging and pride in their ethnic group, accused the teachers of bigotry.

Human Rights Legislation: Minority Protection

Section 15.1 of the Charter of Rights and Freedoms in the Constitution entrenches the illegality of discrimination based on race, national or ethnic origin, colour, religion, and a number of other categories. Moreover, Section 15.2 permits affirmative action programs to ameliorate the conditions of disadvantaged groups. This recognition of equality rights reflects a heightened awareness on the part of both scholars and the Canadian public of the importance of such rights and of Canada's poor record in the past.

The reasoning behind affirmative action programs is that simply equalizing opportunity, de jure, by prohibiting discrimination, will not produce the desired effects for disadvantaged minority groups. This is because structural or institutional discrimination, which is in many ways the cumulative legacy of past discrimination, continues to operate, via old-boy networks, biased entrance examinations, and so on. Former U.S. President Lyndon Johnson argued this position in a 1965 speech, in which he drew an analogy with a race between two runners, one of whom is hobbled by heavy shackles and naturally falls behind. To stop the race, remove the shackles and let the race continue is not enough; to equalize opportunity the disadvantaged runner must be moved up to a position next to the competitor, before the race continues.

Exhibit 15-9 presents some interesting data on the degree of public support for constitutional protection for various types of minority groups, collected before the new Constitution was made law. Groups such as women, seniors, and the physically handicapped were seen as more deserving of protection than ethnic, racial, or religious groups; support for the protection of homosexuals was dramatically lower. Interestingly, women are consistently more supportive of constitutional protection for minorities than are men. Support for such protection decreases as one moves from Atlantic Canada and Quebec westward to Ontario and Western Canada. (It is possible that this question was tapping not only views on minority protection but attitudes about the entire process of patriation of the Canadian Constitution, which faced substantial opposition in Western Canada.)

The shift in emphasis from equality of opportunity to equality of result may cause strains in the Canadian body politic. Majority group members may fear reverse discrimination. Some observers believe that affirmative action will undermine the merit principle as a basis for reward and privilege (though how strictly the merit principle has been observed in the

Exhibit 15-9
Sentiments about the Protection of Specific Groups by a Charter of Rights,
June 1981

Question: "I am going to read you a list of specific groups who could be protected from discrimination by a Charter of Human Rights. For each group, please tell me whether it should be specifically protected or not in the charter."

Specific Group	All Canada	Males	Females	Atlantic	Quebec	Ontario	West
Racial minorities	69	65	73	77	78	66	61
Ethnic minorities	64	60	68	69	76	61	55
Language minorities	61	58	65	71	76	58	48
Religious minorities	58	56	61	67	71	56	46
Senior citizens	89	87	91	92	90	90	84
Women	77	74	80	83	85	78	65
Homosexuals	32	27	37	32	44	30	23
Physically handicapped	92	90	94	91	92	95	87

No. = 1960.
Source: Canadian Human Rights Commission (1981), selected tables from a Survey of Public Opinion on Human Rights. [C.R.O.P. Survey, June 1981, of men and women aged 18 and over in 10 provinces.]

past is open to debate). Some of the groups that are currently economically disadvantaged in Canada are relatively recent arrivals. Their shackles, so to speak, are not Canadian in origin. Should Canadian affirmative action programs address only the wrongs committed here? In that case, would the Japanese Canadians, whose average incomes are among the highest in the country, be eligible? Or should Canadians provide affirmative action programs to those whose disadvantages were forged elsewhere, and thus give them an advantage over groups who had no responsibility for those disadvantages and who have had to overcome their own hardships to achieve their present status?

It is interesting to compare the Constitution's carefully spelled out section on equality rights with the vague provision for multiculturalism. The commitment to cultural survival is less clearly specified than the commitment to ethnic economic equality.

The non-charter ethnic groups can be loosely divided into two sets: those of white or European background, most of whom arrived in Canada some time ago; and non-white groups, most of whom arrived more recently. The former groups are doing rather well economically in Canada and, despite the image of the vertical mosaic, have an average socioeconomic status rivalling that of the English charter group (Darroch 1979). Being relatively successful economically, they are more concerned with cultural survival or matters of policy. The latter groups, however, are still struggling with economic inequality, immigrant adjustment, racial prejudice, and discrimination; their priorities are bread-and-butter issues.

Anti-Hate Laws—A Double-Edged Sword

The ability of any state to legislate intergroup harmony is limited—one cannot legislate love and respect. Moreover, legal attempts to move society toward a harmonious ideal invariably lead to clashes with other important social values, such as freedom of the press and freedom of expression. For example, Canada has existing legislation prohibiting the dissemination of "hate literature." When it was passed in the mid-1960s, Canadian civil libertarians voiced fears that such legislation could be misused to restrict speech. One person's hate message may be another person's free comment; one person's malicious stereotype may be another's presentation of facts.

In 1985, the Canadian public was exposed to drawn-out court prosecutions of two individuals, Ernst Zundel, of Toronto, and James Keegstra, of Eckville, Alberta. Zundel published and distributed, throughout Canada and around the world, neo-Nazi material alleging that records of the murder of roughly six million Jews by the Nazis during the Second World War were a hoax. He was prosecuted and convicted under a little-known section of the criminal code dealing with "spreading of false news."

Keegstra was a schoolteacher who, for 14 years, had been teaching his social studies students that the events of world history could best be understood as the result of a sinister, world-wide Jewish conspiracy. Keegstra was prosecuted and convicted under the hate literature sections of the criminal code for wilfully promoting hatred against an identifiable group.

Both these trials raised issues of restraint of free speech and the effectiveness of laws in restraining purveyors of hate. Moreover, they raised the tactical question of whether it does more harm than good to give the views of bigots such extensive media exposure during the course of a trial. There are no easy answers to such questions.

CONCLUSION

Ethnicity has occupied a central position both as a subject of study for Canadian sociology and as a characteristic of Canadian society. It poses a challenge for both. For sociologists, the challenge lies in finding ways to understand such an extraordinarily varied form of social organization. The Canada of the 1980s has become a living laboratory in which to pursue such studies. For Canadian society, the challenge lies in attempting to take advantage of the cultural and social richness of ethnic diversity, while avoiding the pitfalls of parochialism and discrimination.

FOR FURTHER READING

Anderson, Alan B., and James S. Frideres
1981 *Ethnicity in Canada: Theoretical Perspectives*. Toronto: Butterworths.
This work provides a systematic overview of various theoretical approaches to the study of ethnic relations, with specific reference to Canadian conditions.

Berger, Thomas R.
1981 *Fragile Freedoms: Human Rights and Dissent in Canada*. Toronto: Clarke, Irwin.
This book presents a series of legal case studies on civil liberties in Canada, several of which have direct relevance for ethnic relations. Among the issues discussed by Berger are the internment of Japanese Canadians, the suppression of francophone education rights outside of Quebec, and the struggle of native peoples for land claims and aboriginal rights.

Breton, Raymond, Jeffrey G. Reitz, and Victor Valentine
1980 *Cultural Boundaries and the Cohesion of Canada*. Montreal: The Institute for Research on Public Policy.
This book includes an introductory overview of ethnic composition in Canada and three lengthy essays on the native peoples, French-English relations, and the non-charter groups. Each essay includes a thorough bibliography and presents empirical data interpreted from a policy oriented focus.

Glazer, Nathan, and Daniel P. Moynihan
1970 *Beyond the Melting Pot*. Cambridge: MIT Press.
Beyond the Melting Pot is one of the classics in the field; it describes and analyzes five minority groups in New York City, focusing on the links between ethnicity and participation in political and economic life.

Glazer, Nathan, and Daniel P. Moynihan, eds.
1975 *Ethnicity: Theory and Experience*. Cambridge, Mass.: Harvard University Press.
This reader contains a collection of both theoretical essays and case studies (including a provocative chapter by John Porter on Canada) which attempt to analyze the forces that sustain ethnicity and ethnic attachments in the modern world.

Gordon, Milton
1964 *Assimilation in American Life*. New York: Oxford University Press.
This is a classic exposition of the multidimensional nature of ethnic assimilation that reveals the limits of a simplistic linear theory of assimilation. Gordon traces the rise of three theoretical positions on ethnicity: conformity to the British, the melting pot, and cultural pluralism.

Kallen, Evelyn
1982 *Ethnicity and Human Rights in Canada*. Toronto: Gage.
Kallen gives an overview of general sociological and anthropological concepts of race and ethnicity, as well as particular discussion relevant to Canada. In addition, the book focuses on related human rights issues and the legal-constitutional positions of minority groups, particularly as affected by the Constitution Act of 1982.

Porter, John
1965 *The Vertical Mosaic*. Toronto: University of Toronto Press.
The classic work of Canadian sociology analyzes the relationship between ethnicity and social stratification in Canada, looking at both membership in broad social strata and access to dominant elite positions.

Reitz, Jeffrey G.
1980 *The Survival of Ethnic Groups.* Toronto: McGraw-Hill Ryerson.
Focusing primarily on European groups and the Chinese in Canada, Reitz's book examines the factors that contribute to ethnic group survival and community cohesion.

Ramcharan, Subhas
1982 *Racism: Non-Whites in Canada.* Toronto: Butterworths.
Ramcharan's work on non-whites in Canada presents a clear and cogent summary of the varieties, expressions, and consequences of racism.

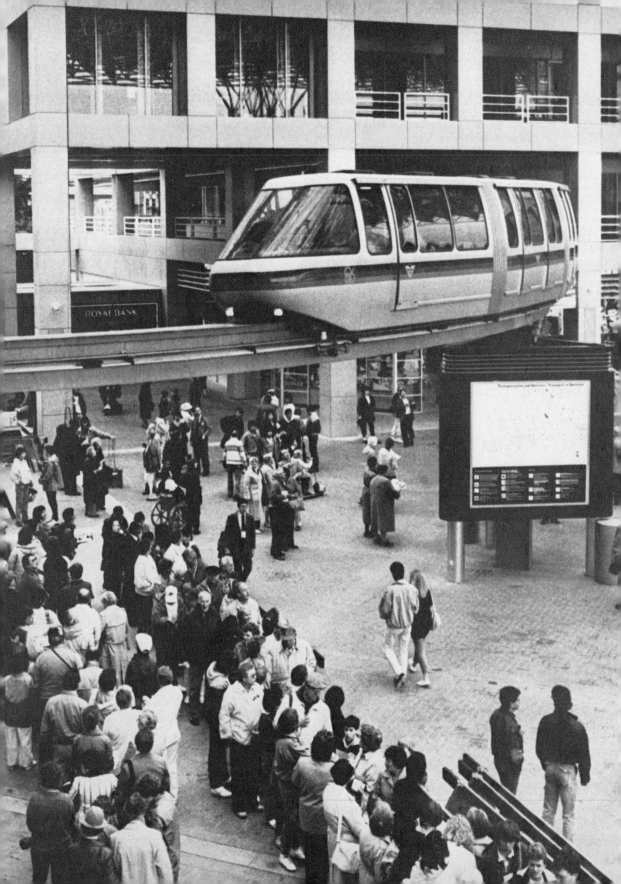

CHAPTER 16

URBAN SOCIOLOGY AND URBANIZATION

Lawrence F. Felt

583

Urban sociology is a bit like Canada—expansive, diverse, and sometimes unsure of where it should be going. Urban sociologists are defined by their desire to understand a particular type of sociospatial system called urban. A **sociospatial system** is simply a geographically (spatially) bounded, relatively permanent settlement and the relationships within it. Understanding it includes looking at its evolutionary features (the processes creating and transforming such a settlement) and structural features (the organized relationships that allow the settlement's continuation into the future), as well as the behavioural and social-psychological consequences associated with—perhaps even caused by—residence in such a settlement. (These consequences include behaviour, attitudes, values, and lifestyles associated with urban living; for example, urban dwellers are allegedly more impersonal and competitive and less religiously inclined than their rural counterparts.)

This focus upon the interplay between human relationships and a particular spatial form is unique to the specialty. In fact, the whole discipline of sociology emerged in the middle of the 19th century as an attempt to decipher that era's tumultuous changes associated with the rise of industrial capitalism. Never before in human history had the social fabric of life been so quickly unravelled. People were pushed off their land and pulled into the growing cities. Wealth and poverty were created on an unheard-of scale. Traditional institutions (such as Church, family, and nobility) and their means for maintaining peace and order appeared to be crumbling, and no viable alternatives were apparent. Since the new industrial city was at the centre of this new life, understanding such new settlements was given priority.

In more recent times, urbanization has become a phenomenon much more pervasive than the city itself. The economic, political, and cultural influences of the process extend to every corner of social life. Largely for this reason, a number of urban sociologists, collectively known as the New Urban Sociologists, have become concerned that the spatial factor imposes too severe limitations on their area of study. They argue against defining the field in geographic terms. The challenge they pose is examined later in this chapter.

Although urban sociology includes a vast expanse of subject matter and a diversity of research, it does, nonetheless, have some common core terms and definitions.

SOME DEFINITIONS AND CONCEPTS

In a common-sense way, everyone knows what an urban settlement is— it's a city! Well, not quite. Sociologically speaking, **urbanization** refers to the process by which increasing numbers of people come to live and work in larger, denser, and more heterogeneous settlements. An **urban settlement** comprises three parts—the city, the suburbs, and the exurbs—which are distinct though functionally interrelated. Before suburban and ex-urban growth took place, "urban" and "city" were almost synonomous.

CANADIAN CENSUS DEFINITION OF "URBAN"

The Canadian census provides the official basis for measuring urbanization in Canada. The precise meaning of "urban" has varied somewhat over the past hundred years, making exact historical comparisons difficult. Moreover, the Canadian definition is less strict than those of other societies, such as Great Britain and the United States, so that Canadian levels are somewhat inflated.

Up to 1951, the census defined an urban area as an incorporated settlement of more than 1,000 inhabitants. Because of the rapid growth of suburbia, much of which was then unincorporated, "urban" was extended in that year to include unincorporated settlements of more than 1,000 as well. As population growth accelerated on the urban fringe in the 1960s and 1970s, the census makers added a requirement of population density (individuals per square mile or kilometre). Thus, in 1961 and 1971 an urban settlement meant any incorporated town, village, or city of more than 1,000 people and any population concentration of 1,000 or more people with a minimum density of 1,000 per square mile. In 1981, to be consistent with the metric system, the density requirement was restated as 400 people per square kilometre.

Two other census definitions are important here. The term **Census Metropolitan Areas (CMAs)** was first used in the 1951 census, re-placing the Canadian Metropolitan Areas that had been categorized as the "great cities of Canada" to reflect the reality of suburban sprawl. According to the 1981 definition—slightly changed from the original—a CMA consists of "the main labour-market area of an urbanized core (or continuously built-up area) having 100,000 or more population." Thus, although expressly urban settlements are contained within the CMA, so are areas that do not meet the definition of urban. As a matter of fact, half the rural growth in Canada between 1976 and 1981 consisted of non-urban growth within a CMA.

A **Census Agglomeration Area** is simply the main labour-market area for a smaller urban population core of 10,000 to 99,000. It too usually contains a number of non-urban areas on its perimeter.

Thus, many of the people classified as non-urban by the census live in a CMA or a CAA and are tied to the urban core for work, culture, leisure activities, and so on. One must approach with caution any statement that these people are not urban people or that the number of urban people is declining in Canada.

This is no longer the case. The city is only one part of an urban settlement pattern. In fact, sociologists restrict use of the term "city" to its definition in the relevant legislation. In other words, **city** is a legal definition of a settlement and nothing more. Many suburbs and even unincorporated townships adjacent to a city may be larger in area and population.

Suburbanization, the process by which suburbs develop, refers to the accelerated growth of smaller settlements adjacent to and surrounding cities. Such suburbs are referred to collectively as the metropolitan area of a city, as in "metropolitan Montreal" or "Metro Toronto." Before the Second World War, suburbs were limited in number and were almost exclusively the preserve of the well-to-do, who wanted to forsake the city for the "country" but still be able to commute daily to work "downtown."

Since the Second World War, this pattern has changed radically. The extensive allocation of public funds for building elaborate expressways and highways, the great increase in automobile ownership, and the significant expansion in real income resulting from the post-war period of economic expansion have led to massive suburban growth during the past 35 years. Today suburban living is not the preserve of even the moderately wealthy. People from virtually every income level and ethnic group can be found in suburbia (though most suburbs, individually, remain relatively homogeneous socioeconomically). Moreover, the revolution in technology that has allowed industries to decentralize has meant that many suburbanites need not even go "downtown" to work. As a result, the populations of many cities have actually declined, while the metropolitan areas have expanded enormously.

Exurbanization is a recent phenomenon. **Exurbs** are those smaller communities beyond the suburbs to which city and, to a lesser extent, suburban dwellers have fled in increasing numbers. Such communities are found as far as 80 to 130 km from a city centre. Collectively, they constitute a second ring of rapidly expanding settlements, with the city and suburbs on one side and rural villages on the other. Exurbs are considered part of the urban pattern because their residents exhibit lifestyles that link them to the city and suburbs much more than to the country. Most exurbanites work in either the city or the rapidly expanding industrial sites within the suburbs. When not commuting to and from the city for employment, they commute for theatre, art, and other cultural pursuits. Their lifestyle is an interesting fusion of the cosmopolitanism and worldliness of the city with the quietness and old traditions of rural life. A recent column in the Toronto *Globe and Mail* captures the sense of it:

> Last August, we moved from old Toronto to a brand new house in Aurora (50 kilometres north of Toronto). Our friends call Aurora the middle of nowhere. It was the kind of move city dwellers make all over Canada. . . . Within a five minute drive we can now see cattle and horses in green pastures . . . The rural paradise does not rule out upscale shopping. We can get Catherine's Antipasto and Honeycup mustard. . . . Commuting costs are $8.50/

day for train and subway. At 8:17 upon arriving in town, I join what they call the "Salmon run" as the crunch of people squeeze through the station doors, buy tickets, a muffin, use a public washroom or just get through the damned subway door. (O'Reilly 1986)

Changing Patterns of Urbanization

The three components of urbanization have exhibited rather different growth rates over the past one hundred years. Before 1945, cities were the dominant type of urban settlement. From 1945 through the 1970s, suburban growth rates quickly outstripped those of cities. So significant was the suburban explosion that the populations of most cities stabilized or even declined, while those of suburbs increased several hundred percent. For example, from 1950 to 1980, Baltimore, Maryland, suffered a population decline of 19 percent, New York City 11 percent, and London, England, 9 percent, while their respective suburban areas expanded. Canadian cities have experienced the same slowdown. From 1976 to 1981, Halifax lost 3.6 percent of its population, Toronto 6.4 percent, Montreal 9.8 percent, and Winnipeg 0.2 percent; Vancouver neither gained nor lost. Meanwhile, the respective metropolitan areas were rapidly expanding.

During the past decade, exurbs have begun to rival suburbs in rates of growth. Although the percentage of urban residents living in exurbs remains relatively small (approximately 15 percent, according to the 1981 census), exurbs have recently overtaken suburbs as the fastest-growing component of urban settlements. Increasing numbers of city and suburban dwellers are attempting to enjoy the advantages of cities, while avoiding the congestion, decay, and ethnic and racial conflicts now found even in some of the larger suburbs. This surge in exurbanization is best understood as a result of the past successes of suburbia. Many suburbs have grown to the point where they resemble a city minus a downtown core. In an important sense, then, a rationale for their existence has been forfeited. Families that still crave the perceived advantages of rural life are now much more likely to be attracted to either villages or medium-sized cities (population 30,000 to 90,000, and especially no more than 40,000) not caught up in what is usually termed "metropolitan sprawl" (in other words, not part of an area immediately adjacent to one of our larger urban centres). In such places, families can have the amenities of urban living with their backs to the country. Evidence for such an interpretation can be found in the fact that small and medium-sized cities are growing much faster than the larger urban metropolitan areas.

This desire for the rural life has been a very significant factor in determining the level of urbanization in recent years. Between 1976 and 1981, the percentage of Canadians living in urban areas declined—from 76.1 percent to 75.7—for the first time in a century. A comparable stabilizing or a slight decline in urban residence has been noted in the United

States, Great Britain, and a number of European countries as well. Berry (1978), among others, terms this a "counter-urbanizing" trend. The word may, however, be something of a misnomer. Nearly half the Canadian rural growth between 1976 and 1981 resulted from exurban growth on the rings of larger cities. A likely conclusion is that, although rural growth has increased significantly enough to stall urbanization as measured by the census, urban influence has increased, insofar as the new exurbanites are more influenced by events and relationships in the cities and suburbs than the country. Until research suggests otherwise, exurban growth is probably best understood as an extension of urban forces to the country, rather than the opposite.

URBANIZATION AS A WORLDWIDE PROCESS

Urban settlement is now the dominant form of settlement in the Western world. Exhibit 16-1 summarizes the growing extent of urbanization in this country. At the time of the 1981 census, 28 percent of Canadians lived in three metropolitan areas with populations of more than one million (Toronto, Montreal, and Vancouver), and 51.7 percent of them lived in urban areas with more than 100,000 people. South of the border in the same year, 42 percent of the United States population was concentrated in thirty-six urban areas that had more than one million people each. Only one in four Americans lived in an area of less than 100,000 people (Westhues 1982, 261).

This urbanizing trend is not limited to North America or even the West. The entire world is urbanizing very rapidly, as Exhibit 16-2 indicates. A 1986 report prepared on world population trends for the United Nations predicts that the urban population of the world will more than double, from 2.01 to 5.1 billion, between 1986 and 2025. Included in this urban projection are five super-cities of more than 15 million inhabitants each (Tokyo, Mexico City, New York, Rio de Janeiro, and London).

A Sociological View of Urbanization

Given such rates and magnitudes of urbanization, today's sociologists are keenly interested in understanding the nature and origin of this process. Building on the work of several of the discipline's founding fathers (whose views we examine later in the chapter), sociologists have traditionally viewed urbanization as resulting from the coming together of three factors:

1. A significant increase in the population of a given territorial space.
2. An increase in social density resulting from such a population increase.
3. An increase in heterogeneity of people as a more diverse population is drawn to a growing urban settlement.

Exhibit 16-1
The Urbanization of Canada (urban population as a percentage of total population)

	1901	1931	1961	1976	1981
Canada[a]	34.9	52.5	70.2	76.0	75.7
Atlantic region	24.5	39.7	49.1	52.8	52.0
Prince Edward Island	14.5	19.5	32.4	37.1	36.3
Nova Scotia	27.7	46.6	54.3	55.8	54.5
New Brunswick	23.1	35.4	46.5	52.3	49.4
Newfoundland			44.8	54.6	53.2
Quebec	36.1	59.5	74.3	79.1	77.0
Ontario	40.3	63.1	77.3	81.1	81.0
Prairies	19.3	31.3	57.6	68.9	70.7
Manitoba	24.9	45.2	63.9	69.9	70.0
Saskatchewan	6.1	20.3	43.0	55.5	57.8
Alberta	16.2	31.8	63.3	75.0	76.4
British Columbia	46.4	62.3	72.6	76.9	75.7

[a]Totals exclude Yukon and Northwest Territories and, before 1947, Newfoundland.

Sources: Stone (1967, table 2:2, p. 29); Statistics Canada, 1971 Census of Canada, *Population, Urban and Rural Distributions*, Bulletin 1.1-9, table 10; Statistics Canada, 1976 Census of Canada, *Urban and Rural Distributions*, cat. no. 92-807; Statistics Canada, 1981 Census of Canada, *Urban Growth in Canada*, cat. no. 99-942; Statistical Office, Government of Newfoundland and Labrador (1984), *Historical Statistics of Newfoundland and Labrador*, vol. II.

Exhibit 16-2
The Urbanization of the World (urban population as a percentage of total population)

	1920	1940	1960	1980	2000[a]
Europe (except USSR)	32.0	37.0	41.0	49.7	56.0
North America	38.0	45.0	57.0	68.1	72.0
East Asia	7.0	13.0	20.0	26.2	34.1
South Asia	6.0	8.0	14.0	19.4	26.0
USSR	10.0	24.0	36.0	52.0	64.0
Latin America (Central and South America)	14.0	19.0	32.0	43.0	54.0
Africa	5.0	7.0	13.0	21.2	29.0
Oceania	34.0	38.0	50.0	57.9	62.0

[a]Estimates

Sources: "Growth of the World's Urban and Rural Population: 1900–2000," *International Social Development Review* 1 (New York: United Nations, 1969). "Selected Demographic Statistics," *United Nations Review* 43 (New York: United Nations, 1983).

A number of organizational consequences flow from these three factors. Perhaps the most important is a significant increase in the division of labour and activity. Durkheim ([1893] 1964), in particular, emphasized the importance of specialization in labour, which arose from an increasing concentration of diverse people. Such a division of labour led, in his opinion, to a much more efficient adaptation to the natural environment, and was the key factor that allowed accelerated economic growth to occur. Thus, in his view, urbanization was a process in which population growth and occupational specialization reinforced each other to create larger and larger settlements.

If urbanization is an organizing process whereby larger concentrations of people come to live in closer and denser relation to one another, **urbanism** refers to a range of beliefs, values, and norms (rules of behaviour) alleged to be associated with urbanization. In other words, urbanism is the cultural component of urbanization. You are doubtless familiar with some popular stereotypes of urbanism, such as aloofness, competitiveness, loneliness, and general lack of interpersonal relationships, compared to the situation in rural living. Since elements of social structure are typically associated with specific cultural forms, many sociologists, such as Simmel ([1950] 1964) and Wirth (1938), have been convinced that urbanization gives rise to particular values, beliefs, and rules. For example:

> The city's size and density also influence the development of impersonal, segmental and superficial relationships between urban residents. . . . These form a defensive mechanism against the potentially overwhelming impositions of the numerous persons with whom some form of contact is possible. Exposure to a wide variety of outlets promotes a certain sense of distance from any single association. An underlying cosmopolitanism emerges. Mutual exploitation—regulated to some extent (by market forces)—along with a relativistic orientation toward belief systems, a general pattern of social distance and the dominance of depersonalization and mass appeals are all products of the heightened mobility, individual variety and social instability characteristic of dense heterogeneous settlements. (McGahan 1982, 22)

At this point we encounter another essential term—community. Popular writers and sociologists alike have used the word with a variety of meanings. Nonetheless, most sociologists would agree that the core meaning refers both to a form of human settlement (and therefore a specific type of social structure) and to a set of values, beliefs, and rules alleged to be associated with such a settlement type. In other words, it has both a structural and a cultural meaning. The major structural features of the form of settlement called **community** are:

1. Relatively small size.
2. Relatively low social density.
3. Homogeneity of residents in ethnicity, language, and religion.

4. Relatively little occupational specialization or social-class differentiation.
5. Frequent and continuous face-to-face interaction among most community members.
6. A much greater proportion of social relations occurring with community members than with outsiders.
7. The relative absence of bureaucratic or highly hierarchical relations among community dwellers.

Culturally, the major features defining a community are said to be:

1. A strong psychological identification with the community and a clear sense of its physical and symbolic boundaries.
2. A significant consensus on the values, beliefs, and rules that define the community.
3. A relatively low evaluation of the importance of privacy in one's personal life.

This picture of a community is what sociologists term an **ideal type** composite—a general prototype or model drawn from varied research carried out on many different populations by several researchers. No single community would actually possess exactly the same amount of all the structural and cultural features listed. An ideal type is useful, however, in that it summarizes, in one example, the various characteristics most frequently mentioned by sociologists in their community studies.

Sociologists have traditionally contrasted urbanization (with its associated urbanism) and community, as types of human settlement. Communities were small, homogeneous, and culturally distinctive. Urban settlements represented a quantitative and qualitative transformation of such communities. Thus, the types have often been posed as two ends of a continuum of settlement possibilities, with the smallest community at one end and the largest urban settlement (usually referred to as a megalopolis) at the other. Such an image often suggests, sometimes directly and at other times by implication, that urban settlement and community are incompatible, that they cannot co-exist in the same space and time. Social scientists now know that such an argument is incorrect in many respects. Communities and large-scale urbanization frequently exist within the same territorial space—one within the other, as it were. Sociologists also know now that urbanization can even create and support types of communities that are different from the ones that the ideal model suggests. (We explore these ideas in the discussion of modern sociological research on urbanization.)

Urbanization in Historical Perspective

How can one explain the magnitude of the urbanizing process throughout the world? Have there always been urban settlements? If so, why? Is the modern trend toward what might be termed mega-scale urbanization a continuation of earlier trends, or is it a recent phenomenon? To answer these questions adequately requires situating urbanization within the history of human evolution.

Human settlements that fit our definition of "urban" have existed for at least 8,000 of the 50-odd thousand years that humans have existed on this planet. (In comparison, writing as a form of communication was initiated only about 3,500 years ago.) By 3500 BC numerous settlements of 4,000 to 6,000 people existed, and by 2500 BC urban units of up to 100,000 people were known.

What factors account for the rise of these early urban units? Until recently, the generally accepted sociological explanation centred on the

A typical street scene in a pre-industrial city.

domestication of animals and seeds and the resultant agricultural surplus. Hamblin captures this view succinctly:

> Once this "food producing revolution" had been accomplished, the old reasoning went, the relative reliability of food supply and the sedentary life increased the life span of childbearing females and made larger families—which made larger villages, which made increased complexity of organization and control, which made intensive agriculture, scholars maintained, and that demanded organization, and then writing. The result was commerce, music, mathematics, architecture, kings, priests and empires—all centered in cities. (1973, 14)

More recent evidence suggests, however, that domestication and surplus may not have had such a direct impact on early urban development and may even have followed, rather than preceded, such settlement. Many seminomadic peoples from Mexico to China were successful in domesticating plants and animals and possessed the capability, at least, to generate agricultural surpluses, yet they never created permanent settlements larger than very small villages.

The prevailing view today is that a complex set of interrelated factors provided the push for urban development. By roughly 8000 BC the effects of the last Ice Age had disappeared from the Near East—the site of the earliest cities. Hamblin (1973) summarizes the work of social researchers who argue convincingly that this geographic area was highly suitable for its hunting-and-gathering inhabitants, providing them an efficient resource base. Population growth increased, and overcrowding gradually occurred. One reaction to crowding was to congregate in the areas most suitable to survival because of their high fertility. As population growth continued, there occurred what Hamblin terms a "second squeeze": as the most desirable areas became overpopulated, people were forced to settle in less desirable areas. Hamblin suggests such secondary settlements had difficulty surviving because they had fewer resources. These settlements began to support themselves partially by providing services—defence, commerce, aqueducts for irrigation, and sites for religious worship—to the surrounding areas.

Defence and commerce functions favoured the growth of settlements into larger units, and such growth contributed to a more complex division of labour, as more and more varied economic and administrative tasks became interdependent within the settlement. With defence and population growth also came a need for coordination and control—that is, a need for a set of procedures for decision-making and a group of individuals authorized to make decisions. From this need emerged ruling classes of varying types, which eventually entrenched themselves with the powers and prerogatives of domination.

Some settlements, because of their favourable location and the ingenuity of their inhabitants (and perhaps historical accident), came to dominate not only the immediately adjacent territory but other, less successful, urban centres as well. The most successful became the imperial cities from which the early empires were controlled and coordinated.

Such **pre-industrial cities**, to use Sjoberg's term (1960), were an interesting mixture of what one might call primitivism and cosmopolitanism. In art, architecture, class distinctions, and military prowess, they reflected a sophisticated and elaborate development. Yet their economic production remained almost entirely dependent on technologically simple, labour-intensive strategies that used slaves and artisans. The use of even primitive machinery was severely limited, and most of these early urban residents were illiterate.

The existence of such cities must be seen in proper context, however. At this time (say, about 3500 BC to AD 500) most of the earth's population lived in non-urban areas. While precise estimates of the number of urban dwellers throughout the period are highly tentative, probably no more than 1 to 3 percent can be said to have been urban, as we have defined the term. Most lived in small, relatively permanent, homogeneous villages or moved as seminomads from one temporary settlement to another. In addition, low levels of medical and other technology and highly inflexible class systems kept most of the urban settlements that did exist to a few thousand people in size—hardly on the scale of today's urban centres.

In Europe, the magnitude of urban settlements increased with the rise of the city states at the end of the so-called Dark Ages (circa AD 700–1300), but only with the rise of industrial capitalism did urbanization become a pervasive social force influencing the lives of vast numbers of people. The development of new technology and the harnessing of existing technology within the factory system created possibilities for economic growth on a scale previously unimagined. Factory organization created unprecedented demands for wage labour and led to massive immigration to the rapidly growing urban centres. Improvements in sanitation, health care, transportation, and communication also reinforced such growth. Some statistics (taken from McGahan 1982, 2) indicate the great increase in urban dwellers as a result of industrial capitalism. In 1800, during the early stages of the Industrial Revolution, approximately 3 percent of the earth's population lived in urban settlements of 20,000 people or more. By 1850 the figure was 20 percent. In 1800 only 50 cities in the world had populations in excess of 100,000. By 1950 the number had increased to 900 and by 1975 it stood at more than 2000.

As these figures suggest, the urbanizing process accelerated following the Second World War. Not only was there increased urban growth, but also the average size of urban settlements increased at a rate barely thought possible at the beginning of the Industrial Revolution. McGahan (1982, 2) summarizes this more recent transformation:

> The movement toward large urban scale is unmistakable. The proportion of the world's population living in cities of 1,000,000 or more doubled between 1950 and 1970. Similarly, the average size of urban place has been consistently

Nineteenth-century Montreal, looking east from the customs house. Shipping, as opposed to industry, was important to Montreal's livelihood.

New York City's Third Avenue elevated railway, around 1895. This woodcut shows how noisy and congested an industrial city could be.

increasing. . . . In 1950 only a small per cent (3.2) of the world's total population lived in cities of 2.6 million or more; by the year 2000 this proportion will have increased to one fifth. In short, "One should not speak simply of the urbanization of the world's population. . . . Instead [one should speak of] the metropolitanization of the population" (Davis 1972, 150).

Canada has, of course, been a participant in this urbanizing process. In fact, since the Second World War it has had the fastest rate of urban growth of any Western industrial nation. By 1981, nearly 76 percent of the population lived in what Statistics Canada (1981b) defines as urban areas, making Canada the 16th most urban nation in the world.

The Phases of Urbanization

This brief overview of urbanization has highlighted three distinct periods or phases: the pre-industrial, the early industrial, and what we might term the post–Second World War industrial. Each phase is characterized by a somewhat different urban organization.

Whenever one thinks of an urban area, the first defining feature to come to mind is usually a downtown area, a city centre where most economic activities are transacted. The terms **central core** or **downtown core** (or central business district) are frequently used to designate this area. Yet one of the basic characteristics of the pre-industrial city was the absence of such a core. The basic organizing principle of these early cities was that people doing similar activities were geographically close to each other. For example, all—or most—carpenters would live in one section of a city, perhaps on the same street. (Thus come references to streets as belonging to particular occupational groups—think of the Street of the Rugmakers in the film *Casablanca*.) Since residence and place of employment were not separated as they are in industrial cities, this arrangement was feasible and reasonable. Merchants lived above their stores in another part of the city—near the transport routes, be they roads, a river, or an ocean, in settlements in which trade was a major economic activity—and administrative offices and courts were found in still another part. The very poor were clustered around the periphery of the site, rather than in the downtown core.

In the 18th and 19th centuries, the early industrial urban settlement evolved to meet the specific needs of an expanding industrial capitalism. The major factor shaping this pattern was the need for large amounts of centrally located land near major transportation routes. Such lands were the sites of the first factories. As capital inputs into the production process increased dramatically and as individual workers came to be treated as a commodity, along with land and machinery, important changes occurred that affected land use and encouraged factory development. Workers could no longer control their labour and were forced to sell it for wages. A greatly expanded division of labour made it increasingly easy to substitute machines for workers and workers for one another.

Urbanization is continuous: neighbourhoods are frequently made over into new neighbourhoods or restructured for new uses.

With workers substitutable and having no control over the products they produced, it was no longer necessary for them to live on the site of their labour.

The result of such an economic revolution was that productive activity could be centralized in the areas most accessible to transportation and workers brought in to work. Typically, workers were housed in districts near the factories. During the early period of industrialization, owners might also live in the core area (in the most desirable locations), but as they became successful, they usually moved out some distance from both the factory and the workers. Similarly, as particular factory workers slightly improved their position, they might also move farther away from the factory and be replaced in the original location by more recent arrivals in the city. Eventually, many early industrial cities assumed the pattern of a series of concentric circles with the inner area occupied by factories, the next circle by the poorest factory workers, the next by moderately successful workers, and so on. Such a pattern provided the basis for some of the early work on the city done by sociologists at the University of Chicago. (See Exhibit 16-3, which we will discuss again.)

Following the Second World War, economic growth was rapid and the size of the typical economic unit increased significantly. As a result, a somewhat different urban pattern emerged. The normative firm is now the corporate giant with headquarters in a large metropolitan area and factories scattered throughout diverse regions. Proliferating multinational corporations have carried decentralization even further. As a result, coordination, administration, and communication functions have become at least as important as productive activities. An important consequence is that economic activity is no longer so tied to a central core

Exhibit 16-3
Chicago as a Series of Concentric Zones

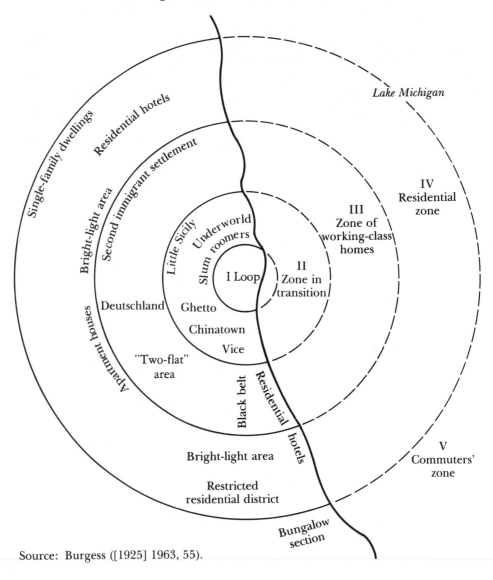

Source: Burgess ([1925] 1963, 55).

area. Many firms have followed suburban development—originally a strategy whereby workers could live in the "country" while commuting daily to the central area for work on heavily subsidized highways or public transit. Increasingly, workers are able to live and work without going downtown.

Regions that have urbanized rapidly during the past 30 years are characterized by the diminished importance of the core area and its replacement by a series of minicentres dispersed throughout the urban area. Los Angeles, with its thousands of miles of expressways and no discernible downtown, typifies this most recent variety of urbanization. As yet, Canada does not have an example of this pattern. Nonetheless, the tendency can be seen in those metropolitan areas experiencing the greatest urban growth in recent years. On a scale considerably less grand than that of Los Angeles, St. John's also exemplifies the process—an interesting phenomenon since it is one of the oldest urban areas in Canada. Since 1975 it has had one of the greatest rates of urban growth in the country, but the expansion has bypassed the old downtown core and the new city lacks a clear central focus or area for business, recreation, or cultural activity.

Thus St. John's, which was founded before the Industrial Revolution, reflects some very old and some very new urban patterns. This phenomenon is not unusual; indeed, depending on their age, most urban areas display some characteristics of at least two and perhaps all three phases of urbanization—pre-industrial, industrial, and post–Second World War.

OLDER SOCIOLOGICAL APPROACHES TO URBANIZATION

Nineteenth-Century Views from Germany and France

As we suggested at the beginning of the chapter, urbanization and its effects on human relationships are at the centre of sociology. In fact, the rise of sociology as a distinct discipline came about because of the efforts of philosophers and political economists to comprehend the stupendous changes associated with the urban-industrial revolution of the 19th century. In the eyes of people living through it, the transition from a largely non-urban society to a decidedly urban one was staggering and bewildering. Countrysides were depopulated as the new economic forces pushed and pulled individuals into the rapidly growing cities. Society, particularly in Europe where sociology was born, was changing profoundly and disturbingly. What was the nature of this change? Where was it leading? These were the first two questions sociology as a discipline tried to answer.

Although the 19th- and early 20th-century sociologists attempting to answer these questions had different emphases, most of the important ones employed a similar underlying strategy: the use of ideal type comparisons between a model of a traditionally organized society on the one hand and the emergent urban society on the other. This approach is most clearly seen in the works of Ferdinand Tönnies ([1887] 1963), Emile Durkheim ([1893] 1964), and Max Weber ([1947] 1967), but it is also present in the writings of Georg Simmel ([1905] 1964) and Karl Marx ([1879] 1964). Collectively, these five Europeans are considered not only the fathers of urban sociology but also the founders of the entire discipline. A few comments on each are in order before proceeding to more scholars.

Ferdinand Tönnies

Tönnies believed that the process of urbanization led to the emergence of a new settlement form with its own particular cultural features. To contrast this new form with the more traditional rural-based one, he used the German terms **Gemeinschaft** and **Gesellschaft**. As McGahan (1982, 16) explains, "*Gemeinschaft* refers to a natural unity, a living organism, involving an underlying consensus or mutual understanding, based on kinship, common locality of residence and friendship." Defined in such a way, the term is similar to "community" as we defined it at the beginning of this chapter. The penultimate form of Tönnies's *Gesellschaft* was the emerging urban-industrial settlement:

> The institutions of the city clearly reflect this trend (toward gesellschaft). Instead of traditional customs and mores appropriate for agricultural villages, there now exist formalized laws of contract. The industrially-based trade economy causes the demise of a general household economy. More impersonal forms of social organization reduce the centrality of the family. Where formerly folkways and customs had served as key pillars of social control in the rural community, now convention and public opinion fulfill this function in the metropolis. (McGahan 1982, 16)

Tönnies saw *Gemeinschaft* and *Gesellschaft* as essentially incompatible forms of human organization, and he believed that *Gesellschaft* would eventually replace *Gemeinschaft* as a model for social organization wherever urban growth occurred.

Emile Durkheim

Durkheim's major concern was to understand what he called the problem of social integration—how human groups are held together. In his work, he contrasted two analytically distinct types of social integration, which he named mechanical solidarity and organic solidarity. **Mechanical solidarity** is the glue, if you will, that holds together traditional, non-urban societies. Based on a similarity of interests, it gives rise to what Durkheim termed a collective conscience—the totality of all the beliefs and values common to the citizenry of the group. The individual is totally immersed in a mechanically solid society; such absorption leaves little room for autonomy and individual discretion (hence the use of "mechanical"). Mechanical solidarity holds together settlements (and even associations of settlements) that possess a high level of homogeneity. Durkheim termed "repressive" the form of law found in such societies, because it is based on an entire community's response to the violator and is frequently violent.

In contrast, **organic solidarity** is based on the functional interdependence of specialized groups ("organs") within the larger unit—be it a city or a country. Such interdependence requires a high degree of individual differences, occupational specialization through an elaborate division of labour, and a lessening reliance on a collective conscience. In such a context, contract law regulating relations between people comes to be more important than repressive law.

In the emerging urban-industrial society of the late 19th century, said Durkheim, this new, organic solidarity would replace the mechanical type. Such a system of coordination would evolve to fill the gap left by the erosion of tradition, the disruption of kinship ties through migration, and the destruction of the craft mode of production as the division of labour expanded. Durkheim looked to the emerging specialized occupational groups to provide the mechanism for tying people to the larger society, while simultaneously giving them meaning in their daily lives. Durkheim, in contrast to Tönnies, was not dismayed by the emerging urban-industrial order. Rather than viewing it as a source of disorganization and pathology, he believed that it might lead to human improvement. For this reason he thought it imperative to intellectually comprehend the emergent social order based on the industrial city.

Georg Simmel

While Durkheim and, to a lesser extent, Tönnies were concerned with the structural characteristics of the new urban order, Simmel attempted to understand how this emerging structure influenced values, beliefs, and rules that individuals use to direct their lives—in short, the cultural and social-psychological consequences of urbanization. Flowing from the increased size, density, and heterogeneity of settlements, as well as from the rise of impersonal market exchange, according to Simmel, were general cultural influences that were affecting the psychology of urban residents. The successful operation of the industrial-urban city requires punctuality, predictability, precision, and the exclusion of irrational tradition. A way of life reflecting such new values was developing, and urban dwellers were internalizing the new values. What was evolving was a certain metropolitanism based, as McGahan (1982, 19) put it, on a "blasé attitude toward new experiences and an underlying sense of reserve and impersonality. This style also serves as a means of protecting the individual from the vast array and demands in the city."

In Simmel's view, the prototypical urbanite was the stranger—but not the apparition associated with evil and the devil in rural mythology. Rather, all urbanites are strangers to one another in the sense that all relationships are compartmentalized and detached. The city dweller knows the salesperson only in the context of an economic transaction, the politician only in a political context, and so on. Urbanites never get to know one another fully because their interaction is always partial and restricted. And this is how it must be if they are to succeed in a situation where the ideology of the marketplace reigns supreme.

Max Weber

In Weber's view, the rise of the city, particularly the Western European medieval city, was a crucial link in the development of industrial capitalism. He listed five defining characteristics of the early city: (1) fortification for protection; (2) a market; (3) a court of its own and at least partially autonomous law; (4) association (citizenship) based on individual allegiance to the city rather than to clan, kin, or religion; and (5) at least partial political independence. Such secular settlements obviously encouraged individual entrepreneurism; more importantly, they provided a fertile setting for a new and highly important form of organizational coordination. This new form, which allowed coordination on a scale unheard of until then, he termed a bureaucracy. Weber's **bureaucracy** is a hierarchical institution based on rational, impersonal rules and procedures. Progression within such an organization is based on merit and professional criteria, as opposed to personal loyalties and favouritism. The virtues of such a type of organization are that it is efficient, can be directed toward virtually any set of goals, and is not tied to the whims, fancies, or life of any particular individual. Such an organization is premised on a type of authority Weber called rational-legal: the justification for and legitimization of a bureaucracy's operation rest on rational, goal-directed, impersonal criteria. Weber contrasted such **rational-legal authority** with earlier types based either on historical tradition alone (**traditional authority**) or the highly special qualities of individual leaders (**charismatic authority**). Thus, he saw bureaucracy, capitalist industrialization, and urbanization as interdependent. (For more on bureaucracy, see Chapter 10.)

Karl Marx

Until recently, the contribution of Karl Marx to urban sociology has been less than one might expect, given his prominence among the founding fathers of the discipline and the fact that urbanization had an important role in his model of society. Although we offer some explanation for this oversight later in the chapter, Marx's stature within the discipline requires inclusion here of a brief overview of his analysis and the centrality of urbanization within it.

Marx is known, of course, for his comprehensive analysis of the rise of industrial capitalism, and he saw urbanization as an important subprocess within it:

> For Marx, the dissolution of the feudal mode of production and the transition to capitalism is attached to a subject, the town. The town breaks up the

medieval system (feudalism) while transcending itself. . . . The town is a "subject" and a coherent force, a partial system that attacks the global system and that simultaneously shows the existence of this system and destroys it. (Lefebvre 1972, 7, my translation)

Although the medieval mercantilist towns and the early industrial ones to which they gave birth were not themselves the cause of the transcendence of feudalism, they were the form it took. The city, said Marx, became the physical site in which capitalist processes were most clearly revealed. And the new industrial city became more than a site; it also served as something akin to a magnifying glass, exaggerating and magnifying capitalism's essential tendencies for self-destruction—what Marx termed its contradictions.

This magnifying process meant that the city was to be the arena within which these contradictions led to the transcendence of capitalism. It was within the urban context that the proletariat's class-consciousness reached its fullest classic expression as a revolutionary force, and the overthrow of capitalism would be decidedly urban-based. Thus Marx gave the city the dialectical status of both heightening the evils of the capitalist system and providing the staging ground for its transformation.

Early Twentieth-Century Contributions

Although the 19th-century European authors just listed provided the basic theoretical background to the study of urbanization, any review must also note the contributions of American sociologists—especially Robert Park, Roderick McKenzie, Ernest Burgess, and Louis Wirth—writing from the University of Chicago during the period 1920 to 1950. Collectively they established what has come to be called the Chicago School of Urban Sociology. Their work was an attempt to understand the emergent American industrial city, so that problems such as poverty and crime could be more successfully addressed by religious reformers and social workers—groups with which the sociologists had close links. At least a brief look at their work is necessary to understand the way urbanization has been studied within sociology, as practised in North America.

Park, McKenzie, and Burgess were primarily concerned with understanding the new American industrial city, which had been growing rapidly since the turn of the century. Specifically, they concentrated on what has come to be known as **urban ecology**—the spatial distribution of people and economic activity within this new urban area. Park and Burgess conceptualized this emerging division of activity and people in terms of zones—a series of expanding concentric circles, each one possessing specialized functions. As the city grew, each zone experienced invasion and succession from the zone adjacent on the inside.

Turn back to Exhibit 16-3 for an illustration of this approach for the city of Chicago. Economic activity is centralized in the core area (the

Loop, as it is called locally) near the river and railway connections. Neigh-bourhoods of recent immigrants (usually ethnically segregated) and skid-row zones for transients, prostitutes, and criminals are located in zones of transition between the central core and the first zone of working people's homes. As workers improve their status, they migrate outward, toward what we now call suburbia, and are replaced by some other group.

In other words, the model used in this **concentric circle approach** shows migrants to the city passing through a number of stages. During the first stage they reside in congested, low-income neighbourhoods near the core; in the final stage, termed assimilation, they (or their children) are able, because of increased education and income levels, to blend into the fairly homogeneous residential areas on the city's margin.

Louis Wirth's main contribution lies in the linking of the mainly structural concerns of Durkheim with the social-psychological focus of Simmel and then applying their insights to a newly emerging American metropolis. An attempt to systematize the effects of density, heterogeneity, and marketplace interdependence upon individual and collective consciousness, his work has been taken as the starting point for analyses of the urban experience and how it influences individual attitudes, beliefs, and world views.

MODERN WORK ON URBANIZATION

The scale of urbanization has led to a great deal of sociological research during the past 40 years. Virtually all of this work begins, even if only for the purpose of criticism, with a consideration of the views of one or more of the authors discussed thus far. The new research has added considerably to an understanding of the urban mode of life and, in so doing, has required modification (and in some cases outright rejection) of certain arguments contained in the earlier approaches. Without attempting to be exhaustive, one can group the newer research into four topical areas. The first of these is a continuation of the analysis of internal urban structure in the tradition of Park and Burgess. The focus here is on the interplay among physical space, alternate land use, and human activity—in other words, on urban ecology, using some sophisticated refinements. The second topical area is the urban environment as a shaper of beliefs and behaviour. Of particular relevance here is the earlier work of Simmel and Wirth, which suggests that a particular complex of values and behaviour come to be associated with urban living. More recent research points to a diversity of values and behaviours much greater than earlier positions implied. The third topical area concerns the nature of suburban and, more recently, exurban living. The fourth area is the interactions among urbanization, community, and kinship. We now know that community and urbanization are related in much more complicated and subtle ways than was seen in the classical, rural/urban contrast of Tönnies, Durkheim, and others.

Urban Ecology Focus

Just before the Second World War, researchers began to question the adequacy of Burgess's model of concentric zones. It was suggested that the black ghetto and other areas of Chicago did not fit into the model of concentric zones; rather they resembled wedges coming from the centre. In 1939, Homer Hoyt completed research that formalized this position, and suggested that activities that were similar in nature occurred along pie-shaped sectors radiating from the core area. Several years later, Harris and Ullman suggested that neither pattern fit most urban areas. They argued that actual living patterns and economic activities can be understood only in terms of what they called the **multiple nuclei approach**. In modern cities, their argument went, location has more to do with a specific group's or activity's requirements for land use than with a predetermined sequence of land use and movement. Inner-city location for industry was efficient and rational in the 18th, 19th, and early 20th centuries. By the middle of this century, however, increased land costs, technological advances, and improved transportation meant that many industries could be located virtually anywhere. Exhibit 16-14 contrasts Hoyt's and Harris and Ullman's focus with the concentric zone model.

Within the past few years have emerged three new research strategies building on these three models. **Social-area analysis** attempts to examine land use and settlement by using an urban population's three main social characteristics: socioeconomic status, family status, and race/ethnicity. **Factorial ecology** builds on social-area analysis; basically, this new technique involves listing all the social characteristics of an urban area and then using a computer to sort and rank the most important ones for explaining land use. Finally, Berry and Rees attempt to synthesize social-area analysis and factorial ecology. Without providing a formal label for their orientation, they argue that the two approaches interact with one another. Moreover, they say, the analysis must include additional factors, such as time of settlement and the symbolic values attached to particular areas within the urban area.

The Urban Experience and the Urban Person

A certain stereotype of cities and their inhabitants pervades the history of Western civilization. Central to this image are the dual themes of excitement and sin. The Greeks and the Romans, despite their elaborate urban-based civilizations, saw country life as more virtuous. Although the city of Jerusalem was the city of peace and the residence of God, the Bible implores the faithful not to be seduced by urban glitter. Sodom and Gomorrah symbolize the prevailing Judeo-Christian representation of the city. Even the literature of Imperial China portrayed the city as a place of corruption, contrasted with the simple, virtuous rural life. The European medieval city was eulogized as a centre of individual freedom and human progress, but writers since the Renaissance—although frequently extolling the freedom, literacy, art, and intelligence of the city as opposed to the idiocy and savagery of the countryside—have viewed the city as the repository of sin and degradation. Rousseau, Dickens, and Balzac are only a few of the well-known writers who have waxed eloquent about the simple, innocent, and "natural" country life.

American, and to a lesser extent Canadian, literature of the 18th and 19th centuries retained such imagery—usually dropping much of the positive view. Thomas Jefferson, the third president of the United States, wrote, "I view great American cities as detrimental to the morals, health and liberties of men" (letter quoted in Boyer 1978, 15). The dominant culture today maintains this vision. For every thrill, excitement, and bit of glamour noted in the city, there is a lament for the rural life—think

Exhibit 16-4
Generalizations about the Internal Structure of Cities

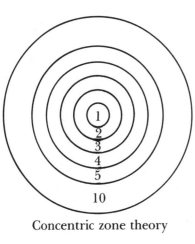

Concentric zone theory

Sector theory

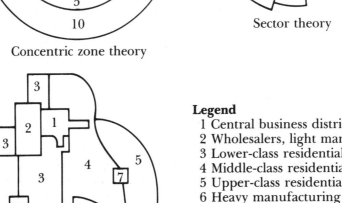

Multiple nuclei theory

Legend
1 Central business district
2 Wholesalers, light manufacturing
3 Lower-class residential
4 Middle-class residential
5 Upper-class residential
6 Heavy manufacturing
7 Outlying business district
8 Residential suburb
9 Industrial suburb
10 Commuters' zone

Source: Harris and Ullman (1945).

about songs such as "Detroit City" and "Eastbound 401." The back-to-the-land and exurban movements illustrate different versions of this negative sense of urban life.

In the past decade, however, the glamorous side of urban imagery seems to have achieved parity with the sinful. Sophistication and excitement (even sin!) seem to be in. The city, particularly its downtown core, is where the action is! Although it is potentially dangerous, its high culture and vitality more than compensate. Television programs such as "Miami Vice" seem to have captured this rediscovered sense. The **gentrification** movement, in which middle- and upper-income young professionals "invade" downtown working-class and impoverished neighbourhoods, purchase buildings, renovate them for their own use, and thereby transform the areas into upper-middle-income neighbourhoods, suggests that this

Much of modern life consists of frenzied — and futile — attempts to "get away from it all."

new sense of the city has a basis in fact. Downtown living is not, of course, a completely new movement for the upper and upper-middle classes. Some urban neighbourhoods never lost their *élan*—one thinks of Toronto's Rosedale and New York's Upper East Side—and even during the 1950s, that period of massive suburban growth, downtown living became desirable and chic for certain groups. What is notable today is the size of the gentrification movement and the breadth of its appeal. Although this central neighbourhood revitalization involves much smaller numbers of people than the exurbanite movement, the return to the city is much in evidence throughout North America, and has received something of a cultural celebration in the media.

How can one account for this rediscovery of downtown and the attendant urban imagery? First, it is important to remember that the view of the city has always been paradoxical. And in recent years, the influx of urban population and the shift toward eulogizing the city have resulted from several evolving conditions:

1. The rebuilding of urban cores with highrise office complexes, thereby offering employment opportunities for the middle and upper-middle classes.

2. The construction of performing arts complexes and other institutions of high culture in the urban core, helping it retain its role as a cultural centre.

3. A significant expansion in the size of the middle and upper-middle class as a highly educated population of baby boomers moves into the middle levels of the occupational hierarchy.

4. Declining birth rates among this group and resulting smaller families, making suburban houses with their three bedrooms, family room, and small yard and their associated lifestyle less appealing for a significant number of couples.

5. An increase in the number of well-educated singles—either divorced or never married—with a taste for the high-culture pursuits associated with downtown living.

6. The success of the gentrification process itself, which reduces the experimental nature of downtown living by providing existing urban neighbourhoods into which to move. Given the disposable incomes represented by such households, families, media exposure, and the advertising and selling of consumer durables are quick to follow.

Many sociologists are interested in discovering the kind of people who inhabit the modern city. The typical image that emerges is only slightly exaggerated in Mordecai Richler's character Duddy Kravitz—street-smart, quick-witted, assertive, adapted to survive in the fast pace of urban life (in sweatshirt or Pierre Cardin jacket, depending on social class background). This prototype is in line with the work of Simmel, Tönnies, and

Wirth, who characterize the successful urban dweller as pragmatic, calculating, and impersonal, with a large amount of egoism.

It is such qualities that collectively convey the image of coldness and impersonality within the urban milieu. Certainly, urban organization requires of people a certain level of detachment and assertiveness beyond what is needed in small, homogeneous settings. That level is easily exaggerated and overgeneralized, however. Areas within the same urban region vary considerably in the aloofness and assertiveness they demand from their residents (contrast, for example, the corner store and a large corporation). Writers on urban life generally fail to distinguish between public and private worlds in the city. From a public view, the city appears large, impersonal, and strange. Yet individuals live in another, much more intimate world of friends, relatives, and neighbours, where they develop networks of intimate contacts and social support that are as real and satisfying as those found in the suburbs or the country. Most urbanites learn the appropriate mix of public and private roles for the city's varying contexts. Thus, the stereotype of the urban person, like all stereotypes, has just enough veracity to prolong its public acceptance.

If a single word can capture the essence of the urban lifestyle, it is diversity. Multiple lifestyles are encouraged by the diverse pressures of the urban milieu. Thus, Herbert Gans (1967) argues that the increased population, density, and heterogeneity are associated with the city, do not necessarily reduce individual urbanites to anything like the stereotype. Even within the city core, Gans notes three social types, each with a distinctive lifestyle:

1 The cosmopolitan, middle-income professionals described by Michelson (1977) and others.
2 The members of villages—ethnic groups living fairly self-contained lives within the urban area.
3 The trapped urban poor.

For each of these social types, says Gans, the factors of race, social class, economic and political power, and ethnic or cultural background all modify the homogenizing pressures suggested by Simmel, Tönnies, and Wirth. Indeed, Gans sees these factors as far more important than the urban experience itself in shaping lifestyles.

Fischer (1975) argues that the views of both Gans and the classical authors have some merit. His own position, which he has termed **subcultural variation** in cities, attempts to bridge the two. Although he agrees with Gans on the importance of race (or ethnicity), social class, and amount of power, he argues that urban areas' special characteristics allow for a range of subcultural variation that could not exist elsewhere. Following the lines suggested by the subcultural approach, Suttles's work (1968) is an incisive examination of how severe economic deprivation and an urban

MAKING SENSE OF THE CITY

It was after 4:00 PM and rapidly getting dark on an early November afternoon in downtown Toronto. Ten-year-old Jamey Strong had stayed after school to play football with his friends and now turned to walk the ten blocks to his home. The fading sun cast long, piercing shadows across the tall buildings that lined the streets. Hundreds— no, millions to Jamey's mind— of people filled the surrounding streets. Here and there, darkened alleyways led off into infrequently used paths. In one direction, the tall buildings gave way to a large park with its lakes and trees. In the fading light and shadows, the nearly deserted park assumed an almost sinister appearance.

Despite the vastness of the setting, Jamey was not particularly nervous or afraid. He had, after all, walked home many times—occasionally even after dark. Coming out of the schoolyard, he walked two blocks east. Jamey knew that this was the safest way home, even though he lived west of the school. By walking east and then north a block, he avoided a small neighbourhood park where older boys frequently accosted him for leftover lunch money. As well, winos from Queen Street sometimes came into this little park to sleep because it was not patrolled. He could always recognize winos by their clothes and how they wore them. After two blocks, he turned north a block to a main street with a trolley line and backtracked west. Although he knew no one

among the hundreds of people on the street, he was satisfied as he randomly inspected passersby that none posed any danger for him. Six blocks down the street, Jamey cut through an alley alongside a Dominion grocery store. Although it was dark now, he had learned from his own and his friends' experiences that this was a "safe" alley. The local drug dealers used the alley on the other side of the grocery store. The alley opened out onto a small street running north. He continued north one block, moved west on the next intersecting street (to avoid a nasty dog) and then turned north again. Two more blocks brought him to his front door.

Why elaborate on a ten-year-old's path home from school? The answer is that we can learn a great deal about the impact of cities on human consciousness through such anecdotes. Cities confront each and every one of us with a vast and strange (and potentially threatening) maze of streets, buildings, and strangers. Each of us must come to terms with this vastness and strangeness. Typically, we do this through familiarization and routinization. In other words, each of us reduces the city to a familiar and predictable environment through our own experiences and those of our acquaintances. In slightly different words, the city (or at least those parts of it with which we deal regularly) becomes internalized within us as part of our own little, intimate worldview.

Lofland (1973) has captured this process very well in a book entitled *A World of Strangers*. Essentially, her argument is that each of us constructs a mental map of those parts of the city in which we spend large amounts of time. This mental or psychological map allows us to understand and relate to our urban environment without feeling overwhelmed or threatened. As we saw with Jamey, urbanites employ various cues based on physical location of places and the appearance of individuals to provide an interpretive guide to the city. Thus, each of us confonts the city and reduces it to our own particular vision of images. It is only through such a process that the urban environment can take on any meaning for those who must dwell within it.

milieu combine to foster special adaptive lifestyles in the city. These findings, as well as extensive supporting research, suggest that urbanization does not reduce individual lifestyles to a single type and thus that classical arguments about urban homogenizing pressures must be at least partially revised. As well, there is no evidence to support the Park-Burgess belief that such lifestyles are only transitory and will eventually be assimilated into a single urban lifestyle.

If the city is not as cold and impersonal as in many stereotypes, it is not necessarily a cauldron of violence and crime. You have probably heard some variation of the story about 37 people passing aimlessly by as an elderly woman is mugged in broad daylight. Similarly, many television shows and movies present a picture of the large urban centres as jungles in which violence and cunning are necessary to survive and few if any guidelines exist on morally proper behaviour. As a result of such images, many people think of urban settlements as hotbeds of violence and crime in which the only morality is one's own and the only way to enforce that morality is with a gun.

Given the large, heterogeneous, and highly mobile population brought together in urban areas under fairly anonymous circumstances, one would expect social control there to be somewhat less effective than in smaller, more homogeneous settlements. Yet the available evidence does not support the view of cities as cauldrons of violence. Although certain crimes, such as armed robbery, do have a slightly urban flavour, a review of federal Department of Justice crime statistics suggests considerable variation across cities; moreover, the rates for many crimes are practically as low in many large Canadian cities as they are in rural areas (Felt 1986). Such a pattern holds in other Western industrial societies as well, particularly if one excludes the statistics from American cities. And there is good reason for excluding cities in the United States. America's long history of violence (going back to its formative frontier period), its acrimonious history of racial subjugation often involving violent repression, the devastating poverty of its inner cities, and a host of other factors give

Calgary's Hillhurst district in the 1940s. Subdivisions featured straight streets and identical houses because they were cheaper to construct.

a unique quality to urban life in America. To support this contention one need only note that rural areas of the United States have levels of violent crime far higher than those of many European and Canadian cities.

The Nature of Suburbia

Suburbia has existed at least since the days of ancient Rome, but as a dominant form of human residence, its history dates only from about 1940. Studies (such as Berger 1960) suggest that the stereotype of suburbia—as a residential pattern centred on the middle-class nuclear family with an orientation toward child-rearing and **voluntarism** (joining and participating in a wide range of social organizations, from clubs to political parties) and a desire for more and more trappings of economic status and success—is vastly overdrawn.

As a result of such research, sociologists are now much more sensitive to the wide range of forms suburbia can take. The two most important bases for such variation are social-cultural characteristics (or ethnicity) and income (or social class). A suburb may be homogeneous with respect to both social class and ethnicity, or it may display considerable variation in either factor or both. Thus, one can find a diverse range of suburbs: Japanese (ethnically homogeneous, class non-homogeneous), upper-class Jewish (class and ethnically homogeneous), and so on. Many suburbanites have a lifestyle more similar to that of their ethnic and class counterparts in the city core than to that of a next-door neighbour who differs in cultural group or income level. Moreover, some suburbs possess an ex-

Calgary, 30 years after the photo of Hillhurst was taken. Apartment buildings have been added to residential districts, office towers have sprouted — and there is urban sprawl.

tensive economic or industrial base, while others are primarily residential enclaves ("bedroom suburbs").

Perhaps the only characteristic all suburbanites share is a desire to escape the congestion, density, and (perhaps) decay of the city for a plot of land, better schools, and the perception (if not necessarily the reality) of a more peaceful, less populated community close enough to the city to allow access but far enough away not to be considered part of it.

The Fate of Community and Kinship

The 19th-century writers left the distinct impression that the small, homogeneous, and relatively undifferentiated settlement we have termed a community is incompatible with and superior to the urban settlement. Many of these analysts noted with regret the inevitable demise of community. Tönnies was the most insistent about this passing (and the most lamenting about it). Durkheim had the most sophisticated response, in his suggestion that evolving occupational groups might take on community functions for urban members of a particular occupation. (What he proposed was a series of urban-based occupational communities mediating between their members and the overarching urban organization. If such a new, mechanically based society had been successful, he would have welcomed it because he saw such a form as enhancing the potential for human progress.)

Having relinquished the possibility of community, the majority of urban researchers during the 1930s, 1940s, and early 1950s turned to the social problems and pathologies of the cities—particularly the inner-city cores—such as poverty, crime, and deviance. The city became, in the eyes of this second generation of urban investigators, almost a magnet for disorder.

In the early 1950s, however, an interesting thing happened. Some sociologists began to uncover a wide range of settlement patterns and human relationships that had decidedly community-like characteristics. For example, Scott Greer (1956), in researching labour unions in Los Angeles, found evidence of viable neighbourhood communities within the rapidly growing metropolis. Countless other researchers have documented the presence of viable, relatively homogeneous, community-like areas within large urban areas, including city cores, which, as you will recall, were viewed as the repository of most urban social problems. Community-like organization has now been extensively documented even in economically deprived neighbourhoods.

Not only can organization with community-like characteristics apparently exist within the urban settlement, but new forms of quasi-communities can even be created as a byproduct of urban growth. Wellman (1973; 1978) and other researchers show various ways in which "communities" arise among individuals who do not live in geographical proximity to each other (many of them dwell in middle-class, urban highrises). Given efficient transportation and communication systems as well as sufficient incomes, people are apparently able to create their own communities of interest while retaining participation in the traditional communities to which they belong by birth or ethnicity. Such arrangements, while meeting basic needs of support and assistance, possess interesting qualities of their own. For example, they allow individuals to belong to a range of communities, some possibly in conflict with each other, since members of one community need not know of an individual's membership in another. Such insights from network analysis have contributed greatly to the current understanding of urban social structure.

The rediscovery of community has been parallelled by the rediscovery of strong kinship bonds within the city. (This phenomenon may not be surprising, since kinship is one of the basic foundations of community relations.) Following Tönnies, Simmel, and particularly Wirth, the sociologists of the early 20th century believed that urbanization meant the replacement of the extended, multigeneration family by the nuclear family of mother, father, and children. Urban life required mobility, which was restricted by the presence of grandparents, aunts and uncles, and even many children. Extensive obligations to kin also cut into the resources available for one's ego satisfaction, the appetite for which was whetted by the freedom and individuality encouraged by the urban environment.

Modern sociological literature, however, suggests a quite different situation. Kinship ties in today's urban areas may, in some cases, be stronger than those existing in rural areas, and in few cases can they be said to be less extensive or emotionally intense. This generalization is based on urban studies—such as that by Butler (1967), among many others, who found that the strength of family ties need not diminish among mobile urbanites—as well as considerable recent work on the history of family relations in non-urban settings. This latter research suggests that the older view of a life centred on the family may overstate the strength of kinship ties in non-urban settings (Spates and Macionis 1982)

THE NEW URBAN SOCIOLOGY

Despite the considerable new research alluded to in the preceding section, social scientists have recently raised a number of serious concerns about urban sociology. As noted in the introduction to this chapter, some believe that overemphasis on the spatial factor in urbanization imposes false limitations. Urban sociology's lack of a clear-cut subject matter has raised the concern that the discipline is not integrated and therefore cannot relate to other powerful social processes, such as stratification and industrialization. The fact that most research has been highly descriptive and undertaken as a response to late-19th-century and early-20th-century writers has made some sociologists fearful that the discipline is looking backward, at least conceptually. Finally, urban sociology appeared to be unaffected by the "rediscovery" of Weberian and particularly Marxian models and their modern reformulations for understanding today's society.

Since the early 1970s, these concerns have led to a number of strategies for defining, describing, and theoretically explaining the urbanizing process. Collectively, these attempts are referred to as the **New Urban Sociology**. Although its advocates frequently disagree with one another as much as they castigate traditional approaches to the field, they are linked by (1) their attempts to use Marxian (and, to a lesser extent, Weberian) sociological analysis to place the urbanizing process in an historical context and to embed it within a larger understanding of present-day society; and (2) their concern with the limitations of defining the subject of the field in terms of geographical space. The best-known advocates of this general approach are Pahl (1970; 1975), Castells (1977; 1978), and Saunders (1982). (It should be noted that Saunders's work is somewhat more recent, and attempts to build upon the insights and critiques of the other two.)

The Reproduction of Labour Power in the Urban Subsystem

In Castells's view (1977; 1978), the urban system is an integrated subpart of the larger capitalist system and performs a specific vital function for that larger system. He terms that function the reproduction of labour power, and the process that maintains it he calls collective consumption. In his view, the urban subsystem comprises three parts: the political (local government and other locally based state agencies); the ideological or symbolic, by which he refers to the meanings attached to the spatial forms that characterize the system; and the economic. The economic is subdivided, in turn, into the elements of (1) production, represented by factories and other sites of production; (2) consumption, represented by consumable items, such as housing and recreation, that are needed to maintain life ("reproduce a labour force" in his formal language); and (3) exchange, represented by market mechanisms. The urban system thus contains all the essential features of the larger capitalist system. It is more than a mere microcosm of this larger environment, however, in that the crucial function of consumption—and through it the reproduction of labour—occurs largely through this subsystem. Thus, in Castells's argument, the provision of such consumer durables as housing, hospitals, recreational facilities, schools, and cultural amenities, which must be consumed if workers are to be available continuously, is best understood in terms of the dynamics peculiar to this part of the capitalist system. Castells's justification for referring to this subsystem as urban rests on the increasing trend in capitalist societies toward concentration of ownership, increased scale of workplace, and the resulting movement of the population into more geographically compressed residential areas.

Castells's work specifically focuses on the contradictions, tensions, and conflicts involved in the reproduction of labour power at the level of the urban subsystem. He provides an illustration from his study of the chronic shortage of inexpensive working-class housing in French urban areas. Even though the need for such housing is obvious and providing it would be in the interests of the larger capitalist system (because labour power must be reproduced cheaply), urban-based French construction companies have found the activity unprofitable and have therefore fallen far behind demand. The first reason he suggests for this situation is that the widespread need cannot easily be translated into a hard demand because even inexpensive housing is beyond the purchasing ability of many who need it. Second, the construction industry is composed of many small firms that cannot tie up capital for long periods of time in rental housing. Finally, the French housing industry, perhaps because of its small-scale, fragmented nature, has been very slow to adopt technological innovations that might improve efficiency. One result of these factors has been considerable political conflict over the housing issue, and the national government has been forced to intervene to alleviate the situation.

A Focus on Urban Managers

A second widely known example of the New Urban Sociology is Raymond Pahl's work on urban managers (1970; 1975). Like Castells, Pahl conceptualizes the urban system as a semiautonomous subsystem of the larger society; although the two cannot be divorced, certain important urban processes can be identified and analyzed within the subsystem, without resort to the larger society. The most important of these processes Pahl calls the "distribution of scarce urban resources" (1975, 10). According to this line of thinking, the urban subsystem generates inequalities additional to those flowing from the general socioeconomic system (be it capitalism or state socialism). For example, people who have to travel long distances to work, such as central-city service workers who cannot afford downtown accommodation, are deprived vis-à-vis people who can afford to choose to live near their employment. Similarly, people who live near positive public resources, such as parks, desirable shops, and good schools, are better off than those who live near railways, motorways, or gasworks.

Although the wages generated through the larger economic system obviously play an important part in determining access to desirable urban resources, it is increasingly true that government intervention plays a considerable role in the distribution of urban inequalities. Therefore, Pahl suggests that the primary task of urban sociology should be the study of the distributional patterns of urban inequalities as these are affected by market and bureaucratic processes. Given the increasing importance of government, Pahl further suggests that the most fruitful line of research is to focus on those individuals who control or mediate state intervention into the urban subsystem. Such individuals he and others have termed **urban managers**, defining them as the people who control and/or manipulate scarce, spatially based resources; housing managers, real estate agents, local government officers, property developers, youth employment officers, judges, and elected municipal officials are all examples. Although researchers disagree on the amount of autonomy or independence urban managers possess (that is, whether they control, mediate, or merely administer the allocative process), this concern with them has generated a considerable amount of research on French and British cities.

The Identity of Urban Problems and Capitalistic Tendencies

Somewhat paradoxically, some advocates of the New Urban Sociology have gone so far as to deny that a distinctively *urban* focus is possible. Harvey (1978), for example, argues that even processes that appear to be pre-eminently urban, such as suburbanization, downtown renewal, and massive transportation infrastructure of expressways and public transportation lines, have less to do with anything distinctly urban than with a perennial problem of capitalism as a whole, which he terms the overaccumulation tendency: the economic system tends to generate profits and productive capacity considerably in excess of investment opportunities. Thus, after the Second World War, the United States and Canada were faced with the problem of how to utilize the capacity created during the war effort. The responses included institution of the Marshall Plan in Europe, suburbanization with its massive transportation and construction outlays, and more recently, urban core renewal. At the present time, these strategies have themselves generated overaccumulation, thereby creating another crisis for capitalism. Such a view is akin to the traditional Marxian view, which saw the industrial city as the arena in which larger forces worked themselves out, rather than as an active, partially independent subsystem with its own ability to shape society.

Castells and Pahl have provided a valuable critique of traditional urban sociology, which Peter Saunders has taken to its most comprehensive level in his book, *Social Theory and the Urban Question* (1982). The argument is quite complex, but in essence Saunders completely severs urban sociology's link to a spatial form and opts for a view of the urban as a semiautonomous local level of state political activity with control over certain resources, which he collectively refers to as "social consumption." (Notice that this concept is similar to Pahl's "collective consumption," but it is somewhat more broadly defined and lacks a spatial factor.) Saunders's urban focus is on the interplay of social consumption, competitive politics, and local government within the larger context of the nation-state. Formally, he defines his subject matter as:

> a specific theoretical and empirical concern with the related processes of social consumption, political competition and local administration within the context of the tensions between private sector profitability and social needs, strategic planning and democratic accountability and centralized direction and local autonomy. (1982, 26)

Saunders feels that, guided by such a focus, social scientists can improve the understanding of the modern nation-state as well as the complex and seemingly fragmented nature of conflict within it.

Overview

Collectively, the New Urban Sociology poses an important challenge for students of urbanization. As well, it adds a necessary corrective to much other work by grounding the urbanizing process more firmly in the classical writings of Weber and Marx, while simultaneously placing it within a set of larger, present-day societal processes.

THE CANADIAN URBAN EXPERIENCE

As a young though ostensibly industrial nation, Canada has experienced the rapid urban growth described earlier. Several special features of Canada's social development have left their imprint on its urbanization. Three come readily to mind: the colonial legacy, the ongoing American influence, and the country's social-democratic and pluralistic orientation.

The Colonial Legacy

Canada is a young nation as Western industrial nations go, and its urbanization is particularly recent. In 1871 approximately 80 percent of the population was rural; by 1981, more than 75 percent was urban; by far the largest part of this change occurred during the past 40 years. Areas with populations of more than 100,000 account for approximately 55 percent of the total urban population—a somewhat higher percentage than in the United States and other highly industrialized Western nations.

The preponderance of large urban areas is partly a result of colonial history, which was characterized by the development of regional centres to facilitate coordination and control. Urban development in Canada was not nearly as much a product of competition and unplanned circumstances as it was in, for example, the United States. Sociologists and historians frequently use this centralizing and coordinating function (usually transmitted to the local populace through the Royal Canadian Mounted Police) as at least a partial explanation for the relative lack of violence on the Western frontier. It also provided for the growth of relatively large regional centres.

The American Influence

Geographical proximity to and extensive political, economic, and social ties with the United States have affected Canadian urban growth in at least four ways. First, of course, is the cultural and media influence. This factor has clearly been important, although its extent and the nature of its impact on urban structure and culture are still extensively debated.

A second factor, which has had rather clear effects, is the underdevelopment of manufacturing capability. That is, because Canada has no economic control over large parts of its economy, it has not developed an extensive manufacturing capability. As a result, it depends disproportionately on selling natural resources abroad and assembling components for manufactured goods that are produced elsewhere ("warehouse assembly"). A direct result of this lack of extensive manufacturing capability is that Canadian cities, with a few notable exceptions, such as Montreal, do not fit the model of the early industrial cities—a central core and adjacent industrial areas. The growth of most Canadian cities—including but not only the oil cities of Alberta—occurred primarily in the post–Second World War period. This newness, in addition to their lack of extensive manufacturing capability, gives them a more diffuse distribution of economic activity than is found in older industrial cities.

A third result of Canada's close ties with the United States is the extensive use of suburbia as a mode of accommodation. The idea of suburbia did not originate in America but, for a variety of reasons including the availability of relatively cheap land, suburban single-family housing has been promoted in that country as the major residential option outside the central city. Lorimer (1978) suggests that close association with the United States (particularly among developers), the important role Canadian governments play in indirectly subsidizing the housing market, and the close ties between Canadian developers and the Canadian political elite have all resulted in a rather narrow and unimaginative housing option.

A fourth impact comes from Canada's dependence on shipping raw materials abroad. An interesting result of such economic organization is that urban communities are frequently created adjacent to valuable mineral or other resource locations but in far-flung settings. The single-industry towns described by Lucas (1971) give Canadian urban development a rather special element. Frequently isolated from any other settlements and lacking road access, such cities often support populations of 10,000 people or more. Although physically isolated, such towns are, of course, economically tied to the larger world, and their inhabitants take on many of the characteristics of urban dwellers in more sizable settlements. No other ostensibly developed Western industrial society has as extensive development of single-industry towns as does Canada.

The Canadian Cultural Heritage

Political culture is a term used by sociologists to refer to the basic values on which a government is based. Although Canada cannot claim to be free of class, sexist, and racial antagonisms and violence, its political institutions, despite their domination by a relatively small elite, are relatively social-democratic. And although ample injustices remain, Canada can be said to be relatively tolerant, and poverty, though present, somehow does not generate as much futility, frustration, and rage as it does in the United States. As well, Canada has no extensive history of racial oppression (the sad exceptions include its treatment of the native peoples and, during the Second World War, of the Japanese). These factors, combined with the tremendous immigration since the Second World War, make Canadian cities a mosaic. Governments and cultural leaders even publicly endorse ethnic diversity and the maintenance of ethnic communities within the cities—perhaps because of Canadians' tolerance, perhaps because Canadian ethnic groups are relatively recent arrivals to the country's cities and thus have not had sufficient time for assimilation. For whatever reason, ethnicity and community seem to be more vital in

Canadian cities than sociological theorists formerly thought possible. (For more on ethnicity in Canada, see Chapter 15.)

Overview

We have discussed Canadian urban structure as if it were monolithic, which of course is not the case. There are considerable variations across Canada in the levels of urbanization and in the particular structure of our cities. Some, such as Edmonton and Calgary, are young and owe much of their growth to the development of modern resources such as oil and gas. Others, such as Montreal, are not only older but reflect a historical succession of economic bases—from trade to manufacturing to service activity. Nevertheless, these three factors of colonial legacy, American influence, and the ethnic mosaic impinge upon all this diversity.

RECENT EMPHASES IN URBAN SOCIOLOGY

Two areas of interest to urban sociologists do not fit readily into our discussion thus far. They are: (1) the influence of culture (the language, beliefs, values, and symbols that distinguish one society or large geographical region from another) on urbanization; and (2) the application of sociological findings to make the socially constructed parts of the urban environment more consistent with peoples' desires. A few comments on each will conclude this introductory essay.

Cities and National Cultures

Urbanization has traditionally been considered a relatively homogeneous process regardless of the society in which it occurs. Is such a view warranted? Could some of the differences between, say, Peking and New York City result from other factors? How do cultural and political traditions unique to a particular society affect its urban appearance? For the beginnings of an answer, consider the factors listed in the commentary on the Canadian urban experience. Are there not ways in which they have shaped an urbanization unique to Canada?

Although cultural influences on particular areas have long provided the basis for travelogues by popular writers, it was only with the work of people such as Peter Lloyd (1967) that the systematic interrelations between urbanization and local culture came to be fully appreciated. (For an example of fascinating recent work, see the discussion of the relationships between Ming Dynasty culture and Peking, Hellenic culture and ancient Athens, and early American industrial capitalism and Chicago in Spates and Macionis [1982].)

A recent series of comparative studies of Japanese, European, and American cities systematically examines this relationship (Umesao et al. 1986). These studies attribute the differences between Japanese cities

NATIONAL CULTURE AND URBAN SPACE

When older Japanese visit European and American cities, they are astonished to learn how simple it is to find one's way around with just the aid of a map. Every street has a name, and if one knows the street name and number, it is generally easy to find an address without any other help. Even medieval European cities with their tortuous street patterns are no exception. In Japanese cities, on the other hand, it is rarely a simple matter to find the address one is seeking. As a look at a Japanese city map will reveal, there are few street names and even fewer numbers. The basic divisions are a hierarchy of irregular geographic areas, descending from the city through various sectors to the smallest area, known as a *machi*, which might be loosely equated with our sense of neighborhood.

This organization of Japanese and Western cities reflects profoundly different conceptions of urban space, directly attributable to the dramatically distinct ways in which each culture provides an understanding of location, space and order. Western cities are best conceived of as a gridwork while Japanese are more like vertical agglomerations. This is most clearly expressed in their respective systems of addresses. In European and North American cities, an *axial* system, whereby addresses are listed by street and number, is standard. Places are located in terms of co-ordinates in two-dimensional space—i.e., along East-West and North-South paths. In Japan, in contrast, a particular address is indicated in terms of a hierarchy of irregular spaces, starting with the *shi* (city), descending through *ku* (ward) and ending with the *machi*. Such a system is a nested one, with smaller units fitting inside the larger. A not uncommon result is that buildings right next door to each other have quite different addresses.

There has been increasing pressure to Westernize Japanese cities along with many other features of Japanese life. This has sometimes resulted in newer cities (or recently built-up areas on the margins of older cities) possessing a *dual* address system of nesting and axial designation. In the worst cases, local idiosyncratic combinations have evolved that are decipherable only to locals. At any rate, next time you have an appointment in a Japanese municipality, give yourself an extra hour to find the location.

—UMESAO ET AL.

such as Kyoto, European cities such as Paris, and American cities such as Boston at least partially to core cultural values that characterize the respective societies. Sonoda (1986), for example, notes that Kyoto has never experienced the suburban sprawl, inner city decay, and unplanned expansion of Boston because of Japanese values of symmetry, order, centrality, and cooperation and the lack of a frontier mentality. These differences in values have had physical consequences. One of the most striking is in the organization of transportation. In Boston, the public transport system, beginning with the electric streetcar, was laid out in a basically centrifugal pattern resembling a set of spokes radiating from the downtown core. In later years, expressways followed the same pattern. In Kyoto, however, public transportation followed established main thoroughfares in all directions. As a result, today's transportation networks resemble a series of rectangles one inside the other—a pattern that has allowed the city core to retain important functions

Another point emphasized in Umesao et al. (1986) is that the American dream of upward mobility and the associated imagery of a frontier to be conquered have encouraged massive movements of people from city to city and region to region. As soon as one improved one's circumstances, one moved—to a "better" neighbourhood, a "better" city, or even a "better" part of the country. American firms have encouraged this mobility with their policy of frequent transfers. By and large, such is not the case in Japan. Promotion and enhanced status do not entail residential change. Thus, Japanese cities have seen much less outmigration of their successful residents.

Applied Urban Sociology

Increasingly, sociologists are involved with practical applications of the sociological understandings gained from their research. Urban sociologists can have important inputs into the planning process. Michelson's (1977) work on housing choice and satisfaction is an excellent example. Perhaps no other feature of the urban environment affects the perceived quality of life as much as the range of housing attainable. His work on social types and their housing preferences and on how the possibility of eventually attaining a preferred housing choice shapes individuals' attitudes is highly important for housing planners in urban areas. Michelson suggests that a majority of renters envision progressing through a sequence of housing options—starting with a small highrise apartment and culminating with a single-family dwelling. People can be relatively happy with their housing at any one step as long as the expectation of eventually getting that single-family house is not jeopardized. This is not to suggest that there is no market for highrise units, townhouses, and other forms of accommodation, particularly in the downtown core. Our earlier discussion of gentrification establishes very clearly that such a market does exist. What the Michelson argument suggests, however, is that the extensive construction of highrise apartment buildings on the peripheries of larger Canadian cities, at the expense of single-family units, is aimed more at developers' bank accounts than at residents' desires. A number of excellent works on the housing industry in Canada reinforce this point. (James Lorimer's *The Developers* [1978] remains a classic in this area.) In such work, urban sociologists have examined how decisions to provide various forms of housing are reached and what interests predominate in making these decisions.

Another, related area for the practical application of urban sociology is the attempt to eradicate urban slums. Previous research indicates that poverty is not a temporary phenomenon. Neither is it restricted to the urban core; although many of the urban poor do live in older areas near city centres, low-income suburbs are appearing in some urban areas. How can the tragedy of slums be eliminated? We now know that tearing down physically blighted neighbourhoods does not solve the problem but merely exports poverty elsewhere. In recent years, many sociologists have turned their attention to strategies of reforming employment and eliminating poverty.

Finally, the kinds of people inhabiting various parts of the urban environment continue to change. In Canada, our central city areas have become increasingly populated by newcomer ethnic groups, as people of British origin (and those of French origin in Quebec) move to suburbs and exurbs. How will this new population pattern affect the nature of Canadian cities? Will these people assimilate over a generation or two, or, as seems more likely, will they retain their distinctive cultural features? If subcultures do remain, how will they affect the structure and experience of life in the central city?

Urban sociologists are increasingly seeking answers to these and related questions. The objective is fuller understanding of the complex processes of urbanization so that the urban environment can be made more consistent with people's needs and desires. As larger numbers of urban sociologists secure employment outside university settings, the emphasis on the practical application of research will increase.

SUMMARY

Human society has existed for approximately 50,000 years. For 48,800 of them, more than 90 percent of the world's inhabitants dwelt in rural settings—either as nomadic groups or in small villages seldom exceeding 200 or 300 individuals. Despite the occasional rise of an urban settlement of considerable size and complexity, such as Rome, Athens, and Constantinople, most human beings lived outside their gates.

In the late 18th and early 19th centuries, tumultuous changes began to occur in the fabric of traditional society, changes summarized today as the Industrial Revolution. One of its central features was the appearance of the industrial urban settlement as the setting in which people lived and worked. As the Industrial Revolution progressed, more and more individuals were pushed from countryside to city. So extensive was this movement that the percentage of urban dwellers increased from about 5 percent of world population in 1780 to nearly 70 percent 200 years later.

The birth of sociology was largely due to a desire to understand this profound change in the basis of human organization. Since industrialization and urbanization appeared to be inseparable and complementary processes, the founding fathers of sociology were of necessity urban sociologists. The questions they raised about the nature of urban life and its effects on family, community, and interpersonal relations remain important issues of investigation.

As the nature of industrialization has dramatically changed in more recent years, so has urban settlement. Suburbs and exurbs have come to rival cities in numbers of people. The heavy industry of the early industrial city of the West is being shifted to emerging industrial cities in the Third World. Medium and light industry is appearing in industrial suburbs on the cities' margins. Many central cities have become redeveloped as administrative and coordinative headquarters for firms that do their manufacturing elsewhere. The demand for middle-class, white-collar workers downtown has helped to fuel a gentrification movement, whereby young professionals move back downtown, taking over lower-income neighbourhoods and transforming them into upper-middle-income ones.

The task of urban sociologists is to understand this complex physical and social environment in its various shapes and forms, and the extent to which it contributes to particular values, attitudes, and lifestyles. An increasing number see a need to understand the urban landscape in the context of its wider political and economic system; those participating in what is called the New Urban Sociology see this task as the most urgent of all.

In recent years, the work of urban sociologists has gone beyond understanding the urban. An applied orientation has evolved; the insights gained from research are being applied to bring the urban environment more into line with the wishes and desires of the increasing number of people who live and work within its boundaries.

FOR FURTHER READING

Hamblin, Dora J.
  1973 *The First Cities*. New York: Time-Life Books.
  This immensely readable, well-illustrated book on the history of cities contains a great deal of archeological information and provides a good, though brief, review of the basic sociological explanations offered for the rise and growth of cities. The discussion of pre-industrial cities is particularly good.

Jacobs, Jane

1970 *The Economy of Cities.* New York: Random House.

This lively account of the rise of cities and their various economic roles in history is good companion reading to another, perhaps more popular book by Jacobs, *The Death and Life of Great American Cities*, which is a commentary on the ways in which the human quality is slowly being removed from the urban environment. Jacobs was so upset with American cities and their increasing dehumanization that she moved to Albany Avenue in Toronto's Annex.

McGahan, Peter

1982 *Urban Sociology in Canada.* Toronto: Butterworths.

McGahan offers everything you ever wanted to know about urbanization generally and Canadian urbanization in particular (except for a discussion of the New Urban Sociology). Encyclopedia-like and not easy reading in places, this book is the most comprehensive statement on urban society in Canada.

Michelson, William

1977 *Environmental Choice, Human Behaviour and Residential Satisfaction.* Toronto: Oxford.

This analysis of housing mobility in Toronto is perhaps the most inclusive study ever done on the relationship of housing to behaviour and attitudes. It is well worth reading.

Saunders, Peter

1982 *Social Theory and the Urban Question.* London: Hutchinson.

Saunders provides the best overall statement of the New Urban Sociology. It is very difficult to read and requires considerable familiarity with classical sociological theory. I can, however, think of no better introduction to the issues, problems and theoretical approaches characterizing this challenge within the field.

Sjoberg, Gideon

1960 *The Preindustrial City.* New York: Free Press.

A fascinating overview of pre-industrial cities, this work captures in considerable detail their elaborate structural features and provides considerable insight into the organization of family and kinship, economic activities, and political decision-making within them.

Umesao, T., et al., eds.

1986 *Japanese Civilization in the Modern World.* Osaka: National Museum of Ethnology.

This easy-to-read and highly informative collection is an excellent illustration of new work being done to trace the impact of cultural traditions on city structure. The studies draw comparisons between American, European, and Japanese cities.

CHAPTER 17

REGIONALISM

David V.J. Bell

Over the past decade, Canadian social scientists, particularly political scientists, have written with great passion about the problems of Canadian unity. The titles of some recent books convey a sense of urgency and concern: *Conflict and Unity* (Gibbins 1985); *Canada in Question* (Smiley 1980); *Unfulfilled Union* (Stevenson 1979); *Canada and the Burden of Unity* (Bercuson 1977); *Must Canada Fail?* (Simeon 1977); and my co-authored book, *The Roots of Disunity* (Bell and Tepperman 1979). These and many other books all grapple with the issue of regionalism. This chapter explains why regionalism has become so central to the question of Canadian unity.

TWO FACES OF REGIONALISM

Like the two faces of drama, regionalism shows two aspects: the smile of harmony and the tragic frown of hostility. Regionalism's happy face reflects pride in the uniqueness of one's region, a sense of cooperation with other groups in the region, and healthy pursuit of the economic and political goals that bring prosperity and stability. These characteristics suggest that regionalism is a great source of strength for Canada. Author and literary critic George Woodcock convincingly affirms regionalism's positive qualities:

> The process by which the regions of this country have emerged into historical-cultural reality has, of course, been coterminous with the process of the making of Canada. In fact, . . . the special character of Canada as a nation is that of a symbiotic union of regions, as organic as a cultural reef, rather than a centralized state constructed according to abstract political concepts. (1981, 21-22)

But what Woodcock calls a symbiotic union has at many periods of Canadian history disintegrated into fractious dispute. Indeed, the other face of regionalism is dark and foreboding, dominated by bitter conflicts, selfishness, and hostile reactions that have led some observers to fear for the very survival of the country. Such alarm was expressed by the Pépin-Roberts Task Force (1979) on Canadian Unity:

> The crisis which the country faces today is not one of Quebec or of French Canada only; it is a crisis of Confederation itself. In this sense, the challenge to the country differs from that of a decade ago and must be considered in much wider terms. To the fundamental challenge of Canadian duality must now be added the other important challenge of Canadian regionalism.

Social scientists in the United States distinguish (positive) **integrative regionalism** from (negative) **disintegrative regionalism**, by calling the latter sectionalism.

> Sectionalism is seen as the nucleus of inter-area antagonism that is centered around the defense of an area's culture or economy against the larger national interest. . . . Regionalism, on the other hand, is portrayed as the effort to meet

an area's needs in such a way as to integrate the area into the national culture and economy. (Sharkansky, quoted in Gibbins 1982, 4)

In Canada, social scientists tend to use the term regionalism to refer to disintegrative forces in Canadian federalism. With the growth in size and autonomy of provincial governments, "regionalism" has become almost synonymous with "provincialism" or "province-building." Except for Gibbins, who is his 1980 book used the term to refer to the movement for an integrated Western region (which he saw as a dead issue), Canadian social scientists have not thought of "regionalism" as connoting cooperation between provinces in a region.

Regionalism and Political Culture

As its suffix suggests, regionalism, like other "isms," involves values, sentiments, and beliefs. The term **regionalism** implies a sense of regional identity, an attachment to one's own region, and usually a belief that it is somehow victimized by other regions or by the larger whole. Thus, Schwartz (1974, 5) states:

> We associate "regionalism" with situations of politically relevant divisiveness and territorial cleavages, often accompanied by some consciousness on the part of the residents that they have distinctive, regionally based interests.

It is this subjective element of awareness that leads to the overt political problems implied by the term regionalism. To describe regionalism as an ideology would be an exaggeration, but it is very closely linked to the concept of **political culture**—the body of politically relevant values, attitudes, beliefs, and symbols that exerts an unseen but important influence on the political life of a society. Political culture helps shape the awareness of both ordinary citizens and political leaders. It affects the way they react to one another, which issues they consider politically relevant, the kinds of solutions prescribed for these problems, and the kinds of government policies deemed legitimate (Bell 1981). When regional identities, allegiances, and grievances are embedded in a society's political culture—especially among the political elite—residents and political leaders of different regions perceive political problems and priorities differently. Thus, oil prices became an issue in the federal elections of 1979 and 1980. Westerners (particularly Albertans) saw higher prices as both economically necessary and a matter of simple fairness. Ontarians, by contrast, viewed this attitude as sheer greed and selfishness on the part of the "blue-eyed Arabs." These contradictory outlooks demonstrate the strength of regionalism in Canadian political culture.

What Is a Region?

But what is a **region**? If "regionalism" connotes subjective elements, the concept of a region at first appears much more objective. Sociologist

REGIONS OF CANADA

The provinces included in a region can vary according to one's perspective. Generally, the Atlantic region (Maritimes) includes New Brunswick, Nova Scotia, Prince Edward Island, and Newfoundland. Central Canada includes Ontario and Quebec. The Prairie provinces are Manitoba, Saskatchewan, and Alberta. The West Coast means British Columbia. However, many Canadians describe as the West all provinces west of Ontario, and as the East, all provinces east of Ontario. The North includes the Yukon and the Northwest Territories, but can also mean anywhere north of the major cities in any of the provinces.

Ralph Matthews is explicit on this point: "Region and regionalism refer to the objective and subjective aspects of the same phenomenon" (1983, 18).

Presumably regions can be identified in terms of empirical characteristics. Geographers use the term region to refer to an area with distinctive natural characteristics—usually physical—that differentiate it from surrounding areas. But political boundaries have a way of overwhelming natural boundaries, so that geographic regions have little relevance to the political phenomenon of regionalism.

How do individuals think about regions in Canada? Some pertinent information is available from the 1974 federal election survey (Clarke et al. 1980, 41), which asked respondents what region they lived in (the researchers provided no definition of "region"). (Unfortunately, these questions were not repeated in subsequent national election surveys.) Many people (41 percent) apparently didn't think of Canada as being divided into regions at all. Younger, more affluent, better-educated respondents displayed a higher awareness of region than the rest of the population. But responses varied enormously: 16 percent named their province as their region; 14 percent seemed to divide the country between East and West. A few (about 7 percent of the sample) thought of their region as a subprovincial local area. (This interpretation is encouraged by such terminology as "regional government," used in Ontario for local administrations that incorporate areas larger than a town. It also reflects the fact that there are obvious regional differences within most provinces—for example, between the highly populated, industrial urban areas and the remote interior or north.) Others applied the term region to a group of provinces: they talked of the Maritime region, the Atlantic region, the Western region, or the Prairie region. This use of the term implies a degree of positive regionalism and, however remotely, the possibility of regional integration, and even of the amalgamation of several different provinces into a single political unit. At the same time, it highlights the political significance of the federal system.

Impact of the Federal System

"To rise much above folklore and to become mobilized as political forces, regional differences must become institutionalized" (Elkins and Simeon 1980, xi-xii). Federalism and regionalism are closely intertwined in the Canadian context. Indeed, to some extent we might say that the existence of separate governments in each province almost guarantees the presence of regional sentiments and politically related movements. Provincial governments, important decision-makers in their own right, provide a framework within which regional sentiments can be mobilized, as well as a core of leaders with prestige and access to the mass media, leaders who are, almost by definition, committed to regional identification. The most significant political sentiments expressed on the issue of regionalism in Canada tend to centre on conflicts between the federal government and various provincial governments. We can therefore speak of negative regionalism as equivalent to or closely related to provincialism.

In effect, the federal system encourages the development of regional conflict and regional aspirations. The provincial governments provide a career structure for politicians whose primary loyalty is to the province rather than to the national government. As provincial governments have grown in strength and maturity, the power of their leaders to mobilize a sense of regional injustice has also grown. It is often convenient for a provincial politician to escape the politically damaging consequences of an unpleasant situation or unpopular policy by blaming it on the federal government. This technique is particularly appealing when different parties hold power at the provincial and the federal levels. In the early part of the 1980s, this situation obtained across the entire country.

The tendency for the federal system in Canada to foster regionalism is increased by the failure of federal political institutions to ensure representation for all regions. Canada has no institution corresponding to the United States Senate, which gives equal representation to each state, irrespective of population. Indeed, as we will show below, the party and the electoral systems encourage the development of political parties that have strong support in one region but virtually no support outside it. (See Exhibit 17-1). Thus, in the early 1980s Canada was governed by a Liberal party that had failed to elect a single member from a riding west of Winnipeg. Sitting in opposition was a Conservative party that had elected only one member from Quebec.

Exhibit 17-1
Regional Representation in the Federal Government:
Canada–United States Comparisons

United States	*Canada*
Bicameral—upper house gives each state equal representation	Essentially unicameral—even in Senate, provinces do not have equal representation
Weak parties permit voting in regional coalitions that are bipartisan	Parliamentary necessity of strong party discipline prevents regional bloc voting
Power fragmented among three major institutions (Congress, presidency, judiciary)	Power concentrated in governing party (which seldom represents all regional interests)
Within Congress, committee system allows legislators from various regions to occupy powerful position and protect regional interests	Committees are much less important, cabinet positions afford individual MPs and senators an opportunity for some leadership on behalf of regional interests

Exhibit 17-2 shows the dramatic reversal of this pattern with the Conservatives' massive federal victory in 1984. Included in the Conservative party's electoral platform and in its first Speech from the Throne was a commitment "to breathe a new spirit into federalism and restore the faith and trust of all Canadians in the effectiveness of our system of government." In pursuit of that aim, the Conservatives changed a number of policies that had offended several provinces, adopted a more accommodative approach to federal-provincial relations, and substantially increased the frequency of top-level meetings with provincial ministers and senior officials. These accomplishments were proudly outlined in a "Progress Report on Federal-Provincial Relations" issued at the Annual Conference of First Ministers held in Halifax 28-29 November 1985.

Within months, however, cracks had begun to appear in the fine edifice of mutual trust and cooperation so magnificently described in the "Progress Report." By 1986, the new Conservative premier of Alberta, Donald

Exhibit 17-2
Valid Votes Obtained by Political Parties,
Federal Election, 1984

Province	Liberals %	Conservatives %	NDP %
Newfoundland	36.40	57.58	5.80
Nova Scotia	33.64	50.74	15.24
Prince Edward Island	40.97	51.98	6.45
New Brunswick	31.89	53.57	14.13
Quebec	35.44	50.23	8.78
Ontario	29.85	47.64	20.78
Manitoba	21.82	43.19	27.25
Saskatchewan	18.20	41.70	38.43
Alberta	12.75	68.79	14.08
British Columbia	16.43	46.64	35.05

Getty, was complaining about the West's lack of clout in Ottawa and suggesting that separatism was again stirring in his province (see the box on the next page). It is questionable, moreover, whether the Conservative government can hold onto its broad base of support; the 1984 vote did not change the lack of assurances of regional representation.

HISTORICAL OVERVIEW

In the early 1980s, partly as a result of the lack of representation just mentioned, Canadians had come to equate regionalism with the grievances of the West. But history shows that regionalism is not a new phenomenon in Canada, and it has not always been confined to the West. Regionalism is older than Confederation itself and at various times in Canadian history has affected virtually every part of the country. In 1784, for example, aspirations for more regional independence led the newly arrived Loyalist settlers to break away from Nova Scotia and found the colony of New Brunswick. Similarly, Upper Canada was carved out of the enormous territory of Quebec in 1791, when Loyalists in that area demanded greater autonomy. Nearly a century later, it was Ontario's premier, Oliver Mowat, who was a leading advocate of the provincial-rights movement. And thus began the long series of confrontations between provincial governments and Ottawa that has continued to this day.

Quebec, of course, has been engaged in intense conflict with the central government throughout much of Canadian history. Many scholars, particularly francophones, consider this conflict to be not a manifestation of regionalism but the expression of Quebec's historical, linguistic, and cultural uniqueness. Others consider Quebec and its many aspirations to be only one dimension of Canadian unity and diversity (Elkins and Simeon

PROVINCES SET TO GANG UP, OTTAWA TOLD

Alberta Premier Donald Getty served warning [20 August 1986] that the provinces would gang up against the federal Government to ensure its policies do not [set] them against one another.

In a toughly worded speech to the Canadian Bar Association, the Progressive Conservative Leader said his federal colleagues are not behaving much differently than their Liberal predecessors.

He said "frustration" with the two-year-old Mulroney Government's failure to assist regions that are struggling now—such as Alberta—has allowed "separatism" to raise its head again.

Deputy Prime Minister Donald Mazankowski, however, dismissed Mr. Getty's suggestion that there is once again separatist sentiment in Alberta. "I don't think it's a big issue. . . . I think it makes good print and titillates the minds of the press.

"If he would examine the record, he would see we have spent a lot of time on the problems of Alberta and the West," Mr. Mazankowski said last night when asked about Mr. Getty's comments. . . .

Mr. Getty told the bar association that, in the past, "we (the provinces) have been played one against another by the federal Government," Mr. Getty said.

"This may give the impression of strength to Ottawa but it weakens the country because of regional wrangling. The message is

this: we can't afford to have our strength dissipated in that way any longer."

He said that at [the recent] Premiers' Conference in Edmonton a momentous agreement was struck when all 10 premiers agreed to submerge their own interests, if necessary, to assist other provinces that are in economic difficulty.

"The provinces will be coming to the defence of any region which is hurt, threatened, or overlooked," he said.

With the Mulroney Government halfway through its mandate "most of us (the premiers) know (its) policies will be geared in the opposite direction of the premiers': to get relected," said Mr. Getty, who was host of the annual conference. Recognizing Ottawa will focus its re-election campaign on the vote-rich provinces of Ontario and Quebec, the premiers have decided to join forces to ensure this does not interfere with the national interest, he said.

"Only by strong provincial leadership can we balance the scales," he said.

He then called for "a new use of political institutions and resources to pull us together.

"I see this as a watershed in Canada. As premiers we are now committed to working together to help (make) national policies, rather than federal policies. I can confirm that at that meeting the premiers agreed to build our country together. The reason this is so important is because the federal Government has failed us so often in that regard."

The first example of provincial unity will be support from Ontario and Quebec to pressure the federal Government to shift its emphasis away from manufacturing regions to regions dependent upon resources and commodities, Mr. Getty said. He understood there was a political risk for provincial politicians from Central Canada, but they had agreed to it, he said.

Mr. Getty said Alberta had supported the Conservatives federally, believing it would lead to a shift away from the centrist policies of successive Liberal governments.

"I get it in my mail, phone calls," he said. "Things are not changing the way they thought they might." . . .

—MATTHEW FISHER and KIRK MAKIN

The Conservative government of Brian Mulroney was elected on a promise of "national reconciliation" between the federal and provincial governments. Nevertheless, issues such as free trade, the location of high-tech industries, falling oil and grain prices, and patronage appointments have all re-emphasized the divergence of federal and provincial interests. Energy minister Pat Carney is seen here responding to Opposition criticism.

1980, vii). Without taking a stand on this debate, I have largely left discussion of Quebec to Hubert Guindon in Chapter 18 of this book. Suffice it to say that regional grievances have touched every part of the country from Newfoundland to British Columbia, from Nova Scotia to the Northwest Territories.

United States

A comparison with the political history of the United States sheds light on the history of regionalism in Canada. The United States came into existence as a result of a war for independence fought by 13 colonies against the central power of the British government. Although the colonies had begun to enjoy integrative experiences and contacts, they also harboured intercolonial rivalries and jealousies. Consequently, their first attempt to form a collective government, under the Articles of Confederation, permitted so much decentralization that it ultimately proved unworkable. Each state retained sovereignty over its economic system and printed its own currency. The federal government had almost no coercive power and relied on state governments to enforce federal law.

Despite the manifest shortcomings of the Articles of Confederation, many influential leaders were extremely wary of instituting a stronger centralized government. The campaign to replace the Articles with what became the United States Constitution barely succeeded. To allay the criticisms of the anti-federalists, the following provisions were included:

1. States were given a strong voice, through the electoral college, in the election of the president.
2. Each state, regardless of size, was given equal representation in the Senate. Federal senators were originally appointed by state governments, a practice that continued in some jurisdictions until the 1930s.
3. States were given a direct role in the ratification of amendments.
4. A bill of rights was inserted to restrain the powers of all government, in particular the federal government.
5. **Residual power**—that is, authority not specifically assigned to any institution—was reserved for the state governments or for individual citizens. (At the same time, however, the Constitution did stipulate that laws passed by Congress enjoyed supremacy over state laws.)

The adoption of the American Constitution by no means ended the conflict between those who supported a strong federal government and those who favoured more state and local autonomy. The conflict was played out philosophically, politically, and finally in armed conflict. Until well into the 19th century, the federal government remained rather weak and ineffectual (Gibbins 1982, 12). Violence silenced debate in 1860, when the United States plunged into a prolonged civil war. Despite enormous costs in human lives and bitterness, the Civil War established beyond question the supremacy of the federal government and set in motion a centralizing trend that has continued to the present, augmented by a variety of Supreme Court decisions and, in this century, by an increasing number of federal grants to the states that are conditional on their taking (or refraining from) some action.

Canada

The fathers of Confederation set about to construct a political system that would avoid what Sir John A. Macdonald called the "flaws and ambiguities" of the American system. The bloody example of the Civil War demonstrated to them the "fatal error" of "making each state a distinct sovereignty." To avoid this mistake, Sir John and the other drafters of the British North America Act (now renamed the Constitution Act 1867) gave to the federal government what they believed were "all the principles and powers of sovereignty," supposedly leaving the provinces with only "minor" matters to administer (cited in Cook 1969, 7). They also gave the residual power to the federal government.

The would-be fathers of Confederation during the Charlottetown Conference in 1864, which formulated the basic structure of Canadian federalism.

Other devices put into the Act to ensure domination by the federal government included:

1. Federal power to disallow provincial legislation and to move into areas of provincial jurisdiction by "declaring" them to be "for the general Advantage of Canada or for the Advantage of Two or more of the Provinces."
2. Appointment of provincial lieutenant governors by the federal government.
3. A double-mandate mechanism that permitted individuals to hold seats simultaneously in both federal and provincial parliaments.

Because of this emphasis on strengthening the federal government at the expense of the provinces, the political arrangement instituted by the Constitution Act 1867 has been described as at best quasi-federal. Ironically, however, the trend in Canadian federalism has been toward decentralization and province-building, especially since 1960. The following factors explain why:

1. Judicial interpretation of the act has tended to expand the powers of the provincial governments and curtail the powers of the federal government.

2. The areas of legislative responsibility assigned to the provinces included health, education, welfare, road construction, resource development, and municipalities—all areas in which government involvement has expanded far more than the fathers of Confederation could have imagined.

3. The provinces were restricted to direct forms of taxation, which were very limited and unpopular in the 19th century. With the introduction of personal income taxes, however, direct taxation has become enormously important in this century, ensuring a major source of revenue for expanding provincial governments.

4. Several provinces have, at various points in Canadian history, challenged the federal government and opposed its efforts to expand (or in some instances merely exercise) its power.[1]

In summary, the United States began with a highly decentralized constitution but has evolved a powerful federal government. Canada began with a highly centralized quasi-federal constitution but has evolved powerful provincial governments.

The dramatic increase in regionalism in Canada is fairly recent. Scholars writing 30 years ago confidently predicted the demise of regionalism and the eclipse of the provincial governments by a burgeoning federal system. Nearly every major scholar assumed that the trend toward greater centralization, very evident during and immediately after the Second World War, was firmly and permanently established. The provinces would shrink while Ottawa would grow in power. Regional differences in outlook and values would be steadily eroded by the forces of modernization—industrialization, mass communications, and so on. Thus, noted political scientist James Corry concluded in 1958:

> Great improvements in transportation and communication within the free trade area that each federation provides have knit the economic life of each federation into an interdependent whole. The separate chambers of the state are insulated no longer. Instead, conduit pipes and high voltage wires link them together, transmitting economic pressures and economic shocks throughout the country. (in Meekison 1968, 52)

Similarly, Corry believed that top leaders in the private sector would increasingly develop a national rather than a regional perspective as they were drawn into organizations and associations that served the country as a whole. Many analysts thought that class differences would become more politically important than ethnic or regional differences.

The Growth of the Provinces

The first real challenge to the assumption that national integration would triumph was a 1966 article by two political scientists. Professors Edwin Black and Alan Cairns had detected centrifugal forces working against the trend toward greater national unification. Even they were surprised by the strength of these forces, especially the remarkable growth of provincial governments relative to the federal government, a growth that has since accelerated. Between 1950 and 1983, the percentage of the GNP accounted for by provincial spending rose from 4.6 to 15.0. (Canadian Tax Foundation 1985, 37). The number of provincial employees has also increased. Indeed, between 1976 and 1984, the number of provincial government employees rose nearly 31.2 percent, to 479,566. During the same period, the number of federal employees increased less than 14 percent, to 460,000 (Statistics Canada 1984d).

This startling expansion at the provincial level has occurred in large part because the areas of provincial responsibility have been among the most important public policy growth areas. The expansion has led to the development of strong provincial bureaucracies capable of matching (and sometimes exceeding) the expertise of the federal government.

Shifting Centres of Regionalism

Growth of the provincial governments alone would not have caused increased regionalism. Regionalism develops when there is a certain degree of common identity, a sense of injustice (economic or otherwise), and political leaders willing to capitalize on the feelings of regional discontent. Given these ingredients, it is obvious that both the prominence and the locus of regionalism will shift according to changes in the federal and provincial economy, in the political culture, and in political elites and institutions. The fact that the dynamic of regionalism moved to the West in the 1970s reflects changes in the balance of economic power in Canada.

With the development of oil and natural gas resources, the West grew enormously in wealth in the 1970s and 1980s, but it had difficulty translating this new economic muscle into political influence, particularly in Ottawa. During the past 35 years, only when the federal governing party has been Conservative has the West elected a majority of its MPs to the government side of the House of Commons. The result was a series of challenges and confrontations between the "feds" and the various provincial governments that assumed the role of the defender and voice of the West—even to the point of replacing the official Opposition as chief critics of the policies of the federal Liberal party until its defeat in 1984.

By 1985, the dynamic of regionalism had shifted again. This time Liberal Ontario (and, to a lesser extent, Quebec) played a leading role in attacking the continentalist policies of the Conservative federal government.

The sight of farms for sale throughout Western Canada is a sign of increasing rather than decreasing regional disparities, as Canada continues to industrialize. The fact that not all regions of Canada share equally in the nation's wealth is a primary cause of regional frustration and national instability.

THE STRUCTURAL UNDERPINNINGS OF REGIONALISM

Despite the mass media's tendency to explain the conflicts between the provinces and Ottawa in terms of the eccentricities of federal and provincial political leaders, much more is at stake than a dispute between parties or individuals, however colourful or inflammatory the personalities happen to be. Of course, it is also true that regional conflict increases or diminishes in cyclical fashion. At its zenith, regionalism can appear to threaten the continued existence of Confederation. At its nadir, regionalism itself appears to be dead.

John Richards summarizes the historical ebb and flow concisely (if, as he admits, "crudely") with the observation:

> The tide has completed one and a half cycles: from federal pre-eminence during the early years of nation-building under the National Policy, to provincial dominance in the 1920s, a return of power to Ottawa during the great depression in the 1930s and the Second World War, and a re-emergence of provincial power since the 1950s. (n.d., 124)

To understand regionalism, we must examine its structural underpinnings—the aspects of the economy, settlement patterns, and other demographic patterns that reinforce territorially based cleavages in Canadian society. These latent divisions become political forces through a process of political socialization and as a result of the activities of political elites and institutions.

Precisely how all these factors are linked together has never been unequivocally established, although several detailed models have been proposed. (For examples, see Mildred Schwartz 1974, 20; and Stephen Ullman 1979, 5). For the purposes of this chapter, it is sufficient to use a rather crude distinction between (1) the environment within which political institutions operate and (2) the institutions themselves. On this basis, I examine the structural aspects of the environment that contribute to or sustain regionalism and then go on to consider the role of political institutions.

Political manifestations of regionalism in Canada do not exist in a vacuum. Neither are they merely the machinations of the political elite acting on whim. Rather, these dramatic and visible events represent the tip of an iceberg made up of complex interactions among economic and demographic patterns and political institutions.

Economic Factors

In his book *Unfulfilled Union* (1979), Garth Stevenson describes the political economy of regionalism, pointing out that the various regions of Canada have historically had different economic bases. Efforts to integrate the regions into an overriding national economy have had some limited success, but regional differences persist. Manufacturing has been the economic mainstay of central Canada; agriculture and, more recently, the production of oil of the Prairies; forestry and mining of British Columbia; fishing of the Atlantic region. Thus, each region has a unique set of economic interests and groups with quite different perspective on Canadian economic policy. As a result, different regions have had markedly different economic fortunes. Some have prospered while others have languished. Unemployment rates, per capita income, and the structure of the economy vary enormously across the country. (See Exhibit 17-3.) Furthermore, differing economies have led to differing political interests and to so much conflict between the governments of the provinces and the federal government, that the development of an overall economic policy for the country has been virtually impossible.

Indeed, by the 1970s, the various provincial governments had begun to adopt policies more appropriate to a common market than to the parts of a supposedly unified sovereign country. In some instances, provincial governments actively discouraged trade with out-of-province suppliers or manufacturers, attempted to prevent non-residents of the province from owning land or taking certain kinds of jobs, and manipulated sales taxes to favour local products.

This type of economic provincialism stems in part from the efforts of business and industry to play the provinces and the federal government

Exhibit 17-3
Provincial Economies, Canada

	B.C.	Alta.	Sask.	Man.	Ont.	Que.	N.B.	N.S.	P.E.I.	Nfld.	Total[a]
Population, 1984 (est.)											
No. (thousands)	2 871	2 349	1 006	1 057	8 937	6 549	713	870	125	580	25 128
% of total	11.4	9.3	4.0	4.2	35.6	26.1	2.8	3.5	0.5	2.3	100
Seats in Commons, 1984											
No.	28	21	14	14	95	75	10	11	4	7	282
% of total	9.9	7.4	5.0	5.0	33.7	26.6	3.5	3.9	1.4	2.5	100
Gross provincial product, 1983 (est.)											
$ (millions)	47 238	56 539	16 281	15 048	151 650	90 432	7 348	9 428	1 198	5 444	402 084
$ per capita	16 715	24 020	16 410	14 382	17 201	13 880	10 399	10 971	9 669	9 448	
% of total	11.7	14.1	4.0	3.7	37.7	22.5	1.8	2.3	0.3	1.4	100
Federal income taxes, 1981											
$ (millions)	3 416	3 103	866	818	9 592	5 627[b]	423	583	59	305	24 928
% of total	13.7	12.5	3.5	3.3	38.5	22.6	1.7	2.3	0.2	1.2	100
Resource revenues, 1982											
Forestry ($ millions)	131	11	3	2	44	34	8	3	0	5	
Oil & gas ($ millions)	232	5 205	484	18	5	0	0	0	0	0	
Other minerals ($ millions)	193	13	1	14	37	39	0	1	0	1	
All resources ($ millions)	596	5 257	570	38	131	115	16	8	0.7	31	
Provincial income tax, 1981											
$ (millions)	1 677	1 284	525	506	4 898	5 703	255	350	38	203	15 477
% of total	10.8	8.3	3.4	3.3	31.6	36.8	1.7	2.3	0.2	1.3	100
Per capita											
Income, 1983 ($)	14 339	14 652	12 686	12 603	14 784	12 531	10 040	10 889	10 056	9 179	
Federal income tax, 1981 ($)	1 245	1 387	894	797	1 112	874[b]	608	688	480	536	
Provincial income tax, 1981 ($)	611	574	542	493	568	886	366	413	306	357	
Equalization entitlement, 1984–5 (est.) ($ millions)	0	0	0	343	0	2 663	538	542	122	568	4 776
Average unemployment rate, 1984 (%)	14.7	11.2	8.0	8.3	9.1	12.8	14.9	13.1	12.8	20.5	

[a]All-Canada figures.
[b]Before deduction from total federal tax payable of $1,044 million for Quebec abatement.
[c]Includes water.
Source: Various publications of Statistics Canada, Department of Finance, Revenue Canada, and Quebec Ministry of Revenue.

The Come-By-Chance oil refinery in Newfoundland, shut down since 1976, recently sold at a bargain basement price. The refinery was a symbol of the failure of the poorer regions such as Newfoundland to free themselves from dependence upon resource-based economies, by promoting industrial development.

against each other. This practice, in turn, has historical roots that reach back to the 19th century—for example when businesses in Ontario turned to the provincial government in an attempt to obtain tariff legislation that the federal government refused to pass. By the 1960s and 1970s alliances between business interests and provincial governments had become both more common and more far-reaching. At the same time, the expanding provincial governments developed a new entrepreneurial aggressiveness, putting a razor-sharp economic edge on provincial-federal conflicts, particularly concerning control over natural resources.

The balkanization of Canada's political economy has been worsened by economic pressure and penetration from the United States. The boundary between the two countries artificially severs geographic regions that have as much potential for economic coherence as the national economy. As long as the railway dominated transportation, the east-west linkages were the most powerful. However, beginning in the 1930s, trucking and airlines strengthened north-south linkages and therefore helped tie each province or region of Canada to its American neighbour. Continental integration of this kind occurs at the expense of national integration. The more provinces look south for markets, finances, products, and services, the less opportunity there is for strong national economic policies or for political arrangements that could complement them.

Finally, recent modernization and industrialization, far from helping to nationalize the Canadian economic elite as Corry had predicted, have given birth to a new middle class that is strongly committed to the interests of the provincial governments, particularly in Quebec and in Alberta. This new middle class was a major force behind the Quiet Revolution and the emergence of the Parti Québécois and provided the backbone of the Alberta Conservative party during the past two decades. Although the political energy generated by these groups has not resulted in a successful separatist movement in either province, it is a crucial under-pinning of provincial power and assertiveness.

Fragment Origins

In his seminal work, *The Founding of New Societies* (1964), Louis Hartz argues persuasively that the culture and institutions of societies founded by immigration are significantly and permanently affected by the early settlers. Because these groups represented but fragments of the larger European whole, they introduced to the new society a particular cultural and ideological slice of Europe. Isolation from their home culture allowed these fragment groups to experience a different pattern of development.

Applying the **fragment hypothesis** to Canada, one immediately detects a source of regional variation. Each region of Canada has had a different fragment origin. Thus, the Maritimes were settled partly by migrants from Europe, but mainly by a wave of American colonists and Loyalists who moved north in the late 18th century. Newfoundland was founded by English and French settlers associated with the fishing trade, who settled as early as the 17th century; a wave of 19th-century Irish immi-gration swelled the population. Quebec was founded by francophone immigrants, who came to Canada in the 17th and 18th centuries from a parent culture that was largely feudal. Ontario was settled by a wave of Loyalists immediately after the American Revolution and then by British immigrants during the early 19th century. Manitoba was initially a bi-cultural society settled by both anglophones and francophones; it received Central-European immigrants in the latter part of the 19th century and the early part of the 20th century. Many different ethnic groups settled in Saskatchewan and Alberta, and in some cases retained their own lan-guages until very recently. Alberta was also strongly influenced by 19th- and 20th-century American immigrants. British Columbia has absorbed several immigrant groups, including the Chinese and the Japanese, but was most influenced by British settlers, again in the late 19th and early 20th centuries.

Given the diversity of the cultural backgrounds of these founding groups, it is not surprising that each region appears to have unique and distinctive cultural traits. This diversity is a source of richness. Socially, it has resulted in wide variations in culture and lifestyle, reflected in such things as divorce rates and crime rates (see Exhibits 17-4 and 17-5). Politically it has created a series of settings in which the various political cultures have played out different policy scenarios. The diversity of Canadians' backgrounds, on the other hand, has made it difficult for an overarching national political culture to emerge. The Western provinces have spawned third parties with distinctive ideological perspectives. Western voters have tended to vote much more along class lines than voters in the rest of the country. Consequently, the traditional parties have had much more difficulty attracting voters in the Prairies than, for example, in Ontario. In every federal election this century save one, the percentage of the popular vote won by the Liberal and Conservative parties has been lower in the Prairies than in Ontario. Throughout much of that period, these two parties have received less than two-thirds of the popular vote.

Exhibit 17-4
Divorce Rates per 100 000 Population, 1966–77

	1966	1968	1970	1974	1976	1977
Newfoundland	2.2	3.0	27.1	55.5	76.0	81.1
Prince Edward Island	16.6	18.2	59.1	82.3	98.1	113.1
Nova Scotia	53.7	64.8	105.2	195.6	211.6	215.7
New Brunswick	25.1	22.9	61.6	114.1	138.5	140.0
Quebec	17.1	10.2	80.9	200.1	243.6	230.8
Ontario	58.9	69.3	164.9	188.7	224.9	235.7
Manitoba	54.4	47.9	125.5	177.6	190.0	202.2
Saskatchewan	33.6	40.0	92.6	114.6	131.0	157.4
Alberta	107.1	125.7	236.4	288.6	309.9	307.6
British Columbia	113.4	110.8	240.2	285.6	333.7	330.4
Yukon	146.0	200.0	241.2	237.1		
Northwest Territories	10.4	36.7	51.5	157.3	194.0	194.4
Canada	51.2	54.8	139.8	200.6	235.8	237.7

Note: Divorce laws were liberalized in Canada in 1968.
Source: Statistics Canada (1976), *Vital Statistics Marriages and Divorces*, cat. no. 84-205.

Exhibit 17-5
Crime Rates per 100 000 Population, 1978

	All Offences		Violent Offences		Property Offences		All Other Offences	
	Rate	% Change 1970–78	Rate	% Change 1970–78	Rate	% Change 1970–78	Rate	% Change 1970–78
Newfoundland	6 402.1	22.8	458.6	27.5	2 676.7	10.3	3 266.8	34.8
Prince Edward Island	9 309.8	39.3	344.2	32.8	2 513.1	43.2	6 452.5	32.2
Nova Scotia	10 207.4	63.0	523.1	20.7	3 285.9	58.6	6 398.4	65.2
New Brunswick	7 217.1	39.3	433.6	35.6	2 712.3	39.9	4 071.2	39.2
Quebec	6 087.2	30.5	400.9	31.9	3 648.0	41.7	2 038.3	14.0
Ontario	10 262.0	61.0	621.1	16.6	4 912.7	31.6	4 728.2	32.5
Manitoba	10 339.2	26.9	567.4	33.3	5 155.3	33.6	4 616.5	19.5
Saskatchewan	13 962.2	60.2	593.1	23.7	4 735.5	33.0	8 633.6	84.6
Alberta	13 784.2	28.2	778.4	14.7	5 486.4	17.7	7 519.4	39.0
British Columbia	13 324.2	18.7	871.0	22.0	7 000.1	24.5	5 453.1	11.3
Canada	9 820.5	33.1	591.8	23.6	4 672.8	33.4	4 555.9	34.6

Note: Statistics for Canada include Yukon and Northwest Territories.
Source: Statistics Canada (1970, 1978) *Crime and Traffic Enforcement Statistics*, cat. no. 35-205.

Demographic Patterns

One force that tends to erode regional difference is interregional migration. Whatever their historical origins, people tend to change their perspective and acculturate to the outlook of their friends and neighbours when they move to another province. But throughout Canadian history, the amount of interregional migration has been relatively small, particularly when compared with that of the United States. Thus, the lack of demographic mobility has reinforced historical regional differences. Canadians tend to live and die in the province or region in which they were born. The 1971 census showed that approximately 90 percent of native-born Canadians living in provinces east of Alberta had been born in the province in which they then lived. Though somewhat lower, the comparable figures for Alberta (75 percent) and British Columbia (63 percent) still constituted a majority.

A study of Canadian migrants between 1966 and 1971 showed that only about 5 percent of all Canadians moved to another province. Ontario and Quebec seemed to serve as a buffer zone between western and eastern migrants. Only a small minority of migrants from the Atlantic provinces moved farther west than Ontario; an even smaller proportion of western migrants moved east of Ontario. Thus, the most geographically remote regions of the country have had very little exchange of population (Bell and Tepperman 1979). During the 1970s, these interprovincial migration patterns changed considerably as a result of several factors, especially the economic boom in the West. For example, the percentage of outmigrants from the Atlantic provinces who headed to the West nearly doubled between 1970 and 1979. In that year more Atlantic residents moved to the West than to other Atlantic provinces. However, the reverse pattern of migration (from the West to the Atlantic provinces) changed very little over the course of the decade.

The West was a popular destination for migrants from Ontario as well. In 1970–71, more than 21,000 Ontarians moved to Quebec, fewer than 17,000 to British Columbia, and fewer than 9,000 to Alberta. By the end of the decade, Ontario migration to Quebec had fallen to less than 16,000, while migration to British Columbia rose to more than 22,000 and migration to Alberta more than quadrupled to over 36,000! In percentage terms, Quebec's share of Ontario outmigration fell from 26.1 to 14.4 percent, while Alberta's rose from 10.8 to 32.7 percent. British Columbia's share stayed about the same at 20.5 percent. Ontario remained the most popular destination for migrant Quebeckers, attracting at least 60 percent of them throughout the decade. It was widely believed that anglophone Quebeckers left the province in droves during the late 1970s and early 1980s, disillusioned by the restrictive, pro-francophone language policies of the Quebec-Nationalist Parti Québécois, which held power until 1985. However, although some large companies moved their head offices—with much publicity—from Montreal, Quebec outmigration figures for the years after 1976 are very similar to those for the first half of the decade. What did change was the number of Canadians moving *to* Quebec from other provinces; this figure fell about 20 percent. It is too early to study internal migration patterns for the 1980s, although it seems that many Ontarians returned from the West in the first half of the decade, when the boom there turned into a bust.

Another important source of demographic change in Canada is immigration. Approximately one Canadian in seven was born outside the country, a ratio that has stayed relatively constant for the past 40 years. Very few of these immigrants have settled in the Atlantic provinces or Quebec. Indeed, for the period 1951 to 1971, fewer than 5 percent of the residents of the Atlantic provinces and 5 to 10 percent of the residents of Quebec were foreign-born. The comparable figure for the Prairies was close to 20 percent; for both Ontario and British Columbia it was more than 20 percent. Hence, the ethnic composition of the five provinces east of Ontario is quite different from the rest.

The Political Dimensions of Regionalism

Although regionalism has its roots in the social and economic environment, it is an intensely *political* phenomenon, and it must be understood in relation to the political institutions of Canadian federalism. So powerful have these institutions become that some leading political scientists emphasize what they call a state-centred view of the relationship between the state and Canadian society. Rather than viewing regionalism as the product of social and economic forces, Alan Cairns (1977, 699) argues that "the support for powerful, independent provincial governments is a product of the political system itself, [and] . . . is fostered and created by provincial government elites employing the policy-making apparatus of their jurisdictions." Taking maximum advantage of their control of education, for example, provincial political elites have at times actively encouraged the development of provincial political symbols and identity, even at the expense of the national identity. Similarly, provincial economic and social policies have frequently encouraged regional patterns of development. Accordingly, this chapter now shifts attention to Canada's political institutions.

Canadian political institutions are the product of a unique constitutional hybrid; the BNA Act in effect grafted federalism onto a British parliamentary structure. Paradoxically, the act states that Canada will have a government similar in form and functioning to that of Britain. Yet the British political system is unitary. Britain has no political structures equivalent to Canadian provincial governments. The parliamentary system is not designed to represent territorially based political interests. The power of the British Parliament is not circumscribed by a constitution that divides legislative authority between different levels of government. Federalism, however, requires both some form of territorial representation within the national political institutions (intrastate federalism) and a division of powers between national and state or provincial government (interstate federalism). Furthermore, there appears to be an inverse relationship between these two mechanisms of federalism; the more successfully regional interests are represented within national political institutions, the less regionally based conflict one finds between levels of government.

A comparison of Canada and the United States supports this proposition. Regional conflicts in the United States are largely played out within and between the national political institutions. Because political power is dispersed among Congress, the presidency, the judiciary, and the bureaucracy, regional interests have many different points of access and strategic strongholds. By contrast, power in Ottawa is concentrated in the governing party. There is no guarantee that all regions will be represented in the party that wins a majority. In fact, the historical record shows that different parties tend to be electorally dominant in different regions of the country.

In a brilliant article published in 1968, Alan Cairns traced this peculiar pattern of regional variation in party support to the electoral system. Because the Canadian system gives all of the electoral spoils (seats in Parliament) to the candidates who get more votes than their opponents in each constituency, in theory a party could technically win every seat in Parliament with very modest support from the electorate. For example, suppose that Party A secured 33.4 percent of the popular vote in every constituency in the country, while Party B and Party C each received 33.3 percent of the vote in every constituency. Party A would thereby win every seat in Parliament, while Parties B and C, which together had attracted two-thirds of the popular vote, would win none.

Such an extreme distortion would almost certainly never occur. But some smaller-scale twists appear in every election. Moreover, the distortions frequently have a pronounced regional flavour. For example, in 1980, the Liberals received approximately 25 percent of the popular vote in the four western-most provinces but won only two seats. Conversely, the Conservatives won only one of Quebec's 75 seats, despite having attracted nearly one-eighth of the popular vote there.

In the 1984 election, the results looked very different for Quebec, where the Conservatives won 50.2 percent of the popular vote and took 58 of the province's 75 seats. But the Liberal party's poor performance in the West remained true to form. The Liberals took only one seat in Manitoba and one in British Columbia and failed to win any in Alberta or Saskatchewan. Nevertheless, the Liberal party received 19.2 percent of the popular vote in the four western provinces.

How this kind of systematic misrepresentation of electoral strength affects party policy is not obvious, but its impact at the level of symbolic politics, particularly regional feeling, is very clear. Lacking representation on the government side of the House until the Conservatives' landslide of 1984, many Westerners felt alienated from Ottawa. If the electoral system were modified to provide some form of proportional representation (PR), no region would be frozen out of elected representation in the ranks of any party that received at least a reasonable fraction (five to 10 percent) of the popular vote.

There are, however, political barriers to substantial electoral reform: the major parties are invariably reluctant to accept proportional representation, which would threaten their current regional electoral bases. Some critics have, therefore, recommended reforming the Senate or replacing it with a body that would assure representation of all regions. Although the Senate does not serve this function in its present form, it is worth noting that, under pressure from aggrieved regions in the early 1980s, Prime Ministers Pierre Trudeau and Joe Clark both appointed senators to the cabinet to ensure a modicum of regional representation for areas that had elected no government MPs.

To summarize, parliamentary majoritarianism has overtaken federal/regional pluralism in Canada's hybrid political system. It should come as no surprise that Canada's parliamentary system does not recognize regional pluralism. In designing our political system, the fathers of Confederation were attempting to respond to a number of pressing challenges: French-English conflict, Catholic-Protestant conflict, economic problems, defence problems, and so on. Regional representation was low on their list of priorities. In fact, as pointed out earlier, they wanted to avoid too much regional autonomy.

VOICES FROM THE CANADIAN PRAIRIE

In the geographical centre of Canada the rugged northern shield of rocks, forests and lakes melts into miles of achingly flat prairie. History seems somehow closer. In Manitoba and Saskatchewan, people still talk of grandparents "turning the first sod," as if settlers, arriving along the partially completed railroad, some pushing farther west in oxcarts, arrived only yesterday instead of in the late 1800s. And here, where grain elevators loom over the sunbaked streets of prairie towns, a deep sense of Canadian nationalism and pride is summed up in the words of a Grenfell, Sask., woman whose family farm was 100 years old in 1982: "We should fight for what our country stands for: freedom and the right to voice your opinions."

And along the Trans-Canada, where the 49th parallel often lies no more than 100 km to the south, past fields with their fresh summer stubble of green crops, people also express their pride in Canada as a more tolerant, accommodating society than the United States. "Americans are very individualistic," said Ed Baker, a Richardson Greenshields of Canada Ltd. stockbroker in Brandon, Man., and a former Canadian Air Force pilot during the Second World War. "Here, we have a feeling for our fellow man that I don't think is reflected across the way. And I think that we're prepared to pay a little extra for that."

The basis for that tolerance may stem from the history of the Canadian Prairie itself, a land and society that has nurtured a mosaic of people from all corners of the globe. Said Winnipeg native Georgina Panting, 25, a park attendant in Manitoba's Whiteshell Provincial Park near the Ontario border: "People still have touch with their backgrounds. You don't feel pressured to become a Canadian."

[. . .] Indeed, many prairie residents view that lack of pressure to assimilate—and conform to a norm—as paramount. In Winnipeg, in a turn-of-the-century brick building that once housed a Bible school, Sophia Kachor, executive director of the Ukrainian Cultural and Educational Centre, said, "I feel that my being Ukrainian is an integral part of my being Canadian." Added Kachor, 37, whose parents emigrated to Canada after the Second World War: "What defines a Canadian is all the cultural baggage that he has—the ability to be able to hold on to values from the past."

Along the main asphalt artery,

many Canadians voice unabashed pride in the nation's accomplishments, from the Canadarm on the U.S. space shuttles to performances in international sporting events. "It gives me a charge when Canada is mentioned internationally," said Chuck Dunning, 32, assistant treasurer for the town of Virden, Man. One special moment for Dunning: the 1984 Summer Olympics, when Canadian swimmers won 10 medals. In many communities—where Canada Day has traditionally been celebrated with sporting events— athletics have a strong symbolic significance. For John Fletcher, 18, this year's class valedictorian at Arthur Meighen High School in Portage la Prairie, Man., hockey, for one, is a living part of his heritage. His grandfather and his father both played minor league hockey, and when Fletcher begins first-year science studies at the University of Manitoba this fall, he says he hopes to play on the university team. "It's part of the Canadian tradition," he said, "like baseball to the Americans."

[. . .] Of course, other, more tangible symbols also stir Canadian emotions: the Peace Tower on Parliament Hill, provincial emblems and the Queen. Yet on the prairie, where the terrain is so flat and empty that a driver on the Trans-Canada can see a complete 100-car-long freight train—from locomotive to caboose—the land itself is a powerful symbol. "There are few countries in the world that have the vast open spaces that we have," said Brandon, Man., fire inspector Frank Watt, a five-year veteran of the Canadian air force and president of one of the city's two Royal Canadian Legion branches. "It is definitely a Canadian symbol."

[. . .] But the overriding focus of Canadian patriotism is the red-and-white Maple Leaf flag, the subject of rancorous debate when the Liberal government of Prime Minister Lester Pearson adopted it in 1965 to replace the Union Jack. Now, it unobtrusively asserts itself in front of post offices, from flag-poles on the tidy lawns of private houses and on spare-tire covers of vans and campers. Ivan Smith, minister at the Bethel United Church in Moosomin, Sask., said that because of his United Empire Loyalist background, he "had a loyalty to the British flag." But, he added, "Canada most definitely had the potential and the right to be a country on its own." Now, Smith concedes, the flag is becoming "a symbol of Canadian patriotism."

For others, that transition is already complete. Although Bruce Penton, editor of the weekly *World-Spectator* in Moosomin, insists that he is not a "flaming patriot," he nonetheless says bluntly: "I love the flag." First-year University of Manitoba commerce student Deanna Smeltz, 18, whose family has farmed the homestead in Cromer, Man., for at least 100 years, declared that the flag "signifies that Canada is a distinct entity all its own." And in Moose Jaw, Sask., where the main street is draped with Canadian and provincial flags, public school superintendent Barclay Cant recalled a recent high school assembly during which a Grade 12 student immediately picked up the flag after it had fallen over. Cant later asked the boy why he had reacted that way. The student's response: "We were talking about it over the dinner table, and my dad said we should be more proud of our flag."

In towns and cities sprinkled along the Trans-Canada, celebrations of Canada Day are perhaps the most obvious indication of increasing national consciousness. While some Canadians say that the day holds no special significance, about 20 percent of Winnipeg's 612,000 people took part in Canada Day events last year. The percentage was even higher in Regina (population 175,000). And Canada Day is also celebrated in many smaller communities—with the aid of federal grants of $80,000 per province. In Grenfell, Sask., population 1,307, the holiday will be marked this year by five days of events that include a parade, community supper and sporting tournaments. Said Frank Clark of Manitoba's Canada Day Committee: "People are becoming much more aware of the country and getting the idea of celebrating Canada's birthday."

PEETER KOPVILLEM

CONCLUSION

With the expansion of governments at all levels, jurisdictional areas have become increasingly complex. In both Canada and the United States, it has become impossible to maintain a strict dividing line between national and state or provincial responsibilities. Instead, there has been an in-eluctable trend toward overlapping jurisdiction, policy interdependence, and complicated joint-financing ventures. The reasons for this trend and its effect on federalism in the two countries illustrate the contrasts between them. In the United States, the dynamic behind this development has been the expansion of the federal governments, which, as Gibbins states:

> drew state governments to Washington in order to protect their interests and participate fully in the newfound bounty of federal programs and aid. The developing web of intergovernmental relations provided a means for federal influence to be exerted on the states and a means by which states had access to the financial and programmatic resources of the national government. (1982, 108)

Although the early Canadian experience was similar, by the middle of the 20th century the impetus had shifted from the federal to the provincial governments, which were beginning to intrude into areas of federal responsibility. Moreover, the pattern of political pressure has been different. Because regional interests are well represented within federal political institutions in the United States, state governments have no special status as a voice for regional interests. They must compete with a wide variety of other groups lobbying Washington. By contrast, the provincial governments have achieved a very high status in our political system. They exert influence directly through a maze of federal-provincial committees and linkages that almost constitute a third layer of government in Canada. Consequently, Ottawa has lost the ability to act unilaterally in many areas.[2] Federal dominance has given way to federal-provincial diplomacy and what Smiley (1980, 91) first called "executive federalism."

Furthermore, provincial politicians have developed what amounts to an ideological justification of regionalist politics that in some ways recalls the American states' rights theories of the pre–Civil War period. For example, at the 1980 First Ministers' Constitutional Conference (the so-called September Summit), Premier Allan Blakeney of Saskatchewan restated a version of John C. Calhoun's "double majority" doctrine:

> The essence of Canada is that it is a federation. The essence of Canada is therefore that on major matters we need a double majority. We need the majority of citizens as expressed by the popular will in the House of Commons and we need the majority, however defined, of the regional will. That is the essence of the federal state. (Bell and Wallace, in Byers 1982, 73)

A keen observer of Canadian federalism, Richard Simeon (1981, 247) notes that "increasingly, federal-provincial conflict over the constitution and other issues has crystallized into sharply different ideological conceptions of the nature of the federal system itself." Blakeney's statement illustrates dramatically the province-centred view. In contrast, Prime Minister Pierre Trudeau articulated the Ottawa-centred vision of Confederation:

> I know that Canadians believe there is a national interest. They do want a strong country, and they do believe that we are more than a collection of provinces, more than a community of communities.
>
> Canadians . . . have a desire that there be national institutions and a national government capable of acting on behalf of all of them. . . . Provincial governments are not constituted to do that. This is not what they are elected for.

Despite the striking contrasts in outlook evident at the September Summit, regional differences were eventually overcome to the extent that all provinces except Quebec gave support to the federal proposal to amend and patriate the Constitution. In this instance, regionalism was not decisive.

What further effects will regionalism have on Canada's political system in the years ahead? The answer depends on many factors. How well will the economy perform? Will the restructuring of our economy bring to the fore new regional or national elites? How will the new Constitution, and particularly the Charter of Rights, affect the distribution of powers between Ottawa and the provinces? Will the Charter weaken regionalism and encourage Canadians to mobilize along lines that cut across territorial divisions, as Smiley and Watts (1985, 35) contend? What effect will the devolution of power and authority to the Yukon and Northwest Territories have in the North, the neglected region? What is the political fate of the Liberal party? Will the parliamentary institutions be restructured to guarantee adequate federal representation in each party for all regions? Will the demand for regional representation extend beyond Parliament to include regulatory agencies, the bureaucracy, and perhaps even the judiciary?[3]

These questions illustrate the range of forces and options that make it impossible to predict the political course of regionalism in Canada. As with so much of Canadian politics, the key players are the members of the political elite. For what it is worth, studies of the attitudes of the Canadian general public provide some rather comforting results. Although residents of every province except Ontario report that they "feel closer" to their provincial government than to the federal government, although extremely high levels of conflict exist between provincial governments and the federal governments, and although politicians at both levels insist that they enjoy strong public support for their demands for change to the federal system, survey data indicate that the majority of citizens have highly positive feelings for *both* levels of government and for the federal system as a whole. Moreover, even during the long tenure of the Liberals in Ottawa, disenchantment in the West did not amount to support for Western separatism or widespread disaffection with Canada itself. The quasi-separatist Western Concept of Canada party failed to elect a single member in the 1982 Alberta election. As for Quebec, which manifests a form of regionalism *"pas comme les autres,"* feelings toward Canada as a whole remained positive throughout the 1970s, and most people (including anglophones) also felt positive toward the province. Given these findings, the defeat of the 1980 referendum on sovereignty-association can be traced to a continuing positive attitude toward Canada among both anglophones and francophones. The defeat of the Parti Québécois in 1985 can be seen as a further vote of confidence in Canada. (It is, however, somewhat disquieting to note that it is Quebec residents under 30 who feel the least affection for Canada.)[4]

Summing up the conclusions these data yield, Jon Pammett (1981, 31) writes, "When serious problems arise in the future, the Canadian people will love their country and their province, consider their government to be important to them, but be not at all confident that their politicians are up to using those governments to solve the problems." One thing is certain: regionalism will continue to pose political problems throughout this decade and beyond. How these problems are handled will in part reflect popular attitudes. But in the final analysis, the actions of political elites will determine the outcomes. In the past, Canada's elites have characteristically ignored public opinion when it was in their interest to do so.[5] Nothing is likely to change this in the future.

NOTES

1. The importance of Quebec cannot be overlooked in this regard. Gibbins (1982, 192) sees this as a major point of contrast between Canada and the United States: "No American state has the importance to its inhabitants that the province of Quebec has to the Québécois, in no state are residents cut off from national mobility and integration by such a fundamental fact as speaking a different language. Quebec, then, has provided a cutting edge for regional politics in the Canadian political system for which there is no American counterpart." At the same time, it would be inaccurate to ignore the role played by other provinces at various points in Canadian history. Nearly every province has taken a turn at providing the "cutting edge for regional politics."

2. Presumably, concern for precisely this development underlay much of the work of the Macdonald Commission. Although the Report of the Commission received media attention almost exclusively with regard to its recommendations concerning free trade, its mandate was much broader than the Canadian economy. Its terms of reference charged the Commission not only to examine "the appropriate allocation of fiscal and economic powers, instruments and resources as between the different levels of governments and administration"; but also to explore "changes in the institutions of national government so as

to take better account of the views and needs of all Canadians *and regions.*"

Under the leadership of co-research director Alan Cairns, the Commission sponsored extensive work on institutional reform and subsequently published 18 volumes under the rubric "Politics and Institutions of Government" and a further 13 volumes under the rubric "Federalism and the Economic Union." A major thrust of this work is to effect better regional representation in Ottawa by reforming the central political institutions, including the party system, the electoral system, the bureaucracy, Crown corporations, the House of Commons, and the Senate.

Despite its limitations, the work of the Commission has expanded dramatically our understanding of the political aspects of the problem of regionalism. Noticeably absent from the work of the Commission, however, is sociological writing (particularly from a radical/Marxist perspective) on the problem of regional inequality.

3. For a brief assessment of provincial demands for direct representation on federal regulatory bodies, see Schultz (1978). For a recent and thorough study of regional representation in the federal bureaucracy, see Peter Aucoin 1985.

4. These data are discussed by Pammett (1981), using the general results of the 1974 and 1979 federal election surveys but drawing as well on the "panel" of identical respondents in both surveys. Note that his survey pre-dates the acrimonious conflict over patriation of the Constitution, which finally took place with the support of every province except Quebec.

A 1983 survey published by the Council for Canadian Unity and conducted by the Centre de recherche sur l'opinion publique (CROP) revealed that a majority of all segments of the Canadian population except francophones think first of the federal government (rather than their provincial government) when the term "government" is used. However, Canadians in almost every group and area (except, among others, Quebec and especially Montreal) feel that the provincial government looks after their needs and interests better than the government of Canada. For a further discussion of regional politics and ideologies, see Michael Ornstein in Brym 1986.

5. Ironically, the relative insulation of Canadian political leaders from the pressures of mass opinion was held to be a great strength of Canadian "consociational democracy." Consociationalism is a form of government that features accommodation between elites who maintain a basic commitment to unity despite the many antagonisms and disunities found at the mass level. If anything, Canada has at times epitomized an anticonsociational state. Political elites are often dangerously divided despite an underlying commitment to unity at the mass level.

FOR FURTHER READING

Bell, David V.J., and Lorne Tepperman
　　1979 *The Roots of Disunity*. Toronto: McClelland and Stewart.
　　This historical-development study of Canadian political culture has several
　　chapters on regionalism. Other topics include Anglo-French relations, iden-
　　tity, and class conflict and ideology.

Brym, Robert J.
　　1986 *Regionalism in Canada*. Toronto: Irwin.
　　This series of essays by leading Canadian sociologists emphasizes the problem
　　of regional inequality.

Elkins, David, and Richard Simeon
　　1980 *Small Worlds*. Toronto: Methuen.
　　This study of "provinces and parties in Canadian life" makes good use of
　　survey and other quantitative data regarding regional identity, public policy
　　preferences, migration, voting, electoral coalitions, and provincial party systems.

Gibbins, Roger
　　1982 *Regionalism: Territorial Politics in Canada and the United States*. Toronto:
　　Butterworths.
　　A comparative study of the institutions and practices of federalism in Canada
　　and the United States, this book is both concise and interesting.
　　1985 *Conflict and Unity*. Toronto: Methuen.
　　This introductory text presents many interesting insights on the problems of
　　regionalism in Canada.

Journal of Canadian Studies
　　1980 "Regionalism" issue *JCS* 15: 2 (Summer).
　　This special issue of an outstanding journal offers an excellent selection of
　　articles on aspects of regionalism in Canada.

Matthews, Ralph
　　1983 *The Creation of Regional Dependency*. Toronto: University of Toronto Press.
　　A good study from the perspective of sociology, this book develops useful
　　conceptual and theoretical insights.

Richards, John, and Larry Pratt
　　1979 *Prairie Capitalism*. Toronto: McClelland and Stewart.
　　This path-breaking study of the historical development of the political econ-
　　omy of Saskatchewan and Alberta was nominated for the Governor-General's
　　Award for non-fiction.

Smiley, Donald
　　1980 *Canada in Question*, 3rd ed. Toronto: McGraw-Hill Ryerson.
　　The standard text on Canadian federalism was written by one of Canada's
　　foremost political scientists.

Smiley, Donald V., and Ronald L. Watts
　　1985 *Interstate Federalism in Canada*. Ottawa: Minister of Supply and Services
　　(with University of Toronto Press).

One of the many excellent volumes published by the Macdonald Commission on the Economic Union and Development Prospects for Canada, this book examines the institutions of intrastate federalism and assesses the prospects for Senate reform.

Westfall, William, ed.
1982 *Perspectives on Regions and Regionalism in Canada.* Proceedings of the Annual Conference of the Association for Canadian Studies, Ottawa, June 8-10 (n.d., n.p.).
This publication is a collection of interesting essays written by scholars from many different disciplines.

CHAPTER 18

QUEBEC AND THE CANADIAN QUESTION

Hubert Guindon

A century and a half ago, after the Rebellion of 1837, Lord Durham observed in his famous report that when he looked for the cause of the unrest, he found, to his astonishment, "two nations warring in the bosom of the same state." He proposed a simple remedy: "I believe that tranquility can only be restored by subjecting the province [of Quebec] to the vigorous rule of an English majority."

Were he to return today, Lord Durham would no doubt be astonished to learn that, despite the application of his proposed remedy, his initial observation holds true. Quebec and English Canada still seem to be "two nations warring in the bosom of the same state." Today the viability of Canada as a political entity remains in question. And for the Québécois it is *the* question, the distinctively *Canadian* question.

How are we to understand Quebec and its place (or lack thereof) in Canada? For most English Canadians, the rise of the separatists in Quebec has been inexplicable. Quebec, that quiescent paragon of rural provincialism, has suddenly been transformed into a seat of rabid nationalists intent on the dismemberment of Canada.

If this change seems inexplicable, it is because it does not fit the political stereotypes and cultural myths that English Canadians long used to interpret Quebec as an archaic, traditional society. Ruled by an autocratic clergy fiercely possessive of its own powers and opposed to democracy, modernization, or social progress, Quebec, it was said, was a rural backwater of poverty, illiteracy, and political despotism.

This political/cultural vision of the French in Canada did not emanate from bigoted Orangemen. Strangely enough, it was the conceptual framework of the politically liberal anglophone academics of the 1950s, and it was shared and disseminated by the "progressive" French-Canadian intellectuals in and around *Cité-Libre* magazine, who then lived in Montreal and went on in the 1960s and 1970s to work mainly in Ottawa. (That move may seem particularly surprising, but it was theoretically predictable. Minorities are often known to internalize the majority's view of themselves, and when people from a minority want to chart a career in the majority setting, it is a necessary precondition that they adopt the common mindset.)

Political fairy tales are always with us, and only belatedly do we become aware of them. It is, therefore, easier to spot distortions of social reality in the older ones than in the current ones. How are we to understand what has really been going on in Quebec these past few decades? What processes have made the Canadian question so urgent for the Québécois?

I have argued elsewhere (Guindon 1978) that the delegitimation of the Canadian state in the eyes of the Québécois is a consequence of the modernization of Quebec, which took off with the provincial government's massive intervention in the areas of health, education, and welfare. In this chapter I explore this issue at somewhat greater length and disentangle some of the separate threads in the modernization process. This necessitates distinguishing between the processes of government involvement, secularization, and political alienation.

The Battle of the Plains of Abraham (1759), in which the British captured Quebec City, and which led to the British conquest of New France, was the single most important — and traumatic — event in the history of Quebec. Almost overnight, the 60,000 French Catholic inhabitants of New France found themselves a small and threatened minority in an overwhelmingly English-speaking Protestant British North America.

The modernization of Quebec was heralded by the beginnings of large-scale government involvement in the structure of Quebec society in the early 1960s—a process now called the Quiet Revolution—and by the overthrow of the Union Nationale party, which had held provincial power. The secularization process became visible six or seven years later, as a massive dropout rate among priests and nuns became noticeable. Finally, political alienation became clear in the late 1960s, as the independence movement took shape: the Mouvement Souveraineté-association, the precursor of the Parti Québécois, was created.

THE QUIET REVOLUTION

Antecedents: Social Unrest in the 1950s

The modernization of Quebec is popularly described as beginning with the Quiet Revolution, as if it had sprung full-blown from the traditional society preceding it. That, of course, is nonsense. The Quiet Revolution was preceded by a decade of unrest, during which more and more Québécois came to question their society and its capacity to meet their needs.

Labour Unrest

The designation of a single event as the beginning of any social change is always arbitrary. Nevertheless, a logical starting point for this history is the strike of the asbestos miners in 1949, a highly symbolic event.

The Asbestos Strike of 1949 was the first in a series of strikes that played major political roles in the evolution of Quebec society. The Asbestos Strike became a rallying point for all those dissatisfied with the political structure of Quebec, when the premier, Maurice Duplessis, openly backed the Johns Manville Corporation and attempted to suppress the strike. This intervention by the Quebec government on behalf of a foreign corporation against Quebec workers outraged a significant sector of the population.

Quebec's asbestos mines, largely American-owned, were virtually closed down by this strike involving some 5,000 workers, who were mainly seeking better job conditions. Their unions were affiliated with the Canadian Catholic Confederation of Labour (the predecessor of the Confédération des syndicats nationaux or CNTU), which until this time had stressed cooperation with management; they received backing from many other Quebec unions, which put aside their history of internecine quarrels and came together to support the asbestos workers. The dispute became particularly bloody, partly because of the goon-squad tactics of the police, who were under orders from the ruling Union Nationale party to aid management and break the strike.

The strike rapidly became much more than a labour dispute. It signalled a questioning of the whole internal political and social order of Quebec society. For many years, the institutional Church had backed the political regime of Maurice Duplessis and the Union Nationale. Now two bishops openly broke with the Church, instituting collections in the parish churches of their dioceses in support of the workers. (One of them, Archbishop Charbonneau of Montreal, was eventually forced to resign his see as a consequence.) Equally significant, the intelligentsia of Quebec, who normally did not choose sides in labour disputes, mainly supported the workers.

The whole event was deeply revealing of the kinds of changes that were beginning to occur in Quebec. Here was an American corporation (at that time we did not have the word multinational to describe it) with English-speaking managers and French-speaking workers who were contracting asbestosis. In retrospect, it seems amazing that under such circumstances it was Maurice Duplessis, not the Johns-Manville Corporation, and the provincial police, not the anglophone management, who became the scapegoats and villains in the political unrest that grew out of this prolonged strike.

The World of the Arts

This unrest spread during the 1950s, through the social, political, and cultural institutions of Quebec's traditional society. The world of the fine arts was ready for it. In 1948, Paul-Emile Borduas, an influential painter, lost his teaching position for writing a manifesto, *Le Refus Global*, that called for artists to reject the ideological hegemony exercised by the institutional Church, and to demand total freedom of expression. Although Borduas subsequently went into self-imposed exile, his message left its imprint.

Social Welfare

Unrest also developed in the area of what is now called social welfare (it was then still called charity). New professionals, such as social workers, were beginning to emerge and become critical of Church control over the welfare institutions and the lack of professional qualifications of many who cared for the socially disadvantaged, the economically deprived, and the mentally disturbed. This growing dissatisfaction with the traditional ways of organizing social activities was an echo from the area of labour, where a growing critique of paternalism foreshadowed a push toward unionization and formalized collective bargaining as the normal way of organizing work.

Education

It was in the area of education that the loudest demands for change were heard. During the mid-1950s, a teaching brother anonymously published a series of letters, collected as *Les Insolences du Frère Untel* (in translation,

The Impertinences of Brother Anonymous), which satirically decried the education system, at the time almost entirely controlled and run by the Church. The articles, which were very funny, attracted broad attention within the middle class, partly because the author castigated the atrocious distortions of his students' spoken and written French, coining the term *joual* (a colloquial pronunciation of *cheval*) to refer to their language. That lower-class French could be spoofed meant that a middle class had been sufficiently developed to constitute a willing audience for such humour. These educated Québécois were equally ready to read the satirical criticism of the "yearly pilgrimage" to Quebec City that was undertaken by each school board in order to have its budget approved. Such mockery was a way of demanding new, more professional bureaucratic structures to handle educational needs.

By the end of the 1950s, educational concerns had shifted to the universities. Three law students of the Université de Montréal staged a sit-in in Premier Duplessis's waiting-room, with the well-publicized purpose of achieving a statutory grant system for the universities—in other words, more automatic transfer of public money to institutions of higher learning. Once again, case-by-case administration was being criticized.

In retrospect, another episode can be seen to herald the secularization of Quebec's public institutions. In reaction to a request by the Jesuits to obtain a charter to start a new French university in Montreal, the newly formed Association des Professeurs de l'Université de Montréal published a booklet entitled *L'Université dit Non aux Jésuites*. The Jesuits failed to obtain the charter.

Health Care

Health institutions were also an object of social dissatisfaction. The costs of health care, which were rising fast, were borne exclusively by the patients of their kin. A twofold demand was emerging: increased involvement of the state in funding and, as a consequence, secularization of health-care institutions. In the meantime, lay people were increasingly questioning the selflessness of the religious orders that oversaw the administration of these institutions.

The End of the Decade

Toward the end of the decade, two events occurred that foreshadowed two political developments: the impending demise of the Duplessis regime, and the eventual rise of the independence movement.

In the first, two priests, Fathers Dion and O'Neil, castigated the political immorality of the Union Nationale party—Duplessis's political vehicle—in a clerical periodical, *Ad Usum Sacerdotum*. The article was leaked and widely publicized and acclaimed. The fact that the charge of immorality was made by clerics who were neither parish priests nor bishops but university professors may have been significant. Certainly, they received no official rebuke. Only the bishop of rural Gaspé made a faint—and inconsequential—rebuttal. Thus, the decade that had begun with the toppling of an archbishop from his see for his expression of sympathies for the workers in a strike declared illegal by the Duplessis regime, ended with a formal, direct attack on the political immorality of that regime— an attack that went unchallenged and its authors unpenalized.

The first ripple of the independence movement, like that of the Quiet Revolution, surfaced in a labour dispute. In 1959, producers at Radio-Canada, the French network of the CBC, tried to start a trade union. The management objected that producers were managers and therefore could not be granted certification as a union. The producers went on a strike that lasted for more than two months and galvanized public attention. Once again, amazingly, the villains of the tale were not the francophone bureaucrats of Radio-Canada but the Canadian Parliament, not the min-

The Radio-Canada Strike of 1959 began when the management of the Canadian Broadcasting Corporation refused to allow producers working for Radio-Canada (the French network of the CBC) to form a trade union. This strike was essentially about the right of Quebecers to organize as they saw fit, politically, economically, or culturally, without interference from English Canada.

ister responsible for the operation of the CBC, but Confederation itself. The asbestos strike had signalled the questioning of the internal socio-political regime of Quebec society. A decade later, the Radio-Canada strike began the eventual questioning of the external political and economic constraints on the development of Quebec society.

Agents: The Emerging Middle Classes

The evolution of the social unrest of the 1950s in the fields of labour, welfare, education, politics, and communications raises the question of who, sociologically speaking, was politically restive and why. The reception given *Les Insolences du Frère Untel* was one indication among many of the existence of a new middle class; in Quebec's increasingly differentiated society, it was this group that felt, articulated, and progressively disseminated social unrest.

"Les Plouffes"/"The Plouffe Family" was a highly successful television series of the 1950s, broadcast in both French and English. The show had the merit of portraying ordinary working-class people through a medium that was then (and still is) devoted to portraying the rich and famous. What the show failed to portray were the powerful changes affecting Quebec society, and this failure made "Les Plouffes" obsolete even when it was on the air.

The massive urbanization that had accompanied the Second World War and immediate post-war period in Quebec had put pressure on the traditional institutions that dealt with education, health care, and welfare. The new demographic conditions required a radical and sudden increase in the scale of these institutions, which, in turn, transformed their nature. New, expensive technologies and increasingly specialized expertise required large-scale organizations in order to service a greatly expanded clientele with up-to-date levels of service. These public and para-public institutions became a major and growing labour market for members of the new middle classes: in contrast to the self-employed petite bourgeoisie of tradition, they were salaried professionals and semiprofessionals developing their careers in large-scale bureaucratic organizations. In the eyes of this new middle class, Quebec institutions urgently required state money if they were to grow and thus modernize Quebec society. And the Duplessis regime was so slow to respond as to be proclaimed reactionary.

When the priorities of the new middle class became the priorities of the state, the Quiet Revolution was officially under way. This happened after Duplessis's death, when Paul Sauvé became premier in 1950. He had been in office barely three months before sudden death ended his term; it was seen as a terrible and personal loss by the whole of Quebec society. Since he had had no time to implement any changes, the deep sense of bereavement was a consequence of his promise of change (*désormais*—"henceforth"), which had included three solemnly declared intentions:

1. To provide statutory grants to universities.
2. To establish a royal commission to study the feasibility of free hospitalization.
3. To revise the pay scale for the civil service.

All three promises were soon met, if not by Sauvé's Union Nationale, then by the Liberals, who won the following election on the slogan "It's time for a change."

Certainly, many of the new Québécois middle class had a sincere commitment to the ideology represented by these goals. But simple sociological analysis shows that the modernization of health and education met the requirements of their career interests, as well as the needs of social progress. Statutory per capita grants to universities and per diem subsidies for hospital beds meant that state money now flowed automatically from the public treasury into educational and health institutions. These institutions were therefore able to plan rapid development. The statutory grants were politically popular because they provided free services to hospital patients as well as subsidized education for university students; they were also, especially in their design, an inducement for institutional growth. At universities, for instance, no limits were set on the number of students—money flowed from the province simply on a head count;

the effect was to induce these institutions to increase their student en-rolments rapidly. With such growth, access was secured for more and more people, thereby democratizing the educational system. Simulta-neously, moreover, as resources soared, these institutions could attract an increasingly qualified (and increasingly specialized) staff and reward them accordingly. Full-time careers in these institutions, once very scarce for the laity, became plentiful, and soon the introduction of the practice of tenure meant that they also became, in the universities, lifetime careers.

That the Quiet Revolution meant social progress is beyond question. It achieved increased accessibility and democratization of education, as well as improvements in the quality and accessibility of health care. It meant greater financial and bureaucratic participation by the state and rapid growth of public and para-public institutions, as well as the growth of new elites. That it also involved the secularization of Quebec society was neither so clearly foreseen nor, probably, intended. Unanticipated consequences of periods of rapid change are, however, the norm rather than the exception.

THE SECULARIZATION OF QUEBEC SOCIETY

Secularization is frequently associated with modernization in sociological literature. But the links between the two are usually far from clear and far from convincing. At the theoretical level, **secularization** is generally defined in terms of the shrinking importance of magic and religion, as a result of the expansion of science and the scientific method. The nar-rowing sphere of the sacred corresponds to the expansion of knowledge, at the expense of faith and myth. Yet to conceive of secularization as a fading of myths rather than an emergence of new ones is to miss the point. Moreover, this idealistic view of secularization fails to take account of how the process takes shape and how it unfolds historically.

If the theoretical perspective on secularization is often rooted in ep-istemology (theories of knowledge), the popular perspective is usually put more crudely in institutional terms of ignorance and education, as a byproduct of increased (mass) education. People erroneously assume that the world of knowledge and the world of meaning are the same thing. In fact, education has or should have something to do with knowledge, while secularization has to do with the world of meaning, quite another matter indeed.

Secularization is a question of politics, not epistemology. Historically, secularization started with the separation of the Church from the state, with constitutional proclamations in France and the United States, not of a churchless society, but of a churchless state. In the case of France, this proclamation was made at the time of the Revolution to formalize the break with a feudal past. In the United States, the American Revo-lution needed to distance the state from an official religion (and therefore from all religions), in order to proclaim freedom of religion and accom-modate the denominational pluralism of the citizens.

No such political imperatives ever existed in Britain or its dominion of Canada, where a break from feudalism never occurred (although the evolution of capitalism did) and where freedom of religion became politically tolerated and practised, not constitutionally proclaimed. Yet one can argue quite correctly that secularization took place in the 19th and 20th centuries in both Britain and English Canada. The process was the institutional consequence of the break from Roman Catholicism.

The term **institutional secularization** refers to the process by which institutions initiated, staffed, or managed by clerics came under lay control. In the 16th and 17th centuries, when the Protestant churches broke from Roman Catholicism, whole societies were deprived of the organizational structure of the religious orders whose missions were to aid the poor, to tend the sick, and to provide education (to the extent that it had been developed). Thus new institutions had to be organized on a community basis under the aegis of the Protestant churches, with increased lay participation through voluntary associations. For these structural reasons, the process of institutional secularization took place much earlier in Protestant countries than in Catholic countries. By the 19th century, voluntary associations were well established in Protestant countries and gradual secularization of institutions was taking place. Higher education in Ontario, for example, followed this pattern (Seeley, Sim, and Loosley 1956). Although denominational rivalry long ensured considerable religious homogeneity among the clients and the administrators of institutions (and will probably continue to do so for some time in many places), effective and legal control by the laity, through non-profit organizations, has become firmly rooted in the social structure of Protestant countries.

In contrast, the secularization of social institutions in most Catholic countries did not take place until after the middle of the 20th century.[1] In fact, both the number of religious orders and their membership increased dramatically during the 19th and early 20th centuries in Catholic countries; the Church became progressively more involved in social institutions during that period of transition when the poor, the sick, and the ignorant, as Everett C. Hughes once put it, no longer belonged to their kin and did not yet belong to the state.

This brief historical outline sets the stage for the analysis of the secularization of Quebec, which, it must be remembered, was—and still is— a Catholic society. We will address three issues: the secularization of institutions, the massive dropout from the ranks of the clergy during the mid-1960s, and finally the substantial drop in religious practice.

The Social Institutions

As the Quiet Revolution swept Quebec, the Church had neither the human nor the financial resources necessary to develop the educational and health-care institutions required to meet social needs as defined by the new middle classes. These needs were broadly defined indeed: nothing short of universal access to free education up to the university level, and heavy subsidies thereafter; free hospitalization for all citizens; and (later in the 1960s) free medical care. When the state accepted such a mandate, it sealed the fate of the Church in the whole area of social institutions. Such massive and rapid investment of public money required the development of a public bureaucracy to act on behalf of the public will (at least theoretically). Neither the Church as an institution nor the traditional community elites could be the agents of this institutional development. New elites—trained in everything from accounting to engineering, from personnel to industrial relations, from purchasing to architectural design—would swell the ranks of the new middle classes in the ever-growing public bureaucracies.

Although massive growth of public institutions took place during the 1960s, the traditional institutions had already felt great demands during the 1950s. Increasing enrolments had put pressure, for instance, on the traditional *collèges*, the institutions that had offered elite youths secondary and undergraduate education from a classical curriculum. (This *cours classique* was generally the only francophone education available beyond the elementary level.) As the number of students rose, these institutions, once staffed almost exclusively by clerics, had to begin hiring lay teachers, who cost much more than clerics. Yet state subsidies amounted to very little—some $15,000 a year per institution. The same pattern was observable in health care. In brief, the demand for education and health care was outstripping the supply. The costs of expanding the existing facilities were essentially borne by their clients and, to a real but undocumented extent, by the Church—most of whose patrimony, one can assume, was spent in this transitional period of growth preceding the financial and administrative takeover by the state and its emerging professional bureaucrats.

Once the state decided to modernize and expand the educational system by the use of incentives, the secularization of the education system was greatly accelerated. This acceleration had nothing to do, as is commonly assumed, with a growing loss of religious belief or decrease in religiosity. Rather, it came from simple economic calculation at the community level. As long as the costs of education were borne locally, through taxes raised from local pockets, it made local economic sense to have clerical teachers, who cost much less than lay teachers because they lived communally and frugally and were low-level consumers. However, once the provincial government bore an overwhelming share of the costs of education, it quickly dawned on local business people (who made up most local school boards) that it made much more sense—if not to the total local community, at least to its merchants—to seek lay people with the highest possible qualifications. Not only were their salaries highly subsidized; they were big spenders with an assured income. In contrast to nuns and priests, lay teachers paid taxes and got married. Everyone— the hairdresser, the car dealer, the real-estate agent, and the insurance salesperson—could expect some share of the action. When principle and

Yet another strike, this one by teachers in 1983, led to the defeat of the Parti Québécois in 1985. The PQ government passed severely repressive legislation to end the strike, losing both its moral claim to champion the rights of workers and its political alliance with the New Middle Class. The long-term effects of this strike, if any, are not yet clear.

self-interest so neatly coincided, no wonder institutional change was both swift and harmonious.

While communities were securing immediate economic advantage, however, their control over local institutions was being sapped. Whether community elites were aware of this erosion or felt it was a fair tradeoff, the fact is that bureaucratic centralization soon eclipsed the importance of the community. Norms as well as subsidies started to come from outside. Since loyalty is most often a function of dependence, the loyalty of the teaching staff belonged no longer to the school board but to the professional association, which bargained with government for working conditions and salary. In the process, school boards came to represent the government more than the community.

Similar analyses could be made in the realm of social welfare. The voluntary agencies that had traditionally been organized, staffed, and managed by the Church in local communities were now to be organized by lay professionals employed by state agencies.

This massive modernization initiated by the growing state bureaucracies was far from unique to Quebec society. It was common to all industrially developed countries, in fact. What was unique to Quebec (and to similar Catholic societies elsewhere in North America) is that the sudden, rapid secularization of social institutions was mostly conflict-free.

The Exodus of Clergy

During the late 1960s and the early 1970s, Quebec, like English Canada, the United States, and some European countries, quite suddenly saw a new phenomenon: priests and nuns left their vocations in droves. Part of the process may be explained by ideological changes within the Catholic Church and part by the fact that the Vatican increasingly facilitated the release of individuals from their clerical vows. Equally facilitating these "defections" in Quebec was the fact that, contrary to the situation before the Quiet Revolution, priests or nuns who left orders could now quite easily find a place for themselves within the social structure. No longer were former clerics—especially priests—viewed as having committed spiritual treason by leaving the sacred calling; no longer could a defector cope only by either leaving the society or concealing his or her previous occupation. Suddenly, with the change in the social order, ex-priests could (and did) enter the growing ranks of the public and semipublic bureaucracies. The change was so thorough and so pervasive that priests who taught religion at the Université de Montréal, which holds a pontifical charter, were able, because of tenure, to keep their positions after quitting the ranks of the clergy and of celibates. Such a situation would have been inconceivable less than a decade earlier.

Paradoxically, the same reasons that had prompted men and women to enter the clergy in remarkable numbers in the none-too-distant past could also explain the sudden, massive exodus. Without doubting the selflessness and sincere motives of those who became priests, brothers, or nuns, one can argue that, in social terms, joining the clergy of Quebec had certainly not involved downward social mobility. For women, it had meant an assurance of comfortable, if austere, living quarters and an escape from the burden of large families and domestic chores, while gaining access to socially esteemed occupations in teaching and nursing. The lifestyle of nuns, although basically other-worldly, certainly matched and often surpassed the conditions under which most married women from the same social backgrounds could expect to live. The social distance that nuns maintained from the civil society was compensated by the deference given them by the laity. The majesty of their convents contrasted with the urban tenements their married sisters occupied. Deprived of the

Brother André (1845–1937, born Alfred Bissette) has been beatified. He is most famous for the healing powers of the shrine he erected to St. Joseph on Mount Royal.

privileges of married life, they were equally spared its burdens; on balance, entering a convent was not—and was not perceived as—an irrational decision.

For men, joining the clergy, regular or secular,[2] meant entering a career that could lead to important institutional positions. In the secular clergy, the career paths mainly involved pastoral duties in the urban and rural parishes of a geographically circumscribed diocese. A young man began as a curate, receiving only a very low stipend beyond room and board, but could fully expect to become a parish pastor some day. Promotions, based primarily on seniority, would lead a parish priest from a small, possibly rural, parish to a large urban parish. As he moved from small to large parish, his income rose substantially because it was a function of both the wealth and the size of his parish. The "good income" years made a relatively secure retirement possible.

For the regular clergy, the career patterns varied according to the kinds of institutions run by the order—from novitiates for the training of future priests to colleges and sometimes universities, as well as shrines, publications, and social agencies involved with cooperatives or credit and trade unions. A man could aspire to positions of leadership, public recognition, and gratitude as his career reached its apex.

Quebec had long had a relatively high percentage of people who chose

to follow these patterns. More or less simultaneously with the Quiet Revolution, decisions to enter the religious life suddenly shrank to a trickle,
and defections increased dramatically, especially among younger nuns
and priests—those who were beginning, not terminating, their careers.
The shrinking role of the Church in the newly emerged social order was
certainly a key factor. The Church, which had previously offered both
full career patterns and social esteem, could now promise neither. One
can also say that the Catholic hierarchy unwittingly helped to curtail the
potential of clerical careers. Bureaucratic centralization of resources and
decision-making, which became hallmarks of the new social organization,
did not spare the Church itself. The career patterns of the secular clergy
were drastically altered. Parish priests were suddenly transformed into
functionaries on a fixed salary—and a low one at that. Any surplus resources were centralized by the bishop, who was, so the rationale went,
in the best position to assess the needs of the various parishes and distribute the resources. Bureaucratically unimpeachable, this doctrine led
to measures that sapped the morale of the secular clergy by suddenly
eliminating the traditional pattern of rewards. Worse, parish priests and
their curates realized that a priest who joined the ranks of the rapidly
growing para-public institutions as a salaried professional made more
than four times their income, was exempt from pastoral duties, could
live in a private apartment, and, as a learned man of science, was more
visible, better known, and socially esteemed in both the lay and the clerical
worlds.

The Decrease in Religious Practice

"Tradition," Everett Hughes once pointed out in conversation, "is sacred
only so long as it is useful." If tradition involves a mix of the sacred and
the utilitarian, it follows that the first people to question its sacred character will be those for whom tradition is no longer useful. And indeed
in mid-20th century Quebec, it was the intelligentsia and the new middle
classes—whose careers and interests were no longer served by the traditional culture, institutions, or leadership—who first challenged the legitimacy of all three.

    For traditional Quebec society, including the elites, visible religious
practices were interwoven with almost every part of life. Many of these
folkways all but disappeared over a very short time. For example, people
had been accustomed to locate themselves by referring to the parish in
which they resided; this custom rapidly disappeared as the majority of
people no longer knew the names or the general locations of parish
churches.

    It would not be misleading to say that most of the population drifted
into secularization through inattention. For the majority, estrangement
from religious practice developed as a result of the Church's growing
irrelevance in meeting their everyday needs. Schools were no longer
linked to the Catholic parish; teachers were more apt to be lay than

clerical; hospitals and clinics were professionally administered by specialists who lived far from where they worked, and neither knew nor cared to know about their clients in other than a professional capacity. The secularization of charity in the professionally operated agencies of the state left the Church not only with a shrinking role but also with half-empty buildings whose material upkeep became increasingly dependent on the continuing popularity of bingo.

The falloff was evident both in the important decisions of life and in the minutiae of daily living. Stanley Ryerson has observed in conversation how deeply Quebec society has changed: nowadays, people no longer doff their hats or cross themselves when passing in front of a church. When what was commonplace has become bizarre, when automatic, unreflecting, customary behaviour becomes unusual over a very short time, one suspects that deep changes separate the present from the immediate past. In every respect except calendar time, centuries—not decades—separate the Quebec of the 1980s from the Quebec of the 1950s.

No longer visible, now basically silent, the Church, once a dominant institution in social and collective life, withdrew to service the spiritual and private needs of those still seeking its counsel. As its political clout faded, the voice of its critics became louder. The political liberals and conservatives maintain that the Church was, in large measure, responsible for the economic underdevelopment of Quebec, because it did not impart to its flock the "right" values, those that inspire entrepreneurial leadership and economic success. Under its leadership, they argue, Quebec's institutions failed to adapt to the requirements of a modern industrial society. The Marxists, on the other hand, take the Church to task for having collaborated with the anglophone bourgeoisie in exploiting its flock, the working class. Both charges are ideologically inspired distortions. The Church, however, no longer answers its critics. Is this a dignified silence, or the sign of its collapse as an institution?

THE CANADIAN QUESTION

By the late 1970s, a modern and secular social order had indeed emerged in Quebec society. Quebec had put its internal house in order, in line with other developed societies. In spite of this—maybe because of this—Quebec remained politically restive. It was readying itself to challenge the legitimacy of another sacred institution: the Canadian state. The internal issue of Church and society having been resolved, the external issue of state and society rose to the top of the political agenda. For Quebec society that was *the* Canadian question.

A Lament for Two Nations

Seldom, if ever, do a conquered people give their consent to a conquering state. Conquered subjects' loyalty to the state is always suspect. This is so

Various small groups of ultra-nationalist independantists calling themselves the Front de Libération du Québec *(FLQ) engaged in violent demonstrations and bombings throughout the 1960s, to dramatize their demand for an independent Quebec.*

true that loyalty oaths are routinely administered to and taken by future civil servants. In times of crisis in national unity, these forgotten oaths become instruments of social control for those who fear for the state's security. The point is raised here not to underscore the vulnerability of those fragile freedoms known as civil liberties, but rather to call attention to the historically enduring price of political domination. Both those who created the state and those who are subject to it are forever condemned to wishful thinking: the first, to the dream of national unity, the latter, to the dream of national independence.

Those who dream of national unity are also forced to lament the absence of a commonly agreed-on history. In Canada in the 1960s, the Royal Commission on Bilingualism and Biculturalism went to great lengths and considerable expense to document this great gap. (On second thought, the commission might have realized it owed its very existence to that regrettable fact.)

Commonly agreed-on history presupposes a common celebration of either a glorious past or a common victory over an undesirable past. France can claim both; Britain can claim the first; the United States, the latter; and Canada neither. The cruelty of this observation is mitigated by the fact that political consensus can also be built on shared visions of the future. Such visions, however, must be based on the correction of history, not its denial. "Unhyphenated Canadianism" is a mirage based on the confusion of individual biography with group history. All immigrants have a biographical break with a past in which the country of origin somehow, to some degree, became undesirable—often because of

The October Crisis of 1970 began with the kidnapping by the FLQ of British diplomat James Cross, followed by the kidnapping and subsequent murder of Quebec's minister of labour and immigration, Pierre Laporte. In response, the federal government suspended civil rights and invoked the War Measures Act, sending troops into Montreal. Prime Minister Trudeau insisted that such drastic action was necessary to prevent the formation of a provisional government.

denied opportunity or political persecution; the country of adoption, by the mere fact of receiving the immigrants, symbolizes a land of opportunity or a refuge from oppression, both of which are good reasons for thanksgiving. In contrast, the French and the English in Canada are burdened with historical continuity. In both cases, the breaking with the biographical past creates not a new citizen but a marginal one. And while marginal people may invent myths and create new visions, a new political order without group consent remains beyond reach.

A political order is a symbolically mediated structure. In other words, the state, to be legitimate, must rely on the substantial—not just formal—consent of the governed. Formal consent can be engineered by manipulation, trickery, propaganda, publicity, and deception, or it can be claimed on the basis of sufficient numbers alone. Shared consent, however, requires shared meanings, shared myths. The French and the English in Canada may have a common fate, but they share no political myths. The closest they have come was the belief that Canada was a partnership between the French and the English, an idea formalized in the **compact theory of Confederation**, which presents dualism as central to the nature of the state. John Porter (1965) spoke of "charter groups"—while admitting the junior status of one of them. Stanley Ryerson called Confederation an "unequal union." Lester Pearson, in striking the Royal Commission on Bilingualism and Biculturalism, spoke of the "two founding races." The commission, sensitive to the connotations that might be evoked by the word "race," preferred to speak of "two societies and two cultures." Pierre Trudeau watered the concept down still further, referring to two language communities (as though language without culture can be the basis of community) and many cultures. One need say no more to illustrate either the inability to define what Canada is or the incapacity of words to cover up an embarrassing social and political reality.

The last person to speak candidly about the social and political reality of Canada in unambiguous, well-established English words was Lord Durham, in his description of "two nations warring in the bosom of the same state." As mentioned at the beginning of this chapter, he recommended the subjugation of the French to the vigorous rule of the British, advice that was heeded but that did not succeed. Before Confederation, following this advice required thwarting democratic principles. With Confederation, those principles ensured political domination of the French nation.

Ever after, the word nation to describe the French fact in Canada was banned from the political vocabulary of Canadian academics and politicians. To make credible this semantic confusion, it became customary to refer not to the Canadian *state* but to the Canadian *nation*—creating unity not politically but semantically.

Such obfuscation obviously requires education. Denying reality rather than assuming it is characteristic of Canadian politicians, not of ordinary Canadian citizens. On leaving or entering Quebec, Québécois and non-Québécois alike quickly perceive the reality of cultural and social differences. Some people are dumbstruck by the differences. Others are paranoid about them. Both types of reaction testify to the reality of social and cultural boundaries. The fact that this dual reality cannot find a political expression in the Canadian political system constitutes its basic vulnerability.

The compact (or dualist) theory of Confederation, the myth that so many French Canadians clung to so that they could symbolically legitimate a dignified commitment to the Canadian state, suffered an ignominious death with the patriation of the Constitution in 1982; one partner, they discovered, could force patriation without the consent of the other. That the death blow was struck by a prime minister who was himself partly French-Canadian made it no less lethal; that it involved political trickery transformed the constitutional process from grand ritual into tragic farce, making the final demise of illusion seem unreal and senseless. Rumour has it that Prime Minister Trudeau's ruthlessness in patriating the Constitution was motivated by his frantic determination to secure a niche for himself in Canadian history. Secure a niche he did indeed;

whether it will be an enviable one is quite another matter.

The destruction of dualism as a shared myth through the forcible patriation of the Constitution constitutes a proof by political action, rather than national argument, of a doctrine close to Trudeau's heart: that Quebec is a province *comme les autres*. In other words, Quebec is not the homeland of a people, it is merely a region of the country, one region among ten.

In legal fiction, Quebec has become a province *comme les autres*; in social reality it has not. It also is different economically; only in the province of Quebec is the economy controlled by a minority who differ socially, culturally, and ethnically from the inhabitants. This social and historical fact has arisen partly because of the Canadian state. Therein lies its tainted legitimacy. Therein, too, lies the reason it gave birth to the dream of national independence among its subjects in Quebec.

The Unreachable Dream

The dream of national independence in Quebec society took root when the "partnership" between French and English in the Canadian state was still a dominant theme in the political rhetoric. In effect, it was the suspicion that English Canadians did not in fact share this political myth that gave rise to the political alienation of the intelligentsia in Quebec society.

While the 1950s were ushered in by the strike in the asbestos mines, the 1960s were opened by the strike at Radio-Canada. Both events heralded basic changes in the sociopolitical order. The asbestos strike led to the Quiet Revolution a decade later. The Radio-Canada strike led, some 15 years later, to the election of the Parti Québécois. With the Quiet Revolution sprang up a modernized and secularized society, founded by the state and managed by bureaucratically employed professionals. With the independence movement was born an enduring, credible challenge to the legitimacy of an externally imposed political order.

As already stated, both strikes at first glance seem paradoxical. The asbestos strike involved a multinational corporation with English-Canadian management and French workers, but it led to a questioning of the Duplessis regime and the social power of the Church. The strike at Radio-Canada involved a conflict between producers and management within the exclusively French network of the CBC but ended by being defined in ethnic terms. Neither interpretation is really paradoxical. The contradiction between objective fact and social response would be real enough in normal times, but in times of social unrest and of heightened tension it is not unusual for an event to be invested with meanings that transcend what actually happens. The discrepancy signals the major redefinitions of historical situations that precede a challenge of a political order.

The strike at Radio-Canada, unlike many strikes, directly affected the intelligentsia and initiated their political alienation. Soon they scrutinized the federal government's institutions to ascertain the amount and level of participation of francophones within them. They found this participation appallingly low, giving substance to the emerging conviction that the Canadian state is "theirs, not ours." Moreover, as the Royal Commission on Bilingualism and Biculturalism eventually substantiated, the few francophones who did work in these institutions had to check their mother tongue at the door. At the Montreal Harbour Board, for example, bilingual civil servants received a routine memo from their francophone boss: "Since everybody in the department is bilingual, from now on all memos must be written in English." It made perfect administrative sense internally. Externally, when leaked to the press, it made no political sense, except as an example of Lord Durham's "vigorous British rule."

The memo was quoted in the first of a series of editorials by André Laurendeau, the prestigious editor of *Le Devoir*. Some months later Prime Minister Lester Pearson struck the Royal Commission on Bilingualism and Biculturalism. Noble men filled with good intentions and alarmed by the strains threatening the state, the commissioners came forth with recommendations that perpetuated, rather than eliminated, those strains. By refusing to recommend a language regime based on territory, which would have ensured the francophone majority in Quebec access in their own language to the large corporate sector of Montreal, they proclaimed Quebec the model for the treatment of "minorities" and urged the rest of Canada to follow suit toward their French minorities. In effect, they recommended leaving Quebec untouched, in terms of language policy, and adopting measures they thought would ensure the viability of French communities outside Quebec.

This viability could not be ensured, however, since postal services and radio and television programming in French were no replacement for a vanishing economic base. Furthermore, they could not convince the politically restive Québécois that Quebec was a model, since within that "model" they had to choose between a public-sector career in French or a private-sector career in English. If Quebec was to be a province *comme les autres*, as Trudeau insisted, it seemed elementary to correct that strange discrepancy. More skilled in provocation than in integration, Prime Minister Trudeau dismissed the terms of reference of the Royal Commission on Bilingualism and Biculturalism and proclaimed Canada to be bilingual and multicultural. While the proclamation pleased those citizens who were neither French nor English, it certainly did not guarantee any substance to ethnic cultures since they would not be celebrated in their own languages; what it did guarantee was state funds to enable colourful celebrations of official pluralism.

The official bilingualism adopted by the Canadian state was politically irrelevant for the modernizing Québécois majority and politically resented in most of English-speaking Canada. In Western Canada it smacked of privilege, since the few French Canadians living there were fully bilingual but now able to get federally funded French-language radio and

The election of the Parti Québécois in 1976 came with a promise to hold a referendum on sovereignty-association. The referendum, held in 1980, was preceded by a dramatic publicity campaign by both the federal and provincial governments to sway the population's sympathy. In the end, the people of Quebec rejected sovereignty-association, but shortly thereafter the Parti Québécois was re-elected with an increased majority. This mixed message indicated the ambivalance of the population in Quebec toward the proposed alternatives.

television, not to mention bilingual labels on their cornflakes, while the overwhelming majority of neo-Canadians could not receive such services in their cultural languages. The reasons of state clashed with the logic of community, and the reasons of state prevailed, pitting the ethnic Canadians against the French Canadians. The very same result was achieved in Quebec by the failure of the senior government to act, leading, in 1974, the junior government under Robert Bourassa—no wild-eyed separatist but a tame Liberal—to introduce Bill 22, *la loi sur la langue officielle.* Replacing a 1969 act that had the same intent but was less comprehensive,

The Constitution Conference, November 1981. Lévesque is disgruntled as Trudeau confers with McEachen.

Bill 22 announced that French was the language of the workplace and of government services. It also restricted anglophone education to children who demonstrated a prior knowledge of the English language. Thus, although the new law was loudly denounced by the anglophone media, one of its most immediate effects was to alienate from the Liberal party many of Quebec's new Canadians, who resented having to learn not one but two languages to qualify for effective citizenship.

The vocal opposition to Bill 22 in English-speaking Quebec was disseminated throughout the rest of Canada, leading the Canadian Air Traffic Controllers' Association to challenge, in 1976, the federal official language policy (described in Chapter 15). Specifically, the air controllers, fearful of eventual bilingual requirements, struck to protest the use of French by francophone pilots when talking to francophone controllers; safety in the air was threatened, the union's public statements suggested, unless both parties had to use English at all times. Until now, implementation of the federal bilingual policy had been passively resisted, as the successive annual reports of the Commissioner of Official Languages ritually attested to. The CATCA strike was, however, an official challenge by a special-interest group. Trudeau responded by solemnly proclaiming in a television address that this challenge constituted a major threat to national unity, packed his bags, went off to Bermuda, and left the whole matter in the hands of Transport Minister Otto Lang—who promptly surrendered to the demands of CATCA.

Only months later, provincial elections brought to power, to the consternation of English Canadians, the Parti Québécois, whose announced goals included the peaceful attainment of independence for Quebec. One of its first actions was to complete the francization of Quebec that Bourassa had begun. It enacted Bill 101, *la charte de la langue française*, which makes French the normal language of work, education, and public life in Quebec. Basically, its authors considered Ontario the model for the treatment of the other official language. But what is normal in Ontario and elsewhere in Canada is considered by those regions to be outrageous in Quebec.

In response to the election of a "separatist" government in Quebec, Trudeau struck a Task Force on Canadian Unity, headed by Jean-Luc Pépin and John Robarts. Its report, however, did not take sufficient umbrage at Bill 101 and was not only ignored but swiftly denounced, on the very day of its release, by Don Johnston, MP for Westmount-St. Henri, then a Liberal backbencher but soon to be promoted to Trudeau's cabinet. Proud of his interview in the electronic media, Johnston eventually had the transcript translated into French and distributed in both languages to his constituents. In it, he solemnly proclaimed his and his constituents' rejection of the Pépin-Robarts Report. The grounds? First, history teaches us one thing: if you leave a minority at the mercy of a majority, its rights will not be protected. And that is what the Pépin-Robarts report did. Second, our French-Canadian compatriots would be "condemned" to live all their lives only in French, a fate presumably worse than death. If Don Johnston was right about the fate of minorities at the hands of majorities, he made it the duty of every self-respecting Québécois to become an *indépendantiste*. By equating living one's life only in French to a sentence, he clearly shows that taking the role of the others is not an automatic consequence of living in their midst.

The Parti Québécois had won its electoral victory preaching **sovereignty-association**—political independence for Quebec within an economic union with Canada—but had promised to seek a specific mandate before attempting to negotiate the change with Ottawa. A referendum was announced for May 1980, and the federal Liberals combined with the provincial party to throw enormous amounts of money and advertising into the campaign. The referendum failed—a joyless victory of national unity. English Canadians stopped holding their breath, even when the PQ unexpectedly won another victory at the polls the next year. What the referendum had done was to make the dream of national independence unreachable.

Then Trudeau delivered on his promise of "renewed federalism"; in 1982 the Constitution was repatriated without Quebec's consent. The PQ resisted federal blandishments to sign, but in its eagerness to retain power, it loosened some requirements of Bill 101 (which even in its original form was felt by some Québécois to give insufficient protection to the French culture and language), and it announced a new, quasi-federalist platform that drove several well-known *indépendantistes* to leave its ranks. Those moves proved too much for the Quebec electorate. Although they had voted overwhelmingly against the Liberals in the federal election of 1984, sweeping the Conservatives to victory, a few months later they voted almost as decisively *for* the provincial Liberals—the party that, after all, had come to power in 1960 under the slogan *maîtres chez nous*.

The outcome of the referendum and the purge of the *indépendantistes* from the Parti Québécois spells not the end of Quebec's "national" movement, but the end of its embodiment by a specific political party. It also means that the strategy to achieve independence will not follow the route of party politics. A return to less institutionalized forms of political mobilization is not to be excluded.

The election of a new Prime Minister, Brian Mulroney, and a new Premier of Quebec, Robert Bourassa, has ended the political tensions and suspicions of the 1970s and early 1980s. How these two leaders deal with the pressing political issues of the day will have a profound impact upon the unity of Canada in the future.

QUEBEC'S NEW ENTREPRENEURS

At the time, it was a clear indication of the declining influence of Canada's once-biggest and busiest city—and of the province it dominated. In 1979 Ultramar Canada Inc., an oil refining and marketing company active in Eastern Canada, moved its head office from Montreal to Toronto. With that, it became one of more than 100 companies to leave the city in the turbulent three-year period that followed the Parti Québécois' rise to power in 1976. But [in July 1986] Ultramar president Jean Gaulin reversed the 1979 decision and announced at a press conference that the firm will return to Montreal in September [1986]. Gaulin denied that there is any connection between the transfer and the PQ's defeat last year. "It is a business decision," he declared, and it reflects a growing confidence within the business community in a recovery that the province has experienced over the past three years.

After more than a decade of political and economic uncertainty, Quebec is undergoing a business revival that is the envy of much of the rest of Canada. Ultramar has been joined by other companies, including Ericsson Communications Inc., a subsidiary of a Swedish telecommunications giant, in deciding to return their head offices to Quebec. There is also an apparent change in thinking on the part of many Quebecers themselves. Over the past five years there has been a growing interest in the private sector, accompanied by criticism of the province's traditional dependence on public spending as the key source of new jobs and economic growth.

Liberal Premier Robert Bourassa concentrated during his successful election campaign last fall on the need to privatize some of Quebec's 65 Crown corporations, reduce regulations and abolish many of the government's 200 commissions. Last week Bourassa told *Maclean's*: "We were elected to reduce the role of the state and, as Ultramar's return to Montreal demonstrates, we have already created some concrete results."

Quebec's economic performance recently has been solid. The Caisse de Dépôt et Placement du Québec estimates that in 1986 the provincial economy—Canada's second largest after Ontario—will grow by 4.3 percent, well above the projected national average of 3.9 percent. Gilles Rhéaume, director of the provincial forecasting group for the Conference Board of Canada, attributes Quebec's continued recovery to a broad range of factors. Rhéaume cites strong spending by consumers, increasing exports to United States, a residential construction surge and continued growth in such businesses as consulting and computer services.

Some indications of the scope of the recovery are dramatic. In Montreal, the engine of the province's economy, housing prices have soared 29 percent in the past year. And the value of commercial construction permits reached $548 million in 1985, up from $360 million in 1984. As well, after a decade in which the yearly exodus from the province exceeded immigration, in 1985 Quebec experienced a net inflow of more than 4,000 people.

Other important factors in the revival have been legislative changes to encourage business growth. The Quebec Stock Savings Plan (QSSP), which PQ Finance Minister Jacques Parizeau created in 1979 as a tax shelter for provincial residents who invest in Quebec firms, has been a key component in raising investment money— and public awareness of the importance of business. Said Parizeau, who resigned from the PQ in 1984 and is now a professor at Université de Montréal's prestigious Ecole des Hautes Etudes Commerciales: "The problem traditionally was that the average French-Canadian chap felt excluded from the financial decision-making process. This plan gave the chap on the street incentive for getting involved."

The prospect of large infusions of new capital is encouraging many Quebec companies that had been privately owned for generations to issue shares. Last year 71 newly listed companies became publicly owned, and in the first six months of this year another 54 companies followed their example. Cascades Inc., a paper products company based in the small Eastern Townships community of Kingsey-Falls, made one of the most successful offerings in 1982. . . . Declared Montreal Exchange president André Saumier: "There is no way

we would have seen this phenomenon before 1979. Private companies were almost hostile to the idea of going public, which was like a foreign concept."

The overall recovery also benefited from the government's reduction of personal income tax for high-income earners to 27.1 from 33 percent, then the highest rate in Canada. Ultramar's Gaulin said that the high tax burden had made executives of national companies reluctant to work in Quebec.

The change in attitude toward business has also underpinned the recovery. Regarded with scorn by many intellectuals during the nationalistic 1970s, business has taken on a powerful allure for young people. Quebec schools currently account for 40 percent of all students enrolled in business administration courses in Canada. Said Daniel Johnson, Quebec's minister of industry and trade, who regularly speaks at high schools and colleges: "I now get 18- and 19-year-old students asking probing questions about mergers and acquisitions. Ten years ago, that kind of stuff was regarded by kids as distasteful." As well, interest in business news—a subject long left to the English-language media—is soaring. Circulation of Quebec's most popular weekly business newspaper, *Les Affaires*, has doubled to 78,000 in the past four years.

Some observers say that Quebecers' current fascination with business is a direct progression from their previous preoccupation with nationalism and the role of government. Said Parizeau: "A large government was once the only place in which French-Canadians felt they could advance without handicaps. That was why, when all those English-Canadian companies were pulling out during the PQ's first few years in power, I maintained my equanimity." He added, "I realized it would simply open the way for French-Canadians to step in and take control of those fields."

The Bourassa government has clearly interpreted the change in mood as a mandate to reduce the size and influence of government. In July a task force into deregulation headed by Reed Scowen, Bourassa's top economic adviser, recommended sweeping reforms. They included reducing the province's regulatory system, with a 25-per-cent cut in the more than 2,000 regulations covering activities and products ranging from the transportation of bees to the purchase of fishing boats. At the same time, Treasury Board President Paul Gobeil and a three-member advisory panel of blue-chip businessmen recommended that Quebec abolish or rework more than 100 of its 200 regulatory boards and commissions.

Among those now urging the government to pare its operations are former civil servants and politicians who once encouraged increased state intervention. One member of Scowen's task force on deregulation was Claude Castonguay, a former civil servant and social affairs minister in the early 1970s who played key roles in creating both the province's pension plan and medicare system. Castonguay, now chief executive officer of Quebec City-based insurance giant Laurentian Group Corp., said that he believes "government has grown beyond a size we ever wanted or envisioned."

Still, some Quebecers say that the role of the state should not be reduced while Ottawa is trying to negotiate a free-trade accord with Washington. Said Parizeau: "The state must still be the incubator of Quebec businesses, particularly if freer trade becomes a reality."

An active business community has become the symbol of Quebec's aspirations. Declared Bourassa: "The presence of strong, dynamic and well-established Quebec enterprises means that economic power will stay in Quebec hands. But instead of resting with the state, it will be in the hands of Quebec businessmen." And in that environment Ultramar and other returning companies have decided to stake their futures.

ANTHONY WILSON-SMITH and
BRUCE WALLACE in MONTREAL

CONCLUSION

This essay ends on a melancholy note of disillusionment with statesman-ship and party politics in this country. It does not claim to be non-partisan or dispassionate. It is a plea, a public and desperate one, for the youth of this country to distance themselves from the political culture they are exposed to. It is especially a plea to young English Canadians not to accept either the new demonology on Quebec or the idea that all is returning to "normal" there, but to resolve to help to bring to birth eventually a state that will truly enjoy the consent of the governed.

NOTES

1. The exception was France, where after the Revolution the state took over the direct organization of education, producing bitter internal conflict that lasted more than a century.
2. Catholic priests may be regular or secular clerics. The regular clerics are those who are members of a particular order, such as the Basilians, the Sulpicians, and the Jesuits, and live under its rule (hence "regular"); they take vows of celibacy, poverty, and obedience (to the hierarchy of the order). Although an order sometimes accepts the responsibility of running a parish, each views itself as having one or more special mandates, which in Quebec before the 1960s was most often education, health, or some form of social service for active orders. (Some orders are strictly contemplative.)

    In contrast, secular clerics take a vow of celibacy, but not of poverty or obedience. They work under the local bishop (whose assignment comes from Rome) and run most parishes, as well as other institutions under direct diocesan control.

    All nuns and religious brothers are regular clerics.

FOR FURTHER READING

Arnopoulos, Sheila McLeod, and Dominique Clift
    1980 *The English Fact in Quebec*. Montreal: McGill-Queen's University Press.
    Arnopoulos and Clift analyze the past, present, and likely future conditions of the English-speaking minority in Quebec.
Dion, Léon
    1976 *Quebec: The Unfinished Revolution*. Montreal: McGill-Queen's University Press.
    A recognized authority offers a provocative assessment of recent social and political changes in Quebec.
Guindon, Hubert
    1978 "The Modernization of Quebec and the Legitimacy of the Canadian State." In Daniel Glenday et al., eds., *Modernization and the Canadian State*. Toronto: Macmillan.
    This article is an interpretation of the federal government's dilemmas in attempting to accommodate Quebec's aspirations.

McRoberts, Kenneth, and Dale Postgate

1980 *Quebec: Social Change and Political Crisis*. Toronto: McClelland and Stewart. This readable account of the evolution of Quebec emphasizes the emergence of the provincial government's role and the interrelations of class structure and Quebec nationalism.

McWhinney, Edward

1979 *Quebec and the Constitution*, 1960–1978. Toronto: University of Toronto Press.

The legal-constitutional issues that have affected Quebec's relations with the federal government are the subject of this concise, lucid review.

Milner, Sheilagh Hodgins, and Henry Milner

1973 *The Decolonization of Quebec*. Toronto: McClelland and Stewart. This sympathetic analysis of left-wing nationalism in Quebec emphasizes the historic and ongoing economic exploitation of the province.

Rioux, Marcel

1978 *Quebec in Question*, 2nd ed. Toronto: Lorimer. This best-selling history of Quebec traces the intellectual foundations of the independence movement.

Rioux, Marcel, and Yves Martin

1964 *French-Canadian Society*. Toronto: McClelland and Stewart. This collection of historical and sociological essays written by a wide range of Quebec scholars traces the evolution of Quebec society and illustrates some of the issues of scholarly debate in the field.

Thomson, Dale

1973 *Quebec Society and Politics: Views from Inside*. Toronto: McClelland and Stewart.

Prominent social scientists wrote this collection of essays dealing with various aspects of Quebec society.

GLOSSARY

Absolute zero point: A reading of "0" on a measurement instrument, which indicates an absence of the quantity being measured (e.g., "0" on a set of scales means that whatever is being weighed is weightless).

Accessibility: Equality of opportunity in a given area, commensurate with one's abilities and irrespective of one's origins, locality, race, or sex.

Accommodation: Some degree of integration of an ethnic group into the broader society and the fullest possible participation in its institutional life.

Achieved characteristics: Qualities that an individual acquires through education, occupation, or voluntary association with particular groups.

Achieved status: A social position attained through personal effort.

Affective individualism: A state resulting from the separation of family life from direct economic production; includes the individual's altered ability to view him or herself in relationship to society (individualism) and the accompanying changed feelings and behaviour toward others (affect).

Affirmative action programs: Programs intended to ameliorate the conditions of disadvantaged groups, usually in regard to employment.

Agents of socialization: Persons who initiate the socialization process; persons with whom one interacts in the process of becoming socialized.

Age-sex-specific mortality rates: The calculation of mortality rates for specific age groups by sex.

Agrarian: A type of society in which the economy iş based almost exclusively on farming.

Alienation: According to Marx, the result of changes in the nature of work due to industrialization, which reduced the worker's involvement in the product he/she helped produce; individual feelings of powerlessness, meaninglessness, isolation, and estrangement from the self and from

society as a whole; a state in which the fundamental human needs to work creatively and to maintain gratifying social relations go unmet.

Anomie: For Durkheim, a state in which clear-cut norms and regulations are lacking: for Merton, a malintegration of individual goals and institutional means.

Anthropology: The study of human culture in all periods and in all parts of the world.

Anticipatory socialization: The preparation for future roles.

Applied research: Research undertaken to satisfy some practical concern.

Applied sociology: A description or explanation of phenomena with findings that can be applied to solve problems of social concern; the application of sociological knowledge or methods to solving real problems.

Arranged free choice: A form of mate selection in which parents arrange the marriage but the children have some sort of veto power.

Arranged marriages: Marriages in which the parents or kin have selected the partners.

Ascribed characteristics: Qualities that are fixed, usually at birth (including sex, racial origin, ethnicity, and age), and over which a person has no control.

Ascribed status: A social position that is assigned to a person (usually at birth but sometimes later), and over which the person has no control.

Assimilation: The process by which an ethnic group loses its distinctive characteristics and becomes indistinguishable from any other segment of the society.

Authority: The legitimate exercise of power.

Autonomism: A form of relationship with the broader society in which the ethnic group is part of a federation of regional ethnic groups.

Back translation: A form of check used by researchers to ensure that questions and response categories have the same meaning in all languages used.

Basic research: Research carried out for the ultimate purpose of developing explanatory theory.

Basic (pure) sociology: Concerned with increasing theoretical understanding of society. A description or explanation of phenomena which is carried out for the ultimate purpose of developing theory.

Biological determinism: The idea that human behaviour is determined by biological inheritance alone.

Blended family: A family in which one or both spouses bring to the union children from a previous marriage.

Boundaries: In the case of ethnic groups, those features, such as language or accent, that set one group apart from another and help it survive as a distinct entity.

Bourgeoisie: The capitalist class that controls the means (forces) of production and purchases labour power in exchange for wages.

Bureaucracy: A hierarchical institution consisting of separate yet interrelated positions that are highly specialized, follow standardized procedures, and are designed to perform some kind of function or work; a type of social organization that is complex and hierarchically structured, characterized by fixed and clear-cut rules, a clearly defined division of labour, and a high degree of impersonal, rational, and routine activity.

Bureaucratic hierarchies: The structures by which societies, whether capitalist or socialist, coordinate divided labour.

Caste systems: Systems in which intergroup marriage and other forms of shifting membership are forbidden.

Census Agglomeration Area: The main labour-market area for an urban population core of 10,000 to 99,000.

Census Metropolitan Area (CMA): a central city and its contiguous suburban and/or exurban area.

Central core: The downtown core or central business district of a city, where most economic activities are transacted.

Charisma: A certain quality of an individual personality, by virtue of which he or she is set apart from ordinary people and treated as endowed with supernatural, superhuman, or at least specifically exceptional powers or qualities.

Charismatic authority: The exercise of power by an individual legitimated by a shared belief that the person possesses unique gifts or characteristics.

Charter groups: Politically and culturally dominant groups whose claim to special privilege is based on their status as the "earliest" arrivals.

Church: A stable, institutionalized organization of religious believers.

City: A legal definition of a settlement.

Class system: A system in which movement between the status groups is both legal and accepted; also referred to as "open system."

Clinical sociology: The offer of professional advice by sociologists to people or organizations with "social problems."

Closed-ended questions: Questions that ask respondents to select from a set of categories predetermined by the researcher.

Cluster sample: A sample in which groups of units (e.g., areas in cities, schools, etc.) are enumerated and selected, even though the individual unit is the object of study.

Cohabitation: A more or less permanent relationship in which two unmarried persons of the opposite sex share a dwelling without legal contract.

Cohort: A group of people who share common life experiences by entering the key transition points in the life cycle at the same time.

Collectivity: A form of social grouping.

Communalism: A strategy of local control in which a group that may be a minority in the society but a majority in a particular region asserts its right to control local institutions.

Community: A specific type of social structure and a set of values, beliefs, and rules alleged to be associated with a settlement type.

Compact theory of Confederation: A belief shared by the English and the French that Canada was a partnership between these two groups.

Composite indicator: A scale devised by taking multiple indicators, expressing them in a common metric, and adding them together to form a scale.

Concentric circle approach: An approach developed by Park and Burgess, who conceptualized the emerging division of activity and people within the city in terms of zones—a series of expanding concentric circles, each one possessing specialized functions.

Conflict perspective: In deviance theory, the view that deviance is the outcome of conflicts between interest groups having different economic and political interests; more generally, a perspective in sociology that sees society as a collection of groups struggling for power.

Conflict theorists: Theorists who focus on the dynamic processes that promote change in a society.

Conflict theory: Theory that argues that segments of society compete with one another for relatively scarce rewards.

Consciousness-raising: A means by which women came to understand their common oppression as women.

Consensus model: The view that the norms and values of a society are shared by almost everyone.

Construct validation: A procedure for validating a new indicator by substituting it for an identical or similar indicator in the test of a theory.

Consumption: Refers to the using of goods and services.

Content analysis: A research technique, using documents of various kinds, in which the frequency of occurrence of certain kinds of information is systematically recorded.

Contracted families: "Empty-nest" families, where the children have all matured and left home, leaving reduced families that consist of just the surviving spouses.

Control group: In an experiment, a selected group identical to the experimental group but not exposed to the experimental stimulus.

Cooperative: A type of participatory organization in which each participant purchases a share and has a vote on all matters requiring decision.

Correlation and regression analysis: A set of procedures for describing how accurately values of a dependent variable can be predicted from knowledge of the values of one or more independent variables, and what the rules are for making such predictions. (*Also see* **gamma, tau**, and **proportional reduction in error**.)

Courtship bargaining: The function of dating as an assessment game, with the participants acknowledging what each has to offer and what each can get from the other.

Crime: A violation of the criminal law.

Crime rates: The number of offences (of a particular kind) as a proportion of the population, as recorded by the police.

Cross-tabulation: A table that indicates the relationship between two variables by listing the distribution of the categories of one variable according to the categories of the other.

Crude death rate: The number of deaths occurring in a specified calendar year in relation to the population exposed to the risk of death.

Crude rate: The number of times a particular event occurs in a calendar year in relation to the mid-year estimate of the total population.

Cultural assimilation: According to Gordon, an ethnic group's incorporation of another group's culture.

Cultural determinism: The idea that human behaviour depends on the society into which the individual is born.

Cultural relativism: The notion that culture can only be understood from the inside, from the actor's viewpoint.

Culture: Anything related to human behaviour that cannot be directly attributed to biology and/or instinct.

Culture/ideology: The meaning people attach to their lives, and the way they understand and justify who they are and what they do.

Debureaucratization: The modification of bureaucratic structures to make them more responsive to democratic concerns.

De facto: In fact, in reality; distinguished from de jure.

Definition of the situation: A phrase coined by W.I. Thomas and Dorothy Swaine Thomas in connection with the idea that reality is socially constructed, and that people respond as much or more to the meaning a situation has for them as to the objective features of the situation.

De jure: Embodied in law.

Demographic analysis: Statistical analysis of demographic variables like fertility and mortality.

Demographic equation: Population at the end of a period = population at start of period + natural increase + net migration.

Demographic variables: The components of population change and variation, such as fertility, mortality, migration, population composition and characteristics, population size and distribution.

Demography: The study of population size, distribution, and composition, as well as population changes.

Denomination: Sociologically, a religious group structured as a voluntary association in a pluralistic society.

Dependent variable: A variable in an asymmetrical relationship that is affected by the independent variable, but does not in turn affect the independent variable.

Descriptive statistics: Statistical analysis that describes the magnitude and form of the relationships among variables in a study.

De-skilling: A tactical option open to employers enabling them to dictate and control the work of their employees.

Deviance: Conduct that fails to meet shared behavioural expectations; a socially constructed reality.

Differential association: A process by which individuals learn criminal behaviour through interaction with others who define such behaviour favourably, and in isolation from those who define it unfavourably.

Discrimination: The treatment of a person differently, usually unfairly, because of his or her membership in a particular group.

Disintegrative regionalism: Regionalism's negative qualities: bitter conflicts and hostile reactions between an area's culture or economy and the larger national interests.

Division of labour: A process by which tasks and roles become increasingly specialized and assigned to specific members of an organization; the specialization of tasks that is found in all human groups.

Divorce rate: The number of divorces versus the number of marriages; the number of recorded divorces per 100,000 population in a calendar year.

Domestic labour: The unpaid labour of women in the home.

Doubling process: A situation (e.g., high mortgage interest rates) where people may be forced to share living arrangements.

Downward occupational mobility: Mobility down the occupational ladder.

Downward social mobility: *See* social mobility.

Dramatic realization: A successful expression, during interaction, of qualities and attributes claimed by the performer; a person's ability to convey a sense of sincerity in a given context.

Dramaturgical model: A sociological model that focuses on the ways people act and interact in everyday life.

Dual-career marriage: The marital arrangement in which both partners are committed to pursuing a career and to maintaining a family.

Dual labour-market: A term traditionally used by economists; argument is that because the job choices of many individuals are grossly constrained, the labour market for working class occupations (blue-collar and lower white-collar) is divided into two substantially non-competing groups.

Dual labour-market theory: A theory that argues that men and women are recruited into different labour markets, to the disadvantage of women.

Dynamic variable: A variable, such as population, that is in a state of continual change.

Economics: The science of the production and consumption of goods and services.

Economism: An economic-determinist argument that states that all events follow naturally from the laws of motion of capitalism.

Education: The organized, collective transmission of knowledge, values, and skills.

Egalitarian model of marriage: Type of marriage in which tasks, responsibility, and privileges are shared equally by both partners, and in which both partners accept responsibility for earning money, caring for the children, and looking after the house.

Elite: The small group of people who fill the top positions in any institutional hierarchy.

Emergent view of ethnicity: The recognition that ethnic groups are not static but dynamic, ever-changing sets of people whose interests, identities, and forms of organization are transformed over time.

Emigrant: As viewed by the country of origin, a person who leaves that country to settle in another country.

Enlightenment: A philosophical movement of the 18th century characterized by beliefs in the power of human reason and by innovations in political, educational, and religious doctrine.

Entrance status: The general status accorded members of an ethnic minority upon their immigration to a new society.

Equal intervals: A unit of measurement representing a constant amount of what is being measured no matter where along the scale it is found.

Equality (Equality of condition): The degree of variation in a society in the distribution of some valued good such as income.

Equity (Equality of opportunity): The extent to which the inequality in a society is distributed fairly.

Estate systems: Social systems in which stratification is a part of law, with distinct rights and duties assigned to each group.

Ethnic community: An ethnic group whose members share ways of acting, thinking, and feeling; usually characterized by the development of organizations to accomplish members' shared objectives.

Ethnic group: A collection of people who share certain ancestral, linguistic, physical and/or religious traits.

Ethnic identity: A feeling of membership in an ethnic group.

Ethnically plural society: A heterogeneous society, such as Canada, that has distinct ethnic groups living within one sociopolitical unit.

Ethnicity: A person's "background," excluding the parents' socioeconomic status.

Ethnocentric approach: Begins with the assumption that one's own culture is right, and others wrong or odd in their differences from it.

Evaluation research: Involves the study of the effectiveness of a project or a program after it has been initiated.

Experimental group: The group exposed to some level of the independent variable, while those in the control group are not.

Exploratory research: Research preliminary to hypothesis-testing research; it involves observing some relatively unstudied phenomenon in order to identify its important features.

Expressive dimension: Actions triggered by strong feelings or emotions and designed to ease tensions and restore emotional balance.

Extended family: A family group that includes groupings of related nuclear families.

Exurbs: Smaller communities beyond the suburbs, found as far as 80 to 130 kilometres from the centre of a city.

Face validation: The agreement of a number of experts that a scale appears (on the "face" of it) to measure a certain variable.

Factorial ecology: A technique that involves listing all the social characteristics in an urban area and then using a computer to sort and rank the most important ones for explaining land use.

False consciousness: An inverted understanding of reality that makes people act against their real interests. Religion is one among many forms of false consciousness that mystify reality.

Family: A group of kin who live together and function as a cooperative unit for economic and other purposes.

Family consumer economy: An economy in which family life revolves around decisions and activities related to the purchase and use of goods produced in specialized work places.

Family economy: An economy, common in pre-industrial societies, in which families operated as mini-manufacturing units.

Family household: A household in which the people are closely related by blood or marriage; a social unit that includes at least one family.

Family of orientation: The nuclear family in which one grows up as a child.

Family of procreation: The family that one creates (usually with a partner) when one has children.

Family wage economy: An economy in which the home was separate from the workplace, as wage labour and business replaced agriculture as a way of life.

Feral children: Children raised in isolation or near-isolated conditions.

Fertility: Reproductive behaviour of women in a society.

Folkways: Social customs that are not considered to be morally significant and are not strictly enforced.

Fragment hypothesis: Louis Hartz's theory that the culture of a new, immigrant society is permanently affected by that brought from the Old World by the early settlers.

Free choice model: The situation in which a person is free to choose a mate without regard to money, occupation, education, age, sex, or family desires.

Free rider: An employee who, while believing that unionization is in his or her best interests, allows fellow workers to strike to achieve unionization but turns up for work and draws a salary.

Frequencies: Raw scores or numbers that show the total number of items in a given category.

Function: Any process that maintains societal integration and solidarity.

Functional definition: As regards the sociology of religion, a definition that accepts Durkheim's argument that any set of beliefs and practices a group uses to give meaning to life may be considered a religion.

Functional equivalents: With respect to the sociology of religion, those beliefs and practices that a group uses to give meaning to life and which, for that group, assume the dimensions of religion.

Functional necessity: A social activity essential to the continued survival of society.

Functionalism: A theoretical perspective that emphasizes the way each part of a society functions to fulfil the needs of the society as a whole.

Functionalists: Sociologists whose primary interest lies in the study of the achievement and maintenance of social order and stability in the society.

Gamma: A measure of how strongly two quantities are related to one another (e.g., people's levels of formal education and annual earnings).

Gemeinschaft: A natural unity, a living organism involving an underlying consensus or mutual understanding, based on kinship, common locality of residence, and friendship.

Gender: The social, cultural, and psychological characteristics assumed appropriate to being male or female.

Gender roles: The expected patterns of behaviour for males and females.

Generalization: The application of an interpretation to other units of the same kind as those studied.

Gentrification: A movement in which middle- and upper-income young professionals invade downtown working-class and impoverished neighbourhoods, purchase buildings, renovate them for their own use, and thereby transform the areas into upper-middle-income neighbourhoods.

Geography: The study of the relationship between human beings and their natural or physical environment.

Gesellschaft: A form of social contract based on formalized rules and relationships.

Gross national product (GNP): A statistic that represents in dollars the overall wealth of a nation; the total dollar value of goods and services produced in a given year.

Hidden curriculum: Unwritten and informal set of values and norms implicitly transmitted to the student by the school.

Hierarchical structure: A critical feature of bureaucracy, in Weber's model, which contributes to the bureaucracy's efficiency.

High culture: The forms of expression defined as high art by an elite.

History: The study of past human interactions and their results.

Hoard labour: To keep on workers during business downturns even though there are not enough orders to keep them busy.

Homogamy: Marriage between individuals having similar characteristics, such as the same economic, racial, ethnic, and religious background.

Homosexual: Refers to either men or women whose primary sexual and affectional orientation is toward partners of their own sex.

Household: People living within the same dwelling place.

Human agency: The importance of people's actions in affecting the course of history.

Human capital theory: The notion that education can contribute to economic growth.

Hypothesis: A prediction of what one expects to find; a testable statement; a possible explanation that may be found to be false; a statement that certain differences or changes in one variable precede and cause certain changes in another variable.

Hypothesis-testing research: A means for checking a proposed explanation against real-world observations.

Ideal type: A general prototype drawn from observation and research on many actual relationships in various societies and situations. (No real-life situation is likely to be as simple as the model or to match it in every respect.)

Idealist approach: An approach that uses the values, beliefs, and attitudes of people to explain the workings of a society; it contrasts with the materialist approach.

Immigrant: As seen by the host country, a person who migrates to the country.

Impersonal relationships: Interactions based on rules and specified procedures, rather than on feelings or personal relationships.

Independent variable: The variable, in an asymmetrical relationship, that can produce changes in the dependent variable, but cannot itself by affected by these changes.

Indicator: A scale used to measure a theoretical variable (*see* **operational definition**).

Industrialization: The mechanization and centralization of certain productive activities away from the home.

Infant mortality: Infant death.

Infant mortality rates: Mortality rates for the first 12 months of life.

Inferential statistics: Statistical analysis of data in order to make an inference as to whether or not relationships between variables, as revealed in the sample, can be generalized to the population from which the sample was drawn.

Institution: An organized aspect of social existence that is established and perpetuated by various norms and rules; reciprocal sets of patterned social relationships.

Institutional completeness: The degree to which an ethnic community can provide a full range of services for its members.

Institutional secularization: The transfer of responsibility for institutions from religious groups to other, non-religious groups, such as government; a process that occurred rapidly in Quebec in the 1960s.

Institutional self-segregation: The establishment by an ethnic group of institutions (for example, schools, churches, residential districts, clubs) enabling the members of the group to avoid coming into contact with outsiders.

Institutions: Reciprocal sets of patterned social relationships.

Instrument decay: A decrease in the reliability of an instrument caused by sheer repetition of use.

Instrumental dimension: Task- or goal-oriented actions focused on the needs of the general social system.

Integrationist: Describes a group determined to participate as fully as possible in a society.

Integrative regionalism: Regionalism's positive qualities: pride in the uniqueness of one's region, a sense of cooperation with other groups in the region, and a healthy pursuit of the economic and political goals that bring prosperity and stability.

Interaction: The public interplay, verbal or non-verbal, between two or more individuals or groups.

Interdependence norm: A new norm of marital power that implies both mutual dependence and the capacity to be independent.

Internal consistency approach: A method used to assess reliability, in which two or more similar (but not identical) scales are applied to the same objects or events, at essentially the same time.

Internal job ladder: The organization of jobs in a hierarchy of desirability, up which workers may progress.

Internal migrant: A person who crosses a country line irrespective of distance.

Internal migration: Movement within a country's borders, whether it be between cities or from rural to urban areas or vice versa.

Internalization: A process by which individuals are socialized to play respectable roles.

International migration: The movement of people across national boundaries.

International unions: Unions whose headquarters are located in the United States.

Intervening variable: A variable interposed between an independent variable, A, and a dependent variable, C, so that A only affects C through B.

Invisible religion: Religion as a private, individual matter, rather than a collective, socially shared system; a consequence of modernization and secularization; a term introduced by Luckmann, pointing to the consequences of modernization and secularization.

Irredentism: A strategy whereby an ethnic community seeks reunification and the recovery of the "lost" or "unredeemed" territories occupied by its members.

Isolationist: Describes a group that closes itself off from other groups in an effort to retain its traditions and institutions.

Jurisdictions: Sets of responsibilities.

Labelling: A perspective within the sociology of deviance; hypothesizes that individuals will behave according to the expectations of others and the "labels" they have been given.

Labour market: The distribution of people among available jobs.

Latent functions: Unintended or unanticipated results.

Laws: Norms that are codified into formal rules or regulations by a government.

Learning: The process, frequently informal and unorganized, through which a person acquires knowledge.

Learning structure: Environments in which an individual learns social techniques from others; in deviance theory, refers to access to the illegitimate means required to engage in deviance.

Level of statistical significance: The probability level chosen (e.g., probability of 0.05 indicates five chances in one hundred draws) in order to determine that a particular value of statistical measure would not be likely to occur by chance.

Likert-type item: A common variety of the closed-ended question, used in research, in which respondents are asked to react to some statement in terms of graded response. Categories range from "strongly agree" to "strongly disagree."

Limited free choice model: A model that takes into account such sociocultural factors as occupation, education, age, sex, and family desires in the course of mate selection.

Lone-parent family: Single-parent family.

Looking-glass self: Term used by Cooley to express the idea that a person's self-image and self-esteem are directly related to the feedback received from others.

Lumpenproletariat: The unemployed who have no power because they are shut out from the mode of production.

Macrosociology: The study of patterns of human interaction with social institutions.

Managerial ideologies: Explanations that justify the possession and exercise of authority by owners and managers.

Manifest functions: Intended and anticipated results; recognized and acccepted consequencces of social behaviour.

Marginal: The characteristic of belonging to two ethnic groups or feeling estranged from one's own ethnic group.

Marital dissolution: The dissolving of marital unions through divorce, separation, or death.

Markers: In the study of ethnicity, synonymous with group characteristics.

Market: A set of social arrangements whereby supply and demand determine price.

Marriage rate: The number of marriages per 1,000 population in a given calendar year.

Marriage squeeze: A situation in which the relevant male and female age groups are in imbalance, thus altering the frequency of marriage.

Matching: An alternative to random assignment; two units are chosen that are the same in some respect, then one unit is assigned to one group and another to the other group.

Materialist approach: An approach that explains the workings of society and the relationships between people in terms of the ways in which they reproduce themselves, especially economically; it contrasts with the idealist approach.

Materialists: Social scientists who focus on the economic system, which is believed to condition social relationships within the familial, political, and cultural arenas.

Mating gradient: The average usual age difference between the sexes at the time of marriage.

Measure: To assign numbers to objects or events according to certain rules; to apply some calibrated instrument to an object or event to determine its membership in a particular category or its location along some continuum.

Measure of association (correlation): A statistic indicating the strength and (where relevant) direction of the relationship(s) among two or more variables.

Mechanical solidarity: As found in traditional, agricultural societies, a social cohesiveness based on role similarities, which lead people to identify with each other and to share the same values and beliefs.

Mechanistic: Bureaucratic, as opposed to organic.

Media literacy: The ability to respond critically to media messages in order not to be manipulated by them.

Melting pot ideology/theory: An ideology/theory that expects ethnic groups to assimilate into the dominant culture.

Meritocracy: A hierarchy based not on inheritance but on ability as signalled by educational achievement; a system in which the most talented and able are given the powerful and privileged positions.

Microsociology: The study of how persons interact in social relationships.

Migration: Geographical movement across a specified boundary involving a change of residence.

Minority power groups: Groups with insufficient power to promote their interests and purposes in the legislative process.

Misrepresentation: The creation of a false impression through impersonation, innuendo, strategic ambiguity, crucial omissions, or lies.

Mode of production: A society's economic base.

Modernization: The process of enormous change, including industrialization, urbanization, and technological innovations, that has substantially altered public and private relationships and transformed Western society in the past two centuries.

Morbidity: Sickness, disease, and disability.

Mores: Norms that provide the moral standards of a social system and are strictly enforced.

Mortality: Death or termination of the life cycle.

Motivation: Peoples' willingness, in the context of a bureaucracy, to conform to organizational norms and organizational role expectations.

Mover: A person who changes residence within a country.

Multimethod approach: The use of two or more methodological approaches for collecting data.

Multiple nuclei approach: A model developed by Harris and Ullman for understanding patterns and economic activity in the city.

Multiple regression analysis: A statistical technique used to estimate the collective and separate effects of two or more independent variables on a dependent variable.

Multistage sample: A sampling carried out in two or more stages; a sample of clusters is selected, then units within each cluster are selected, and so on until a sample of individual units has been drawn.

Natural increase: The net balance between births and deaths; can be either a loss or a gain.

"Nature versus nurture" debate: Debate over whether individuals become what they are primarily because of their biology and genetic inheritance ("nature") or because of their environment—how others behave toward them and what opportunities they have ("nurture").

Negative social control: The achievement of conformity to the norms through various threats.

Neotraditional marriage: Also called quasi- or pseudoegalitarian marriage; a marital relationship in which the spouses endorse egalitarian principles but relate to each other unequally.

Net migration: The difference between the numbers of people moving into an area and the numbers of people moving out of that area.

New Urban Sociology: A set of strategies developed since the 1970s for defining, describing, and theoretically explaining the urbanizing process.

Noblesse oblige: The belief that high status confers special obligations as well as privileges.

Nominal scales: A measurement of qualitative variables in which objects or events are "named" in terms of their category membership rather than assigned ranks or numbers.

Nominal scale: An instrument to measure qualitative variables.

Non-family household: An economic arrangement in which one person lives alone or a group of unrelated persons share a dwelling.

Norms: Expectations about how people should act, think, or feel in specific situations; rules of behaviour.

Nuclear (Conjugal) family: The smallest form of family unit; usually includes a husband, a wife, and their children.

Null hypothesis: A hypothesis that there is no association between one variable and another.

Nuptiality: The rate of marriage, the characteristics of the marital partners, and marital dissolution in a society.

Occupational licensure: Effective professional control over who qualifies to practise; a common aspiration of would-be professions.

Occupational prestige: The social rating or standing given to occupations.

Offices: Positions within an organization.

Official crime rates: The number of offences of a particular kind as a proportion of the population, as recorded by the police.

Open-ended question: A question that the respondent is free to answer as he/she chooses; contrasts with closed-ended questions.

Operational definition (indicator): A scale used to measure a theoretical variable; for example, the operational definition of intelligence is the IQ test.

Opportunity structures: Environments or situations that enable individuals to express newly learned anti-social behaviour and techniques.

Optimum population concept: Idea that in order for the land to be utilized properly, to yield maximum productivity, it must have the right number of people.

Organic organization: A type of organization that does not have a strict division of labour: employees accept whatever tasks and responsibilities, relevant to their expertise, are necessary to solve a problem.

Organic solidarity: The functional interdependence of specialized groups (or organs) within larger units such as cities and countries.

Organization: A collectivity that is formed to achieve explicit goals.

Orientation-to-work perspective: The view that an individual has the option of taking or not taking any particular job.

Panel study: A longitudinal survey in which measurements of a set of variables are taken on a sample of cases at two or more points in time.

Participant observation: A method in which the researcher becomes, to some extent, a member of a group for the purpose of studying it.

Party: As used by Weber, a politically based collectivity with a role of sheer power in the structure of a society.

Path coefficients: Numbers, ranging from 0.00 to 1.00, that measure the strength of presumed causal relationships.

Path diagram: A type of statistical presentation used in sociology and other disciplines.

Patriarchy: A society in which men are dominant and rule over women; the control of women by men.

Pearson product-moment correlation coefficient: A statistic, denoted by r, that measures the strength, or predictive power, of the relationship between two quantitative scales.

Peer group: A grouping of individuals of the same general age with approximately the same interests.

Per capita GNP: The GNP divided by the number of people in the society; a figure that roughly measures average individual affluence.

Percentage difference: A measure of association between two variables; a percentage difference of 100 shows a perfect association, while a percentage difference of 0 shows no association at all.

Performance team: A set of individuals who cooperate in staging a single routine.

Petite bourgeoisie: Small business owners, shopkeepers, and professionals who generally support the power of the bourgeoisie.

Policy-oriented study: A study designed to generate data that relate to specific topics.

Political culture: The body of politically relevant values, attitudes, beliefs, and symbols that exert an important influence on the political life of a society.

Political economy: An interdisciplinary blend of the history of economics and political and cultural relations.

Political-economy perspective on sociology: The understanding of the relationships between people as the development of economic, political, and cultural phenomena combined.

Political science: The study of political behaviour and institutions.

Politics: In the context of political economy, all power relations, whether they involve nations, workers, or family members.

Polity: A mini political system with selected leaders, constituencies, decision-making and representative functions; a useful way to study ethnic groups and their organizations.

Population: In a research study, the total group of people to be studied.

Population census: A national survey of the residents of a country conducted at regular intervals.

Population projections: What is likely to occur with respect to three components: fertility, mortality, and migration.

Population study: Unlike demographic analysis, it includes both demographic and non-demographic variables in the analytic equation.

Positive checks: Factors, such as war, pestilence, disease, and starvation, that would increase the number of deaths in a population.

Positive social control: The achievement of conformity to the norms through various rewards.

Post-industrial age (information age): The stage of development where a society's centre of economy is the transfer of information, not production of manufacturing goods.

Poverty lines: Estimates of the minimum amount of money needed for households of various sizes.

Pre-industrial cities: Settlements whose economic production depended on labour-intensive, technologically simple strategies.

Prejudice: An attitude in which individuals are pre-judged on the basis of characteristics assumed to be common to all members of a group.

Preventive checks: Factors, such as moral restraint, celibacy, and postponement of marriage, that would decrease the number of births in a population.

Primary ethnic group: A group that has retained intimate and warm relationships among its members through close contact with family or friends.

Primary market jobs: Jobs characterized by mobility potential, good working conditions, high wages, good benefit packages, and provisions for job security.

Primary sector: Refers to jobs provided by firms that have an internal job ladder.

Primary socialization: The process through which a child becomes familiar with and a member of society.

Private interaction: An individual's inner conversation with him or herself; a self-reflection in which an individual engages.

Product market: A set of arrangements whereby goods and services are traded.

Production/consumption division: As applied to the sexes, a particular feature of capitalist development; a distinction between real work (which produces a wage or salary) and housework (which results in the spending of money).

Profane: Characterized by irreverence for God or sacred things.

Profession: A group whose practitioners have succeeded in laying claim to a monopoly over a specialized body of knowledge related to the work they do.

Professionalization: The process by which an occupation attempts to secure professional recognition, complete with the legal authority to license practitioners.

Proletariat: A Marxist term for the people who sell their labour to the owners of the means of production.

Proportional reduction in error: The increased accuracy in predicting values on a variable that occurs with knowledge of units' scores on some other variable (e.g., I can predict a person's social status better if I know how well educated that person is.)

Psychology: The science of the human mind and personality.

Qualitative data: Data that are usually derived from participant observation and informal interviews; data on variations in type, as opposed to variations in quantity.

Qualitative variables: Variables that exhibit variation in form or type; these variables are measured by nominal scales.

Quality of Working Life approach: Modification of the division of labour in an organization to increase the number and variety of tasks that workers perform and to provide an opportunity to engage in collective decision-making.

Quantitative scale: An instrument to measure quantitative variables.

Quantitative variables: Variables that exhibit differences in degree or magnitude, such as weight, temperature, etc.; these variables can be numerically coded.

Racism: A belief that racial differences reflect not only physical traits, but also personality characteristics, and that these differences have—or ought to have—social consequences.

Random assignment: A selection process employed to ensure that two or more groups differ initially only in ways that could be expected to occur by chance alone.

Rational authority: Authority resting upon the existence of rules and regulations legally enacted as the means to a socially agreed-upon end.

Rational-legal authority: The exercise of power legitimated by the rational, demonstrable relevance of directions and orders to the achievement of a group's shared goals or values.

Rationality: The demonstrable relevance of directions and orders to the achievement of a group's shared goals or values.

Reconstituted or blended families: Families in which one or both spouses bring to the union children from a previous relationship; the couple may also have children of their own.

Region: A geographical area with distinctive natural characteristics that differentiate it from surrounding areas; also a group of provinces, e.g. the Atlantic region.

Regionalism: A sense of regional identity, an attachment to one's own region, and usually a belief that it is victimized by other regions or by the larger whole; also, the effort to meet an area's needs in such a way as to integrate the area into the national culture and economy.

Relative income hypothesis: Theory that a large baby boom cohort will be relatively disadvantaged and hence, produce smaller birth cohorts, which, in turn, will become relatively advantaged, as competition for employment, income, and the necessities of life becomes less severe.

Relativism: In deviance theory, the recognition that deviance is not absolute but consists of an interpretation by one person of another person's deeds.

Reliability: The extent to which a scale yields consistent results when applied repeatedly to the same objects or events within a short space of time.

Religion: *Functionally defined as* any set of beliefs and practices used by a group to give meaning to life; *substantively defined as* only those sets of beliefs and practices that make reference to a supernatural reality.

Research design: The procedures used in selecting the objects or events studied and the conditions under which they are observed.

Reserve army of labour: A Marxist concept used to explain women's labour-force participation.

Residential segregation: A situation where ethnic group members live close together.

Residual power: Authority not specifically assigned to any institution.

Reverse discrimination: Discrimination that results from an attempt, usually by government, to correct past differential treatment of ethnic minorities, in the society.

Revolving door pattern: The movement of individuals in and out of crime.

Role: Expected pattern of behaviour connected with a social position.

Role conflict: Opposing demands between two or more roles.

Sacralization: A process that stabilizes personal identity and social structure by giving them qualities of untouchability and awe.

Sacred: That which is set apart from everyday life and evokes deep respect and awe.

Sample: A selection assumed to be representative of the total population that one desires to study.

Science: Systematic observation of the real world for the purpose of developing theories to describe the occurrence of certain events as originating in the prior occurrence of certain other events.

Scientific method: The persistent critique of arguments in light of tried canons for judging the reliability of the procedures by which evidential data are obtained.

Secondary ethnic group: A group that results from the migration of isolated individuals whose ties with fellow group members are mainly limited to participation in common institutions.

Secondary sector: Refers to jobs provided by firms that do not have an internal job ladder.

Secondary sector jobs: Jobs characterized by low wages, poor working conditions, instability, and few opportunities for advancement.

Secondary socialization: Processes that initiate an already socialized person into new areas of social life.

Sect: Exclusive congregation with doctrines and practices distinct from the surrounding society.

Secularization: The process by which sectors of society and culture are removed from the domination of religious institutions and symbols; the process whereby magic and religion become less significant in society, as science and the scientific method expand in significance.

Self: An individual's awareness of ideas and attitudes about his or her own personal and social identity.

Self-fulfilling prophecy: A definition of a situation that sets into motion several mechanisms leading to behaviour that fulfils the prediction.

Self-image: One's awareness of one's own personal and social identity.

Semantic differential: A seven-point, bipolar adjectival type of closed-ended question.

Separatism: "Ethno-national self-determination," in which the goal is to remove the group from the society in which it is an ethnic minority and to create a new state in which it is a national majority.

Sex: The ascribed status of being male or female, determined by chromosomal, hormonal, anatomical, and physiological characteristics.

Sex ratio: The numerical relationship of males to females.

Significant others: People who are emotionally or symbolically important to an individual.

Simple random sample: A sample drawn from a population in which each case has an equal probability of being chosen.

Social area analysis: Attempts to examine land use and settlement by using an urban population's three main social characteristics: socioeconomic status, family status and race/ethnicity.

Social class: According to Marxists, groups that are independently defined by reference to their relationship to the mode of production; a status group based on a distinctive relationship to the mode of economic production.

Social cohesion: According to Blau, the product of interpersonal commitments among employees in a bureaucratic structure.

Social control: The formal and informal mechanisms that support desired behaviour and discourage undesirable behaviour.

Social control agents: Those people who are officially or semi-officially responsible for the maintenance of acceptable, moral behaviour in society; for example, the police, the judiciary, the clergy, teachers, and sometimes parents.

Social Darwinism: The claim that human society evolves in the same manner as other living species.

Social experiment: The setting up of a research design before a program is initiated, to test whether it has achieved the desired results.

Social history: A sub-discipline of history concerned with social conditions or large, often non-elite groups in a society.

Social location: The complex of status and roles assigned to and/or achieved by each individual.

Social mobility: The movement of people from one position in a society's class structure to another, either within a generation or across generations.

Social psychology: A subdiscipline of psychology that studies how psychological characteristics (attitudes and behaviour) are influenced by social background.

Social reality of crime: The definitions of crime, their applications, the criminal behaviour patterns, and the communicated conceptions of crime.

Social relationships: The mutual involvement of persons belonging to a social collectivity.

Social self: A person's awareness of others and their expectations.

Social status: The level of prestige accorded to an individual as a result of the value placed on the role he/she plays; refers to more than inequality in income, in education, or in occupation or even in any simple combination of these three.

Social stratification: A pattern based on the ranking of people in social positions according to their access to desirables.

Socialization: The process through which an individual learns the ways and rules of a society or group; the process of development or change that a person experiences as a consequence of social influence.

Societal agents: People authorized by society to make judgments about certain human activities.

Societal reaction: The community's response to an individual's actions defined by that community as deviant.

Society: An abstract term that refers to a set of social institutions that channel behaviour in everyday life.

Sociology: The scientific study of society and the social relationships of which it is composed.

Sociology of religion: An explanation or interpretation, based upon the systematic gathering and presentation of data, of religious belief and action as a social phenomenon.

Sociospatial system: A geographically (spatially) bounded, relatively permanent settlement and the relationships within it.

Sovereignty-association: A political platform of Quebec's Parti Québécois, arguing for political independence for Quebec within an economic union with Canada.

Standard metric: Units of measurement (e.g., litres, kilopascals) that are generally agreed upon and have the same meaning for everyone who uses them.

Standardized questions: Questions or stimuli presented in exactly the same way to each respondent to ensure reliability and validity.

Staples thesis: That Canada, as a white settler society, was developed in order to exploit a series of raw materials for advanced metropolitan nations.

Stationary population: One in which fertility is in balance with mortality, resulting in a zero natural increase.

Status: Position within the social system; a non-economic criterion referring to a socially defined position in a group or society; a place in society with culturally defined obligations and rights.

Status attainment approach: A theoretical approach which examines the primacy of educational achievement as the common denominator for both sexes in their occupational statuses.

Status attainment theory: A theory that focuses on the importance of educational achievement for occupational status, regardless of the person's sex.

Status groups: Groups that occupy a socially defined position in a society.

Status-production work: Work that is undertaken to enhance the family's social standing.

Stem family: The smallest form of extended family; comprises two nuclear families generationally and economically linked and co-residing.

Stigma: A mark of discredit or unworthiness; the opposite of a status symbol.

Stratified sample: A sample in which the population is first classified into categories or strata (e.g., high-school education, university, post-graduate, etc.) and separate samples are drawn from within each stratum.

Structural assimilation: According to Gordon, the admission of minority and immigrant groups into the institutional, occupational, and social structures of the host society.

Structural discrimination: Discrimination that results not necessarily from racist motivations or from specific acts, but from traditions or forces built into the social system, which are hard to eliminate.

Structural features: The patterned ways in which social institutions are integrated to make up and stabilize the society.

Structural functionalism: A view of society as consisting of parts or institutions, with each part contributing to the maintenance of the system as a whole.

Structured observation: A method of research in which a non-participant observer systematically notes the occurrence of certain aspects of the behaviour of individuals, according to a predetermined schedule.

Subcultural variation: A term, introduced by Fischer, arguing that urban areas' special characteristics allow for a range of subcultural variation that could not exist elsewhere.

Subculture: A social group whose norms, values, and ideology differ in some respects from those of the dominant culture.

Substantive definition: As regards the sociology of religion, a definition that considers as religions only those sets of beliefs and practices that make reference to a supernatural quality.

Suburbanization: The process by which suburbs develop; the accelerated growth of smaller settlements adjacent to and surrounding cities.

Survivalist perspective: A perspective, developed by Glazer and Moynihan, that sees ethnicity as a fundamental basis on which political, economic, and cultural interest groups organize.

Symbol: Anything that meaningfully represents something else; can be either verbal or non-verbal.

Symbolic interactionism: A sociological perspective that emphasizes the importance of symbols and meaning in human interaction; the view that human behaviour depends on the meanings that objects or situations have for the individual.

System rationalization: In the context of education, an attempt to rationalize (to make more efficient) educational spending, and to achieve cost effective use of educational facilities.

Taking the role of the other: The process in which individuals try to see themselves as others see them and adjust their behaviour accordingly.

Task specialization: The first characteristic of a bureaucracy identified by Weber; division of labour.

Tau: A measure of association between two variables (*Also see* **gamma**).

Technical competence: According to Weber, the single most important criterion for staffing a highly differentiated role or occupational structure.

Test-retest approach: The application of some scale to the same object or events at two or more points in time, to test reliability.

Testing effect: The process by which an indicator of a sociological variable changes due to repeated measuring of it.

Theory of social and cultural homogamy: A theory suggesting that "like marries like" with regard to age, education, social class, race, religion, and area of residence.

Third variables: Additional variables considered in examining how sets of empirical measurements are connected.

Time budget studies: Studies, often using self-reports, of how much time respondents devote to particular tasks.

Time-series analysis: A form of analysis in which observations are taken on two or more variables for a single case on several separate occasions.

Total fertility rate: The average number of children that would be born to a woman if she survived through her reproductive years and bore children in accordance with the age-specific fertility rates observed in a given year.

Traditional authority: The exercise of power legitimated by longstanding custom.

Traditional model of marriage: Type of marriage in which there is a rigid division of labour by gender, with the man assuming total responsibility for financial provision and the woman for homemaking.

Two-person career: A situation in which the husband's success depends upon the joint efforts of him and his wife.

Unit of analysis: The object or event whose behaviour or characteristics the theory purports to explain and which the investigator will observe.

Unobtrusive measures: Measures that do not interfere with the objects or events being studied (e.g., observation of graffiti on walls, fingerprints, etc.).

Unstandardized questions: Questions or stimuli shaped by the context of the interview with the respondent.

Unstandardized regression coefficient: A statistic used to predict values on a dependent variable from values on an independent variable. (*See* correlation and regression analysis.)

Upward occupational mobility: Mobility up the occupational ladder.

Upward social mobility: *See* **social mobility.**

Urban ecology: The spatial distribution of people and activities within industrial areas.

Urban managers: People who control and/or manipulate scarce, spatially based resources; examples include housing managers, real estate agents, local government officers, property developers, youth employment officers, judges, and councillors.

Urban settlement: A settlement that comprises three functionally interrelated parts: the city, the suburbs, and the exurbs.

Urbanism: A range of beliefs, values, and rules of behaviour that are associated with urbanization.

Urbanization: The process by which increasing numbers of people come to live and work in larger, denser, and more heterogeneous settlements; from the perspective of population study, a process involving three interrelated trends: the multiplication of points of concentration, the growth of these concentrations, and the increasing proportion of the total population living in these concentrations.

Validity: The degree to which a scale actually measures what it is intended to measure.

Values: Those norms that are particularly important to the integration of a society; ideas shared by members of a society as to what is good and bad, right and wrong, desirable and undesirable.

Variables: Aspects of objects or events that can vary or change.

Vertical mosaic: Porter's term, describing Canada as a nation in which ethnicity is inextricably intertwined with stratification.

Victimless crimes: The illegal exchange between willing partners of goods or services.

Violence: An act carried out with the intention of injuring another person.

Vital registration system: A population monitoring system that concerns itself with the day-to-day recording of vital events.

Vocabularies of motive: Regulations that govern an organization or an occupation.

Voluntarism: Joining and participating in a wide range of social organizations, from clubs to political parties; often seen as typical of the nuclear family living in suburbia.

Weighting: A process used to make a sample representative of the entire population.

Work: The production of goods and services.

Workers' control: A complex form of participation for all employees in all decisions concerning an organization.

Workers' council: A council representing workers and sharing with management the power to make decisions about matters such as wage-payment procedures and working conditions.

REFERENCES

Abella, Irving, and Harold Troper
1982 *None Is Too Many.* Toronto:
Lester and Orpen Dennys.

Abella, Rosalie S.
1984 *Equality in Employment: A Royal
Commission Report,* Vol. 1. Ottawa:
Supply and Services.

Abrahamsson, Bengt
1977 *Bureaucracy or Participation.*
Beverley Hills, Calif.: Sage
Publications.

Acker, Joan
1978 "Issues in the Sociological Study
of Women's Work." In Ann Stromberg and Shirley Harkess, *Women
Working: Theories and Facts in Perspective.* Palo Alto, Calif: Mayfield.
134–61.

Acock, Alan C., and John H. Edwards
1982 "Egalitarian Sex-Role Attitudes
and Female Income." *Journal of
Marriage and the Family* 44 (August):
581–89.

Adams, Bert N.
1980 *The Family,* 3rd ed. Chicago:
Rand McNally.

Adams, Roy J., and C.H. Rummel
1977 "Workers' Participation in
Management in West Germany:
Impact on the Worker, the Enterprise
and the Trade Union." *Industrial
Relations Journal* 8: 4–22.

Allen, Richard
1971 *The Social Passion: Religion and
Social Reform in Canada.* Toronto:
University of Toronto Press.

Ambert, Anne-Marie
1975 *Sex Structure,* 2nd ed. Don Mills,
Ont.: Longman.
1986 "Being a Step-Parent: Live-in
and Visiting Stepchildren." *Journal of
Marriage and the Family* November.

Andelin, Helen B.
1965 *Fascinating Womanhood.* New
York: Bantam Books.

Anderson, Alan B., and James S. Frideres
1981 *Ethnicity in Canada: Theoretical
Perspectives.* Toronto: Butterworth.

Antony, A.E.C.
1980 "Radical Criminology." In
R.A. Silverman and J.J. Teevan, Jr.,
eds., *Crime in Canadian Society,*
2nd ed. Toronto: Butterworth.

Apostle, Richard, Don Clairmont and
Lars Osberg
1985 "Segmentation and Labour
Force Strategies." *Canadian Journal
of Sociology* 10: 253–75.

Araji, Sharon K.
1977 "Husbands' and Wives' Attitude-
Behavior Congruence on Family
Roles." *Journal of Marriage and the
Family* 39: 309–320.

Aries, Philippe
1962 *Centuries of Childhood.* New
York: Vintage.
1980 "Two Successive Motivations for
the Declining Birth Rate in the
West." *Population and Development
Review* 6 (4)

Armstrong, Hugh
1977 "The Labour Force and State
Workers in Canada." In Leo Panitch,
ed., *The Canadian State: Political
Economy and Political Power.*
Toronto: University of Toronto
Press.

Armstrong, Hugh, and Pat Armstrong
1975 "Women in the Canadian
Labour Force, 1941–71." *Canadian
Review of Sociology and Anthropology* 12
(4): 370–84.

Armstrong, Pat
1984 *Labour Pains: Women's Work in
Crisis.* Toronto: Women's Press.

Armstrong, Pat, and Hugh Armstrong
1978 *The Double Ghetto: Canadian
Women and Their Segregated Work.*
Toronto: McClelland and Stewart.
1983 *A Working Majority: What Women
Must Do for Pay.* Ottawa: Advisory
Council on the Status of Women.

Atwood, Margaret
1972 *Survival: A Thematic Guide to
Canadian Literature.* Toronto: House
of Anansi.

Aucoin, Peter
1985 *Regional Responsiveness and the
National Administrative State.* Toronto:
University of Toronto Press. Vol. 37
in a series of studies commissioned by

the Royal Commission on the Economic Union and Development Prospects for Canada (Macdonald Commission).

Avery, Donald
1979 *"Dangerous Foreigners": European Immigrant Workers and Labour Radicalism in Canada, 1896–1932*. Toronto: McClelland and Stewart.

Badertscher, John
1977 "Response to Sinclair-Faulkner." In Peter Slater, ed., *Religion and Culture in Canada*. Canadian Corporation for Studies in Religion. 407–20.

Badgley, Robin F.
1984 *Sexual Offenses Against Children*. Ottawa: Minister of Supply and Services Canada.

Bahr, Steven J.
1974 *Effects on Power and Division of Labor in the Family*. In Lois Wladis Hoffman and F. Ivan Nye, eds., *Working Mothers*. San Francisco: Jossey-Bass.

Bain, George
1978 *Union Growth and Public Policy in Canada*. Ottawa: Labour Canada.

Bain, George, and Farouk Elsheikh
1976 "Trade Union Growth in Canada: A Comment." *Relations Industrielles/Industrial Relations* 31: 482–90.

Baker, Maureen
1984 *The Family: Changing Trends in Canada*. Toronto: McGraw-Hill Ryerson.

Balakrishnan, T.R., Karol Krotki, and Evelyne Lapierre-Adamcyk
1985 "Contraceptive Use in Canada, 1984." *Family Planning Perspectives* 17 (5): 209–15.

Baldamus, W.
1961 *Efficiency and Effort*. London: Tavistock.

Barron, R.D., and G.M. Norris
1976 "Sexual Divisions and the Dual Labour Market." In S. Allen and D. Barker, eds., *Dependence and Exploitation in Work and Marriage*. London: Longman.

Baum, Gregory
1975 *Religion and Alienation: A Theological Reading of Sociology*. New York: Paulist Press.
1980 *Catholics and Canadian Socialism:*

Political Thought in the Thirties and Forties. Toronto: Lorimer.

Beattie, Christopher
1975 *Minority Men in a Majority Setting*. Toronto: McClelland and Stewart.

Beaujot, Roderic, and Kevin McQuillan
1982 *Growth and Dualism: The Demographic Development of Canadian Society*. Toronto: Gage.

Becker, Howard S.
1963 *The Outsiders: Studies in the Sociology of Deviance*. New York: Free Press.

Bell, A.P., and N.S. Weinberg
1978 *Homosexualities: A Study of Diversity Among Men and Women*. New York: Simon and Schuster.

Bell, David V.J.
1981 "Social Change and the Political Culture of Problem-Posing in Advanced Societies: The Case of Canada." In G. Dlugos et al., eds., *Management Under Differing Value Systems*. Berlin: DeGruyter.

Bell, David V.J., and Lorne Tepperman
1979 *The Roots of Disunity*. Toronto: McClelland and Stewart.

Bell, David V.J., and Donald Wallace
1982 "Parliament and Politics." In R.B. Byers, ed., *Canadian Annual Review, 1980*. Toronto: University of Toronto Press.

Bellah, Robert N.
1970 "Civil Religion in America." In *Beyond Belief: Essays on Religion in a Post-Industrial World*. New York: Harper and Row
1975 *The Broken Covenant: American Civil Religion in Time of Trial*. New York: Harper and Row.

Bendix, Reinhard
1960 *Max Weber: An Intellectual Portrait*. Garden City, New York: Doubleday.
1974 *Work and Authority in Industry*. Berkeley: University of California Press.

Benedict, Ruth
1934 *Patterns of Culture*. Boston: Houghton and Mifflin

Bercuson, David J.
1977 *Canada and the Burden of Unity*. Toronto: Macmillan.
1981 "Through the Looking Glass

of Culture: An Essay on the New Labour History and Working-Class Culture in Recent Canadian Historical Writing." *Labour/Le Travailleur* 7 (Spring).

Bercuson, David J., ed.
1977 *Canada and the Burden of Unity.* Toronto: McClelland and Stewart.

Berg, Ivar, Marcia Freedman, and Michael Freeman
1978 *Managers and Work Reform: A Limited Engagement.* New York: Macmillan.

Berger, Bennett
1960 *Working Class Suburb.* Berkeley: University of California Press.

Berger, Peter
1967 *The Sacred Canopy: Elements of a Sociological Theory of Religion.* New York: Doubleday.

Berger, Thomas
1977 *Northern Frontier, Northern Homeland: The Report of the Mackenzie Valley Pipeline Inquiry.* Ottawa: Minister of Supply and Services Canada.

Bergeron, Léandre
1971 *The History of Quebec: A Patriote's Handbook*, rev. ed. Toronto: NC Press.

Berheide, Catherine White
1984 "Women's Work in the Home: Seems Like Old Times." In Beth Hess and Marvin Sussman, "Women and the Family: Two Decades of Change." *Marriage and Family Review* 7 (3/4): 37.

Bernard, Jessie
1972 *The Future of Marriage.* New York: World.
1974 *The Future of Motherhood.* New York: Penguin Books.
1981 *The Female World.* New York: Free Press.

Bernstein, Basil
1973 *Class, Codes and Control*, 2 vol. London: Routledge and Kegan Paul.
1974 "Sociology and the Sociology of Education: A Brief Account." In John Rex, ed., *Approaches to Sociology.* London: Routledge and Kegan Paul.

Bernstein, Judy, Peggy Morton, Linda Sees, and Myrna Wood
1972 "Sister, Brothers, Lovers . . . Listen . . . " In *Women Unite!* Toronto: Canadian Women's Educational Press. 31–39.

Bernstein, Paul
1980 *Workplace Democratization—Its Internal Dynamics.* New Brunswick, N.J.: Transaction Books.

Berry, B.
1978 "The Counterurbanization Process: How General?" In Niles Hansen, ed., *Human Settlement Systems.* Cambridge: Ballinger.

Berry, J.W., R. Kalin, and D.M. Taylor
1977 *Multiculturalism and Ethnic Attitudes in Canada.* Ottawa: Minister of Supply and Services Canada.

Bibby, Reginald W.
1983 "Religionless Christianity: A Profile of Religion in Canada in the 80s." *Social Indicators Research* 13 (1):1–16.
1985 "Religious Encasement in Canada: An Argument for Protestant and Catholic Entrenchment." *Social Compass* 32: 287–303.

Bibby, Reginald W., and Harold R. Weaver
1985 "Cult Consumption in Canada: A Further Critique of Stark and Bainbridge." *Sociological Analysis* 46 (4): 445–60.

Bidney, David
1953 *Theoretical Anthropology.* New York: Columbia University Press.

Bierstedt, Robert, ed.
1959 *The Making of Society*, rev. ed. New York: Random House.

Bird, Frederick
1977 "A Comparative Analysis of the Rituals Used by Some Contemporary 'New' Religious and Para-Religious Movements." In Peter Slater, ed., *Religion and Culture in Canada.* Waterloo, Ont.: Canadian Corporation for Studies in Religion.

Bird, Frederick, and William Reimer
1976 "New Religious and Para-Religious Movements in Montreal." In Stewart Crysdale and Les Wheatcroft, eds., *Religion in Canadian Society.* Toronto: Macmillan.
1982 "Participation Rates in New Religious Movements." *Journal for the Scientific Study of Religion* 21: 1–14.

Black, D.J.
1970 "Production of Crime Rates." *American Sociological Review* 35: 733–47.

Black, Don, and John Myles
1986 "Dependent Industrialization and the Canadian Class Structure: A Comparative Analysis of Canada, the United States and Sweden." *Canadian Review of Sociology and Anthropology* 23 (2): 157–83.

Black, D.J., and A.J. Reiss
1970 "Police Control of Juveniles." *American Sociological Review* 35: 63–77.

Black, Edwin R., and Alan Cairns
1966 "A Different Perspective on Canadian Federalism." *Canadian Public Administration* 9: 27–45.

Black, H.C.
1968 *Black's Law Dictionary*, 4th ed. St. Paul, Minn.: West.

Blackburn, R.M., and M. Mann
1979 *The Working Class in the Labour Market*. London: Macmillan.

Blau, Peter M.
[1955] 1963 *The Dynamics of Bureaucracy*, rev. ed. Chicago: The University of Chicago Press.

Blau, Peter M., and Otis Dudley Duncan
1967 *The American Occupational Structure*. New York: John Wiley and Sons.

Blauner, Robert
1964 *Alienation and Freedom: The Factory Worker and His Industry*. Chicago: University of Chicago Press.

Blishen, B.R.
1967 "A Socio-Economic Index for Occupations in Canada." *Canadian Review of Sociology and Anthropology* 4: 41–53.

Blishen, B.R., and Hugh A. McRoberts
1976 "A Revised Socio-Economic Index for Occupations in Canada." *Canadian Review of Sociology and Anthropology* 13: 71–79.

Blumberg, Paul
1968 *Industrial Democracy: The Sociology of Participation*. London: Constable.

Blumer, Herbert
1962 "Society as Symbolic Interaction." In Arnold Rose, ed., *Human Behavior and Social Processes: An Interactionist*. Boston: Houghton Mifflin.
1969 *Symbolic Interactionism: Perspective and Method*. Englewood Cliffs, N.J.: Prentice-Hall.

Bock, Philip K.
1976 "The Religion of the Micmac Indians of Restigouche." In Stewart Crysdale and Les Wheatcroft, eds., *Religion in Canadian Society*. Toronto: Macmillan. 141–50.

Bong, Nguyen Quy
1980 "The Vietnamese in Canada: Some Settlement Problems." In K. Victor Ujimoto and Gordon Hirabayashi, eds., *Visible Minorities and Multiculturalism: Asians in Canada*. Toronto: Butterworth.

Booth, Alan
1977 "Wife's Employment and Husband's Stress: A Replication and Refutation." *Journal of Marriage and the Family* (November): 645–50.

Borins, Sandford
1981 *The Language of the Air*. Toronto: Faculty of Administrative Studies, York University, mimeo (February).

Bottomore, T.B., and Maximilien Rubel, eds.
1961 *Karl Marx: Selected Writings in Sociology and Social Philosophy*. Harmondsworth: Penguin.

Bourdieu, Pierre
1973 "Cultural Reproduction and Social Reproduction." In Richard Brown, ed., *Knowledge, Education and Cultural Change*. London: Tavistock.

Bourgault, Pierre
1972 *Innovation and the Structure of Canadian Industry*. Background Study 23. Ottawa: Science Council of Canada.

Bourque, Gilles
1980 "The New Parameters of the Quebec Bourgeoisie." *Studies in Political Economy* 3 (Spring): 67–92.

Bourque, Susan, and Jean Grossholtz
1984 "Politics an Unnatural Practice: Political Science Looks at Female Participation." In Janet Siltanen and Michelle Stanworth, eds. *Women and the Public Sphere*. London: Hutchinson. 103–21.

Bowles, Samuel, and Herbert Gintis
1976 *Schooling in Capitalist America*. London: Routledge and Kegan Paul.

Boyd, Monica
1977 "The Forgotten Minority: The Socio-Economic Status of Divorced

and Separated Women." In Patricia Marchak, ed., *The Working Sexes*. Vancouver: Institute of Industrial Relations, University of British Columbia.

Boyd, Monica, John Goyder, F.E. Jones, H.A. McRoberts, P.C. Pineo, and J. Porter
1985 *Ascription and Achievement: Studies in Mobility and Status Attainment in Canada*. Ottawa: Carleton University Press.

Boyer, P.
1978 *Urban Masses and Moral Order in America: 1820-1920*. Cambridge, Mass.: Harvard University Press.

Brannigan, A.
1979 "Some Observations Regarding the Problem of Integration and the Cumulative Effects of Discretionary Decisions." In J.L. Wilkins, ed., *The Prosecution and the Courts*. Toronto: University of Toronto, Centre of Criminology.

Braverman, Harry
1974 *Labor and Monopoly Capital: The Degradation of Work in the Twentieth Century*. New York: Monthly Review Press.

Brenton, Myron
1976 "The Breadwinner." In Debora S. David and Robert Brannon, eds., *The Forty-Nine Percent Majority*. California: Addison-Wesley.

Breton, Raymond
1968 "Institutional Completeness of Ethnic Communities and the Personal Relations of Immigrants." In Bernard Blishen et al., *Canadian Society: A Sociological Prospectus*. Toronto: Macmillan.
1972 *Social and Academic Factors in the Career Decisions of Canadian Youth*. Ottawa: Manpower and Immigration.
1981 "The Ethnic Community as a Resource in Relation to Group Problems: Perceptions and Attitudes." Research Paper No. 122. Toronto: University of Toronto, Centre for Urban and Community Studies.

Breton, Raymond, et al.
1980 *Cultural Boundaries and the Cohesion of Canada*. Montreal: The Institute for Research on Public Policy.

Brinkerhoff, Merlin B., and Eugen Lupri
1983 "Conjugal Power and Family Relationships: Some Theoretical and Methodological Issues." In K. Ishwaran, ed., *The Canadian Family*. Toronto: Gage.

Britton, John, and James Gilmour
1978 *The Weakest Link: A Technological Perspective on Canadian Industrial Underdevelopment*. Background Study 43. Ottawa: Science Council of Canada.

Brotz, Howard
1980 "Multiculturalism in Canada: A Middle." *Canadian Public Policy* VI (1): 41–46.

Brown, C.
1974 "Memoirs of an Intermittent Madman." In J. Haas and W. Shaffir, eds., *Decency and Deviance*. Toronto: McClelland and Stewart.

Brym, Robert, and James Sacouman, eds.
1979 *Underdevelopment and Social Movements in Atlantic Canada*. Toronto: Hogtown Press.

Brym, Robert J.
1986 *Regionalism in Canada*. Toronto: Irwin.

Burawoy, Michael
1979 *Manufacturing Consent*. Chicago: University of Chicago Press.

Burgess, Ernest W.
1925 "The Growth of the City: An Introduction to a Research Project." In R.E. Park, E.W. Burgess, and R.D. McKenzie, eds., *The City*. Chicago: University of Chicago Press.

Burnet, Jean
1961 "The Urban Community and Changing Moral Standards." In S.D. Clark, ed., *Urbanism and the Changing Canadian Society*. Toronto: University of Toronto Press. 70–79.

Burns, Tom, and G.M. Stalker
1961 *The Management of Innovation*. London: Tavistock.

Burnstein, M., et al.
1975 *Canadian Work Values*. Ottawa: Department of Manpower and Immigration.

Bursten, B., and R. D'Esopo
1965 "The Obligation to Remain Sick." *Archives of General Psychiatry* 12: 402–07.

Burstyn, Varda
1985 "Masculine Dominance and the State." In Varda Burstyn, Dorothy Smith, and Roxanna Ng, *Women, Class, Family and the State*. Toronto: Garamond Press.

Butler, Peter M.
1967 "Migrants and Settlers: Geographical Mobility and Kinship Ties." M.A. thesis, University of New Brunswick.

Byers, R.B., ed.
1982 *Canadian Annual Review of Politics and Public Affairs*. Toronto: University of Toronto Press.

Cain, Glen G.
1976 "The Challenge of Segmented Labour Market Theories to Orthodox Theories: A Survey." *Journal of Economic Literature* 14: 1215–57.

Cairns, Alan
1968 "The Electoral System and the Party System in Canada." *Canadian Journal of Political Science* I: 55–80.
1977 "The Governments and Societies of Canadian Federalism." *Canadian Journal of Political Science* 10: 695–726.

Cameron, D.
1974 "Tim Crawford Meets the Mind Police." In J. Haas and W. Shaffir, eds., *Decency and Deviance*. Toronto: McClelland and Stewart.

Campbell, Kenneth
1978 "Regional Disparity and Inter-regional Exchange Imbalance." In D. Glenday, H. Guindon, and A. Turowetz, eds., *Modernization and the Canadian State*. Toronto: Macmillan.

Canadian Tax Foundation
1985 *Report of the Proceedings of the 37th Tax Conference*.

Caplow, Theodore
1954 *The Sociology of Work*. New York: McGraw Hill.

Cappon, Paul, ed.
1978 *In Our Own House: Social Perspectives on Canadian Literature*. Toronto: McClelland and Stewart.

Cargan, Leonard
1981 "Singles: An Explanation of Two Stereotypes." *Family Relations* 30 (3): 377–85.

Carlton, R.A.
1983 "Education Policies and the Labour Force: An Historical Perspec-tive on the Ontario Case." Guelph: University of Guelph, mimeo.

Carter, Hugh, and Paul C. Glick
1976 *Marriage and Divorce: A Social and Economic Study*, rev. ed. Cambridge, Mass.: Harvard University Press.

Castells, Manuel
1977 *The Urban Question*. London: Edward Arnold.
1978 *City, Class and Power*. London: Macmillan.

Cate, Rodney M., June M. Henton, James Koral, F. Scott Christopher and Sally Lloyd.
1982 "Premarital Abuse: A Social-Psychological Perspective." *Journal of Family Issues* 3 (March): 72–90.

Chatelaine
1986 10 Best Bodies in Canada. January: 60–67.

Cherlin, A., and P.B. Walters
1981 "Trends in United States Men's and Women's Sex-Role Attitudes: 1972 to 1978." *American Sociological Review* 46: 453–60.

Chodorow, Nancy
1978 *The Reproduction of Mothering*. Berkeley: University of California Press.

Clark, S.D.
1948 *Church and Sect in Canada*. Toronto: University of Toronto Press.
1976 *Canadian Society in Historical Perspective*. Toronto: McGraw-Hill Ryerson.

Clarke, Harold D., et al.
1980 *Political Choice in Canada*, abridged ed. Toronto: McGraw-Hill Ryerson.

Clarke, Juanne N.
1978 "The Unmarried Marrieds: The Meaning of the Relationship." In J. Ross Eshleman and Juanne N. Clarke, eds., *Intimacy, Commitments and Marriage: Development of Relationships*. Toronto: Allyn and Bacon, 149–53.

Clement, Wallace
1975 *The Canadian Corporate Elite: An Analysis of Economic Power*. Toronto: McClelland and Stewart.
1978a "Canada and Multinational Corporations." In D. Glenday, H. Guindon, and A. Turowetz, eds.,

Modernization and the Canadian State. Toronto: Macmillan.

1978b "A Political Economy of Regionalism in Canada." In D. Glenday, H. Guindon, and A. Turowetz, eds., *Modernization and the Canadian State.* Toronto: Macmillan.

1980 "The Subordination of Labour in Canadian Mining." *Labour/Le Travailleur* 5 (Spring): 133–48.

1981 *Hardrock Mining: Industrial Relations and Technological Change at Inco.* Toronto: McClelland and Stewart.

1986 *The Struggle to Organize: Resistance in Canada's Fishery.* Toronto: McClelland and Stewart.

Clement, Wallace, and Daniel Drache
1979 *A Practical Guide to Canadian Political Economy.* Toronto: Lorimer.

Clifford, Keith
1977 "His Dominion: A Vision in Crisis." In Peter Slater, ed., *Religion and Culture in Canada.* Canadian Corporation for Studies in Religion.

Cloward, R.A.
1959 "Illegitimate Means, Anomie, and Deviant Behavior." *American Sociological Review* 24: 164–76.

Codere, Helen
1950 *Fighting with Property.* Monographs of the American Ethnological Society, No. 18. New York: J.J. Augustin.

Cole, C.L.
1977 "Cohabitation in Social Context." In R. Libby and R. Whitehurst, eds., *Marriage and Alternatives.* Glenview, Ill.: Scott, Foresman. 62–79.

Coleman, James C.
1984 *Intimate Relationships, Marriage and the Family.* Indianapolis: Bobbs-Merrill Educational Publishing.

Coleman, James S.
1961 *The Adolescent Society.* New York: The Free Press.

Coleman, James S., et al.
1966 *Equality of Educational Opportunity.* Washington, D.C.: U.S. Government Printing Office.

Coleman, John A.
1970 "Civil Religion." *Sociological Analysis* 31: 67–77.

Collier, Jane, Michelle Z. Rosaldo, and Sylvia Yanagaisako

1982 "Is There a Family? New Anthropological Views." In Barrie Thorne with Marilyn Yalom, eds., *Rethinking the Family: Some Feminist Questions.* New York: Longman. 25–29.

Collins, Randall
1975 *Conflict Sociology.* New York: Academic Press.

Commission on Post-secondary Education in Ontario
1972 *The Learning Society.* Toronto: Ministry of Government Services of Ontario.

Conklin, J.E.
1986 *Criminology,* 2nd ed. New York: Macmillan.

Connelly, Patricia
1978 *Last Hired, First Fired: Women and the Canadian Work Force.* Intro. by Margaret Benston. Toronto: The Women's Press.

Cook, Ramsay
1969 *Provincial Autonomy, Minority Rights, and the Compact Theory.* Ottawa: Queen's Printer.

Cook, Ramsay, and Wendy Mitchinson, eds.
1976 *The Proper Sphere.* Toronto: Oxford University Press.

Cook, Ramsay, with John Saywell and John Ricker
1971 *Canada: A Modern Study.* Toronto: Clarke, Irwin.

Cooley, Charles Horton
[1922] 1964 *Human Nature and the Social Order.* New York: Schocken.

Coon, C.S.
1954 *The Story of Man.* New York: Alfred A. Knopf.

Corliss, Richard
1982 "Coming on Strong: The New Ideal of Beauty." *Time Magazine,* 30 August: 72–77.

Coser, Lewis F.
1975 "Presidential Address: Two Methods in Search of a Substance." *American Sociological Review* 40: 691–700.

Cott, Nancy
1977 *The Bonds of Womanhood.* New Haven: Yale University Press.

Craven, Paul
    1980 *"An Impartial Empire": Industrial Relations and the Canadian State 1900–1911*. Toronto: University of Toronto Press.

Craven, Paul, and Tom Traves
    1979 "The Class Politics of the National Policy, 1872–1933". *Journal of Canadian Studies* 14 (3): 14–38.

Crean, Susan M.
    1976 *Who's Afraid of Canadian Culture?* Don Mills, Ont.: General Publishing.

Creighton, Donald G.
    [1937] 1956 *The Empire of the St. Lawrence*. Toronto: Macmillan.

Crysdale, Stewart
    1965 *The Changing Church in Canada: Beliefs and Social Attitudes of United Church People*. Toronto: United Church of Canada.
    In press *Families Under Stress: Conflict Through Time in East Side, a Worker's Area*.

Crysdale, Stewart, and Les Wheatcroft, eds.
    1976 *Religion in Canadian Society*. Toronto: Macmillan.

cummings, e.e.
    1972 *Complete Poems, 1913–1962*. New York: Harcourt Brace Jovanovich.

Cuneo, Carl J.
    1978a "Class Exploitation in Canada." *Canadian Review of Sociology and Anthropology* 15: 284–300.
    1978b "A Class Perspective on Regionalism." In D. Glenday, H. Guindon, and A. Turowetz, eds., *Modernization and the Canadian State*. Toronto: Macmillan.
    1982 "The Politics of Surplus Labour in the Collapse of Canada's Dependence on Britain, 1840–49." *Studies in Political Economy* 7 (Winter): 61–88.

Dahl, Robert
    1976 *Democracy in the United States: Promise and Performance*, 3rd ed. Chicago: Rand McNally.

Dalton, Melville
    1959 *Men Who Manage: Fusions of Feeling and Theory in Administration*. New York: John Wiley and Sons.

Darroch, A.G.
    1979 "Another Look at Ethnicity, Stratification and Social Mobility in Canada." *Canadian Journal of Sociology* 4 (1): 1–25.

Davis, Fred
    1966 *The Nursing Profession: Five Sociological Essays*. New York: John Wiley and Sons.

Davis, Kingsley
    1972 *World Urbanization 1950–1970*. Berkeley: University of California Institute of International Studies.

Davis, Kingsley, and Wilbert E. Moore
    1945 "Some Principles of Stratification." *American Sociological Review* 10: 242–49.

Daymont, Thomas N.
    1980 "Racial Equity or Racial Equality." *Demography* 17: 379–93.

de Beauvoir, Simone
    [1949] 1974 *The Second Sex*. New York: Vintage Books.

De Fleur, Melvin L., and Sandra Ball-Rokeach
    1975 *Theories of Mass Communication*, 3rd ed. New York: David McKay.

de Tocqueville, Alexis
    [1835] 1945 *Democracy in America*, vol. II. Phillips Bradley, ed.; Henry Reeve, trans. New York: Vintage.

Deaton, Rick
    1972 "The Fiscal Crisis of the State and the Revolt of the Public Employee." *Our Generation* 8 (4): 11–51.

Deckard, Barbara Sinclair
    1979 *The Women's Movement*. New York: Harper and Row.

Delphy, Christine
    1984 *Close to Home*. Diana Leonard, ed. and trans. London: Hutchinson in association with The Explorations in Feminism Collective.

Denzin, Norman K.
    1979 "Children and Their Caretakers." In Peter I. Rose, ed., *Socialization and the Life Cycle*. New York: St. Martin's Press.

Deverell, John
    1975 *Falconbridge: Portrait of a Canadian Mining Multinational*. Toronto: Lorimer.

Dobbelaere, Karel
    1981 "Secularization: A Multi-Dimensional Concept." *Current Sociology* 29 (2): 1–216.

Doerr, Audrey
    1984 "Women's Rights in Canada:

Social and Economic Realities."
Atlantis 9 (2): 35–49.

Drache, Daniel
1979 "Rediscovering Canadian Political Economy." In Wallace Clement and Daniel Drache, *A Practical Guide to Canadian Political Economy*. Toronto: Lorimer.
1982 "Harold Innis and Canadian Capitalist Development." *Canadian Journal of Political and Social Theory* 6 (1–2): 35–60.

Drache, Daniel, ed.
1972 *Quebec—Only the Beginning: The Manifestoes of the Common Front*. Toronto: New Press.

Drache, Daniel, and Wallace Clement
1985 *The New Practical Guide to Canadian Political Economy*. Toronto: James Lorimer.

Dressler, D. and W. Willis, Jr.
1976 *Sociology: The Study of Human Interaction*. New York: Alfred A. Knopf.

Driedger, Leo
1980 "Nomos-building on the Prairies: Construction of Indian, Hutterite and Jewish Sacred Canopies." *Canadian Journal of Sociology* 5 (4): 341–56.

Dumas, Jean
1985 *Report on the Demographic Situation in Canada 1983*. Current Demographic Analysis Series. Statistics Canada. Cat. no. 91–209E. Ottawa: Minister of Supply and Services Canada.

Durkheim, Émile
[1893] 1933 *The Division of Labor in Society*. George Simpson, trans. New York: Free Press.
[1897] 1951 *Suicide: A Study in Sociology*. J.A. Spaulding and G. Simpson, trans; George Simpson, ed. New York: Free Press.
[1912] 1961 *The Elementary Forms of the Religious Life*. J.W. Swain, trans. New York: Collier Books.
[1893] 1964 *The Division of Labour in Society*. George Simpson, trans. New York: Macmillan.

Easterlin, Richard A.
1978 "What Will 1984 Be Like? Socioeconomic Implications of Recent Twists in Age Structure." *Demography* 15 (4): 397–432.

Economic Council of Canada
1967 *The Canadian Economy From the 1960's to the 1970's*. Fourth Annual Review. Ottawa: Information Canada.
1976 *People and Jobs*. Ottawa: Information Canada.

Eichler, Margrit
1975 "Sociological Research on Women in Canada." *Canadian Review of Sociology and Anthropology* 12 (4): 474–81.
1983 *Families in Canada Today: Recent Changes and Their Policy Consequences*. Toronto: Gage.
1984 "Sexism in Research and its Policy Implications." In Jill McCalla Vickers, *Taking Sex into Account*. Ottawa: Carleton University Press. 17–39.

Eisenstein, Zillah, ed.
1979 *Capitalist Patriarchy and the Case for Socialist Feminism*. New York: Monthly Review Press.

Elbing, Peter
1973 "God is Dead." *The Mitchell Trio: Alive*. California: Reprise Records, Warner Bros. Sound recording.

Elderidge, Hope T.
1942 "The Process of Urbanization." *Social Forces* 20 (March): 311–16.

Elkins, David, and Richard Simeon
1980 *Small Worlds: Provinces and Parties in Canadian Political Life*. Toronto: Methuen.

Emery, Fred, and Einar Thorsrud
1976 *Democracy at Work*. Leiden: Marinus Nijhoff.

Engels, Friedrich
[1884] 1902 *The Origin of the Family, Private Property and the State*. Chicago: Charles H. Kerr.

Eshleman, J. Ross
1985 *The Family: An Introduction*, 4th ed. Boston: Allyn and Bacon.

Falardeau, Jean-Charles
[1949] 1976 "The Seventeenth-Century Parish in French Canada." In Stewart Crysdale and Les Wheatcroft, eds., *Religion in Canadian Society*. Toronto: Macmillan.

Fallding, Harold
1974 *The Sociology of Religion*. Toronto: McGraw-Hill Ryerson.

Farb, Peter
1974 *Word Play: What Happens When*

People Talk. New York: Alfred A. Knopf.

Farrell, Michael P., and Stanley D. Rosenberg
1981 *Men at Midlife*. Boston: Auburn House.

Fee, Elizabeth
1983 "Women's Nature and Scientific Objectivity." In Marian Lowe and Ruth Hubbard, eds., *Woman's Nature: Rationalizations of Inequality*. New York: Pergamon Press. 9–27.

Fels, Lynn
1981 *Living Together: Unmarried Couples in Canada*. Toronto: Personal Library.

Felt, Lawrence F.
1986 *Take the "Bloods of Bitches" to the Gallows: Levels of Interpersonal Crime in Newfoundland Compared to the Canadian Mainland*. Policy Paper No. 5. St. John's: Institute for Social and Economic Research.

Feree, Myra M.
1984 "The View from Below: Women's Employment and Gender Equality in Working Class Families." In Beth B. Hess and Marvin B. Sussman, eds., "Women and the Family: Two Decades of Change." *Marriage and Family Review* 7: 3/4.

Feshbach, Seymour, and Robert Singer
1971 *Television and Aggression*. San Francisco: Jossey Bass.

Festinger, L., H.W. Riecken, and S. Schachter
1956 *When Prophecy Fails*. Minneapolis: University of Minnesota Press.

Firestone, Shulamith
1971 *The Dialectic of Sex*. New York: William Morrow.

Fischer, Claude S.
1975 "Towards a Subcultural Theory of Urbanism." *American Journal of Sociology* 80: 1319–41.

Flandrin, Jean-Louis
1975 "Contraception, Marriage, and Sexual Relations in the Christian West." In Robert Forster and Orest Ranum, eds., *Biology of Man in History*. Baltimore: Johns Hopkins University Press.

Fletcher, Susan, and Leroy O. Stone
1982 *The Living Arrangements of Canada's Older Women*. Statistics Canada.

Cat. no. 86–503. Ottawa: Minister of Supply and Services Canada.

Fogarty, Michael, Rhona Rapoport, and Robert Rapoport
1971 *Sex, Career and Family*. Beverly Hills, Calif.: Sage.

Ford, Clellan S., and F. Beach
1951 *Patterns of Sexual Behavior*. New York: Harper.

Foucault, Michel
1978 *The History of Sexuality*. New York: Pantheon Books.

Fournier, Pierre
1980 "The New Parameters of the Quebec Bourgeoisie." *Studies in Political Economy* 3 (Spring): 67–92.

Fox, Bonnie
1980 *Hidden in the Household: Women's Domestic Labour Under Capitalism*. Toronto: The Women's Press.

Fox, John, and Timothy F. Hartnagel
1979 "Changing Social Roles and Female Crime in Canada: A Time Series Analysis." *Canadian Review of Sociology and Anthropology* 16: 96–104.

Freedman, Jim
1983 "Will the Sheik Use His Blinding Fireball?" In Frank E. Manning, ed., *The Celebration of Society: Perspectives on Contemporary Cultural Performance*. London, Ontario: Congress of Social and Humanistic Societies, University of Western Ontario.

Freeman, Jo
1975 *The Politics of Women's Liberation*. Don Mills, Ont.: Longman.
1984 *Women: A Feminist Perspective*, 3rd ed. Palo Alto, Calif.: Mayfield Publishing.

Freeman, R.
1978 "The Effect of Trade Unionism on Fringe Benefits." Working Paper 292. National Bureau of Economic Research.

Friedan, Betty
1963 *The Feminine Mystique*. New York: Dell.

Friedenberg, Edgar
1983 "Culture in Canadian Context." In M. Rosenberg, W.B. Shaffir, A. Turowetz and M. Weinfeld, eds., *An Introduction to Sociology*, 1st ed. Toronto: Methuen.

Friedman, Milton
1962 *Capitalism and Freedom.* Chicago: University of Chicago Press.
Furstenberg, Frank F. Jr.
1966 "Industrialization and the American Family: A Look Backward." *American Sociological Review* (June): 326–37.
Gaffield, Chad.
1984 "Wage Labour, Industrialization and the Origins of the Modern Family." In Maureen Baker, ed., *The Family: Changing Trends in Canada.* Toronto: McGraw-Hill Ryerson, 21–34.
Galbraith, John Kenneth
1967 *The New Industrial State.* Boston: Houghton Mifflin.
1978 *The Affluent Society,* 3rd ed. New York: New American Library.
Gallup Poll
1981 June. Canadian Institute of Public Opinion.
1983 Monday, 2 May, and Monday, 15 October.
Gannagé, Charlene
1986 *Double Day, Double Bind: Women Garment Workers.* Toronto: Women's Press.
Gans, Herbert
1967 *The Levittowners.* New York: Pantheon.
Garson, Barbara
1975 *All The Livelong Day: The Meaning and Demeaning of Routine Work.* Garden City, N.Y.: Doubleday.
Gecas, Viktor
1981 "Contexts of Socialization." In M. Rosenberg and Ralph H. Turner, eds., *Social Psychology: Sociological Perspectives.* New York: Basic Books.
Geis, Frances, and Joseph Geis
1980 *Women in the Middle Ages.* New York: Barnes and Noble Books.
Gibbins, Roger
1980 *Prairie Politics and Society.* Toronto: Butterworth.
1982 *Regionalism: Territorial Politics in Canada and the United States.* Toronto: Butterworth.
1985 *Conflict and Unity.* Toronto: Methuen.
Gilbert, Sid, and Hugh A. McRoberts
1975 "Differentiation and Stratification: The Issue of Inequality." In Dennis Forcese and Stephen Richer,

eds., *Issues in Canadian Society.* Toronto: Prentice-Hall of Canada.
1977 "Academic Stratification and Education Plans: A Reassessment." *The Canadian Review of Sociology and Anthropology* 14 (1): 34–47.
Glaberman, Martin
1975 *The Working Class and Social Change: Four Essays on the Working Class.* Toronto: New Hogtown Press.
Glass, David V., et al.
1954 *Social Mobility in Britain.* London: Routledge and Kegan Paul.
Glazer, Nathan, and Daniel P. Moynihan
1970 *Beyond the Melting Pot.* Cambridge, Mass.: MIT Press.
1975 *Ethnicity: Theory and Experience.* Cambridge, Mass.: Harvard University Press.
Glazer-Malbin, Nona
1976 "Housework." *Signs: A Journal of Women in Culture and Society* 1 (4): 906–22.
Glazer, Nona, and Helen Youngelson Waehrer, eds.
1977 *Women in a Man-Made World,* 2nd ed. Chicago: Rand McNally.
Glick, Paul, and Graham Spanier
1981 "Cohabitation in the United States." In Peter J. Stein, ed., *Single Life: Unmarried Adults in Social Context.* New York: St. Martin's. 194–209.
Godfrey, David, and Mel Watkins
1970 *Gordon to Watkins to You.* Toronto: New Press.
Goffman, Erving
1959 *The Presentation of Self in Everyday Life.* Garden City, N.Y.: Doubleday.
1961a *Asylums.* Garden City, N.Y.: Doubleday.
1961b *Encounters.* Indianapolis: Bobbs-Merrill.
1962 *Stigma.* Englewood Cliffs, N.J.: Prentice-Hall.
1963 *Behavior in Public Places.* New York: Free Press.
Goldstein, Jay E.
1985 "The Prestige Dimension of Ethnic Stratification." In Rita Bienvenue and J.E. Goldstein, *Ethnicity and Ethnic Relations in Canada,* 2nd ed. Toronto: Butterworth.
Goldthorpe, J.H., and D. Lockwood
1969 *The Affluent Worker in the Class*

Structure. Cambridge: Cambridge University Press.

Goldthorpe, John H., et al.
1968 *The Affluent Worker: Industrial Attitudes and Behaviour*. Cambridge: Cambridge University Press.

Goode, William J.
1963 *Work, Revolution and Family Patterns*. Glencoe, Ill.: Free Press.

Gordon, Milton
1964 *Assimilation in American Life*. New York: Oxford University Press.

Gorz, André
1965 "Work and Consumption." In Perry Anderson and Robin Blackburn, eds., *Towards Socialism*. London: Fontana.

Gough, Kathleen
1986 "The Origin of the Family." In Arlene S. Skolnick and Jerome H. Skolnick, *The Family in Transition*, 5th ed. Boston: Little, Brown. 22–39.

Gouldner, Alvin W.
1954a *Patterns of Industrial Bureaucracy*. New York: The Free Press.
1954b *Wildcat Strike: A Study in Worker-Management Relationships*. New York: Harper and Row.

Goyder, John C.
1981 "Income Differences Between the Sexes: Findings from a National Canadian Survey." *Canadian Review of Sociology and Anthropology* 18 (3): 321–42.

Grabb, Edward G.
1980 "Differences in Sense of Control Among French- and English-Canadian Adolescents." *Canadian Review of Sociology and Anthropology* 17, 169–75.

Grant, George
1967 *Lament for a Nation: The Defeat of Canadian Nationalism*. Toronto: McClelland and Stewart.

Grant, John Webster
1977 "Religion and the Quest for a National Identity: The Background in Canadian History." In Peter Slater, ed., *Religion and Culture in Canada*. Canadian Corporation for Studies in Religion. 7–21.

Greeley, Andrew M.
1972a *Unsecular Man: The Persistence of Religion*. New York: Schocken.
1972b *The Denominational Society*.

Glenview, Ill.: Scott, Foresman.
1982 *Religion: A Secular Theory*. New York: Free Press.

Greer, Scott
1956 "Urbanism Reconsidered: A Comparative Study of Areas in a Metropolis." *American Sociological Review* 21: 19–25.

Grindstaff, Carl
1975 "The Baby Bust: Change in Fertility Patterns in Canada." *Canadian Studies in Population* 2: 15–22.
1985 "The Baby Bust Revisited: Canada's Continuing Pattern of Low Fertility." *Canadian Studies in Population* 12 (1): 103–10.

Guindon, Hubert
1968 "Two Cultures: An Essay on Nationalism, Class and Ethnic Tension." In R.H. Leach, ed., *Contemporary Canada*. Toronto: Macmillan.
1978 "The Modernization of Quebec and the Legitimacy of the Canadian State." In Daniel Glenday et al., eds., *Modernization and the Canadian State*. Toronto: Macmillan.

Guppy, L. Neil
1982 "On Intersubjectivity and Collective Conscience in Occupational Prestige Research." *Social Forces* 60: 1178–82.
1984 "Access to Higher Education in Canada." *The Canadian Journal of Higher Education* 14 (3): 79–93.

Haas, J., and William Shaffir
1974 *Decency and Deviance*. Toronto: McClelland and Stewart.
1978 *Shaping Identity in Canadian Society*. Toronto: Prentice-Hall Canada.

Hagan, J.
1984 *The Disreputable Pleasures*, 2nd ed. Toronto: McGraw-Hill Ryerson.

Hall, Edward
1966 *The Hidden Dimension*. Garden City, N.Y.: Doubleday.

Hall, Richard H.
1982 *Organizations—Structure and Process*, 3rd ed. Englewood Cliffs, N.J.: Prentice-Hall.

Hamblin, Dora J.
1973 *The First Cities*. New York: Time-Life Books.

Hamilton, Richard F., and James D. Wright

1986 *The State of the Masses*. Chicago: Aldine.

Hamilton, Roberta
1978 *The Liberation of Women*. London: George Allen and Unwin.

Hann, Russel G., et al., eds.
1973 *Primary Sources in the Canadian Working Class*. Kitchener, Ont.: Dumont Press.

Hardin, Herschel
1974 *A Nation Unaware: The Canadian Economic Culture*. Vancouver: J.J. Douglas.

Harlow, H.F., and R.R. Zimmerman
1959 "Affectional Responses in the Infant Monkey." *Science* 130: 421–23.

Harrington, Michael
1983 *The Politics at God's Funeral*. New York: Holt, Rinehart and Winston.

Harris, Chauncey D., and Edward L. Ullman
1945 "The Nature of Cities." *The Annals* 242 (Nov. 1945): 7–17.

Harris, Howell John
1982 *The Right to Manage: Industrial Relations Policies of American Business in the 1940s*. Madison: University of Wisconsin Press.

Hartmann, Heidi
1976 "Capitalism, Patriarchy, and Job Segregation." *Signs: Journal of Women in Culture and Society* 1 (3): 137–69.
1981 "The Family as the Locus of Gender, Class, and Political Struggles. The Example of Housework." *Signs: Journal of Women in Culture and Society* 6 (3): 366–94.

Hartsock, Nancy
1979 "Feminist Theory and the Development of Revolutionary Strategy." In Zillah R. Eisenstein, *Capitalist Patriarchy and the Case for Socialist Feminism*. New York: Monthly Review Press.

Hartz, Louis, et al.
1964 *The Founding of New Societies*. New York: Harcourt, Brace.

Harvey, David
1978 "The Urban Process Under Capitalism: A Framework for Analysis." *International Journal for Urban and Regional Research* 2: 101–31.

Hauser, Philip M., and Dudley Otis Duncan, eds.
1959 *The Study of Population: An Inventory and Appraisal*. Chicago: University of Chicago Press.

Hawkins, Elizabeth Bates
1978 "Effects of Empty Nest Transition on Self-report of Psychological and Physical Well-being." *Journal of Marriage and the Family* 40: 549–56.

Hebdige, Dick
1979 *Subculture: The Meaning of Style*. London: Methuen.

Hein, Hilde
1981 "Women and Science: Fitting Men to Think About Nature." *International Journal of Women's Studies* 4 (4): 369–77.

Henripin, Jacques
1972 *Trends and Factors of Fertility*. 1961 Census Monograph. Ottawa: Information Canada.

Henslin, James M.
1975 *Introducing Sociology: Toward Understanding Life in Society*. New York: Free Press.

Herskovits, M.J.
1960 *Economic Anthropology*. New York: Alfred A. Knopf.

Hirschi, T.
1969 *Causes of Delinquency*. Berkeley, Calif.: University of California Press.

Hoestetler, John
1974 *Hutterite Society*. Baltimore: Johns Hopkins University.

Holmstrom, Lynda Lytle
1973 *The Two-Career Family*. Cambridge, Mass.: Schenkman.

Horowitz, Gad
1968 *Canadian Labour in Politics*. Toronto: University of Toronto Press.

Hubbard, Ruth
1983 "Have Only Men Evolved?" In Sandra Harding and Merril B. Hintikka, eds., *Discovering Reality: Feminist Perspectives on Epistemology, Metaphysics, Methodology, and Philosophy of Science*. Dordrecht, Holland: D. Reidel Publishing Company. 45–69.

Hughes, David, and Evelyn Kallen
1974 *The Anatomy of Racism: Canadian Dimensions*. Montreal: Harvest House.

Hughes, Everett C.
1958 *Men and Their Work*. New York: Free Press.
[1945] 1963 *French Canada in Transition*. Chicago: University of Chicago Press.

Hughey, Michael
1983 *Civil Religion and Moral Order: Theoretical and Historical Dimensions.* Westport, Conn.: Greenwood Press.

Hum, Derek P.J.
1981 *Unemployment Insurance and Work Effort: Issues, Evidence, and Policy Directions.* Toronto: Ontario Economic Council.

Humphreys, L.
1970 *Tearoom Trade: Impersonal Sex in Public Places.* Chicago: Atherton.
1972 *Out of the Closets.* Englewood Cliffs, N.J.: Prentice-Hall.

Hunt, Janet G., and Larry L. Hunt
1982 "The Dualities of Careers and Families: New Integrations or New Polarizations?" *Social Problems* 29 (June): 499–510.

Hunter, Alfred A.
1976 "Class and Status in Canada." In G.N. Ramu and S. Johnson, eds., *Introduction to Canadian Society.* Toronto: Macmillan.
1986 *Class Tells: On Social Inequality in Canada*, 2nd ed. Toronto: Butterworths.

Ichniowski, C.
1980 "Economic Effects of the Fire-fighters' Union." *Industrial and Labour Relations Review* 33: 198–211.

Information Canada
1972 *Foreign-Direct Investment in Canada (The Gray Report).* Ottawa: Information Canada.

Innis, Harold
1936 "Settlement in the Mining Frontier." In W.A. Mackintosh and W.L.G. Joerg, eds., *Canadian Frontiers of Settlement.* Toronto: Macmillan.
[1930] 1956a *The Fur Trade in Canada: An Introduction to Canadian Economic History.* Toronto: University of Toronto Press.
[1930] 1956b *Essays in Canadian Economic History*, rev. ed. Toronto: University of Toronto Press.
1972 *Empire and Communication.* Toronto: University of Toronto Press.
[1940] 1978 *The Cod Fisheries: The History of an International Economy.* Toronto: University of Toronto Press.

International Labour Office
1984 *Yearbook of Labour Statistics.* Geneva: International Labour Organization.

Janeway, Elizabeth
1980 "Who is Sylvia: On the Loss of Sexual Paradigms." *Signs: Journal of Women in Culture and Society* 5 (4): 573–89.

Jencks, Christopher, et al.
1972 *Inequality.* New York: Basic Books Inc.

Johnson, Terrence
1972 *Professions and Power.* London: Macmillan.

Johnstone, John C.
1969 *Young People's Images of Canadian Society.* Studies of the Royal Commission of Bilingualism and Biculturalism. Ottawa: Information Canada.

Jourard, Sidney
1974 "Some Lethal Aspects of the Male Role." In Joseph Pleck and Jack Sawyer, *Men and Masculinity.* Englewood Cliffs, N.J.: Prentice-Hall.

Joy, Richard J.
1972 *Languages in Conflict.* Toronto: McClelland and Stewart.
1978 *Canada's Official Language Minorities.* Montreal: C.D. Howe Research Institute.

Kafka, Franz
1930 *The Castle.* Edwin and Willa Muir, trans. New York: Alfred A. Knopf.

Kahn, Robert L.
1972 "The Meaning of Work." In Angus Campbell and Phillip Converse, eds., *The Human Meaning of Social Change.* New York: Russel Sage Foundation.

Kalbach, Warren
1978 "Growth and Distribution of Canada's Ethnic Population." In Leo Driedger, ed., *The Canadian Ethnic Mosaic.* Toronto: McClelland and Stewart.

Kammeyer, Kenneth C.W.
1971 *An Introduction to Population.* Toronto: Chandler Publishing.

Kanter, Rosabeth Moss
1977 *Men and Women of the Corporation.* New York: Basic Books.

Karabel, Jerome, and A.H. Halsey
1977 *Power and Ideology in Education.*

New York: Oxford University Press.

Katz, Michael, and Ian E. Davey
1978 "Youth and Early Industrialization in a Canadian City." In John Demos and Sarane Spence Boocock, eds., *Turning Points: Historical and Sociological Essays on the Family.* Chicago: University of Chicago Press.

Kay, Herma Hill
1965 "The Outside Substitute for the Family." In Seymour M. Farber, Piero Mustacchi and Roger H.L. Wilson, eds., *Man and Civilization: The Family's Search for Survival.* New York: McGraw-Hill.

Kealey, Gregory S.
1980 *Toronto Workers Respond to Industrial Capitalism, 1867–1892.* Toronto: University of Toronto Press.
1981 "Labour and Working-Class History in Canada: Prospects in the 1980s." *Labour/Le Travailleur* 7 (Spring).

Keith, P.M., and R.B. Schafer
1980 "Role Strain and Depression in Two-Job Families." *Family Relations* 29: 483–88.

Kernaghan, Kenneth
1978 "Representative Bureaucracy: The Canadian Perspective." *Canadian Public Administration* 21: 489–511.

Kessler, Ronald C., and James A. McRae Jr.
1982 "The Effect of Wives' Employment on the Mental Health of Married Men and Women." *American Sociological Review* 47: 216–27.

Kierans, Eric
1973 Report on the Natural Resource Policy in Manitoba. Winnipeg: Queen's Printer.

Klapp, Orrin E.
1969 *A Collective Search for Identity.* New York: Holt, Rinehart and Winston.

Knight, Ralf
1975 *Work Camps and Company Towns in Canada and the U.S.: An Annotated Bibliography.* Vancouver: New Star Books.

Komarovsky, Mirra
1976 *Blue-Collar Marriage.* New York: Vintage Books.

Korman, Sheila K.
1983 "Nontraditional Dating Behavior: Date-initiation and Date

Expense-sharing Among Feminists and Nonfeminists." *Family Relations* 32: 575–81.

Kornhauser, Arthur
1965 *Mental Health of the Industrial Worker.* New York: Wiley.

Kumar, Pradip
1972 "Differentials in Wage Rates of Unskilled Labor in Canadian Manufacturing Industries." *Industrial and Labor Relations Review* 26: 631–45.

Lakoff, Robin
1975 *Language and Woman's Place.* New York: Harper and Row.

Lakoff, R.T., and R.L. Scherr
1984 *Face Value: The Politics of Beauty.* London: Routledge and Kegan Paul.

Lamb, Matthew
1980 "The Challenge of Critical Theory." In Gregory Baum, ed., *Sociology and Human Destiny.* New York: Seabury Press. 183–213.

Lambert, Ronald D., and James E. Curtis
1979 "Education, Economic Dissatisfaction and Nonconfidence in Canadian Social Institutions." *Canadian Review of Sociology and Anthropology* 16: 47–59

Landsberg, Michelle
1985 *Guide to Children's Books.* Markham, Ont.: Penguin Books.

Lane, Christel
1981 *The Rites of Rulers: Ritual in Industrial Society—The Soviet Case.* Cambridge: Cambridge University Press.

Langton, Anne
1964 *A Gentlewoman in Upper Canada: The Journals of Anne Langton.* H.H. Langton, ed. Toronto: Clarke, Irwin.

LaPiere, R.T.
1954 *A Theory of Social Control.* New York: McGraw-Hill.

Lasch, Christopher
1977 *Haven in a Heartless World.* New York: Basic Books.

Laslett, Peter
1970 "The Comparative History of Household and Family." *Journal of Social History* 4: 75–87.

Laxer, James, and Robert Laxer
1977 *The Liberal Idea of Canada.* Toronto: Lorimer.

Lazarsfeld, Paul F., Bernard Berelson, and Hazel Gauder

1948 *The People's Choice*. New York: Columbia University Press.

Leacock, Eleanor
1983 "Ideologies of Male Dominance as Divide and Rule Politics: An Anthropologist's View." In Marion Lowe and Ruth Hubbard, eds., *Woman's Nature*. New York: Pergamon Press. 111–21.

Lebowitz, Michael
1982 "The General and the Specific of Marx's Theory of Crisis." *Studies in Political Economy* 7 (Winter): 5–26.

Lefebvre, Henri
1972 *La pensée marxiste et la ville*. Paris: Casterman.

Leffler, Ann, Dair L. Gillespie, and Elinar Lerner Ratner
1973 "Academic Feminists and the Women's Movement." *Insurgent Sociologist* IV: 44–55.

Lemert, E.M.
1951 *Social Pathology*. New York: McGraw-Hill.
1982 "Issues in the Study of Deviance." In M.M. Rosenberg, R.A. Stebbins, and A. Turowetz, eds., *The Sociology of Deviance*. New York: St. Martin's Press.

Lengermann, Patricia Madoo, and Ruth A. Wallace
1985 *Gender in America: Social Control and Social Change*. Englewood Cliffs, N.J.: Prentice-Hall.

Lenski, Gerhard E.
1966 *Power and Privilege: A Theory of Social Stratification*. New York: McGraw-Hill.

Lévesque, René
1968 *An Option for Quebec*. Toronto: McClelland and Stewart.

Levitt, Kari
1970 *Silent Surrender: The Multinational Corporation in Canada*. Toronto: Macmillan.

Lipset, Seymour Martin
1960 *Political Man: The Social Bases of Politics*. Garden City, N.Y.: Doubleday.
1965 "Canada and the United States: A Comparative View." *Canadian Review of Sociology and Anthropology* 1 (4).

Livingston, J.
1974 *Compulsive Gamblers*. New York: Harper and Row.

Lloyd, Peter C.
1967 *Africa in Social Change*. Baltimore: Penguin.

Lopata, Helen Z.
1971 *Occupation Housewife*. New York: Oxford University Press.

Lorimer, James
1978 *The Developers*. Toronto: Lorimer.

Lovell, John
1964 "The Professional Socialization of the West Point Cadet." In Morris Janowitz, ed., *The New Military*. New York: Russel Sage Foundation.

Lucas, Rex
1971 *Minetown, Milltown, Railtown*. Toronto: University of Toronto Press.

Luckman, Thomas
1967 *The Invisible Religion*. New York: Macmillan.

Lumsden, Ian, ed.
1970 *Close the 49th Parallel, Etc.: The Americanization of Canada*. Toronto: University of Toronto Press.

Lundberg, Ferdinand, and Marynia F. Farnham
1947 *Modern Woman: The Lost Sex*. New York: Harper & Brothers.

Lupri, Eugen, and James Frieders
1981 "The Quality of Marriage and the Passage of Time." *Canadian Journal of Sociology* 6 (3): 283–305.

Luxton, Meg
1980 *More Than a Labour of Love. Three Generations of Women's Work in the Home*. Toronto: The Women's Press.
1981 "Taking on the Double Day." *Atlantis* 7 (2): 12–22.
1984 "Conceptualizing 'Women' in Anthropology and Sociology." In Ursula M. Franklin, *Knowledge Reconsidered: A Feminist Overview*. Ottawa: Canadian Research Institute for the Advancement of Women.

Luxton, Meg, and Harriet Rosenberg
1986 *Through the Kitchen Window: The Politics of Home and Family*. Toronto: Garamond Press.

MacDonald, G., and J. Evans
1981 "The Size and Structure of Union-nonunion Wage Differentials in Canadian Industry." *Canadian Journal of Economics* 14: 216–31.

Mackie, Marlene
1983 *Exploring Gender Relations: A Canadian Perspective*. Toronto: Butterworth.

MacKinnon, Neil J., and Paul Anisef
1979 "Self Assessment in the Early Educational Attainment Process." *The Canadian Review of Sociology and Anthropology* 16 (3): 305–19.

Macklin, Eleanor
1980 "Nontraditional Family Forms: A Decade of Research." *Journal of Marriage and the Family* 42 (4): 905–22.
1983 "Nonmarital Heterosexual Cohabitation: An Overview." In Eleanor Macklin and R. Rubin, eds., *Contemporary Families and Alternative Lifestyles*. Beverly Hills: Sage.

MacLeod, Linda
1980 *Wife Battering in Canada: The Vicious Circle*. Prepared for the Canadian Advisory Council on the Status of Women. Ottawa: Minister of Supply and Services Canada.

Macpherson, C.B.
1962 *The Political Theory of Possessive Individualism: Hobbes to Locke*. London: Oxford University Press.
[1955] 1968 *Democracy in Alberta: Social Credit and the Party System*, 2nd ed. Toronto: University of Toronto Press.
1977 *The Life and Times of Liberal Democracy*. London: Oxford University Press.
1978 *Property: Mainstream and Critical Positions*. Toronto: University of Toronto Press.
1985 *The Rise and Fall of Economic Justice and Other Essays*. Oxford University Press.

Makepeace, James M.
1983 "Life Events, Stress and Courtship Violence." *Family Relations* 32: 101–09.

Maki, D., and S. Christensen
1980 "The Union Wage Effect Reexamined." *Relations Industrielles/Industrial Relations* 35: 210–29.

Malinowski, Bronislaw
1913 *The Family Among the Australian Aborigines*. London: University of London Press.
1944 *A Scientific Theory of Culture*.
Chapel Hill: University of North Carolina Press.

Malmo, Cheryl
1984 "Sexism in Psychological Research." In Jill McCalla Vickers, ed., *Taking Sex into Account*. Ottawa: Carleton University Press. 116–32.

Mandell, Nancy
In press "Marital Roles in Transition." In K. Ishwaran, ed., *The Modern Family: A Cross-Cultural Introduction*. Toronto: Oxford.

Mandell, Nancy, and Rose Hutchens
1986 "Juggling the Load: Women and Work." Paper presented at the Society for the Study of Social Problems, August, 1986, New York.

Manis, Jerome, and Bernard Meltzer
1967 *Symbolic Interaction: A Reader in Social Psychology*. Boston: Allyn and Bacon.

Mann, W.E.
1955 *Sect, Cult and Church in Alberta*. Toronto: University of Toronto Press.

Marchak, Patricia
1972 "Labour in a Staples Economy." *Studies in Political Economy* 2 (Autumn): 7–36.
1983 *Green Gold: The Forest Industry in British Columbia*. Vancouver: University of British Columbia Press.

Martin, David
1978 *A General Theory of Secularization*. Oxford: Basil Blackwell.

Marx, Karl
1956 *Selected Writings in Sociology and Social Philosophy*. T.B. Bottomore, trans. London: C.A. Watts.
[1879] 1964 *Precapitalist Economic Formations*. New York: International Publishers.
[1884] 1969 "Religion, Illusion and the Task of History." In Norman Birnbaum and Gertrud Lenzer, eds., *Sociology and Religion: A Book of Readings*. Englewood Cliffs, N.J.: Prentice-Hall; originally "Contribution to the Critique of Hegel's Philosophy of Right."

Marx, Karl, and Friedrich Engels
[1848] 1969 *The Communist Manifesto*. New York: Regnery.

Maslow, Abraham
1970 *Motivation and Personality*, 2nd ed. New York: Harper and Row.

Mathias, Phillip
1971 *Forced Growth: Five Studies of Government Involvement in the Development of Canada*. Toronto: James, Lewis and Samuel.

Matras, Judah
1977 *Introduction to Population: A Sociological Approach*. Englewood Cliffs, N.J.: Prentice-Hall.

Matthews, Ralph
1978 "Economic Viability vs. Social Vitality in Regional Development." In D. Glenday, H. Guindon, and A. Turowetz, eds., *Modernization and the Canadian State*. Toronto: Macmillan.
1983 *The Creation of Regional Dependency*. Toronto: University of Toronto Press.

McCallum, John
1980 *Unequal Beginnings: Agriculture and Economic Development in Quebec and Ontario Until 1870*. Toronto: University of Toronto Press.

McGahan, Peter
1982 *Urban Sociology in Canada*. Toronto: Butterworths.

McHugh, Peter
1968 *Defining the Situation: The Organization of Meaning in Social Interaction*. New York: Bobbs-Merrill.

McLuhan, Herbert Marshall
1964 *Understanding Media: The Extensions of Man*. New York: McGraw Hill.

McNally, David
1981 "Staple Theory as Commodity Fetishism: Marx, Innis and Canadian Political Economy." *Studies in Political Economy* 6 (Autumn): 56–57.

McNamara, JoAnn, and Suzanne F. Wemple
1977 "Sanctity and Power: The Dual Pursuit of Medieval Women." In Renate Bridenthal and Claudia Koonz, *Becoming Visible! Women in European History*. Boston: Houghton Mifflin. 92–118.

McRoberts, Kenneth, and Dale Postgate
1976 *Quebec: Social Change and Political Crisis*. Toronto: McClelland and Stewart.

McVey, Wayne W. Jr., and Barrie W. Robinson
1981 "Separation in Canada: New Insights Concerning Marital Dissolution." *Canadian Journal of Sociology* 6 (3): 353–66.

Mead, George Herbert
1938 *The Philosophy of the Act*. Charles Morris, ed. Chicago: University of Chicago Press.

Mead, Margaret
1949 *Male and Female*. New York: Dell.

Meekison, Peter J., ed.
1968 *Canadian Federalism: Myth or Reality*. Toronto: Methuen.

Meier, R.F.
1982 "Perspectives on the Concept of Social Control." In R.H. Turner and J.F. Short, Jr., eds., *Annual Review of Sociology* vol. 8. Palo Alto, Calif.: Annual Reviews.

Meissner, Martin
1976 "Women and Inequality: At Work—At Home." *Our Generation* 11 (2): 59–71.

Meissner, Martin, et al.
1974 "No Exit for Wives: Sexual Division of Labour and the Culmination of Household Demands." *Canadian Review of Sociology and Anthropology* 12 (4): 424–39.

Meltz, Noah M.
1982 *Economic Analysis of Labour Shortages: The Case of Tool and Die Makers in Ontario*. Toronto: Ontario Economic Council.

Merton, Robert K.
1949 "Bureaucratic Structure and Personality." In Robert K. Merton, *Social Theory and Social Structure*. Glencoe, Ill.: Free Press.
1957 *Social Theory and Social Structure*, rev. ed., Glencoe, Ill.: Free Press.
1968 *Social Theory and Social Structure*, rev. and enlarged ed. New York: Free Press.

Michelson, William
1977 *Environmental Choice, Human Behaviour and Residential Satisfaction*. Toronto: Oxford.

Michels, Robert
1959 *Political Parties*. New York: Dover.

Milgram, Stanley
1963 "Behavioral Study of Obedience." *Journal of Abnormal and Social Psychology* 67: 371–78.

Miller, S.M.
1972 "The Making of a Confused, Middle-aged Husband." In Constantina Safilios-Rothschild, *Toward a Sociology of Women*. Lexington, Mass.: Xerox College Publishing.

Miller, S.M., ed.
1963 *Max Weber: Selections From His Work*. New York: Crowell.

Millet, David
1969 "A Typology of Religious Organizations Suggested by the Canadian Census." *Sociological Analysis* 30: 108–19.

Mills, C. Wright
1956 *The Power Elite*. Oxford: Oxford University Press.
1959 *The Sociological Imagination*. New York: Oxford University Press.

Milner, Henry
1973 *Politics in the New Quebec*. Toronto: McClelland and Stewart.

Milner, Sheilagh, and Henry Milner
1973 *The Decolonization of Quebec*. Toronto: McClelland and Stewart.

Mol, Hans
1976 *Identity and the Sacred: A Sketch for a New Social-Scientific Theory of Religion*. Oxford: Basil Blackwell.
1985 *Faith and Fragility: Religion and Identity in Canada*. Burlington, Ont.: Trinity Press.

Money, John, and Anke Ehrhardt
1974 *Man and Woman/Boy and Girl*. New York: Signet.

Montagu, Ashley
1960 *Introduction to Physical Anthropology*, 3rd ed. London: Thomas.

Morley, Terry
1979 "Canada and the Romantic Left." *Queen's Quarterly* 86.

Morris, Desmond
1965 *The Mammals: A Guide to the Living Species*. London: Hodder and Stoughton.
1983 *The Book of Apes*. New York: Viking Press.

Multiculturalism Canada
1986 *Socio-Economic Profiles of Selected Ethnic/Visible Minority Groups*. Ottawa.

Murphy, Raymond
1979 *Sociological Theories of Education*. Toronto: McGraw-Hill Ryerson.

Naegele, Kaspar D.
1961 "Some Observations on the Scope of Sociological Analysis." In Talcott Parsons et al., eds., *Theories of Society*, vol. I. New York: Free Press.

Nagel, Ernest
1961 *The Structure of Science*. New York: Harcourt, Brace and World.

National Council of Welfare
1982 *Poverty in Canada: 1980 Preliminary Statistics*. Ottawa: Minister of Supply and Services Canada.
1985 *Poverty Lines*. Ottawa: Minister of Supply and Services Canada.

Naylor, R.T.
1975 *The History of Canadian Business 1867–1914*, 2 vols. Toronto: Lorimer.

Nelles, H.V.
1972 "Empire Ontario: The Problems of Resource Development." In Donald Swainson, ed., *Oliver Mowat's Ontario*. Toronto: Macmillan.
1974 *The Politics of Development: Forests, Mines and Hydro-Electric Power in Ontario, 1849–1941*. Toronto: Macmillan.

Nett, Emily M.
1979 "Marriage and the Family: Organization and Interaction." In G.N. Ramu, ed., *Courtship, Marriage and the Family in Canada*. Toronto: Macmillan of Canada: 4–17.
1983 "The Family." In Robert Hagedorn, ed., *Sociology*, 2nd ed. Toronto: Holt, Rinehart and Winston.
1984 "The Family and Aging." In Maureen Baker, ed., *The Family: Changing Trends in Canada*. Toronto: McGraw-Hill Ryerson. 129–61.

Niebuhr, H. Richard
1929 *The Social Sources of Denominationalism*. New York: Henry Holt and Company.

Niosi, Jorge
1979 "The New French-Canadian Bourgeoisie." *Studies in Political Economy* 2 (Autumn): 129–58.

Nunnally, J.C.
1961 *Popular Conceptions of Mental Health*. New York: Holt, Rinehart and Winston.

Oakeshott, Robert
1978 *The Case for Co-workers' Co-ops*. London: Routledge and Kegan Paul.

Oakley, Ann
1974 *The Sociology of Housework*. New York: Pantheon Books.

O'Brien, Mary
1979 "The Politics of Reproduction." *Resources for Feminist Research* Spring 1979: 27–32.
1981 "Feminist Thought and Dialectical Logic." *Signs: Journal of Women in Culture and Society* 7 (1): 144–57.

Ogburn, William F.
1933 "The Family and Its Functions." In Wm. F. Ogburn, ed., *Recent Social Trends.* New York: McGraw-Hill.

Ogmundson, Richard
1982 "Good News and Canadian Sociology." *Canadian Journal of Sociology* 7: 73–78.

Ollman, Bertell
1971 *Alienation.* Cambridge: Cambridge University Press.

Olsen, Dennis
1980 *The State Elite.* Toronto: McClelland and Stewart.

Olson, Mancur
1965 *The Logic of Collective Action: Public Goods and the Theory of Groups.* Cambridge, Mass.: Harvard University Press.

O'Reilly, K.
1986 "The Joys of Commuting from the Middle of Nowhere." Toronto *Globe and Mail,* 2 May, A13.

Ornstein, Michael, et al.
1980 "Region, Class and Political Culture in Canada." *Canadian Journal of Political Science* 13, 227.
1981 "The Occupational Mobility of Men in Ontario." *Canadian Review of Sociology and Anthropology* 18 (2): 183–215.

Osgood, Charles E., W.H. May, and M.S. Miron
1975 *Cross-Cultural Universals of Affective Meaning.* Urbana: University of Illinois Press.

Oster, Gerry
1979 "A Factor Analytic Test of the Theory of the Dual Economy." *Review of Economics and Statistics* 61: 33–9.

Ostry, Sylvia
1967 *The Occupational Composition of the Canadian Labour Force.* Ottawa: Statistics Canada.
1984 "Competition Policy and the Self-Regulating Professions." In Audrey Wipper, ed., *The Sociology of Work.* Ottawa: Carleton University Press.

O'Toole, Roger
1977 *The Precipitous Path: Studies in Political Sects.* Toronto: Peter Martin.

Pahl, Raymond
1970 *Patterns of Urban Life.* London: Longman.
1975 *Whose City,* 2nd ed. Harmondsworth: Penguin.

Palmer, Bryan D.
1979a *A Culture of Conflict: Skilled Workers and Industrial Capitalism in Hamilton, Ontario, 1860–1914.* Montreal: McGill University Press.
1979b "Working-Class Canada: Recent Historical Writing." *Queen's Quarterly* 86.
1983 *Working-class Experience: The Rise and Reconstitution of Canadian Labour, 1800–1980.* Toronto: Butterworth.

Pammett, Jon
1981 *Public Evaluations of the Canadian Federal System.* Mimeo.

Papanek, Hanna
1979 "Family Status Production: The 'Work' and 'Non-work' of Women." *Signs: Journal of Women in Culture and Society* 4 (4): 775–81.

Pareto, Vilfredo
1935 *The Mind and Society.* London: Jonathon Cape.

Park, Robert
1950 *Race and Culture.* Glencoe, Ill.: Free Press.

Parkin, Frank
1979 *Marxism and Class Theory.* New York: Columbia University Press.

Parsons, Talcott
1940 "An Analytical Approach to the Theory of Social Stratification." *American Journal of Sociology* 45: 841–62.
1951 *The Social System.* Glencoe, Ill.: Free Press.
1953 "A Revised Analytical Approach to the Theory of Social Stratification." In Reinhard Bendix and Seymour, eds., *Class, Status and Power.* Glencoe, Ill.: Free Press.
1960 "A Sociological Approach to the Theory of Organizations." In Talcott Parsons, *Structure and Process in Modern Societies.* Glencoe, Ill.: Free Press.
1970 "Equality and Inequity in Modern Society, or Social Stratification Revisited." In Edward O. Laumann,

ed., *Social Stratification: Research and Theory for the 1970s.* New York: Bobbs-Merrill.
1971 *The System of Modern Societies.* Englewood Cliffs, N.J.: Prentice-Hall.
1977 *The Evolution of Societies.* Englewood Cliffs, N.J.: Prentice-Hall.

Patterson, T.T.
1955 *Morale and Work: An Experiment in the Management of Men.* New York: Clarke, Irwin.

Pentland, H. Clare
1959 "The Development of a Capitalistic Labour Market in Canada." *Canadian Journal of Economics and Political Science* 25 (4).
1968 *A Study of the Changing Social, Economic and Political Background of the Canadian System of Industrial Relations.* Ottawa: Task Force on Labour Relations.
[1961] 1981 *Labour and Capital in Canada, 1650–1860.* Paul Phillips, ed. Toronto: Lorimer.

Perrow, Charles
1979 *Complex Organizations*, 2nd ed. Glenview, Ill.: Scott, Foresman.

Person, Ethel Spector
1980 "Sexuality as the Mainstay of Identity: Psychoanalytic Existence." *Signs: Journal of Women and Culture in Society* 5 (4).

Peters, John F.
1983 "The Single Female." In K. Ishwaran, ed., *Marriage and Divorce in Canada.* Toronto: Methuen.

Petersen, William
1968 "The Ideological Background to Canada's Immigrations." In Blishen et al., eds., *Canadian Society.* Toronto: Macmillan.

Phillips, Paul
1978 *Regional Disparities.* Toronto: Lorimer.

Piaget, Jean
[1932] 1965 *The Moral Judgment of the Child.* New York: Free Press.

Pike, Robert
1978 "Equality of Educational Opportunity: Dilemmas and Policy Options." *Interchange* 9 (2): 30–39.
1980 "Education, Class and Power in Canada." In Richard J. Ossenberg, ed., *Power and Change in Canada.* Toronto: McClelland and Stewart.

Pineo, Peter
1977 "The Social Standing of Ethnic and Racial Groupings." *Canadian Review of Sociology and Anthropology* 14: 147–57.

Pineo, Peter C., and John Porter
1967 "Occupational Prestige in Canada." *Canadian Review of Sociology and Anthropology* 4: 24–40.
1985a "Revisions of the Pineo-Porter-McRoberts Socioeconomic Classification of Occupations for the 1981 Census." Research Report No. 125, Program for Quantitative Studies in Economics and Population, McMaster University.
1985b "Ethnic Origin and Occupational Achievement." In M. Boyd, et al., *Ascription and Achievement: Studies in Mobility and Status Attainment in Canada.* Ottawa: Carleton University Press.

Pineo, Peter C., John Porter, and Hugh A. McRoberts
1977 "The 1971 Census and the Socioeconomic Classification of Occupations." *Canadian Review of Sociology and Anthropology* 14, 91–102.

Pleck, Joseph
1979 "Men's Family Work: Three Perspectives and Some New Data." *Family Coordinator* 28: 481–88.

Pollack, J.
1981 *Connecticut Mutual Life Insurance Report on American Values in the 80s.* New York: Research and Forecasts Inc.

Poloma, Margaret M., and T. Neal Garland
1971 "The Married Professional Woman: A Study in the Tolerance of Domestication." *Journal of Marriage and the Family* 33 (3): 531–40.

Population Reference Bureau
1972 *The World Population Dilemma.* Washington, D.C.: Population Reference Bureau.
1985 *1985 Population Data Sheet.* Washington, D.C.: Population Reference Bureau.

Porter, J.
1970 "Canadian Universities: Democratization and the Need for a National System." *Minerva* 8 (3): 325–56.

Porter, John
1965 *The Vertical Mosaic: An Analysis of Social Class and Power in Canada.* Toronto: University of Toronto Press.
1975 "Ethnic Pluralism in Canadian Perspective." Nathan Glazer and Daniel P. Moynihan, eds., *Ethnicity: Theory and Experience.* Cambridge, Mass.: Harvard University Press.
1979 *The Measure of Canadian Society: Education, Equality, and Opportunity.* Toronto: Gage.

Porter, John, Marion Porter, and Bernard R. Blishen
1973 *Does Money Matter?* Toronto: Institute for Behavioural Research, York University.
1982 *Stations and Callings: Making It Through the School System.* Toronto: Methuen.

Porter, Marion
1981 "John Porter and Education: Technical Functionalist or Conflict Theorist?" *Canadian Review of Sociology and Anthropology* 18: 627–38.

Posner, Judith
1985 "Closing the Muscle Gap: Pumping Iron II: The Women." *Canadian Woman Studies* 6 (3).

Power, Eileen
1975 *Medieval Women.* M.M. Postan, ed. London: Cambridge University Press.

Pratt, Larry
1976 *The Tar Sands: Syncrude and the Politics of Oil.* Edmonton: Hurtig.

Pratt, Larry, and Garth Stevenson, eds.
1981 *Western Separatism: The Myths, Realities and Dangers.* Edmonton: Hurtig.

Prentice, Allison
1977 *The School Promoters: Education and Social Class in Mid-nineteenth Century Upper Canada.* Toronto: McClelland and Stewart.

Presthus, Robert
1978 *The Organizational Society,* rev. ed. New York: St. Martin's Press.

Preston, James J.
1982 *Mother Worship: Theme and Variations.* Chapel Hill, N.C.: University of North Carolina Press.

Proulx, Monique
1978 *Five Million Women: A Study of the Canadian Housewife.* Ottawa: Advisory Council on the Status of Women.

Quinney, R.
1970 *The Social Reality of Crime.* Boston: Little, Brown.

Radcliffe-Brown, A.R.
[1952] 1956 *Structure and Function of Primitive Society.* Glencoe, Ill.: Free Press.

Rapoport, Rhona, and Robert N. Rapoport
1971 *Dual-Career Families.* Harmondsworth: Penguin.

Raynauld, A., G. Marion, and R. Beland
1967 "La Répartition des Revenus Selon les Groupes Ethniques au Canada." A Study for the Royal Commission on Bilingualism and Biculturalism. Ottawa: Queen's Printer.

Reiss, A.J., Jr.
1951 "Delinquency as a Failure of Personal and Social Controls." *American Sociological Review* 16: 196–206.

Reitz, Jeffrey G.
1974 "Language and Ethnic Community Survival." *Canadian Review of Sociology and Anthropology*: 104–22.

Resnick, Philip
1977 *The Land of Cain: Class and Nationalism in English Canada.* Vancouver: New Star Books.

Rice, David G.
1979 *Dual-Career Marriage: Conflict and Management.* New York: Free Press.

Rich, Adrienne
1980 "Compulsory Heterosexuality and Lesbian Existence." *Signs: Journal of Women and Culture in Society* 5 (21).

Richards, John
n.d. "The Democratic Potential of Federalism" in William Westfall, ed., *Perspectives on Regions and Regionalism in Canada,* Proceedings of the Annual Conference of the Association for Canadian Studies, June 1982.

Richards, John, and Larry Pratt
1979 *Prairie Capitalism: Power in the New West.* Toronto: McClelland and Stewart.

Richer, S.
1982 "Equality to Benefit from Schooling: The Issue of Educational Opportunity." In Dennis Forcese and Stephen Richer, eds., *Social Issues:*

Sociological Views of Canada. Scarborough, Ont.: Prentice-Hall.

Richler, Mordecai
1964 *The Apprenticeship of Duddy Kravitz*. New York: Paperback Library.

Riesman, David
1950 *The Lonely Crowd*. New York: Basic Books.

Rinehart, James W.
1975 *The Tyranny of Work*. Don Mills, Ont.: Longman Canada.
1978 "Contradictions of Work-Related Attitudes and Behaviour: An Interpretation." *Canadian Review of Sociology and Anthropology* 15: 1–15.

Rioux, Marcel
1978 *Quebec in Question*, 2nd ed. Toronto: Lorimer.

Roberts, Keith A.
1984 *Religion in Sociological Perspective*. Homewood, Ill.: Dorsey Press.

Roberts, Wayne
1978 *The Hamilton Working Class 1820–1977, A Bibliography*. Hamilton, Ont.: Labour Studies Program, McMaster University.

Robinson, Lillian
1978 *Sex, Class and Culture*. Bloomington, Ind.: Indiana University Press.

Roethlisberger, Felix J., and W.J. Dickson
1939 *Management and the Worker*. Cambridge, Mass.: Harvard University Press.

Rogoff, Natalie
1953 *Recent Trends in Occupational Mobility*. Glencoe, Ill.: Free Press.

Rosaldo, Michelle Zimbalist, and Louise Lamphere, eds.
1974 *Women, Culture and Society*. Stanford, Calif.: Stanford University Press.

Rosenberg, Stuart G.
1970 *The Jewish Community in Canada*. Toronto: McClelland and Stewart.

Rosenhan, D.L.
1973 "On Being Sane in Insane Places." *Science* 179: 250–58.

Rosenthal, Robert, and Lenore Jacobsen
1968 *Pygmalion in the Classroom: Teacher Expectation and Pupil's Intellectual Development*. New York: Holt, Rinehart and Winston.

Rosow, I.
1974 *Socialization to Old Age*. Berkeley: University of California Press.

Ross, James B., and Mary M. McLaughlin, eds.
1949 *The Portable Medieval Reader*. New York: Viking.

Rothman, Sheila
1978 *Woman's Proper Place: A History of Changing Ideals and Practices, 1870 to the Present*. New York: Basic Books.

Rowbotham, Sheila M.
1973 *Hidden from History*. London: Pluto Press.

Roy, Donald F.
1967 "Quota Restriction and Goldbricking in a Machine Shop." In W.A. Faunce, ed., *Readings in Industrial Sociology*. New York: Appleton-Century-Crofts.

The Royal Bank Reporter
1986 (spring).

Rubin, Gayle
1975 "The Traffic in Women." In Rayna Rapp Reiter, ed., *Toward an Anthropology of Women*. New York: Monthly Review Press. 157–210.

Ryerson, Stanley B.
1960 *The Founding of Canada: Beginnings to 1815*. Toronto: Progress Books.
1968 *Unequal Union: Confederation and the Roots of Conflict in the Canadas*. Toronto: Progress Books.
1972 "Quebec: The Concept of Class and Nation." In Gary Teeple, ed., *Capitalism and the National Question in Canada*. Toronto: University of Toronto Press.

Sacouman, R. James
1979 "The Differing Origins, Organization and Impact of Maritime Prairie Cooperative Movements in 1940." In Robert Brym and James Sacouman, eds., *Underdevelopment and Social Movements in Atlantic Canada*. Toronto: Hogtown Press.
1981 "The 'Peripheral' Maritimes and Canada-Wide Marxist Political Economy." *Studies in Political Economy* 6 (Autumn): 135–50.

Sadker, M.P., and D.M. Sadker
1982 *Sex Equity Handbook for Schools*. New York: Longman.

Samuelson, Paul
1976 *Economics*, 10th ed. New York: McGraw-Hill.

Sapir, Edward
[1929] 1962 "The Status of Linguistics as a Science." In D. Krech, R. Crutchfield and E. Ballachey, eds. "Selections from Language and Communication," in *Individual and Society*. New York: McGraw Hill, 273–307.

Sattel, Jack
1982 "The Impressive Male: Tragedy or Sexual Politics?" In Rachel Kahn-Hut, Arlene Kaplan Daniels and Richard Colvard, eds., *Women and Work: Problems and Perspectives*, New York: Oxford University Press.

Saunders, Peter
1982 *Social Theory and the Urban Question*. London: Hutchinson.

Sawatsky, Rodney
1985 "Evangelical and Fundamentalist Movements." In *The Canadian Encyclopedia*. Edmonton: Hurtig. 599.

Scanzoni, Letha Dawson, and John Scanzoni
1981 *Men, Women and Change: A Sociology of Marriage and the Family*, 2nd ed. New York: McGraw-Hill.

Scheff, T.J.
1975 *Labelling Madness*. Englewood Cliffs, N.J.: Prentice-Hall.
1984 *Being Mentally Ill*, 2nd ed. Chicago: Aldine.

Schlesinger, Benjamin
1970 "Remarriages and Family Reorganization for Divorced Persons: A Canadian Study." *Jounal of Comparative Family Studies* 1, 101–18.

Schmidt, Ray
1981 "Canadian Political Economy: A Critique." *Studies in Political Economy* 6 (Autumn): 65–92.

Schudson, Michael
1984 *Advertising, the Uneasy Persuasion*. New York: Basic Books.

Schultz, Richard
1978 "The Regulatory Process and Federal-Provincial Relations." In G. Bruce Doern, ed., *The Regulatory Process in Canada*. Toronto: Macmillan.

Schur, E.M.
1974 "A Sociologist's View." In E.M. Schur and H.A. Bedau, eds., *Victim-less Crimes: Two Sides of a Controversy*. Englewood Cliffs, N.J.: Prentice-Hall.
1984 *Labeling Women Deviant*. New York: Random House.

Schütz, Alfred
1964 *Collected Papers II*. Maurice Natanson, ed. The Hague: Martinus Nijhoff.

Schwartz, Mildred A.
1974 *Politics and Territory: The Sociology of Regional Persistence in Canada*. Montreal: McGill-Queen's University Press.

Schweikert, Patrocinio
1983 "What If . . . Science and Technology in Feminist Utopias." In Joan Rothschild, ed., *Machina Ex Dea: Feminist Perspectives on Technology*. New York: Pergamon Press.

Seeley, John R., R. Alexander Sim, and Elizabeth W. Loosley
1956 *Crestwood Heights: A Study of the Culture of Suburban Life*. Toronto: University of Toronto Press.

Seeman, Melvin
1972 "The Signals of '68: Alienation in Pre-crisis France." *American Sociological Review* 7: 385–402.

Sennett, R., and J. Cobb
1972 *The Hidden Injuries of Class*. New York: Vintage.

Shaffir, William B.
1974 *Life in a Religious Community: The Lubavitcher Chassidim in Montreal*. Toronto: Holt, Rinehart and Winston.

Shahar, Shulamith
1983 *The Fourth Estate*. London: Methuen.

Sheppard, H.L., and N.Q. Herrick
1973 *Where Have All the Robots Gone? Worker Dissatisfaction in the 70's*. New York: The Free Press.

Shimpo, Mitsuru
1976 "Native Religion and Sociocultural Change: The Cree and Salteaux in Southern Saskatchewan, 1830 to 1900." In Stewart Crysdale and Les Wheatcroft, eds., *Religion in Canadian Society*. Toronto: Macmillan.

Shulman, Alix Kates
1980 "Sex and Power: Sexual Bases of Radical Feminism." *Signs: Journal of Women in Culture and Society* 5 (4): 590–604.

Sibley, Elbridge
1942 "Some Demographic Clues to Stratification." *American Sociological Review* 7: 322–30.

Siltanen, Janet, and Michelle Stanworth, eds.
1984 *Women and the Public Sphere: A Critique of Sociology and Politics.* London: Hutchinson.

Simeon, Richard
1979 *Must Canada Fail?* Montreal: McGill-Queen's University Press.
1981 "Constitutional Development and Reform." In M.S. Whittington and Glen Williams, eds., *Canadian Politics in the 1980s.* Toronto: Methuen.

Simmel, Georg
[1905] 1964 "The Metropolis and Mental Life." In K. Wolff, ed., *The Sociology of Georg Simmel.* New York: Free Press.

Simmons, J.L.
1969 *Deviants.* Berkeley, Calif.: Glendessary Press.

Sinclair-Faulkner, Tom
1977 "A Puckish Look at Hockey in Canada." In Peter Slater, ed., *Religion and Culture in Canada.* Waterloo, Ont.: The Canadian Corporation for Studies in Religion.

Singelmann, Joachim
1978 *From Agriculture to Services: The Transformation of Industrial Employment.* Beverly Hills: Sage.

Singh, J.A.L., and Robert M. Zingg
1942 *Wolf Children and Feral Man.* New York: Harper and Row.

Sjoberg, Gideon
1960 *The Preindustrial City.* New York: Free Press.

Skinner, Denise A.
1980 "Dual-career Family Stress and Coping: A Literature Review." *Family Relations* 29: 473–81.

Skolnick, Arlene
1983 *The Intimate Environment,* 3rd ed. Boston: Little, Brown.

Slater, Peter
1977 *Religion and Culture in Canada.* Waterloo, Ont.: Wilfrid Laurier University Press (Canadian Corporation for Studies in Religion).

Smiley, Donald
1980 *Canada in Question,* 3rd ed. Toronto: McGraw-Hill Ryerson.

Smiley, Donald, and Ronald L. Watts
1985 *Interstate Federalism in Canada.* Ottawa: Minister of Supply and Services (with University of Toronto Press.)

Smith, Anthony D.
1981 *The Ethnic Revival in the Modern World.* Cambridge: Cambridge University Press.

Smith, Dorothy
1973 "Women, the Family and Corporate Capitalism." In Marylee Stephenson, ed., *Women in Canada.* Toronto: New Press.
1975 "Ideological Structures and How Women are Excluded." *Canadian Review of Sociology and Anthropology* 12 (4): 353–69.

Smith, Michael R.
1979 "Characterizations of Canadian Strikes: Some Critical Comments." *Relations Industrielles/Industrial Relations* 34: 592–605.

Smucker, Joseph
1980 *Industrialization in Canada.* Toronto: Prentice-Hall Canada.

Sokoloff, Natalie
1979 *Bibliography on the Sociology of Women and Work: 1970's.* Vol. VIII, 4. Toronto: Resources for Feminist Research, Ontario Institute for Studies in Education.

Sonoda, H.
1986 "Boston and Kyoto: City Versus Suburb in Two Civilizations." In T. Umesao et al., eds., *Japanese Civilization in the Modern World.* Osaka: Museum of Ethnology.

Spanier, Graham B.
1980 "Married and Unmarried Cohabitation in the United States." *Journal of Marriage and the Family* 45: 277–88.

Spates, James, and John Macionis
1982 *The Society of Cities.* New York: St. Martin's Press.

Spender, Dale
1983 *There's Always Been a Women's Movement This Century.* London: Routledge and Kegan Paul, Pandora Press.

Stanley, Liz, and Sue Wise
1983 *Breaking Out: Feminist Consciousness and Feminist Research.* London: Routledge and Kegan Paul.

Stark, Rodney, and William Sims Bainbridge

1985 *The Future of Religion: Secularization, Revival and Cult Formation.* Berkeley: University of California Press.

Starr, G.
1973 *Union-Nonunion Wage Differentials.* Toronto: Ontario Ministry of Labour.

Statistics Canada
1921 *Vital Statistics, 1921.* Ottawa: Minister of Supply and Services Canada.

1971 *Vital Statistics Vol. III, Deaths, 1971.* Cat. no. 84–204. Ottawa: Minister of Supply and Services Canada.

1971b *Census of Canada.* Ottawa: Minister of Supply and Services Canada.

1975 *Crime and Traffic Enforcement Statistics.* Cat. no. 85–205. Ottawa: Minister of Supply and Services Canada.

1976 *Vital Statistics. Vol. 1, Births, 1976.* Cat. no. 84–204. Ottawa: Minister of Supply and Services Canada.

1978 *Historical Compendium of Educational Statistics.* Cat. no. 81–568. Ottawa: Minister of Supply and Services Canada.

1980a *Perspectives Canada III.* Cat. no. 11–511E. Ottawa: Minister of Supply and Services Canada.

1980b *Vital Statistics, Vol. 1, Births and Deaths.* Cat. no. 84–204. Ottawa: Minister of Supply and Services Canada.

1981a "One in Eight: Mental Illness in Canada." Ottawa: brochure.

1981b *Census Metropolitan Areas and Census Agglomerations with Components.* Cat. no. 95–903. Ottawa: Minister of Supply and Services Canada.

1982a *Advance Statistics of Education.* Cat. no. 81–220. Ottawa: Minister of Supply and Services Canada.

1982b *Education in Canada 1980–1981.* Cat. no. 81–229. Ottawa: Minister of Supply and Services Canada.

1982c *Census of Canada News Release.* Ottawa: Minister of Supply and Services Canada.

1983a *Vital Statistics, Vol. I, Births and Deaths, 1983.* Cat. no. 84–204. Ottawa: Minister of Supply and Services Canada.

1983b *Vital Statistics, Vol. III, Mortality: Summary List of Causes, 1983.* Cat. no. 84-206. Ottawa: Minister of Supply and Services Canada.

1983c *Vital Statistics, Vol. II, Marriages and Divorces.* Cat. 84–205. Ottawa: Minister of Supply and Services Canada.

1983d *Vital Statistics, Vol. I, Births and Deaths, 1982, 1983.* Cat. no. 84–204. Ottawa: Minister of Supply and Services Canada.

1984a *Fertility in Canada: From Babyboom to Baby-bust.* A. Romaniuc. Cat. no. 91–524E. Ottawa: Minister of Supply and Services Canada.

1984b *Crime and Traffic Enforcement Statistics.* Cat. no. 85–205. Ottawa: Minister of Supply and Services Canada.

1984c *Causes of Death, 1983, Provinces by Sex and Canada by Sex and Age.* Annual Cat. no. 84–203. Ottawa: Minister of Supply and Services Canada.

1984d *Federal Government Employment, January–March 1984.* (August 1984) Ottawa: Minister of Supply and Services Canada.

1985a *Advance Statistics of Education.* Cat. no. 81–220. Ottawa: Minister of Supply and Services Canada.

1985b *Education in Canada 1984: A Statistical Review.* Cat. no. 81–229. Ottawa: Minister of Supply and Services Canada.

1985c *Report on the Demographic Situation in Canada.* Cat. no. 91–209E. Ottawa: Minister of Supply and Services.

1985d *Canadian Statistical Review* (July 1985). Cat. no. 11–003E. Ottawa: Minister of Supply and Services Canada.

1985e *National Income and Expenditure Accounts, Second Quarter.* Cat. no. 13–001. Ottawa: Minister of Supply and Services Canada.

1985f *Women in Canada: A Statistical Report.* Ottawa: Minister of Supply and Services Canada.

1985g *Canada Yearbook 1985.* Cat. no. 11–402E. Ottawa: Minister of Supply and Services Canada.

1985h *Population Projections for Can-*

ada, Provinces and Territories: 1984–2006. M.V. George and J. Perreault, Demography Division, Population Projections Section. Cat. no. 91–520. Ottawa: Minister of Supply and Services Canada.
1986 *Causes of Death, 1985*. Cat. no. 84–203.

Stebbins, Robert A.
1967 "A Theory of the Definition of the Situation." *Canadian Review of Sociology and Anthropology* 4:3, 148–64.
1987 *Deviance: Tolerable Differences.* Scarborough, Ont.: McGraw-Hill Ryerson.

Stein, Peter
1983 "Singlehood." In E. Macklin and R. Rubin, eds., *Contemporary Families and Alternative Lifestyles.* Beverly Hills: Sage.

Steinmetz, Suzanne K., and Murray A. Strauss, eds.
1974 *Violence in the Family.* New York: Harper and Row.

Stevenson, Garth
1979 *Unfulfilled Union: Canadian Federalism and National Unity.* Toronto: Macmillan.

Stokes, Bruce
1978 *Worker Participation—Productivity and Quality of Work Life.* World Watch Paper 25. Washington, D.C.: World Watch Institute.

Stone, Gregory P., and Harvey A. Farberman
1970 *Social Psychology through Symbolic Interaction.* Waltham, Mass.: Xerox College Publishing.

Stone, Lawrence
1977 *The Family, Sex and Marriage in England, 1500–1800.* London: Weidenfeld and Nicholson.

Stone, Leroy O.
1967 *Urban Development in Canada.* 1961 Census monograph. Ottawa: Dominion Bureau of Statistics.

Sutherland, E.H., and D.R. Cressey
1978 *Principles of Criminology*, 10th ed. Philadelphia: Lippincott.

Suttles, G.
1968 *The Social Order of the Slum.* Chicago: University of Chicago Press.

Swift, Jamie
1977 *The Big Nickel: Inco at Home and Abroad.* Kitchener, Ont.: Between the Lines Press.

Szasz, T.S.
1970 *The Manufacture of Madness.* New York: Dell.

Szinovacz, Maximiliane
1984 "Changing Family Roles and Interactions." In Beth B. Hess and Marvin B. Sussman, "Women and the Family: Two Decades of Change." *Marriage and Family Review* II (3/4): 163–201.

Tanner, D.M.
1978 *The Lesbian Couple.* Lexington, Mass.: Heath.

Task Force on Canadian Unity (Pépin-Robarts Report)
1979 *A Future Together.* Hull: Canadian Government Publishing Centre.

Task Force on Child Care
1986 Status of Women Canada. Ottawa: Minister of Supply and Services Canada.

Task Force on Foreign Direct Investment in Canada
1972 *Foreign Direct Investment in Canada (the Gray Report).* Ottawa: Queen's Printer.

Task Force on Labour Market Development
1981 *Labour Market Development in the 1980's (the Dodge Report).* Ottawa: Ministry of Employment and Immigration.

Task Force on the Structure of Canadian Industry
1970 *Foreign Ownership and the Structure of Canadian Industry (the Watkins Report).* Privy Council Office. Ottawa: Information Canada.

Thomas, W.I., and Dorothy Swaine Thomas
1928 *The Child in America.* New York: Alfred A. Knopf.

Thomlinson, Ralph
1976 *Population Dynamics: Causes and Consequences of World Demographic Change*, 2nd ed. New York: Random House.

Thompson, John F., and Norman Beasley
1960 *For the Years to Come: A Story of International Nickel of Canada.* New York: Putnam, 1960.

Thorne, Barrie, with Marilyn Yalom
1982 *Rethinking the Family: Some Feminist Questions.* New York: Longman.

Thornton, A., D.F. Alwin, and P. Camburn
1983 "Causes and Consequences of Sex-Role Attitude Change." *American Sociological Review* 48: 211–27.

Tönnies, Ferdinand
[1887] 1963 *Community and Society.* Charles P. Loomis, trans. and ed. New York: Harper and Row.

Troeltsch, Ernst
1931 *The Social Teaching of the Christian Churches.* 2 vols. Olive Wyon, trans., with an introduction by H. Richard Niebuhr. New York: Macmillan.

Tucker, R.C.
1978 *The Marx-Engels Reader.* New York: Norton.

Tumin, Melvin
1953 "Some Principles of Stratification: A Critical Appraisal." *American Sociological Review* 18: 387–94.

Turner, Jonathan
1986 *The Structure of Sociological Theory.* Homewood, Ill.: Dorsey Press.

Tylor, E.B.
1871 *Primitive Culture.* London: John Murray Publishers Ltd.

Tyree, Andrea, Mose Semyonov, and Robert W. Hodge
1979 "Gaps and Glissandos: Inequality, Economic Development and Social Mobility." *American Sociological Review* 44: 410–24.

Ullman, Stephen
1979 "Regional Political Cultures in Canada: A Theoretical and Conceptual Introduction." *American Review of Canadian Studies* VII: 2.

Umesao, T., H. Smith, T. Moriya, and R. Ogawa, eds.
1986 *Japanese Civilization in the Modern World.* Osaka: National Museum of Ethnology.

United Nations
1978 "Death Rates and Birth Rates, 1950–75." *UN Population Studies* *78.* United Nations.

Vaillancourt, François
1978 "La charte de la langue française du Québec." *Canadian Public Policy* 4 (3): 284–308.

Valentine, Victor
1980 "Part Two: Native Peoples and Canadians, A Profile of Issues and Trends." *Cultural Boundaries and the Cohesion of Canada.* Montreal: Institute for Research on Public Policy.

Vallee, Frank G.
1976 "Religion of the Kabloona and Eskimo." In Stewart Crysdale and Les Wheatcroft, eds., *Religion in Canadian Society.* Toronto: Macmillan. 151–60.

Vallières, Pierre
1971 *White Niggers of America.* Toronto: McClelland and Stewart.

van de Berghe, Pierre L.
1981 *The Ethnic Phenomenon.* New York: Elsevier.

Vanek, Joann
1974 "Time Spent in Housework." *Scientific American* 231: 116–20.
1978 "Housewives as Workers." In Ann Stromberg and Shirley Harkess, eds., *Working: Theories and Facts in Perspective.* Palo Alto, Calif.: Mayfield.

Vaz, Edmund W.
1984 "Institutionalized Stealing Among Big-City Taxidrivers." In Audrey Wipper, ed., *The Sociology of Work: Papers in Honour of Oswald Hall.* Ottawa: Carleton University Press.

Veevers, Jean
1977a *The Family in Canada.* 1971 Census of Canada Profile Series, Bulletin 5: 3–3. Statistics Canada. Ottawa: Minister of Supply and Services Canada.
1977b *Childless by Choice.* Toronto: Butterworth.
1979 "Voluntary Childlessness: A Review of Issues and Evidence." *Marriage and Family Review* 2 (2).

Verbrugge, Lois M.
1979 "Marital Status and Health." *Journal of Marriage and the Family.* May: 267–85.

Viscusi, W. Kip
1983 *Risk by Choice: Regulating Health and Safety in the Workplace.* Cambridge, Mass.: Harvard University Press.

Vold, G.B., and T.J. Bernard
1986 *Theoretical Criminology,* 3rd ed. New York: Oxford University Press.

Walker, Kathryne E.
1969 "Homemaking Still Takes Time." *Journal of Home Economics* 61 (8): 621–24.

Waller, Willard
[1938] 1951 *The Family: A Dynamic Interpretation*. Rev. ed. by Reuben Hill. New York: Holt, Rinehart and Winston.

Walum, Shirley
1977 *Sex Roles: Biological, Psychological and Social Foundations*. New York: Oxford University Press.

Warburton, T. Rennie
1976 "Religion and the Control of Native Peoples." In Stewart Crysdale and Les Wheatcroft, eds., *Religion in Canadian Society*. Toronto: Macmillan. 412–22.

Wargon, Sylvia
1979 *Canadian Households and Families*. Statistics Canada. Cat. no. 99–753E. Ottawa: Minister of Supply and Services Canada.

Warner, W. Lloyd, J.O. Low, Paul S. Lunt, and Leo Srola
1963 *Yankee City*. New Haven: Yale University Press.

Watkins, Mel
1967 "A Staple Theory of Economic Growth." In W.T. Easterbrook and Mel Watkins, *Approaches to Canadian Economic History: A Selection of Essays*. Toronto: McClelland and Stewart.
1977 "The Staple Theory Revisited." *Journal of Canadian Studies* 12 (5): 83–95.
1982 "The Innis Tradition in Political Economy." *Canadian Journal of Political and Social Theory* 6 (1–2): 12–34.

Watkins, Mel, ed.
1977 *Dene Nation: The Colony Within*. Toronto: University of Toronto Press.

Watson, J.B.
1924 *Behavior*. New York: Norton.

Webb, Eugene J., Donald T. Campbell, Richard D. Schwartz, and Lee Sechrest
1966 *Unobtrusive Measures: Nonreactive Research in the Social Sciences*. Chicago: Rand McNally.

Weber, Max
1946 *Essays in Sociology*. Hans H. Gerth and C. Wright Mills, eds. and trans. New York: Oxford University Press.
[1925] 1946 "Class, Status and Party." In H.H. Gerth and C. Wright Mills, eds. and trans., from Max Weber, *Essays in Sociology*. New York: Oxford University Press.
[1922] 1947 *The Theory of Social and Economic Organization*. A.R. Henderson and Talcott Parsons, trans.; revised and edited with an Introduction by Talcott Parsons. London: William Hodge.
[1930] 1958 *The Protestant Ethic and the Spirit of Capitalism*. Talcott Parsons, trans. New York: Charles Scribner's Sons.
[1927] 1961 *General Economic History*. New York: Allen and Unwin.
[1922] 1963 *The Sociology of Religion*. Ephraim Fischoff, trans. Boston: Beacon Press.
[1947] 1967 *The Theory of Economic and Social Organization*. New York: Free Press.

Weinfeld, Morton
1981a "The Development of Affirmative Action in Canada." *Canadian Ethnic Studies* XIII: 2.
1981b "Myth and Reality in the Canadian Mosaic: Affective Ethnicity." *Canadian Ethnic Studies* XIII: 3.

Weingarten, Kathy
1978 "Interdependence." In Robert Rapoport and Rhona Rapoport, eds., *Working Couples*. New York: Harper and Row.

Wellman, Barry
1973 "The Network Nature of Future Communities: A Predictive Synthesis." Research Paper No. 58. Toronto: Centre for Urban and Community Studies, University of Toronto.
1978 *The Community Question: The Intimate Networks of East Yorkers*. Toronto: Centre for Urban and Community Studies, University of Toronto.
1985 "Domestic Work, Paid Work and Network." In Steve Duck and Daniel Perlman, eds., *Understanding Personal Relationships*. London: Gage.

Westhues, Kenneth
1982 *First Sociology*. Toronto: McGraw-Hill Ryerson.

Westley, Frances
1983 *The Complex Forms of the Religious Life.* Chico, Calif.: Scholars Press.

Westoff, Charles
1978 "The Predictability of Fertility in Developed Countries." *Population Bulletin of the United Nations* 11: 1–5. New York: United Nations.

White, Leslie
1949 *The Science of Culture.* New York: Grove Press.

White, Lynn K.
1979 "Sex Differentials in the Effect of Remarriage on Global Happiness." *Journal of Marriage and the Family* 41: 869–76.

Whitehurst, R.N.
1975 "Alternative Life-Styles and Canadian Pluralism." In S.P. Wakil, ed., *Marriage, Family and Society.* Toronto: Butterworth.

Whitmont, Edward C.
1984 *Return of the Goddess.* New York: Crossroad.

Whyte, Donald R.
1965 "Sociological Aspects of Poverty: A Conceptual Analysis." *Canadian Review of Sociology and Anthropology* 2, 175–89.

Whyte, William H., Jr.
1956 *The Organization Man.* Garden City, N.Y.: Doubleday.

Williams, Rick
1979 "Inshore Fishermen, Unionization, and the Struggle Against Underdevelopment Today." In Robert Brym and James Sacouman, eds., *Underdevelopment and Social Movements in Atlantic Canada.* Toronto: Hogtown Press.

Williamson, Oliver
1975 *Markets and Hierarchies: Analysis and Antitrust Implications.* New York: Free Press.

Wilson, Bryan
1982 *Religion in Sociological Perspective.* New York: Oxford University Press.

Wilson, S.J.
1986 *Women, the Family and the Economy,* 2nd ed. Toronto: McGraw-Hill Ryerson.

Wirth, Louis
1938 "Urbanism as a Way of Life." *American Journal of Sociology* 44: 1–24.

Wood, Adrian
1978 *A Theory of Pay.* London: Cambridge University Press.

Woodcock, George
1981 *The Meeting of Time and Space: Regionalism in Canadian Literature.* Edmonton: NeWest.

Woolf, Virginia
[1938] 1977 *Three Guineas.* Middlesex: Penguin.

Wrong, Dennis
1961 "The Oversocialized Conception of Man in Modern Sociology." *American Sociological Review* 26: 183–93.

Yancey, William L., Eugene P. Erickson, and Richard N. Juliani
1976 "Emergent Ethnicity: A Review and Reformulation." *American Sociological Review* 41, 391–403.

Yogev, S.
1981 "Do Professional Women Have Egalitarian Marital Relationships?" *Journal of Marriage and the Family* 43: 865–71.

Yorburg, Betty
1975 "The Nuclear and the Extended Family: An Area of Conceptual Confusion." *Journal of Comparative Family Studies* 6 (Spring).

Young, Michael D.
1958 *The Rise of Meritocracy.* Harmondsworth: Penguin.

Zaretsky, Eli
1976 *Capitalism, the Family and Personal Life.* New York: Harper and Row.
1982 "The Place of the Family in the Origins of the Welfare State." In Barrie Thorne with Marilyn Yalom, *Rethinking the Family: Some Feminist Questions.* New York: Longman.

INDEX OF NAMES

perspectives of, 15
on religion, 242-46
on social organization, 300-301
sociology influenced by, 17-18
on urbanization, 602
Wellman, Barry, 614

Westley, Frances, 260
Whyte, William H., Jr., 367
Woodcock, George, 629
Wright, James D., 397

Yanagisako, Sylvia, 330

INDEX OF SUBJECTS

CREDITS

CHAPTER 1

Excerpts from *The Presentation of Self in Everyday Life*, by Erving Goffman. Copyright © 1959 by Erving Goffman. Reprinted by permission of Doubleday & Co. Inc.

Excerpts from *Social Theory and Social Structure*, by Robert K. Merton. Revised and Enlarged Edition. Reprinted by permission of The Free Press, a Division of Macmillan Publishing Company, 1968.

Excerpt from *Conflict Sociology* by Randall Collins. Reprinted by permission of Academic Press Inc.

Excerpts from *"In the Maze of Bureaucracy"* in *The Castle* by Franz Kafka, translated by Edwin & Willa Muir. Copyright 1930, 1954 and renewed 1958 by Alfred A. Knopf, Inc. Reprinted by permission of the publisher.

From the *Apprenticeship of Duddy Kravitz* by Mordecai Richler, used by permission of The Canadian Publishers, McClelland and Stewart Limited, Toronto.

Excerpts from *Democracy in America* by Alexis de Tocqueville. Copyright 1945 and renewed 1973 by Alfred A. Knopf, Inc.

From *The Vertical Mosaic* by John Porter. Reprinted courtesy of University of Toronto Press.

From *The Sociological Imagination* by C. Wright Mills. Copyright © 1959 by Oxford University Press, Inc. Reprinted by permission.

CHAPTER 2

Lines from "voices to voices, lip to lip" from *Is 5, poems by e.e. cummings*, are reprinted by permission of Liveright Publishing Corporation. Copyright 1926 by Horace Liveright. Copyright renewed 1953 by e.e. cummings.

"The Median Isn't the Message" by Stephen Jay Gould, *Discover*, June 1985. Reprinted by permission of the author.

CHAPTER 3

From *Word Play: What Happens When People Talk* by Peter Farb. Copyright © 1973 by Peter Farb. Reprinted by permission of Alfred A. Kopf, Inc.

"Cabby-ese and The Social World" reprinted with permission of The Free Press, a Division of Macmillan, Inc. from *Introducing Sociology: Toward Understanding Life in Society* by James M. Henslin. Copyright © 1975 by The Free Press.

Excerpts from *Language and Woman's Place* by Robin Lakoff. Copyright © 1975 by Robin Lakoff. Reprinted by permission of Harper & Row, Publishers, Inc.

From *Advertising, the Uneasy Persuasion: Its Dubious Impact on American Society* by Michael Schudson. Copyright © 1984 by Michael Schudson. Reprinted by permission of Basic Books, Inc., Publishers.

CHAPTER 4

From *The Portable Medieval Reader*, edited by James B. Ross and Mary M. McLaughlin. Copyright 1949 by James B. Ross and Mary M. McLaughlin. Copyright renewed 1977 by James B. Ross and Mary M. McLaughlin. Reprinted by permission of Viking Penguin Inc.

Excerpt from *Theories of Mass Communication*, 3rd edition by Melvin L. De Fleur and Sandra Ball-Rokeach. Copyright © 1966, 1970 and 1975 by Longman Inc. Reprinted by permission of Longman Inc., New York.

Reprinted from Paula L. Dressel and David M. Petersen, "Becoming a Male Stripper: Recruitment, Socialization, and Ideological Development," *Work and Occupations* 9:3 (August 1982), pp. 387-406, © Sage Publications, Inc., with permission.

From "The Fate of Idealism in Medical

747

School," by Howard S. Becker and Blanche Geer. *American Sociological Review* 23 (1958), pp. 50-56.

CHAPTER 5

Excerpts from "The Changing Family," *The Royal Bank Reporter* (1986, 2). Reprinted by permission.

Table from Arlene S. Skolnick, *The Intimate Environment: Exploring Marriage and the Family*, 3rd ed., p. 116. Copyright © 1983 by Arlene S. Skolnick. Reprinted by permission of Little, Brown and Company.

Table, 'A Typology of Family Structures,' from "The Nuclear and the Extended Family: An Area of Conceptual Confusion," by Betty Yorburg, *Journal of Comparative Family Studies* (1975, 6). Reprinted by permission.

"Married Women in the Labour Force, Canada, 1961-84," *The Royal Bank Reporter* (1986, 19). Reprinted by permission.

"Traditional versus Egalitarian Marital Scripts," reprinted with permission of Macmillan Publishing Company from *Intimate Relationships, Marriage, and Family* by James C. Coleman. Copyright © 1984 by Macmillan Publishing Company.

"The Cost of Raising a Child," *The Royal Bank Reporter* (1986, 18). Reprinted by permission.

CHAPTER 6

Excerpts from "Inequalities in the Opportunity Structure" (originally titled "Access to Higher Education in Canada") by Neil Guppy, *The Canadian Journal of Higher Education* 14:3 (1984, 80, 93). Reprinted by permission.

Excerpts from *The Measure of Canadian Society: Education, Equality and Opportunity* by John Porter. Reproduced by permission of Gage Publishing Ltd.

Excerpts from "The Hidden Curriculum of Schooling" (originally titled "Equality to Benefit from Schooling: The Issue of Educational Opportunity") by Stephen Richer, in Dennis Forcese and Stephen Richer, eds., *Social Issues: Sociological Views of Canada*, 1982, pp. 354-56. Reproduced by permission of Prentice-Hall Canada Inc.

Excerpt from "Academic Stratification and Education Plans: A Reassessment" by Gilbert and McRoberts, reprinted from *The Canadian Review of Sociology and Anthropology* 14:1 (1977), by permission of the authors and the publisher.

CHAPTER 7

"God Is Dead" by Peter Elbling. © 1967 Cherry Lane Music Publishing Co. Inc. All rights reserved. Used by permission.

"For one strong public school system" poster. Reproduced courtesy of the Ontario Secondary School Teachers' Federation.

Exhibit from *Religion in Sociological Perspective* by Keith A. Roberts, Homewood, Ill. Dorsey Press, 1984, p. 228. Reprinted by permission of The Dorsey Press.

"Christianity and Canadian Indians: A Critical View" (originally titled "Native Religion and Sociocultural Change: the Cree and Salteaux in Southern Saskatchewan, 1830 to 1900") by Mitsuru Shimpo, in Stewart Crysdale and Les Wheatcroft, eds., *Religion in Canadian Society*, Toronto: Macmillan of Canada, 1976, pp. 135-36. Reprinted by permission of the author and editors.

"Churches practising too much institutional coercion" by Tom Harpur, *Toronto Star*, January 26, 1986. Reprinted with permission – The Toronto Star Syndicate.

"A Saint and His Shrine in the Soviet Union," *The Rites of Rulers: Ritual in Industrial Society – The Soviet Case* by Christel Lane. Cambridge: Cambridge University Press, pp. 210-11. Reprinted by permission of the publisher.

CHAPTER 8

"Occupational Prestige in Canada," by Peter C. Pineo and John Porter, reprinted from *The Canadian Review of Sociology and Anthropology* 4:1 (1967), by permission of the authors and publisher.

CHAPTER 10

"Industrial Democracy in Action," *Industrial Democracy: Yugoslav Style* by I. Adizes. New York: The Free Press,

1971, 116-21, 126-27. Reprinted by permission of the author.

CHAPTER 11

Excerpts from "CLC set for white-collar drive" by James Bagnall, *Financial Post*, April 26, 1986. Reprinted by permission.

CHAPTER 12

"Chickens slaughtered to ease kin's spirits," *Calgary Herald*, October 27, 1985. Reprinted by permission of The Canadian Press.

From *Social Theory and Social Structure*. Revised and Enlarged Edition, by Robert K. Merton, adapted with permission of Macmillan Publishing Co., Inc. Copyright © 1957, The Free Press, a Corporation.

Excerpts from "Crack's Deadly Cycle," *Maclean's*, September 29, 1986. Reprinted by permission.

Excerpts from "Why the Boss Steals," *Maclean's*, June 30, 1986. Reprinted by permission.

CHAPTER 14

"Toward a world of ten billion people" by Gwynne Dyer, *Edmonton Journal*, July 22, 1982. Reprinted by permission of the author.

Excerpts from "Canada's population will fall greatly without more immigrants – Tory," *Edmonton Journal*, September 15, 1986. Reprinted by permission of The Canadian Press.

CHAPTER 15

Extract from "Mon Pays" by Gilles Vigneault, Les Nouvelles Editions de l'Arc, Montreal, Quebec.

From *Introduction to Physical Anthropology*, 3rd ed., by Ashley Montagu, 1960. Courtesy of Charles C. Thomas, Publisher, Springfield, Illinois.

Excerpts from "Desperate Voyage," *MacLean's*, August 25, 1986. Reprinted by permission.

Excerpts from "A Canadian Tragedy," *Maclean's*, July 14, 1986. Reprinted by permission.

CHAPTER 16

From *The City* by Ernest W. Burgess & Robert Park, 1963. Copyright © 1925, 1967, by the University of Chicago Press. All rights reserved. Published 1925. Seventh impression 1974.

From "The Nature of Cities" by Chauncy D. Harris and Edward L. Ullman in volume no. 242 of *The Annals of the American Academy of Political and Social Science*. Copyright, 1945, by The American Academy of Political and Social Science. All rights reserved.

From *A World of Strangers: Order and Action in Urban Public Space*, by Lyn H. Lofland. Copyright © 1973 by Basic Books, Inc., New York. Reprinted by permission of the publisher.

CHAPTER 17

Excerpts from "Provinces set to gang up, Ottawa told," by Matthew Fisher and Kirk Makin, *The Globe and Mail*, August 21, 1986. Reprinted by permission.

Excerpts from "Voices from the Canadian Prairie," *Maclean's*, July 7, 1986. Reprinted by permission.

CHAPTER 18

"Quebec's New Entrepreneurs," *Maclean's*, August 4, 1986. Reprinted by permission.

Note

Statistics Canada material reproduced by permission of the Minister of Supply and Services Canada.

PHOTOGRAPHS AND ILLUSTRATIONS

TO THE OWNER OF THIS BOOK:

Please help improve future editions of this book. Complete and return the following questionnaire.

1. Why did you purchase this book?
    _____university course   _____continuing education course
    _____college course   _____personal interest

2. How much of the book did you read?
    _____all   _____ 3/4   _____ 1/2   _____ 1/4

3. Which chapters did you find most interesting or useful?
    _____
    _____
    _____

4. How could the book be improved?
    _____
    _____
    _____

5. Will you keep or re-sell this book? _____

6. Did you or do you intend to purchase the Study Guide which accompanies this text?
    _____yes   _____ no

Return To:

METHUEN PUBLICATIONS
College Division
150 Laird Drive
Toronto, Ontario
M4G 9Z9